The Routledge Companion to Career Studies

The Routledge Companion to Career Studies is an in-depth reference for researchers, students, and practitioners looking for a comprehensive overview of the state of the art of career studies. Split into five parts, the volume looks at major areas of research within career studies and reflects on the latest developments in the areas of theory, empirical studies, and methodology.

The book's five parts cover (1) major theoretical and methodological debates and approaches to studying careers; (2) careers as dynamic, ongoing processes covering such issues as time, shaping careers, career outcomes and patterns, and the forces shaping careers; (3) the local, national, and global context of careers, (4) implementing career research to design practical interventions in areas such as education, counseling, and national policy; and (5) a commentary on the current state of career scholarship and its future development as represented in this volume, by founding scholars in the field.

This book will be a sourcebook for scholars studying careers, research students intending to take up the study of careers, and anyone – scholars and practitioners – with an interest not only in understanding careers, the factors shaping them and where they lead, but also in how this understanding might be used in practice.

Hugh Gunz is Professor Emeritus of Organizational Behaviour and Human Resource Management at the University of Toronto, Canada.

Mila Lazarova is Associate Professor of International Business and Canada Research Chair in Global Workforce Management at Simon Fraser University, Canada.

Wolfgang Mayrhofer is Full Professor and Head of the Interdisciplinary Institute of Management and Organizational Behaviour, Vienna University of Economics and Business, Austria.

Routledge Companions in Business, Management and Accounting

Routledge Companions in Business, Management and Accounting are prestige reference works providing an overview of a whole subject area or sub-discipline. These books survey the state of the discipline including emerging and cutting-edge areas. Providing a comprehensive, up to date, definitive work of reference, Routledge Companions can be cited as an authoritative source on the subject.

A key aspect of these Routledge Companions is their international scope and relevance. Edited by an array of highly regarded scholars, these volumes also benefit from teams of contributors which reflect an international range of perspectives.

Individually, Routledge Companions in Business, Management and Accounting provide an impactful one-stop-shop resource for each theme covered. Collectively, they represent a comprehensive learning and research resource for researchers, postgraduate students and practitioners.

Published titles in this series include:

THE ROUTLEDGE COMPANION TO THE HISTORY OF RETAILING
Edited by Jon Stobart and Vicki Howard

THE ROUTLEDGE COMPANION TO INNOVATION MANAGEMENT
Edited by Jin Chen, Alexander Brem, Eric Viardot and Poh Kam Wong

THE ROUTLEDGE COMPANION TO THE MAKERS OF GLOBAL BUSINESS
Edited by Teresa da Silva Lopes, Christina Lubinski and Heidi J. S. Tworek

THE ROUTLEDGE COMPANION TO ACCOUNTING IN EMERGING ECONOMIES
Edited by Pauline Weetman and Ioannis Tsalavoutas

THE ROUTLEDGE COMPANION TO CAREER STUDIES
Edited by Hugh Gunz, Mila Lazarova, and Wolfgang Mayrhofer

For more information about this series, please visit: www.routledge.com/Routledge-Companions-in-Business-Management-and-Accounting/book-series/RCBMA

The Routledge Companion to Career Studies

Edited by
Hugh Gunz, Mila Lazarova,
and Wolfgang Mayrhofer

Routledge
Taylor & Francis Group

LONDON AND NEW YORK

First published 2020
by Routledge
4 Park Square, Milton Park, Abingdon, Oxon OX14 4RN

and by Routledge
605 Third Avenue, New York, NY 10017

First issued in paperback 2023

Routledge is an imprint of the Taylor & Francis Group, an informa business

Publisher's Note
The publisher has gone to great lengths to ensure the quality of this reprint but points out that some imperfections in the original copies may be apparent.

British Library Cataloguing-in-Publication Data
A catalogue record for this book is available from the British Library

Library of Congress Cataloging-in-Publication Data
Names: Gunz, Hugh, editor. | Lazarova, Mila B., editor. | Mayrhofer, Wolfgang, editor.
Title: The Routledge companion to career studies / edited by Hugh Gunz, Mila Lazarova and Wolfgang Mayrhofer.
Description: Abingdon, Oxon ; New York, NY : Routledge, 2020. | Includes bibliographical references and index. |
Identifiers: LCCN 2019022909 (print) | LCCN 2019022910 (ebook) | ISBN 9781138939776 (hardback) | ISBN 9781315674704 (ebook)
Subjects: LCSH: Vocational guidance—Study and teaching. | Career development—Study and teaching.
Classification: LCC HF5381 .R7745 2020 (print) | LCC HF5381 (ebook) | DDC 331.702071—dc23
LC record available at https://lccn.loc.gov/2019022909
LC ebook record available at https://lccn.loc.gov/2019022910

ISBN 13: 978-1-032-65231-3 (pbk)
ISBN 13: 978-1-138-93977-6 (hbk)
ISBN 13: 978-1-315-67470-4 (ebk)

DOI: 10.4324/9781315674704

Typeset in Bembo
by Apex CoVantage, LLC

Contents

Contents

Tables

Figures

About the authors

Jos Akkermans is Associate Professor at the Vrije Universiteit Amsterdam, The Netherlands. His research mainly focuses on career sustainability, career success, employability, and career transitions. He has a special interest in studying career shocks, examining how these events can impact on peoples' career development. He adopts a multidisciplinary focus, for example studying careers of blue-collar workers, entrepreneurs, and project workers. He currently serves as Associate Editor for the *Journal of Vocational Behavior*, as editorial board member of *Career Development International*, and as an executive board member of the Academy of Management Careers Division.

Tracy Anderson explores how careers are shaped by features of modern employment, investigating how practices like independent contracting and collaborative working shape individual outcomes such as performance, pay, and mobility. Currently, she is focusing on understanding the career consequences of intra-organizational social networks and their dynamics. She is Assistant Professor in the Department of Management and Technology at Bocconi University (starting September 2019), and has a PhD in Management (Human and Social Capital) from the Wharton School at the University of Pennsylvania.

Maike Andresen, PhD, is Professor of Human Resource Management and Organisational Behaviour at University of Bamberg in Germany. She has served as a visiting scholar at Copenhagen Business School and Deakin University. She is a faculty member of the joint European Human Resource Management programme together with five European universities. She has contributed numerous peer-reviewed articles to leading academic journals and to edited volumes and has published and edited 17 books. She currently serves on several editorial boards of academic journals including *Human Resource Management Journal* and the *International Journal of Human Resource Management*. Her primary research interests are in the area of international mobility, (global) careers, and work flexibilization.

Michael B. Arthur is Emeritus Professor of Strategy and International Business at Suffolk University, Boston, USA, and Visiting Professor at Cranfield School of Management, UK. His books include the *Handbook of Career Theory, The Boundaryless Career, The New Careers, Knowledge at Work*, and most recently *An Intelligent Career: Taking Ownership of Your Life and Your Work*, aimed directly at career owners. He sits on the editorial boards of *Career Development International, Journal of Organizational Behavior*, and *Journal of Vocational Behavior*. He is a regular speaker about contemporary career phenomena and a contributor to the business magazine website Forbes.com.

Silvia Bagdadli (PhD, Bocconi University) is Associate Professor of Human Resource Management at Bocconi University. Her research focuses on the areas of career, talent, and human resource management and she is interested in the intersection of the individual and the organizational perspective. Recent international projects include global talent management and the understanding of career meanings, determinants and outcomes around the world. Her research appeared in *Human Resource Management, Human Resource Management Journal, International Journal of Human Resource Management, Journal of Organizational Behavior,* and *Journal of Business and Psychology.*

Roxana Barbulescu is Associate Professor of Management at HEC Paris. Her research focuses on the career trajectories of managerial and professional workers, particularly the ways in which gender and prior experience shape individuals' subsequent mobility outcomes. Her work has appeared in premier academic journals, including *Organization Science, Academy of Management Review,* and *Strategic Management Journal* as well as the popular press. At HEC she serves as academic director of the Advanced Management Specialization in the MBA program. A native of Romania, she holds a BA in Economics from Stanford University and MSc and PhD degrees in Management from INSEAD.

Frans Bévort, PhD, is Associate Professor at the Department of Organization, Copenhagen Business School. His research focuses on HRM, professions, and management. A special research interest is the tensions between management as a professional discipline and other disciplines. The development of HRM as a professional discipline is another research interest. Over the past 25 years he has contributed to research, practice and debate within HRM, organization theory and management as researcher, consultant and manager. He has authored more than 10 books and his research has been published in journals such as *German Journal of Research in Human Resource Management, Journal of Professions and Organization,* and *International Studies in Management and Organization.*

Matthew Bidwell is Associate Professor of Management at the Wharton School. His research explores topics of careers and employment, with a particular focus on causes, consequences and patterns of internal and external job mobility. He also studies the careers of highly skilled contingent workers. He currently serves as a senior editor at *Organization Science.* Originally from the UK, he received a PhD from the MIT Sloan School and worked at INSEAD in Singapore before moving to Philadelphia.

Torsten Biemann is Professor of Human Resource Management and Leadership at the University of Mannheim, Germany. He holds BA and MA degrees in Business Administration and in Psychology, and received his PhD from Kiel University. His current research and teaching interests center on occupational careers and career patterns, leadership effectiveness, international human resource management, and methods in management research. He has published many articles in leading academic journals and is frequently cited in practitioner outlets.

Nikos Bozionelos is Professor of IHRM and OB in EMLyon Business School (France). He received his PhD from the University of Strathclyde (UK). His research interests include careers, mentoring and social capital, employability, and individual differences in the workplace. He has nearly 200 publications and conference presentations, which culminate in an individual research impact index hI = 27. His research has repeatedly attracted practitioner and media attention including the *Wall Street Journal, CNN, BBC, Ouest France, Boston Globe*, the *Times*, the *Guardian, Davos Economics Forum*, and *India Today*. He acts as senior editor for *Asia Pacific Journal of Management*.

Forrest Briscoe is Frank and Mary Jean Smeal Research Professor of Management at the Smeal College of Business, Pennsylvania State University. He conducts research in the broad domain of organizational theory, including the topics of careers, networks, organizational change, diffusion, social movements, and strategy. His empirical careers research tends to focus on professional occupations, such as lawyers and doctors, where career structures that were historically shaped by highly institutionalized norms are now changing. New projects ask how these careers are being reshaped by organizations' strategic actions, and by use of new technologies. He received his PhD in management from the MIT Sloan School.

Jon P. Briscoe is Professor of Management at Northern Illinois University. A co-founder of the 5C (Cross-Cultural Collaboration on Contemporary Careers) Group, much of his research effort revolves around comparative research around the world. In addition he studies self-directed career management, leadership development, and value expression. He is an active member and past chair of the Careers Division of the Academy of Management.

Gerard A. Callanan is Professor of Management in the School of Business at West Chester University. He received his PhD in Organizational Behavior from Drexel University. A member of the Academy of Management and the American Psychological Association, his research on a variety of management topics has appeared in a number of scholarly publications. He is coeditor (with Jeffrey H. Greenhaus of Drexel University) of the *Encyclopedia of Career Development*, published in 2006 by Sage. He is also the co-author (with Jeffrey H. Greenhaus of Drexel University and Veronica M. Godshalk of Penn State University) of the fifth edition of *Career Management for Life*, published in 2019 by Routledge.

Priscilla Claman has seen careers from the vantage point of both individuals and employers. She worked on a team researching careers at TERC and then spent years in human resources specializing in hiring, career development, and merger-related programs. Since founding Career Strategies, Inc. in 1989, she has worked with well over 100 employers and thousands of individuals in many fields. She is the author of, *ASK . . . How to Get What You Want and Need at Work* and is a regular contributor to Harvard Business School publications. She has an AB from Harvard College and a master's degree from Harvard's Graduate School of Education.

Laurie Cohen is Professor of Work and Organisation at Nottingham University Business School. Her research focuses on career-making over the lifespan, and research methods in the study of career, focusing on interpretive approaches and the use of narrative. Much of her research revolves around women's working lives and careers, and for several years she has explored how gender plays out in scientific research, engineering and higher education sectors. She has published in academic and practitioner journals. Her research monograph, *Imagining Women's Careers*, was published by Oxford University Press in September, 2014.

Ans De Vos, PhD, is the SD Worx Professor on Sustainable Careers at Antwerp Management School and professor at the University of Antwerp in Antwerp, Belgium. She investigates careers at the intersection of individuals and organizations and the conditions that affect the sustainability of careers over time. She is co-editor of the *Handbook of Research on Sustainable Careers* (EE Publishing). Her work has been published in diverse peer-reviewed journals including *Academy of Management Review, Journal of Vocational Behavior*, and *Career Development International*. She is associate editor of the *European Journal of Work and Organizational Psychology* and editorial board member of *Career Development International* and *Journal of Managerial Psychology*.

Michael Dickmann is Professor of International Human Resource Management, Cranfield University, School of Management, UK. He lectures in the areas of international and strategic HRM. His research focuses on human resource strategies, structures and processes of multinational organizations, cross-cultural management, international mobility and global careers. He has published in many different academic journals and he is the senior editor in chief of the *International Journal of Human Resource Management*. He is the lead author of several books on international HRM and global careers. His latest edited book is *The Management of Global Careers* (with Vesa Suutari and Olivier Wurtz).

Katja Dlouhy is Assistant Professor of Human Resource Management and Leadership at the University of Mannheim, Germany. She received her PhD in Management from the University of Mannheim and her diploma in work and organizational psychology from the University of Koblenz-Landau, Germany. Her research interests include individuals' career development, the emergence of career patterns, and occupational risk-taking. Methodologically, she studies these topics from a person-centered perspective, oftentimes using novel approaches that are tailored to the analysis of career trajectories.

Gina Dokko holds a PhD in Management from the Wharton School of the University of Pennsylvania, an MS in Industrial Administration from Carnegie Mellon GSIA, and a BS in Economics, also from the Wharton School. Her research focuses on the consequences of job mobility and careers for individuals and organizations, including its effects on innovation, learning, performance, and social capital. Her research has been published in *Strategic Management Journal, Research Policy, Organization Science, Organization Studies*, and the *Academy of Management Journal*. She is an Associate Professor at the University of California, Davis.

Nicky Dries is Senior Research Professor at KU Leuven and a Visiting Professor at BI Norwegian Business School. She has been a visiting scholar at University of Tilburg, Wirtschaftsuniversität Vienna, Reykjavik University, IESE, TUM München, and University of Victoria; and a Fulbright scholar at Boston University. Her research interests are talent management, untapped employee potential, and the future of work – and more broadly, employee reactions to organizational inequalities, secrecy, and ambiguity. She is an active member of the two largest cross-cultural projects in career studies, i.e. 5C (Consortium for the Cross-Cultural Study of Contemporary Careers) and the Career Adaptability/Life Design project.

Joanne Duberley is Professor of Organisation Studies at the University of Birmingham. Her research focuses on the ways that gender, age, ethnicity, and social class impact upon access to and experience of careers. She has been involved in research projects exploring careers in a variety of contexts, including elite professions, academic scientists, engineering, women entrepreneurs, NHS managers, and women approaching retirement. She generally adopts a qualitative approach towards research, although she enjoys working in multidisciplinary teams and maintains an interest in innovative approaches towards research methodology.

Anders Dysvik is Professor of Organizational Behavior at BI Norwegian Business School. His work has been accepted for publication in journals such as *Academy of Management Journal, Journal of Management Studies, Journal of Organizational Behavior, Leadership Quarterly, Journal of Vocational Behavior*, and *Human Resource Management*. He is one of two Norwegian ambassadors to the HR Division of the Academy of Management and the Norwegian representative to the Cross-Cultural Collaboration on Contemporary Careers (5C) and an associate editor of *Human Resource Management Journal*.

Margie Elley-Brown is Senior Lecturer in Management at AUT University, Auckland, Aotearoa New Zealand. She has had a variety of career transitions in business and education prior to joining academia. Her doctoral research was impelled by her long-standing commitment to social and human capital formation and used hermeneutic phenomenology to explore the meaning of career for women working in education. She is particularly invested in creating platforms for women to tell their career stories, giving voice to their lived experiences: how do women find meaning in their careers?

Ariane Froidevaux is Assistant Professor of Management at the University of Texas at Arlington. She received her PhD in Psychology from the University of Lausanne, then worked as a postdoctoral researcher at the University of Florida. Her research interests include career transitions, aging and late-careers, and identity negotiation. She received the Award for Best Young Researcher by the European Society of Vocational Designing and Career Counseling (2017), the Michael Driver Best Applied Paper Award by the Academy of Management Careers Division (2015), and two Excellence Awards for her doctoral (2017) and Master (2012) dissertations by the University of Lausanne.

Marina Gianecchini (PhD, Business Management, University of Udine) is Associate Professor of Human Resource Management at the Department of Economics and Management at the University of Padova, Italy. She is Scientific Director of the Executive Master in Human Resource Management at CUOA Business School. Her main research interests regard career management and labour market dynamics. She is a member of the international research group 5C (Cross-Cultural Collaboration on Contemporary Careers), which aims at understanding meanings and determinants of career success around the world.

Jeffrey H. Greenhaus is Professor Emeritus of Management in Drexel University's LeBow College of Business. His research focuses on work-family relationships and career dynamics. He is the author of numerous journal articles and books, including most recently *Career Management for Life with Gerry Callanan and Ronnie Godshalk*, now in its fifth edition (Routledge, 2019), and *Making Work and Family Work: From Hard Choices to Smart Choices* with Gary Powell (Routledge, 2017).

Hugh Gunz is Professor Emeritus at the University of Toronto. He has published on the careers of managers, professionals and others, the management of professionals, and management education, has authored or co-authored monographs on career scholarship, and co-edited the 2007 Sage *Handbook of Career Studies*. He serves or has served on the editorial boards of a number of journals, including *Journal of Professions and Organization, Academy of Management Journal, Journal of Managerial Psychology*, and *Emergence*, is a former chair of the Careers Division of the Academy of Management and a co-convenor of a former EGOS Standing Working Group on careers.

Douglas T. (Tim) Hall is the Morton H. and Charlotte Friedman Professor of Management Emeritus in the Questrom School of Business at Boston University. He has held faculty positions at Yale, York, Michigan State, and Northwestern Universities, as well as visiting positions at Columbia, Minnesota, the US Military Academy at West Point, Boston College, the University of Canterbury (NZ), and the Center for Creative Leadership. His research deals with retirement, success, global careers, work-family dynamics, and leadership development.

Peter A. Heslin is Associate Professor of Management and UNSW Scientia Education Fellow at the UNSW Sydney Business School in Australia. His research focuses on self-regulatory dynamics (especially mindsets) in careers and leadership development. In collaboration with Lauren Keating and Sue Ashford, he recently developed and studies the concept of being "in learning mode" to enable experiential learning. He is a multi-award-winning executive educator who relishes facilitating leaders' discovering useful insights and competencies regarding their learning mode, responses to frustrations, employee development, career sustainability, and career success. He is Past Chair of the Academy of Management Careers Division.

Monica Higgins is the Kathleen McCartney Professor of Education Leadership at Harvard Graduate School of Education where her research and teaching focus on leadership, teaming, learning, and entrepreneurship. In addition to education, she has conducted research on the careers of leaders in other industries, including biotechnology, which culminated in a book called *Career Imprints: Creating Leaders Across an Industry*. Prior to academia, she held consulting positions with Bain & Company and Harbridge House. She earned her PhD in Organizational Behavior and MA in Psychology from Harvard University, her MBA from Tuck Business School, and her AB from Dartmouth College.

Andreas Hirschi, PhD, is a full professor and chair of the department of Work and Organizational Psychology at the University of Bern, Switzerland. He obtained his PhD from the University of Zurich and a post-master degree as Master of Advanced Studies in Psychology of Career Counseling and Human Resources Management from the Universities of Zurich, Berne, and Fribourg, Switzerland. He previously worked at the Pennsylvania State University, USA, the Leuphana University of Lueneburg, Germany, and at the University of Lausanne, Switzerland. His major research interests are career development, career counseling, and the work-nonwork interface.

Johanna Hofbauer is Associate Professor of Sociology at the Department of Socioeconomics and a member of the research institute 'Economics of Inequality' at WU Vienna in Austria. Her research focus lies on issues of power and domination in work organizations, with a particular emphasis on the theories of Pierre Bourdieu. A general concern for issues of gender inequality has more recently taken her to investigate public sector reform, for example in labor market agencies and higher education. Key issues of this research are the turn to managerialism and quantitative performance measurement, and their impact on working and career conditions.

Robert Kaše is Associate Professor of Management and Organization at the School of Business and Economics, University of Ljubljana. His research interests include social network, strategic HRM, talent management, careers, compensation and emergence. His work has been published in journals such as *Organization Science, Journal of Organizational Behavior, Human Resource Management, Human Resource Management Journal,* and *International Journal of Human Resource*

Management. He has served on editorial boards of several HRM journals and is a board member of the Slovenian HR Association.

Markus Latzke is Professor for Management at IMC University of Applied Sciences Krems. In one of his two main research areas he focuses on organizational learning, organizational culture and organizational change, especially in the context of health care management. His other field of research is in career studies, where he investigates individual and contextual influences on careers and career transitions. His work has been published in journals like *Human Relations, Health Care Management Review,* and *Journal of Vocational Behavior.*

Mila Lazarova (Beedie School of Business, Simon Fraser University) is the Canada Research Chair in Global Workforce Management. Her research interests include global careers, the role of organizational career development and mobility practices in organizations; repatriation and career impact of international assignments; and HR issues related to workplace integration of skilled migrants. She has published in journals such as the *Academy of Management Review, Journal of International Business Studies, Journal of World Business, Organizational Science, Journal of Organizational Behavior, Human Resource Management,* and *Human Resource Management Journal.* She is currently an associate editor at *Human Resource Management Journal* and sits on several editorial boards.

Wolfgang Mayrhofer is Full Professor and Head of the Interdisciplinary Institute of Management and Organisational Behaviour, WU Vienna, Austria. He previously has held full-time positions at the University of Paderborn, Germany, and at Dresden University of Technology, Germany. He conducts research in comparative international human resource management and careers, and systems theory and management and has received national and international awards for outstanding research and service to the academic community. He has widely published, serves as editorial or advisory board member of several international journals and research centres, and regularly consults with organizations in the for-profit and non-profit world.

Kevin McKouen is a doctoral candidate at the University of Wisconsin, Milwaukee. He holds a BS in mechanical engineering from Purdue University, West Lafayette, an MS in management from Rensselaer at Hartford, and an MA in humanities and social thought from New York University. In addition to studying expatriates and other global workers, his research interests include team diversity, constructive and destructive organizational behaviors, and adult attachments both within and outside of organizations.

Barbara Myers is Senior Research Lecturer in the Management Department at Auckland University of Technology. Her research and teaching philosophy centres on narrative storytelling methodologies. She believes there is real value in personal and organizational story telling to support wider business strategy, incorporating history and change into the way we look at a changing world of work. Core research interests include gender and diversity, aging, careers, and life development. Through her PhD on older women who have worked and travelled abroad, Barbara has identified changing views on what becoming "older" means and the possibilities and opportunities for how older people might live their lives differently.

Emma Parry is Professor of Human Resource Management and Head of the Changing World of Work Group at Cranfield School of Management. UK. She is also Visiting Fellow at Westminster Business School, Academic Fellow of the Chartered Institute of Personnel and Development

(CIPD) and Honorary Fellow of the Institute for Employment Studies (IES). Her research focuses on the impact of the changing external context on people management, particularly the influence of national context, technological advancement and workforce demographics. She has produced several books and papers on these topics.

Maury A. Peiperl, PhD FAcSS, is Dean of George Mason University's School of Business and author/editor of many works on careers, including the *Handbook of Career Studies* (with Hugh Gunz). He has published in *AMR, HBR, JIBS, JOM, HRM*, and *GOM*, and is co-author of the leading text *Managing Change* (with Todd Jick). Previously, he was Director of Cranfield School of Management, professor at IMD and LBS, and visiting faculty at MIT, Maryland, Georgetown, HEC Paris and Templeton College, Oxford. Earlier, he worked for IBM, Merrill Lynch, LEK Consulting and as a research fellow at Harvard, where he earned his MBA and PhD. He holds a BS in Engineering from Princeton.

Judith K. Pringle, Professor of Organisation Studies, initiator of the Gender and Diversity Research Group at Auckland University of Technology. Her research focuses on reframing career theory, workplace diversity, intersections of social identities (gender/ethnicity/sexuality/age). She is a co-editor and co-author of *Handbook of Research Methods on Diversity Management, Equality and Inclusion at Work* (2018), *Handbook for Workplace Diversity* (2006), and *The New Careers* (1999). She has published numerous book chapters and in journals including *Gender, Work and Organization, Sociological Review, British Journal of Management, Equality, Diversity and Inclusion*, and *Career Development International*. She is currently enjoying post paid work life.

B. Sebastian Reiche is Professor and Department Chair of Managing People in Organizations at IESE Business School. His research focuses on the forms, prerequisites and consequences of global work, international HRM, global leadership, and knowledge transfer, and has appeared in outlets such as *Journal of International Business Studies, Organization Science, Personnel Psychology, Journal of Management Studies*, and *Academy of Management Discoveries*. He is co-editor of *Readings and Cases in International Human Resource Management* (6th edition, Routledge) and *International Human Resource Management* (5th edition, Sage). He serves as associate editor of *Human Resource Management Journal*, co-editor of *Advances in Global Leadership*, and regularly blogs about global work (http://blog.iese.edu/expatriatus).

Lynette Reid is a senior lecturer in the School of Education at AUT University, New Zealand. She is of Ngati Konohi decent, is the eldest of her siblings, and is from a small community called Whangara. Whangara is located on the East Coast of the North Island of New Zealand. Each of these identities have a significant influence on her perspective of career. She is an active researcher who continues to have a strong focus on problematizing "career," using a Māori and interdisciplinary lens. She teaches at the undergraduate and postgraduate levels.

Iben Sandal Stjerne is Assistant Professor at Copenhagen Business School at Department of Organization. Her primary research focus is in the intersection between temporality, transient forms of organizing and temporality and human resource management. Her research publications explore the organizing and managing of careers, people and strategy in and across projects, which has primarily been studies in creative industries.

Eva Repovš is a PhD student and teaching assistant at the Entrepreneurship department at the University of Ljubljana, School of Economics and Business. She obtained her master's degree in management from the University of Ljubljana, focusing on careers. Her research interests include human capital, psychological capital, careers, entrepreneurship, and change management, with a current research focus on the role of contextual, cognitive and emotional aspects that shape employees' change readiness.

Marina A. Schmitz works as Research Associate and Lecturer at the Center for Advanced Sustainable Management (CASM) at the Cologne Business School. She also works for M3trix GmbH as Director of Analytics in various consulting projects on the topic of sustainability and transformation of business models. After graduating at the University of Trier in Business Administration and Sinology, she worked as a Research Associate at the Chair of Human Resources Management and Asian Business at the University of Goettingen. Her dissertation deals with the voluntary labor turnover phenomenon of Chinese factory workers.

Thomas M. Schneidhofer is currently Full Professor for HR, Management, and Organization at the Seeburg Castle University, Austria. Interested in Bourdieu's theory of practice, he studies careers from a relational perspective, with special emphasis on reconstructing careers as serious social games (currently: games of male and female midwives). He has published in journals such as the *Journal of Occupational and Organizational Psychology, Journal of Vocational Behavior*, and *Equality, Diversity and Inclusion* − an international journal.

Margaret A. Shaffer is the Michael F. Price Chair of International Business at the Price College of Business, University of Oklahoma. Her research interests are in the areas of global mobility, expatriation, and work-life interplay. Her publications have appeared in the *Academy of Management Review, Academy of Management Journal, Journal of Applied Psychology, Personnel Psychology, Journal of Management*, and *Journal of International Business Studies*. She is an associate editor for the *Journal of Global Mobility* and serves on several editorial boards.

Ahu Tatli is Professor of International Human Resource Management at Queen Mary University of London. She conducted research into equality and diversity at work for nearly two decades working with a number of practitioner bodies. Her current work focuses on understanding the workings of privilege in organizations and reproduction of status quo and potentials for agency towards progressive change. With her research, Ahu is particularly interested in contributing to the debate on intersectionality, privilege, equality and diversity through multi-layered sociological theorizing. Her research is widely published in academic journals, edited collections, and practitioner and policy outlets.

Soo Min Toh is Director and Associate Professor of organizational behavior and human resource management at the Institute for Management and Innovation, University of Toronto Mississauga, cross-appointed to the Rotman School of Management, and Professorial Fellow at the University of Edinburgh Business School. She received her PhD from Texas A&M University. Her research interests include cross-cultural management, leadership, and cooperation. She has published in the *Academy of Management Journal, Academy of Management Review, Journal of Applied Psychology*, and *Psychological Science*, and serves on the editorial board of the *Journal of International Business Studies*.

Jennifer Tosti-Kharas is Associate Professor of Organizational Behavior at Babson College. Her research program explores the psychological resources people draw upon to manage their work lives and careers over time, focusing in particular on the meaning of work, work as a calling, and work identity. Her work has appeared in outlets such as *Personnel Psychology, Journal of Vocational Behavior, Journal of Business Ethics*, and *Journal of Career Development*. She is currently co-editing the *Handbook for Research Methods in Careers*.

John Van Maanen is the Erwin Schell Professor of Organization Studies in the Sloan School of Management at MIT. He is an ethnographer of occupations and organizations focusing on socialization practices, careers and cultures. The settings in which he has worked include police organizations, fisheries, educational institutions, Disneylands, and business firms. He is the author of numerous articles and books including *Tales of the Field* (University of Chicago Press, 2011, 2nd edition) and, with Edgar Schein, *Career Anchors* (Wiley, 2013, 4th edition).

Beatrice Van der Heijden is Professor of Strategic HRM at the Radboud University, Institute for Management Research, Nijmegen, the Netherlands, and Head of the Department Strategic HRM. Moreover, she occupies chairs in SHRM at the Open University of the Netherlands, at Ghent University, Belgium, at Kingston University, London, UK, and at Hubei University, Wuhan, China. Her main research areas are sustainable careers, employability, and aging at work. She is associate editor for the *European Journal of Work and Organizational Psychology* and co-editor for the *German Journal of Human Resource Management*. She co-edited the *Handbook of Research on Sustainable Careers* (EE Publishing).

Itai Vardi is Lecturer in Sociology at the University of Massachusetts–Boston. He is interested in the sociology of science and technology and social problems. He is also a freelance journalist, whose writings appeared in such outlets as the *Guardian, Huffington Post*, and *Mother Jones*.

Yoav Vardi is retired from the Department of Labour Studies, Faculty of Social Sciences, Tel Aviv University where he served since 1980. He currently heads the Society and Behavior program at Ramat Gan College. Yoav received his PhD in organizational behavior from the ILR School at Cornell University in 1978. Since 1998 he holds a visiting professorship at the University of Ljubljana. His main areas of interest are organizational careers and organizational misbehaviour. He has published papers in the *Academy of Management Journal, Academy of Management Review, Organization Science, Psychological Reports*, and *Journal of Business Ethics*. In 2016 he co-authored *Misbehavior in Organizations: A Dynamic Approach*, published by Routledge.

Claartje J. Vinkenburg, PhD, is an independent expert consultant and researcher specialized in (gender) diversity in careers. Her area of expertise is careers in academia and professional service firms, where she looks at the impact of implicit bias, normative beliefs, and discursive practices on career patterns and outcomes. She spent 25 years studying and writing on this subject at Vrije Universiteit Amsterdam. She is committed to developing evidence-based interventions to promote diversity in organizations. Claartje is an affiliated research consultant with VU Amsterdam, Atria Institute for Gender Equality, and Portia Ltd.

Ivan Župić is Lecturer in Entrepreneurship at Kingston Business School, London. He received his PhD degree in Management and Organisation from the School of Economics and Business, University of Ljubljana. His research interests include digital economy, high-growth firms, entrepreneurial ecosystems, and research methods. His research has been published in peer-reviewed journals such as Organizational Research Methods, Management Decision, and European Management Journal. Before entering academia he worked as a consultant in the IT industry and as a journalist/photographer in the media.

Forward

What follows are a few brief remarks on career studies made visible by the sweeping array of state-of-the-art chapters that make up this ambitious handbook – the intention of which is to bring readers up to date on the how this broad and still widening field is more or less forming and progressing. I will leave it in the competent hands of the editors Hugh Gunz, Mila Lazarova and Wolfgang Mayrhofer in Chapters 1 and 2 to elaborate on the whys and wherefores behind the organization of this volume and to provide a crisp take on the varied roots and routes of career studies. While I will touch on themes developed in many of the chapters to follow, I purposely will not remark on any of the specific chapters, leaving it to the lively commentary that closes this volume put forth by former career studies handbook editors to weigh in on what they take away from the chapters and what it may mean going forward.

Since it has been over 10 years since the last handbook of this size appeared, I want to first quickly trace some of the unsettling shifts that have taken place in the career landscape of late that appear to have real social consequences. Second, I want to say something about what I see as a currently undervalued approach to career studies but needed in part to more precisely address some of the changes taking place. Third and last, I want to remind readers by way of a personal anecdote of the role chance and serendipity play as individual careers develop over time. It is a warning of sorts to treat theoretical notions related to agency and structure skeptically; as rather abstract concepts, of value certainly but always circumscribed by the way particular careers play out.

The changing context of careers

What is perhaps most salient and felt throughout the world is the decline and in some cases the utter demise of the bureaucratic and psychological contract in which employees traded off their labor for employment security. Jobs and hence work careers in organizations have become much less stable, predictable, and ordered. In the United States, this coincides with the plummeting of manufacturing and other well-paying working and middle class jobs, an issue that figured prominently in the rise of populist politics and the election of Donald Trump. Among other consequences, this has led to increased relevance of the occupational instead of the organizational context of careers.

Equally important has been the growth of contingent and project work, often part-time forms of employment tied to the completion of specific tasks and consequently of limited duration. Contingent work covers a variety of working situations including, for instance, independent contractors who are self-employed, temporary workers placed by staffing or temp agencies, and the rapidly growing – and latest addition the contingent work force – those spot workers of the "gig economy" who typically land jobs through online platforms. Estimates of

Americans holding at least one contingent and possibly two or three contingent jobs in parallel run anywhere from 15 to 30 percent. As contingent work expands, so too do project forms of organizing – in high tech industries, in consulting, in retail, in construction. We know little of the career experiences of those involved in these pursuits but we do know people are increasingly jumping from job to job, city to city as steady work becomes harder to find and hence the contingent workforce grows.

Relatedly, the financial meltdown of 2007 and 2008 followed by the ever so slow economic convalescence along with the all too visible growth in income inequality has led to a painful and bitter divide between the comfortable elites in society, the haves, and those struggling to make ends meet, the have-nots. Executive salaries and corporate profits soar while union membership and power decline and real wages remain stagnant or slump. As framed by the popular media, the vast majority of people, an envisioned 99 percent, feel they are losing ground to the 1 percent and are feeling vulnerable, precarious and angry as a result. The coming of a new Gilded Age in many Western societies seems to be on the horizon as social supports and safety nets are experienced as inadequate or seen as being dismantled piece by piece. In many regions around the world, higher education has become the great stratifier, the golden passport to the precious but few rewarding careers in society. But, apparent from the growing divide among economic classes, to achieve a position in top tier of wealth, power and status in society, it helps enormously to start there. Meritocracy may have begun as a way to combat privilege but has increasing become a mechanism for the transmission of wealth, power and status across generations.

Finally, I must mention the undeniable role that technology and the rise of artificial intelligence has played – and is playing – in shaping careers over the past decade. The rapid establishment of huge social media companies, the growth of so-called big data analytics along with statistical learning theory, and the ubiquity of smart phones and other hand held device has altered the way we communicate with one another, protect our privacy (or lack thereof) while allowing for the explosion of various forms of formal and informal networking organizations along with the invention of numerous instruments of mass deception ("fake news"). Economists point out that as a result of the increasing sophistication and proficiency of new technologies, jobs that used to go to men and women, now go to robots who never take a vacation, show up late, never slip or fall or file a sex or race discrimination case. Along with what we have now, such as fully automated oil rigs and robotic harvesting in agriculture, we may soon see the proliferation of clerk-free stores and self-driving trucks. Even where human labor or oversight is still required, technology marches on and it appears fewer and fewer people are needed each year to do these jobs. These changes in the employment realm, both realized and foreseen, are enough to bring the devil howling out his black hole.

And this is but a short list. I've not mentioned shifts in the career landscape as a result of corporate restructuring and aggregation (leading to monopolistic practices), the decay of large public and private institutions, climate change and the geographic relocations it necessitates, and massive human migrations taking place across national borders a result of war, extreme poverty or local violence. One disquieting concern associated with all the changes of the past several decades – but surprisingly little discussed by career researchers – is how will people make enough money in the post-industrial world to sustain a life, let alone a family? What are people to do when the available career paths and institutions no longer meet their needs?

Everett Hughes (1958) wisely observed that careers are not necessarily – or commonly – hierarchical nor need they be tied to paying jobs. Indeed, the homeless have careers as do down on their luck actors, poets and artists, freelance writers and web designers, itinerant academics and carpenters, and unemployed coal miners and auto mechanics. Careers are constructed within the varied social worlds in which an individual participates, whether that participation is by choice or not. In the not too distant future, contingent work as a main source of income or as a side hustle may well mark half of the American workforce. Lyft drivers, street vendors, E-Bay merchants, TaskRabbit operatives, seasonal workers of all sorts, cannot often count on a steady or sufficient income even when they are able somehow to construct the semblance of a career through such undertakings. These edgy and all too insecure work worlds cry out for sustained attention from both career researchers and policy makers. But we are unlikely to speak with knowledge and authority unless we have some close studies of these rapidly expanding pursuits. And here I have a modest suggestion.

Careers and culture

It seems that these days everyone has a culture – more likely, multiple cultures – from which to draw meaning. Thus we have accounts of pockets of culture as built, sustained and interrogated by Second Life enthusiasts, by doormen of the upper-east side in New York City, by beat patrolmen on the High Street in rural English villages, by the Masters of the Universe on Wall Street, by slick, youthful Silicon Valley entrepreneurs, and by those abducted by Martians but mercifully returned to us (curiously, only Americans are abducted). For ethnographers, for whom the study of culture is their raison d'être, this is a rather welcome development, expanding traditional fields of inquiry and opening up new ones.

For students of careers this is good news as well. Culture presumes membership and membership presumes careers – within and perhaps beyond cultural boundaries. But contemporary ethnographic perspectives on culture – both organizational and occupational – have shifted a good deal from the time the classic anthropological and sociological studies were conducted to the present. To wit, culture is represented today as far more open-ended, flexible, internally contested, less (and less) precisely situated in space and time, ambiguous and constantly reordering itself in the continually changing environment. This is rather well suited to the changing context of careers as put forth in the previous section. The notion of a coherent, homogeneous, stable and highly integrated culture – a sort of "cultural island" or "essentialist" view – is distinctly out of fashion (for good reason).

Partly as a result of these changes, we now live in what might be called a Cambrian period for ethnographic studies and an expanding number of lively (and, alas, dull) research monographs appear each year. Like any other social practice, ethnography doesn't remain the same because its topics, problems, facts, methods, theories, genres remain the same, but because in the midst of changes an audience still looks to it for the performance of a given task. In this case, the given task is the close study of culture as constructed and construed by particular people, in particular places, at particular times, doing particular things.

A number of career relevant ethnographic studies come to mind in this regard. They point of course to the problematic nature of such careers but also to the innovative ways ethnographers have stumbled on to study them. A few examples of recent vintage will have to suffice although there are many. Consider Shehzad Nadeem's (2013) close multi-organizational look at the way the outsourcing industry for call centers works and just how globalization has opened up new careers and opportunities (and lives) for young people in India that are full of both hope and disappointment. And Karen Ho's (2009) timely examination of the work of young Wall Street bankers and traders and the culture of greed associated with their positions is a superb example of a study of careers carried out in fierce competitive fields. Consider too Ofer Sharone's (2013) moving portrait of the troubled careers experienced by long-term unemployed workers in the United States and Israel. I am also particularly fond of Robin Nagel's (2013) study of a reviled occupation, garbage collecting. She convincingly shows how those in a vast and essential city bureaucracy – the New York Sanitation Department – manage to maintain their pride and dignity over the course of one of the few remaining long and stable careers while keeping the city clean, navigable and safe. Finally, consider Graham Jones's (2010) cunning investigation of the making of magicians in France and the career opportunities that open and close for them via his own hard earned attempts the master this trade of tricks.

As an ethnographer approaching the end of my tour of duty, I could easily add to this list of exemplary ethnographically informed career studies. My view is that ethnography is a logic, a stance if you will, rather than a given method or particular type of study. It calls out an epistemology – a way of knowing and the kind of knowledge that results. It is anything but a recipe. It involves fieldwork and results in a written representation of the cultural understandings held by others – meanings about work, about careers, about life – that are intimately tied to a specific context and are always provisional and partial. Moreover, ethnography is improvisational, not procedural. It is path-dependent because we learn more about the subjectivity and intentionality of those we encounter in the field after our work has begun and, the longer we are at it, the more we learn about what we need to learn next. Our knowledge accumulates and changes over time as we come closer to understanding the perspectives – the venerable if mythical "native's point of view" – of the people from whom we are learning.

I am struck however that ethnographic work of the sort I'm highlighting here is so often ignored, egregiously so, in what I take to be the mainstream career literature in organizational and management studies – at least in the research that shows up in journal article form where a variable and measurement approach is still so dominant. Yet a career, like a culture, is not a variable, it is a pattern and an increasingly complex one. Arguably, it is best and most faithfully evoked and made visible – if infrequently so – though lengthy, hard slogging fieldwork alongside those who enact the career. The logic is one of discovery, not verification. Thus, I issue a plea to career researchers of all sorts to be attentive to what organizational and occupational ethnographers have to say. Our cultural islands have been left far behind and many of us are deeply entangled in messy and changing work worlds – of Uber drivers, of lab scientists, of seasonal tax preparers – trying to bring back the news of what's happening in these worlds and how careers take shape within them.

On chance and contingency

Let me end this Forward by going backward. I'll conclude with a cautionary tale from my past told in the present. The unexpected journey I call my career began over 50 years ago when I came in 1965 to the then notably isolated, treeless, bare campus still under construction of the University of California, Irvine. A political science grad from Long Beach State, I came as a 22-year-old, uninspired "special student" in the social sciences ostensibly to sort out various inchoate career possibilities, avoid the draft, and perhaps hang out at the beach.

Worth noting is that I never applied to the school. In fact, I never applied to any graduate school including UCI. Wondering what I would do in the coming fall, I just more or less wandered on to the campus one day during the late summer and, by chance, met with some people who happened to be around, available and willing to spend a little time with me. Fortunately, among those with whom I met was the young dean of the brand new social science department, Jim March. We had what I recall as a delightful informal chat and, miraculously, I was told that very day that I could be admitted to the small, seemingly novel social science program designed by and large by Jim. Provisions were attached of course. I had to send on my undergraduate records, I had to take the GREs in October, and, left unsaid, I was to pass whatever classes I was to take in the coming fall. All very casual, informal and impossible to imagine today.

Little did I know at the time that this was a daring and one-off experimental program – one without a history or disciplinary boundaries. The first year got me reading, taught me some basic probability and statistics and left me slightly computer literate. The following year the Graduate School of Administration opened and initiated a master's degree program. Five students enrolled, myself included, and five managed to graduate two years later. Four went on to useful public and private management careers but I figured I'd stick around and once again try a new program, this time a PhD program. Needless to say, this was a highly consequential choice, for the program as I experienced it as a cohort of one was nothing less than a free fall into an esoteric scholarly world that shaped the vocation and way of life I've been following ever since.

Let me pause and use this occasion of 'serendipitous happenstance' as an example of the role of luck or chance plays in life and the careers we follow. It plays I would argue a far, far greater role than most people recognize. Had I come a day or an hour earlier or later, I might not have met with Jim March or had the university been more advanced in its bureaucratic procedures, I never would have been admitted. The roll of the dice certainly turned in my favor. But I realize most people don't like to hear of success – especially their own – explained away as luck. There is a strong hindsight bias to think after the fact that an event – in this case, my career – was predictable even when it wasn't. There are no counterfactuals to tell us what would have happened had I not been so lucky at various points in my career. Of course, most of us are vividly aware of how hard we work and the difficult problems we face, but our day-to-day environment provides few reminders of how fortunate we are to have not been born in Northern Nigeria or Outer Mongolia or some remote Appalachian hollow. Or, to put forth another example, how fortunate we have been to have had access to an exceptional teacher, coach, or friend steering us the right direction.

Our personal career narratives are biased in another way as well. Events that work to our disadvantage are rather easier to recall than those that affect us in a positive way. A runner's sense of headwinds and tailwinds is helpful here. We are acutely aware and struggle against headwinds. But, when the winds are at our back, we're largely unaware of them – being pushed along by invisible and largely unheeded forces. If I were more conscious of the tailwinds at my back, such an awareness would bring to light that throughout my career I've been blessed with a privileged institutional position: Light teaching loads, enormous intellectual help from patient colleagues who were – and are – supportive of my work; small classes; superb graduate students full of energy and wonder; generous leave policies; relatively easy access to grants and fellowship that allowed me to pursue my research interests wherever they led (even if straight into a writer's block). These are indulgences, the tailwinds pushing me onward. Had I been at another institution or even at MIT some 10 or 20 years later, there might have been more pressure, sooner, to "cut to the chase" and submit to the sort of normal science that the publish-or-perish academic world of today demands, I might well have done very different work. These intergenerational and institutional differences are real and I recognize that my career – like all careers – developed in a rather specific time and place with advantages that were and are, sadly, hardly widespread.

The biases I've highlighted here work to overestimate our own role in whatever success we achieve. Most personal histories of the sort I am displaying here almost certainly exaggerate the casual significance of the individual. True, overlooking the part chance or luck plays in life may be (perversely) adaptive – encouraging us to work hard, carry on and fight in the face of challenges. But, turning a blind eye to the role chance plays, serves also to make personal narratives of career success highly unreliable. Success stories based on an n of one are something of an exercise in imagination. History does not run controlled experiments. Career histories retrospectively link rather vague and uncertain intentions to specified and realized outcomes when, in between the two, are a multitude of contingencies at play.

At the same time however I would be remiss were I not to mention the real work that goes into successful careers and, paradoxically, the effort we put into hiding such work. Along with Malcolm Gladwell (2008), I hold that success is largely a matter of grit or following a rule that says becoming proficient at anything takes dedication and practice – be it archery, surgery, or ethnography. Yet, invariably, we seem to chalk up success to talent: Some have it, some don't. The cognitive bias here says that "natural talent" in the end trumps effort and hard work. One function of such a bias is to avoid ever having to say in the presence of accomplished practitioners: "There but for the grace of grit go I."

The partiality that is displayed for so-called natural talent however encourages many of us to cover up all the laborious, time-consuming, and potentially embarrassing effort we put into getting good at what we do. For example, I still have something of deep terror of anyone seeing my half-written, grammatically flawed, poorly reasoned, cringe worthy drafts of paper thus perpetuating the myth that I am a natural at what I do – *the rightful words and bon mots just fly out folks, as fast as I can type.* The truth of the matter is that they come fitfully, woodenly thus obscuring the amount of failure that goes into success. Such predilections make for confusing career advice: "Try hard enough and you can do anything but don't let anyone know that you are trying so hard."

With these human foibles in mind, let me as a way of closing out this prologue remind you dear readers that what follows is based on the murky but optimistic premise that there is a structure to the world. Or, to be more specific to our career interests, an organizational and occupational order. Moreover, the concepts we develop to decode this order promise to bring forth understandings that will help us act wisely and knowledgeably in the world. But remember too what the playful ghost of Everett Hughes might say: That when all is said and done and we are all properly admonished as to the infinite complexity of our social world and its ever-changing workings, the precepts and assurances of our intellectual fields appear rather fragile and weak and thus we must always return to the flickering, messy, cross-purposed, unknown and unknowable surroundings and circumstances that our empirical and analytic work seeks to tame. Words – and the concepts they carry – will hardly hold back the wind. But we continue to try. Read on.

John Van Maanen

References

Gladwell, M. 2008. *Outliners: The Story of Success.* New York: Little Brown.

Ho, K. 2009. *Liquidated: An Ethnography of Wall Street.* Durham, NC: Duke University Press.

Hughes, E.C. 1958. Cycles, turning points and career. *In:* E.C. Hughes (ed.) *Men and Their Work.* Glencoe, IL: Free Press, 11–22.

Jones, G. 2011. *Trade of the Tricks: Inside the Magician's Craft.* Berkeley: University of California Press.

Nadeem, S. 2013. *Dead Ringers: How Outsourcing in Changing the Way Indians Understand Themselves.* Princeton, NJ: Princeton University Press.

Nagel, R. 2013. *Picking Up: On the Streets and Behind the Trucks with the Sanitation Workers of New York City.* New York: Farrar, Straus and Giroux.

Sharone, O. 2013. *Flawed System/Flawed Self: Job Searching and Unemployment Experiences.* Chicago: University of Chicago Press.

Preface

It is now over 10 years since the last handbook on career studies was published, and a lot has happened both to the world and to the field since then. So when we were approached by Routledge to see whether we had any publishing projects in mind, the notion of a new handbook – this *Companion* – sprang immediately to mind. Of course, a reasonable observer might be tempted to enquire into the soundness of such a mind. Most normal people would regard a sensible time frame for editing a volume like this as perhaps once or twice per millennium, and each member of the putative editorial team had more than used up their quota in this respect. But as has been noted elsewhere, normal people are harder to find than you'd think. So here we go (again).

Actually, editing a work such as this is quite a privilege. There aren't many opportunities that one has to be able to collaborate with some of the best people in one's field to shape, in however minor a way, its development. So when such an opportunity arises, it's hard, foolish even, to resist the temptation to grab it with both hands. And in this case, it has been an absolute delight to be able to work on the project.

That said, what are the aims of this volume? To quote our commissioning editor at Routledge, *Companions* "provide a thematic overview of the current state of the discipline, including newly emerging areas. When taken as a whole, the chapters should cover all the key topics within the field." That is a pretty steep hill to climb. In essence, the book should arrogate to itself the right to enunciate what the key topics are in the field of career studies. This, of course, implies a clear understanding of what belongs in the field, what doesn't, and which of the topics that belong in the field are key.

As we note in Chapter 1, in a field such as career studies in which there is little consensus about what really matters most and how it all fits together, any attempt to suggest such a structure for that field is bound to be the source of substantial controversy. But that is pretty much what comes with the job of volume editor when laying out the architecture for a book of this kind. In this case we decided to structure the book around four themes: (1) the enterprise of studying careers; (2) examining careers as developing entities; (3) the contexts in which careers develop; and (4) in the light of all this, what might one do about careers? We also decided to invite editors of previous volumes in what we think of as this series to comment on the material in the book. More of all that in Chapter 1.

Then we were faced with the invidious task of selecting a set of authors to invite. In any project like this, there are too few slots for far too many scholars who have contributed greatly to the field; there are so many able colleagues we would have liked to bring in but simply weren't able to. Conversely, we were gratified by the generous responses of those we *were* able to invite, all of whom are busy people with a million other calls on their time. Invariably they reacted with alacrity, making it easy to assemble an outstanding team of contributors. Not only that, but each writing team proved themselves ready and willing to accede to our no doubt seemingly endless requests for revisions. It was evident that everyone wanted their chapters not only to be the best they could be, but also a good fit with the aims of the *Companion* as a whole. There's a well-worn saying about managing academics being like herding cats; if that's so, then we were privileged to have assembled an amazingly helpful and supportive herd of cats. Actually, one aspect of the team that may mark it out for distinction is that not one but two chapters were written by parent-child pairings. We leave it to you, the reader, to figure out who they are. In sum, we owe each member of our authorial team a very great debt of gratitude. Thank you for all your hard work. Without it, this project could never have become a reality.

There are many others whom we need to thank. Several anonymous referees provided valuable feedback on our proposal. Any failure on our part to implement all of the excellent suggestions we received should be seen in the same light as our inability to include everyone we would have liked to invite as authors. Natalie Thompson at Routledge played a key role as commissioning editor in nurturing the project in its early stages and taking us through the process of getting it ready for Routledge's editorial board, for which we are most grateful. Her able assistants Nicola Cupit, Izzy Fitzharris, and Judith Lorton did a wonderful job of keeping things on the rails, as did Lucy McLune, who subsequently took over from Natalie, and Rebecca Marsh and Sophie Peoples saw the book through its closing stages. Michaela Schreder and Gisela Ullrich-Rosner from ivm at WU Wien were always more than willing to go the extra mile when dealing with the inevitable broad variety of subjective views about what are formally correct citations and chapter headers and tirelessly and in good humor hunted for corrections. An enormously big thank you goes to both of them.

All writing projects like this come at great cost to the families of everyone involved. We owe our spouses – Elizabeth Badley, Gancho Armianov, and Andrea Mayrhofer – a debt of gratitude for their tolerance and support while we postponed real life and, in HG's case something resembling a proper retirement, in order to complete the project.

Finally, editing this volume has also been a lot of fun. Given the scholarly nature of this publication, it is probably a good idea not to go into any detail about the frivolity that accompanied the various forms of electronic communication that were used to keep the project on track, more or less. Suffice it to say that we are uncomfortable about having to put the names of the editors in any kind of order, partly because "order" is rather a strong term to use to describe the way the team operated, but more importantly because nobody's contribution was more important than anyone else's (and indeed each of us is convinced that the others' contributions were much more significant). So the order of the names is strictly alphabetic.

HG
ML
WM
Toronto, Vancouver, and Vienna

1
Career studies
A continuing journey

Hugh Gunz, Mila Lazarova, and Wolfgang Mayrhofer

Those who study career come from a very broad set of disciplines and interests. Indeed careers have been a central interest of people in general, probably since humans emerged as sentient beings. For much if not most of humankind, this interest springs from the existential question: who am I? Particularly in what Max Weber labels more traditional societies – but not only there – it can be boiled down to the more straightforward question: where do I come from? Increasingly, though, it also leads in a different direction, towards reflection on the question: what is my life story? How has what has happened to me and what I have done made me what I am today? And this, in turn, leads to reflection on career.

A brief history

Career means many different things to different people. In this *Companion*, our focus is on the study of work career in its richness and complexity, with particular reference to careers associated with organizations and their management. Much of the interest in looking at work careers can be traced to the contributions of an influential group of Chicago sociologists, in particular those working with Everett Hughes, who brought the study of people's stories to the social sciences (Barley, 1989). Their accounts of the life histories of inhabitants of Chicago – ordinary people, often but not always those living at the edges of society – introduced concepts to sociology such as "career contingencies (Becker, 1953b), career timetables (Roth, 1963), and career lines (Hughes, 1937, 1958)" (ibid.: 45). These, in turn, involved linking the concept of career to the social structures within which the careers were lived. But the rise in interest also has a lot to do with two groups, one "mainly based in Boston at institutions such as MIT and Harvard, and led by figures such as Edgar Schein and Donald Super, and . . . [one] organized by George Milkovich at Cornell" (Gunz and Peiperl, 2007a: 5).

These two North American groups, together with others in Europe for example (e.g., Sofer, 1970; Eckardstein, 1971; Bauer and Cohen, 1981; Berthel and Koch, 1985; Gerpott, 1988) inspired a burgeoning literature on careers, in particular those of members of organizations and those who manage the organizations. By 1989 the editors of the first handbook on career scholarship (Arthur et al., 1989a) were observing that "career theory has 'gone legitimate'. We (people who study careers) have become established. We have become a *field*" (Arthur et al., 1989b: xv, emphasis in the original).

Others have questioned the nature of this field, or rather, what it means to talk about the "field of career studies." As Moore et al. (2007) suggest, scholarly social science interest in career can be traced to at least three streams in the literature – in the fields of sociology, developmental psychology, and vocational psychology – each bringing with it a particular approach to understanding career. These streams reach back a long way to figures such as Freud, Weber, and even Cicero, and have a lot to do with why it is that there are so many literatures on career. It also explains why, although scholars contributing to the literature tend to be somewhat aware that the others exist, they spend very little time interacting with each other. We raise this point not because the issue of the multidisciplinary origins of career studies is specifically addressed in the present volume, but because it is important to note that these multidisciplinary origins are closely related to the divisions that run through the field. There are, in fact, several fields that on the surface one would expect to be closely allied with the work of organization and management scholars but which in practice are not. For example, the vast and complex vocational psychology literature is the principal focus of only one chapter of this book (Chapter 20), and the equally large life course literature makes little appearance (nor does "career" appear much in the life course literature: Mortimer and Shanahan, 2003; Shanahan et al., 2016).

That there are divisions in the field is not a new observation. Edgar Schein, one of the seminal contributors to the study of careers in organizational settings, observes:

> What is most amazing to me is that when I got into the field in the late '50s there was almost zero overlap between the psychologists (Strong, Super, Osipow, Holland) and the sociologists (Hughes, Becker, Goffman, White). . . . Hughes and the sociologists were working on careers as they are lived and had literally no overlap with Super, Osipow, and others who were completely focused on the Strong Interest Inventory and trying to predict, like good psychologists, who would be suitable for what kind of career and, based on psychometric and interview data who would succeed (usually measured narrowly by income). . . . Not a single reference in either group to the other group. This state of affairs led to my paper, "The Individual, the Organization and the Career," which I believe broke the ice and started some thinking about psychological contracts and how organizations (work) and individuals each have to take the other into account.
>
> *(E.H. Schein, personal communication, January 13, 17, 2005;*
> *cited in Moore et al., 2007: 21)*

This gulf between disciplines with an interest in career is one that has been repeatedly commented on, lamented even, since then – nor is it the only one (Chapter 2).

The question of whether the study of career is a field in itself or just a label that is used by scholars from many different disciplines stretching from the social sciences to the humanities (Arthur et al., 1989c) has been widely discussed and probably will continue to be so for as long as social scientists in particular retain their interest in people's life stories. Indeed the matter of what the word "career" means has been debated extensively; we shall not get into this debate here, although it is addressed in Chapter 2 of this volume. For now we should return to the stream of literature that sprang from the work of the Chicago sociologists, that grew as a result of the contributions of, for example, the Boston and Cornell groups and that was landmarked by the 1989 handbook edited by Michael Arthur, Tim Hall, and Barbara Lawrence. For convenience, and following Gunz and Mayrhofer (2018), we shall refer to the focus of this stream of research as "organization and management careers" (OMC).

The 1989 handbook proved highly influential, providing a springboard for increasing interest in the OMC field over the following decades. The 1980s saw historic upheavals on a global scale, for example the collapse of the Soviet Union and its subservient administrations across Eastern and Central Europe. Immense change in corporate structures had profound effects on the lives of the people working for these corporations. By the 1990s an influential school of thought within OMC was pointing to the changing nature of career boundaries (Arthur and Rousseau, 1996), and many writers were claiming that the organizational career was now dead (e.g., Hall, 1996). Although this view was not universally accepted (e.g., Rodrigues and Guest, 2010; Jacoby, 1999), it was evident by the early 2000s not only that the OMC field had become more established, but that the issues being discussed in it were substantially different from those in the 1989 handbook. That in turn led to the publication of a second handbook (Gunz and Peiperl, 2007b) that attempted to provide an overview of the state of the field as it was in 2007, nearly 20 years after the production of the first such publication. Almost simultaneously, an encyclopedia covering OMC and much more was published (Greenhaus and Callanan, 2006), further cementing the position of the field within organization studies generally.

Almost immediately after these two volumes were published – the 2006 encyclopedia and 2007 handbook – the world changed drastically.[1] First came the international financial catastrophe of 2008, and then the lengthy economic recovery that followed and its accompanying growth in inequality. By 2016 it became painfully evident in a series of unexpected political events that those left behind by globalization and many others who, though largely unaffected nevertheless feared its effects, were easily persuaded that this was leading their countries to disaster. They proved highly responsive to the wild claims of demagogues and populists, whose appeal was enhanced by the largest displacement of people across national borders since the Second World War. During the following two years, in an unsettling echo of the events in 1930s Europe, impervious national boundaries started to become reasserted and concern grew about the future of the world economic and political order. In addition, the extraordinary technological change during the past decade, involving for example the appearance of now ubiquitous handheld information technology (IT) devices, the establishment of social media and big data analysis, and the growth of artificial intelligence, has transformed the way people communicate, their privacy, and the way social movements and polities grow and change. This combination of a long period of economic growth and political and social upheaval sets the scene for the present volume. First, these changes mean that the context of careers has changed considerably. Second, they have had substantial impact on the academic world in many ways. The consequence has been a noticeable shift in the character of work within the OMC field from the broad, almost encompassing coverage of researchers such as the Chicago sociologists to approaches that focus on a narrower range of perspectives (Schein, 2007; Gunz and Mayrhofer, 2018: 130–145).

It seemed to us, the editors, that the world has changed so much since 2007 that it was well worth the effort to examine what has happened to the OMC field. Add to that a generational change involving the emergence of a new and very productive international cohort of OMC researchers and the need to revisit the 2007 *Handbook of Career Studies* became even more salient.

Handbooks such as this provide an opportunity for scholars deeply embedded in the field to reflect on its state as they see it and consider what that might mean for its future. This kind of book provides a useful reference point for other scholars in the field and those interested in joining it, a collective statement about what the field is in the view of some of its leading scholars and what is interesting to them about it. Of course, the choice of subjects is inevitably a personal one reflecting the views of the editors, and anyone in this role is acutely aware that their choices – of approach, range of topics, and authors – is theirs alone. Given that compendia of writing in the careers field rarely if ever overlap much in their choice of topics (Peiperl and

Gunz, 2007), it would be surprising if there would be much agreement that the subjects covered in, for example, this volume, were the right ones. Many readers will be baffled that certain topics were left out and others included. But, of course, publishers place limits on how long these works can be, so choices have to be made. And in a field that has been described as a "fragmented adhocracy" (Whitley, 1984) – one in which there is no consensus around a central organizing theoretical framework, nor any around which topics matter most – there is no basis for agreement across the field on what should be in a handbook, what shouldn't, and how it should be organized. Each group of editors makes their own choices and hopes that they have not upset too many of their colleagues in the process.

The choices we made were based on a five-part concept. First, we wanted the book to examine the nature of career and the approaches, theoretical and methodological, that affect the development of its study. Next, it should consider the processual side of career: how career choices are made, where careers lead, and what affects the routes people take during their careers. Then, as careers are always careers in context (Mayrhofer et al., 2007), it needed to examine context at several levels of analysis from organizational to global. We also thought it important to bring the focus closer to praxis: in the light of all this research, what can people do about their careers, and about the careers of the members of their organization or even the citizens of their country? Finally, we wanted to find a way of reflecting on the volume as a whole.

That was the basis of the brief that we invited our authors to consider: what has changed in their particular subfield within OMC, and what in their view does this mean for the future of that sub-field? Where do they see it going? Furthermore, given the extraordinary level of change to which we refer above, we decided to invite an international group of authors who were in the early to middle stage of their careers rather than established "senior" academics, because we wanted this volume to be the product of those who have been and are closest to the changes that are happening, who are now shaping and will continue to shape the field over at least the next decade and possibly much longer. It didn't turn out like this in every case; there are some areas of the field which have not yet attracted the interest of early career stage scholars. However, that was our basic approach as we invited contributions to this volume. Next, we briefly preview the material in each of the book's parts.

Overview of the handbook

The book is in five parts.

Part I, "Studying Careers," develops the idea to which we refer above, namely that career studies, even when defined as OMC, has attracted a broad range of disciplinary and theoretical approaches. It begins (Chapter 2) by examining the concept of career and what is involved in its study; that is, what do career researchers do? It moves on to look at the range of theory that is invoked in the study of career (Chapter 3), drawing on the oft-noted point that career as a phenomenon bridges micro- and macro-levels of analysis. Subsequent chapters examine what can be learned about careers by reviewing the approaches of different disciplines (Chapter 4), the contribution of the agency-structure debate to the study of careers (Chapter 5), how diversity provides a useful perspective to the field (Chapter 6), and the range of methodologies that researchers employ (Chapter 7).

Part II, "Developing Careers," addresses a range of issues to do with the processual side of career. Although, as we see in Chapter 2, there are many approaches taken in the literature to defining career, there is a general consensus that a key element of career is that of time: careers are things that take place over time. The time in question may be the individual's lifespan (or lifespan to date), the time they spend working in a particular occupation or profession, or in a particular organization. But if what is being studied does not play out over time, it is not a career. So the chapters in Part II address many aspects of this temporal feature of career, starting with a direct examination of how time is approached in a range of literatures and what implications these differing approaches might have for the study of career (Chapter 8). Subsequent chapters examine the process of choosing an occupation (Chapter 9), the many different ways in which career outcomes can be conceptualized and measured (Chapter 10), the various intrapersonal (Chapter 11) and extrapersonal (Chapter 12) antecedents that might affect these career outcomes, the role of mentorship and development networks in career development (Chapter 13), the consequences for organizations of the way in which careers within them are managed (Chapter 14), the various career patterns that emerge as a result of these various career processes (Chapter 15), and the possibility that not all careers, or not all of any given career, may be positive experiences – the dark side of careers (Chapter 16).

Part III, "Contextualizing Careers," addresses a point that has been made many times, albeit without as much impact as it arguably should have, namely that careers are always lived in context. They involve a path through space, both geographical and social. Not only does the context shape the path, but careers themselves shape the social spaces through which they are made. Chapter 17 addresses this from an organizational perspective, examining how careers are affected by the institutions in and through which they are acted out, and how in turn careers affect the institutions. The following two chapters take an international perspective. Chapter 18 looks at recent research that questions universalistic assumptions about careers in given occupations and describes ways in which they may in fact vary from one national context to another. Chapter 19 analyzes global careers specifically: what they are, how they vary, and where they lead.

Part IV, "Implementing Career Research: Interventions," moves from the analytical stance in Parts I–III to the prescriptive: what does the literature say about what can be done about careers? It begins with the class of intervention that most people will probably think of most immediately when they are concerned with their career: career counseling (Chapter 20). Chapter 21 maintains the focus on the individual, reviewing the many ways in which people can be taught about career issues, and the learning processes that are involved. Next, the focus turns to the organizational level of analysis: the human resource management and other organizational policies and practices that are available to manage the career flows of employees. Chapter 22 shows how career management systems can be aligned with organizations' career and leadership development policies and practices. Finally, Chapter 23 moves to the national level, addressing the question: what happens when national governments adopt policies that are intended to direct the movement of people in their country, and what can go wrong?

Part V, "Commentary," concludes the volume. We noted earlier that the authors we invited to contribute chapters to the book are largely drawn from the ranks of scholars in early and mid-career. We thought that it might make an intriguing conclusion to invite some of our old friends and colleagues, namely those who have preceded us in this ongoing journey of drawing together the threads of the field of career studies, to share with our readership their thoughts on the present volume. So we invited the editors of the 1989 and 2007 handbooks, and the 2006 encyclopedia, to meet and discuss the chapters that had been contributed to this handbook. This distinguished group – Michael Arthur, Gerald Callanan, Jeff Greenhaus, Tim Hall, Barbara Lawrence, and Maury Peiperl – met with two of the present editors (Hugh Gunz, who for the purposes of the exercise overlooked the fact that he had co-edited with Maury the 2007 handbook, and Wolfgang Mayrhofer). The lively discussion of all former editors led to a decision that some members of the group would reflect and comment on what they saw in the chapters and what they thought this meant for the future of the field. The chapters comprising Part V are the results of those reflections.

We noted earlier how much the world has changed since the last handbook was published. We suspect that it will keep changing in very much the same way in the decade to follow. As we go to press, much of the world is consumed by threats to its democracies and to the global order coming from the forces to which we briefly allude together with many others. Not the least of these is, of course, global climate change. We are just beginning to really notice its impact. In a decade or so, unless something extraordinary happens to the will of the world's politicians, even larger-scale population shifts may be in progress than now, driven by the increasing uninhabitability of currently highly populated regions and accompanying damage to national economies (and none of this takes into account the increasing risks of catastrophic runaway climate change).

To quote the old cliché, forecasting is a hazardous process, especially when it involves the future. That said, the world that will provide the context for the next handbook, assuming that career studies continues to fascinate and absorb as it does now, is likely to be as different a place, if not more different, from the present than the present is from 2007. What all of these shifts imply for careers by the time of the next handbook is impossible to imagine, but it is equally impossible to imagine that they will account for nothing. We hope that the ideas in this *Companion* will provide a springboard to new thinking about careers, about how the world shapes careers and they, in turn, reshape the world, and that this thinking will play at least some part in preparing for the changes to come.

Note

1 We do not think it very likely that the books were responsible for this change; but adherents to the butterfly effect (attributed to the mathematical meteorologist E.N. Lorenz) might differ on this.

References

Arthur, M.B., Hall, D.T. & Lawrence, B.S. (eds.) 1989a. *Handbook of Career Theory*. Cambridge: Cambridge University Press.

Arthur, M.B., Hall, D.T. & Lawrence, B.S. 1989b. Preface. *In:* Arthur, M.B., Hall, D.T. & Lawrence, B.S. (eds.) *Handbook of Career Theory*. Cambridge: Cambridge University Press.

Arthur, M.B., Hall, D.T. & Lawrence, B.S. 1989c. Generating new directions in career theory: The case for a transdisciplinary approach. *In:* Arthur, M.B., Hall, D.T. & Lawrence, B.S. (eds.) *Handbook of Career Theory*. Cambridge: Cambridge University Press.

Arthur, M.B. & Rousseau, D.M. (eds.) 1996. *The Boundaryless Career: A New Employment Principle for a New Organizational Era*. New York and Oxford: Oxford University Press.

Barley, S.R. 1989. Careers, identities, and institutions: The legacy of the Chicago school of sociology. *In:* Arthur, M.B., Hall, D.T. & Lawrence, B.S. (eds.) *Handbook of Career Theory*. Cambridge, England: Cambridge University Press.

Bauer, M. & Cohen, E. 1981. *Qui Gouverne les Groupes Industriel?* Paris: Seuil.

Berthel, J. & Koch, H-E. 1985. *Karriereplanung und Mitarbeiterförderung*. Stuttgart: Expert Taylorix.

Eckardstein, D.V. 1971. *Laufbahnplanung für Führungskräfte*. Berlin: Duncker & Humblot.

Gerpott, T.J. 1988. *Karriereentwicklung von Industrieforschern*. Berlin et al.: de Gruyter.

Greenhaus, J.H. & Callanan, G.A. (eds.) 2006. *Encyclopedia of Career Development*. Thousand Oaks, CA: Sage Publications.

Gunz, H. & Mayrhofer, W. 2018. *Rethinking Career Studies: Facilitating Conversation Across Boundaries with the Social Chronology Framework*. Cambridge: Cambridge University Press.

Gunz, H. & Peiperl, M. 2007a. Introduction. *In:* Gunz, H. & Peiperl, M. (eds.) *Handbook of Career Studies*. Thousand Oaks, CA: Sage Publications.

Gunz, H. & Peiperl, M. (eds.) 2007b. *Handbook of Career Studies*. Thousand Oaks, CA: Sage Publications.

Hall, D.T. 1996. *The Career Is Dead – Long Live the Career: A Relational Approach to Careers*. San Francisco: Jossey–Bass Publishers.

Jacoby, S.M. 1999. Are career jobs headed for extinction? *California Management Review*, 42, 123–145.

Mayrhofer, W., Meyer, M. & Steyrer, J. 2007. Contextual issues in the study of careers. *In:* Gunz, H. & Peiperl, M. (eds.) *Handbook of Career Studies*. Thousand Oaks, CA: Sage Publications.

Moore, C., Gunz, H.P. & Hall, D.T. 2007. Tracing the historical roots of career theory in management and organization studies. *In:* Gunz, H.P. & Peiperl, M.A. (eds.) *Handbook of Career Studies*. Thousand Oaks, CA: Sage Publications.

Mortimer, J.T. & Shanahan, M.J. (eds.) 2003. *Handbook of the Life Course*. New York: Kluwer Academic Publishers.

Peiperl, M. & Gunz, H. 2007. Taxonomy of career studies. *In:* Gunz, H. & Peiperl, M. (eds.) *Handbook of Career Studies*. Thousand Oaks, CA: Sage Publications.

Rodrigues, R.A. & Guest, D. 2010. Have careers become boundaryless? *Human Relations*, 63, 1157–1175.

Schein, E.H. 2007. Career research: Some issues and dilemmas. *In:* Gunz, H. & Peiperl, M. (eds.) *Handbook of Career Studies*. Thousand Oaks, CA: Sage Publications.

Shanahan, M.J., Mortimer, J.T. & Kirkpatrick Johnson, M. (eds.) 2016. *Handbook of the Life Course*. New York: Springer.

Sofer, C. 1970. *Men in Mid-Career*. Cambridge: Cambridge University Press.

Whitley, R.D. 1984. The development of management studies as a fragmented adhocracy. *Social Science Information / Information sur les Sciences Sociales*, 23, 775–818.

Part I
Studying careers

2

The concept of career and the field(s) of career studies

Hugh Gunz, Wolfgang Mayrhofer, and Mila Lazarova

Introduction

In this chapter we briefly explore the concept of career. It is a commonplace to say that career is a concept that is found almost everywhere in the social sciences, not to mention a substantial part of the humanities. Arthur et al. (1989) list psychology, economics, sociology, demography, organization studies, anthropology, political science, history, and geography as disciplines in which careers are studied; Moore et al. (2007) trace the origins of the field of organizational careers to what they call sociological, vocational, and developmental streams, each with its own distinct literature. Careers appear in the humanities, too, most obviously in history in terms of the lives of historic figures, in biography, and so on. On top of that, since everyone has a career, there is a vast industry publishing advice on how to navigate that career successfully. Perhaps not surprisingly, then, the term "career" gets used in many different senses – Hall (2002: 8) refers to it as "suffer[ing] from surplus meaning" – so it is important that we are clear about how we use it in this chapter.

We begin by touching on two issues fundamental to our task: how career is conceptualized, and the question of whether it is possible to define a "field" in which it is studied. In so doing, and in much of what follows here, we draw on Gunz and Mayrhofer (2018).

Career

So what is this "thing" called "career"[1] that is studied and written about in so many different places? It is clearly something to do with a person's passage through life, although the life course literature (Mortimer and Shanahan, 2003; Shanahan et al., 2016) rarely uses the term. It is connected in the minds of many with work, as in the "work career" (although "work" is rarely used as a qualifier), yet an important thread within this research tradition attends to the relationship between work and *non*-work (e.g., Greenhaus and Foley, 2007; Chapter 25, this volume). It is often used, sometimes disparagingly, in an evaluative sense as in someone being "career-minded," meaning that they are ambitious and have an eye to their future. This sense of future-mindedness, of career as the future that is the consequence of decisions and actions taken now, is central to the vast vocational literature, directed at understanding how to help people make sense of their careers and make choices about addressing their future. It can refer to a part of a work life, as in someone's career as a student or a professional football player, a whole work life (something that is becoming harder to define with precision as, for example, retirement becomes a more complex experience; Sargent et al., 2013), or even the entire lifespan (Hughes, 1958; Sullivan and Baruch, 2009). The term can also have strong connections with certain kinds of occupation, as when careers are thought to be something that, for example, professionals, executives, artists or professional sportspeople have but ordinary working people do not.

Hall (2002) captures much of this profusion of perspective in four distinct meanings of the term: career as (1) advancement; (2) profession; (3) a lifelong sequence of jobs; and (4) a lifelong sequence of role-related experiences. The distinction between the third and fourth meanings rests on the well-established concept of so-called objective and subjective careers. The objective career is the "sequence of work-related positions occupied throughout a person's life" (London and Stumpf, 1982: 4), and goes under a variety of labels, including objective (Hughes, 1958: 63), external (Schein, 1980: 357), or orderly (Wilensky, 1961: 522). The subjective career, by contrast, is "the moving perspective in which the person sees his life as a whole and interprets the meaning of his various attributes, actions, and the things which happen to him" (Hughes, 1958: 63). The familiar definition of career from the 1989 *Handbook of Career Theory*, "the evolving sequence of a person's work experiences over time" (Arthur et al., 1989: 8), captures something of the objective career but with a strong sense (in "experiences") of subjectivity as well.

Gunz and Mayrhofer (2018) extend these views of career by listing five extensions of the construct:

1   Career as retrospective sense-making, concerned with understanding what careers mean to people: "[m]any in our complex and highly differentiated society use [career] to attribute coherence, continuity, and social meaning to their lives" (Young and Collin, 2000: 1). Nicholson and West (1989: 181) use sense-making to distinguish between work history ("sequences of job experiences") and career ("the sense people make of them") (see also Patton, 2008: 147; Savickas, 2005; Parker et al., 2004; Cohen and Mallon, 2001; Young and Valach, 1996; Herr, 1990: 4).

2   Career as a means of linking different levels of social complexity: "the moving perspective in which persons orient themselves with reference to the social order" (Hughes, 1958: 67), or career "falling at the intersection between the individual and society" (Schein, 1980: 357; see also Young and Collin, 2000; Gunz, 1989; Grandjean, 1981; Mills, 1959).

3   Career as a path through space and time (Gowler and Legge, 1989; Nicholson and West, 1989; Schein, 1977) or across a complex landscape (Nicholson and De Waal-Andrews, 2005). The space can be geographical or social, in particular occupational or organizational, such that the "movement is contextualized, anchored in a specific space" (Collin, 2006: 62–63).

4   Career as self-construction, as an organizing and regulative principle in modern society: "Career can offer one of the most obvious sites for realizing the project of self" (Grey, 1994: 482). The self is construed as a self-governing entity where each actor, in work as much as outside, is engaged in a project to shape his or her life as an autonomous individual driven by motives of self-fulfillment (cf. Giddens, 1991: 75; Rose, 1989: 115; Sennett, 1980: 84ff).

5   Career as a product rather than a process: as a product of a life's work as typified in a résumé or CV, rather than the process, the results of which are summarized in that document. A widely cited example of this is Bird's (1996) concept of careers as repositories of knowledge.

Clearly there is a lot packed into the term "career." Before we unpack it in what we suggest is a more systematic way, looking for unifying themes across the many perspectives referred to here, we briefly consider the nature of the field of career studies, the field that is the focus of this volume.

The "field" of career studies

The field of career studies has a curiously mirage-like quality. At first sight it seems obvious that there is such a field; there are, after all, plenty of scholars who think of themselves as students of career, and various scholarly bodies such as the Academy of Management and the European Group for Organizational Studies (EGOS) have established divisions or interest groups focusing on careers. There are many professional and other bodies for scholars and practitioners in the field of vocational psychology or career counseling. But the closer one examines what is happening, the fuzzier the picture becomes. Whitley (1984: 776) views fields as "particular kinds of work organizations which produce intellectual novelty by working on intellectual artifacts to solve intellectual problems." So what are the intellectual artifacts that career studies deals with?

In an earlier handbook Peiperl and Gunz (2007) attempt to construct a taxonomy of career studies and find little agreement in the literature on what belongs "within" the field. No two publications in their review that attempt to provide an overview of the field concur on the topics that constitute career studies; there are some themes that recur more often than others, in particular adult development, but that is about it. Some collections of writing on careers are organized by discipline (for example psychology, sociology, or management studies; e.g. Arthur and Lawrence, 1984) or research topic (for instance career stage, life cycle, career shape, career choice; e.g. Collin and Young, 1986; Van Maanen, 1977). Others are structured by issue (for example career planning, gender, self-designing careers; e.g. Glaser, 1968; Hall, 1976). Of course, the boundaries of even clearly structured disciplines such as the physical and life sciences shift over time and become blurred as the questions being asked, for example those concerning the chemistry of life, become more transdisciplinary. But Peiperl and Gunz suggest that what we see in the field of career studies is what Whitley (1984) calls a "fragmented adhocracy," characterized by

> a low degree of interdependency between researchers, which implies a rather "loose" or flat research organization . . . a relatively fragmented knowledge structure and the existence of much disagreement about the relative importance of different problems to be solved by the field. As a result, the problem solving activity within the field takes place in a rather arbitrary and ad hoc manner, with limited attempts to integrate new solutions with the existing structure of knowledge.
>
> *(Knudsen, 2003: 278)*

Knowledge does not build cumulatively, and there is no accepted and authoritative view on what constitutes "good" research, who is leading the field, or in which direction. If so, then it is no surprise that there is no accepted and authoritative view of what belongs "inside" the field of career studies.

All of this sounds rather depressing; but as Van Maanen (1995: 689) argues for the similar and related case of organization studies, paradigmatic consensus of the kind that Pfeffer (1995) proposes and which is characteristic of less fragmented fields "would be a most uncomfortable place to reside. It would be a world with little emancipatory possibilities, a world with even tighter restrictions on who can be published, promoted, fired, celebrated, reviled than we have now." In this view, a lack of clear and well-understood structure with an accompanying lack of clear boundaries becomes a cause for celebration, albeit one in which the need for conversations between scholars active in the field becomes crucial (Arthur, 2008; Gunz and Mayrhofer, 2018).

To summarize, then, we have a view of the "field" of career studies as something that lacks both a clear intellectual structure and a clear sense of social organization. There are also significant divisions between career scholars with different interests in career, the one probably most widely commented on (e.g., Collin and Patton, 2009; Schein, 2007) being between what Gunz and Mayrhofer (2018) call organizational and managerial career (OMC) studies and vocational career studies. Perhaps less commented on but equally striking is the gap we note above between research on the life course and the careers literature. The life course literature clearly focuses on a phenomenon that is closely related to – or, depending on one's view of career, is indistinguishable from – career, but it rarely refers to career. Furthermore, the literature associated with OMC studies or vocational studies rarely refers to the life course. In addition, as we noted earlier, the construct of career is widely used in research in a range of fields outside anything that self-identifies as being about careers or an obvious synonym. Within disciplines that fall within the social sciences, for instance, Gunz and Mayrhofer point to examples that can be found in fields as diverse as strategic management (e.g., Sorensen, 1999; Boeker, 1997; Haveman and Cohen, 1994), human resource management (HRM; e.g. Mayrhofer et al., 2004; Ferris and Rowland, 1990), international business (e.g., Cappellen and Janssens, 2010; Carraher et al., 2008; Vance, 2005), and health sciences (Boadi-Kusi et al., 2015; Gigliotti and Makhoul, 2015).

Gunz and Mayrhofer (2018) summarize these observations in a figure we reproduce in Figure 2.1. They distinguish between (1) fields of study, for example OMC or life course studies; (2) proto-fields of study, for example one encompassing any field that focuses on career or an obvious synonym; and (3) a broader nascent commonality of interest in career. The label "proto-field" indicates that there is no social organization connecting the various fields within it (other than, perhaps, occasional links between individual researchers), which does not exclude

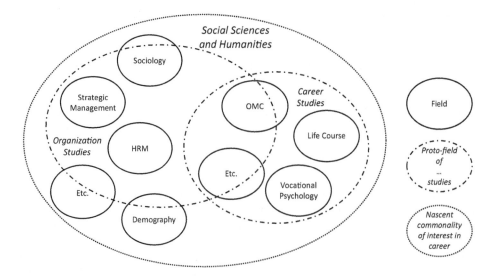

Figure 2.1 Fields, proto-fields, and nascent commonalities of interest
Source: From Gunz and Mayrhofer, 2018: 13.

the possibility that such an organization might develop over time. The "nascent commonality of interest" refers to any research activity in which careers appear as an object of interest, with "nascent" implying that there is potential for an awareness to grow about the possibility that there is indeed such a commonality of interest between scholars working with careers in disparate fields with different interests.

Having considered the breadth of meaning associated with the term career, and the character of the interrelationships (if any) between scholars interested in this phenomenon, the time has come to try to pull things together and suggest a view that can cope with the complex set of ideas about career that we have been reviewing.

Conceptual pillars of career studies

Space does not allow us here to review all the many different ways in which career has been defined in the literature, although our preceding account gives a reasonably clear picture of the situation. It is evident that, regardless of how career is viewed and defined, there are three themes common to each approach to career outlined above (the account that follows also draws on the analysis of Gunz and Mayrhofer, 2018). Each approach to career involves a *career actor* who "has" the career, attention to the *context* in which the career happens, and the *time* over which the career takes place (cf. Collin's view of "time, social space, and the individual" (2007: 560) as being central for careers). For example, the context of a work career is the social and geographical space that the career actor occupies over their working career: the organizations they have worked in, the occupational communities they may be part of, the countries their careers have taken them through, and so forth. It is axiomatic that a career involves a career actor, and any account of their career involves an account of what has happened to them over the course of their career. Finally, time is fundamental to career in the sense that a career is something that happens over time.

The study of career, then, involves "the examination of what happens to career actors as they move through a given geographical and social space over time" (Gunz and Mayrhofer, 2018): 28). Drawing on a suggestion that career studies "may not be a field at all, but a *perspective on social enquiry*" (Gunz and Peiperl, 2007: 4; emphasis in original), Gunz and Mayrhofer (2018: 29) develop this idea by suggesting that "career studies involves the simultaneous application of *three* perspectives to social phenomena, focusing on (1) the – primarily social – space(s) surrounding the career actor, (2) the career actor, and (3) the time over which the career happens" (emphasis added). They label these perspectives spatial, ontic,[2] and temporal, respectively. These three perspectives form the foundation of what they call the Social Chronology Framework (SCF), namely a framework that provides a view of career and an approach to studying it. Next, we examine these three fundamental aspects of career in a little more detail.

The career actor

As we noted earlier, it is axiomatic that career requires a career actor. We follow Meyer and Jepperson (2000) by using the term "actor" in contrast to many other possibilities, such as individual, human being, subject, or person, because of two key characteristics of the construct of actor:

> First . . . the natural human entity with valid and lawful functions and interests . . . the human individual or group that can be represented as behaving in terms of natural (scientifically expressible) laws. Second, devolving from rationalized spiritual authority . . . the legitimated agent and carrier of authority, responsibility, and capacity to act in history. The

integration of these two elements in a single imagined natural-and-spiritual entity is what moderns mean by the term "actor."

(ibid.: 106)

This view of an actor combines the sense of a competent actor having responsible agency with constraints coming from the institutional context. In this way, it focuses on the notion of actor-in-context, one who balances actorhood and contextual influences: actors are not the "boundaryless, autonomous individuals steering their career with aplomb, largely unfazed by what goes on around them. Instead, intricate, dynamic relationships exist between actor and their environments" (Gunz and Mayrhofer, 2018: 33). This is compatible with a view of career that focuses on the actor and their environment.

A further benefit of using the term actor is that it directs our attention to a feature of career that is not widely discussed in the careers literature. The term "career" has been used not only in connection with actors as individuals (i.e., people) but also as collectivities (Barley, 1989: 51). Historians, for example, have been known to use it in this way, as in "the career of France, Prussia, etc." (OED, 2016: entry "career"). Although most careers researchers would not immediately recognize this sense of the term as being relevant to their work, career contexts are often social entities such as organizations, occupational bodies, families, or countries. These are not static entities: they change over time. They have, in other words, careers of their own. Barley (1989), drawing on Giddens's model of structuration in which "institutions jointly 'constitute' and are 'constituted by' the actions of individuals" (ibid.: 52), derives a view of career in which institutions and individual action and interaction mutually evolve over time, mediated by what he calls career scripts that "encode contextually appropriate behaviors and perceptions" (ibid.: 54). For now, however, we shall stay with career actors as individuals.

Actor, then, is a useful word to use in connection with careers. Any examination of an objective or subjective career involves an examination of some aspect of that actor: their status, income, sense of well-being or career satisfaction, their age, and so on. Following Gunz and Mayrhofer, we call these aspects elements of the actor's condition, a portmanteau used to describe anything about the actor that is of interest to the researcher. In the example just given, that might be the actor's status, income, sense of well-being or career satisfaction, or age. So the actor's condition is what is "seen" when the ontic perspective is applied.

The "seeing" is performed by means of a process of comparison: we make sense of any aspect of an actor's condition by comparing it with something else. For example, height is measured by comparing it with a standard measure of length such as a meter or foot, and the various elements of compensation are typically compared with a unit of currency of some kind. Psychometric measures such as general mental ability or the Big Five personality factors are measured using appropriate standardized instruments, the results of which are compared with the results from a selected comparison population, perhaps a national one. Self-report measures such as the widely used subjective career success scale of Greenhaus et al. (1990) provide a raw number or numbers which only make sense when the results are compared with those from other selected groups of subjects. For example, a response that having time for non-work interests is "somewhat important" (4 on a 5-point scale) to one's career success is hard to make sense of by itself. Perhaps everyone would say this; perhaps only a few would; perhaps it is characteristic of people in particular occupations or particular countries, while in other occupations or countries it is more common to say that it is "not important." These questions can only be answered by having a comparison group, such as the 17,000+-strong sample of respondents from more than 27 countries in the 5C study (Briscoe et al., 2012a; Mayrhofer et al., 2016; see also Chapter 18, this volume).

A career actor's condition can be viewed in many different ways depending on the purpose at hand. A researcher might be interested, for example, in actors' educational level, age, technical skills, managerial capabilities, or combinations of any of these with other aspects of their condition. But this is only part of the story; the context within which the actor is embedded matters too, and we turn to this next.

The contextual embeddedness of career

Career implies context, in the sense that at any given time a career actor has to be somewhere: careers are always careers in context (Collin, 1997; Schein, 1984). Grandjean (1981: 1057) locates them at the "intersection of societal history and individual biography," linking micro- and macro-frames of reference (Barley, 1989). This much seems obvious, yet despite calls for a greater recognition of the need to examine context (Mayrhofer et al., 2007), it is probably fair to say that for many years the career actor has been the center of attention to the neglect of context. To the extent that context is considered, organizations are probably the most commonly studied, or they were until the mid-1990s when it was suggested that a richer perspective on context, moving beyond simply the organization, was necessary to reflect changes that were happening in the nature of work (Arthur and Rousseau, 1996). More recently, interest in context has encompassed boundaries (e.g., Rodrigues et al., 2016), the integration of institutional contexts in career analysis (e.g., Kaulisch and Enders, 2005), and the growing field of international comparative career studies (e.g., Briscoe et al., 2012b).

We view the context of career here as a composite of the geographic and social space occupied by the career actor. Sometimes metaphorically referred to as the landscape through which the career actor travels (Nicholson and De Waal-Andrews, 2005), this space is the social and physical world that they move through over the course of their career. It is most evident when the objective career is being considered. In the case of the work career, we see this in the phrase "sequence of work-related positions" (London and Stumpf, 1982: 4), the positions defining where the actor is in their geographical and social space. Position might be mapped in terms of, for example, formal position within a hierarchy, relationships with other members of a community of practice (Barley, 1996), location within a social or kinship network, socioeconomic status, geographic location, or political affiliation. Subjectively, when career actors measure their success by reference to others (Heslin, 2003), they almost invariably measure their relationship to those others by reference to how they both fit into the social order, as for example, colleagues, fellow alumni and former teachers (Higgins et al., 2008), or family members.

It is the spatial perspective that provides a view of the geographical and social space through which the actor moves. Whereas in the ontic perspective we construe careers through a process of comparison, in the spatial perspective the corresponding operation is mapping – mapping the position of the actor in geographical and social space. In the ontic perspective, the construct "seen" is the actor's condition; in the spatial perspective, it is boundary that provides the necessary orientation. Boundaries provide structure to maps. Physical geography maps show boundaries between land and sea; they define features such as rivers, lakes, and mountains; political geography maps show boundaries between national and sub-national jurisdictions; and so on. In the social space, boundaries shape careers in fundamental ways (Inkson et al., 2012). They constrain careers by restricting the kinds of changes people can make in their working lives (Vardi, 1980), enable them by structuring status passages (Glaser and Strauss, 1971), and punctuate them by providing the markers that help structure people's careers into episodes (Roth, 1963) and develop rites of passage (van Gennep, 1960 [Orig. 1909]). It has often been argued that boundaries come before, and define, structure (e.g., Nicholson and De Waal-Andrews, 2005; Heracleous, 2004; Abbott, 1995).

Career boundaries begin as subjective impressions about how possible it is to make a transition from one position to another (Gunz et al., 2007); the less possible it seems, the less permeable the boundary. These boundaries can be mapped on to organizations, in the sense that an actor crosses a boundary when joining an organization; they can also be internal to organizations, as in Schein's (1971) conical model comprising hierarchical, functional, and inclusional boundaries. They can separate occupations and levels of inclusion within occupations (for example, between novices and established members). They may surround temporary groups (Bechky, 2006) and occupations within them. The greater the consensus about the nature of a particular boundary, the more it takes on aspects of an objective boundary (Gunz et al., 2007), such as those separating members of various professions from laypeople. In most countries, for example, there is a general understanding, usually backed by legislation, about what is required to become a physician, and the boundary feels very "real" to both those who cross it and those who aren't able to.

As we noted earlier, other career actors – both individual and collective (Coleman, 1990) – are part of the social space. Examples include (Gunz and Mayrhofer, 2018: 53) individuals such as peers and supervisors; collectivities such as organizations that offer career opportunities, facilitate career opportunities (Fernandez-Mateo, 2007) or constitute major players in the field such as trade unions; or even nation states undergoing roller coaster experiences as debtors. Indeed the careers of both a career actor and others in their social space can be thought of as coevolving as a result of the complex relationships that connect them (Gunz and Mayrhofer, 2018). For example, a mentor (an actor in the career actor's social space) may provide advice that allows their protégé, the career actor, to get promoted to a more senior role in their organization. This, in turn, may result in the protégé being able to help their mentor with some other agenda, helping the mentor to get ahead. Similarly, universities' reputations benefit from the success of their faculty, whose careers as a result benefit from finding their institution gaining in prestige.

We should note, finally, that power relations play a critical role in the way that the social space is governed (Emerson, 1962). The rules of the social space, influencing the behavior of career actors as well as their interactions, form these power relations and, at the same time, are their expression (Bourdieu, 1989). Boundaries are an obvious indication of rules and the underlying power relations, in particular as they channel the movement of career actors within the social space. Various types of boundaries exist. Legal boundaries determine who can access a certain profession, for example becoming a medical doctor (all around the globe) or a plumber (in some countries). Boundaries of meaning (Luhmann, 1995: 194ff) create collective identities and indicate demarcation lines between "us" and "them," for example by signaling the limits and the possibilities of crossing this boundary, as in the case of a technical expert with no leadership responsibility accepting the promotion to first-line supervisor. Cultural boundaries regulate the social access to an organization or a group as expressed, for example, by the despicable rites of some college fraternities in the United States when admitting new members.

Implicit in the discussion thus far has been time: the time over which changes in condition and moves across boundaries take place. Lastly, we turn to this third perspective that is essential when talking about careers.

The role of time in career

It is the temporal perspective that converts a view of an actor's condition and position into a view of a career (Gunz and Mayrhofer, 2018). What we "see" through this perspective is a chronology of changes in condition and position, assembled through a process of sequencing, that allows us to make sense of how these changes connect – the retrospective sense-making to which we referred earlier – although it is easy to be misled by this chronology, a point to which we will return.

Time as it can be visualized with respect to careers is a surprisingly complex construct. At a very simplistic level, positions and their corresponding condition can appear to exist simultaneously or sequentially depending on the level of resolution, or granularity, of the chronology. For example, a CV or resumé usually operates at a fairly coarse-grained level of resolution, so that an actor may appear to occupy several positions simultaneously. Their CV may record the fact that at any given time they may be a member of professional body, a law firm partner, a director of one or more companies, a spouse, parent, daughter, a member of one or more voluntary bodies, and so on. But if we were to examine in finer-grained detail how they manage to play all these roles apparently simultaneously, we will in all probability discover that they are not occupied simultaneously at all, but sequentially. This is accomplished through a series of micro-transitions (Ashforth et al., 2000) as the actor moves from one situation to another in their professional and home lives. Indeed the rarity with which these different roles genuinely overlap is underlined by the awkwardness and embarrassment that can result when an angry spouse storms into the office during a delicate negotiation with a client, or that can be seen in the faces and actions of the people in the famous live BBC interview interrupted by the interviewee's young children (Anonymous, 2017).

Changing levels of resolution of time can also change the way in which a transition between positions across a career boundary – typically, a work role transition (Nicholson, 1984) – appears. Again at the level of resolution of a CV, transitions are represented as instantaneous: one moment the actor is in this position, and the next, they are in another one. But as the granularity of the resolution becomes finer, it may become apparent that the transition itself has a time scale which may be longer or shorter (Glaser and Strauss, 1971), during which the actor may be in a liminal state (van Gennep, 1960) in which they are neither on one side of the boundary nor on the other. A probationary period can feel like this, and under certain circumstances, such as the rather odd world of academic life in some countries such as Germany or the United States, it can last for as long as 10 years while a junior scholar attempts to prove themselves worthy of inclusion in a given university's faculty by being awarded their habilitation or tenure.

We note above that assembling changes in condition and position into a chronology allows us to make sense of a career. Attributing meaning and causality works both prospectively and retrospectively. Prospective sensemaking is about predicting future events, or about intentions to make these future events happen. It is, in a sense, "a probability statement at time ti_n of the likelihood of occurrence of an event at some time later than ti_n" (Jaques, 1982: 99). It assumes teleological behavior which is goal-directed and purposeful. Retrospectively, attributing meaning and causality has often been referred to as retrospective sensemaking (Young and Collin, 2000: 1; Weick, 1995: 25ff; Nicholson and West, 1989: 181). We cannot go back and unmake the past, but we can construct a narrative which reinterprets our past perhaps, following typical attribution tendencies (e.g., self-serving bias; Miller and Ross, 1975; or fundamental attribution error; Ross, 1977), framing unsuccessful outcomes as being caused by events that were out of our control and successful outcomes as being the result of our initiative. As events unfold, these interpretations can change. Kierkegaard (1960: 111) notes, however, that

> [i]t is quite true what Philosophy says: that Life must be understood backwards. But that makes one forget the other saying: that it must be lived – forwards. The more one ponders this, the more it comes to mean that life in the temporal existence never becomes quite intelligible, precisely because at no moment can I find complete quiet to take the backward-looking position.

While the time dimension is crucial for the issue of causality, sequencing (i.e., the ordering of events on a time axis) in itself does not necessarily imply causality. We follow the view of Jaques (1982), who differentiates between two dimensions of time that he calls the axes of succession and intention. The former one – succession – differentiates between earlier and later and sorts various events accordingly. While superficially it might evoke a sense of directional development where one thing leads to another, a closer look reveals that you can do this only in retrospect. It does not make any sense to argue that Barack Obama's joining the Trinity United Church of Christ in 1988 (and leaving it in 2008 again) led to him becoming the 44th president of the United States, since the latter did not even exist as a possibility at that time. However, Jaques's second dimension, the axis of intention, allows causality into the picture since it acknowledges that actions have consequences in the future. Usually, however, this does not imply strict path-dependence where "singular historical events ... may, under certain conditions, transform themselves into self-reinforcing dynamics, and ... possibly end up in a ... lock-in" (Sydow et al., 2009: 690).

Conclusion

In this chapter our intention was to explore the concept of career and the field of studies that examines it. First, we described some of the many different ways in which the term is used. Next, we discussed the nature of the field of career studies and its complex relationship with other fields, especially in the social sciences, in which "career" appears even though it may not be the main focus for the research. We then looked for commonalities in the various views of career in the literature, suggesting, following Gunz and Mayrhofer's (2018) Social Chronology Framework, that the study of career involves the simultaneous application of three perspectives: ontic, spatial, and temporal.

The ontic perspective, an awkward term drawing on existential philosophy and meaning to do with the facts about some entity, draws attention to the career actor and what we know about them, namely their condition. It does this by a process of comparison: condition is measured by comparing specific facets, such as age, personality, status, compensation, ethnicity, or gender with a measurement standard or the same facet in a comparison population. The spatial perspective focuses on the geographical and social space through which the career actor moves over their career. It does so by mapping the actor's position in these spaces, using boundaries, typically career boundaries, as structuring devices. Finally, the temporal perspective puts changes in condition as boundaries are crossed on a time base by means of a process of sequencing, to form a chronology.

Taken together, these three perspectives give a view of career as *a pattern of a career actor's positions and condition within a bounded social and geographic space over their life to date* (Gunz and Mayrhofer, 2018: 70). A work career is a subset of this, namely the pattern in a bounded work-related social and geographical space, over a working life to date. Career, seen in this way, is a very broad statement about the life of a career actor, as seen both from "outside" (i.e., the so-called objective career) and "inside" (the subjective career), because condition can be any view of the actor that we want it to be. And "pattern" implies that there is something there to be analyzed and made sense of (even if, as in a pattern of raindrops, the pattern is entirely random). The extraordinarily broad range of phenomena that this view of career directs our attention towards provides the incredibly broad canvas on which career scholarship can work, and explains why this scholarship is so pervasive across the social sciences and humanities.

Notes

1 With apologies to Cole Porter.
2 Ontic "refers to the traditional approach of the sciences, including psychology, of categorizing, labeling, and objectifying that which is studied. It is the explaining of "things" and their generalized ways of being" (Karcher, M.J. & Nakkula, M.J. 1997. Multicultural pair counseling and the development of expanded worldviews. *In:* Selman, R., Watts, C. & Schultz, L. (eds.) *Fostering friendship: Pair therapy for treatment and prevention.* New York: Aldine de Gruyter.: 211).

References

Abbott, A. 1995. Things of boundaries. *Social Research*, 62, 857–882.

Anonymous. 2017. Children interrupt BBC news interview – BBC news. *YouTube: BBC News* [Online]. Available: https://www.youtube.com/watch?v=Mh4f9AYRCZY [Accessed 25 September 2018].

Arthur, M.B. 2008. Examining contemporary careers: A call for interdisciplinary enquiry. *Human Relations*, 61, 163–186.

Arthur, M.B., Hall, D.T. & Lawrence, B.S. 1989. Generating new directions in career theory: The case for a transdisciplinary approach. *In:* Arthur, M.B., Hall, D.T. & Lawrence, B.S. (eds.) *Handbook of Career Theory.* Cambridge: Cambridge University Press

Arthur, M.B. & Lawrence, B.S. 1984. Perspectives on environment and career: An introduction. *Journal of Occupational Behaviour*, 5, 1–8.

Arthur, M.B. & Rousseau, D.M. (eds.) 1996. *The Boundaryless Career: A New Employment Principle for a New Organizational Era.* New York and Oxford: Oxford University Press.

Ashforth, B.E., Kreiner, G.E. & Fugate, M. 2000. All in a day's work: Boundaries and micro role transitions. *Academy of Management Review*, 25, 472–491.

Barley, S.R. 1989. Careers, identities, and institutions: The legacy of the Chicago school of sociology. *In:* Arthur, M.B., Hall, D.T. & Lawrence, B.S. (eds.) *Handbook of Career Theory.* Cambridge, England: Cambridge University Press.

Barley, S.R. 1996. Technicians in the workplace: Ethnographic evidence for bringing work into organization studies. *Administrative Science Quarterly*, 41, 404–441.

Bechky, B.A. 2006. Gaffers, gofers, and grips: Role-based coordination in temporary organizations. *Organization Science*, 17, 3–21.

Bird, A. 1996. Careers as repositories of knowledge: Considerations for boundaryless careers. *In:* Arthur, M.B. & Rousseau, D.M. (eds.) *The Boundaryless Career: A New Employment Principle for a New Organizational Era.* Oxford: Oxford University Press.

Boadi-Kusi, S.B., Kyei, S., Mashige, K.P., Abu, E.K., Antwi-Boasiako, D. & Halladay, A.C. 2015. Demographic characteristics of Ghanaian optometry students and factors influencing their career choice and institution of learning. *Advances in Health Sciences Education*, 20, 33–44.

Boeker, W. 1997. Executive migration and strategic change: The effect of top manager movement on product-market entry. *Administrative Science Quarterly*, 42, 213–236.

Bourdieu, P. 1989. Social space and symbolic power. *Sociological Theory*, 7, 14–25.

Briscoe, J.P., Chudzikowski, K., Demel, B., Mayrhofer, W. & Unite, J. 2012a. The 5C project: Our story and our research. *In:* Briscoe, J.P., Hall, D.T. & Mayrhofer, W. (eds.) *Careers around the world.* New York and London: Routledge Taylor & Francis Group.

Briscoe, J.P., Hall, D.T. & Mayrhofer, W. (eds.) 2012b. *Careers around the world: Individual and contextual perspectives.* New York and Oxon: Routledge.

Cappellen, T. & Janssens, M. 2010. Enacting global careers: Organizational career scripts and the global economy as co-existing career referents. *Journal of Organizational Behavior*, 31, 687–706.

Carraher, S.M., Sullivan, S.E. & Crocitto, M.M. 2008. Mentoring across global boundaries: An empirical examination of home- and host-country mentors on expatriate career outcomes. *Journal of International Business Studies*, 39, 1310–1326.

Cohen, L. & Mallon, M. 2001. My brilliant career? *International Studies of Management & Organization*, 31, 48–68.

Coleman, J.S. 1990. *Foundations of Social Theory*. Cambridge, MA: Harvard University Press.

Collin, A. 1997. Career in context. *British Journal of Guidance & Counselling*, 25, 435–446.

Collin, A. 2006. Career. *In:* Greenhaus, J.H. & Callanan, G.A. (eds.) *Encyclopedia of Career Development*. Thousand Oaks, CA: Sage Publications.

Collin, A. 2007. The meanings of career. *In:* Gunz, H.P. & Peiperl, M.A. (eds.) *Handbook of Career Studies*. Thousand Oaks: Sage Publications.

Collin, A. & Patton, W. (eds.) 2009. *Vocational Psychological and Organisational Perspectives on Career: Towards a Multidisciplinary Dialogue*. Rotterdam: Sense Publishers.

Collin, A. & Young, R.A. 1986. New directions for theories of career. *Human Relations*, 39, 837–853.

Emerson, R.M. 1962. Power dependence relations. *American Sociological Review*, 27, 31–41.

Fernandez-Mateo, I. 2007. Who pays the price of brokerage? Transferring constraint through prices setting in the staffing sector. *American Sociological Review*, 72, 291–317.

Ferris, G.R. & Rowland, K.M. 1990. *Career and Human Resources Development*. Greenwich, CT: Jai.

Giddens, A. 1991. *Modernity and Self-Identity: Self and Society in the Late Modern Age*. Cambridge, UK: Polity Press.

Gigliotti, J. & Makhoul, N. 2015. Demographics, training satisfaction, and career plans of Canadian oral and maxillofacial surgery residents. *International Journal of Oral and Maxillofacial Surgery*, 44, 1574–1580.

Glaser, B.G. 1968. *Organizational Careers: A Sourcebook for Theory*. Chicago: Aldine.

Glaser, B.G. & Strauss, A.L. 1971. *Status Passage: A Formal Theory*. Chicago: Aldine, Atherton.

Gowler, D. & Legge, K. 1989. Careers, reputations and the rhetoric of bureaucratic control. *In:* Arthur, M.B., Hall, D.T. & Lawrence, B.S. (eds.) *Handbook of Career Theory*. Cambridge: Cambridge University Press.

Grandjean, B.D. 1981. History and career in a bureaucratic labor market. *American Journal of Sociology*, 86, 1057–1092.

Greenhaus, J.H. & Foley, S. 2007. The intersection of work and family lives. *In:* Gunz, H. & Peiperl, M. (eds.) *Handbook of Career Studies*. Thousand Oaks, CA: Sage Publications.

Greenhaus, J.H., Parasuraman, S. & Wormley, W. 1990. Effects of race on organizational experiences, job performance evaluations, and career outcomes. *Academy of Management Journal*, 33, 64–86.

Grey, C. 1994. Career as a project of the self and labour process discipline. *Sociology*, 28, 479–497.

Gunz, H. & Mayrhofer, W. 2018. *Rethinking Career Studies: Facilitating Conversation Across Boundaries with the Social Chronology Framework*. Cambridge: Cambridge University Press.

Gunz, H. & Peiperl, M. 2007. Introduction. *In:* Gunz, H. & Peiperl, M. (eds.) *Handbook of Career Studies*. Thousand Oaks, CA: Sage Publications.

Gunz, H., Peiperl, M. & Tzabbar, D. 2007. Boundaries in the study of career. *In:* Gunz, H. & Peiperl, M. (eds.) *Handbook of Career Studies*. Thousand Oaks, CA: Sage Publications.

Gunz, H.P. 1989. The dual meaning of managerial careers: Organizational and individual levels of analysis. *Journal of Management Studies*, 26, 225–250.

Hall, D.T. 1976. *Careers in Organizations*. Santa Monica, CA: Goodyear.

Hall, D.T. 2002. *Careers in and Out of Organizations*. Thousand Oaks, CA: Sage Publications.

Haveman, H.A. & Cohen, L.E. 1994. The ecological dynamics of careers: The impact of organizational founding, dissolution, and merger on job mobility. *American Journal of Sociology*, 100, 104–152.

Heracleous, L. 2004. Boundaries in the study of organization. *Human Relations*, 57, 95–103.

Herr, E.L. 1990. Issues in career research. *In:* Young, R.A. & Borgen, W.A. (eds.) *Methodological Approaches to the Study of Career*. New York: Praeger.

Heslin, P. 2003. Self- and other-referent criteria of career success. *Journal of Career Assessment*, 11, 262–286.

Higgins, M.C., Dobrow, S.R. & Chandler, D. 2008. Never quite good enough: The paradox of sticky developmental relationships for elite university graduates. *Journal of Vocational Behavior*, 72, 207–224.

Hughes, E.C. 1958. *Men and Their Work*. Glencoe, IL: The Free Press.

Inkson, K., Gunz, H., Ganesh, S. & Roper, J. 2012. Boundaryless careers: Bringing back boundaries. *Organization Studies*, 33, 323–340.

Jaques, E. 1982. *The Form of Time*. New York and London: Crane Russak, Heinemann.

Karcher, M.J. & Nakkula, M.J. 1997. Multicultural pair counseling and the development of expanded worldviews. *In:* Selman, R., Watts, C. & Schultz, L. (eds.) *Fostering Friendship: Pair Therapy for Treatment and Prevention*. New York: Aldine de Gruyter.

Kaulisch, M. & Enders, J. 2005. Careers in overlapping institutional contexts: The case of academe. *Career Development International*, 10, 130–144.

Kierkegaard, S. 1960. *The Diary of Soren Kierkegaard*. London: Peter Owen Limited.

Knudsen, C. 2003. *Pluralism, Scientific Progress and the Structure of Organization Studies*. Oxford: Oxford University Press.

London, M. & Stumpf, S.A. 1982. *Managing Careers*. Reading, MA: Addison-Wesley.

Luhmann, N. 1995. *Social Systems*. Stanford: Stanford University Press.

Mayrhofer, W., Briscoe, J.P., Hall, D.T., Dickmann, M., Dries, N., Dysvik, A., Kaše, R., Parry, E. & Unite, J. 2016. Career success across the globe – insights from the 5C project. *Organizational Dynamics*, 45, 197–205.

Mayrhofer, W., Meyer, M., Iellatchitch, A. & Schiffinger, M. 2004. Careers and human resource management – a European perspective. *Human Resource Management Review*, 14, 473–498.

Mayrhofer, W., Meyer, M. & Steyrer, J. 2007. Contextual issues in the study of careers. *In:* Gunz, H. & Peiperl, M. (eds.) *Handbook of Career Studies*. Thousand Oaks, CA: Sage Publications.

Meyer, J.W. & Jepperson, R.L. 2000. The 'actors' of modern society: The cultural construction of social agency. *Sociological Theory*, 18, 100–120.

Miller, D.T. & Ross, M. 1975. Self-serving biases in the attribution of causality: Fact or fiction? *Psychological Bulletin*, 82, 213–225.

Mills, C.W. 1959. *The Sociological Imagination*. London: Oxford University Press.

Moore, C., Gunz, H.P. & Hall, D.T. 2007. Tracing the historical roots of career theory in management and organization studies. *In:* Gunz, H.P. & Peiperl, M.A. (eds.) *Handbook of Career Studies*. Thousand Oaks, CA: Sage Publications.

Mortimer, J.T. & Shanahan, M.J. (eds.) 2003. *Handbook of the Life Course*. New York: Kluwer Academic Publishers.

Nicholson, N. 1984. A theory of work role transitions. *Administrative Science Quarterly*, 29, 172–191.

Nicholson, N. & de Waal-Andrews, W. 2005. Playing to win: Biological imperatives, self-regulation, and trade-offs in the game of career success. *Journal of Organizational Behavior*, 26, 137–154.

Nicholson, N. & West, M. 1989. Transitions, work histories and careers. *In:* Arthur, M.B., Hall, D.T. & Lawrence, B.S. (eds.) *Handbook of Career Theory*. Cambridge, England: Cambridge University Press.

OED. 2016. *Oxford English Dictionary*. Oxford University Press.

Parker, P., Arthur, M.B. & Inkson, K. 2004. Career communities: A preliminary exploration of member-defined career support structures. *Journal of Organizational Behavior*, 25, 489–514.

Patton, W. 2008. Recent developments in career theories: The influences of constructivism and convergence. *In:* Athanasou, J.A. & Esbroeck, R.V. (eds.) *International Handbook of Career Guidance*. London: Springer.

Peiperl, M. & Gunz, H. 2007. Taxonomy of career studies. *In:* Gunz, H. & Peiperl, M. (eds.) *Handbook of Career Studies*. Thousand Oaks, CA: Sage Publications.

Pfeffer, J. 1995. Mortality, reproducibility, and the persistence of styles of theory. *Organization Science*, 6, 681–686.

Rodrigues, R., Guest, D. & Budjanovcanin, A. 2016. Bounded or boundaryless? An empirical investigation of career boundaries and boundary crossing. *Work, Employment & Society*, 30, 669–686.

Rose, N. 1989. *Governing the Soul: The Shaping of the Private Self*. London: Free Association Books.

Ross, L.D. 1977. The intuitive psychologist and his shortcomings: Distortions in the attribution process. *In:* Berkowitz, L. (ed.) *Advances in Experimental Social Psychology*. New York: Academic Press.

Roth, J.A. 1963. *Timetables: Structuring the Passage of Time in Hospital Treatment and Other Careers*. Indianapolis: Bobbs-Merrill.

Sargent, L., Lee, M., Martin, B. & Zikic, J. 2013. Reinventing retirement: New pathways, new arrangements, new meanings. *Human Relations*, 66, 3–21.

Savickas, M.L. 2005. The theory and practice of career construction. *In:* Brown, S.D. & Lent, R.W. (eds.) *Career Development and Counselling: Putting Research and Theory to Work*. Hoboken, NJ: Wiley.

Schein, E.H. 1971. The individual, the organization and the career: A conceptual scheme. *Journal of Applied Behavioral Science*, 7, 401–426.

Schein, E.H. 1977. Career anchors and career paths: A panel study of management school graduates. *In:* van Maanen, J. (ed.) *Organizational Careers: Some New Perspectives*. London: Wiley.

Schein, E.H. 1980. Career theory and research: Some issues for the future. *In:* Derr, C.B. (ed.) *Work, Family, and the Career: New Frontiers in Theory and Research*, New York: Praeger, 357–365.

Schein, E.H. 1984. Culture as an environmental context for careers. *Journal of Occupational Behavior*, 5, 71–81.

Schein, E.H. 2007. Career research: Some issues and dilemmas. *In:* Gunz, H. & Peiperl, M. (eds.) *Handbook of Career Studies*. Thousand Oaks, CA: Sage Publications.

Sennett, R. 1980. *Authority*. New York: Norton.

Shanahan, M.J., Mortimer, J.T. & Kirkpatrick Johnson, M. (eds.) 2016. *Handbook of the Life Course*. New York: Springer.

Sorensen, J.B. 1999. Executive migration and interorganizational competition. *Social Science Research*, 28, 289–315.

Sullivan, S.E. & Baruch, Y. 2009. Advances in career theory and research: A critical review and agenda for further exploration. *Journal of Management*, 35, 1542–1571.

Sydow, J., Schreyogg, G. & Koch, J. 2009. Organizational path dependence: Opening the black box. *Academy of Management Review*, 34, 689–709.

Vance, C.M. 2005. The personal quest for building global competence: A taxonomy of self-initiating career path strategies for gaining business experience abroad. *Journal of World Business*, 40, 374–385.

van Gennep, A. 1960. *The Rites of Passage*. Chicago, IL: University of Chicago Press.

van Gennep, A. 1960 [Orig. 1909]. *Rites of Passage*. Chicago: University of Chicago Press.

van Maanen, J. (ed.) 1977. *Organizational Careers: Some New Perspectives*. London: John Wiley & Sons.

van Maanen, J. 1995. Fear and loathing in organization studies. *Organization Science*, 6, 687–692.

Vardi, Y. 1980. Organizational career mobility: An integrative model. *Academy of Management Review*, 5, 341–355.

Weick, K.E. 1995. What theory is not, theorizing is. *Administrative Science Quarterly*, 40, 385–390.

Whitley, R.D. 1984. The development of management studies as a fragmented adhocracy. *Social Science Information/Information sur les Sciences Sociales*, 23, 775–818.

Wilensky, H.L. 1961. Orderly careers and social participation: The impact of work history on social integration in the middle mass. *American Sociological Review*, 26, 521–539.

Young, R.A. & Collin, A. 2000. Introduction: Framing the future of career. *In:* Collin, A. & Young, R.A. (eds.) *The Future of Career*. Cambridge: Cambridge University Press.

Young, R.A. & Valach, L. 1996. Interpretation and action in career counseling. *In:* Savickas, M.L. & Walsh, W.B. (eds.) *Handbook of Career Theory and Practice*. Palo Alto, CA: Davies-Black.

3

Bridging micro and macro

An interdisciplinary review of theories used in career studies

Gina Dokko, Jennifer Tosti-Kharas, and Roxana Barbulescu

Introduction

Theory used in careers research is more diverse than ever. The range of theories reflects the diversity of scholars who recognize the importance of careers to many questions from across the field of management. Hughes (1937) observed 80 years ago that careers connect individuals and larger social structures. Individuals make career choices in institutional environments that enable, constrain, and give the choices meaning. At the same time, these choices reproduce and reinforce institutions (Barley, 1989; Jones and Dunn, 2007; Hughes, 1937). Management scholars have long recognized the unique potential of careers research as a hub to illuminate processes and outcomes at multiple levels of analysis (Gunz, 1989), and have called for fulfillment of the promise of careers research to become a predominant element of studies of organizations and work (Arthur et al., 1989a; Jones and Dunn, 2007; Van Maanen, 1977). Because careers link individuals to organizations, occupations, institutions, and society in general, they speak to both micro and macro concerns. Accordingly, careers research appears across virtually all of the sub-fields of management, from organizational behavior to strategy, as well as in the sub-field that specializes in careers studies.

Recently, there has been an uptick in interest about careers across management sub-fields, driven in part by increasing interest in micro-foundations of organizational phenomena (Felin et al., 2015) and in part by increasing availability of matched employer-employee data that enable better understanding of careers within and across organizations (e.g., Campbell, 2005). Careers work is being presented at the annual Wharton People and Organizations conference that started in 2007 and the Strategic Management Society's Strategic Human Capital Interest Group, founded in 2011, as well as across many divisions of the Academy of Management. The broadening base of interest has resulted in a stream of recent work in the management literature that speaks to careers issues from a variety of theoretical perspectives. Representing a range of disciplines, these studies are a step toward a more central place for careers research in the field of management. At the same time, we echo Arthur et al. (1989b) in proposing that the strongest contribution that careers research can make to the understanding of work and organizations is in developing interdisciplinary theory that can explain complex phenomena.

In this chapter, we discuss the use of theory from multiple disciplines in careers research. To provide a framework to organize our discussion, we reviewed recent literature with an eye toward identifying themes. We inductively derived three major areas of interest to careers scholars: career success, job mobility, and career patterns and progressions.[1] Though several studies address multiple categories, we find these categories encompass most recent research conversations in Management. *Career success* refers to research about objective and subjective outcomes of careers (e.g., salary, promotion, and career satisfaction). *Job mobility* refers to questions about the causes and consequences of career moves (i.e. what causes individuals to make a job or career change) and how change affects mobile individuals and their employers. *Career patterns and progressions* is about the shape of a whole career, and refers to questions about why people's careers might follow particular sequences of jobs, and the consequences of having certain careers (e.g., boundaryless, erratic careers, or careers with spells of unemployment). For each of these areas, we discuss how theories from the main disciplinary perspectives that inform careers research in the field of management (i.e., psychology, sociology, and economics) have been used. Though careers research can be found across the social sciences, in fields as diverse as anthropology, philosophy, communications, education, social work, and others (Agergaard and Ungruhe, 2016; Care, 1984; Kramer, 1995), each with their own disciplinary bases, we focus on the disciplines most central to the field of management (Agarwal and Hoetker, 2007). We primarily consider studies published in roughly the last 15 years, acknowledging similar previous reviews (e.g., Arthur et al., 1989a; Sullivan, 1999; Sullivan and Baruch, 2009). We also emphasize empirical work in order to show theory in use. Finally, we discuss the continuing need for interdisciplinary theory and research in careers.

Career success

Career success is a central concern of careers research (see Ng et al., 2005 for a meta-analysis). Understanding the sources of career success and what careers success means to individuals can enrich our understanding of the role that careers play in individuals' lives. The careers literature has conceptualized career success as having both objective and subjective aspects (Arthur et al., 2005). Objective career success is about the tangible aspects of a person's career situation, such as salary, promotions, and high-status occupational attainment. By contrast, intangible factors like career satisfaction are subjective, primarily from the point of view of the career holder. A great deal of attention has been paid to career success by careers scholars (Chudzikowski, 2012; Mayrhofer et al., 2016; Verbruggen, 2012) and also in the broader management literature. It is interesting to note, though, that researchers using different disciplinary perspectives do not necessarily consider both aspects of career success. Those using theory from economics or sociology almost exclusively study objective career success, while those using psychological theories are interested in objective and subjective success. In addition, the specific career success outcomes of interest vary across disciplinary perspectives. Economics-based studies use wages and promotions almost exclusively as measures of career success, while sociology-based studies also consider occupational or job attainment, and psychologists might view an unsatisfactory new job as even worse than being unemployed (e.g., Feldman et al., 2002).

Economics

Despite a large number of studies in the field of labor economics that focus on objective career success outcomes like wages or promotions (see Gibbons and Waldman, 1999 for a review), relatively little of this research has migrated into the management literature. Though some earlier management studies use theory imported directly from economics, like tournaments or signaling theory, to explain career success in internal labor markets (e.g., Cappelli and Cascio, 1991), more recent work using economic theory has focused on human capital as a determinant of objective career success. A human capital perspective holds that the knowledge and skills that individuals accrue through work experiences, education, and training can be considered a form of capital, because they are productive, like other forms of capital (Becker, 1962). A central aspect of human capital theory is the notion of specificity (i.e. accrual of expertise that is especially valuable to specific firms, industries, or occupations), which should lead to higher rewards in those contexts. Though numerous studies have shown a relationship between expertise, measured by firm or job tenure, and career success (Ng et al., 2005), recent studies have begun to unpack aspects of work experience that affect career success. Along these lines, certain types of experience, such as entrepreneurial experience or experience in similar firms, can positively affect subsequent earnings (Campbell, 2013; Sturman et al., 2008).

Sociology

Understanding career success in sociology has a long tradition, notably via the sociology of labor markets (Granovetter, 1995, 1974; Marsden and Gorman, 2001), and its attendant focus on social networks as means for career attainment (i.e., success in obtaining job offers). Management research has increasingly highlighted the mechanisms by which social contacts contribute to individuals' job search success. Thus we have made great progress in understanding the role of referrers and other organizational insiders on chances of being offered jobs (Sterling, 2014; Yakubovich and Lup, 2006), the characteristics of social networks that have a differential influence on job search success (e.g., strong versus weak ties; Obukhova, 2012; Yakubovich, 2005) or centrality versus brokerage (Kilduff and Brass, 2010), and how different tie configurations may be beneficial in various stages of the job search process (Barbulescu, 2015). Interest is also increasing in how social networks matter to people's career success beyond getting a job, such as for salary negotiations (Belliveau, 2005) or compensation, promotions, and career satisfaction (e.g., Seibert et al., 2001).

A second vibrant stream of sociology-based research on career success draws on theories of status and reputation in economic exchange (Podolny, 1993) to understand the effects of employer status on the career outcomes of employees. Phillips (2001) showed that the more likely a firm is to fail, the easier it is for people to get promoted internally. On the external labor market, having worked for a firm that failed has negative effects on status attainment in the future, but the effect is also moderated by other forms of status affiliation, such as educational prestige (Rider and Negro, 2015). Also, association with high-status firms seems to bring people qualified career benefits: high-status firms can hire higher ability workers without having to pay for the full value of their ability early in the career, but must raise wages relatively more rapidly for later career workers (Bidwell et al., 2015). There are also trade-offs between pecuniary benefits and the status of the employing organizations (Rider and Tan, 2015).

A third stream we identify also has a respected history in the sociology of organization – research on the impact of organizational structure, market structure, and demography on career outcomes (Lawrence and Tolbert, 2007; Rosenfeld, 1992). This stream is perhaps best known in management for its classic theory and research on internal labor markets (Doeringer and Piore, 1971). Though attention has mostly shifted to external labor markets instead of organizational ones, there has been a very recent renewal of interest in internal hiring practices and their associated career success outcomes, with studies that contrast the job attainment, performance, and wages of internal versus external hires (Bidwell and Keller, 2014; Gaba and Dokko, 2016). In external labor markets, brokers that mediate the employment relationship can also affect gender segregation, or the tendency for men to end up in better jobs than women, for example by enabling anticipatory gendered sorting (Fernandez-Mateo and King, 2011) and creating gendered consideration sets for top executive positions (Fernandez-Mateo and Fernandez, 2016). Inequality in distribution of rewards in organization is also being studied as a factor influencing career success (Bidwell et al., 2013), along with a revival of demography studies (Cohen et al., 1998), in which organizational demographic composition influences career outcomes, for example when women or racial minorities experience different promotion chances relative to white men (McGinn and Milkman, 2013).

Psychology

Psychological research on career success generally seeks to understand people's perceptions about career success, in particular the various factors that influence career success. A key departure of the psychology perspective from that of economics and sociology is that people themselves define what it means to be successful rather than having success defined by an objective standard. Subjective career success is by definition psychologically determined, yet the same holds for objective career success (Gunz and Heslin, 2005; Seibert and Kraimer, 2001).

Psychological inquiries into what factors contribute to career success often start with stable individual differences, such as personality and cognitive ability. Along these lines, a comprehensive meta-analysis by Ng and colleagues (2005) found that "Big Five" and other personality characteristics, such as proactivity and internal locus of control, influenced salary, promotions, and career satisfaction. Further, these stable individual differences were more strongly related to subjective than objective career success. Recent work has extended these findings by considering additional traits, such as occupational self-efficacy, which predicted salary and status increases (Abele and Spurk, 2009). Several studies have also examined how the changing career context might redefine career success (Arthur et al., 2005; Grote and Raeder, 2009).

A second stream of research stems from the notion that career success is defined in relative rather than absolute terms (Gunz and Heslin, 2005). This research builds on self-categorization theory, which posits that people evaluate their outcomes in part by comparison to relevant others (Festinger, 1957). Research along these lines has sought to understand which reference groups will be salient and why (Heslin, 2005), whether upward or downward social comparisons are beneficial (Eddleston, 2009), and the types and functions of career reference groups (Grote and Hall, 2013).

A third thriving area of study considers "extreme" subjective career success: work as a calling (Hall and Chandler, 2005; Wrzesniewski et al., 1997). People who experience work as a strong calling feel that it is a deeply meaningful, consuming passion (Dobrow and Tosti-Kharas, 2011). Research has considered both the antecedents (Dobrow, 2013) and consequences (Bunderson and Thompson, 2009) of perceiving work as a calling. While a strong calling is typically viewed as positive for employees and organizations, scholars have recently explored the "dark side" of calling, such as the potential for mistreatment by employers (Bunderson and Thompson, 2009) and overestimation of one's objective abilities (Dobrow and Heller, 2015).

Job mobility

Job mobility is an interest area that has received substantial attention from multiple disciplinary perspectives. Modern career theories are based on the observation that job mobility can occur at all stages of a career and in all directions (Sullivan and Baruch, 2009). While the causes of job mobility and the ease of transitions continues to be an important area of research (e.g., Ng et al., 2007), recent years have seen an increase in studies that consider consequences of job mobility. Because job moves represent change, mobility events can represent changes in occupation and identity for individuals, and capabilities and social networks for organizations. In addition, the mobility event is the point where the relationship between people and organizations is most clear. It is at the point when individuals change jobs that we can understand the nature of their attachments to larger social structures like organizations or occupations, as well as the implications of changing affiliations. Moreover, unlike career success studies, job mobility studies are also concerned with organizational or institutional outcomes and individual level outcomes beyond obtaining job offers. Because of mobility's direct implications for individuals, firms, and larger social structures, the study of job mobility is of interest to scholars from all disciplines of management, and theories from multiple disciplines have been used to understand mobility and its implications (for recent reviews, see Dokko and Jiang, 2017; Mawdsley and Somaya, 2016).

Economics

Like studies of career success, job mobility studies use human capital specificity as the primary theory from economics. Job mobility, especially across organization boundaries, potentially disrupts human capital, as skills that are tailored to jobs, firms, industries, and so forth lose value. Accordingly, numerous studies using human capital theory have focused on the consequences of mobility for individuals. For example, Groysberg et al. (2008) and Huckman and Pisano (2006) showed that job performance degrades as individuals move across organizational boundaries, suggesting that mobility can have negative consequences for individuals; however, it can also lead to greater career success in terms of wages (Sturman et al., 2008). For firms, changing job function can be beneficial to innovation outcomes, as mobile workers carry diverse knowledge into new firms (Dokko and Wu, 2017). There have also been recent advances in human capital theory that consider the value of human capital for competitive advantage in terms of constraints on mobility (Campbell et al., 2012).

Another economic theory used to show the effects of job mobility is matching theory. In a matching framework (Heckman and Sedlacek, 1985), mobility occurs when individuals' preferences better match employers' willingness to pay for their skills. This framework has been used to explore matching in internal versus external moves that lead to promotions within firms, but increased wages when moving to another firm (Bidwell and Mollick, 2015) and when individuals move into independent contracting versus permanent jobs (Bidwell and Briscoe, 2009).

Sociology

Job mobility has been of significant interest to scholars who take a sociological view of careers. The most commonly used sociological perspective in job mobility studies is imprinting. Theories of imprinting hold that job experiences, especially those in sensitive periods of a person's career, can have a lasting influence on work and outcomes, as individuals carry mental models about appropriate behaviors or modes of organizing into new contexts (Dokko et al., 2009; Higgins, 2006; Marquis and Tilcsik, 2013). Accordingly, scholars have considered how individuals' job mobility affects the employers they leave and join. For example, studies of entrepreneurship have shown that founders carry models of organizing and employment relationships from their prior job experiences into their new ventures (Beckman and Burton, 2008; Phillips, 2005).

Another stream of work has used social network theories to explore the implications of mobility. When individuals move between firms, they can carry social relationships with them.

Individuals' careers choices, then, can affect interfirm relationships. Individual relationships that are maintained after job moves can lead to organizational learning, such that knowledge flows increase between old and new employers (Corredoira and Rosenkopf, 2010; Ganco, 2013). Individuals can also carry social capital as they move across firms, enabling their new employers to benefit from the social position of the ex-employer (Dokko and Rosenkopf, 2010). Exiting employees can even break links between firms altogether (Broschak and Block, 2014), though this effect is contingent on whether the individual moves to competitors or clients (Somaya et al., 2008).

Psychology

From a psychological perspective, two main questions surround job mobility. The first question is what makes people likely to initiate job change, and the second is what factors facilitate mobility when people decide to change jobs. To answer the first question, a comprehensive review identified several dispositional factors related to the likelihood of seeking mobility, including personality traits, career interests, values, and attachment styles (Ng et al., 2007). For example, people high in neuroticism may exhibit nervousness and emotional instability that makes them unlikely to seek upward transitions (Ng et al., 2005), yet they might seek external lateral transitions due to low self-esteem (Judge and Bono, 2001).

The decision to search for a new job can also be analyzed using decision-making theories. The theory of planned behavior identifies the factors that lead to behavioral intentions, which are predictive of subsequent behavior (Ajzen, 1991). This theory has gained traction as a means to explain efforts around job searching and job mobility (see Ng et al., 2007 for a review). More recently, cybernetic decision theory has been employed to posit that people have a sense of their own employability, which in turn drives their job search and voluntary turnover behavior (Direnzo and Greenhaus, 2011). An emergent finding across studies, then, is that people construct a sense about their own mobility potential that contributes to their desire to turnover above and beyond feelings of fit (Wheeler et al., 2007).

Individual differences also factor into addressing questions about determinants of successful job changes. Job mobility is facilitated when the new position is a match for the employee's personality, career interests, and values (Ng et al., 2007). Additionally, there is initial evidence that identity theories may play an important role in job moves. Relational identity may inform post-mobility job performance in determining how hard to compete when former employers become current rivals (Grohsjean et al., 2015). Identity is also a useful, though largely untapped, lens through which to understand whether people decide to leave a job or not (an exception is Rothausen et al., 2015).

Career patterns and progressions

While job mobility research encompasses the causes and effects of discrete career changes, a related stream of recent research considers career patterns and progressions across a broader time span. Perhaps the most generative and influential perspective in recent careers research is the boundaryless career (Arthur and Rousseau, 1996). Boundaryless careers, along with related concepts like protean careers (Hall, 2002) and kaleidoscope careers (Mainiero and Sullivan, 2005), describe patterns and progressions of modern careers that depart sharply from older conceptions of careers in terms of the direction and speed of movement over the course of a career (see Sullivan and Baruch, 2009 for a comprehensive review). These new characterizations have described a phenomenon of less predictable careers that researchers are just beginning to explore. Building on these ideas, recent research has explored the consequences of these less orderly careers.

Though the upper echelons literature has a history of explaining firm outcomes via CEOs' careers (Higgins and Dillon, 2007), recent work has considered a broader set of workers, using more readily available and comprehensive biographical career data from sources like LinkedIn (Bidwell and Mollick, 2015; Gaba and Dokko, 2016) or more standardized and objective records of work experiences (e.g., online labor markets; Leung, 2014). The increasing availability of these data provides increasing opportunities to explore career patterns and progressions.

Economics

As in the previous sections on economic theory, human capital theory has been used to consider the consequences of career patterns and progressions. Interestingly, a great deal of this work has focused on the careers of entrepreneurs or organizational leaders, expanding human capital theory to include the idea of diverse skills (Lazear, 2004). Studies have shown that diverse career backgrounds and prior entrepreneurial experience are associated with becoming an entrepreneur (Astebro and Thompson, 2011; Shane and Khurana, 2003). Further, performance of new ventures, a career success outcome for entrepreneurs, is associated with prior entrepreneurial experience (Hsu, 2007; Paik, 2014), as well as within-industry experience (Chatterji, 2009; Dahl and Reichstein, 2007).

Sociology

From a sociology standpoint, probably the most influential perspective for scholars of career patterns has been Barley's (1989: 53) adaptation of structuration theory to career studies. Building on the early Chicago School studies of careers, Barley proposed the notion of career scripts that "encode contextually appropriate behaviors and perceptions" as an intermediate link between the institutions that structure people's work lives and the actions of individuals who enact those institutions. Using career structuration theory, scholars have examined the coexistence of organizational and global managerial career scripts (Cappellen and Janssens, 2010), career transitions (Duberley et al., 2006b), the construction of scientific careers (Duberley et al., 2006a), and patterns for promotion in academia (Dany et al., 2011). These studies share an interest in how pre-existing scripts influence people's career actions and how people's decisions and actions may in turn shape the scripts they use, making these studies among the most theoretically ambitious that career research offers today.

Another growing stream of research on career patterns originates from work in economic sociology on the valuation of social objects in critics-mediated markets (Hsu, 2006). Employers are seen here as critics, or evaluators, of an individual's prior career, and their valuation of certain job sequences over others depends on what the employers are looking for when they seek a new hire. Scholars have applied this theory in particular to specialized versus diverse career patterns. While seminal work in sociology found that early-career individuals were rewarded more for specialism in a line of work and later career individuals for generalism across lines of work (Zuckerman et al., 2003), subsequent studies have nuanced this conclusion. Ferguson and Hasan (2013) found that specialism benefits workers throughout their career in the Indian Administrative Service. Leung (2014) identified coherence in career history as a key factor for subsequent success in a market for freelance programmers. In addition, Merluzzi and Phillips (2016) found that generalists may be preferred when specialists are the modal candidate rather than the rare one. In qualitative work, O'Mahony and Bechky (2006) also showed that contract workers engage in "stretchwork" to construct labor market identities that appeared coherent to potential employers.

Another stream of work draws on micro-sociological theories of cultural and social roles-based beliefs, norms, and identities as influences on people's decisions and actions, especially as these contribute to inequality in careers outcomes (e.g., Ridgeway and Correll, 2000). On the one hand, individuals choose courses of action consistent with norms and values implied by the identities they are committed to (e.g., Foote, 1951). Cultural beliefs about gender-appropriate jobs, for instance, are found to constrain women's job application decisions, such that women's and men's propensity to identify with different types of jobs explains some of the difference in occupational choices (Barbulescu and Bidwell, 2013). On the other hand, internalized beliefs about group differences and anticipation of how those differences will play out in the future career also shape individuals' occupational aspirations; gay men and lesbians tend to concentrate in occupations that provide task independence or require social perceptions, or both (Tilcsik et al., 2015).

Finally, research on patterns in careers also draws on micro-sociological theory about social referents. Social referents affect the likelihood of changing careers (Higgins, 2001) and influence people's notions about whom they might aspire to emulate (Gibson and Lawrence, 2010; Grote and Hall, 2013). Reciprocally, prior career patterns have been shown to influence employees' subsequent positioning in informal social structures (e.g., people with atypical careers are more likely to become brokers; Kleinbaum, 2012) and managers' reference groups for adoption and abandonment of practices (Gaba and Dokko, 2016).

Psychology

Scholars drawing upon psychological theories have examined what outlooks facilitate careers in the new economy. For example, protean career orientation is a career mindset in line with the flexibility, self-direction, and values that define some modern careers (Briscoe and Finkelstein, 2009). This orientation contains an attitudinal, cognitive, and behavioral component and is thought to be somewhat stable, in that some people appear more naturally to embrace new career models.

A second active stream of research explores how people navigate their careers at pivotal junctures. Given the deeply personal and self-defining nature of work for many people, especially professionals, identity theories are often employed to understand how people handle both intended and unintended career changes. Some of the groundbreaking work in this vein is conceptual; for instance, the notion that people's narrative identity work – their social efforts to craft identity-consistent self-narratives – may enable completion of major work role transitions (Ibarra and Barbulescu, 2010). Much of this work develops theory inductively by examining rich qualitative data situated within a specific population. For example, research has investigated how medical residents develop a sense of who they are in their profession (Pratt et al., 2006) and the identity shifts that occur as working women transition through pregnancy to motherhood (Ladge et al., 2012). Key studies have also examined how people navigate professional careers through gender (e.g., Reid, 2015) and race lenses (e.g., Slay and Smith, 2011). There has also been an examination of how people respond when their careers did not work out as planned, for example because of missed callings (Berg et al., 2010) or lost jobs (Tosti-Kharas, 2012; Zikic and Klehe, 2006).

Discussion

As we have shown in the preceding sections, the major disciplinary bases of management have all been used to explore questions about careers, reflecting the breadth and flexibility of careers research. Table 3.1 summarizes our findings about the major theories used from the disciplinary bases of management. As the table shows, all three disciplines have been actively represented in career studies in recent years. Particularly notable is that many theories carry over across themes. Human capital was the dominant theory used for economic inquiries into careers, regardless of the interest area. Within sociological careers studies, social network theories were used to explore both career success and job mobility. In psychology, the dominant theories across all three themes were individual differences and identity. Thus we get a sense of what is being used as well as opportunities that exist.

We also note increased prevalence of sociological theories to explain career phenomena. One reason for this could be the changing context in which work is experienced. As career ladders become less prescribed, and the influence of a single organization weakens, other institutions may come in to help define modern careers (Osterman, 1996). These institutions might include occupations (Van Maanen and Barley, 1984) and communities of practice (Wenger and Snyder, 2000), as well as novel contemporary forms, such as co-working spaces, new venture incubators,

Table 3.1 Key theories in recent careers studies

	Career Success	Job Mobility	Career Patterns and Progressions
Economics	• Human capital (e.g., Ferguson and Hasan, 2013; Ng et al., 2005)	• Human capital (e.g., Campbell et al., 2012; Dokko and Wu, 2017; Groysberg et al., 2008) • Matching (e.g., Bidwell and Mollick, 2015)	• Human capital (e.g., Chatterji, 2009; Dahl and Reichstein, 2007; Paik, 2014)
Sociology	• Social networks (e.g., Barbulescu, 2015; Seibert et al., 2001; Sterling, 2014) • Status and reputation (e.g., Rider and Negro, 2015) • Organization/ market structure and demography (e.g., Bidwell et al., 2013; Fernandez-Mateo and King, 2011)	• Social networks (e.g., Broschak and Block, 2014; Dokko and Rosenkopf, 2010) • Imprinting (e.g., Beckman and Burton, 2008; Higgins, 2006)	• Career scripts (e.g., Cappellen and Janssens, 2010; Duberley et al., 2006a) • Categorization and valuation (e.g., Leung, 2014; Merluzzi and Phillips, 2016) • Social roles and referents (e.g., Barbulescu and Bidwell, 2013; Gaba and Dokko, 2016; Tilcsik et al., 2015)
Psychology	• Individual differences (e.g., Abele and Spurk, 2009; Fang et al., 2015) • Identity and social categorization (e.g., Grote and Hall, 2013; Heslin, 2005) • Calling (e.g., Bunderson and Thompson, 2009; Dobrow and Tosti-Kharas, 2011)	• Individual differences (e.g., Ng et al., 2005; Judge and Bono, 2001) • Identity and social categorization (e.g., Grohsjean et al., 2015; Rothausen et al., 2015) • Decision-making theory (e.g., DiRenzo and Greenhaus, 2011; van Hooft et al., 2004)	• Individual differences (e.g., Briscoe and Finkelstein, 2009; Briscoe and Hall, 2006) • Identity and social categorization (e.g., Ladge et al., 2012; Slay and Smith, 2011)

and participants in the sharing economy. The question of which groups are meaningful reference points for careers becomes increasingly significant even as it becomes harder to determine (e.g., Grote and Hall, 2013). Another reason sociological theories have become more relevant is that careers are becoming more diverse, not only in their patterns and progressions but also in the people developing careers. Accordingly, sociocultural lenses of gender, race, national culture, sexual orientation, disability, and socioeconomic class become essential to understanding the forces that shape careers.

The recent discourse around careers has been lively, and the pool of scholars interested in careers questions has been widening; however, careers studies still have tremendous opportunities for cross-disciplinary work. Scholars focusing on careers studies have always been open to and inclusive of multiple disciplinary perspectives, despite the many barriers to interdisciplinary work (Chudzikowski and Mayrhofer, 2011). For instance, a recent review of global mobility covers research that goes from the individual level to the country level and from psychological to sociological to economic (Baruch et al., 2016). Similarly, the intelligent career framework (e.g., Arthur et al., 2017) explicitly considers three ways of knowing: how, who, and why, that cover multi-disciplinary considerations. Though cross-disciplinary research is hard to conduct and even harder to publish in top journals, careers research is well positioned to contribute in this way. Integrating disciplinary perspectives can yield insights that are qualitatively different than single-discipline or even multi-discipline studies. Consider Lawrence (2011), who analyzed career success through single, multi-, and interdisciplinary perspectives. She shows how a single data set and outcome construct can lead to different questions and conclusions when viewed through these different lenses.

Among the many papers we reviewed, a few already bridge disciplinary boundaries. For example, Crossland et al. (2014) showed that CEOs whose careers include a diversity of industry, functional, and firm experiences lead firms that are more strategically dynamic and distinctive. In linking career patterns of CEOs with firm-level outcomes, they combine theory on individual dispositions, social influence, and corporate governance. Another example is Barbulescu and Bidwell (2013), who use matching theory from economics as well as theory about gender roles from sociology in order to understand why men and women self-sort into different jobs. Examining how individuals' careers interact with organizational or higher level conditions or outcomes seems propitious for using multi- or interdisciplinary approaches. Yet we also noticed how the scarcity of interdisciplinary research in our field slows progress. For instance, working at the intersection of individual differences and social networks, Fang et al. (2015) use meta-analysis to study the joint effects of personality and social networks on career success and job performance attempts. The authors set out to investigate both independent and interactive effects, but while they could show the interaction effects of personality and social network position for job performance, they could not do so for career success because of the paucity of relevant interdisciplinary research (Fang et al., 2015: 1256).

Finally, in a chapter dedicated to theory in careers research, we are bound to address the issue of whether or not it is useful to think in terms of "career theory" as opposed to theories that are used in careers studies. We believe this question arises because careers are both an important factor in many social questions and a valid arena for focused inquiry. Playing this dual role, careers can be implicated in theories of identity (e.g., Ibarra and Barbulescu, 2010; Tosti-Kharas, 2012), institutions (e.g., Dokko and Gaba, 2012; Jones, 2001), work and occupations (e.g., O'Mahony and Bechky, 2006; Zabusky and Barley, 1996), human resources (e.g., Bidwell and Briscoe, 2010), strategy (e.g., Crossland et al., 2014; Gunz and Jalland, 1996), and many more organizational and social subjects, while still being itself a subject of theoretical inquiry. Volumes like the *Handbook of Career Theory* (Arthur et al., 1989b) and the *Handbook of Career*

Studies (Gunz and Peiperl, 2007) contain essays and theoretical contributions that point to the breadth of theoretical interest and possibilities for research in careers. Therefore, rather than thinking solely about career theories that explain particular constructs with particular predictors, careers can be thought of as a perspective from which to examine social phenomena that can lead to questions or insights that have not been previously explored. For example, well-established streams of literature that have not incorporated careers, such as institutional work (Lawrence and Suddaby, 2006), structural holes (Burt, 1992), or prosocial motivation (Grant, 2007) when viewed through a careers lens might lead to new questions about the role of career experience in enabling action, or career goals in choosing when to act, and so forth. Similarly, ideas like boundaryless, protean, kaleidoscope, and intelligent careers have been called career theories but have acted more as powerful concepts or frameworks (as Sullivan and Baruch (2009) call them) that inspire specific research questions inside and outside of the careers community of scholars (e.g., Bidwell and Mollick, 2015; Briscoe and Hall, 2006; Joseph et al., 2012; O'Mahony and Bechky, 2006).

In this chapter, we have shown that the disciplines underlying the field of management have been well represented in recent careers research, with a renewed excitement and energy. The increasing number and diversity of scholars interested in careers as an object of study point to increased opportunities for joint research. More emphasis on inter- and multi-disciplinary research would advance the field of career research and also strengthen the field's contributions back to the disciplinary theory bases on which it is founded, making careers more central to organization studies.

Note

1 Though we focused primarily on general field journals in management, the topics we derive are consistent with a recent review of trending topics in journals focused on careers research (Akkermans, J. & Kubasch, S. 2017. #Trending topics in careers: A review and future research agenda. *Career Development International,* 22, 586–627).

References

Abele, A.E. & Spurk, D. 2009. The longitudinal impact of self-efficacy and career goals on objective and subjective career success. *Journal of Vocational Behavior*, 74, 53–62.

Agarwal, R. & Hoetker, G. 2007. A Faustian bargain? The growth of management and its relationship with related disciplines. *Academy of Management Journal*, 50, 1304–1322.

Agergaard, S. & Ungruhe, C. 2016. Ambivalent precarity: Career trajectories and temporalities in highly skilled sports labor migration from West Africa to Northern Europe. *Anthropology of Work Review*, 37, 67–78.

Ajzen, L. 1991. The theory of planned behavior. *Organizational Behavior and Human Decision Processes*, 50, 179–211.

Akkermans, J. & Kubasch, S. 2017. #Trending topics in careers: A review and future research agenda. *Career Development International*, 22, 586–627.

Arthur, M.B., Hall, D.T. & Lawrence, B.S. 1989a. Generating new directions in career theory: The case for a transdisciplinary approach. *In:* Arthur, M.B., Hall, D.T. & Lawrence, B.S. (eds.) *Handbook of Career Theory*. Cambridge, UK: Cambridge University Press.

Arthur, M.B., Hall, D.T. & Lawrence, B.S. 1989b. *Handbook of Career Theory*. New York: Harper Collins.

Arthur, M.B., Khapova, S.N. & Richardson, J. 2017. *An Intelligent Career: Taking Ownership of Your Work and Your Life*. Oxford and New York: Oxford University Press.

Arthur, M.B., Khapova, S.N. & Wilderom, C.P.M. 2005. Career success in a boundaryless career world. *Journal of Organizational Behavior*, 26, 177–202.

Arthur, M.B. & Rousseau, D.M. 1996. *The Boundaryless Career: A New Employment Principle for a New Organizational Era*. New York: Oxford University Press.

Astebro, T. & Thompson, P. 2011. Entrepreneurs, Jacks of all trades or Hobos? *Research Policy*, 40, 637–649.

Barbulescu, R. 2015. The strength of many kinds of ties: Unpacking the role of social contacts across stages of the job search process. *Organization Science*, 26, 1040–1058.

Barbulescu, R. & Bidwell, M. 2013. Do women choose different jobs from men? Mechanisms of application segregation in the market for managerial workers. *Organization Science*, 24, 737–756.

Barley, S.R. 1989. Careers, identities and institutions: The legacy of the Chicago school of sociology. *In*: Arthur, M.B., Hall, D.T. & Lawrence, B.S. (eds.) *Handbook of Career Theory*. New York: Harper Collins.

Baruch, Y., Altman, Y. & Tung, R.L. 2016. Career mobility in a global era. *The Academy of Management Annals*, 10, 1–49.

Becker, G.S. 1962. Investment in human capital: A theoretical analysis. *Journal of Political Economy*, 70, 9–49.

Beckman, C.M. & Burton, M.D. 2008. Founding the future: Path dependence in the evolution of top management teams from founding to IPO. *Organization Science*, 19, 3–24.

Belliveau, M.A. 2005. Blind ambition? The effects of social networks and institutional sex composition on the job search outcomes of elite coeducational and women's college graduates. *Organization Science*, 16, 134–150.

Berg, J.M., Grant, A.M. & Johnson, V. 2010. When callings are calling: Crafting work and leisure in pursuit of unanswered occupational callings. *Organization Science*, 21, 973–994.

Bidwell, M. & Briscoe, F. 2009. Who contracts? Determinants of the decision to work as an independent contractor among information technology workers. *Academy of Management Journal*, 52, 1148–1168.

Bidwell, M. & Briscoe, F. 2010. The dynamics of interorganizational careers. *Organization Science*, 21, 1034–1053.

Bidwell, M., Briscoe, F., Fernandez-Mateo, I. & Sterling, A. 2013. The employment relationship and inequality: How and why changes in employment practices are reshaping rewards in organizations. *Academy of Management Annals*, 7, 61–121.

Bidwell, M. & Keller, J. 2014. Within or without? How firms combine internal and external labor markets to fill jobs. *Academy of Management Journal*, 57, 1035–1055.

Bidwell, M. & Mollick, E. 2015. Shifts and ladders: Comparing the role of internal and external mobility in managerial careers. *Organization Science*, 26, 1629–1645.

Bidwell, M., Won, S., Barbulescu, R. & Mollick, E. 2015. I used to work at Goldman Sachs! How firms benefit from organizational status in the market for human capital. *Strategic Management Journal*, 36, 1164–1173.

Briscoe, J.P. & Finkelstein, L.M. 2009. The 'new career' and organizational commitment: Do boundaryless and protean attitudes make a difference? *Career Development International*, 14, 242–260.

Briscoe, J.P. & Hall, D.T. 2006. The interplay of boundaryless and protean careers: Combinations and implications. *Journal of Vocational Behavior*, 69, 4–18.

Broschak, J.P. & Block, E.S. 2014. With or without you: When does managerial exit matter for the dissolution of dyadic market ties? *Academy of Management Journal*, 57, 743–765.

Bunderson, J.S. & Thompson, J.A. 2009. The call of the wild: Zookeepers, callings, and the double-edged sword of deeply meaningful work. *Administrative Science Quarterly*, 54, 32–57.

Burt, R.S. 1992. *Structural Holes: The Social Structure of Competition*. Cambridge, MA: Harvard University Press.

Campbell, B.A. 2005. Using linked employer-employee data to study entrepreneurship issues. *In*: Alvarez, S.A., Agarwal, R. & Sorenson, O. (eds.) *Handbook of Entrepreneurship Research*. New York: Springer.

Campbell, B.A. 2013. Earnings effects of entrepreneurial experience: Evidence from the semiconductor industry. *Management Science*, 59, 286–304.

Campbell, B.A., Coff, R. & Kryscynski, D. 2012. Rethinking sustained competitive advantage from human capital. *Academy of Management Review*, 37, 376–395.

Cappellen, T. & Janssens, M. 2010. Enacting global careers: Organizational career scripts and the global economy as co-existing career referents. *Journal of Organizational Behavior*, 31, 687–706.

Cappelli, P. & Cascio, W. F. 1991. Why some jobs command wage premiums: A test of career tournament and internal labor market hypotheses. *Academy of Management Journal*, 34, 848–868.

Care, N. S. 1984. Career choice. *Ethics*, 94, 283–302.

Chatterji, A. K. 2009. Spawned with a silver spoon? Entrepreneurial performance and innovation in the medical device industry. *Strategic Management Journal*, 30, 185–206.

Chudzikowski, K. 2012. Career transitions and career success in the 'new' career era. *Journal of Vocational Behavior*, 81, 298–306.

Chudzikowski, K. & Mayrhofer, W. 2011. In search of the blue flower? Grand social theories and career research: The case of Bourdieu's theory of practice. *Human Relations*, 64, 19–36.

Cohen, L. E., Broschak, J. P. & Haveman, H. A. 1998. And then there were more? The effect of organizational sex composition on the hiring and promotion of managers. *American Sociological Review*, 63, 711–727.

Corredoira, R. A. & Rosenkopf, L. 2010. Should auld acquaintance be forgot? The reverse transfer of knowledge through mobility ties. *Strategic Management Journal*, 31, 159–181.

Crossland, C., Zyung, J. Y., Hiller, N. J. & Hambrick, D. C. 2014. CEO career variety: Effects on firm-level strategic and social novelty. *Academy of Management Journal*, 57, 652–674.

Dahl, M. S. & Reichstein, T. 2007. Are you experienced? Prior experience and the survival of new organizations. *Industry & Innovation*, 14, 497–511.

Dany, F., Louvel, S. & Valette, A. 2011. Academic careers: The limits of the 'boundaryless approach' and the power of promotion scripts. *Human Relations*, 64, 971–996.

Direnzo, M. S. & Greenhaus, J. H. 2011. Job search and voluntary turnover in a boundaryless world: A control theory perspective. *Academy of Management Review*, 36, 567–589.

Dobrow, S. R. 2013. Dynamics of calling: A longitudinal study of musicians. *Journal of Organizational Behavior*, 34, 431–452.

Dobrow, S. R. & Heller, D. 2015. Follow your heart or your head? A longitudinal study of calling and ability in the pursuit of a challenging career. *Journal of Applied Psychology*, 100, 695–712.

Dobrow, S. R. & Tosti-Kharas, J. 2011. Calling: The development of a scale measure. *Personnel Psychology*, 64, 1001–1049.

Doeringer, P. B. & Piore, M. J. 1971. *Internal Labor Markets and Manpower Analysis*. Lexington, MA: Heath.

Dokko, G. & Gaba, V. 2012. Venturing into new territory: Career experiences of corporate venture capital managers and practice variation. *Academy of Management Journal*, 55, 563–583.

Dokko, G. & Jiang, W. 2017. Managing talent across organizations. *In*: Cascio, W., Collings, D. & Mellahi, K. (eds.) *The Oxford Handbook of Talent Management*. Oxford, UK: Oxford University Press.

Dokko, G. & Rosenkopf, L. 2010. Social capital for hire? Mobility of technical professionals and firm influence in wireless standards committees. *Organization Science*, 21, 677–695.

Dokko, G., Wilk, S. L. & Rothbard, N. P. 2009. Unpacking prior experience: How career history affects job performance. *Organization Science*, 20, 51–68.

Dokko, G. & Wu, G. A. 2017. Boundary-crossing job mobility, new product area entry, and the performance of entrepreneurial ventures. *Emergence*, 419–448.

Duberley, J., Cohen, L. & Mallon, M. 2006a. Constructing scientific careers: Change, continuity and context. *Organization Studies*, 27, 1131–1151.

Duberley, J., Mallon, M. & Cohen, L. 2006b. Exploring career transitions: Accounting for structure and agency. *Personnel Review*, 35, 281–296.

Eddleston, K. A. 2009. The effects of social comparisons on managerial career satisfaction and turnover intentions. *Career Development International*, 14, 87–110.

Fang, R. L., Landis, B., Zhang, Z., Anderson, M. H., Shaw, J. D. & Kilduff, M. 2015. Integrating personality and social networks: A meta-analysis of personality, network position, and work outcomes in organizations. *Organization Science*, 26, 1243–1260.

Feldman, D. C., Leana, C. R. & Bolino, M. C. 2002. Underemployment and relative deprivation among re-employed executives. *Journal of Occupational and Organizational Psychology*, 75, 453–471.

Felin, T., Foss, N. J. & Ployhart, R. E. 2015. The microfoundations movement in strategy and organization theory. *Academy of Management Annals*, 9, 575–632.

Ferguson, J.P. & Hasan, S. 2013. Specialization and career dynamics: Evidence from the Indian administrative service. *Administrative Science Quarterly*, 58, 233–256.

Fernandez-Mateo, I. & Fernandez, R.M. 2016. Bending the pipeline? Executive search and gender inequality in hiring for top management jobs. *Management Science*, 62, 3636–3655.

Fernandez-Mateo, I. & King, Z. 2011. Anticipatory sorting and gender segregation in temporary employment. *Management Science*, 57, 989–1008.

Festinger, L. 1957. *A Theory of Cognitive Dissonance*. Stanford, CA: Stanford University Press.

Foote, N.N. 1951. Identification as the basis for a theory of motivation. *American Sociological Review*, 16, 14–22.

Gaba, V. & Dokko, G. 2016. Learning to let go: Social influence, learning, and the abandonment of corporate venture capital practices. *Strategic Management Journal*, 37, 1558–1577.

Ganco, M. 2013. Cutting the Gordian knot: The effect of knowledge complexity on employee mobility and entrepreneurship. *Strategic Management Journal*, 34, 666–686.

Gibbons, R. & Waldman, M. 1999. Careers in organizations: Theory and evidence. *In:* Ashenfelter, O. & Card, D. (eds.) *Handbook of Labor Economics*. Amsterdam: Elsevier Science B.V.

Gibson, D.E. & Lawrence, B.S. 2010. Women's and men's career referents: How gender composition and comparison level shape career expectations. *Organization Science*, 21, 1159–1175.

Granovetter, M.S. 1974. *Getting a Job: A Study of Contacts and Careers*. Cambridge, MA: Harvard University Press.

Granovetter, M.S. 1995. *Getting a Job: A Study of Contacts and Careers*. Chicago: University of Chicago Press.

Grant, A.M. 2007. Relational job design and the motivation to make a prosocial difference. *Academy of Management Review*, 32, 393–417.

Grohsjean, T., Kober, P. & Zucchini, L. 2015. Coming back to Edmonton: Competing with former employers and colleagues. *Academy of Management Journal*, 59, 394–412.

Grote, G. & Hall, D.T. 2013. Reference groups: A missing link in career studies. *Journal of Vocational Behavior*, 83, 265–279.

Grote, G. & Raeder, S. 2009. Careers and identity in flexible working: Do flexible identities fare better? *Human Relations*, 62, 219–244.

Groysberg, B., Lee, L-E. & Nanda, A. 2008. Can they take it with them? The portability of star knowledge workers' performance. *Management Science*, 54, 1213–1230.

Gunz, H.P. 1989. The dual meaning of managerial careers – organizational and individual levels of analysis. *Journal of Management Studies*, 26, 225–250.

Gunz, H.P. & Heslin, P.A. 2005. Reconceptualizing career success. *Journal of Organizational Behavior*, 26, 105–111.

Gunz, H.P. & Jalland, R.M. 1996. Managerial careers and business strategies. *Academy of Management Review*, 21, 718–756.

Gunz, H.P. & Peiperl, M. 2007. *Handbook of Career Studies*. Thousand Oaks, CA: Sage Publications.

Hall, D.T. 2002. *Careers in and Out of Organizations*. Thousand Oaks, CA: Sage Publications.

Hall, D.T. & Chandler, D.E. 2005. Psychological success: When the career is a calling. *Journal of Organizational Behavior*, 26, 155–176.

Heckman, J.J. & Sedlacek, G. 1985. Heterogeneity, aggregation, and market wage functions – an empirical-model of self-selection in the labor-market. *Journal of Political Economy*, 93, 1077–1125.

Heslin, P.A. 2005. Conceptualizing and evaluating career success. *Journal of Organizational Behavior*, 26, 113–136.

Higgins, M.C. 2001. Changing careers: The effects of social context. *Journal of Organizational Behavior*, 22, 595–618.

Higgins, M.C. 2006. *Career Imprints: Creating Leaders Across an Industry*. San Francisco: Jossey-Bass.

Higgins, M.C. & Dillon, J.R. 2007. Career pattern and organizational performance. *In:* Gunz, H. & Peiperl, M. (eds.) *Handbook of Career Studies*. Thousand Oaks, CA: Sage Publications.

Hsu, D.H. 2007. Experienced entrepreneurial founders, organizational capital, and venture capital funding. *Research Policy*, 36, 722–741.

Hsu, G. 2006. Evaluative schemas and the attention of critics in the US film industry. *Industrial and Corporate Change*, 15, 467–496.

Huckman, R.S. & Pisano, G.P. 2006. The firm specificity of individual performance: Evidence from cardiac surgery. *Management Science*, 52, 473–488.

Hughes, E.C. 1937. Institutional office and the person. *American Journal of Sociology*, 43, 404–413.

Ibarra, H. & Barbulescu, R. 2010. Identity as narrative: Prevalence, effectiveness, and consequences of narrative identity work in macro work role transitions. *Academy of Management Review*, 35, 135–154.

Jones, C. 2001. Co-evolution of entrepreneurial careers, institutional rules and competitive dynamics in American film, 1895–1920. *Organization Studies*, 22, 911–944.

Jones, C. & Dunn, M.B. 2007. Careers and institutions: The centrality of careers to organizational studies. *In: Handbook of Career Studies*. Los Angeles: Sage Publications.

Joseph, D., Boh, W.F., Ang, S. & Slaughter, S.A. 2012. The career paths less (or more) trafeled: A sequence analysis of it career histories, mobility patterns, and career success. *Mis Quarterly*, 36, 427–452.

Judge, T.A. & Bono, J.E. 2001. Relationship of core self-evaluations traits-self-esteem, generalized self-efficacy, locus of control, and emotional stability-with job satisfaction and job performance: A meta-analysis. *Journal of Applied Psychology*, 86, 80–92.

Kilduff, M. & Brass, D.J. 2010. Organizational social network research: Core ideas and key debates. *Academy of Management Annals*, 4, 317–357.

Kleinbaum, A.M. 2012. Organizational misfits and the origins of brokerage in intrafirm networks. *Administrative Science Quarterly*, 57, 407–452.

Kramer, M.W. 1995. A longitudinal-study of superior-subordinate communication during job transfers. *Human Communication Research*, 22, 39–64.

Ladge, J.J., Clair, J.A. & Greenberg, D. 2012. Cross-domain identity transition during liminal periods: Constructing multiple selves as professional and mother during pregnancy. *Academy of Management Journal*, 55, 1449–1471.

Lawrence, B.S. 2011. Careers, social context and interdisciplinary thinking. *Human Relations*, 64, 59–84.

Lawrence, B.S. & Tolbert, P.S. 2007. Organizational demography and careers: Structure, norms and outcomes. *In:* Gunz, H. & Peiperl, M. (eds.) *Handbook of Career Studies*. Thousand Oaks, CA: Sage Publications.

Lawrence, T.B. & Suddaby, R. 2006. Institutions and institutional work. *In:* Clegg, S.R., Hardy, C., Lawrence, T.B. & Nord, W.R. (eds.) *Handbook of Organization Studies*, 2nd ed. London: Sage Publications.

Lazear, E.P. 2004. Balanced skills and entrepreneurship. *The American Economic Review*, 94, 208–211.

Leung, M.D. 2014. Dilettante or renaissance person? How the order of job experiences affects hiring in an external labor market. *American Sociological Review*, 79, 136–158.

Mainiero, L.A. & Sullivan, S.E. 2005. Kaleidoscope careers: An alternate explanation for the 'opt-out' revolution. *Academy of Management Executive*, 19, 106–123.

Marquis, C. & Tilcsik, A. 2013. Imprinting: Toward a multilevel theory. *Academy of Management Annals*, 7, 195–245.

Marsden, P.V. & Gorman, E.H. 2001. Social networks, job changes and recruitment. *In:* Berg, I. & Kalleberg, A.L. (eds.) *Sourcebook of Labor Markets: Evolving Structures and Processes*. New York: Plenum Press.

Mawdsley, J.K. & Somaya, D. 2016. Employee mobility and organizational outcomes: An integrative conceptual framework and research agenda. *Journal of Management*, 42, 85–113.

Mayrhofer, W., Briscoe, J.P., Hall, D.T., Dickmann, M., Dries, N., Dysvik, A., Kase, R., Parry, E. & Unite, J. 2016. Career success across the globe: Insights from the 5C project. *Organizational Dynamics*, 45, 197–205.

Mcginn, K.L. & Milkman, K.L. 2013. Looking up and looking out: Career mobility effects of demographic similarity among professionals. *Organization Science*, 24, 1041–1060.

Merluzzi, J. & Phillips, D.J. 2016. The specialist discount: Negative returns for MBAs with focused profiles in investment banking. *Administrative Science Quarterly*, 61, 87–124.

Ng, T.W.H., Eby, L.T., Sorensen, K.L. & Feldman, D.C. 2005. Predictors of objective and subjective career success: A meta-analysis. *Personnel Psychology*, 58, 367–408.

Ng, T.W.H., Sorensen, K.L., Eby, L.T. & Feldman, D.C. 2007. Determinants of job mobility: A theoretical integration and extension. *Journal of Occupational and Organizational Psychology*, 80, 363–386.

Obukhova, E. 2012. Motivation vs. relevance: Using strong ties to find a job in Urban China. *Social Science Research*, 41, 570–580.

O'Mahony, S. & Bechky, B.A. 2006. Stretchwork: Managing the career progression paradox in external labor markets. *Academy of Management Journal*, 49, 918–941.

Osterman, P. (ed.) 1996. *Broken Ladders: Managerial Careers in the New Economy*. Oxford, UK: Oxford University Press.

Paik, Y. 2014. Serial entrepreneurs and venture survival: Evidence from U.S. venture-capital-financed semiconductor firms. *Strategic Entrepreneurship Journal*, 8, 254–268.

Phillips, D.J. 2001. The promotion paradox: Organizational mortality and employee promotion chances in Silicon Valley law firms, 1946–1996. *American Journal of Sociology*, 106, 1058–1098.

Phillips, D.J. 2005. Organizational genealogies and the persistence of gender inequality: The case of Silicon Valley law firms. *Administrative Science Quarterly*, 50, 440–472.

Podolny, J.M. 1993. A status-based model of market competition. *American Journal of Sociology*, 98, 829–872.

Pratt, M.G., Rockmann, K.W. & Kaufmann, J.B. 2006. Constructing professional identity: The role of work and identity learning cycles in the customization of identity among medical residents. *Academy of Management Journal*, 49, 235–262.

Reid, E. 2015. Embracing, passing, revealing, and the ideal worker image: How people navigate expected and experienced professional identities. *Organization Science*, 26, 997–1017.

Rider, C.I. & Negro, G. 2015. Organizational failure and intraprofessional status loss. *Organization Science*, 26, 633–649.

Rider, C.I. & Tan, D. 2015. Labor market advantages of organizational status: A study of lateral partner hiring by large US law firms. *Organization Science*, 26, 356–372.

Ridgeway, C.L. & Correll, S.J. 2000. Limiting inequality through interaction: The end(s) of gender. *Contemporary Sociology: A Journal of Reviews*, 29, 110–120.

Rosenfeld, R.A. 1992. Job mobility and career processes. *Annual Review of Sociology*, 18, 39–61.

Rothausen, T., Henderson, K., Arnold, J. & Malshe, A. 2015. Should I stay or should I go? Identity and well-being in sensemaking about retention and turnover. *Journal of Management*, 43, 2357–2385.

Seibert, S.E. & Kraimer, M.L. 2001. The five-factor model of personality and career success. *Journal of Vocational Behavior*, 58, 1–21.

Seibert, S.E., Kraimer, M.L. & Liden, R.C. 2001. A social capital theory of career success. *Academy of Management Journal*, 44, 219–237.

Shane, S. & Khurana, R. 2003. Bringing individuals back in: The effects of career experience on new firm founding. *Industrial and Corporate Change*, 12, 519–543.

Slay, H.S. & Smith, D.A. 2011. Professional identity construction: Using narrative to understand the negotiation of professional and stigmatized cultural identities. *Human Relations*, 64, 85–107.

Somaya, D., Williamson, I.O. & Lorinkova, N. 2008. Gone but not lost: The different performance impacts of employee mobility between cooperators versus competitors. *Academy of Management Journal*, 51, 936–953.

Sterling, A.D. 2014. Friendships and search behavior in labor markets. *Management Science*, 60, 2341–2354.

Sturman, M.C., Walsh, K. & Cheramie, R.A. 2008. The value of human capital specificity versus transferability. *Journal of Management*, 34, 290–316.

Sullivan, S.E. 1999. The changing nature of careers: A review and research agenda. *Journal of Management*, 25, 457–484.

Sullivan, S.E. & Baruch, Y. 2009. Advances in career theory and research: A critical review and agenda for future exploration. *Journal of Management*, 35, 1542–1571.

Tilcsik, A., Anteby, M. & Knight, C.R. 2015. Concealable stigma and occupational segregation: Toward a theory of gay and lesbian occupations. *Administrative Science Quarterly*, 60, 446–481.

Tosti-Kharas, J. 2012. Continued organizational identification following involuntary job loss. *Journal of Managerial Psychology*, 27, 829–847.

van Hooft, E. A. J., Born, M. P. H., Taris, T. W., van der Flier, H. & Blonk, R. W. B. 2004. Predictors of job search behavior among employed and unemployed people. *Personnel Psychology*, 57, 25–59.

van Maanen, J. 1977. Introduction: The promise of career studies. In: van Maanen, J. (ed.) *Organizational Careers: Some New Perspectives*. New York: Wiley.

van Maanen, J. & Barley, S.R. 1984. Occupational communities: Culture and control in organizations. In: Cummings, L.L. & Staw, B.M. (eds.) *Research in Organizational Behavior*. Greenwich, CT: Jai Press.

Verbruggen, M. 2012. Psychological mobility and career success in the 'new' career climate. *Journal of Vocational Behavior*, 81, 289–297.

Wenger, E.C. & Snyder, W.M. 2000. Communities of practice: The organizational frontier. *Harvard Business Review*, 78, 139–146.

Wheeler, A.R., Gallagher, V.C., Brouner, R.L. & Sablynski, C.J. 2007. When person-organization (mis)fit and (dis)satisfaction lead to turnover. *Journal of Managerial Psychology*, 22, 203–219.

Wrzesniewski, A., Mccauley, C., Rozin, P. & Schwartz, B. 1997. Jobs, careers, and callings: People's relations to their work. *Journal of Research in Personality*, 31, 21–33.

Yakubovich, V. 2005. Weak ties, information, and influence: How workers find jobs in a local Russian labor market. *American Sociological Review*, 70, 408–421.

Yakubovich, V. & Lup, D. 2006. Stages of the recruitment process and the referrer's performance effect. *Organization Science*, 17, 710–723.

Zabusky, S.E. & Barley, S.R. 1996. Redefining success: Ethnographic observations on the careers of technicians. *In:* Osterman, P. (ed.) *Broken Ladders: Managerial Careers in the New Economy*. Oxford: Oxford University Press.

Zikic, J. & Klehe, U.C. 2006. Job loss as a blessing in disguise: The role of career exploration and career planning in predicting reemployment quality. *Journal of Vocational Behavior*, 69, 391–409.

Zuckerman, E.W., Kim, T.Y., Ukanwa, K. & Von Rittmann, J. 2003. Robust identities or nonentities? Typecasting in the feature-film labor market. *American Journal of Sociology*, 108, 1018–1074.

4

New horizons

What we can learn from career's travels in different disciplinary lands

Laurie Cohen and Joanne Duberley

Some concepts seem to be indelibly fused to their foundation disciplines: society and sociology, culture and anthropology, the market and economics. Indeed, it is almost impossible to envisage these fields of knowledge in the absence of their core, defining constructs. Other concepts are more eclectic. Sliding between disciplines, in different times and places they are picked up and used to illuminate particular aspects of the social world, only to be left aside when the problem is solved or when researchers' interests move on to other things.

Career is one of these eclectic and elastic concepts. Although it is typically associated with vocational psychology and human resource management (Collin and Patton, 2009) and institutionalized through the various practices established within these fields, career's reach draws upon and is used in a wide variety of disciplinary settings. For example, close to home, critical management studies scholar Chris Grey (1994) used the concept of career to elucidate the power of self-discipline in contemporary organizational life. Further afield, for scholars of sports science (Adams et al., 2015), art history (White and White, 1965), construction engineering (Tutt et al., 2013) and dance (Daly, 1995), career is a valuable conceptual vehicle for illuminating the recursive relationship between people and their social contexts, and examining how these play out through time and across space. Within these works, though, the concept of career itself is rarely problematized or interrogated. Rather, its function is to shed light on other things: sport as social practice; the role of social, political and economic dimensions in the construction of 'taste' in art and music; the relationship between migration and the built environment. Thus, like the character Zelig in the 1983 Woody Allen film of the same title, career itself becomes camouflaged, morphing into other shapes and sizes, taking on the look and feel of the wherever it happens to be, blending in.

However, we would argue that unlike the character Zelig, who appears to move through time and space unfettered and untouched by experience, for career, immersion in diverse disciplinary settings matters. Careers look different when examined by art historians, musicologists or sports scientists. Furthermore, as career scholars, who not only use career as a conceptual vehicle for pursuing our particular research puzzles but rather are interested in the concept per se, we have a lot to learn from career's sojourns into other disciplinary lands. In this chapter we examine how disciplinary open-mindedness can (a) raise questions about our taken-for-granted understandings and (b) offer the potential to contribute new insights.

This is not a traditional empirical chapter, as it does not systematically report on research findings. However, we do use a recent study that we undertook into the careers of senior managers in a social services department in an English local authority to illustrate our points (Cohen and Duberley, 2015). It tracks the experiences of senior staff who retired from a UK county council. Between 2008 and 2011 the nature of English local government was transformed. In the wake of the global financial crash and the austerity agenda that followed, local authorities faced large cuts to budgets and huge swathes of public sector workers were made redundant. We are privileged to have been given unique access to a group of senior employees who had worked together for over two decades in the social services department of an English local authority (which we are calling Starling County Council – SCC) and who left between 2010 and 2011, mainly taking advantage of early retirement packages that were available for a short time at the height of the budget cuts.

Developing interdisciplinary perspectives

Examining these individuals' stories, it quickly becomes apparent that although the established careers literature can offer some valuable insights into their experiences, to more fully understand both the context of these changes and their impact upon individuals we might usefully turn to disciplines outside our familiar stomping ground. Career studies typically draw from psychology and sociology. By contrast, in this chapter we highlight the relevance of a broader set of disciplines that afford insights not only into our particular cohort but also into career-making more generally.

However, travelling outside the conventional boundaries immediately raises some uncomfortable problems. First, where do we look? Second, how do we avoid the charge of being 'intellectual dilettantes' – skipping between disciplines, taking what we want from each to suit today's puzzle, but without the kind of deep understanding we associate with academic rigour and quality? We have debated this question long and hard and have arrived at an approach which makes the task possible, and which we hope will go some way to satisfying potential critics. For several years now, many of the important academic publishing houses have introduced series of 'handbooks'. The purpose of these series is to amass current thinking about a particular topic. By definition, this is an interdisciplinary endeavour.

Given the extent of scholarly activity dedicated to handbooks, in this analysis we will unabashedly use them. Our focus on career and retirement led us to three in particular: *The Oxford Handbook of Work and Aging* (Hedge and Borman, 2012), the *Routledge Handbook of Cultural Gerontology* (Twigg and Martin, 2015) and the Academic Press *Handbook of Aging and the Social Sciences* (Ferraro and George, 2015). We will draw on these to examine our questions from four disciplinary perspectives: demography, economics, gerontology and cultural studies.

Methodological approach and research design

As noted, this chapter is based on in-depth accounts of 11 senior managers who developed their careers within the social services department of an English local authority and who left in late 2010 and early 2011 as a consequence of deep public sector budget cuts.

The qualitative data were generated in three broad stages during 2015 and 2016. The first stage was through the generation of individual career narratives based on in-depth interviews (Kvale, 1996). The second stage was a group interview in order to enable our participants to create a collective account (Patton, 2005), follow up key issues and discuss our developing insights. This included 8 of the original 11 respondents. This was followed by a third stage in which we met with the three remaining respondents. In addition to these formal stages, throughout the period of data generation several respondents participated in email exchanges and discussions about their experiences and their developing thoughts of the project.

Interviews were fully transcribed and analyzed using a 'bottom-up' approach (Shepherd and Sutcliffe, 2011) in which descriptive, open coding techniques were used to fully examine the data, and then moving on to axial coding to develop second-order themes (Van Maanen, 1979; Silverman, 2000). These themes were used to construct the guide for the group interview – the second stage of data generation. Our purpose here was to test out our interpretations and gain further insight into our respondents' collective memory. In line with Bansal and Corley's (2011) recommendations concerning transparency, we showed transcripts to respondents and discussed our evolving analysis with them.

In the sections that follow, we will consider four disciplines included in the three handbooks noted above: demography, economics, gerontology and cultural studies, briefly highlighting some insights that these perspectives can offer into our SCC retirement data. Given the constraints of this chapter, this will not systematically report on our data. Rather we will provide illustrative examples which we hope will provide a flavour of each perspective, their differences, and the potential richness that can result from their melding but also the limitations of these transdisciplinary endeavours.

Demography

Using large-scale datasets (produced by organizations such as the OECD,[1] the UN,[2] US Census Bureau[3] and the British Office of National Statistics[4]) to elucidate aspects of populations, demography has a great deal to offer our understandings of career. On the one hand, macro demographic patterns of ageing, economic activity, movement, education and training create the conditions in which people conduct their working lives. From a slightly different angle, although they are often conceptualized as individual phenomena and examined on the micro level, it is illuminating to consider how individuals' career journeys work together to form more macro patterns that play out across both time and space. Together these pictures become the landscapes on which people's trajectories are evaluated, legitimated or cast as somehow aberrant. We discuss both perspectives below: briefly highlighting some of the macro- and meso-level factors that led to individuals making their particular career moves, and also considering how our respondents' SCC careers map onto larger-scale trends. We consider three key issues: patterns in intention to retire versus 'realized' retirement, reasons for the retirement decision, and lives after 'official' retirement.

Demographic studies of retirement often delineate intention to retire from actual retirement – and the disparity between the two can be revealing. For example, Skirbekk et al. (2012) explain that although survey findings suggest a general European preference for early retirement (with the exception of the British), OECD (2006) data suggest that 'realized' retirement is often considerably later, dependent on a spectrum of factors including workplace expectations and demands, organizational factors, family circumstances, health, skill levels and peer group intentions. Considering US patterns of actual retirement, Cahill et al. (2016) highlight a similar pattern. A further, significant dimension Cahill et al. highlight is women's steady increase in labour market activity in the last half of the 20th century, such that their retirement patterns are beginning to converge with men's.

It is revealing to examine our data against these patterns. Asked about their retirement intentions, nine respondents had expected to carry on working until what they considered to be 'normal' retirement age or beyond. This is consistent with UK survey data, and as Skirbekk and colleagues (2012) highlight, diverts from trends in continental Europe. As Laura and Michael explain:

> I would have expected to retire probably at 65 and to hopefully have still been well and then to have some time for me. (Laura)
>
> The treadmill. I was going to go on. That would go on. I hadn't ever thought of getting out. (Michael)

In contrast another respondent, Josie, had always intended to retire at 55 because she had assumed that by that point her energy levels would have begun to dwindle. However, upon reaching 55 she realized that she was not quite finished, and decided to carry on.

All 11 respondents actually retired from SCC well before they had planned to. Although this is clearly at odds with demographic patterns that highlight ever-longer working lives, it echoes Skirbekk et al.'s (2012) findings that people's reasons for retiring are multiple and complex and often triggered by external individual, institutional and societal factors. Likewise, George and Ferraro (2016) argue that proximal events, like Hurricane Katrina in the US state of Louisiana in 2005, and the 2008 recession, significantly impact on patterns of working life and retirement.

Our respondents' accounts of their decisions to retire were multi-dimensional. The first quote below highlights individual, the second family, and the third organizational factors:

> I had a lot of interests and hobbies anyway, so I think I felt that it would just give me more time to do those things. . . . I did look forward to having more time to do what I enjoyed and wanted to do really. (Roger)
>
> I suppose it just felt like the right time to go. I mean my husband was already retired. He had retired five years before that, I think, so it wasn't an issue of sort of I'll be knocking about at home on my own kind of thing or anything. (Penny)
>
> [The decision to leave] was pressured voluntary; I could see the writing on the wall and I always said to myself that the bottom line is I'm not competing for a job again and especially I'm not competing with people I've managed for the last five to ten years who needed the job more than me because they were younger. That was a bottom line and my other bottom line was if I didn't think the service was going to be manageable in the way it was. I suppose both things happened and I just said 'I'll go'. (Josie)

Consistent with George and Ferraro's emphasis on proximal events, 9 of our 11 respondents accepted/were pressured into accepting voluntary retirement packages introduced after the 2008 banking crisis and the recession that followed in its wake.

Skirbekk and colleagues (2012) suggest that as people enjoy longer, healthier lives, it is useful to examine average remaining lifetime at retirement. Unsurprisingly, UN figures (2007) suggest that this too is rising. Because it is based on a snapshot, our study offers little insight into this trend. However, it does shed light on the implications. Barring unforeseen health problems, we can speculate that in general, people's long post-retirement lives will look very different to the traditional notion of retirement as denouement. Thus our respondents' accounts depict retirement not as an ending, but as a new beginning: full of diverse plans and aspirations, and hopefully stretching out over years and even decades.

Not only has the duration of retirement changed, but what retired people actually do is being reconfigured. Social scientists have argued that that we need new terminology to more adequately represent these shifts. For demographers, this has become an interesting but thorny methodological problem (Cahill et al., 2016). Instead of 'retirement', which as a social category has become increasingly problematic, US Health and Retirement Study (HRS) data are now gathered according to a different set of categories: not retired, partially retired, completely retired and not working but not retired. However, even this revised classification raises questions about the nature and status of 'bridge' positions, volunteering and domestic caring and about the status of leisure activities. Morrow-Howell and Greenfield (2016) offer a different set of categorical clusters: formal volunteer work, informal help, unpaid domestic work, caregiving and paid work.

At first glance we expected that these categories could be usefully applied to the SCC data. However, respondents' reported activities do not fit neatly into Morrow-Howell and Greenfield's clusters. For example, 'caregiving' was sometimes unpaid and sometimes paid – within and between accounts. Second, there was a blurred line between formal volunteering and informal help, with many activities sitting at the cusp. Third, although leisure pursuits permeated several categories and were central to participants' accounts, they are not explicitly included in the framework. Arguably, this makes them both invisible and ubiquitous. Mindful of these limitations, we have classified what respondents' described as their one or two main activities as follows:

Formal volunteering	4
Informal help	3
Unpaid domestic work	0 (but all 11 did it some of the time)
Caregiving	4 (in one case, this was paid)
Paid work (in a different capacity)	5
Leisure	9

The following quotes give a flavour of the clusters and participants' diverse post-SCC lives:

Formal volunteering. I was a trustee for two charities. I resigned from one because, unlike my usual situation, I fell out with the Chief Exec, which is very odd for me, but anyway, that's another whole story. I'm very involved in another charity for people with learning disabilities called Reach and I'm using all the skills that I ever used really when I do work with them. (Penny)

Informal help. I do a bird watching group and I run a supper club and I run the games evenings – so that's canasta, crib, dominoes and whist – and then I run an afternoon crib group. (Tanya)

Caregiving. I mean for instance, we took over looking after our grandson. So we've been doing that. We did it quite a lot to start with because my daughter-in-law's father had a heart attack, so her mum who did most of the childcare then couldn't, so we just stepped in. . . . So that's been lovely to spend more time with them. And then my mum's been ill, so that takes a lot of time. (Caroline)

Paid work. I got hooked back into this kind of voluntary sector [organization]. What is really good about this is that in the set-up of this in terms of developing policies, recruiting staff, the board, how we deal with the media we simply do not have the bureaucratic constraints of the large bureaucracy which is represented in the NHS or county council or local government. The decision making process that we go through here every day is fast, fluid, lean, effective, untrammelled, unconstrained. (Jim)

Leisure. Well, I wanted to have a go at archery. So I did and I found I liked it, so now I'm in an archery club. There were opportunities in [neighbourhood] for a textile workshop and I thought 'Oh, I wouldn't mind having a go at that'. I had a go at stained glass and then said 'Oh, I'll do some stained glass work now'. They're some things I've had a go at and it gives me chance to do pilates. It's just the time available, but most of all I absolutely adore gardening. . . . And it'll give me time to be and spend time with friends. (Josie)

Our sample thus resonates with recent, large-scale surveys (e.g., SHARE: Survey of Health, Ageing and Retirement in Europe) that highlight retirement as a period which is longer, more complex and more diverse than the traditional view of retirement might connote.

Importantly, how people think about retirement and the choices they can (and do) make are inextricably linked to the resources they can draw on. In the next section we turn to economics, considering what insights the discipline can offer into our respondents' experiences of retirement and into careers more generally.

Economics

Economics is the branch of social science that describes the factors that determine the production, distribution and consumption of goods and services (Gans et al., 2011). Demographic statistics can offer vivid insights into economic issues, including individual agents, how they interact, and the outcomes of those interactions. In contrast, macroeconomics analyzes the economy as a whole and issues affecting it, such as the employment and unemployment of resources (labour, capital and land), inflation, economic growth and the public policies that address these issues. Concerns such as unemployment levels, inflation, trade, taxation and other fiscal policies will have a major influence on people's decisions to retire and their experiences of retirement. Clearly, in a short chapter section it is impossible to do justice to all of these debates. Thus we will highlight a few key economic issues that our respondents raised in discussion of their careers and the transition to retirement.

Economics is of central importance to careers as the state of the economy provides an important context or backdrop against which careers are played out. The original incentive for this study was to examine the impact of the financial crisis, so economics looms large. And because our respondents were based in the public sector, this was linked to politics and ideology. They talked at length about introduction of a neoliberal market philosophy enacted through new public management. Jim, for example, related how change evolved:

The new managerialism in the late 1980s and the 90s was impacting on the county council, and at the same time the huge impact of performance culture emanating from central government under New Labour was beginning to impact on the way the county council and the social services department saw itself. . . . The times I heard we must learn from the business sector. (Jim)

After the financial crisis hit and the Conservative coalition came to power, that change became more dramatic:

Well, obviously things started to get very difficult financially. I mean there were very big telephone numbers [very big numbers] spoken about savings and we were already working on savings. (Caroline)

The last year or so I'd kind of worked ridiculous hours in the job because I was doing the Supporting People job, but I was also acting up as assistant director. So I was trying to do both jobs half time, but actually I was really doing both jobs full-time, if you like. It was just a crazy time in my life, but also it was all devoted to making savings, cutting services. (Paul)

Eventually the cuts to the public sector meant that these individuals were able to take voluntary redundancy and retire early – something they would previously not have considered. But the wider context, coupled with their privileged positions in terms of pension provision, made this option more attractive.

Price and Livsey (2015) discuss the role of the state and markets in structuring the life course. They point to the neoliberal economic policies of recent governments and the shrinking of the state sector leading to an 'increased individualization of risk' (ibid.: 306), as citizens are reconceptualized as consumers. In this context, scholars such as Chan (Chan, 2012) and Cahill et al. (2016) highlight the impact of social security provision, access to pensions, savings rates, technology and health changes and demographic changes upon labour participation rates amongst older workers. Cahill and colleagues argue that the influence of the macro-economy has become more pronounced in recent years and discuss how the stock market crash of 2008–2009 impacted on workers' retirement plans as a result of decreased financial wealth and decreased property values. They also examine the impact of the economy on older people's wages and unemployment levels (Coile and Levine, 2011; Gorodnichenko and Schnitzer, 2013).

The respondents in this study were all in a fortunate position with regard to pensions as they benefited from a 'final salary' pension scheme. Although several left before they had planned to, they had access to good pension provision, enabling them to take an agentic view of retirement.

> I still feel embarrassed actually about getting a gold-plated local authority pension at 55, but not embarrassed enough to be too upset. (Michael)
>
> I felt so lucky. I'd got my pension, I paid off the mortgage because second marriage, longer mortgage. It would have gone into 67 before I finished it, but I paid it off. Thank you very much and good night. [laughter] So I felt good about leaving. I felt okay about it. (Roger)

That said, as the quote below illustrates, finances remained a concern for some and the majority of our respondents, particularly those who were younger, continued to work in some capacity to supplement their pensions:

> It was later on in the year. They offered me a reasonable return on my hours and I think I was quite up for it actually. I felt there was a bit of a gap there maybe. Maybe there was a little bit of a gap there in terms of what I wanted to do. I hadn't particularly thought I was going to finish work altogether, whether it was voluntary work or paid work, and I think I was looking for a little bit of paid work just to top up the pension. (Roger)

An additional area where we can see the insight offered by an economics perspective on our understandings of career in the literature is in the idea of productive ageing. According to Morrow Howell and Greenfield (2016), the most commonly accepted definition of productive involves monetary value, in terms of producing goods and services. However, when we are looking at older workers and retirement, we have to recognize that productive activities include unpaid activities. Typically these are valued by multiplying the time spent on them by a financial value attributed to the activity. Morrow-Howell and Greenfield (2016: 294) suggest that estimation techniques such as this lead to calculations for example that older adults provide $1 billion worth of care to parents, spouses and grandchildren. Although none of our respondents would categorize themselves as full-time carers, the majority was involved in some form of unpaid care at some point and volunteering was also common. The variety of activities that individuals take part in as they age and the factors which enable and constrain this participation is a key issue for the next discipline we are considering: gerontology.

Gerontology

Gerontology refers to the scientific study of the ageing process at the individual and the societal level. It is an interdisciplinary field including social, psychological and physical perspectives. Moen and Spencer (2006: 129) propose that the third age is outside of what is normally seen as institutional careers, starting with a period of education, followed by years of productive work and then retirement, seen from this perspective as the onset of old age. However, demographic changes discussed earlier point to a changing conception of old age, and life course approaches have been modified to take account of the varied experience of retirement which now exists.

Whilst it might seem unusual to consider gerontology as an element of career, the field provides a number of conceptual models and tools that enhance our understandings, potentially offering new insights into the interrelationship between the physical, psychological and social elements of work. Life course perspectives (Lynch and Danely, 2013; Shanahan et al., 2016) have particular resonance for the study of career:

> Understanding the life course perspective is about describing individual and collective experiences and statuses over long stretches of time and explaining the short- and long-range causes of and consequences of these patterns. It is also about addressing a range of social, historical and cultural forces that determine the structure and content of life experiences and pathways.
>
> *(Settersten, 2006: 4)*

Of central concern here is the importance of life course capital and risks (O'Rand, 2006). Capital refers to the interdependent stocks of resources that are accumulated and/or dissipated over the life course (O'Rand, 2006: 146), while risks include differential likelihoods of exposure to adverse conditions (disadvantages) or structural opportunities (advantages) that enable the accumulation, protection or depletion of these capitals. Moen and Spencer (2006: 130) argue that the life course is not merely a process of accumulation but rather involves strategic selection as individuals 'adapt to their changing situations'. These adaptive strategies are core to life course research, with important implications for career.

According to Settersten (2006), five principles underpin the life course approach:

1   *Lifespan development*: a key finding from this perspective relates to the cumulative career disadvantage experienced by women (Allen and Shockley, 2016) as a result of greater informal caring responsibilities and potentially discontinuous fragmented careers.
2   *Agency*: a concern with the choices people make within structures of opportunity and constraint and how decisions made early on impact on what happens later. This is illustrated in the following quotes. The first, from Jim, presents a highly agentic picture. This is in stark contrast to Josie's feelings of having very little room for manoeuvre in the second:

> I viewed this as an absolutely fantastic opportunity to try and bang some heads together because I knew how to do it. . . . That was very strong for me. (Jim)
> I think I hated the way it was and what had changed. I just didn't want to be a part of dismantling services that I'd spent a lifetime building up. . . . They were all things that I just couldn't politically or idealistically actually agree with and struggled to actually feel that I was doing anything meaningful when I had to co-operate. (Josie)

3   *Time and place*: contextualization is a core element of the life course perspective (Moen, 2012; George, 1993), providing insights into linkages between individuals, institutions,

social structural disparities and social change in the shaping of social behavior. When discussing why she had chosen to be a social worker, Josie highlights the cultural context in which she grew up:

> It was a combination of things like it was for an awful lot of people in the late '60s/early '70s, which was a combination of, I would say, left wing idealism, really a sense in which we wanted to build a fairer, less stigmatising society with greater equality for all and a sense that if we went into this area of work, social work in particular, that there was something about it being empowering, enabling people to improve their lives and to enable them to do that in a supportive way. (Josie)

4   *Timing*: as this quote highlights, the effects of events and other experiences vary depending on age/life stage:

> I didn't have [my daughter] till I was 40 and I'd waited a long time for her, so I wasn't going to miss her once I'd got her. . . . So I didn't actively seek progression really because if I'd gone for that it would have had different requirements and I didn't feel I wanted to do that. (Caroline)

5   *Linked lives*: a key element of the life course approach concerns the social networks and relationships that structure opportunities and constraints available to individuals. Women, in particular, have been found to take a relational perspective on their careers. In the following quote, Laura highlights both the relational nature of her decision and the effect of others' ill-health on her own perceptions:

> So pretty much at the time my marriage was breaking up and my life was changing at work, my sister was quite poorly. . . . So that was a bit of a, you know, we think we've got a lot of life left and maybe we haven't. They were looking for people to take voluntary redundancy and I just thought maybe the life I've got is rather more limited than I'd previously thought. (Laura)

This quote raises another important element of a life course/gerontological perspective – the consideration of biology. Gerontology highlights the important influence of physical health upon career and also recognizes that physical and psychological health is an outcome of career experiences (Morrow-Howell and Greenfield, 2016; Wang, 2012). Whilst this is implicit in much career theorizing, it is rarely explicitly examined.

A number of our respondents discussed their health when talking about their decision to leave the organization.

> The other thing that did was I thought my. . . . Well, I knew my memory was failing. One thing I won't forget when I talk about David who became my boss, he could tell me details about my budgets and what I was responsible for and I thought 'Goodness, I can't remember that'. . . . My mum got demented, not badly demented but demented around that sort of time and I did actually go to my GP and say I'm worried about my memory. (Michael)

Through their focus on physical well-being, gerontological studies introduce alternative methodologies and more diverse measurement procedures, such as the use of biomarkers and other clinical data (Morrow-Howell and Greenfield, 2016). In contrast to these objective, medical approaches, the following section on cultural studies focuses on subjectivity and meaning-making.

Cultural studies

Cultural studies is a field of academic enquiry and analysis that emerged (primarily in the UK) in the 1970s and '80s, drawing on insights from political theory, history, literature and linguistics, anthropology and sociology. In the face of large-scale social and economic change in the post-war era, cultural studies challenged the association of culture with elites, attendant notions of 'the canon' and the apparent inevitability of meaning. Highlighting meaning as a 'site of struggle', Stuart Hall, a leading theorist within the field, sees the field as converging around its conceptualization of culture:

> [The field] stands opposed to the residual and merely reflective role assigned to 'the cultural'.... It defines 'culture' as *both* the meanings and values which arise amongst distinctive social groups and classes, on the basis of their given historical conditions and relationships... *and* as the lived traditions and practices though which those 'understandings' are expressed and in which they are embodied.
>
> *(Hall, 1980: 9)*

With respect to career, cultural studies perspectives pose a challenge to our core concepts, models and theories, and the deeply embedded assumptions upon which they are based, and offer new ways of seeing. They invite us to question how people with different histories and in different social locations experience working life and career. Indeed, the concept of career itself could be usefully examined as a cultural sign, representing and reproducing certain meanings and prescriptions, resisting others and offering possibilities of change.

For careers research, the cultural turn involves an appreciation of how the conditions of late modernity have destabilized patterns of career-making and thinking, more dynamic relationships between people and social structures, and the idea that careers are contingent, fundamentally shaped by cultural phenomena and processes (Bauman, 2000; Ulrich, 2000). It leads to a move away from realist ontological and epistemological positions to a focus on people's working lives and career-making as socially constructed.

Bornat (2015) explains that, from a methodological point of view, the cultural turn necessitates approaches that enable researchers to access 'little narratives' (Lyotard, 1984), challenge normative assumptions about working life and hear frequently silenced voices about how careers are developed and legitimated within particular, local conditions. She suggests that narrative methods, which seek to generate insights into people's subjective experiences, are well suited to this task. As we noted earlier, our SCC study was based on the generation of career narratives. Embedded within these narratives were issues of language and meaning-making, and about the creation and re/creation of identity. Both offered insights into retirement lives that were often eclipsed or ignored by other disciplinary perspectives.

Whereas previously gerontologists typically focused on ageing processes in terms of fixed stages and phases, the cultural turn takes issue with what was assumed to be a 'natural' progression (Grenier, 2015), emphasizing fluidity and permeability and destablizing familiar scripts. These ideas resonate in our data. Several respondents were uncertain about how to talk about their new phase of life. 'Retirement' did not effectively describe their experience, but neither did any other term. Penny and Paul explain:

> I took voluntary redundancy. I mean I refer to myself as retired because I am in effect, but I wasn't at an age where I had to retire or when I thought, 'I am going to retire' and I think there may be a difference between the two. (Penny)

> It's funny because you spend your whole life thinking that at one point you will be either retired or, I mean I don't regard myself as retired anyway or even semi-retired because as far as I'm concerned I'm still working, but I just work part-time now. Some people would argue that it's a kind of semi-retirement. . . . I suppose the difference for me personally is that with my other job, all through my whole career I never ever left it behind at five o'clock. (Paul)

For Penny, the uncertainty related to her age, her prior intention, the 'deal' she struck with her employer and her current work status. Paul's uncertainty, on the other hand, was linked to others' views of his status and to where he drew the boundary between work and personal life. This lack of adequate terminology (Cahill et al., 2016) mattered because it connected to fundamental issues of identity: how respondents saw themselves, how others saw them, how they retrospectively accounted for their SCC years and what all this meant for their sense of purpose and self-worth.

The issue of identity loomed large in people's accounts, and several respondents recounted their feelings of loss having left SCC. As Josie explained:

> For the first year one of the things I talked about to friends was I said, 'I find there's lots of things to do, but what I feel is I've lost a purpose', and it was the loss of purpose that puzzled me. I've always had a purpose being either a mum or a manager or a social worker or whatever and a lot of the things when you identify what your purpose is are work related. 'So what's my purpose now?' And actually, just by puzzling about it, it lost its importance. A purpose is to, if you like, make as positive impact on the world and people around me. So you know, I'm an avid environmentalist and I do the things I can now to make an impact. (Josie)

Although she initially experienced a rupture in her sense of self, over time Josie regained this by recognizing an overarching set of values and commitments that served to create a link between her years at SCC and her current situation. Indeed, this story of identity lost and rediscovered recurred in respondents' accounts. In weaving together past and present in their course of their narratives, most respondents created a sense of coherence about who they were and what their careers were for.

Many respondents were unsure about their post-SCC status and the lack of words to describe it. As Caroline explained, 'There is no label that says I go and visit my friend who's 51 and demented'. In her analysis of retirement, Vickerstaff (2015) offers two salient images: one of 'agency and choice, and new beginnings', and a contrasting image of 'deprivation, failing health and dependency'. In many ways our narratives depict the former: these are highly agentic people with significant cultural and social capital and enough financial capital to make lifestyle choices. However, at the same time they have ongoing concerns about what all this amounts to in identity terms, and much of the 'work' they did in their interviews was about constructing a sense of coherence. Perhaps this is because there are as yet few blueprints about 'third-age careers' (Lloyd, 2015) and because in some ways our respondents were the trailblazers.

However, there was at the same time a sense that norms were beginning to be established and agreed. In the preceding quote, Josie talked about being very busy. We noted that statements like this were repeated across the dataset. Our respondents had lots to do, and some even wondered how they had ever had time to go to work. Often these comments had distinctly moral overtones which to us suggested a social, collective imperative about what 'good' retirement looks like, echoing some fascinating new research into what has been called 'productive ageing'

(Morrow-Howell and Greenfield, 2016). Being busy was important, and so was being adventurous. Jim, for example, was proud of the fact that unlike his busy colleagues, he was happy 'drifting' around the city centre for a year after leaving SCC. Significantly, two respondents who had no wish to travel or pursue dangerous sports apologized for their lack of spirit.

As they referenced their own experience against these ideals, respondents compared themselves to others in the group. For example, Jonathon explained how the men and the women in the group had very different post-SCC experiences (Twigg and Martin, 2015). He added that because the men's identities were fundamentally tied up with work, most ended up going back to paid employment, while the women felt able to explore a wider range of options. What we saw in our data, thus, was an ongoing interplay of gender, occupational role, age, family circumstances and so forth, which together produced 'diverse life stories' (Hearn and Wray, 2015: 204). Importantly, amongst our respondents there was a sense that these diverse approaches were not necessarily accorded equal value. Rather, alongside the emergence of difference, there was an emergent hierarchy of worth within which certain lifestyles were seen to be more highly valued than others.

Discussion and conclusions

As the preceding sections have shown, different disciplines have the potential to offer important and, we would argue, refreshing alternative insights into the concept of career, utilizing concepts and methodologies that may be seen as alien to traditional careers research. The choice of appropriate disciplines to consider should be determined by the issue or problem being studied. This chapter focused on a study of retirement, but one could easily imagine that other disciplines would be more appropriate for studies of other aspects of career.

That said, our application of demography, economics, gerontology and cultural studies to our SCC retirement study offers insights that are pertinent to the wider career field. From demography we come to appreciate the importance of extending our gaze beyond our field's usual levels of analysis, the individual and/or the organization, to populations situated in time and space. Analyses at the macro level illuminate how careers work, as patterns that are inextricably linked to their wider contexts (Bornat, 2015; Cahill et al., 2016). These patterns are used as reference points against which individuals make sense of and judge their own (and others') career-making.

We have argued that demographic studies of retirement intention versus 'realized' retirement, reasons for retirement and post 'official' retirement lives (Morrow-Howell and Greenfield, 2016) highlight the limitations of the terms we use to describe working and post-working life and the increasing blurriness of the boundaries between them. This is clearly relevant to the career field more generally where key concepts are subject to ongoing scrutiny and contestation. Importantly, demography provides us with methodological tools to examine and evaluate this dynamism as expressions of wider social, economic and cultural trends.

Economics gives us further insights into the contexts within which careers are conceived and played out, and in particular into the structures of opportunity available to individuals as they seek to develop meaningful working lives. Our application of perspectives from economics to our SCC study highlighted the salience of current economic conditions to individuals' career options and the importance of economic policies on social security and pension arrangements for their career decision-making. Crucially, such perspectives remind us of the inextricable relationship between the state, markets and the life course (Price and Livsey, 2015; Cahill et al., 2016).

Furthermore, economics draws our attention to the idea of productivity: a concept that lurks implicitly in much of our career thinking, but which rarely surfaces. Not only do economists quantify the value of our working lives in terms of the production of goods and services, but the concept of monetarizing an individual's contribution has also been extended to retirement (Morrow-Howell and Greenfield, 2016). In that context the notion of 'value' becomes much wider, extending beyond paid work to a whole range of activities, including caregiving. Here two important points emerge. First, considering career in terms of productivity elucidates powerful but often hidden ideological assumptions that underpin our frameworks for understanding. We career researchers like to talk about meaning, purpose, adaptability, competence and success – but we rarely associate these with productivity. And yet, both formally and informally our careers are judged (and we judge others) on the basis of what we produce. Second, the extension of the concept of productivity into retirement taps into calls for greater inclusivity in what constitutes a career, and in particular the need to extend our thinking beyond the traditional boundaries of home and work, or paid and unpaid work.

Insights from gerontology further contribute to the breaking down of boundaries, providing tools that help us to understand careers as they extend over the life course. In recent decades career theorists have called for more holistic approaches which seek to avoid the reductionism of excessive voluntarism and excessive determinism (Duberley et al., 2006; Chudzikowski and Mayrhofer, 2011; see also Chapter 5, this volume). We see life course approaches which examine the interplay of changing individuals and changing environments (Settersten, 2006) as a rich and valuable resource in this endeavour.

We have shown how central themes in life course research emphasize important dimensions of our respondents' retirement lives and, most importantly, how these connect in time and space. Outside of this particular setting, the interplay of lifespan development, agency, time and place, timing and linked lives could provide a fruitful framework for understanding an individual's career development more broadly. In particular, such a framework could help us to understand recurring cycles of advantage and disadvantage related to social identity positions such as gender, ethnicity and able-bodiedness. In a field which has been criticized for its celebration of the individual and its lack of attention to structures of opportunity and constraint, this represents a significant research opportunity. Similarly, although we career researchers recognize the importance of time and place, in practice these dimensions have often proven difficult to incorporate into our research programmes. Life course research, based largely on approached used in gerontology, could help us out of this impasse.

Underpinning the eclectic 'pick and mix' we have taken in this chapter is a call for careers researchers to engage in critical scholarship: to continually question the assumptions upon which we build our frameworks for understanding and the (largely implicit) ideological positions on which they are based. We have shown how cultural studies concepts (contingency, subjectivity, identity and reflexivity) help us to challenge established notions of retirement and what it means to have a meaningful retirement life. Similarly, such concepts can provide invaluable insights into our ongoing debates on careers and career change and highlighting lacunae in our current theorizing.

Methodologically, cultural studies resonate with careers researchers' current interest in stories, the idea that as people 'narrate' their careers they infuse them with meaning and continuity – but recognizing that these achievements are at best contingent, temporary accomplishments or performances (Cohen and Duberley, 2013). Such approaches offer a powerful antidote to the 'grand narratives' – bureaucracy, organization, person-organization fit, success, failure – that continue to resonate in our thinking. Crucially, they also inspire us to question how we evaluate research itself and our definitions of value, quality and significance. In cultural studies terms, our research processes, practices and products thus work as texts. Although we often treat them as fixed and reified – as 'the way research happens' – cultural studies perspectives remind us of their fluidity, permeability and instability.

Calls for multi- or interdisciplinary research to study career are not new (see for example Arthur, 2008; Crow et al., 1992; Khapova and Arthur, 2011). However it has been argued that its uptake remains fairly limited (Arthur, 2008; Jacobs and Frickel, 2009), partially as a result of a lack of clear means of evaluating interdisciplinary research (Chudzikowski and Mayrhofer, 2011; Klein, 2006; Pautasso and Pautasso, 2010). Reflecting on the different disciplines and their approaches to understanding career, some notable challenges come to the fore. First, the boundaries between perspectives are often blurred, and it is difficult to ascertain where one begins and the other ends. Language and understanding pose additional challenges. Terms used in one field can mean something quite different in other field (Jacobs and Frickel, 2009) – for example, an economist's understanding of the term 'capital' would potentially be somewhat different to the ways in which it is often used in career studies. Such difficulties are not insurmountable, but they do require a willingness from researchers to learn the language of other fields and to work to ensure that they provide clear definitions of their own constructs.

Perhaps a thornier question relates to the commensurability of these disciplines. For example, much economic theorizing and empirical work is underpinned by a search for causal relations and a positivist philosophy. On the other hand, informed by postmodernism and poststructuralism, cultural approaches challenge correspondence theories of truth and positivistic epistemologies, looking critically and more relativistically at how we constitute our realities and at the process of knowing. Whilst we would argue that in order to understand social problems we need to draw on a range of disciplines, given these very different starting points it is clear that bringing such perspectives together both theoretically and practically poses a challenge (Romm, 1998).

Weick (1995) argues that most of us 'oscillate ontologically', at least some of the time. We are encouraged by this view because it supports the kind of eclecticism and open-mindedness that we find enriching. It also encourages critical thinking, and a challenge to our taken-for-granted, 'go to' positions that limit and inhibit new ways of thinking. Yet we need to be mindful when we combine disciplines and be reflexive about the claims we make and on what basis. Lewis and Keleman suggest that multi-paradigm researchers should apply an 'accommodating' ideology valuing each perspective for its potential to illuminate aspects of human life. They also suggest a stratified ontology, assuming multiple dimensions of reality and a pluralist epistemology which 'rejects the notion of a single reference system in which we can establish truth' (Lewis and Kelemen, 2002: 258).

For successful multi-disciplinary research, it is important that researchers gain knowledge of each other's perspectives and methodologies, not necessarily as experts but to enable them to see the value in alternative perspectives and begin conversations with academics from alternative fields (Brocklesby, 1997). It is also vital that scholars engaging in these interdisciplinary meanderings maintain respect for the knowledge and skill levels inherent in different disciplines and we do not forsake the depth of understanding offered by alternative approaches in favour of a 'pick and mix', superficial analysis. Scholars must remain aware of their own socialization in their home discipline which may make it difficult or uncomfortable to fully acknowledge the value brought by other perspectives. Back in 1973, Gouldner talked about this in his call for greater reflexivity, arguing that developing reflexivity would involve

> the deepening of the self's capacity to recognize that it views certain information as hostile, to recognize the various dodges that it uses to deny, ignore or camouflage information that is hostile to it.

(495)

Lewis and Keleman utilize Holland's (1999) typology of reflexivity to elucidate the levels of self-interrogation and awareness that are required for successful multi-paradigm research. Holland identifies four levels of reflexivity. Level 1 is a weak form which remains within a single discipline and fails to draw on resources offered by other disciplines. Levels 2, 3 and 4, in contrast, involve researchers scrutinizing the underpinning assumptions of their own and others' viewpoints, appreciating different languages and methodologies through experimenting with new research practices and exploring the intricate differences in researcher identity, and the subjects and audiences for research. Holland considers level 4 the highest level of analytical reflexivity to be transdisciplinary and argues that researchers operating at this level must be willing to transcend disciplinary boundaries and their associated paradigms in order to further understanding. However, such reflexivity should not be a (potentially self-indulgent) end in itself. Instead, it should be a dynamic process used to enable a 'multilayered appreciation' (Romm, 1998: 65) and more effective multi- or interdisciplinary theorizing (Johnson and Duberley, 2003).

Returning to our earlier point, despite the promise and attractiveness of multi-disciplinary work, it remains relatively scarce. There are a number of reasons for this, including the training of social scientists, institutional structures of promotion and reward, publishing and reviewing norms. Lewis and Kelemen (2002: 259) suggest that researchers attempting to bridge paradigms 'live in a glass house' open to attack from all sides. It is perhaps ironic that the career structures that we operate within deter us from adopting a more holistic approach to the study of career!

Notes

1 http://www.oecd-ilibrary.org/finance-and-investment/data/oecd-pensions-statistics_pension-data-en.
2 http://www.un.org/popin/data.html.
3 https://www.census.gov/population/international/files/ipc95_2.pdf.
4 https://www.ons.gov.uk/aboutus/transparencyandgovernance/freedomofinformationfoi/averageageofretirement.

References

Adams, C., Coffee, P. & Lavallee, D. 2015. Athletes' perceptions about the availability of social support during within-career transitions. *Sport and Exercise Psychology Review*, 11, 37–48.

Allen, T.D., & Eby, L.T. (Eds.) 2016. *The Oxford Handbook of Work and Family*. Oxford University Press.

Arthur, M.B. 2008. Examining contemporary careers: A call for interdisciplinary inquiry. *Human Relations*, 61, 163–186.

Bansal, P. & Corley, K. 2011. From the editors: The coming of age for qualitative research: Embracing the diversity of qualitative methods. *The Academy of Management Journal*, 54, 233–237.

Bauman, Z. 2000. *Liquid Modernity*. Cambridge: Polity Press.

Bornat, J. 2015. Ageing, narrative and biographical methods. *In:* Twigg, J. & Martin, W. (eds.) *Routledge Handbook of Cultural Gerontology*. London and New York: Routledge.

Brocklesby, J. 1997. Becoming multimethodology literate: An assessment of the cognitive difficulties of working across paradigms. *In:* Mingers, J. & Gill, A. (eds.) *Multimethodology: The Theory and Practice of Combining Management Science Methodologies: Towards Theory and Practice for Mixing and Matching Methodologies*. Chichester: Wiley.

Cahill, K.E., Giandrea, M.D. & Quinn, J.F. 2016. Evolving patterns of work and retirement. *In:* George, L. & Ferraro, K. (eds.) *Handbook of Aging and the Social Sciences*, 8th ed. San Diego: Academic Press.

Chan, S. 2012. The fiscal challenge of an aging population in the United States. *In:* Hedge, J.W. & Borman, W.C. (eds.) *The Oxford Handbook of Work and Aging*. Oxford: Oxford University Press.

Chudzikowski, K. & Mayrhofer, W. 2011. In search of the blue flower? Grand social theories and career research: The case of Bourdieu's theory of practice. *Human Relations*, 64, 19–36.

Cohen, L. & Duberley, J. 2013. Constructing careers through narrative and music: An analysis of desert island discs. *Journal of Vocational Behavior*, 82, 165–175.

Cohen, L. & Duberley, J. 2015. Three faces of context and their implications for career: A study of public sector careers cut short. *Journal of Vocational Behavior*, 91, 189–202.

Coile, C.C. & Levine, P.B. 2011. The market crash and mass layoffs: How the current economic crisis may affect retirement. *The BE Journal of Economic Analysis & Policy*, 11.

Collin, A. & Patton, W.A. 2009. *Vocational Psychological and Organisational Perspectives on Career: Towards a Multidisciplinary Dialogue*. Rotterdam: Sense Publishers.

Crow, G.M., Levine, L. & Nager, N. 1992. Are three heads better than one? Reflections on doing collaborative interdisciplinary research. *American Educational Research Journal*, 29, 737–753.

Daly, A. 1995. *Done into Dance: Isadora Duncan in America*. Indiana University Press.

Duberley, J., Cohen, L. & Mallon, M. 2006. Constructing scientific careers: Change, continuity and context. *Organization Studies*, 27, 1131–1151.

Ferraro, K. & George, L. 2015. *Handbook of Aging and the Social Sciences*. San Diego: Academic Press.

Gans, J., King, S., Stonecash, R. & Mankiw, N.G. 2011. *Principles of Economics*. Boston, MA: Cengage Learning.

George, L.K. 1993. Sociological perspectives on life transitions. *Annual Review of Sociology*, 19, 353–373.

George, L.K. & Ferraro, K.F. 2016. Aging and the social sciences: Progress and prospects. *In:* George, L. & Ferraro, K. (eds.) *Handbook of Aging and the Social Sciences*, 8th ed. Cambridge, MA: Academic Press.

Gorodnichenko, Y. & Schnitzer, M. 2013. Financial constraints and innovation: Why poor countries don't catch up. *Journal of the European Economic Association*, 11, 1115–1152.

Grenier, A. 2015. Transitions, time and later life. *In:* Twigg, J. & Martin, W. (eds.) *Routledge Handbook of Cultural Gerontology*. London: Routledge.

Grey, C. 1994. Career as a project of the self and labour process discipline. *Sociology*, 28, 479–497.

Hall, S. 1980. Cultural studies: Two paradigms. *Media, Culture & Society*, 2, 57–72.

Hearn, J. & Wray, S. 2015. Gender. Implications of a contested area. *In:* Twigg, J. & Martin, W. (eds.) *Handbook of Cultural Gerontology*. London: Routledge.

Hedge, J.W. & Borman, W.C. 2012. *The Oxford Handbook of Work and Aging*. Oxford: Oxford University Press.

Holland, R. 1999. Reflexivity. *Human Relations*, 52, 463–484.

Jacobs, J.A. & Frickel, S. 2009. Interdisciplinarity: A critical assessment. *Annual Review of Sociology*, 35, 43–65.

Johnson, P. & Duberley, J. 2003. Reflexivity in management research. *Journal of Management Studies*, 40, 1279–1303.

Khapova, S.N. & Arthur, M.B. 2011. Interdisciplinary approaches to contemporary career studies. *Human Relations*, 64, 3–17.

Klein, J.T. 2006. Resources for interdisciplinary studies. *Change: The Magazine of Higher Learning*, 38, 50–56.

Kvale, S. 1996. *InterViews: An Introduction to Qualitative Research Interviewing: Steinar Kvale*. Thousand Oaks, CA: Sage Publications.

Lewis, M.W. & Kelemen, M.L. 2002. Multiparadigm inquiry: Exploring organizational pluralism and paradox. *Human Relations*, 55, 251–275.

Lloyd, L. 2015. The fourth age. *In:* Twigg, J. & Martin, W. (eds.) *Routledge Handbook of Cultural Gerontology*. London: Routledge.

Lynch, C. & Danely, J. 2013. *Transitions and Transformations: Cultural Perspectives on Aging and the Life Course*. New York: Berghahn Books.

Lyotard, J-F. 1984. *The Postmodern Condition: A Report on Knowledge*. Minneapolis: University of Minnesota Press.

Moen, P. 2012. Retirement dilemmas and decisions. *In:* Hedge, J.W. & Borman, W.C. (eds.) *The Oxford Handbook of Work and Aging*. Oxford: Oxford University Press.

Moen, P. & Spencer, D. 2006. Converging Divergences in age, gender, health, and well-being: Strategic selection in the third age. *In:* Binstock, R. & George, L. (eds.) *Handbook of Aging and the Social Sciences.* Burlington: Elsevier Academic Press.

Morrow-Howell, N. & Greenfield, E.A. 2016. Productive engagement in later life. *In:* George, L. & Ferraro, K. (eds.) *Handbook of Aging and the Social Sciences,* 8th ed. Cambridge, MA: Academic Press.

OECD. 2006. *Live Longer, Work Longer. Ageing and Employment Policies.* Paris: OECD.

O'Rand, A.M. 2006. Stratification and the life course: Life course capital, life course risks, and social inequality. *In:* George, L. & Ferraro, K. (eds.) *Handbook of Aging and Social Science.* Cambridge, MA: Academic Press.

Patton, M.Q. 2005. *Qualitative Research.* Wiley Online Library.

Pautasso, M. & Pautasso, C. 2010. Peer reviewing interdisciplinary papers. *European Review,* 18, 227–237.

Price, D. & Livsey, L. 2015. Money and later life. *In:* Twigg, J. & Martin, W. (eds.) *Handbook of Cultural Gerontology.* London: Routledge.

Romm, N.R. 1998. Interdisciplinary practice as reflexivity. *Systemic Practice and Action Research,* 11, 63–77.

Settersten, R.A. 2006. Aging and the life course. *In:* George, L. & Ferraro, K. (eds.) *Handbook of Aging and the Social Sciences,* 6th ed. Cambridge, MA: Academic Press.

Shanahan, M.J., Mortimer, J.T. & Johnson, M.K. 2016. *Handbook of the Life Course.* Heidelberg: Springer.

Shepherd, D.A. & Sutcliffe, K.M. 2011. Inductive top-down theorizing: A source of new theories of organization. *Academy of Management Review,* 36, 361–380.

Silverman, D. 2000. *Doing Qualitative Research: A Practical Guide.* London: Sage Publications.

Skirbekk, V., Loichinger, E. & Barakat, B.F. 2012. The aging of the workforce in European countries. *In:* Hedge, J.W. & Borman, W.C. (eds.) *The Oxford Handbook of Work and Aging.* Oxford: Oxford University Press.

Tutt, D., Pink, S., Dainty, A.R. & Gibb, A. 2013. Building networks to work: An ethnographic study of informal routes into the UK construction industry and pathways for migrant up-skilling. *Construction Management and Economics,* 31, 1025–1037.

Twigg, J. & Martin, W. 2015. *Routledge Handbook of Cultural Gerontology.* London: Routledge.

United Nations, 2007. *World Population Aging 2007,* New York: United Nations, Department of Economic and Social Affairs, Population Division.

Ulrich, B. 2000. *What Is Globalization?* Cambridge: Polity Press.

van Maanen, J. 1979. The fact of fiction in organizational ethnography. *Administrative Science Quarterly,* 24, 539–550.

Vickerstaff, S. 2015. Retirement: Evolution, revolution or retrenchment. *In:* Twigg, J. & Martin, W. (eds.) *The Routledge Cultural Gerontology Handbook.* London: Routledge.

Wang, M. 2012. Health and fiscal and psychological well-being in retirement. *In:* Hedge, J.W. & Borman, W.C. (eds.) *The Oxford Handbook of Work and Aging.* Oxford: Oxford University Press.

Weick, K.E. 1995. *Sensemaking in Organizations.* Thousand Oaks, CA: Sage Publications.

White, H.C. & White, C.A. 1965. *Canvases and Careers: Institutional Change in the French Painting World.* New York: John Wiley & Sons.

5

On the agency/structure debate in careers research

A bridge over troubled water

Thomas M. Schneidhofer, Johanna Hofbauer, and Ahu Tatli

"My career," Nobel Prize winner Herbert Simon (1916–2001) said, "was settled at least as much by drift as by choice" (*Economist*, March 20, 2009).[1] However, most of us (at least want to) believe that our careers depend largely on our decisions, which are themselves allegedly grounded on concepts such as free will, deliberate choice, or rational consideration. In this chapter we delve into the unresolved debate on how careers of individuals are constructed and shaped, and how or why they do change and evolve over time. We ask: How are we to conceive the drivers of careers at the intersection of agency or structure? Is there a dualism, a duality, or a divide between the role of agency and structure in generating and shaping careers?

Agency most broadly refers to an individual's capacity to act and to make their own choices, while structures designate relationships and institutions that create as well as constrain the choices that agents are actually able or inclined to make (see Afiouni and Karam, 2014). This analytical distinction of agency and structure, however, does not highlight the problem of "free will" versus "determination" (Emirbayer and Mische, 1998). It rather points to the question of how actors are capable (at least in principle) of critically evaluating and reconstructing the conditions of their own lives. These two processes – evaluation of trajectories and reconstruction of possibilities – are essential also for understanding careers, understood as patterns of movements within a social space over time (Gunz and Mayrhofer, 2018).

Today, hardly any career scholar seriously denies that careers take shape through the influence of both agency and structure (Mayrhofer et al., 2007). It is more difficult to assess, however, whether one or the other – agency or structure – is more important, or whether the former precedes the latter. Indeed, different streams within careers research offer heterogeneous answers to these questions often owing to their tributaries (for an overview, see e.g., Moore et al., 2007; Sullivan and Baruch, 2009; Sullivan and Crocitto, 2007; see also Gunz and Mayrhofer, 2018 for a recent review of career studies). Unfortunately careers researchers seldom address issues of agency and structure explicitly and head on. Implicitly, however, these issues are "running through the entire literature on career" (Moore et al., 2007: 30). As we cannot offer an exhaustive reconstruction of these approaches here, we suggest identifying three analytical positions towards the "structure and/or agency" debate and map out careers research accordingly:

1   Prioritizing *either* agency *or* structure. In both cases, researchers acknowledge stable entities behind actors and context. More precisely, while career actors and career context are both perceived as "things," their substances are distinguishable. Additionally, one or the other (i.e., agency or structure) is either perceived as more important and/or determining the other. We will argue that this position represents the mainstream of careers research.

2   Neglecting the influence of both. Instead of stable entities, then, unpredictable events pave the way to the "evolving sequence of a person's work experiences over time" (the career definition most frequently borrowed from and developed by Arthur et al., 1989: 8), such as luck, chance, or happenstance. Career, then, is an erratic process. Unsurprisingly, very few of the careers researchers takes this position as the explanation lies in the metaphysical domain.

3   Acknowledging interdependence between agency and structure. Hence, the whole social world, of which careers are a part, may be perceived as being generated through the processes of the structuring or shaping of careers – processes that are embedded in dynamic, unfolding social relations (Emirbayer, 1997). For instance, employment relations, gender relations, or other relations constituted within or beyond organizational or otherwise "contextual" settings come into play. Instead of opposite poles, then, agency and structure are regarded as mutually constituent. In this case, careers are contextualized and "anchored in a specific social space" (with reference to Collin, 2006), and the social dynamics within this space leaves a trace on the individuals who progress (or do not) therein. Herbert Simon seems to insinuate this notion when describing his own career as a matter of drift and choice, thereby acknowledging that he had to move in the right space at the right time to make the choices it took for him to progress in academia and take his research further, which reversely impacted on the social space of academia. This last position towards the agency vs. structure debate in careers research has been becoming more popular in the recent years although it still remains at the margins of the mainstream of careers research. We propose in this chapter that there is much promise in this third position in opening up new avenues for careers research. It represents a bridge over the troubled water of disputes on ontological, epistemological, and methodological issues in careers research.

This chapter makes four contributions. (a) It sheds light on the question whether and to what extent structure and agency are interwoven in a way that allows acknowledging that careers are outcomes of both structural and agentic forces. That is, the chapter explores how careers may be dependent on contextual developments but also how they feed back to the context (and the individuals therein). (b) The chapter contests the way that careers are predominantly seen as an individual phenomenon to be analyzed psychologically (Schein, 2007). Hence it follows the call for including important variables for analyzing careers, such as organizational structure/culture, ethnicity, gender, class/social origin, labour markets, or life context (Mayrhofer et al., 2007). (c) The chapter proposes that the more structure and agency are perceived as interdependent, the more we are able to acknowledge power and domination as an integral component of analyzing careers. (d) Finally, we account for the fundamental importance of the research philosophies underlying current debates in careers research by assessing past and current approaches with respect to their ontological, epistemological, and methodological claims. These labels can be associated with three questions: (1) the ontological question of what is the nature of reality, (2) the epistemological question of what is the nature of the knowledge of reality, and (3) the methodological question of what are the ways of attaining the knowledge of reality. Furthermore it also helps to map career theories in the agency-structure debate, which seems necessary in times of a danger of a diversified careers research field getting fragmented "with scholars speaking to sympathetic sub communities and oblivious to those challenging their view" (Dany, 2014: 728). In particular, we emphasize the merits of critical realism for bridging structure and agency, providing fruitful avenues for the study of careers.

An age-old debate: structure versus agency

Our discussion in this chapter aims to revisit careers research in terms of the popular research philosophies adopted. Thus we start with a brief section on research philosophy to carve out the distinct ontological, epistemological, and methodological positions, which are to a varying degree implicitly or explicitly built in the past and current approaches within careers research. In Table 5.1, we categorize the literature in relation to ontological, epistemological, and methodological positions taken. Subsequently we further delineate how the three approaches we identified in the literature (either/or, neither/nor, and both/and) are used in careers research tracing its particular features such as of blind spots, roots, discipline, and unit of analysis. Therefore, Table 5.1 will act as a road map to which we will refer through the rest of the chapter.

Returning to the task of setting the scene of the age-old paradigm wars, we open with a point that is made by Collier (1994) and which we think constitutes a strong warning for careers research: "A good part of the answer to the question 'why philosophy?' is that the alternative to philosophy is not *no* philosophy, but *bad* philosophy" (Collier, 1994: 16; italics in original). This quote succinctly points to the fact that understanding different positions in career studies requires us to acknowledge the underlying philosophical tensions and divides between scholars from different traditions. Since careers research is embedded in the wider space of social science, we may take a look at the fundamental problems arising there as a starting point.

The domain of social science is characterized by unsettled and unresolved disputes on the three interrelated questions that establish the background of scientific inquiry mentioned in Table 5.1. The answers given to these questions draw the lines of broad divisions of research philosophy in the social sciences. In that respect, it is possible to identify four philosophical strands: rationalism, empiricism, idealism, and realism. The key difference between these four approaches is their ontological assumptions about reality.

Rationalist philosophy deems the reality dependent on a priori categories of human mind (i.e., reality is bound with what we can think). Empiricist philosophy assumes that reality is what we can observe, whilst idealist philosophy defines reality in terms of what we can conceptualize and experience. Bhaskar (1979: 38), the founder of critical realism, criticizes these three standpoints as they commit an "epistemic fallacy" by reducing the question of ontology to the question of epistemology (i.e., reducing the reality to the knowledge of reality; Bhaskar, 1979; see also Archer, 2000). These three standpoints (rationalism, idealism, and empiricism) then inform the two broad methodological standpoints: positivism and interpretivism. Positivist tradition presents an objectivist view of reality in limiting scientific inquiry to observable regularities in the empirical domain. However, this focus often results in a failure to account for unobservable entities and processes that are "behind or beyond the phenomena revealed to us by sensory experience" (Keat and Urry, 1975: 4). Furthermore, positivism is criticized for its inability to "recognise that the social world is constituted by the actions of meaning-conferring human beings whose behaviour is quite unlike that of the inanimate phenomena of natural world which is law-like, predictable and generalisable" (Layder, 1998: 139). Translated to careers research, positivist methodologies underplay the role of both underlying structures that do not

Table 5.1 Careers research discourse over time

	Either-Or (mainstream)			Neither-Nor	Both-And
	1950–1970	1970–1990	1990–now		
Ontology: What is the nature of reality?	(a) Reality is bound to what we can observe (b) Reality is bound to what we can conceptualize and experience	Reality is bound to what we can conceptualize and experience	Reality is bound to what we can conceptualize and experience	Reality is bound to what we can observe	Reality exists twice (things/minds)
Epistemology: What is the nature of the knowledge of reality?	(a) Empiricism (b) Idealism	Idealism	Idealism	Empiricism	(Critical) Realism
Methodology: What are the ways of attaining the knowledge of reality?	(a) Positivism (b) Interpretivism	Interpretivism	Interpretivism	Positivism	Structuralist constructivism, which is at the same time a constructivist structuralism
What is the main focus?	(a) Individuals from the perspective of organizations (b) Organizations from the perspective of individuals	Individuals within the organization	Individuals within, outside and across organizations	Trajectories	(Net of) Relations, power, domination, communication, fields/habitus/capital
What is the unit of inquiry?	(a) People/jobs (b) Institutions, work environments	Employees	Mindsets, values, beliefs, employability	Erratic processes	Relations
Which discipline might this refer to?	(a) Psychology – Developmental – Vocational (b) Sociology	Organization studies Ethno-methodology	Interdisciplinary	Psychology	Transdisciplinary

Who may serve as paradigmatic examples in careers research?	(a) Psychology
	  – Super, Osipow
	  – Parsons, Holland
	(b) Sociology
	  – Caplow, Goffman
	  – Becker/Strauss
		Bailyn, Barley, Kunda, Van Maanen, Schein, Hall	Arthur, DeFillipi, Rousseau, Lawrence, Hall, Peiperl, Briscoe, Baruch, Blustein, Ibarra	Rojewski, Miller, Bright/ Pryor/ Harpham	Gunz, Inkson, Mayrhofer, Schneidhofer

Where do the roots lie?	(a) Erikson, Alderfer – Plato, Cicero (b) Durkheim, Weber	Hughes	Schein	Erikson, Alderfer	Bourdieu, Gergen, Giddens, Luhmann
What is the blind spot?	(a) Processes behind or beyond the phenomena revealed to us by sensory experience (b) Acknowledgement of influences of social structures and systems, forms of domination, cultural symbols, ideology	Contexts other than organizations – problematic in times of change, drivers such as globalization	Claims of universality, boundaries are missing	Structures, institutions or decisions that generate or inhibit opportunities	Empirical feasibility
Structure or agency?	(a) Agency (b) Structure	Primacy of agency	Dominance of agency	Neither of the two	Interdependence between the two

lend themselves to easy empirical observation and agentic ability of meaning-making in development and emergence of careers.

At the other end of the spectrum, interpretivist tradition focuses on the "reality" as it is experienced and interpreted by the actors. As opposed to positivists, interpretivists argue that social reality can be only understood from the point of view of the people (e.g., Blumer, 1969). Consequently, the subjectivist stance of interpretivism relies heavily on individuals' conceptions and interpretations of social phenomena as the basic source of the knowledge of the reality. Layder (1998: 139) presents a strong criticism of interpretivists who, he argues, envision

> the social world as entirely composed of intersubjective meaning and communication. This leaves out of account many features of social life, such as social structures and systems, forms of domination, cultural symbols, ideology, which cannot be understood solely in this fashion.

Notwithstanding the fact that interpretivist approaches potentially expand careers research by providing rich description of career experiences and choices of individuals through in-depth stories and narrations, they are unable to explain "why such conceptions are held, how they are shaped by the world in which the actors operate and the extent to which such conceptions are more or less useful" (Mutch, 1999: 329). Thus, having criticized objectivist and positivist accounts that underestimate human agency, interpretivist schools overestimate the individuals' capacity to independently interpret the world, thereby ignoring that agents "have not constructed the categories they put to work" in their everyday construction of reality (Bourdieu and Wacquant, 1992: 10).

Against the single-dimensional ontological focus of positivism and interpretivism, realism offers a third way by stressing that social scientific analysis should go beyond "mere appearances" and investigate the underlying structures and mechanisms that generate the observable phenomena or experiences (Keat and Urry, 1975). Thus realism insists on the explanation of deep structures which exist at a different level of reality than the empirically observable phenomena. Hence the reality is deep, complex, and layered, and social scientists should be aware that the real world is not explainable either by referring to some observable empirical regularities or to our experiences. For example, within that scope of stratified ontology proposed by critical realism, "attention turns away from the flux of perceived and actual events towards the mechanisms, social structures, powers and relations that causally govern these events" (Brown et al., 2001: 6).

It is this very distinction at the level of ontology and epistemology which then shapes and informs the theoretical standpoints with respect to the "dualities" of structure versus agency, which have long been a demarcation line between different social science traditions. Mutch (1999), a realist, identifies the central problem in the agency and structure debate as "the need to avoid, on the one hand, collapsing all social structures into aggregations of individual behaviours and, on the other hand, creating extra-human structures which mould and direct human actions without their conscious choice" (329). Similarly, Roberts (2001) notes that Bhaskar's realism "suggests that social structures exist only through individual agency, but that social structures provide the (un)conscious context for individual agency" (Roberts, 2001: 675). Bhaskar avoids any subjectivist conception of social structures by maintaining that dependency of social structures on consciousness of individuals for their reproduction does not mean that they are reducible to this consciousness. The value of realism for careers research lies in its conception of structure and agents as ontologically different from and irreducible to each other, whilst at the same time emphasizing the existence of relationality and interdependence between the two spheres. The principle of relationality is a key particularly in understanding careers as phenomena that are co-constituted through the particular set of relationships between agentic and structural influences. Thus realism has a potential to helps us move beyond substantialist approaches of idealism and positivism, objectivism and subjectivism, and focus on the dynamic relationality between agency and structure in constructing careers.

In the context of the fundamental social science debate on objectivism versus subjectivism, our chapter aims to provide a review of the dividing lines in career studies by explicating to what extent careers research explicitly or implicitly engages in position taking across the spectrum of structure and agency. As indicated above, this endeavour will take three directions. (1) Structure and agency as separate entities. The emphasis thus lies on either objectivism or subjectivism. (2) Structure and agency as dynamic, yet separable processes. In this case, neither of the two accounts for the emergence of careers, but something else does (such as chance, luck, or happenstance). (3) Structure and agency as interwoven dynamic processes. Here, both standpoints are merged and transcended for the sake of realism. We will delineate these directions hereinafter.

Either-or: structure and agency as separate entities

Most of the literature on careers indicates that structure and agency are separate entities, which get divided from and studied in isolation of one another (Tams and Arthur, 2010). This is most clearly visible in the so-called mainstream of careers research. In general, this tradition may be classified in three research phases (Lawrence et al., 2015): 1950–1970, 1970–1989, and from 1989 until now. Retrospectively, the first period was characterized by the focus on either the individual, the organization, or the occupation. To a certain extent, this mirrors the perspectives originally influential to the careers research field: developmental, vocational, and sociological (Sonnenfeld and Kotter, 1982; cf. Moore et al., 2007: 15).

Sigmund Freud (1856–1939), Carl Gustav Jung (1875–1961), Abraham Maslow (1908–1970), or Erik Erikson (1002–1994) may serve as founding fathers [*sic*] of the first of these tributaries, together with life course psychologists (such as Clayton Alderfer, 1940–2015; George Vaillant, 1934–; and Daniel Levinson, 1920–1994). Their heritage may be subsumed under the term "developmental theories." They have informed approaches of career stages (Donald Super, 1910–1994) or careers development (Samuel H. Osipow, born 1934).

The vocational stream shows the longest history, for its roots may be located with the early philosophers (Plato, 428–438 BC; Cicero, 106–43 BC) and psychologists (Francis Galton, 1822–1911; James Cattell, 1860–1944; Charles Spearman, 1863–1945). They have found their way into the works of Frank Parsons (1854–1908, choosing a vocation), or John Holland (1919–2008; the Holland Codes). The sociological stream can be traced back to Emile Durkheim (1858–1917), the Chicago School of Sociology (e.g., Erving Goffman (1922–1982), Howard S. Becker (1928–), and Anselm Strauss (1916–1996), but also Everett Hughes (1897–1983, although his rather bracing eclectic style may bounce any categorization) or Max Weber (1864–1920). While these origins are much younger than the ones of the vocational perspective, the sociological approach to careers is interestingly the oldest direct ancestor for career studies as a discipline itself. Starting with studies on taxi-hall dancers (Cressey, 1932) or medical doctors (Becker et al., 1961), these studies have strongly emphasized the contextual parameters shaping careers. Their insights arguably inspired the works of Lotte Bailyn (1930–), Steve Barley (1953–), Gideon Kunda (1952–), Edgar Schein (1928–), and John Van Maanen (1943–). Some observers argue that their work has somehow fallen off the field's radar these days (Van Maanen, 2015: 38).

These three perspectives – developmental, vocational, and sociological – have in common that they allow for separating the individual and their context more or less easily. Psychological approaches often stress the individual's capacity to act. This ranges from vocational psychology, whose agentic focus is often explicit, to developmental theories that are more difficult to categorize. However, even though Super's influential book is called "The Psychology of Careers" (Super, 1957), and although the book distinguishes between four career stages referring to the self-concept of individuals, he also acknowledges the importance of social roles and a recursive relation between the two (cf. Moore et al., 2007: 30). However, most developmental approaches share an empirical epistemology with vocational psychologists. This is in contrast to sociological approaches which are based on an idealistic ground. Hence we find both positivism and interpretivism as bases for early careers research. It is difficult to generally assess whether agency or structure is more strongly emphasized in either of these sub-categories: this research phase seems the most balanced with respect to the structure-agency divide, for some approaches prioritize the motivations and skills of individuals while others point out the importance of the nature of the work to be done.

With the second research phase at the latest, this balance faded away in favour of the agency perspective. Between 1970 and 1989 the attention shifted to individuals within the organization. At that time, vocational and developmental perspectives gained momentum together with the focus on what is contemporarily referred to as "traditional," or bureaucratic, careers. Chimney careers metaphorically capture their nature from humble beginnings to more senior positions. Although the individual now comes into focus more strongly, s/he moves within the organizational context. Of course, these contexts enable and restrict careers. Other institutions besides the employer are seldom addressed. Increasingly it is individual human action that is the elementary unit of social life.

> Indeed, the major career choice and development theories throughout the 20th century, for the most part, were rooted in an individualistic ethos, based on an assumption that the work-based plans and choices that people established were relatively isolated from other people in their lives and communities.
>
> *(Blustein, 2011: 2)*

Finally, beginning with the 1990s career studies put its emphasis definitely on individuals (and their capacity to act) within, outside, and across organizations. Consequently, the tension between structure and agency in careers research is now disarmed with an almost exclusive focus on the latter, not only through the concentration on individual career agents but also due to the focus on their abilities to craft their trajectories based upon their capacities and matching skills. The former (focus on the individual) is best mirrored by the contemporarily most common definition of career as "the unfolding sequence of any person's work experiences over time" (Arthur et al., 1989: 8). In an attempt to emancipate the notion of careers from older ones, which have argued that managers and professionals have careers while blue-collar workers have jobs, careers research now pointed out that people create meanings out of life experiences to build a sense of psychological success (Mirvis and Hall, 1989). The latter (emphasis on capacities) on the other hand gets visible as soon as you try to answer the question: "who is responsible for the genesis of these experiences?" Again exemplified by the most prominent career concept of boundaryless careers (Arthur, 1994), the careers discourse now seems to represent a "manifestation of wider neoliberal discourse that emphasizes individual rather than societal or organizational responsibility for economic and career outcomes" (Roper et al., 2010: 673). Hence institutional constraints are downplayed by many (boundaryless) careers researchers (I nkson et al., 2012). Arguably, this accounts for other "new career concepts" as well, because the concept of protean careers also highlights the "strong sense of identity and values as well as adaptability [. . .] needed to successfully navigate the course of one's life" (Briscoe and Hall, 2006: 5). This indicates an emphasis on individualism (Arnold and Cohen, 2008), which arguably characterizes the majority of the "new careers" literature, not only on a conceptual but also on an empirical level. According to a Delphi study conducted among "experts within the field," individual-related concepts dominate the contemporary discourse, emphasizing foremost insecurity (Baruch et al., 2014: 10). Based on a longitudinal historical study of the literature revealing yearly numbers of publication trends, Baruch et al. (2014) conclude that the most influential concepts that shape the field of career studies are (in this order) "employability," "career success," and "career track" (ibid.: 9). Yet sociological determinants shape the social stage, within which careers are played out, initiated, developed, stagnated, and ended. Unfortunately, the influence the social stage exerts on the performance of careers is overlooked. As a result, this orientation gets increasingly criticized (Arnold and Cohen, 2008; Baruch et al., 2014; Dany, 2014; Inkson et al., 2012; Rodrigues and Guest, 2010).

Recently, in an introduction to a special issue of the *Journal of Organizational Behavior*, Tams and Arthur (2010) re-introduced sociological thinking (mostly with reference to Emirbayer and Mische, 1998) to re-define career agency as "a process of work-related social engagement, informed by past experiences and future possibilities, through which an individual invests in his or her career" (ibid.: 630). This is followed by six features of agency (individual variation, social referencing, practice, outcomes, contexts, and learning), which get acknowledged from both an independent and interdependent perspective (ibid.: 636). However, despite capturing the context as multi-layered and mutually enacted through practice, power and domination only indirectly influence career agency (through dimensions such as gender, which shape values and beliefs or priorities and which are themselves derived from normative expectations, responsibilities to significant others, reference groups, institutions, and society). The relational aspect – that careers might be games for and over power and domination as well, played with other individuals, and that the very concept of gender, or priorities, might be at stake in the course of playing (let alone that the individual career agent may be the result of career-related investments) – remains necessarily rather unexplored. Hence their concept of agency focuses almost exclusively upon reflexivity.

To sum it up, the either-or approach is most prevalent within careers research mainstream and strongly influenced by the two basic ontological positions: positivism on the one hand and interpretivism on the other. It seems that the former is more important, for psychological views are very dominant (Lawrence et al., 2015: 438). However, the latter is more influential for careers research as a discipline, and there is a flavour of the subjectivist stance of interpretivism in the new careers literature (although it is predominantly psychological as well). Both standpoints enable distinguishing between agency and structure and prefer one or the other in the course of their interplay. Consequently an empirical, variable-centred approach fits well as epistemological and methodological extension of this perspective (Bradbury and Bergmann Lichtenstein, 2000). Either the individual or the context remain more or less fixed, and both appear as stable entities, which are more or less independent of the existence of the other. The latter parallels the second approach.

Neither-nor: luck, chance, and happenstance

There is some evidence that careers depend on "unplanned, accidental, or otherwise situational, unpredictable, or unintentional events or encounters" (Rojewski, 1999: 269). Referred to as chance (Roe and Baruch, 1967), serendipity (Betsworth and Hanson, 1996), happenstance (Miller, 1983), or synchronicity (Guindon and Hanna, 2002), many individuals report that such events have influenced their career decision-making significantly (Bright et al., 2005). It might also be argued that the real impact of them is much higher, suggesting that they are even ubiquitous (Krumboltz, 1998).

However, luck, chance, and happenstance are beyond the powers of agency. It is difficult to argue that individuals may control the roll of the dice (in most cases at least). At the same time, these concepts cannot be explained as products of structural forces either. The Oxford English Dictionary points out that chance is fortuitous, and neither the descriptive nor the prescriptive meaning suggests that it is produced by collective human action. For example, provided that it is not the concurrence of many dysfunctional contextual effects that are merely reconstructed as "bad luck," from this perspective neither structure nor agency is responsible for the development of careers but unpredictable processes are instead.

Unsurprisingly perhaps, there are relatively few empirical investigations in this area available (Bright et al., 2005), and these studies do not represent the mainstream of careers research (for more details, see Betsworth and Hanson, 1996; Hart et al., 1971; Roe and Baruch, 1967; Williams et al., 1998).

Both-and: structure and agency as interdependent

The (critical) realist approach argues for moving beyond positivist or rationalist notions of agency and accounting for deep structures shaping conduct, such as past events and experiences, or structures of power and domination. Furthermore, scholars sharing the view of a relational ontology argue for the interconnectedness of structure and agency. Structure and agency are thus seen as inseparably interwoven, making theories of middle range (Merton, 1968) especially interesting in their application for explaining careers. We will concentrate on four approaches in translating the works of Anthony Giddens (1938–), Niklas Luhmann (1927–1998), Ken Gergen (1934–) and Pierre Bourdieu (1930–2002) for careers research here.

Structuration theory (Giddens, 1971, 1984, 1991) provides both a theoretical and a methodological approach for connecting structure and agency. In a recursive process, every behaviour (co-)constitutes the context within which it is taken (or not), which in return has consequences for future actions ("duality"). This idea was translated to the issue of career first by Barley (1989), who blends Giddens with interpretative perspectives of sense-making, and it was then further developed by Duberley et al. (2006) to make sense of career transitions and to show that individuals' enactment of career scripts is a dynamic process impacting back upon those scripts in return. In a similar vein, Halford et al. (1997) argue that individuals not only passively enact gendered career scripts but also actively reshape those scripts in ways that tend to allow for a renewal of gender boundaries. Lately Afiouni and Karam (2014) developed a career success framework grounded on the idea that individuals experience tensions due to misaligned mandated structures and that this prompts individual agency, and in turn the emergence of what the authors call agentic processes shaping structure. Following that idea, individuals may conform to mandated rules and stereotypes, shape/adjust/reject them or create alternate, more idiosyncratically acceptable roles and responsibilities. Either way, this decision feeds back to structures which have them made necessary at first hand.

With reference to social systems theory (Luhmann, 1973, 1994, 1995) Becker and Haunschild (2003) argued that careers have an impact on several actors. They may serve as a basis of individualization for the career actor and operate as a means of complexity reduction for organizations at the same time. Consequently, new forms of careers (the authors explicitly refer to the concept of boundaryless careers at this point) raise new challenges especially for organizations.

The authors suggest distinguishing between five ways of coping with those challenges (ibid.: 722): (1) restricting the spreading of boundaryless careers; (2) supporting the evaluative capacity of the form "career"; (3) facilitating the construction of persons; (4) attributing motives and assigning personnel in spite of little knowledge about persons; and (5) enforcing other devices for what they call de-paradoxization (i.e. the difficulty of reducing one's own blind spot, which is a prerequisite of human recognition). Inspired more generally by von Bertalanffy (1948), Patton and McMahon (2014) developed the systems theory framework of careers development (STF). First aimed at understanding adolescent career decision-making, it finally seeks to integrate the whole careers development literature (ibid.: 11).

Arguing that interpersonal relationships as well as internalized relational objects play essential roles in the development of a viable and meaningful work life, Blustein (2011) presents a relational theory of working. It is grounded in social constructivism (Gergen, 2001) and extends the works of authors who point out the relevance of families, peers, social networks, and cultural factors for careers (Flum, 2001; Richardson, 2000; Schultheiss, 2007). Additionally, this approach acknowledges that other people's careers have impact on the career of the focal agent as well, which makes individual agency a process depending on social processes.

Eventually, developing theories of practice (Bourdieu, 1977, 1984; Bourdieu and Wacquant, 1992), Iellatchitch et al. (2003) distinguish four different career fields, each of which demands specific guises of capital for developing and applying career habitus, which in turn enables or restricts movements of individuals within the social space. This idea is taken up by Schneidhofer et al. (2015), who stress that Bourdieu's theoretical cornerstones make careers to serious social games for and over the social order on the one hand and the individuals' bodies and brains on the other.

Especially the Bourdieu-inspired approach indicates that power and domination are important facets of careers. Indeed, chances of access to schooling and education are not equally distributed from the beginning (Hodkinson, 2008), every staffing and recruitment process is potentially subject to discrimination and inequities (Graves and Powell, 1988; Tatli and Özbilgin, 2012), being evaluated is not objective (Eagly et al., 1992; Tatli et al., 2017), getting training and professional development is more probable when you are male and/or higher up the hierarchy (Frey and Flörcken, 2011), and compensation and benefits are the result of negotiations between two parties with varying degrees of power (Townley, 1993). All these examples show that power and domination as well as structural influences are always part and parcel of the career landscape, although they often are overlooked or treated in a deterministic fashion. Relational approaches, such as theories of practice, broach the issue of dominated and dominants within any social space (Emirbayer and Johnson, 2008). For example, a career field appears in this case as a terrain of contestation between individuals making a career equipped with the resources necessary for gaining and safeguarding an ascendant position within that terrain to varying degrees. Power, then, is both an engine of career field dynamics and the primary interest of career-related practice (with reference to Friedland, 2009). Pursuing a trajectory consequently means to decide whether to conform to or challenge the nexus of domination – the former through playing the game in accordance to the rules of the game determined by the powerful within a career field (see Tatli's (2011), work on diversity managers' careers through a Bourdieusian lens), and the latter through trying to influence the game to one's own interest, and to become powerful, in order to make the rules in the future, and to keep making the rules from that point on (Golsorkhi et al., 2009). Careers are consequently sites of power (Schneidhofer et al., 2015) where the social order is negotiated – and power is to career like oxygen is to breathing.

Discussion and conclusion

According to its "genealogic tree" (Barley, 1989: 60) careers research has two important branches: sociology on the one hand and psychology on the other. While the former focuses primarily on the social and class determinants of careers, the latter emphasizes how dispositional differences influence career choice and success (Moore et al., 2007). As a heritage of this, we currently witness a "polarized debate" (Tams and Arthur, 2010: 632) about the relative independence or dependence of careers from contextual characteristics on one side and individual determinants on the other side. Linked with this are questions about choice, self-determination, and individual agency (Tams and Arthur, 2007: 95). To be sure, agency in some sense is universal, and it is part of a fundamental humanness (Ortner, 2006: 136). More precisely, all humans have a capacity to act, but the specific forms it takes will vary in different times and places. In other words, agency and structure are connected at least in some way or the other. And they are the subject of debates that will never be fully resolved.

We have shown that the discussion about the prevalence, and relative importance of structure and/or agency is linked with fundamental problems within social science (see Table 5.1). Hence it is not surprising that careers research struggles with this debate as well. There are three perspectives available in contemporary literature (either-or, neither-nor, and both-and), with the first representing the mainstream.

The perspective of "either-or" implies a one-way chain of influence. On the one hand, careers may then be shaped by the context within which they emerge. This is paradigmatic for the origins of careers research. Ontologically, this represents empiricism with an emphasis on observing empirical regularities with quantitative methods. Here, the structure precedes the agency. More common, on the other hand, is to argue that careers have impacts on society reflected by both developmental and vocational approaches. They are mainly based on idealism and informed by interpretivism. This is the mainstream in careers research at the moment, stressing the agentic dimension of careers. Meanings, interpretations, and experiences are subjects of research. Careers are then about the "path to the heart" (Briscoe and Hall, 2006; Gubler et al., 2014). Interestingly it seems, though, that this is not accompanied by an emphasis on qualitative methods, as is usual in the subjective paradigm of social sciences.

The "neither-nor" approach shares with the axes on "either-or" that structure and agency are distinct entities. But between the two there is a process (although a one-directional one), making careers the result of luck, chance, or happenstance. In this case, the structure just precedes the agency, but the agency has a negligible influence on structures.

Finally, and this is where we see promising new beginnings for careers research, the "both-and" approach starts from a recognition that careers have societal impacts in that they are the result of the duality of structures (Giddens), the web of communications (Luhmann), the nexus of interactions (Gergen), or the net of relations (Bourdieu). In return, they also have impacts on society, for feedback channels challenge the social order and the people living therein. The more closely structure and agency are aligned, the more important power and domination will get, because careers are consequently subject to negotiation processes performed by many people, all of whom having varying degrees of influence on this negotiation process, and the process has consequences on further acting of individuals. Hence the question of structure *versus* agency does not matter anymore, and instead the focus is re-oriented towards the space of interplay *between the two*. Layder (1998: 141–142), a realist, emphasizes the relational nature of agency and structure, their interdependency on and relative autonomy from each other at the same time:

> Social activity is conditioned and significantly shaped by systemic phenomena . . . while simultaneously activity itself serves to reproduce, sustain or transform these social systemic

features and social arrangements. . . .The idea that the social world comprises both objective and subjective features and various "mixtures" or amalgams of their effects and influences means that . . . the social world is complex and dense. Furthermore, . . . the texture of this complexity and density is formed from the multifarious interconnections between agency and structure.

In this vein, careers are outcomes of the co-generative relationship between agentic choices and actions and structural constraints and opportunities. Career decisions of agents take place in the complex plane of structural influences or relational spaces, as Bourdieu would call it. This space of relations engenders relations of power and domination, competition for access to scarce resources and legitimacy, and agents who consciously or habitually make choices and invest resources in order to enhance their career trajectories. Thus careers materialize in a complex and layered societal domain, and we suggest that ontological realisms, genetic or generative structuralisms, relational theories and methodologies offer an alternative third way to understand careers, the ways in which they emerge, evolve, or stagnate. We argue that those approaches will open up new avenues for research into careers. But again, our proposed approach is not the end but a continuation of an age-old debate in social sciences in the specific context of careers research. The waters will continue to be troubled between the allegedly opposed shores of structure- and agency-centred careers research. The ontological, epistemological, and methodological currents are historical and strong and thus will prevail, but there will be many bridges, of which our chapter is an example. To us, relational approaches promise an inspiring and robust tool to navigate careers.

Note

1 http://www.economist.com/node/13350892, last retrieved 2 February 2018.

References

Afiouni, F. & Karam, C.M. 2014. Structure, agency, and notions of career success: A process-oriented, subjectively malleable and localized approach. *Career Development International*, 19, 548–571.

Archer, M. 2000. For structure: Its reality, properties and powers: A reply to Anthony King. *Sociological Review*, 48, 464–472.

Arnold, J. & Cohen, L. 2008. The psychology of careers in industrial and organizational settings: A critical but appreciative analysis. *In:* Hodgkinson, G. & Ford, K. (eds.) *The International Review of Industrial and Organizational Psychology*. Chichester: Wiley and Sons.

Arthur, M.B. 1994. The boundaryless career: A new perspective for organizational inquiry. *Journal of Organizational Behavior*, 15, 295–306.

Arthur, M.B., Hall, D.T. & Lawrence, B.S. 1989. Generating new directions in career theory: The case for a transdisciplinary approach. *In:* Arthur, M.B., Hall, D.T. & Lawrence, B.S. (eds.) *Handbook of Career Theory*. Cambridge: Cambridge University Press.

Barley, S.R. 1989. Careers, identities, and institutions: The legacy of the Chicago school of sociology. *In:* Arthur, M.B., Hall, D.T. & Lawrence, B.S. (eds.) *Handbook of Career Theory*. Cambridge, UK: Cambridge University Press.

Baruch, Y., Szücs, N. & Gunz, H.P. 2014. Career studies in search of theory: The rise and rise of concepts. *Career Development International*, 20, 3–20.

Becker, H.S., Geer, B., Hughes, E.C. & Strauss, A.L. 1961. *Boys in White: Student Culture in Medical School*. Chicago, IL: Chicago University Press.

Becker, K.H. & Haunschild, A. 2003. The impact of boundaryless careers on organizational decision-making: An analysis from the perspective of Luhmann's theory of social systems. *The International Journal of Human Resource Management*, 14, 713–727.

Bertalanffy, L. von. 1948. Zu einer allgemeinen Systemlehre. *Biologia Generalis*, 195, 114–129.

Betsworth, D.G. & Hanson, J.C. 1996. The categorization of serendipitious career development events. *Journal of Career Assessment*, 4, 91–98.

Bhaskar, R. 1979. *The Possibility of Naturalism*, New York: Humanities Press.

Blumer, H. 1969. *Symbolic Interactionalism: Perspective and Method*. Englewood Cliffs, NJ: Prentice-Hall.

Blustein, D.L. 2011. A relational theory of working. *Journal of Vocational Behavior*, 79, 1–17.

Bourdieu, P. 1977. *Outline of Theory of Practice*. Cambridge: Cambridge University Press.

Bourdieu, P. 1984. *Distinction: A Social Critique of the Judgement of Taste*. Cambridge, MA: Cambridge University Press.

Bourdieu, P. & Wacquant, L. 1992. *An Invitation to Reflexive Sociology*. Chicago: The University of Chicago Press.

Bradbury, H. & Bergmann Lichtenstein, B.M. 2000. Relationality in organizational research: Exploring the space between. *Organizational Science*, 11, 551–564.

Bright, J.E.H., Pryor, R.G.L. & Harpham, L. 2005. The role of chance events in career decision making. *Journal of Vocational Behavior*, 66, 561–576.

Briscoe, J.P. & Hall, D.T. 2006. The interplay of boundarylessness and protean careers: Combinations and implications. *Journal of Vocational Behavior*, 69, 4–18.

Brown, A., Fleetwood, S. & Roberts, J. 2001. The marriage of critical realism and Marxism: Happy, unhappy or on the rocks? *In*: Brown, A., Fleedwood, S. & Roberts, J. (eds.) *Critical Realism and Marxism*. London, UK: Routledge.

Collier, A. 1994. *Critical Realism: An Introduction to Roy Bhaskar's Philosophy*. London, UK: Verso.

Collin, A. 2006. Career. *In*: Greenhaus, J.H. & Callanan, G.A. (eds.) *Encyclopedia of Career Development*. Thousand Oaks, CA: Sage Publications.

Cressey, P.G. 1932. *The Taxi-Dance Hall: A Sociological Study in Comercialized Recreation and City Life*. Chicago, IL: University of Chicago Press.

Dany, F. 2014. Time to change: The added value of an integrative approach to career research. *Career Development International*, 19, 718–730.

Duberley, J., Mallon, M. & Cohen, L. 2006. Exploring career transitions: Accounting for structure and agency. *Personnel Review*, 35, 281–296.

Eagly, A.H., Makhjani, M. & Konski, B.G. 1992. Gender and the evaluation of leaders: A meta-analysis. *Psychological Bulletin*, 111, 3–22.

Emirbayer, M. 1997. Manifesto for a relational sociology. *American Journal of Sociology*, 103, 281–317.

Emirbayer, M. & Johnson, V. 2008. Bourdieu and organizational analysis. *Theory & Society*, 37, 1–44.

Emirbayer, M. & Mische, A. 1998. What is agency? *American Journal of Sociology*, 103, 962–1023.

Flum, H. 2001. Relational dimensions in career development. *Journal of Vocational Behavior*, 59, 1–16.

Frey, R. & Flörcken, T. 2011. *Gender-Aspekte in der betrieblichen Weiterbildung*. Berlin: Agentur für Gleichstellung im ESF.

Friedland, R. 2009. The endless fields of Pierre Bourdieu. *Organization*, 16, 887–917.

Gergen, K.J. 2001. Psychological science in a post modern context. *American Psychologist*, 56, 803–813.

Giddens, A. 1971. *Capitalism and Modern Social Theory: An Analysis of the Writings of Marx, Durkheim and Max Weber*. Cambridge: Cambridge University Press.

Giddens, A. 1984. *The Constitution of Society*. Cambridge: Polity Press.

Giddens, A. 1991. *Modernity and Self-Identity: Self and Society in the Late Modern Age*. Cambridge: Polity Press.

Golsorkhi, D., Leca, B., Lounsbury, M. & Ramirez, C. 2009. Analysing, accounting for and unmasking domination: On our role as scholars of practice, practitioners of social science and public intellectuals. *Organization*, 16, 779–797.

Graves, L.M. & Powell, G.N. 1988. An investigation of sex discrimination in recruiters' evaluations of actual applicants. *Journal of Applied Psychology*, 73, 20–29.

Gubler, M., Arnold, J. & Coombs, C. 2014. Reassessing the protean career concept: Empirical findings, conceptual component, and measurements. *Journal of Organizational Behavior*, 35, 23–40.

Guindon, M.H. & Hanna, F.J. 2002. Coincidence, happenstance, serendipity, fate, or the hand of god: Case studies in synchronicity. *Career Development Quarterly*, 50, 195–209.

Gunz, H.P. & Mayrhofer, W. 2018. *Rethinking Career Studies: Facilitating Conversation Across Boundaries with the Social Chronology Framework*. Cambridge: Cambridge University Press.

Halford, S., Savage, M. & Witz, A. (eds.) 1997. *Gender, Careers and Organisations*. Houndsmills: Palgrave Macmillan.

Hart, D.H., Rayner, K. & Christensen, E.R. 1971. Planning, preparation, and chance in occupational entry. *Journal of Vocational Behavior*, 1, 279–285.

Hodkinson, P. 2008. Understanding career decision-making and progression: Careership revisited. *John Killeen Memorial Lecture* [Online]. Available: http://www.crac.org.uk/CMS/files/upload/fifth_johnkilleenlecturenotes.pdf [Accessed 7 October 2014].

Iellatchitch, A., Mayrhofer, W. & Meyer, M. 2003. Career fields: A small step towards a grand career theory? *International Journal of Human Resource Management*, 15, 728–750.

Inkson, K., Gunz, H.P., Ganesh, S. & Roper, J. 2012. Boundaryless careers: Bringing back boundaries. *Organization Studies*, 33, 323–340.

Keat, R. & Urry, J. 1975. *Social Theory as Science*. London and Boston: Routledge & Kegan Paul.

Krumboltz, D. 1998. Serendipity is not serendipitous. *Journal of Counseling Psychology*, 4, 390–392.

Lawrence, B.S., Hall, D.T. & Arthur, M.B. 2015. Sustainable careers then and now. *In:* de Vos, A. & van der Heijden, B. (eds.) *Handbook of Research on Sustainable Careers*. Cheltenham: Edward Elgar.

Layder, D. 1998. *Sociological Practice: Linking Theory and Social Research*. London: Sage Publications.

Luhmann, N. 1973. Die Zurechnung von Beförderung im öffentlichen Dienst. *Zeitschrift für Soziologie*, 2, 326–351.

Luhmann, N. 1994. Copierte Existenz und Karriere. *In:* Beck, U. & Beck-Gernsheim, E. (eds.) *Riskante Freiheiten*. Frankfurt a. Main: Suhrkamp.

Luhmann, N. 1995. *Social Systems*. Stanford, CA: Stanford University Press.

Mayrhofer, W., Meyer, M. & Steyrer, J. 2007. Contextual issues in the study of careers. *In:* Gunz, H.P. & Peiperl, M. (eds.) *Handbook of Career Studies*. Los Angeles: Sage Publications.

Merton, R.K. 1968. *Social Theory and Social Structure*. New York: Free Press.

Miller, M.J. 1983. The role of happenstance in career choice. *Vocational Guidance Quarterly*, 32, 16–20.

Mirvis, P.H. & Hall, D.T. 1989. Psychological success and the boundaryless career. *In:* Arthur, M.B. & Rousseau, D.M. (eds.) *The Boundaryless Career: A New Employment Principle for a New Organizational Era*. New York: Oxford University Press.

Moore, C., Gunz, H.P. & Hall, D.T. 2007. Tracing the historical roots of career theory in management and organization studies. *In:* Gunz, H.P. & Peiperl, M. (eds.) *Handbook of Career Studies*. Los Angeles: Sage Publications.

Mutch, A. 1999. Critical realism, managers and information. *British Journal of Management*, 10, 323–333.

Ortner, S.B. 2006. *Anthropology and Social Theory: Culture, Power, and the Acting Subject*. Durham and London: Duke University Press.

Patton, W. & Mcmahon, M. 2014. *Career Development and Systems Theory: Connecting Theory and Practice*. Rotterdam: Sense Publishers.

Richardson, M.S. 2000. A new perspective for counselors: From career ideologies to empowerment through work and relationship practices. *In:* Collin, A. & Young, R.A. (eds.) *The Future of Career*. New York: Cambridge University Press.

Roberts, J.M. 2001. Critical realism and the dialectic. *British Journal of Sociology*, 52, 667–685.

Rodrigues, R.A. & Guest, D.E. 2010. Have careers become boundaryless? *Human Relations*, 63, 1157–1175.

Roe, A. & Baruch, R. 1967. Occupational changes in the adult years. *Personnel Administration*, 30, 26–32.

Rojewski, J.W. 1999. The role of chance in the career development of individuals with learning disabilities. *Learning Disability Quarterly*, 22, 267–278.

Roper, J., Ganesh, S. & Inkson, K. 2010. Neoliberalism and knowledge interests in boundaryless careers discourse. *Work, Employment and Society*, 24, 661–679.

Schein, E.H. 2007. Afterword: Career research – some issues and dilemmas. *In:* Gunz, H.P. & Peiperl, M. (eds.) *Handbook of Career Studies*. Los Angeles: Sage Publications.

Schneidhofer, T.M., Latzke, M. & Mayrhofer, W. 2015. Careers as sites of power. A relational understanding of careers based on Bourdieu's cornerstones. *In:* Tatli, A., Özbilgin, M.F. & Karatas-Özkan, M. (eds.) *Bourdieu, Organisation and Management*. New York: Routledge.

Schultheiss, D.E.P. 2007. The emergence of a relational cultural paradigm for vocational psychology. *International Journal for Educational and Vocational Guidance*, 7, 191–201.

Sonnenfeld, J.A. & Kotter, J.P. 1982. The maturation of career theory. *Human Relations*, 35, 19–46.

Sullivan, S.E. & Baruch, Y. 2009. Advances in career theory and research: A critical review and agenda for future exploration. *Journal of Management*, 35, 1542–1571.

Sullivan, S.E. & Crocitto, M. 2007. The developmental theories – A critical examination of their continuing impact on careers research. *In:* Gunz, H.P. & Peiperl, M. (eds.) *Handbook of Career Studies*. London: Sage Publications.

Super, D.E. 1957. *The Psychology of Careers*. New York: Harper & Row.

Tams, S. & Arthur, M.B. 2007. Studying careers across cultures: Distinguishing international, cross-cultural and globalization perspectives. *Career Development International*, 12, 86–98.

Tams, S. & Arthur, M.B. 2010. New directions for boundaryless careers: Agency and interdependence in a changing world. *Journal of Organizational Behavior*, 31, 629–646.

Tatli, A. 2011. A multi-layered exploration of the diversity management field: Diversity discourses, practices, and practitioners in the UK. *British Journal of Management*, 22, 238–253.

Tatli, A. & Özbilgin, M.F. 2012. Surprising intersectionalities of inequality and privilege: The case of the arts and cultural sector. *Equality, Diversity and Inclusion: An International Journal*, 31, 249–265.

Tatli, A., Ozturk, M.B. & Woo, H.S. 2017. Individualization and marketization of responsibility for gender equality: The case of women managers in China. *Human Resource Management*, 56, 407–430.

Townley, B. 1993. Foucault, power/knowledge and its relevance for human resource management. *Academy of Management Review*, 18, 518–545.

van Maanen, J. 2015. The present of things past: Ethnography and career studies. *Human Relations*, 68, 35–53.

Williams, E.N., Soeprato, E., Like, K., Touradji, P., Hess, S. & Hill, C.E. 1998. Perceptions of serendipity: Career paths of prominent academic woman in counseling psychology. *Journal of Counseling Psychology*, 45, 379–389.

6

Diversity as a perspective on career

Judith K. Pringle, Barbara Myers, Margie Elley-Brown, and Lynette Reid

Among the various theoretical and conceptual developments in the social sciences over the past decades, diversity has a prominent place. Beyond describing a social phenomenon including dimensions such as sex and gender, ethnicity, religion and spirituality, or culture and social origin, it has also become a perspective on social reality in its own right. Arguably gender as part of this perspective shows this most clearly. This chapter looks at the concept of diversity and discusses the potential of this perspective to generate new and more differentiated insights when applied to studying careers.

Introduction

Diversity in the career research literature has remained tied to what is known as "traditional" career theory (Moore et al., 2007). In spite of substantive critiques (Collin, 2007; Inkson et al., 2012; Pringle and Mallon, 2003), career theory continues to privilege professionals and paid work (Atkinson et al., 2015; Sullivan and Baruch, 2009). Even when diversity dimensions such as sex, gender, ethnicity, age, disability and religion are considered, the features of a traditional career – linearity, continuity, masculinity, individuality – are retained. Arguably, the boundaryless career concept (Arthur and Rousseau, 1996) has disrupted assumptions of linearity in career trajectories, but the other aspects remain entwined in the career discourse. Consequently much careers research on the "marginalized other" (Prasad et al., 2007) describes continuing biases resulting in exclusion from career processes. Implicit are assumptions that career progression is based on succeeding within the norms of the dominant culture.

In this chapter, we examine contemporary career theory and practice (e.g., Baruch and Vardi, 2016; Gunz and Peiperl, 2007; Sullivan and Baruch, 2009) from a critical diversity perspective. Critical diversity studies and critical career studies refer explicitly to the power relations and struggles between and within the social identity group(s) studied (Zanoni et al., 2010). Research methodologies used in the existing literature are limited, emphasizing homogeneity over heterogeneity. Most commonly, careers have been researched through group data aggregated from individual experiences, the aim being to create explanatory models which reduce complexity and increase generalizability as part of an agenda to develop an overarching or "grand theory" (Iellatchitch et al., 2003) that in turn reduces potential influences of diversity. In order to illustrate a diversity perspective in critical career studies in the later sections, we describe three local studies that lie within the interpretive and the critical research paradigms (Grant and Giddings, 2002).

As we bring together the two strands of careers and diversity scholarship, we outline how diversity research emerged. We then provide a short, critically nuanced overview of the career research from a diversity perspective (Prasad et al., 2006), noting major diversity identity groups and the recent focus on immigration (often intersecting with ethnicity and religious belief). It is impossible to review the burgeoning literature on the careers of separate identity groups (e.g., women, people with disabilities, careers of sexual minorities, different ethnic groups). Rather we direct our discussion of diversity perspectives on careers by drawing on recent careers research of the authors: careers of professional women, race/ethnicity amplified through the experiences of indigenous peoples and the diversity of older workers' careers, examined through the experiences of women who go on self-initiated expatriation. Aspects of intersectional identities are necessarily embedded within the discussion. We close by discussing new influences and insights that a diversity perspective brings to career research: highlighting context, interdependence, heterogeneity, navigating two worlds and future considerations for a more diverse career studies.

Diversity studies: struggles for influences of power

The sub-discipline of diversity studies evolved from organizational equal employment opportunity (EEO) research that has been well theorized (Pringle and Strachan, 2015). The managing diversity discourse arose from a nexus of social movements, anti-discrimination legislation and public policy initiatives in the United States. A key spark was a report analyzing contemporary workforce trends (Johnston and Packer, 1987) and incremental societal demographic changes in the United States. New entrants would be minority ethnic groups, women and immigrants; consequently, white men were predicted to be just 15 percent of hires in the United States by 2000. Changes in organizational socialization processes and ultimately the organizational culture would no doubt result. The shift to the business case for diversity was also fuelled by a backlash against the social justice agenda of affirmative action/EEO by business leaders, consultants (Thomas, 1991) and arguably human resource (HR) practitioners. The movement away from social justice to the business case for diversity quickly spread to other Western countries (Jones et al., 2000; Kandola and Fullerton, 1994) and beyond (Klarsfeld et al., 2014). The business case argued that organizations could gain a competitive advantage by leveraging advantages brought by employee differences. Employees from diversity groups – ethnicity, gender, sexualities, disabilities – could provide entry into previously ignored or inaccessible niche markets. This shift to instrumental thinking about diversity groups has not been uncontested, with calls for analyses of power relations (Zanoni et al., 2010) between minorities and the dominant group(s).

Contemporary diversity studies (Bendl et al., 2015) have also been nudged along by critical race theory and women's studies to embrace the concept of intersectionality in identity (Rodriguez et al., 2016). Some prominent gender scholars now argue that any analysis of identity politics needs to consider more than a single diversity dimension such as gender, ethnicity and age. Intersectional identity effects, for example from being an older women or a male refugee, are recognized as fluid, shifting across situations. The key social identity characteristics in any situation are the result of the relevant socio-political contextual factors at the time of enquiry (Pringle and Ryan, 2015). Analysis of diversity effects has become more complex than the study of careers of the "marginalized other" (Prasad et al., 2007).

Critical career studies: places for multiple faces

Our work emerges partly in response to the perpetuation of career research that brings detailed information on the dominant group: white, male, middle class professionals. A pattern of masculine careers generally denotes a primary earner supported by a second person in a (stable) coupled relationship who provides emotional and physical support. This second person is usually a woman who has primary responsibility for the care of any offspring or wider familial responsibilities at the cost of reduced career involvement and financial rewards (Wheatley, 2017). Society reinforces this norm through the continuation of a gender pay gap that disadvantages women and those in female-dominated occupations. Diversity perspectives on careers are important because the experiences of those people outside of this group are largely ignored in research, teaching and subsequent career counselling. Societal norms, explicitly and implicitly, guide the relative positioning of women and men in workplaces. Similarly, prejudice towards minority diversity groups spills over into workplace relations and associated opportunities for career development. Two diversity groups that have been the focus of recent research attention are people with disabilities and people of different sexual orientations.

Much of the research on people with disabilities is not on careers but on work in general, with a recurring finding that they are less likely to be employed (Pope and Bambra, 2005). The study of the careers of people with disabilities has shown the importance of supportive employer attitudes (Nota et al., 2014). Significant research into the careers of academics with disabilities highlights the crucial role of agency to actively negotiate boundaries – not only from situational constraints but also from physical or psychological impairments (Williams and Mavin, 2015).

The need to actively negotiate one's career is also pivotal for people with diverse sexual orientations. Research into the careers of non-heterosexual people have been dominated by research on gay men and lesbians, focusing on whether or not to be visible, or to "come out" (Kaplan, 2014). As societal norms have shifted, there is recent enquiry into the career experiences and prospects for transgender and gender non-conforming people (Dickey et al., 2016). As Kaplan notes, "how individuals manage their sexual identity impacts their careers" (2014: 119).

These studies indicate the increasing research into groups of workers that are often marginalized and to a large extent aim for acceptance and assimilation into normative careers (Trau, 2015). They are affected by legislative contexts guiding discrimination in employment practices that in turn affect decisions around an individual's visibility in workplaces. Currently the individual-in-context is not central to careers research, which we believe distorts understanding of career aspirations and progression. Context includes the local situation and increasingly, global influences.

Diversity and global careers

Globalization, demographic changes, technological innovations and shifting geographic and economic borders have led to growth in an international labour market and fostered international mobility. Changing political and social contexts (e.g., the Syrian crisis) have also forced some individuals and families to flee their home countries while others (e.g., Brexpats; Munk, 2016) elect to leave their home country to pursue employment opportunities and the promise of a better life. These global mobility patterns are variously labelled as immigration, migration and expatriation and are further sub-categorized by terms such as immigrant, refugee, flexpat, expat, self-initiated expatriate (Doherty et al., 2013), skilled, semi-skilled and low skilled (Al Ariss et al., 2012). The increasing impact of international mobility, particularly forced immigration, is particularly salient for Western European countries. With shifts in population through immigration and refugees, there is a shake-up of existing cultural patterns that previously have gone back generations.

International careers research has generally come from one of three streams: corporate or organizational expatriation, self-initiated expatriation and migration studies. There is a well-established literature in international human resource management (HRM) and management of corporate expatriation (McNulty and Brewster, 2016), and more recently self-initiated expatriation (Andresen et al., 2013a; Doherty et al., 2013; Myers, 2016). These literatures generally privilege professional and managerial groups, who move from and to developed nations to enhance individual career profiles. In contrast, migration studies have tended to focus on lower skilled migrants, often coming from a developing to a developed nation, seeking a secure refuge and work rather than aiming to develop a career (Al Ariss et al., 2012). A special issue of the *Journal of Management Development* on the careers of skilled migrants (Al Ariss et al., 2012) sought to redress this imbalance in the migrant literature.

Additionally, there has been ongoing discussion of definitional terms such as expatriate, migrant and self-initiated expatriation (SIE) within the management literature, highlighting continuing terminological dilemmas (Andresen et al., 2013b: 237). Al Ariss et al. (2012) argue for greater reflexivity and cognisance of "context" so that more "comprehensive and inclusive" (ibid.: 99) research is developed to better understand the careers of skilled migrants. In future research, "migrant" identity may be studied alongside religion and ethnicity.

Altogether we concur with scholars arguing for greater diversity in the study of international careers (Tatli, 2011). We also suggest more intersectional, contextual, cross-cultural, reflexive, cross-disciplinary and critical approaches to international mobility studies (Al Ariss et al., 2012; McNulty and Brewster, 2016) and to careers more generally.

In the following sections we discuss specific diversity groups and how they enact careers – indigenous Māori, women and older workers (specifically women) – bringing a criticality to the careers literature. The three studies are presented by individual co-authors (Elley-Brown, 2015; Myers, 2016; Reid, 2010), with each author bringing a different methodology and their unique voice, thus embedding diversity within a critical careers discourse.

Ethnicity and indigeneity

It is accepted that careers are influenced by cultural values and practices, however a career theory fully immersed in a cultural space has yet to be realized. Career theories have responded to culture primarily as a moderator with the search for sameness minimizing cultural differences. It is often through multicultural models that indigenous and non-indigenous career practitioners work "across" cultures (Triandis, 2000).

More recently, there have been moves by indigenous scholars to situate culture within localized knowledge and practices (Leong and Flores, 2015). A localized perspective of career argues for an indigenous identity independent from a westernized view of culture. One of the distinguishing characteristics of an indigenous model of careers is its collective or interdependent orientation (Hartung et al., 2010). An indigenous identity denotes a way of being that is culturally situated, premised on the knowledge brought through relationships with others and also connected to wider physical and spiritual worlds. Thus identity embodies a web of relationships that exist within many indigenous communities.

Career researchers (e.g., Bingham et al., 2014; Erueti and Palmer, 2014) advocate examining the sometimes contradictory nature of an indigenous identity living in two competing worlds (i.e., an indigenous worldview and the westernized dominant culture that attempts to acculturate the other; Juntunen and Cline, 2010). Using a positivist methodology, researchers

(Haar and Brougham, 2013) have supported the exploration of career aspirations within an indigenous worldview and within diverse indigenous identities. Results affirm positive career satisfaction by indigenous employees when workplaces espouse and practice cultural well-being and collectivism.

The career literature continues to propagate a view that people will find satisfaction primarily from their career identity rather than one drawn from a cultural (or other) space. Yet for indigenous communities, the currently constructed notion of a career restricts discovery and imagination. The objective of creating a more inclusive career theory and practice is less about predicting and controlling future career development and more about accepting the ambiguities inherent in living within an indigenous worldview as a minority culture. Existing among ambiguities and contradictions are part of the fibre of many indigenous communities, yet career literature continues to seek a definitive effect of culture.

There is a continuing need for careers to be interpreted from an indigenous viewpoint, not only for indigenous peoples but also to expand career knowledge. New career research (Staniland et al., 2019) is already influencing the shift from an adaptation of career models "for" culture, to reconstructing careers to have culture "in" career. Even as the notion of careers continues to be a contestable space for indigenous communities, Mitra (2015) challenges career scholars to probe such intersections and paradoxes in more depth, to question their own universally held assumptions of culture and career.

An emerging indigenous perspective in career comes from Māori research in Aotearoa New Zealand (Aotearoa is the island nation's Māori name). Indigenous identities are increasingly recognized as heterogeneous and shaped by the contexts in which they exist. For example, Māori identities are constituted from location, community interests and class structures, resulting in urban Māori identities and more fluid identities of Māori youth (McIntosh, 2005). Significant career research focusing on a Māori worldview (McNicholas and Humphries, 2005; Reid, 2010) has been underpinned by indigenous research paradigms such as *kaupapa Māori* (Smith, 1999), which presents synchronicities between the methodology used and a Māori worldview. This research paradigm emerged from a wider Māori cultural renaissance and its accompanying critique of colonization (Durie, 2012). *Kaupapa Māori* has been succinctly described as research by Māori, for Māori and with Māori, speaking directly to the core of a culture-based identity. This methodology formed the basis of a career study that explored a culturally constructed notion of career from participants who had a range of perspectives on what it meant to be Māori (Reid, 2010). The cultural identity of the participants remained the centre from which to enact careers. Both cultural and career identities emerged from relationships between a people and their context (Mitra, 2015). For indigenous communities, a cultural identity is enduring, discovered from the past, present and future, and through the experiences of others, both living and dead. A significant feature of this research was the conceptualization and development of a cultural identity that shaped and informed a career identity. In other words, the diverse experiences of being Māori supported, subsumed or hindered a career identity.

The narrative study (Reid, 2010) used life history accounts from 22 Māori volunteers drawn across the lifespan. The enquiry into multiple and overlapping identities was prompted by questions such as "who are you?" or "who are you, alongside others?" (Reid, 2011). A typology of three categories was developed that focused on a culturally constructed identity and how this was enacted within and alongside a career identity.

The first of the three typology groups was identified as "the cloaked." This group of Māori indicated a preference for protecting or shielding their cultural identity and expected to be in control of when and where this identity was revealed. A career identity among the cloaked was an individual endeavour and aligned with Western conceptualizations of career as future-oriented.

The second group was identified as "the seekers." In contrast to the previous group, the seekers openly expressed a strong cultural identity. A common theme from this group was the need to seek out new cultural and career experiences as part of the process of understanding who they were. A career identity served as just one vehicle for an exploration of their cultural identity. For this group, being in the present was very important, providing an immediately gratifying search for self-discovery. The final group was described as "the keepers." This group were characterized as the keepers of traditional Māori values and viewed a cultural identity as the only way to identify as Māori. A career identity was accepted only as a space from which the keeper could continue to live and work in a Māori world. For this group, the past was seen as a time where cultural wisdoms and practices prevailed and their role was to maintain traditional knowledge.

An indigenous identity could be described as a journey without an itinerary or destination, supported by a cultural compass that delivers a point for direction (Reid, 2015). As an indigenous identity shifts and moves in response to a changing world, it is this identity that reconfigures life's purpose. Hitherto career concepts and measures have been unable to construct the depth of indigenous knowing, experiences and wisdoms. More diversity is needed in career theories to realize indigenous identity discourses, drawing together a range of indigenous experiences, to support relational practices, that include collective wisdoms from past, present and future worlds.

Gender and women's careers

This section moves from considering indigenous careers to theorizing women's careers. Arguably, the first initiatives to consider diversity in careers came through a gender analysis with an emphasis on women's career models. Women's career research affirmed women's careers as different from and more holistic than men's careers (Gallos, 1989). A stream of research that reaches back to the 1980s (Gutek and Larwood, 1987) has strongly argued for difference, a discourse influenced by Marshall's landmark piece (1989) invoking a radical feminist analysis that focuses on difference. Marshall differentiated between Bakan's (1966) female and male principles of agency and communion to highlight the "othering" of women's career experience.

Recent models offer alternative conceptualizations of women's career patterns. The most dominant 21st-century women's career model is Mainiero and Sullivan's (2005) Kaleidoscope Career Model (KCM). The authors place gender at the forefront of their analytical framework and argue that the KCM accommodates "career interruptions, employment gaps, top-outs, opt outs, as well as the new values of the current generation" (ibid.: 108). In the KCM research, women's career patterns and transitions have been described as opting in or opting out (Cabrera, 2007), following kaleidoscope or protean careers (Cabrera, 2009) and enacting "alpha" or "beta" careers (Sullivan and Mainiero, 2007). Findings from KCM research showed that women exhibited a beta pattern, namely, challenge followed by balance then authenticity, whereas men typically demonstrated an alpha pattern, challenge followed by authenticity then balance (Mainiero and Sullivan, 2005). Assumptions of men's career as the benchmark is implicit in use of the alpha label.

In a significant review, and following the development of the KCM, O'Neil et al. (2008) sought to understand "what is known and what is still left to be known" (ibid.: 727) about women's careers. Examining the extant literature, they found four patterns. Firstly, women's careers are embedded in women's larger life contexts, namely women's careers are contextual; secondly, families and careers are central to women's lives; thirdly, women's career paths offer a wide range and variety of patterns. Fourthly, although numerous research studies have reinforced the critical importance of human and social capital for women's career progress, these factors do not necessarily translate to career advancement (O'Neil et al., 2008). Updating their review five years later, O'Neil et al. (2013) found little deviation from the previously established patterns.

There is a danger that generating alternate conceptualizations of career risks propagating an essentialist gender view (Cabrera, 2007). Gender ideology adheres to valuing traditional gender roles and abilities in some countries and cultures (Hutchings et al., 2012) pointing to diversity within women's careers as a group (Afiouni and Karam, 2014).

Nevertheless, subtle but significant shifts are occurring. Dual careers, once described as an atypical pattern (Rapoport and Rapoport, 1969), have become a new norm and an established construct in the career literature. What were well-defined gender roles have become more ambiguous (Litano et al., 2014). There is a merging of female and male careers as dual-career couples address the challenges of managing not just individual, but shared career-life goals (Clarke, 2015). These findings indicate a greater sharing of work and family responsibilities for these professional couples. In particular, Generation Y couples (born 1980–2000) navigating dual careers have been shown to be less constrained by gender stereotypes than previous generations (Clarke, 2015; Rusconi et al., 2013).

A recent interpretive study of one of the authors reflects the impact of these emergent models and patterns (Elley-Brown, 2015). The study used hermeneutic phenomenology (Heidegger, 1962), a methodology novel in management studies, to enable an emic view of the careers of 14 professional women working in the education industry. Three themes emerged. The first theme revealed how sociological aspects of a woman's life, such as culture and heritage, were key in shaping her career identity. Women made sense of their present situation by being aware of how their past, culture and heritage influenced them. This was particularly potent for Māori women in the study.

A second theme involved the power of an "ethic of care" (Gilligan, 1982). Distinguishable from feminist ethics, a feminine ethic of care has a primary concern to define the moral experiences and insights of women, given that traditional approaches have failed to include women's perspectives (Sherwin, 1992). Being shown attentive care or concern caused a positive change in women's subjective and objective career experience; it increased both career meaningfulness and career agency (Elley-Brown and Pringle, 2019).

The third theme related to women's search for authenticity. These women's careers felt more meaningful when they could follow their own pathway and become increasingly reflective (Murphy and Volpe, 2015). Strong ties, the reciprocal relationships shared with their partner were pivotal in their career behaviour and enabled them to "hold it lightly" whilst staying true to themselves. Participants' adherence to non-traditional gender beliefs and adopting egalitarian practices in their dual-career partnerships contributed to their positive well-being (Elley-Brown, et al., 2018). A woman's partner was seen as an "ally" to career progression (Litano et al., 2014: 365).

Gaining additional qualifications throughout a career was the norm (Vaccaro and Lovell, 2010), seeking study leave to keep their career "on track" rather than seeking an "off ramp" (Sullivan and Mainiero, 2007). Some women had attained significant positions with no evidence that they had "hit" any ceiling. Yet other participants experienced blockages to their career progression which limited their career advancement, and in spite of significant human and social capital accumulation, this was no guarantee of ongoing career advancement (O'Neil et al., 2008). Participants did not opt out or enact a beta-KCM career pattern, but their career paths were instead labyrinthine (Eagly and Carli, 2007) as they pursued complex challenges throughout their career, a finding that differentiates their careers from the "normal" career trajectory defined for men.

These findings reflect shifts in the role of gender and how these have influenced women's career decisions through the life course. Being enmeshed in a web of relationships has been a distinguishing trademark of women's careers, seen to constrain women's career progression

(O'Neil et al., 2008). This interpretive study reveals the significance of pivotal relationships in sustaining well-being and enabling meaning-making for women through their careers. Further, the study confirms the emergence of challenges to gender stereotypes of women's careers as necessarily different from men's careers. These shifts indicate a need for re-conceptualizations of career to enable flexible and diverse understandings of career experiences within gendered perspectives.

Age, gender and work-centrism

This section focuses on the lives of older women in relation to the careers and ageing literatures. It explores whether or not the extant literature is sufficient to theorize and explain the increasingly diverse pathways that people follow in later life (Van der Heijden et al., 2008).

Traditional career theory reflects a structured social context where a career path consists of a series of incremental roles that suggest increasing status and extrinsic rewards. Social and demographic change, an increasingly diverse workforce, and changing organizational contexts have significantly affected how individuals perceive and manage their career, retirement options and later life plans (Wang and Shultz, 2010). In a more fluid societal structure, contemporary careers are perceived more broadly as "an individual's work-related and other relevant experiences . . . over the individual's life-span" (Sullivan and Baruch, 2009: 1453). Yet limited attention is given to "later careers," particularly to women's later careers.

Reconceptualizing careers has given rise to a life course perspective (Shanahan et al., 2016) that attends to the changing career needs of individuals, shifting the historical narrative of decline in later life (Super, 1957). There is a growing awareness that individuals are seeking more flexible or different work and life options to accommodate individual needs. Disillusionment with profit-driven organizational practices is perceived to be responsible for a range of social and environmental concerns (Tams and Marshall, 2011) that may be linked to an older person's search for generativity in their careers (Myers and Douglas, 2017; Newman, 2011).

Inkson et al. (2013) point to the ageing stereotypes of previous adult development literature and suggest four types of more flexible work options (Inkson et al., 2015) for later careers. The first three – phased retirement, bridge employment and self-employment – are discussed in the retirement literature (Wang and Shultz, 2010), where work is still a central "life" anchor. The fourth option, "encore careers" (Freedman, 2007), explores another aspect, recognizing that some older individuals seek different and sometimes unpaid work contexts "to contribute to the well-being of others, for example through voluntary work in a charitable institution, and/or develop their self-knowledge and wisdom" (Inkson et al., 2015: 108). Other variations on later life career transitions are career recycling (Sullivan et al., 2003), career exit and rebirth (Murphy and Volpe, 2015) and career reinvention (Broadbridge and Moulettes, 2015).

Although career changes for older women and men are not always driven by a search for authenticity (Baugh and Sullivan, 2015), the later life careers literature suggests that older individuals may want different things compared to earlier career stages. Nevertheless, most careers research of later life remains centred on a "work and organisational construct," even as personal values gain increasing attention. The new generation of career theory suggests frameworks to explore ageing and careers from a more "cumulative" perspective (Dany, 2014).

A societal driver for considering a more "whole of life" perspective on career are the demographic changes impacting on social and economic contexts of OECD countries resulting in the formulation of government policy to retain older people in the labour market beyond the traditional (60–65 years) retirement age. Ageing, work and retirement has been researched from a range of perspectives, but as with the positive ageing strategy, the economic imperative is still privileged over social context (Moulaert and Biggs, 2013). This emphasis contradicts the World Health Organization, which advocates a more holistic lifestyle strategy for older people (Post et al., 2013).

The influence of gender in ageing and retirement studies is not yet well understood. Loretto and Vickerstaff (2013) posit that "retirement may mean very different things for women and for men" (ibid.: 65), and as more older women continue in paid work, they are likely to experience greater work-life imbalance and disadvantage (Moen, 1996). Other strands of career literature includes women's concerns around career advancement (Metz, 2011), reasons women leave organizational employment (Cohen, 2014) and gendered experiences of self-employment in later life (Loretto et al., 2013).

Given the limited research on women's careers in later life experiences, we draw on a study of one of our authors (Myers, 2016) to indicate directions for more diversity. The interpretive narrative study explores the career experiences and outcomes of 21 older (50-plus) New Zealand women who exited their established working lives to undertake self-initiated expatriation (SIE), an autonomous and extended period of travel and work overseas.

Findings indicate that SIE by older women brings a diversity of work and non-work (personal) experiences. The extant literature on SIE addresses a broad range of types, and there is still an active debate around conceptualizations of the SIE construct (Doherty et al., 2013; Cerdin and Selmer, 2014; McNulty and Brewster, 2016). As with other SIE studies, participants undertook SIE for personal and work-related reasons, although personal reasons were more important for women in the study. Participants' SIE was a broader "international experience" when compared to other SIE research focusing on careers and international talent management (Vaiman et al., 2015). While the development of career capital was an unexpected outcome (Dickmann and Doherty, 2010), participants also experienced significant personal development, clarified their values and priorities, and began to realize that a range of diverse life paths was open to them, rich with possibilities. Many participants eschewed paid work, took on university studies and unpaid roles where they felt more valued and autonomous. Economic imperatives no longer shaped participants' lives, and for those who worked, it was invariably a stepping stone towards a more holistic and authentic life path (Myers et al., 2017).

While the study draws primarily on the careers and older worker literatures (including ageing and retirement), the work-centred focus of the literatures does not fully account for the radical changes in participants attitudes to paid work, nor does it account for the major changes in life direction enacted as a result of SIE (Myers, 2016). These findings contribute to an emergent discourse about later life disengagement from employment that challenges society's acceptance of paid work as the main source of individual revenue and identity (Weeks, 2011).

Age and gender remain under-researched (Loretto and Vickerstaff, 2015), and there is a particularly limited understanding of older women's careers, the significance of the turning points and timing of their life transitions and their search for identity and meaning. This study highlights the holistic nature of the evolving life paths of these older women and provides additional insights from which to argue for greater diversity in the study of careers (Collin, 2007).

Discussion and future directions

In this chapter we have engaged with a dual agenda, discussing and demonstrating a diversity perspective on careers. Previous careers research has been somewhat monolithic, valorizing a particular kind of career: one situated within paid work on a trajectory of increasing responsibilities and material rewards. Bringing a diversity perspective to careers shifts the discussion beyond sameness or differences from this ideal. An openness to differences is very important for working with all diversity groups. Accommodating differences requires employers, managers and policy makers to be flexible and open to a range of career paths countering a tendency to universalize policy and practice. A call for diversity in careers is not new (Doherty et al., 2013), but we advocate more extreme action. We have provided research evidence indicating some implications for understanding careers from a diversity perspective. These features include the importance of analyzing context, interdependence, appreciating multiple worldviews, heterogeneity and intersectionality in identities. Considering implications of diversity for future careers research, we question the nature of power and control implicit in career decisions and the confinement of career to paid work.

When career research is more open to diversity, then the study of careers in context will become the norm. Analysis of the local context becomes a conceptual thread to tie together diverse experiences. Studying careers in context (Mayrhofer et al., 2007) necessarily requires defining which boundaries are salient – which groups are included and excluded in specific geographic places and times. Accordingly, historical and contemporary power relations must be scrutinized to allow the most salient intersecting identities in any particular research study (Pringle and Ryan, 2015).

Another result of a diversity perspective on careers is disruption to an emphasis on the individual. Interdependence centralizes a relational component to the career experience. Interdependence is a notable feature of women's careers that can have not only positive (Elley-Brown, 2015) but also negative consequences for the women. Expectations of relationships as primary for women is evident when recruiters and assessors question women's commitment to paid work. Relationships in women's lives provide ebb and flow of competing priorities that can lead to career choices of satisficing and compromise. Connections between people also become more complex when we include people from more collective cultures, such as the indigenous Māori. This cultural collectivity translates to people journeying relationally in their careers; each is not journeying alone. Collectivism also speaks to the interplay between dependent, interdependent and independent relations. For Māori, this refers to the integral place of kinship (relational) in career experiences. But interdependence and collectivism are characteristic of some women and some cultures.

Extensive research on women's careers over decades has sharpened our understanding of the heterogeneity across and within diversity identity groups. Heterogeneity is a feature of "diversity groups," for example, differences within older women (and men) workers become more varied as they age, demanding a need to accommodate differences. While a focus on ethnicity has the potential to produce single models of "indigenous career," integrating knowledge and practices of a local context opens up understanding of multiple ways of expressing identity. For example, study of Māori careers identified that "the keepers" support traditional measures of being Māori, while Māori "seekers" are open to learning new expressions of their cultural identities. The research studies reported in this chapter highlight heterogeneity, demanding the ability to live in (at least) two worlds – a feature for all people who are not members of the dominant group.

Moving between two (or more) worlds is work required of diversity group members to enact careers. Navigating two worlds means negotiating the power relationships with the dominant group to progress one's career. Negotiating a place within an "other" work culture includes the hidden work of educating the dominant group, coupled with ongoing decision-making on how much to be "out," revealing aspects of one's identity that are not aligned or valued by the dominant culture. These identity characteristics may be visible (such as race) or less visible, embodied through different sexualities, ethnicities, religions and abilities.

Future directions

A diversity perspective on career research includes an analysis of power and resources, requiring a more critical and interdisciplinary approach. The example of Māori careers demonstrates aspects of the power dynamic within different expressions of identity. Within dual career couples there is often negotiation of power and position at a micro-level, even as organizations are slow to accommodate different ways of working. "Critical" research also recognizes that scholarship takes place within a Western worldview with its emphasis on paid work, implying that other activities are inferior. Career theory that continues to promote the power position of a dominant group truncates differences, limiting diversity group members to an agenda of assimilation to prevailing career norms.

Our discussion of diversity perspectives critiques the assumption that career knowledge brings increased prediction and control. An implicit objective within much established career research is to decrease uncertainty by creating predictive models of career progression and "success," which reinforce sameness. Such research enables workplaces and their agents to exert greater control over their human resources. In contrast, traditional indigenous communities live more comfortably with an unfolding way of being; for Māori, the unknowing is an accepted part of their worldview (Reid, 2015). For the older women on SIE, stepping out from their established work and home lives created an initial nervousness (Myers, 2016) but as they experienced more present-centred living rather than concern about past and future, they developed a learned ease with "unknowingness." Trusting serendipitous events can help people work with change and strengthen resilience.

The three empirical studies outlined in this chapter illustrate the importance of studying holistic careers and careers more holistically. Intersectionality also becomes central to careers research when a diversity perspective is adopted. For example, the study of immigration includes culture and social origin nuanced by politics. When career research is more open to a diversity perspective, then a close study of the context becomes a necessity. Taking a diversity perspective on careers also results in the use of a critical lens, with an examination of the power relations within the structures of careers, who defines them, lives them and rewards them. Altogether, a diversity perspective on careers will disrupt narrow conceptions, enabling careers to become more inclusive of a variety of identity groups, situations and local contexts.

References

Afiouni, F. & Karam, C.M. 2014. Structure, agency, and notions of career success: A process-oriented, subjectively malleable and localized approach. *Career Development International*, 19, 548–571.

Al Ariss, A., Koall, I., Özbilgin, M. & Suutari, V. 2012. Careers of skilled migrants: Towards a theoretical and methodological expansion. *Journal of Management Development*, 31, 92–101.

Andresen, M., Al Ariss, A. & Walther, M. (eds.) 2013a. *Self-Initiated Expatriation: Individual, Organizational, and National Perspectives*. New York: Routledge.

Andresen, M., Bergdolt, F. & Margenfeld, J. 2013b. What distinguishes self-initiated expatriates from assigned expatriates and migrants. *In:* Andresen, M., Al Ariss, A. & Walther, M. (eds.) *Self-Initiated Expatriation: Individual, Organizational and National Perspectives*. New York: Routledge.

Arthur, M.B. & Rousseau, D.M. 1996. The boundaryless career as a new employment principle. *In:* Arthur, M.B. & Rousseau, D.M. (eds.) *The Boundaryless Career: A New Employment Principle for a New Organizational Era*. New York: Oxford University Press.

Atkinson, C., Ford, J., Harding, N. & Jones, F. 2015. The expectations and aspirations of a late-career professional woman. *Work, Employment and Society*, 29, 1019–1028.

Bakan, D. 1966. *The Duality of Human Existence*. Chicago: Rand McNally.

Baruch, Y. & Vardi, Y. 2016. A fresh look at the dark side of contemporary careers: Toward a realistic discourse. *British Journal of Management*, 27, 355–372.

Baugh, S.G. & Sullivan, S.E. 2015. Introduction to the research in careers series. *In:* Baugh, S.G. & Sullivan, S.E. (eds.) *Searching for Authenticity*. Charlotte, NC: Information Age Publishing.

Bendl, R., Bleijenbergh, I., Henttonen, E. & Mills, A.J. (eds.) 2015. *The Oxford Handbook of Diversity in Organizations*. Oxford, England: Oxford University Press.

Bingham, J.L., Adolpho, Q.B., Jackson, A.P. & Alexitch, L.R. 2014. Indigenous women college students' perspectives on college, work, and family. *Journal of College Student Development*, 55, 615–632.

Broadbridge, A.M. & Moulettes, A. 2015. Retirement – a new beginning or the beginning of the end? *In:* Broadbridge, A.M. & Fielden, S.L. (eds.) *Handbook of Gendered Careers in Management: Getting in, Getting On, Getting Out*. Cheltenham, England: Edward Elgar Publishing.

Cabrera, E.F. 2007. Opting out and opting in: Understanding the complexities of women's career transitions. *Career Development International*, 12, 218–237.

Cabrera, E.F. 2009. Protean organizations: Reshaping work and careers to retain female talent. *Career Development International*, 14, 186–201.

Cerdin, J-L. & Selmer, J. 2014. Who is a self-initiated expatriate? Towards conceptual clarity of a common notion. *International Journal of Human Resource Management*, 25, 1281–1301.

Clarke, M. 2015. Dual careers: The new norm for gen Y professionals? *Career Development International*, 20, 562–582.

Cohen, L. 2014. *Imagining Women's Careers*. Oxford, England: Oxford University Press.

Collin, A. 2007. The meanings of career. *In:* Gunz, H. & Peiperl, M. (eds.) *Handbook of Career Studies*. London: Sage Publications.

Dany, F. 2014. Time to change: The added value of an integrative approach to career research. *Career Development International*, 19, 718–730.

Dickey, L.M., Walinsky, D., Rofkahr, C., Richardson-Cline, K. & Juntunen, C. 2016. Career decision self-efficacy of transgender people: Pre- and posttransition. *The Career Development Quarterly*, 64, 360–372.

Dickmann, M. & Doherty, N. 2010. Exploring organizational and individual career goals, interactions, and outcomes of developmental international assignments. *Thunderbird International Business Review*, 52, 313–324.

Doherty, N., Richardson, J. & Thorn, K. 2013. Self-initiated expatriation and self-initiated expatriates: Clarification of the research stream. *Career Development International*, 18, 97–112.

Durie, M. 2012. Kaupapa Māori: Shifting the social. *New Zealand Journal of Educational Studies*, 47, 21–29.

Eagly, A.H. & Carli, L.L. 2007. Women and the labyrinth of leadership. *Harvard Business Review*, 85, 63–71.

Elley-Brown, M.J. 2015. *Career as Meaning Making: A Hermeneutic Phenomenological Study of Women's Lived Experience*. Auckland University of Technology. Available: http://aut.researchgateway.ac.nz/handle/10292/9159.

Elley-Brown, M.J., Pringle, J.K. & Harris, C. 2018. Women opting in?: New perspectives on the Kaleidoscope Career Model. *Australian Journal of Career Development*, 27(3), 172–180.

Elley-Brown, M.J. & Pringle, J.K. 2019. Sorge, Heideggerian ethic of care: Creating more caring organizations. *Journal of Business Ethics*, 1–13. doi:10.1007/s10551-019-04243-3

Erueti, B. & Palmer, F.R. 2014. Te Whariki Tuakiri (the identity mat): Māori elite athletes and the expression of ethno-cultural identity in global sport. *Sport in Society*, 17, 1061–1075.

Freedman, M. 2007. *Encore: Finding Work That Matters in the Second Half of Life*. New York: Public Affairs.

Gallos, J.V. 1989. Exploring women's development: Implications for career theory, practice. *In:* Arthur, M.B., Hall, D.T. & Lawrence, B.S. (eds.) *Handbook of Career Theory*. Cambridge, MA: Cambridge University Press.

Gilligan, C. 1982. *In A Different Voice: Psychological Theory and Women's Development*. Cambridge, MA: Harvard University Press.

Grant, B.M. & Giddings, L.S. 2002. Making sense of methodologies: A paradigm framework for the novice researcher. *Contemporary Nurse*, 13, 10–28.

Gunz, H.P. & Peiperl, M. (eds.) 2007. *Handbook of Career Studies*. London: Sage Publications.

Gutek, B.A. & Larwood, L.E. 1987. *Women's Career Development*. Newbury Park, CA: Sage Publications.

Haar, J.M. & Brougham, D.M. 2013. An indigenous model of career satisfaction: Exploring the role of workplace cultural wellbeing. *Social Indicators Research*, 110, 873–890.

Hartung, P.J., Fouad, N.A., Leong, F.T. & Hardin, E.E. 2010. Individualism-collectivism: Links to occupational plans and work values. *Journal of Career Assessment*, 18, 34–45.

Heidegger, M. 1962. *Being and Time*. New York: Harper and Row.

Hutchings, K., Lirio, P. & Metcalfe, B.D. 2012. Gender, globalisation and development: A re-evaluation of the nature of women's global work. *International Journal of Human Resource Management*, 23, 1763–1787.

Iellatchitch, A., Mayrhofer, W. & Meyer, M. 2003. Career fields: A small step towards a grand career theory? *International Journal of Human Resource Management*, 14, 728–750.

Inkson, K., Dries, N. & Arnold, J. 2015. *Understanding Careers*. London: Sage Publications.

Inkson, K., Gunz, H., Ganesh, S. & Roper, J. 2012. Boundaryless careers: Bringing back boundaries. *Organization Studies*, 33, 323–340.

Inkson, K., Richardson, M. & Houkamau, C. 2013. New patterns of late-career employment. *In:* Field, J., Burke, R. & Cooper, C. (eds.) *The Sage Handbook of Aging, Work and Society*. London: Sage Publications.

Johnston, W.B. & Packer, A.E. 1987. *Workforce 2000: Work and Workers for the 21st Century*. Indianapolis, IN: Hudson Institute.

Jones, D., Pringle, J. & Shepherd, D. 2000. 'Managing diversity' meets Aotearoa/New Zealand. *Personnel Review*, 29, 364–380.

Juntunen, C.L. & Cline, K. 2010. Culture and self in career development: Working with American Indians. *Journal of Career Development*, 37, 391–410.

Kandola, R.S. & Fullerton, J. 1994. *Managing the Mosaic: Diversity in Action*. London: Institute of Personnel and Development.

Kaplan, D.M. 2014. Career anchors and paths: The case of gay, lesbian, & bisexual workers. *Human Resource Management Review*, 24, 119–130.

Klarsfeld, A., Booysen, L.A.E., Ng, E., Roper, I. & Tatli, A. (eds.) 2014. *International Handbook on Diversity Management at Work: Country Perspectives on Diversity and Equal Treatment*. Cheltenham: Edward Elgar Publishing.

Leong, F.T.L. & Flores, L.Y. 2015. Career interventions with racial and ethnic minority clients. *In:* Hartung, P.J., Savickas, M.L. & Bruce, W. (eds.) *APA Handbook of Career Intervention*. Washington, DC: US American Psychology Association.

Litano, M.L., Myers, D.P. & Major, D.A. 2014. How can men and women be allies in achieving work-family balance? The role of coping in facilitating positive crossover. *In:* Burke, R.J. & Major, D.A. (eds.) *Gender in Organizations: Are Men Allies or Adversaries to Women's Career Advancement?* Cheltenham, UK: Edward Elgar.

Loretto, W., Lain, D. & Vickerstaff, S. 2013. Rethinking retirement: Changing realities for older workers and employee relations? *Employee Relations*, 35, 248–256.

Loretto, W. & Vickerstaff, S. 2013. The domestic and gendered context for retirement. *Human Relations*, 66, 65–86.

Loretto, W. & Vickerstaff, S. 2015. Gender, age and flexible working in later life. *Work, Employment and Society*, 29, 233–249.

Mainiero, L.A. & Sullivan, S.E. 2005. Kaleidoscope careers: An alternate explanation for the 'opt-out' revolution *Academy of Management Perspectives*, 19, 106–123.

Marshall, J. 1989. Re-visioning career concepts: A feminist invitation. *In:* Arthur, M.B., Hall, D.T. & Lawrence, B.S. (eds.) *Handbook of Career Theory*. Cambridge, MA: Cambridge University Press.

Mayrhofer, W., Meyer, M. & Steyrer, J. 2007. Contextualising issues in the study of careers. *In:* Gunz, H. & Peiperl, M. (eds.) *Handbook of Career Studies*. London: Sage Publications.

Mcintosh, T. 2005. Māori identities: Fixed, fluid, forced. *In:* Liu, J.H., Mccreanor, T., Mcintosh, T. & Teaiwa, T. (eds.) *New Zealand Identities: Departures and Destinations*. Wellington, NZ: Victoria University Press.

Mcnicholas, P. & Humphries, M. 2005. Decolonisation through critical career research and action: Māori women and accountancy. *Australian Journal of Career Development*, 14, 30–40.

Mcnulty, Y. & Brewster, C. 2016. The meanings of expatriate. *In:* Mcnulty, Y. & Selmer, J. (eds.) *Research Handbook of Expatriates*. London: Edward Elgar.

Metz, I. 2011. Women leave work because of family responsibilities: Fact or fiction? *Asia Pacific Journal of Human Resources*, 49, 285–307.

Mitra, R. 2015. Proposing a culture-centered approach to career scholarship: The example of subsistence careers in the US Arctic. *Human Relations*, 68, 1813–1835.

Moen, P. 1996. A life course perspective on retirement, gender, and well-being. *Journal of Occupational Health Psychology*, 1, 131–144.

Moore, C., Gunz, H. & Hall, D.T. 2007. Tracing the historical roots of career theory in management and organization studies. *In:* Gunz, H. & Peiperl, M. (eds.) *Handbook of Career Studies*. London: Sage Publications.

Moulaert, T. & Biggs, S. 2013. International and European policy on work and retirement: Reinventing critical perspectives on active ageing and mature subjectivity. *Human Relations*, 66, 23–43.

Munk, K. 2016. Brexpats after Brexit: Impacts for British expats in Europe. *Global Risks Impact: Know Your World* [Online]. Available: http://globalriskinsights.com/2016/07/brexpats-brexit-british-expats-risk/.

Murphy, W.M. & Volpe, E.H. 2015. Enacting authentic careers: An identity salience and social network approach. *In:* Baugh, S.G. & Sullivan, S.E. (eds.) *Research in Careers*. Charlotte, NC: Information Age Publishing.

Myers, B. 2016. *Self-Initiated Expatriation (SIE) and Older Women: Motivations, Experiences and Impacts*. Auckland University of Technology. Available: https://aut.researchgateway.ac.nz/handle/10292/9693.

Myers, B. & Douglas, J. 2017. Older women: Employment and wellbeing in later life. *New Zealand Journal of Employment Relations*, 42, 7–28.

Myers, B., Inkson, K. & Pringle, J.K. 2017. Self-initiated expatriation (SIE) by older women: An exploratory study. *Journal of Global Mobility*, 5, 158–173.

Newman, K.L. 2011. Sustainable careers: Lifecycle engagement in work. *Organizational Dynamics*, 40, 136–143.

Nota, L., Santilli, S., Ginevra, M.C. & Soresi, S. 2014. Employer attitudes towards the work inclusion of people with disability. *Journal of Applied Research in Intellectual Disabilities*, 27, 511–520.

O'Neil, D.A., Hopkins, M.M. & Bilimoria, D. 2008. Women's careers at the start of the 21st century: Patterns and paradoxes. *Journal of Business Ethics*, 80, 727–743.

O'Neil, D.A., Hopkins, M.M. & Bilimoria, D. 2013. Patterns and paradoxes in women's careers. *In:* Mcmahon, M. (ed.) *Conceptualising Women's Working Lives*. Rotterdam: Sense Publishers.

Pope, D. & Bambra, C. 2005. Has the disability discrimination act closed the employment gap? *Disability and Rehabilitation*, 27, 1261–1266.

Post, C., Schneer, J.A., Reitman, F. & Ogilvie, D. 2013. Pathways to retirement: A career stage analysis of retirement age expectations. *Human Relations*, 66, 87–112.

Prasad, P., A'Bate, C. & Prasad, A. 2007. Organizational challenges at the periphery: Career issues for the socially marginalized. *In:* Gunz, H. & Peiperl, M. (eds.) *Handbook of Career Studies*. London: Sage Publications.

Prasad, P., Pringle, J.K. & Konrad, A.M. 2006. Examining the contours of workplace diversity. *In:* Konrad, A.M., Prasad, P. & Pringle, J.K. (eds.) *Handbook of Workplace Diversity*. London: Sage Publications.

Pringle, J.K. & Mallon, M. 2003. Challenges for the boundaryless career odyssey. *International Journal of Human Resource Management*, 14, 839–853.

Pringle, J.K. & Ryan, I. 2015. Understanding context in diversity management: A multi-level analysis. *Equality, Diversity and Inclusion: An International Journal*, 34, 470–482.

Pringle, J.K. & Strachan, G. 2015. Duelling dualisms: A history of diversity management. *In:* Bendl, R., Bleijenberg, I., Hentonnen, E. & Mills, A.J. (eds.) *The Oxford Handbook of Diversity in Organizations*. Oxford, England: Oxford University Press.

Rapoport, R. & Rapoport, R.N. 1969. The dual career family: A variant pattern and social change. *Human Relations*, 22, 3–30.

Reid, L.A. 2010. *Understanding How Cultural Values Influence Career Processes for Maori*. Auckland University of Technology. Available: http://aut.researchgateway.ac.nz/handle/10292/1036.

Reid, L.A. 2011. Looking back to look forward: Māori cultural values and the impact on career. *International Journal for Educational and Vocational Guidance*, 11, 187–196.

Reid, L.A. 2015. *Who I am is what I do: An indigenous perspective*. Paper presented at the 17th International Conference on Higher Education, World Academy of Science, Engineering, and Technology, London UK.

Rodriguez, J.K., Holvino, E., Fletcher, J.K. & Nkomo, S.M. 2016. The theory and praxis of intersectionality in work and organisations: Where do we go from here? *Gender, Work & Organization*, 23, 201–222.

Rusconi, A., Moen, P. & Kaduk, A. 2013. Career priorities and pathways across the (gendered) life course. *In:* Major, D.A. & Burke, R.J. (eds.) *Handbook of Work-Life Integration Among Professionals: Challenges and Opportunities*. Cheltenham: Edward Elgar.

Shanahan, M.J., Mortimer, J.T. & Kirkpatrick Johnson, M. (eds.) 2016. *Handbook of the Life Course*. Switzerland: Springer International Publishing.

Sherwin, S. 1992. *No Longer Patient: Feminist Ethics and Health Care*. Philadelphia: Temple University Press.

Smith, L.T. 1999. *Decolonising Methodologies: Research and Indigenous Peoples*. Dunedin, NZ: University of Otago Press.

Staniland, N. A, Harris, C. & Pringle J.K. 2019. 'Fit' for whom? Career strategies of Indigenous (Maori) academics. *Higher Education*, 1–16. doi.org/10.1007/s10734-019-00425-0.

Sullivan, S.E. & Baruch, Y. 2009. Advances in career theory and research: A critical review and agenda for future exploration. *Journal of Management*, 35, 1542–1571.

Sullivan, S.E. & Mainiero, L.A. 2007. The changing nature of gender roles, alpha/beta careers and work–life issues: Theory-driven implications for human resource management. *Career Development International*, 12, 238–263.

Sullivan, S.E., Martin, D.F., Carden, W.A. & Mainiero, L.A. 2003. The road less traveled: How to manage the recycling career stage. *Journal of Leadership & Organizational Studies*, 10, 34–42.

Super, D.E. 1957. *The Psychology of Careers*. New York: Harper.

Tams, S. & Marshall, J. 2011. Responsible careers: Systemic reflexivity in shifting landscapes. *Human Relations*, 64, 109–131.

Tatli, A. 2011. A multi-layered exploration of the diversity management field: Diversity discourses, practices and practitioners in the UK. *British Journal of Management*, 22, 238–253.

Thomas, R. 1991. *Beyond Race and Gender: Unleashing the Power of Your Total Workforce by Managing Diversity*. New York: AMACOM.

Trau, R.N. 2015. The impact of discriminatory climate perceptions on the composition of intraorganizational developmental networks, psychosocial support, and job and career attitudes of employees with an invisible stigma. *Human Resource Management*, 54, 345–366.

Triandis, H.C. 2000. Dialectics between cultural and cross-cultural psychology. *Asian Journal of Social Psychology*, 3, 185–195.

Vaccaro, A. & Lovell, C.D. 2010. Inspiration from home: Understanding family as key to adult women's self-investment. *Adult Education Quarterly*, 60, 161–176.

Vaiman, V., Haslberger, A. & Vance, C.M. 2015. Recognizing the important role of self-initiated expatriates in effective global talent management. *Human Resource Management Review*, 25, 280–286.

van der Heijden, B.I.J.M., Schalk, R. & Van Veldhoven, M.J. 2008. Ageing and careers: European research on long-term career development and early retirement. *Career Development International*, 13, 85–94.

Wang, M. & Shultz, K.S. 2010. Employee retirement: A review and recommendations for future investigation. *Journal of Management*, 36, 172–206.

Weeks, K. 2011. *The Problem with Work: Feminism, Marxism, Antiwork Politics, and Postwork Imaginaries*. Durham, NC: Duke University Press.

Wheatley, D. 2017. Employee satisfaction and use of flexible working arrangements. *Work, Employment and Society*, 31, 567–585.

Williams, J. & Mavin, S. 2015. Impairment effects as a career boundary: A case study of disabled academics. *Studies in Higher Education*, 40, 123–141.

Zanoni, P., Janssens, M., Benschop, Y. & Nkomo, S.M. 2010. Unpacking diversity, grasping inequality: Rethinking difference through critical perspectives. *Organization*, 17, 9–21.

7

Methodologies in organizational career research

Past, present, and future

Robert Kaše, Ivan Župić, Eva Repovš, and Anders Dysvik

The extent and quality of accumulated knowledge within a research field depends largely on how it has been produced (cf. Gibbons et al., 1994). Similar to many other fields in social sciences, over the last two decades career research has witnessed a strong increase of research output and notable changes in the manner of how knowledge is produced. The number of published papers in organizational and management career research has almost quadrupled (from about 35 papers per year in 1995 to about 131 papers per year in 2015), with empirical articles being the most voluminous driver of the increasing research output (currently amounting to about 80 percent of yearly output). However, just increasing the quantity of output is usually not sufficient to ensure that a field is making progress. Future formation of knowledge in the field is contingent upon appropriate use and upgrading of existing methodology and upon careful adoption of emerging methodologies that could provide new insights into careers in a highly dynamic, interconnected, and increasingly digitalized world.

In this chapter, we review knowledge creation in organizational and management career research in the two decades between 1995 and 2015 and discuss methodological approaches that we consider promising for further developing our knowledge about careers. We first offer a robust overview of the development, current state, and use of approaches for producing knowledge in academic journals that publish career research. We continue by describing emerging methods in social sciences and beyond that have the potential to facilitate further creation of knowledge on careers. We discuss their potential along with identifying areas within the career research field where they could most likely be applied. We conclude by a summary of current state and future directions of organizational and management career research methodology.

The domain of career research in management and organization and the scope of our methodological overview

In its broadest sense, career research is a highly fragmented, multidisciplinary research field with several taxonomic approaches trying to make sense of the vast landscape (Peiperl and Gunz, 2007). The most recent attempt to classify career research by Lee et al. (2014) used bibliometric techniques (science mapping) to distinguish between *global* and *local* career research. The global view encompasses career research done in all social science disciplines and includes research areas such as education and social policy, while the local view only includes career studies in the domain of management and organization research. For the 1990–2012 period, Lee et al. (2014) identified more than 16,000 publications using the global view and 3,141 publications if they considered the local view within the relevant Web of Science categories (ibid.: 340).

Similar to Lee et al. (2014), we adopt the narrower view and examine the knowledge base about careers in the organization and management research domain. In particular, we draw on what Gunz and Mayrhofer (2018) refer to as "organizational and management career (OMC) studies." They describe the OMC field as the (ibid.: 16) "area of scholarship, where the primary interest is in individuals as career actors, where their career is seen from the three perspectives, ontic, spatial, and temporal, and where the implicit or explicit frame of reference is management and organization studies." In addition, we considered what Gunz and Mayrhofer (2018: 3) characterized as a career study following four criteria. First, it has an identifiable career actor (i.e., an individual); second, it addresses at least two "conditions" of the career actor (e.g., a personality trait such as extraversion and a state such as career satisfaction); third, it includes a temporal dimension (unfolding in time is at least implied); fourth, it at least implicitly addresses the social space within which the career unfolds (e.g., organizations). This represents the general scope for our review of career research methodology for the 1995–2015 period.

Data and procedure

The selection of publications (academic articles) used in our review is based on the Thomson Reuters Web of Science (WoS) database, which includes the vast majority of the world's quality academic journals. To find studies that satisfy our criteria we used a multi-step process that involved journal category selection, keyword search, and manual filtering. The first step was to search the WoS database for publications published in the 1995–2015 period in the business and management categories that have "career" in their abstract, keywords, or title. This search returned 8,244 articles published in specialized career journals and other journals publishing career research.

Consistently with the domain of our research, we further filtered the articles by excluding those that were published in professional-focused journals (e.g., *Fortune, Harvard Business Review*), in journals that have not been published continuously throughout the period, and in journals that were not listed on the *Academic Journal Guide* 2015 (AJG) high-quality journals lists (to ensure sufficient quality, we considered only journals with AJG ranking 2 or higher). Further, we excluded articles published in journals focusing on career counseling (e.g., *Journal of Employment Counseling, Journal of Counseling Psychology, British Journal of Guidance and Counselling*), and journals from other social science disciplines (i.e., education, sport, public relations, tourism, migrations). We also excluded all commentaries, book reviews, and teaching cases. This further reduction resulted in 4,107 articles published in 47 quality scholarly journals publishing career research.

The final stage of the funneling process was done by reviewing titles and abstracts of all remaining articles using the criteria introduced in the previous section. In order to develop a coding protocol, two raters first independently examined 200 randomly drawn papers (100 from specialized career journals and 100 from other journals) from the remaining articles. Based on inductive reasoning, they developed a selection protocol by jointly discussing their individual selections of career papers from the sample. A third independent rater reviewed the initial (pilot) selection and provided feedback, which was jointly discussed before final selection criteria were set.

The general inclusion rule was that papers where career (or mobility) was the central and explicit focus of the article are included in the final sample. Articles that addressed very early

Table 7.1 The overview and rank ordering of journals publishing OMC research between 1995 and 2015

Journal rank	Total number of publications		Total number of citations		Mean citations per paper	
1	**JVB**	357	**JVB**	8,752	PP	138
2	**JCA**	165	**JCA**	2,312	JOM	94
3	**CDI**	81	JAP	2,251	AMJ	91
4	**CDQ**	78	JOB	2,194	JAP	90
5	IJHRM	77	PP	1,936	AMR*	69
6	JOB	52	**CDQ**	1,453	JBV*	50
7	HR	45	AMJ	1,094	AME*	50
8	PR	41	IJHRM	1,048	JWB	42
9	GWO	32	HR	741	JOB	42
10	JOOP	27	JOOP	670	ASQ	38
11	IJM	26	JOM	659	ETP*	34
12	JAP	25	HRM	518	JIBS	29
13	HRM	24	PR	499	SMJ*	29
14	PP	14	**CDI**	414	HRMR	27
15	RP	14	GWO	411	JOOP	25
Totals OMC field		1,251		29,023		23

Notes: List of full journal names is available in the Appendix; * denotes five or fewer papers published in the journal in the observed period; bold text denotes specialized career journals.

(i.e., before school-to-work transition) or very late career (i.e., post-retirement time) were considered outside of the scope and thus were not included. In addition, as the focus was on the long-term issues of individuals associated with working in organizations, we excluded studies with exclusively short-term focus (e.g., job-search and turnover studies). Papers on related topics (e.g., mentoring, expatriates, work-life balance, professional identity, talent management) were included only if they were explicitly career focused. Two raters independently read and coded the abstracts of all 4,107 articles and indicated whether an article fits the criteria for final selection. After coding all articles, the inter-rater agreement was 92 percent. Disagreements were settled by discussion between the raters. For especially difficult decisions, an additional evaluation was sought within the research team. The final sample included 1,251 articles published in the 1995–2015 period. The abstracts of these articles were content analyzed, which allowed us to categorize them with regard to their type and methodology used.

An overview of most relevant journals, where OMC research was published in the 1995–2015 period, is available in Table 7.1. We rank-ordered them by total number of publications, total citations and mean citations per paper. Specialized career journals top the rankings by the total number of publications and total number of citations. They are, however, not listed among the 15 journals with the highest mean citations per career paper (the closest is the *Journal of Vocational Behavior*, ranked 17, with 24.5 citations per paper).

Overview of knowledge creation in the OMC field in the 1995–2015 period

The field of organizational and management career (OMC) is renowned for cohabitation of a diversity of research traditions spanning from the positivist epistemological position and quantitative research designs to constructivist epistemological position and corresponding qualitative research designs (cf. Gunz and Peiperl, 2007; Gunz and Mayrhofer, 2018). Based on content

Table 7.2 The knowledge created in the OMC field in the 1995–2015 period by publication type

Type of paper	Number of papers	Share of papers	Mean citations per paper	Share of total citations	Ratio
Quantitative	590	47.4%	24	49.4%	1.04
Qualitative	202	16.2%	12	8.6%	0.53
Method Instrument development	179	14.4%	16	9.5%	0.66
Conceptual	101	8.1%	37	13.0%	1.60
Review	83	6.7%	35	10.3%	1.54
Mixed methods	36	2.9%	17	2.2%	0.77
Method review	34	2.7%	13	1.5%	0.56
Meta-analysis	20	1.65%	38	5.4%	3.36

Note: Six papers from our final sample that could not be classified in any of the above categories were not considered in the calculations.

analysis of articles published in the 1995–2015 period, we offer a general overview of how knowledge was produced in the field (see Table 7.2).

Scholarly articles using quantitative approaches accounted for almost 50 percent of the field's aggregated publications, followed by qualitative papers (16.2 percent), method and instrument development papers (14.4 percent), conceptual papers (8.1 percent), review papers (6.7 percent), mixed methods papers (2.9 percent), method review papers (2.7 percent), and meta-analysis papers (1.6 percent). Whereas quantitative papers have had almost the same position in the publication and in the citation space (i.e., the share of total citations received relative to the share of the number of publications is almost the same), other types of papers have had asymmetric representations. Notably, meta-analysis papers (e.g., Ng et al., 2005) have had by far the strongest relative impact ratio. They are followed by conceptual and review papers, which also exhibit strong relative impact ratio, while qualitative papers, method papers, and mixed methods papers are on the other side of the continuum with low relative impact ratio.

It is also worth looking into the relative importance of different ways of how knowledge was produced across the observed period. In Figure 7.1 we can see that the percentage of yearly knowledge production in the field by means of empirical papers (including quantitative, qualitative, mixed method, and meta-analysis papers) has increased considerably over the last 20 years and amounted to almost 80 percent in 2015. The share of conceptual (including review) papers, on the other hand, has shrunk drastically to as little as 5 percent in 2015, while the share of methodological contributions (including instrument development and method review papers) is on the rise again after exhibiting the lowest shares among the three types in the 2008–2011 period.

A more in-depth view into the empirical papers throughout the period reveals that the share of empirical papers using quantitative approach has decreased and stabilized in the last 10 years at about 65 percent (Figure 7.2). The share of papers adopting qualitative approaches, on the other hand, has increased and in 2015 represented around 25 percent of yearly empirical contributions within the OMC research. The share of papers using meta-analyses and mixed methods approaches, however, remains at very low levels. Mixed methods papers in particular have shrunk in the recent years after signs of stronger adoption in the 2009–2012 period.

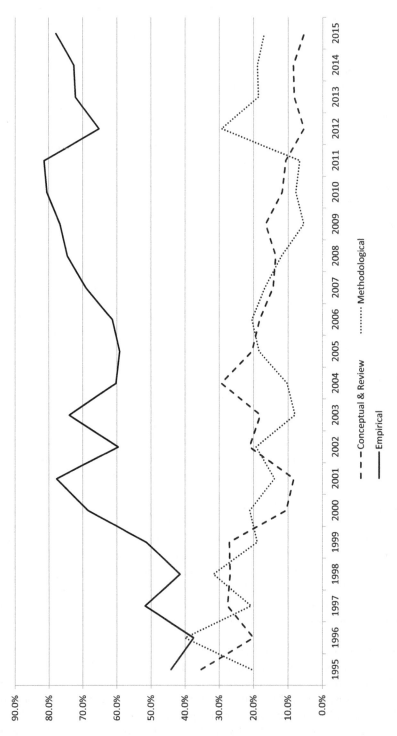

Figure 7.1 The share of empirical, methodological, and conceptual (including review) papers in the OMC field in the 1995–2015 period

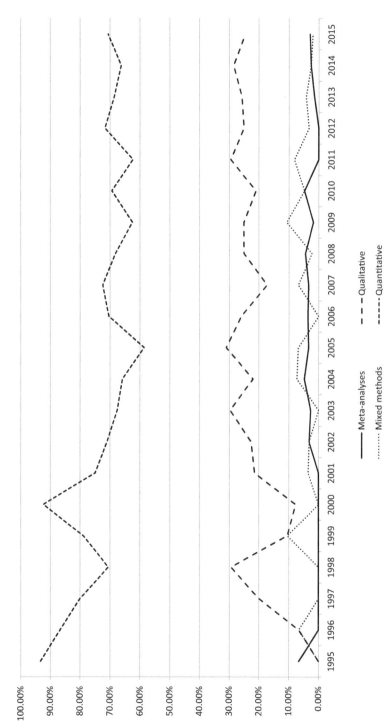

Figure 7.2   The share of different types of empirical papers in the OMC field in the 1995–2015 period

A typical *quantitative paper* in our sample follows deductive reasoning and adopts survey-based (field) data gathering methods in combination with (hierarchical) linear regression or structural equation modelling for data analysis. For example, in a well-cited *Journal of Vocational Behavior*[1] paper, Seibert and Kraimer (2001) examined the relationship between the Big Five personality dimensions and career success by surveying approximately 500 employees and adopting hierarchical regression analyses along with observing incremental variance to test hypotheses. Some contributions, especially more recent ones, used more advanced structural equation modeling, mediation and conditional process analyses (e.g., Russo et al., 2014; De Vos et al., 2011), and multilevel (random coefficient) modeling (Eby et al., 2005; Biemann et al., 2015). However, the adoption of these more sophisticated quantitative methods appears to be less prevalent in the OMC field in comparison to some other areas of management and organization research.

Recently the field has also offered more quantitative research papers adopting longitudinal research designs (i.e., since 2009 the field has on average produced about 10 quantitative papers with longitudinal designs per year in comparison to about 4 per year in the 1995–2008 period). However, the share of papers adopting these research designs (about 1 in 5) is not growing and can still be considered not high enough. While more intense use of longitudinal designs is consistent with the need for stronger research designs in management and organization research in general (cf. Ployhart and Vandenberg, 2010), it is even more important for career studies because the focal phenomenon – career – is inherently time-bound and should also be studied as such. A relevant positive pattern that we have observed in OMC research output is that between 2008 and 2015 the share of longitudinal research stabilized at about 22 percent of quantitative research output after being highly volatile in the 1995–2007 period. Stable presence of longitudinal designs in OMC research output might be a good signal for facilitating stronger growth of this type of research in the future. Longitudinal designs in our sample included panel (e.g., Judge et al., 2010; Biemann et al., 2012), follow-up (e.g., Salmela-Aro and Nurmi, 2007), cohort (e.g., Higgins et al., 2010), and even diary studies (Zacher, 2015). A nice example of the application of longitudinal designs in career research is the work by Abele and Spurk (Abele and Spurk, 2009; Spurk and Abele, 2014) on inter-temporal aspects of subjective and objective career success. In particular, Spurk and Abele (2014) used four-waves of data from a nine-year longitudinal study to explore feedback loops between occupational self-efficacy and objective and subjective career success over time. The design of the study allowed the authors not only to deal with typical problems stemming from survey research employing cross-sectional designs (cf. Podsakoff et al., 2012; Arnulf et al., 2014), but also to truly capture the dynamic nature of the focal variables and their interrelationships and make advancements that would not be feasible with a cross-sectional design.

Quantitative papers also built on archival (i.e., occupational records, job search portal data, labor market data) and biographical data (e.g., Shah et al., 2014). Optimal matching analysis is a good example of a method that has been used several times to analyze sequences in archival data (e.g., Biemann and Wolf, 2009; Kovalenko and Mortelmans, 2014). In a similar way, researchers studied how various events affected careers of individuals. For example, Hamori (2007) gathered media coverage of organizations in daily business press to examine how stigmatizing events at the level of the current organization (e.g., lawsuits, downsizing, resignations of key representatives) affected outgoing individuals' mobility (upward, downward, lateral) as they joined subsequent organizations.

While pure experimental design has rarely been adopted in OMC research, we were able to identify several (mostly recent) papers building on quasi-experimental (e.g., Spurk et al., 2015; Rider and Negro, 2015; Kossek et al., 1998) and scenario designs (e.g., Bright et al., 2009). These papers examined how exposure of study participants to various interventions (e.g., training in self-management and networking, providing coaching), organizational career circumstances (e.g., organizational failure), or scenarios affected (or would affect) their career outcomes.

Our analyses indicated that research designs using multisource designs are rare in OMC research. We only found a few dyad/multisource studies (e.g., Rodrigues et al., 2015; Gentry and Sosik, 2010; Lyness and Judiesch, 2008), where multiple respondents (e.g., self, peer, and supervisor rating) reported about focal career concepts. By and large, this is a line with subjective conceptualization of career (i.e., protean, boundaryless career) in OMC. Subjective aspects of careers are primarily in the domain of the individual, who should then also report on career-related concepts. However, this approach might be less suitable for studying objective or objectivized views on (other's) careers in an organizational setting. It also represents another deviation from the broader social sciences research, where multisource data is considered a research design's strength (Podsakoff et al., 2012; Heidemeier and Moser, 2009).

Finally, although we observed an increasing number of quantitative studies that collected and analyzed cross-cultural data (e.g., Willner et al., 2015; Newbury et al., 2008; Gunkel et al., 2010), these studies predominately narrowly reported results from two or three countries/cultures (often using business or executive students as respondents). Broad cross-cultural (comparative) designs such as the one adopted by Lyness and Judiesch (2008), who explored international perspectives on work-life balance and career advancement potential across 33 countries, are still largely missing in the OMC research (see also Smale et al., 2018).

A typical *qualitative paper*, on the other hand, follows inductive reasoning, builds on interviews, and uses various types of content analysis to create new knowledge. For example, in the *International Journal of Human Resource Management*, where a notable share of the qualitative papers has been published, Mäkelä and Suutari (2009) examined the social capital paradox of global careers by interviewing 20 Finnish multinational corporation (MNC) managers and content analyzing answers about their career and their social capital development. Alternatively, in a less typical, highly cited example in the *Journal of Organizational Behavior*, Hall and Chandler (2005) address subjective career success in circumstances where career represents a calling by presenting a real-life case example. The example of an unfolding career of a person with a strong calling serves as an illustration of the authors' conceptualization and as an introduction to stipulating the propositions. The differences between the two aforementioned papers show that although both papers were classified as qualitative in our sample, there is considerable diversity in how qualitative research is executed. The prototypicality is weaker than in the case of quantitative papers.

Papers adopting qualitative designs often combine multiple sources of qualitative data (e.g., biographical and interview data, direct observation) and use a grounded theory approach to develop new theory inductively (e.g., O'Mahony and Bechky, 2006; Simosi et al., 2015). Some qualitative studies also had explicit longitudinal design. Brodsky (2006), for instance, interviewed 54 British symphony orchestra musicians eight times over a 10-month period. Also, researchers adopting qualitative designs used some alternative research methods such as Q-sorting (Dries et al., 2008), analysis of symbolic networks (Jones, 2010), and even a pre- and post-career related developmental project video analysis of career-related conversations (Young et al., 2003) to generate new knowledge about careers.

Finally, we would like to discuss a typical *mixed methods paper*. In our sample, mixed method papers most often combined (field) survey with interview, focus group or case study. For example, in a *Gender, Work and Organization* article, Probert (2005) studied gender inequity in academic employment using mixed methods. In particular, she combined a large-scale nationally representative survey to gather information about human capital, family responsibilities, career preferences, workloads and objective experiences of appointment and promotion with a detailed case study of an organization. The latter adopted among other focus group method to study women identified with the survey as potentially "just under the glass ceiling." The two methods were used to mutually corroborate findings. In addition, the focus group helped to identify specific explanations that were not at the forefront in the quantitative part of the research. Further, we also identified a paper that combined panel data with biographical interviews (López-Andreu and Miquel Verd, 2013) and a paper combining survey, case and geographical data (Wheatley, 2013). A general observation is that mixed methodologies contribute to a more comprehensive understanding of careers in their contexts, but are very rare in the OMC research.

Emerging methodologies in social sciences and implications for the OMC research

In recent years we have seen an increased attention of researchers in social sciences to how knowledge is being produced, both from the viewpoint of validity and replicability of findings (e.g., Open Science Collaboration, 2015) and from the viewpoint of introducing new methodologies for tackling problems that researchers have not yet been able to address successfully or efficiently. The emergence and increasing adoption of new methodologies stem mostly from increasing computing power, new technologies for continuous unobtrusive observation, accumulation of big data, and opportunities for digitalization and automatic processing of qualitative data. In addition, cross-fertilization and transfer of methodologies between disciplines and fields of research, availability of outlets that disseminate knowledge about methods (methodological sections and special issues of high-quality journals, specialized journals such as *Organizational Research Methods*, etc.), and ever-increasing demands for sophistication of methods at the top-rated journals have helped to excel these processes. Below we succinctly review selected emerging methodologies that in our view are relevant for future OMC research and discuss their implications.

The Internet has opened new avenues for research on careers that have to date not yet been sufficiently exploited by career researchers. Several approaches exist that provide researchers with access to career data from the World Wide Web. One example is individual voluminous career data available through online career networks such as LinkedIn, which provides self-reported information about current employment but also previous postings and developments (Ge et al., 2016). Of particular interest for career researchers is that LinkedIn readily provides career profiles as complementary measures of objective career success beyond number of promotions. LinkedIn includes profiles from professionals across a wide range of occupations and industries that can be helpful with respect to sample criteria for career research. Furthermore, both technical and managerial positions are identified, which may aid researchers in investigating horizontal career developments and not only the more traditional vertical trajectories associated with objective career success. Since LinkedIn provides detailed information with respect to employment, location, education and interpersonal connections, future quantitative OMC research could combine this data and investigate issues such as the effects of an individual's social networks on her job or geographical mobility, or the effects of her formal education on both horizontal and/or vertical career advancement (Ge et al., 2016).

Further, qualitative OMC researchers could resort to *netnography* – an online, systematic study of people and cultures – to study career-related phenomena. Netnography has its origins in the traditional observation techniques of anthropology and extends these to the study of the interactions and experiences that manifest themselves through digital communications (Kozinets, 1998). It was first applied in consumer research (e.g., Schau and Gilly, 2003) and has since spread to a range of other disciplines in the social sciences, yet its influence on career research remains limited. Netnography is a naturalistic and immersive approach – it focuses on examining what actually unfolds in individuals' online social lives by involving the researcher in naturally occurring public online conversations directly. Collecting and interpreting publicly available digital communications is complemented with methods including but not limited to interviews, social network analysis, and big data analytic tools and techniques (Kozinets, 2015). Since technology is becoming more important for shaping individuals' (digital) identities and influencing their decision-making, netnography could be a fertile approach for understanding people's career-related behaviors and decisions. For example, observing people's posting on social media sites such as LinkedIn, Twitter, and Facebook, their communications in virtual communities, or monitoring their activity using other online social sharing formats could be used to examine their career decisions and behaviors and gain insight into their views of career-related phenomena. Use of online narratives allows researchers to access rich data about a vast range of individuals from different contexts and across time. Empowered with new methods for (quantitative) analysis of text using computer-aided approaches and machine learning techniques (cf. Pollach, 2012; Althoff et al., 2016), this methodological approach provides a very promising opportunity for a large-scale analysis of career narratives publically available on the Web.

Finally, publicly available career data on the Web can also be transformed into a relational database for further analysis by using web crawler and extractions along with text analyzer and codifier algorithms (e.g., Geuna et al., 2015). These algorithms search for webpages and metadata from the whole Internet for a combination of provided search terms, such as names and affiliations of individuals, to extract their biographical information (CV) and transform it into a relational database. Geuna et al. (2015) developed such a tool to build a database and studied careers and productivity of biomedical scientists using only information publicly available on the Internet. This kind of method is especially valuable where biographical information of individuals in question is available online and when commercial sites such as online career networks (platforms) are not restricting access to such data.

We could see in our review that use of longitudinal research designs is now more stable in OMC research. A recent development in longitudinal designs are *intensive longitudinal methods* (ILMs, see Beal and Weiss, 2003; Fisher and To, 2012). ILMs assess individuals repeatedly within short intervals (i.e., by administering measures on multiple occasions during the same day). They are particularly useful for in-depth analyses of momentary and defining moments evolving over shorter periods. In contrast to retrospective self-reports, ILMs are less prone to retrospective recall bias, which influences the accuracy of information through blurred memories and self-justification processes. They are also better in following participants in their natural context (in contrast to more artificial lab settings). The third and final advantage of ILMs is the possibility to investigate dynamic within-subject processes through a higher level of specificity of temporal events (Bamberger, 2016). ILM data sources include but are not limited to daily diaries and experience sampling (Bamberger, 2016). The method is gaining in popularity since the ability to employ such designs has increased recently, due to intense use of smartphones (Raento et al., 2009) and because the statistical tools for conducting data analysis have become more available. With the increased use of sensors embedded in everyday objects and wearable devices (cf. Chaffin et al., 2017) and movements like "Quantified Self" – whose members proactively, willingly and continuously use technology to record data about various aspects of their daily lives (Wilson, 2012) – this approach seems to only grow in prospects for career researchers. For instance, a more detailed analysis of events preceding, accompanying, and following important career events or career transitions could be made more readily available through ILM rather than retrospective perceptual measures comparing previous employment with current employment.

For example, Zacher (2015) already adopted the method for career research and studied daily manifestations of career adaptability.

Our review also showed that while experimental research is very rare in career studies, there is an increased use of *quasi-experimentation* (cf. Grant and Wall, 2009). Given that organizations invest time and resources in facilitating career developmental activities for their employees (Kraimer et al., 2011), this methodology could be used more frequently since studies examining the actual influence of these activities on, and not mere covariation with, important employee outcomes such as career success, job embeddedness, and turnover remain limited. Even though careers is a challenging topic to study within an experimental framework, given the numerous challenges associated with confounding variables stemming from the broad range of influences on individual careers, attempts to use more experimental research are welcome. There are several strengths found in (quasi-)experimental designs in terms of establishing causal claims. For instance, interventions in one or several groups compared to control groups would allow researchers and organizations to assess the influence of differing inducements on career-related outcomes and ensure better control over temporal progression. As noted previously, classical experimental designs are rare in OMC research. Some papers using quasi-experimental approaches are available (e.g., Kossek et al., 1998), evaluating the effects of career self-management training on consecutive employee engagement in career self-management activities.

Another benefit from (quasi-)experimental designs is increased collaboration between academia and practitioners and thereby reduced research/practice divide. HR managers should be interested in nurturing career development of their employees in ways that ensure they experience perception of uniqueness and belongingness (Guest and Rodrigues, 2012). But without in-depth knowledge of current career research and with limited methodological skills, the same practitioners might experience difficulties running interventions as controlled experiments and learning from them. Therefore, helping practitioners make the interventions they are planning to do anyhow more in line with the best available evidence should be beneficial for them and for generating new knowledge on careers. A final advantage of intervention studies is the ability to take into account the impact of particular contexts on careers and career development. Organizations operating globally, for instance, may be interested in whether their career developmental programs are perceived and welcomed similarly across different country contexts, or whether important cultural differences should be taken into account, and if so how. Interventions in the form of selected pilots could reduce the probability that scarce resources are washed away on initiatives with little or no value.

One of the observations of our review was that comparative studies are missing in OMC research, especially quantitative comparative research. However, *qualitative comparative analysis* (QCA) also has the potential to offer valuable contributions for comparative career research. The optimal situation for adopting QCA (Rihoux, 2006; Ragin, 1987) is when the availability of units of observation is limited, the study subject is complex and difficult to examine using quantitative analytical methods, and in-depth qualitative data using traditional qualitative methods was not collected. QCA was developed by Ragin as a methodological approach for small-*n* comparative research (Meuer and Rupietta, 2017) as opposed to more quantitative-oriented methods. QCA is a case-sensitive approach which retains a holistic-analytic perspective in that cases are regarded as parts of a more complex entity. Analyses are based on minimization procedures and Boolean algebra rather than correlational matrices. As such, QCA allows for more complex causal models to be investigated in that several conditions may jointly cause changes in the outcome (Rihoux, 2006). Given the potential complexity involved, a central tenet of such comparative case analysis is that of analytical control, implying the need for the researcher to have in-depth knowledge of the relevant cases as well as of relevant theory/theories to make meaningful interpretations and conclusions of the observed material. Career studies adopting QCA could thus be positioned somewhere in between large-scale quantitative (i.e., Lyness and Judiesch, 2008) and qualitative comparative career research (i.e., Shen et al., 2015). Researchers have, for example, examined which theoretically plausible combinations of institutional and/or cultural conditions shape career success schemas across countries (cf. Kaše et al., in press).

Further, recent advances in neurosciences and the emerging organizational neuroscience research area could offer new opportunities for OMC research, especially for studying career decisions. Since the beginning of the decade there have been efforts to introduce neuroscience in studies of management and organizations (e.g., Becker et al., 2011; Becker and Cropanzano, 2010) and a continued debate about its promises and limitations (Lindebaum and Zundel, 2013; Ashkanasy et al., 2014). Its main promise is that it offers new (relatively accessible) methods for studying and understanding people's cognitive processes by examining their brain functions/ activity (Waldman et al., 2016). In particular, *neuroscanning or neurosensing technologies* such as functional magnetic resonance imaging (fMRI) and quantitative electroencephalogram (qEEG) have been frequently mentioned and already adopted in studies within the broader management and organizational research (e.g., Laureiro-Martínez et al., 2015). These studies typically examine the difference between ongoing intrinsic brain activity and brain activity which occurs as a reaction to stimuli, by identifying particular brain region(s) activated by the stimuli or imitating others (Waldman et al., 2016). For example, Laureiro-Martínez et al. (2015) used fMRI to identify brain regions that are associated with exploitation and exploration decisions. In the OMC field, neurosensing technologies could be used to study sensemaking of career-related situations and career decision-making as well as emotional reactions to (expected and unexpected) career events and transitions. These methods would be particularly valuable as complementary to existing methods in OMC research (i.e., interviews and surveys). When the methods are used together, researchers could compare findings derived by using traditional methods with those derived using these innovative interdisciplinary techniques and increase confidence in using them. We think that studies using both traditional and neuroimaging methods could invigorate the stagnating mixed method research in OMC research.

Finally, one of the observations in our review was that the share of conceptual papers is decreasing. One possibility of advancing theoretical development is *simulation modeling* (Davis et al., 2007; Harrison et al., 2007), which is defined as the use of algorithmic programming to model organizational behaviors and processes. Simulation models can address longitudinal, nonlinear, and process phenomena (Davis et al., 2007) and provide formal modeling of complex relationships among constructs. It is particularly suitable for developing dynamic theories. Simulation modeling forces a theorist to explicitly deal with assumptions and theoretical logic (i.e., they need to be expressed formally) with much greater precision than verbal theory. It also allows a researcher to engage in a fast iterative cycle of developing, testing, and refining theory. Overall, simulation modeling is still underutilized in organizational psychology along with management and organization research (see Weinhardt and Vancouver, 2012)

A simulation method with highest potential for OMC research is agent-based modeling (ABM) (Fioretti, 2013). It is based on computational agents representing social actors and models their behavior and interaction. ABMs are a great tool for conceptual experiments – by explicitly showing the theorist where different assumptions and hypotheses might lead to. Theorists can explore the consequences of their conceptual models by simulating interaction dynamics among theoretical constructs in a computer-based artificial laboratory. This can be done in two ways: (1) as a series of "what if" simulation experiments using theoretically relevant parameter values and/ or (2) basing the simulation on real-world data and trying to reproduce the data artificially in a simulation. For example, Vancouver and colleagues (2016) used simulation model to examine potential sources of skews in distributions of job performance. Although simulation methods remain neglected in career research, they hold great promise for modeling of career decisions and behaviors of individuals and consequently further development of career theory.

Conclusion: building on traditional and emerging methodologies for further progress of the OMC research

In this chapter, we have reviewed how knowledge was produced in OMC research between 1995 and 2015. Our findings show that empirical research has emerged as the prevailing manner of producing knowledge in the OMC field and that researchers are gradually adopting more complex research and data designs. We also established that the proportion between quantitative and qualitative approaches has stabilized and now stands at about 3 to 1 in favor of the former, while mixed research designs remain scarce.

The introduction of new methodologies and a more stable use of longitudinal designs in OMC studies are in line with calls for increasing data and research quality in general in organization and management research. This development is even more welcome for OMC research given the longitudinal character of careers that, ideally, warrants research designs where data is collected over longer periods of time. An interesting observation is that a large share of studies that use novel methodological approaches has been done by a limited number of researchers (e.g., Biemann, Spurk, Dries). By identifying several methodological possibilities that could be used to enrich OMC studies in the future, we encourage current and emerging scholars within the field to add additional names to this list.

The selected emerging technologies presented above, several of them building on technological developments and interdisciplinarity, have the potential to facilitate further quantitative, qualitative, and mixed study approaches in the areas such as career management (quasi-experiments), career decision-making (neuroimaging), career transitions (intensive longitudinal methods), and comparative career research (QCA). We urge researchers in the field to be open to these new methodologies and (cautiously) embrace them for new knowledge creation.

In the end, we have to mention some limitations of the review presented in this chapter. The most obvious limitations are that we only considered papers published in academic journals (in the English language) and used relatively strict inclusion criteria. Consistently with the conventions of the field, it is likely that we may have neglected work published in other academic outlets such as monographs/books and edited (hand)books. Future work on analyzing the use of methodology in OMC research should therefore also include these outputs. Further, although we carefully examined methodological approaches our high-level large-scope review prevented us from examining the epistemological positions adopted in the field and the dynamics of their use in more depth. Whereas we think that some observations about the use of epistemological positions could be inferred from our review (we could, for example, suggest that the interpretative position has emerged as a valid alternative to the dominant positivistic approach in the OMC field's research landscape), we call for future work to address the relationship between methodologies used and epistemological positions in OMC research. That said, we hope that scholars will welcome our review of extant and emerging methodologies as an inspiration for using most appropriate and strong methods for future generation of knowledge on careers in management and organization.

Appendix
List of abbreviations and full journal names for Table 7.1

AME: *Academy of Management Executive*
AMJ: *Academy of Management Journal*
AMR: *Academy of Management Review*
ASQ: *Administrative Science Quarterly*
CDI: *Career Development International*
CDQ: *Career Development Quarterly*
ETP: *Entrepreneurship Theory and Practice*
GWO: *Gender Work and Organization*
HR: *Human Relations*
HRM: *Human Resource Management*
HRMR: *Human Resource Management Review*
IJHRM: *International Journal of Human Resource Management*
IJM: *International Journal of Manpower*
JAP: *Journal of Applied Psychology*
JBV: *Journal of Business Venturing*
JCA: *Journal of Career Assessment*
JIBS: *Journal of International Business Studies*
JOB: *Journal of Organizational Behavior*
JOM: *Journal of Management*
JOOP: *Journal of Occupational and Organizational Psychology*
JVB: *Journal of Vocational Behavior*
JWB: *Journal of World Business*
PP: *Personnel Psychology*
PR: *Personnel Review*
RP: *Research Policy*
SMJ: *Strategic Management Journal*

Note

1 Where we mention a journal explicitly, it is because it is representative outlet for the paper type.

References

Abele, A.E. & Spurk, D. 2009. How do objective and subjective career success interrelate over time? *Journal of Occupational and Organizational Psychology*, 82, 803–824.

Althoff, T., Clark, K. & Leskovec, J. 2016. Large-scale analysis of counseling conversations: An application of natural language processing to mental health. *Transactions of the Association for Computational Linguistics*, 4, 463–476.

Arnulf, J.K., Larsen, K.R., Martinsen, Ø.L. & Bong, C.H. 2014. Predicting survey responses: How and why semantics shape survey statistics on organizational behaviour. *PloS One*, 9.

Ashkanasy, N.M., Becker, W.J. & Waldman, D.A. 2014. Neuroscience and organizational behavior: Avoiding both neuro-euphoria and neuro-phobia. *Journal of Organizational Behavior*, 35, 909–919.

Bamberger, K.T. 2016. The application of intensive longitudinal methods to investigate change: Stimulating the field of applied family research. *Clinical Child and Family Psychology Review*, 19, 21–38.

Beal, D.J. & Weiss, H.M. 2003. Methods of ecological momentary assessment in organizational research. *Organizational Research Methods*, 6, 440–464.

Becker, W.J. & Cropanzano, R. 2010. Organizational neuroscience: The promise and prospects of an emerging discipline. *Journal of Organizational Behavior*, 31, 1055–1059.

Becker, W.J., Cropanzano, R. & Sanfey, A.G. 2011. Organizational neuroscience: Taking organizational theory inside the neural black box. *Journal of Management*, 37, 933–961.

Biemann, T., Kearney, E. & Marggraf, K. 2015. Empowering leadership and managers' career perceptions: Examining effects at both the individual and the team level. *The Leadership Quarterly*, 26, 775–789.

Biemann, T. & Wolf, J. 2009. Career patterns of top management team members in five countries: An optimal matching analysis. *The International Journal of Human Resource Management*, 20, 975–991.

Biemann, T., Zacher, H. & Feldman, D.C. 2012. Career patterns: A twenty-year panel study. *Journal of Vocational Behavior*, 81, 159–170.

Bright, J.E., Pryor, R.G., Chan, E.W.M. & Rijanto, J. 2009. Chance events in career development: Influence, control and multiplicity. *Journal of Vocational Behavior*, 75, 14–25.

Brodsky, W. 2006. In the wings of British orchestras: A multi-episode interview study among symphony players. *Journal of Occupational and Organizational Psychology*, 79, 673–690.

Chaffin, D., Heidl, R., Hollenbeck, J.R., Howe, M., Yu, A., Voorhees, C. & Calantone, R. 2017. The promise and perils of wearable sensors in organizational research. *Organizational Research Methods*, 20, 3–31.

Davis, J.P., Eisenhardt, K.M. & Bingham, C.B. 2007. Developing theory through simulation methods. *Academy of Management Review*, 32, 480–499.

de Vos, A., de Hauw, S. & van der Heijden, B.I. 2011. Competency development and career success: The mediating role of employability. *Journal of Vocational Behavior*, 79, 438–447.

Dries, N., Pepermans, R. & Carlier, O. 2008. Career success: Constructing a multidimensional model. *Journal of Vocational Behavior*, 73, 254–267.

Eby, L.T., Allen, T.D. & Brinley, A. 2005. A cross-level investigation of the relationship between career management practices and career-related attitudes. *Group & Organization Management*, 30, 565–596.

Fioretti, G. 2013. Agent-based simulation models in organization science. *Organizational Research Methods*, 16, 227–242.

Fisher, C.D. & To, M.L. 2012. Using experience sampling methodology in organizational behavior. *Journal of Organizational Behavior*, 33, 865–877.

Ge, C., Huang, K.W. & Png, I.P.L. 2016. Engineer/scientist careers: Patents, online profiles, and misclassification bias. *Strategic Management Journal*, 37, 232–253.

Gentry, W.A. & Sosik, J.J. 2010. Developmental relationships and managerial promotability in organizations: A multisource study. *Journal of Vocational Behavior*, 77, 266–278.

Geuna, A., Kataishi, R., Toselli, M., Guzmán, E., Lawson, C., Fernandez-Zubieta, A. & Barros, B. 2015. SiSOB data extraction and codification: A tool to analyze scientific careers. *Research Policy*, 44, 1645–1658.

Gibbons, M., Limoges, C., Nowotny, H., Schwartzman, S., Scott, P. & Trow, M. 1994. *The New Production of Knowledge: The Dynamics of Science and Research in Contemporary Societies*. London: Sage Publications.

Grant, A.M. & Wall, T.D. 2009. The neglected science and art of quasi-experimentation: Why-to, when-to, and how-to advice for organizational researchers. *Organizational Research Methods*, 12, 653–686.

Guest, D.E. & Rodrigues, R. 2012. Can the organizational career survive? An evaluation within a social exchange perspective. *In:* Shore, L.M., Coyle-Shapiro, J.A. & Tetrick, L.E. (eds.) *The Employee-Organization Relationship: Applications for the 21st Century.* London: Routledge Academic.

Gunkel, M., Schlaegel, C., Langella, I.M. & Peluchette, J.V. 2010. Personality and career decisiveness: An international empirical comparison of business students' career planning. *Personnel Review*, 39, 503–524.

Gunz, H.P. & Mayrhofer, W. 2018. *Career and Organization Studies: Facilitating Conversation Across Boundaries with the Social Chronology Framework.* Cambridge: Cambridge University Press.

Gunz, H.P. & Peiperl, M. (eds.) 2007. *Handbook of Career Studies.* Thousand Oaks, CA: Sage Publications.

Hall, D.T. & Chandler, D.E. 2005. Psychological success: When the career is a calling. *Journal of Organizational Behavior*, 26, 155–176.

Hamori, M. 2007. Career success after stigmatizing organizational events. *Human Resource Management*, 46, 493–511.

Harrison, J.R., Lin, Z., Carroll, G.R. & Carley, K.M. 2007. Simulation modeling in organizational and management research. *Academy of Management Review*, 32, 1229–1245.

Heidemeier, H. & Moser, K. 2009. Self – other agreement in job performance ratings: A meta-analytic test of a process model. *Journal of Applied Psychology*, 94, 353–370.

Higgins, M., Dobrow, S.R. & Roloff, K.S. 2010. Optimism and the boundaryless career: The role of developmental relationships. *Journal of Organizational Behavior*, 31, 749–769.

Jones, C. 2010. Finding a place in history: Symbolic and social networks in creative careers and collective memory. *Journal of Organizational Behavior*, 31, 726–748.

Judge, T.A., Klinger, R.L. & Simon, L.S. 2010. Time is on my side: Time, general mental ability, human capital, and extrinsic career success. *Journal of Applied Psychology*, 95, 92–107.

Kaše, R., Dries, N., Briscoe, J.P., Cotton, R.D., Apospori, E., Bagdadli, S., Çakmak-Otluoğlu, O., Chudzikowski, K., Dysvik, A., Saxena, R., Shen, Y., Verbruggen, M., Adeleye, I., Babalola, O., Casado, T., Cerdin, J.-L., Kim, N., Kumar, M., Unite, J. & Fei, Z. In press. Career success schemas and their contextual embeddedness: A comparative configurational perspective. *Human Resource Management Journal.*

Kossek, E.E., Roberts, K., Fisher, S. & Demarr, B. 1998. Career self-management: A quasi-experimental assessment of the effects of a training intervention. *Personnel Psychology*, 51, 935–960.

Kovalenko, M. & Mortelmans, D. 2014. Does career type matter? Outcomes in traditional and transitional career patterns. *Journal of Vocational Behavior*, 85, 238–249.

Kozinets, R.V. (ed.) 1998. *On Netnography: Initial Reflections on Consumer Research Investigations of Cyberculture.* Provo, UT: Association for Consumer Research.

Kozinets, R.V. 2015. *Netnography: Redefined.* Los Angeles: Sage Publications.

Kraimer, M.L., Seibert, S.E., Wayne, S.J., Liden, R.C. & Bravo, J. 2011. Antecedents and outcomes of organizational support for development: The critical role of career opportunities. *Journal of Applied Psychology*, 96, 485–500.

Laureiro-Martínez, D., Brusoni, S., Canessa, N. & Zollo, M. 2015. Understanding the exploration – exploitation dilemma: An fMRI study of attention control and decision-making performance. *Strategic Management Journal*, 36, 319–338.

Lee, C.I., Felps, W. & Baruch, Y. 2014. Toward a taxonomy of career studies through bibliometric visualization. *Journal of Vocational Behavior*, 85, 339–351.

Lindebaum, D. & Zundel, M. 2013. Not quite a revolution: Scrutinizing organizational neuroscience in leadership studies. *Human Relations*, 66, 857–877.

López-Andreu, M. & Miquel Verd, J. 2013. Employer strategies, capabilities and career development: Two case studies of Spanish service firms. *International Journal of Manpower*, 34, 345–361.

Lyness, K.S. & Judiesch, M.K. 2008. Can a manager have a life and a career? International and multisource perspectives on work-life balance and career advancement potential. *Journal of Applied Psychology*, 93, 789–805.

Mäkelä, K. & Suutari, V. 2009. Global careers: A social capital paradox. *The International Journal of Human Resource Management*, 20, 992–1008.

Meuer, J. & Rupietta, C. 2017. Integrating QCA and HLM for multilevel research on organizational configurations. *Organizational Research Methods*, 20, 324–342.

Newburry, W., Belkin, L.Y. & Ansari, P. 2008. Perceived career opportunities from globalization: Globalization capabilities and attitudes towards women in Iran and the US. *Journal of International Business Studies*, 39, 814–832.

Ng, T.W., Eby, L.T., Sorensen, K.L. & Feldman, D.C. 2005. Predictors of objective and subjective career success: A meta-analysis. *Personnel Psychology*, 58, 367–408.

O'Mahony, S. & Bechky, B.A. 2006. Stretchwork: Managing the career progression paradox in external labor markets. *Academy of Management Journal*, 49, 918–941.

Open Science Collaboration. 2015. Estimating the reproducibility of psychological science. *Science*, 349, aac4716.

Peiperl, M. & Gunz, H.P. 2007. Taxonomy of career studies. *In:* Gunz, H.P. & Peiperl, M. (eds.) *Handbook of Career Studies*. Thousand Oaks, CA: Sage Publications.

Ployhart, R.E. & Vandenberg, R.J. 2010. Longitudinal research: The theory, design, and analysis of change. *Journal of Management*, 36, 94–120.

Podsakoff, P.M., Mackenzie, S.B. & Podsakoff, N.P. 2012. Sources of method bias in social science research and recommendations on how to control it. *Annual Review of Psychology*, 63, 539–569.

Pollach, I. 2012. Taming textual data: The contribution of corpus linguistics to computer-aided text analysis. *Organizational Research Methods*, 15, 263–287.

Probert, B. 2005. 'I just couldn't fit it in': Gender and unequal outcomes in academic careers. *Gender, Work & Organization*, 12, 50–72.

Raento, M., Oulasvirta, A. & Eagle, N. 2009. Smartphones: An emerging tool for social scientists. *Sociological Methods & Research*, 37, 426–454.

Ragin, C.C. 1987. *The Comparative Method: Moving Beyond Qualitative and Quantitative Strategies*. Los Angeles and London: University of California Press.

Rider, C.I. & Negro, G. 2015. Organizational failure and intraprofessional status loss. *Organization Science*, 26, 633–649.

Rihoux, B. 2006. Qualitative comparative analysis (QCA) and related systematic comparative methods: Recent advances and remaining challenges for social science research. *International Sociology*, 21, 679–706.

Rodrigues, R., Guest, D., Oliveira, T. & Alfes, K. 2015. Who benefits from independent careers? Employees, organizations, or both? *Journal of Vocational Behavior*, 91, 23–34.

Russo, M., Guo, L. & Baruch, Y. 2014. Work attitudes, career success and health: Evidence from China. *Journal of Vocational Behavior*, 84, 248–258.

Salmela-Aro, K. & Nurmi, J-E. 2007. Self-esteem during university studies predicts career characteristics 10 years later. *Journal of Vocational Behavior*, 70, 463–477.

Schau, H.J. & Gilly, M.C. 2003. We are what we post? Self-presentation in personal web space. *Journal of Consumer Research*, 30, 385–404.

Seibert, S.E. & Kraimer, M.L. 2001. The five-factor model of personality and career success. *Journal of Vocational Behavior*, 58, 1–21.

Shah, P.P., Bechara, J.P., Kolars, J., Drefahl, M., Larusso, N., Wood, D. & Spurrier, B. 2014. Temporal elements in career selection decisions: An archival study investigating career decisions in medicine. *Organization Science*, 25, 245–261.

Shen, Y., Demel, B., Unite, J., Briscoe, J.P., Hall, D.T., Chudzikowski, K., Mayrhofer, W., Abdul-Ghani, R., Bogicevic Milikic, B., Colorado, O., Fei, Z., Las Heras, M., Ogliastri, E., Pazy, A., Poon, J.M., Shefer, D., Taniguchi, M. & Zikic, J. 2015. Career success across 11 countries: Implications for international human resource management. *The International Journal of Human Resource Management*, 26, 1753–1778.

Simosi, M., Rousseau, D.M. & Daskalaki, M. 2015. When career paths cease to exist: A qualitative study of career behavior in a crisis economy. *Journal of Vocational Behavior*, 91, 134–146.

Smale, A., Bagdadli, S., Cotton, R., Dello Russo, S., Dickmann, M., Dysvik, A., Gianecchini, M., Kaše, R., Lazarova, M. & Reichel, A. 2018. Proactive career behaviors and subjective career success: The moderating role of national culture. *Journal of Organizational Behavior*, 1–18.

Spurk, D. & Abele, A.E. 2014. Synchronous and time-lagged effects between occupational self-efficacy and objective and subjective career success: Findings from a four-wave and 9-year longitudinal study. *Journal of Vocational Behavior*, 84, 119–132.

Spurk, D., Kauffeld, S., Barthauer, L. & Heinemann, N.S. 2015. Fostering networking behavior, career planning and optimism, and subjective career success: An intervention study. *Journal of Vocational Behavior*, 87, 134–144.

Vancouver, J.B., Li, X., Weinhardt, J.M., Steel, P. & Purl, J.D. 2016. Using a computational model to understand possible sources of skews in distributions of job performance. *Personnel Psychology*, 69, 931–974.

Waldman, D.A., Wang, D. & Fenters, V. 2016. The added value of neuroscience methods in organizational research. *Organizational Research Methods*, 1–27.

Weinhardt, J.M. & Vancouver, J.B. 2012. Computational models and organizational psychology: Opportunities abound. *Organizational Psychology Review*, 2, 267–292.

Wheatley, D. 2013. Location, vocation, location? Spatial entrapment among women in dual career households. *Gender, Work & Organization*, 20, 720–736.

Willner, T., Gati, I. & Guan, Y. 2015. Career decision-making profiles and career decision-making difficulties: A cross-cultural comparison among US, Israeli, and Chinese samples. *Journal of Vocational Behavior*, 88, 143–153.

Wilson, H.J. 2012. You, by the numbers. *Harvard Business Review*, 90, 119–122.

Young, R.A., Ball, J., Valach, L., Turkel, H. & Wong, Y.S. 2003. The family career development project in Chinese Canadian families. *Journal of Vocational Behavior*, 62, 287–304.

Zacher, H. 2015. Daily manifestations of career adaptability: Relationships with job and career outcomes. *Journal of Vocational Behavior*, 91, 76–86.

Part II

Developing careers

8

Time is of the essence

The temporal dimension of careers

Wolfgang Mayrhofer and Hugh Gunz

Time is both fundamental and, for the past nearly 40 years, the least studied of major constructs associated with career. It is fundamental because, as Arthur et al. (1989: 8) point out when proposing their widely used definition of career ("the evolving sequence of a person's work experiences over time"):

> A central theme in this definition is that of work and all that work can mean for the ways in which we see and experience other people, organizations, and society. However, *equally central to this definition is the theme of time*, along which the career provides a 'moving perspective' (Hughes, 1958: 67) on the unfolding interaction between a person and society.
>
> *(emphasis added)*

In a previous handbook, Gunz and Peiperl (2007: 4) note that "whichever way one looks at it, career and the passage of time are inextricably entangled." Viewing career involves the simultaneous application of three perspectives (Chapter 2, this volume; Gunz and Mayrhofer, 2018). One is interested in the condition of the individual (the ontic perspective), the positions they occupy within their social and geographic space (the spatial perspective), and the time over which the career happens (the temporal perspective). In the absence of the temporal perspective, no career is visible. Time figures in pretty much any definition of career, either explicitly, for example in Arthur et al.'s (1989: 8) definition cited above, or implicitly, for example in Hughes's (1958: 63) "moving perspective in which the person sees his life as a whole."

If time is fundamental to the understanding of career, then it is somewhat surprising that it has not played a more notable role in career research since the early 1980s (Gunz and Mayrhofer, 2018: 144). That is not to say that it has not been studied (recent examples of research in which the temporal perspective plays an important role include Koch et al., 2016; Bidwell and Mollick, 2015; Kattenbach et al., 2014; Schneidhofer et al., 2012; Bidwell and Briscoe, 2010), nor that it is ignored in studies in which it does not play a central role. It becomes less of a surprise when one considers the difficulties associated with including the temporal perspective in a research study, as it involves either a retrospective design, subject to all the fallibilities of memory and the difficulties in gaining access to historical archives, or a prospective design, something that is expensive and dependent on a research team that can count on its funding being sustained for a significant period of time. Indeed one of the great clichés of writing in the organization sciences is the call, at the end of so many papers, for the study's findings to be further substantiated by means of longitudinal designs that were not available to the authors.

Time is not only fundamental for careers, but it has also been conceptualized in many strikingly different ways in the social sciences. In this chapter, after briefly reviewing how time has been addressed in classic career studies, we reflect on ways that the many different approaches to understanding time can contribute to a richer understanding of careers. Space limitations allow only so much. Therefore, we restrict ourselves to pointing towards the core aspects of a number of concepts. For some, this might come across as superficial or "name-dropping style"; our hope is that this is a teaser to get readers interested in a more in-depth exploration of this fascinating area.

Searching for traces: time in classic career studies

Time permeates all work on careers, but it has played a particularly prominent role in two distinct traditions in career research. They focus respectively on (1) the developmental stages through which career actors pass during their lives and (2) the timetables that actors develop in order to make sense of portions of their lives.

Probably the most obvious way in which time appears in classic career studies takes the form of the various developmental and career stage models that trace their origins at least to the work of Freud. Indeed the speech by the melancholy Jacques in Shakespeare's *As You Like It* (Act II, Scene vii: "And one man in his time plays many parts / His acts being seven ages."), could be seen in this tradition. The basic concept behind these approaches is that the individual passes through a series of predictable developmental stages as they pass through life (Sullivan and Crocitto, 2007). Some models, such as that of Erikson (1963), focus more on the earlier stages. Erikson, for example, depicts development as an eight-stage process, at each of which the individual must cope with a dilemma peculiar to that stage. Others, such as Super (1957), Levinson et al. (1978), and Bateson (1989), are more concerned with the adult stages. Some models focus on particular aspects of the individual's development, most notably those that look at their moral development (Kohlberg, 1969; Gilligan, 1982). Given increasing life expectancy throughout nearly the entire world, recent models also focus on the final stages of life (e.g., Bateson, 2011). Finally, there are models (e.g., Schein, 1978) that view the development of the individual in the context of the organization(s) in which they develop their work career.

The use of time in the empirical study of careers also takes on more complex forms than the already complex stage/developmental theories to which we have been alluding. For example, Baltes and Nesselroade (1984), responding to Dannefer's (1984) critique of their work as neglecting social influences on development, draw attention both to ontogenetic (age-graded) time (i.e., the aging of the individual actor) but also to what they term evolutionary (history-graded) time, namely "fairly general (normative) events or event patterns experienced by a given cultural unit in connection with biosocial change, for example, as evidenced by cohort effects" (ibid.: 843).

Timetables (Zerubavel, 1976) provide a different angle on the way in which time appears in careers. In his classic study of the experience of tuberculosis (TB) patients, Roth (1963) argues:

> People will not accept uncertainty. They will make an effort to structure it no matter how poor the materials they have to work with and no matter how much the experts try to discourage them. One way to structure uncertainty is to structure the time period through which uncertain events occur. Such a structure must usually be developed from

information gained from the experience of others who have gone or are going through the same series of events. As a result of such comparisons, norms develop for entire groups about when certain events may be expected to occur. When many people go through the same series of events, we speak of this as a career and of the sequence and timing of events as their career timetable.

(ibid.: 93)

The TB patients in Roth's study – he himself was one such – make sense of their time in hospital by means of the "benchmarks" (ibid.: 3) that they pass through over the course of their treatment. The timing of the benchmarks may be arbitrarily defined by the particular hospital's regulations, or they may relate to the treatment process that all TB patients at that time went through, aimed at assessing whether the disease was still active, whether surgery was required, how long the patient remained in hospital after surgery, and so on. Patients falling behind the usual timetable would realize that their condition was more serious and would adjust their perspective on their future timetable accordingly. Roth extends the idea of career timetables to many other situations: medical (polio convalescence, psychiatric illness), "standardized" (the draftee army, the educational system), and what he terms "vertical occupational careers" (the business executive, the airline pilot). Managers in particular (Sofer, 1970) but also people in general (Collin, 2000) can be extremely sensitive to their positioning on their career timetable – whether they are on schedule or falling behind. If they feel that they are ahead of the "normal" timetable, they tend to have more positive attitudes to their work than if they feel – rightly or wrongly – that they are falling behind (Lawrence, 1984).

We note above that the temporal perspective has played less of a central role in career research in recent years. In our previous work (Gunz and Mayrhofer, 2018: 130ff), we traced the history of the field of what is labeled "organizational and managerial careers" (OMC), dividing it into four periods called (1) the Chicago School (1920s–1950s), (2) the age of the organization (1960s–1970s), (3) a period of transition (1980s), and (4) boundarylessness and beyond (1990s to date). We suggested that the first two periods paid considerable attention to the temporal perspective. The Chicago School, for example, was "fascinated by the stages through which their subjects pass as their careers progress (perhaps the best-known of these studies being Roth, 1963); the concept of status passage (Glaser and Strauss, 1971) is central to their thinking" (p. 132). Similarly, scholars in the second period paid great attention to "timetables, stages/phases, and the interest in the development of careers over extended periods of time" (p. 137). The third period is dominated by an interest in structure and its impact on careers, but – with some exceptions, such as Lawrence's (1984) study of timetables – interest in the temporal perspective is not as strong. By the final period, the temporal perspective (again, as we note above) with exceptions puts in even less of an appearance because, we speculated, "longitudinal research is both too expensive and risky for junior faculty trying to establish a foothold in the academic world" (p. 144).

Time has been examined from many different angles, and in the next section we look at some of them.

Sources of refreshment: discourses providing conceptualizations of time

Looking at conceptualizations of time reveals an interesting tension. On the one hand, in many scientific disciplines, there is some considerable lamentation that despite its importance, time is not adequately acknowledged in the respective discourses. As an example from the psychological realm, Roe (2008: 37) states "that while time is a salient facet of everyday life, its role is barely acknowledged in the psychological literature." In similar manner, Bergmann (1992: 82) reports that "[i]f one skims the literature on the subject of 'social time', one finds complaints everywhere about the neglect and marginality of the time problem in sociology."

On the other hand, a closer look reveals that, though dispersed across many disciplines and cross-disciplinary discourses, a substantial amount of thought has been given to this topic (see, e.g., Birx, 2009). Hence, and again quoting Bergmann (1992: 82):

> one comes, contrary to the neglect asserted everywhere, upon a quite extensive body of literature – although it is advisable to look beyond the borders of sociology and to take into account numerous works in the related disciplines of ethnology, cultural anthropology, psychology and history. Given the wealth of material, the thesis that the category of "time" has been neglected proves in part to be a protective assertion that allows many authors to begin right at the beginning without having to take note of existing studies to any great extent. Because of this "solipsistic" approach, a look through the literature gives the impression of a very large but barely interconnected number of studies.

Against this backdrop, in this section we give a selective overview of major thinking about time.[1] We start with concepts that, while inevitably framed by the authors' disciplinary heritage, aim at presenting a 'generic' view on time. Following that, we will look at major scientific disciplines adjacent to career studies that have dealt with time in their respective manner before looking at time-related views in organization studies. This provides the basis for our final section where we outline major routes for reintegration time more strongly into career studies.

Theories of time

What some would call "philosophy of time" deals with very fundamental issues, such as what time is, how it can be perceived, how human life is related to it, and whether time is real (Ryan, 2007). For example, Heath (1956 [Orig. 1936]) points towards three major issues of temporal philosophy: one has to address the issue whether time is subjective or located in the objective world as something real and concrete; whether time units are equivalent or of different length and experienced in a different way; and how to measure time (see also Hassard, 2001). Among others, these considerations point towards a number of classical dualities such as "*chronos* (time/ interval/while) vs. *kairos* (opportunity, critical/right moment in time), *aeternitas* (spreading out of time) vs. *tempus* (differentiation between past and future), *temps* (objective time) vs. *durée* (flow of duration), and linear vs. cyclical time" (Heath, 1956 [Orig. 1936]: 838, italics in original) that were picked up and further developed in different areas of time research.

Close to these considerations are works that deal with various phenomena from a mono-, multi-, or cross-disciplinary perspective, but assign time a central place in their theorizing. Again, by means of exemplifying major but by no means all works, we illustrate the breadth as well as depth of these conceptualizations.

Time as culture

Hall (1983) looks at time from a cultural angle and argues that time and culture are closely intertwined. As time is "a core system of cultural, social, and personal life . . . and nothing occurs except in some kind of time frame" (ibid.: 3), cultures formulate, use, and pattern time in different ways, both consciously and unconsciously. Among others, time is essential for organizing activities, for categorizing experiences and determining priorities and also for evaluating individual and collective efforts and achievements. Hall differentiates between eight forms of time that he groups in the form of a mandala: sacred vs. profane; micro vs. sync; personal vs. biological; physical vs. metaphysical. The ninth form, meta time, is a synthesis of these eight forms.

A and B series of time

Starting with the assertion that time is unreal, McTaggart (1908) focuses on the relative ordering of positions in time and presents two ways of distinguishing such positions:

> Each position is Earlier than some, and Later than some, of the other positions. And each position is either Past, Present, or Future. The distinctions of the former class are permanent, while those of the latter are not. If M is ever earlier than N, it is always earlier. But an event, which is now present, was future and will be past.
>
> *(458)*

The distinction between earlier and later is what McTaggart calls the B series of time, which also relates to the duration of events and their frequency. The A series of time relates to the distinctions between past, present, future, pointing towards an inevitable fluidity as present becomes past, future becomes present and so on.

Two axes of time

Jaques (1982) argues that time allows one to organize events along two axes. The axis of succession is "a statement of a reconstruction of what has already succeeded what, and cannot be a statement of what *will* at some time in the future succeed what" (Jaques, 1982: 99, italics in original). It leads to the relative temporal positioning of events with respect to each other. While this axis appears to be directional, it is not since only a retrospective angle allows us to say that one thing led to another. It does not make any sense to imply that A leads to B when B does not even exist yet at a certain point in time. Causality comes into the picture with the axis of intention. On this axis, events are related to each other in a meaningful way. This assigns (lack of) causality, both prospectively and retrospectively.

Open versus closed system of time

Put forward by Wax (1959; cited in Roth, 1963: 96), this differentiation points towards an important aspect of how societies view time. Open systems primarily rely on calendar and clock to govern and evaluate their activities. Development is closely related to time-related measures (e.g., years spent in an organization) or age as threshold for access (e.g., entering a night club or having the right to vote). For the biblical Hebrews, their linear sense of history also means progress and has a final endpoint (i.e., the coming of the Messiah and the resurrection of the Kingdom of God). Conversely, closed systems of time bank on conditions to determine development (e.g., by relating to changing weather conditions or seasons). For example, the Pawnee, a tribe of Native Americans, view life as a series of cycles that are not linked with progress but marked by changes in condition.

Being and time

Heidegger (1962 [German orig. 1927]; Heidegger, 1985) links time inextricably with being (*Dasein*). Analyzing the core of being requires one to view being interwoven with time. Since humans are futural beings, we never are fully and only in the present as such, but always look ahead through plans, worries, and hopes. *Sorge* (care) plays a central role, as "[m]an's perfectio – his transformation into that which he can be in Being free for his ownmost possibilities (projection) – is 'accomplished' by 'care'" (Heidegger, 1962 [German orig. 1927]: 243) and the "authentic correlation of world and Dasein . . . is . . . care and meaningfulness" (Heidegger, 1985: 221). Based on this and deviating from a more traditional view of temporality with its objective-physical concept of time that leads to, in Heidegger's terms, a "vulgar" notion of time, he develops the notion of originary temporality, a basic structure of the being of *Dasein*. Time, then, is to be understood in itself as the unity of three ecstases (i.e. dimensions of present, past, and future). It cannot be reduced to the mere subjective experience of time or as differentiated from eternity.

Time in scientific disciplines adjacent to career studies

As a topic, time plays a crucial role in a number of disciplines in close proximity to career studies, in particular sociology, psychology, and organization studies. The respective discourses are extensive as well as highly differentiated and there is no way to give a comprehensive overview. Rather, by means of example we want to highlight a few prominent contributions that give the reader not familiar with those fields an impression about a few major threads of these discussions.

To be sure, time also plays a role in other but more distant disciplines leading to an anthropology of time (e.g., Gell, 1992; Munn, 1992) or a geography of time (Levine, 1997; Thrift, 2011). Given the restrictions of this chapter, however, we focus on career studies' closest disciplinary neighbors, sociology and psychology, before turning to organization studies in the next step.

Sociology

When looking at the theoretical treatment of time in sociology, three broad strands emerge (Ryan, 2007; see also Bergmann, 1992). A first group of theories refers to time as an important but only implicitly acknowledged factor. Examples include theories that target phenomena such as change or deciphering operations (e.g., ecological modernization theory; Huber, 2008; Mol et al., 2014) and theory of art perception (Bordieu, 1968).

A second group theorizes a broad variety of social phenomena, in particular comprehensive analyses of society or parts of it, and assigns time an important role in their analyses (see, for example, the overview in Nowotny, 1992). Examples include the Marxian analysis of capitalism with its stage-oriented concept of evolution towards the classless society (Marx, 1859); Weber's core interest in historical developments and the specifics of modern capitalism and its iron cage of rationality (Weber, 2000 [Orig. 1904/05]); and Luhmann's view of time as *conditio sine qua non* for linking communications – his core element of organizations – and for selection, one of the core operations of social systems and the different forms of time (*Eigenzeit*) that (various) social systems and their environment have (Luhmann, 1995; Luhmann, 1997).

In its most elaborate form, major works of prominent figures in the sociological discourse focus on time through various aspects of a sociology of time, focusing on a broad range of issues. Three examples may suffice.

SOCIAL VERSUS CLOCK/ASTRONOMICAL TIME

Pointing towards the role that time-related considerations have for social functioning, Sorokin and Merton (1937) differentiate between social and clock/astronomical time. The former is firmly rooted in social specifics as it refers to one social phenomenon through another. Social time is essentially discontinuous as it relates to specific social events. For examples, the concept of "week" varies greatly depending on the society and group you look at, ranging from a mere three days with the Muysca in Bogotá to 10 days with the Inca, often closely linked to the respective market cycles and the complexity of the economy. As interaction and contact spread and grew beyond physically and socially confined circles, locally colored time concepts turned out to be inadequate. Clock/astronomical time follows the dictum that Newton has set in terms of objectivity of time (i.e., time being continuous, infinitely divisible, and uniform). It provides a common standard for actors to synchronize their action. Note, however, that even astronomical time can be "colored" by social considerations:

> witness the new convention of "daylight-saving time." The desired result, an increased number of daylight hours for recreation and leisure, could have been attained simply by shifting working hours to 8:00 a.m.–4:00 p.m. But the "9:00 to 5:00" designation has become so deeply rooted in our economy that the presumably less violent innovation of changing the numerical designations of units within the twenty-four-hour cycle was deemed preferable.
> *(Sorokin and Merton, 1937: 626)*

SOCIOTEMPORAL ORDER

Zerubavel (1982) wants to bring temporality to the forefront of sociological thinking. He points out that going beyond the individual experience leads to social time that we collectively adhere to, and "if time is to be shared as an intersubjective social reality, it ought to be *standardized*" (Zerubavel, 1982: 2; italics in original). Arguing that much of our everyday world is quite structured, he focuses on the sociotemporal order that regulates various social units such as organizations, families, or nations. His point of departure is temporal regularity expressing the orderliness of time. From a temporal perspective, all situations can be described by four parameters: the order in which they take place (sequential structure); how long they last (duration); when they happen (temporal location); and, finally, how often they occur (rate of recurrence). Based on this, temporal regularity takes four distinct forms, i.e., "rigid sequential structures, fixed durations, standard temporal locations, and uniform rates of recurrence" (Zerubavel, 1981: 1), across a broad variety of different contexts, ranging from Benedictine monasteries and Orthodox Judaism to Revolutionary France and modern-day hospitals.

PLURALITY OF SOCIAL TIMES

Gurvitch (1964) emphasizes the plurality of social times and argues that cultures not only have different social times, but also that these different social times are conflicting with each other and that various social groups within a society are in continuous competition over what constitute appropriate times. He differentiates between the micro-level of social groups and communities and their times and the times of macro-level of society and its institutions. Regarding the latter, he identifies various types of societies such as charismatic theocracies (e.g., Babylonia or the Caliphate of Islam under the dynasties of the Ammeyades and Abbasides (8th–12th centuries)), ancient city-states such as the Greek polis and the Latin civitas, and fascist societies (e.g.,

Argentina during the Perón era), and analyzes the respective social times. In addition, Gurvitch also differentiates between eight different forms of time (enduring, deceptive, erratic, cyclical, retarded, alternating, pushing forward, and explosive).

Psychology

Time is essential for a psychological view on individuals and their context, since "no form of behavior could possibly be defined without reference to time, and no behavior could be observed if the time interval were limited to zero" (Roe, 2008: 37). A time-related psychological view can focus on a broad range of topics such as developmental stages of individuals through their life course; learning processes; duration of emotional responses to internal and external events; self-concept in relation to position in the individual life cycle, the time-orientation (past, present, future), and the influence of remembrance (past) and anticipation (future); multi-tasking by doing more than one thing at a time; and developmental stages of teams and related performance issues (McGrath, 1988, 1994; Roe, 2008).

Work in this area implicitly or explicitly refers to one of the basic differentiations related to time (i.e., the dichotomous nature of time already hinted at earlier). Arguably going back at least to ancient Greece and the opposing views of Heraclitus and Zeno about time and the reality of change, the difference between time as something with an objective quality and as something that is experienced within the individual is nicely represented by the views of Sir Isaac Newton and St. Augustine. While the former sees time as a container for all events existing with or without them (Boniwell, 2009), St. Augustine captures the subjective quality by asking:

> What then is time? If no one asks me, I know; if I want to explain it to a questioner, I do not know. But at any rate this much I dare affirm I know: that if nothing passed there would be no past time; if nothing were approaching, there would be no future time; if nothing were, there would be no present time. But the two times, past and future, how can they be, since the past is no more and the future is not yet? On the other hand, if the present were always present and never flowed away into the past, it would not be time at all, but eternity.
>
> *(Augustine, 2006 [Orig. around AD 400]: Book 11, chapter XIV,*
> *section 17; italics in the original, translation F.J. Sheed)*

Much of the time-related work in psychology relates to the subjective view of time. Of course, the labels vary, including, for example, "time as it is processed by the human mind" or "subjective estimation of duration" (Levin and Zakay, 1989: 2). Three examples may suffice to illustrate work in this area.

TIME PERSPECTIVE

Time perspective (TP; also "time orientation") denotes the preferences that individuals have in their thinking towards the present, future, or past. This influences how they experience themselves and their environment, their motivation, and various other aspects of behavior (De Volder, 1979). A number of factors such as socialization, education, and modeling influence TP. One important facet of TP is future time perspective (FTP), that is the present anticipation of future goals (Simons et al., 2004). People differ with regard to how short or long they reach to the future. FTP has a cognitive and a dynamic aspect.

> The dynamic aspect of FTP is formed by the disposition to ascribe high valence to goals in the distant future. The cognitive aspect of FTP is formed by the disposition to grasp the

long-term consequences of actual behavior, as reflected in the concept of instrumental value of a behavioral act.

(De Volder and Lens, 1982: 567)

Consequently, individuals with a long FTP are able to reach further into the future, which not only "makes it possible to anticipate the more distant future; to dispose of longer time intervals in which one can situate motivational goals, plans, and projects; and to direct present actions toward goals in the more distant future" (Simons et al., 2004: 123). It also leads to higher utility values and a higher instrumental value of current activities. FTP is no general disposition, but related to different areas of behavior, for example personal development, family, occupation, politics, economics, and environment (Lamm et al., 1976).

INFLUENCING FUTURE ORIENTATION

Marko and Savickas (1998) focus on an individual's orientation to the future in relation to career planning. They start from the idea "that a future orientation is a critical dimension in career development and that this time perspective can be learned through experience" (ibid.: 108). Focusing on career planning and on future orientation, the study used the three-phased Time Perspective Modification Intervention (TPMI) to influence participants' levels of future orientation and career planning. In the orientation phase, participants reflect on their relationship to past, present, and future. The differentiation phase aims at making the future feel real, supports existing positive attitudes towards planning, and encourages goal setting. The integration phase is intended to link present behavior with future outcomes, heighten career awareness, and practice with planning skills. Results show that interventions can influence time orientations and career planning.

TEMPORALISM

Roe (2008) suggests temporalism as an approach that starts from the phenomenon, that is "an observable event, or series of events, happening to a particular object (e.g., individual, group, organization) during a certain time interval" (ibid.: 41). Every phenomenon is bounded in time (i.e., it has a beginning, an end and emerges and vanishes within the interval that is demarcated by points in time). These intervals are not set by coincidence or arbitrarily but are an integral part of the phenomenon, meaningful and important to understand because they provide insight about the phenomenon and its underlying characteristics. For example, major exams at certain points during one's studies demarcate the phenomenon "being educated at a university," indicating, among others, assumptions about the field of study, relationships between areas of knowledge, and so forth. Against this backdrop, Roe not only advocates using verbs instead of nouns in order to emphasize and capture the dynamics of phenomena but also suggests an analytic framework for temporally sensitive general descriptions of phenomena. Core pillars of such descriptions are onset, offset, duration (i.e., the time between on- and offset), and dynamics (i.e., the emerging shape of the phenomenon as it unfolds).

Organization studies

Calls for a better integration of the temporal dimension into organization studies have a long tradition and are part of the more general efforts to contextualize research in order to better understand what goes on in organizations (e.g., Johns, 2001; Rousseau and Fried, 2001; Johns, 2006).

There are a number of significant contributions in the organization studies discourse related to time (see, e.g., the chapters in Roe et al., 2009). They broadly fall into four groups.

A first group of contributions draws on basic works about time and develops various conceptualizations of time (e.g., McGrath and Rotchford, 1983; George and Jones, 2000; Mosakowski and Earley, 2000; Ancona et al., 2001b; Mitchell and James, 2001; Ofori-Dankwa and Julian, 2001). By and large, these contributions use the more generic literature on time as springboard for taking a more in-depth look at segments of these conceptualizations that are especially relevant in the context of organizations, groups, and individuals. A second group focuses on the theoretical realm and looks for ways of emphasizing the temporal aspects in building theories about phenomena in the world of organizations (e.g., Bluedorn and Denhardt, 1988; Ancona et al., 2001a, 2001b; Goodman et al., 2001; Orlikowski and Yates, 2002; Whipp et al., 2002; Bluedorn and Jaussi, 2007; Sonnentag, 2012; Shipp and Fried, 2014b; Shipp and Fried, 2014a). Areas that receive specific attention are, for example, organizational improvisation (Crossan et al., 2005), leadership (e.g., Bluedorn and Jaussi, 2008), and organizational identity (Schultz and Hernes, 2013). The third group takes a methods angle and discusses the implications that the temporal dimension has for the design of empirical studies and the formulation of hypotheses (e.g., Mitchell and James, 2001; Shipp and Fried, 2014a). A final group picks up the problem of time in the world of work from an empirical point of view. Examples range from the link between CEOs' feelings and perceptions about time and the consequences for organizational strategies (Jianhong and Nadkarni, 2017) to the use of visual artifacts in organizations to represent time (Yakura, 2002). One example from each of the categories may suffice to illustrate the work in these areas.

RELEVANT TIME DIMENSIONS FOR ORGANIZATIONAL ANALYSES

George and Jones (2000) identify six time dimensions that are critical when theorizing organizations. The subjective experience of time seems to be an intrinsic part of consciousness and the way individuals link past, present, and future with regard to continuation, inseparability, and connection influences how they experience time. Time aggregations are similar to bracketing processes in which individuals assemble their time experiences into one or several episodes that help to assign meaning. Duration of steady states and rates of change address how long a specific kind of aggregation lasts and to what degree it changes in order to capture a more dynamic view of the matter at hand. Incremental versus discontinuous change points towards the form of change and whether it occurs gradually. Frequency, rhythm, and cycles take note of the fact that phenomena often do not only occur once but more often and with a detectable underlying temporal pattern. Spirals and intensity reflect the fact that phenomena not only oscillate around some kind of (quasi-)equilibrium but can develop in a spiral form with increasing intensity (e.g., an escalating conflict between two parties).

TEMPORAL STRUCTURING

Orlikowski and Yates (2002) propose looking at the everyday action of organizational actors as a way of producing and reproducing various temporal structures that mold the form and rhythm of their ongoing practices. These structures serve to coordinate, orient, and guide their various activities. Examples include academic calendars, financial reporting periods, meeting schedules, and project deadlines. These temporal structures are not merely an objective expression of an underlying phenomenon or the socially shaped product of collective sensemaking. Rather, they limit acceptable action and, at the same time, are influenced by the very action they are trying to inform. People use these temporal structures to shape their everyday work practices. "In turn, such legitimized temporal structures – while always potentially changeable because they are constituted in action – become taken for granted, serving as powerful templates for the timing and rhythm of members' social action within the community" (ibid.: 685). This view offers a theoretical alternative to the classic objective/subjective divide of conceptualizing time, since it focuses on human practices and neither on subjective construction nor objective external forces.

BANANA TIME

In a classic study on social interaction in a small group of factory workers ("clicker operators") with extremely monotonous and repetitive work, Roy (1960) focuses on the informal social activities of the workers. Through participatory observation Roy was able to show that typical themes and times of dense social interaction emerged that structured the otherwise rather uneventful day of work. The times he identifies

> featured the consumption of food or drink of one sort or another. There was coffee time, peach time, banana time, fish time, coke time, and, of course, lunch time. Other interruptions, which formed part of the series but were not verbally recognized as times, were window time, pickup time.
>
> *(ibid.: 162)*

Each of these times and themes had its own specific choreography with distributed roles and script-like interaction between the clicker operators. The predictable temporal structuring of the day provided orientation, allowed structured interaction, and constituted an important element of the cultural glue necessary for group cohesion.

TIME SCALES AND ITS EFFECTS ON RESEARCH

Zaheer et al. (1999) direct our attention to the importance of specifying the respective time scale when doing organizational analyses. By time scale they

> refer to the size of the temporal intervals, whether subjective or objective, used to build or test theory about a process, pattern, phenomenon, or event. Two fundamental properties define time scales: (1) time scales partition or differentiate the temporal continuum into units of different sizes, and (2) time scales may have either a socially constructed or an objectively determined nature.
>
> *(ibid.: 725)*

The choice of the time scales heavily influence what one can observe and how researchers can relate to and understand the phenomenon at hand. They present five time scales they call existence, validity, observation, recording, and aggregation interval, which are crucial for the research process.

Back to the future: reintegrating time into career studies

In the previous sections we have pointed towards the breadth and depth of insight from various scientific discourses with regard to time. In this section, we will briefly outline some major ways forward in assigning time a more appropriate place in career studies. Of course, we are not here to tell the field of career studies what to do. Yet we think that we can identify three major routes for a stronger integration of time in career theorizing, strengthening the temporal dimension when designing empirical studies, and addressing time across different levels of social complexity. We will deal with these issues in turn.

Including the temporal dimension in career theorizing

Perhaps the most fundamental request is to make the temporal dimension more explicit when building theories and conceptual frameworks. It is good scientific practice to be as explicit as feasible about the underlying theoretical and epistemological assumptions in one's work. In career theory, using time in one way or another as part of an overall theoretical framework, at least two issues have to be addressed to strengthen the temporal aspect of career theories.

A first issue is to clarify the notion of time that underlies the framework. A minimum requirement would be to take a position in the simple dichotomy of Newton-like objective time and St. Augustine–like subjectively experienced time. Beyond that, the existing literature on time, roughly sketched in the previous sections, offers a number of approaches that one can draw upon in order to clarify which approach to time one takes.

A second issue is to assign time an adequate place in the architecture of the theory or framework used for one's studies. To be sure, constructs and variables closely related to time are common practice in career studies as the regular use of variables such as biological age, organizational tenure, and time orientation testify. However, we argue that it is worth exploring whether these variables have their adequate place in the overall theoretical reasoning and whether time as the underlying concept is hidden under the constructs used, thus contributing to the deviation from and/or rendering invisible the temporal dimension underlying careers and one's theoretical frame.

Strengthening the temporal dimension in empirical research designs

Related to the above but directly targeting empirical research designs is the issue of reflecting the temporal qualities of careers in how one sets up empirical studies, which involves matching the theoretical conceptualization of time with the empirical approach. Continuing with the objective-subjective divide as an example, very different data collection and analysis methods have to be used in order to align theory, methods, and, for that matter, epistemology. Building on time as an objective entity that can be divided and measured, much if not all of the standard toolbox of quantitative empirical research is available. If one leans towards the more subjective perspective on time, these methods are hardly adequate. Instead, methods of data gathering and analyses that provide inroads into personal perception of and emotions and cognitions about time and its relationship to action are required. Examples include in-depth interviews, narrative studies, and hermeneutic text analyses based on subjective reconstruction.

Beyond that, the usual shorthand for strengthening the temporal dimension in empirical research on careers is a call for more longitudinal studies. While this is not wrong, a closer look reveals that this is a header for a number of different things.

The basic reading of this is to have at least two points in time when you collect data. Beyond this being essential for career-related issues that include development or change (e.g. when analyzing whether mentoring has any effect on career satisfaction or how early career experiences relate to mid-career occupational change), it also creates the foundations for causal explanations where a differentiation between "cause" and "effect" requires some time lag.

Expanding on that, strengthening the temporal dimension in empirical research design goes beyond a basically straightforward data collection at two points in time by conducting studies at multiple points in time – for example, studying graduate careers by not only surveying the graduates when they leave university and enter the labor market and then again, say, 20 years later, but asking them on a yearly basis about core parameters of their development allows one to discern patterns and reveals twists and turns that are not detectable in a two-points-in-time study. Another example would be diary studies that, often by relying on recent technology such as mobile phone apps or smart clothing, allow one to gather data at several points in time or even continuously.

Very much like in other areas of empirical research, one has at least to differentiate between three different kinds of longitudinal designs. Trend studies look at the same population, but at different sample participants over time. For example, Cranet (www.cranet.org) looks at broadly representative national samples of organizations to analyze HRM and career issues since 1989. Panel studies focus on the same population *and* on the same sample participants in different points in time. Examples of this include various national household-studies such as the German Socio-Economic Panel (SOEP) or, from an opposite side of the globe, the Household, Income and Labour Dynamics in Australia (HILDA) survey. Finally, cohort studies target a specific population characterized by joint core characteristics such as university graduates of specific years. Examples include a well-known study of MBA graduates or various studies on graduates looking at the role of gender (e.g., Schneer and Reitman, 1995; Schneidhofer et al., 2012).

Addressing time across different levels of social complexity

Finally, reintegrating time more strongly into career studies also suggests the need to address various temporal aspects across different levels of social complexity. Time is not only an issue relevant for the individual that can be analyzed purely at the individual level. Quite the contrary, it is often, if not regularly, located at other levels or spans across them. A few examples may suffice to illustrate the broad variety of research issues that arise when taking a multilevel view. They all focus on the conceptual framing of time as a point of reference to illustrate that such a singular angle already allows for a broad variety of fascinating topics.

At the individual level, career actors' conceptualizations of time are crucial for a number of career related issues. For example, one can further dive into the question whether and how career actors' conceptualizations of time influence their views of career success and also, vice versa, how views of career success influence their conceptualizations of time. In a broader view, one might also further analyze the moderating effects of different individual conceptualizations of time on seemingly well-established insights in career (success) research, such as perceived career stages or the relationship between objective and subjective career success.

At the organizational level, every organization implicitly or explicitly has views on time, for example as expressed in various elements of organizational culture at the level of artifacts, values, and basic assumptions. With respect to exploring careers, one issue could be the relationship between organizational time perspectives and organizational career management (e.g., whether available career paths within organizations and the expected or required rate of promotions is linked to particular organizational views on time). In a similar vein, it would be interesting to explore whether individual career aspirations are linked to organizational views on time (e.g., through self-selection of new members with particular aspirations or through socialization effects once individuals have become members of the organization).

At the level of occupations, different occupations have different views on temporal issues such as length of feedback cycles for one's action or time horizons for planning. While, for example, day traders on the financial markets act within a very short time perspective, restorers of applied arts and crafts have to take a much longer-term view both into the past and the future when, for example, exploring the materials used by Pieter Bruegel the Elder in his oil on wood panel painting *The Hunters in the Snow* from the 16th century, displayed in Vienna's Kunsthistorisches Museum, and considering the potential long-term effects of restoration efforts. We know very little about how such occupation-specific time aspects are related to general expectations about careers, for example the kind of career progress and rate of advancement, and to the decision-making criteria that individuals use during their career.

At the societal level, cultures have different concepts of time (e.g., long-term vs. short-term or linear vs. cyclical). A theoretical and empirical analysis of the relationship between this macro-variable and various career-related issues could shed further light on the contextual contingencies that play a role in careers. Such issues include, for example, effects of culture-based time conceptualizations on the design of organizational career management systems and the (non-) use of various organizational career development tools, such as high-flyer programs or assignments abroad. Likewise, the relationship between such time conceptualizations and salient career success dimensions for individuals is an important topic.

Closing remark

The temporal dimension of career deserves more – and more explicit – attention in career studies. This was the starting point of our chapter. We argued that in classic career studies, time played an important role and that a number of disciplines make frameworks available that can help to assign time the place in career studies that it, at least in our view, deserves. Our brief suggestions about reintegrating time in theoretical and empirical works across different levels of social complexity point towards a potentially rich and fruitful field of research. Time will tell whether someone will cultivate and harvest this field. We, at least, hope so.

Note

1 We should acknowledge in passing a massively important literature on time that we do not consider, namely that of relativistic time dilation, even though its impact on life as it is lived now is far from unimportant (see, e.g., Ashby, N. 2003. Relativity in the Global Positioning System. *Living Reviews in Relativity* [Online], 6. Available: https://link.springer.com/article/10.12942/lrr-2003-1, for a discussion on how it affects the Global Positioning System).

References

Ancona, D.G., Goodman, P., Lawrence, B. & Tushman, M. 2001a. Time: A new research lense. *Academy of Management Review,* 26, 645–663.
Ancona, D.G., Okhuysen, G.A. & Perlow, L.A. 2001b. Taking time to integrate temporal research. *The Academy of Management Review,* 26, 512–529.
Arthur, M.B., Hall, D.T. & Lawrence, B.S. 1989. Generating new directions in career theory: The case for a transdisciplinary approach. *In:* Arthur, M.B., Hall, D.T. & Lawrence, B.S. (eds.) *Handbook of Career Theory.* Cambridge: Cambridge University Press.
Ashby, N. 2003. Relativity in the global positioning system. *Living Reviews in Relativity* [Online], 6. Available: https://link.springer.com/article/10.12942/lrr-2003-1.
Augustine. 2006 [Orig. around 400]. *Confessions.* Indianapolis and Cambridge: Hackett.
Baltes, P.B. & Nesselroade, J.R. 1984. Paradigm lost and paradigm regained: Critique of Dannefer's portrayal of life-span developmental psychology. *American Sociological Review,* 49, 841–847.

Bateson, M. C. 1989. *Composing a Life*. New York: Penguin.

Bateson, M. C. 2011. *Composing a Further Life: The Age of Active Wisdom*. New York and Toronto: Vintage.

Bergmann, W. 1992. The problem of time in sociology: An overview of the literature on the state of theory and research on the 'sociology of time', 1900–82. *Time & Society*, 1, 81–134.

Bidwell, M. & Briscoe, F. 2010. The dynamics of interorganizational careers. *Organization Science, 21*, 1034–1053.

Bidwell, M. & Mollick, E. 2015. Shifts and ladders: Comparing the role of internal and external mobility in managerial careers. *Organization Science, 26*, 1629–1645.

Birx, H.J. (ed.) 2009. *Encyclopedia of Time: Science, Philosophy, Theology, & Culture. Vol. 1*. Thousand Oaks, CA: Sage Publications.

Bluedorn, A.C. & Denhardt, R. 1988. Time and organizations. *Journal of Management*, 14, 299–320.

Bluedorn, A.C. & Jaussi, K.S. 2007. Organizationally relevant dimensions of time across levels of analysis. *Research in Multi-Level Issues*, 6, 187–223.

Bluedorn, A.C. & Jaussi, K.S. 2008. Leaders, followers, and time. *The Leadership Quarterly*, 19, 654–668.

Boniwell, I. 2009. Perspectives on time. *In:* Lopez, S.J. & Snyder, C.R. (eds.) *Oxford Handbook of Positive Psychology*, 2nd ed. New York: Oxford University Press.

Bordieu, P. 1968. Outline of a sociological theory of art perception. *International Social Science Journal*, 20, 589–612.

Collin, A. 2000. Dancing to the music of time. *In:* Collin, A. & Young, R.A. (eds.) *The Future of Career*. Cambridge: Cambridge University Press.

Crossan, M., Cunha, M.P.E., Vera, D. & Cunha, J. 2005. Time and organizational improvisation. *Academy of Management Review*, 30, 129–145.

Dannefer, D. 1984. Adult development and social theory: A paradigmatic reappraisal. *American Sociological Review*, 49, 100–116.

De Volder, M. 1979. Time orientation: A review. *Psychologica Belgica*, 19, 61–79.

De Volder, M.L. & Lens, W. 1982. Academic achievement and future time perspective as a cognitive – motivational concept. *Journal of Personality and Social Psychology*, 42, 566–571.

Erikson, E.H. 1963. Eight ages of man. *In:* Erikson, E.H. (ed.) *Childhood and Society*. New York: Norton.

Gell, A. 1992. *The Anthropology of Time: Cultural Constructions of Temporal Maps and Images*. Oxford: Berg.

George, J. & Jones, G. 2000. The role of time in theory and theory building. *Journal of Management*, 26, 657–684.

Gilligan, C. 1982. *In a Different Voice*. Cambrige, MA: Harvard University Press.

Goodman, P., Lawrence, B., Ancona, D. & Tushman, M. 2001. Introduction to the special issue. *Academy of Management Review*, 26, 507–511.

Gunz, H. & Mayrhofer, W. 2018. *Rethinking Career Studies. Facilitating Conversation Across Boundaries with the Social Chronology Framework*. Cambridge: Cambridge University Press.

Gunz, H. & Peiperl, M. 2007. Introduction. *In:* Gunz, H.P. & Peiperl, M.A. (eds.) *Handbook of Career Studies*. London: Sage Publications.

Gurvitch, G. 1964. *The Spectrum of Social Time*. Dordrecht: D. Reidel.

Hall, E.T. 1983. *The Dance of Life*. Doubleday: Anchor Books.

Hassard, J. 2001. Commodification, construction and compression: A review of time metaphors in organizational analysis. *International Journal of Management Reviews*, 3, 131–140.

Heath, L.R. 1956 [Orig. 1936]. *The Concept of Time*. Chicago: University of Chicago Press.

Heidegger, M. 1962 [German orig. 1927]. *Being and Time*. Oxford, UK and Cambridge, MA: Blackwell.

Heidegger, M. 1985. *History of the Concept of Time. Prolegomena*. Bloomington: Indiana University Press.

Huber, J. 2008. Pioneer countries and the global diffusion of environmental innovations: Theses from the viewpoint of ecological modernisation theory. *Global Environmental Change*, 18, 360–367.

Hughes, E.C. 1958. *Men and Their Work*. Glencoe, IL: The Free Press.

Jaques, E. 1982. *The Form of Time*. New York and London: Crane Russak, Heinemann.

Jianhong, C. & Nadkarni, S. 2017. It's about Time! CEOs' Temporal Dispositions, Temporal Leadership, and Corporate Entrepreneurship. *Administrative Science Quarterly*, 62, 31–66.

Johns, G. 2001. In praise of context. *Journal of Organizational Behavior*, 22, 31–42.

Johns, G. 2006. The essential impact of context on organizational behavior. *Academy of Management Review*, 31, 386–408.

Kattenbach, R., Schneidhofer, T.M., Lücke, J., Latzke, M., Loacker, B., Schramm, F. & Mayrhofer, W. 2014. A quarter of a century of job transitions in Germany. *Journal of Vocational Behavior*, 84, 49–58.

Koch, M., Forgues, B. & Monties, V. 2016. The way to the top: Career patterns of Fortune 100 CEOs. *Human Resource Management*. Doi:10.1002/hrm.21759.

Kohlberg, L. 1969. Stage and sequence: The cognitive-developmental approach to socialization. *In:* Goslin, D.A. (ed.) *Handbook of Socialization Theory and Research*. Chicago: Rand McNally.

Lamm, H., Schmidt, R.W. & Trommsdorff, G. 1976. Sex and social class as determinants of future orientation (time perspective) in adolescents. *Journal of Personality and Social Psychology*, 34, 317–326.

Lawrence, B.S. 1984. Age grading: The implicit organizational timetable. *Journal of Occupational Behaviour*, 5, 23–35.

Levin, I. & Zakay, D. 1989. Introduction. *In:* Levin, I. & Zakay, D. (eds.) *Time and Human Cognition. A Life-Span Perspective*. Amsterdam: North Holland.

Levine, R. 1997. *A Geography of Time: The Temporal Misadventures of a Social Psychologist, or How Every Culture Keeps Time Just a Little Bit Differently*. New York: Basic Books.

Levinson, D.J., Darrow, C., Klein, E., Levinson, M. & Mckee, B. 1978. *The Seasons of a Man's Life*. New York: Knopf.

Luhmann, N. 1995. *Social Systems*. Stanford: Stanford University Press.

Luhmann, N. 1997. *Die Gesellschaft der Gesellschaft*. Frankfurt am Main: Suhrkamp.

Marko, K.W. & Savickas, M.L. 1998. Effectiveness of a career time perspective intervention. *Journal of Vocational Behavior*, 52, 106–119.

Marx, K. 1859 *Zur Kritik der Politischen Ökonomie*. Berlin: Franz Duncker.

McGrath, J.E. (ed.) 1988. *The Social Psychology of Time: New Perspectives*. Newbury Park, CA: Sage Publications.

McGrath, J.E. 1994. Social Psychology. *In:* Macey, S.L. (ed.) *Encyclopedia of Time*. New York and London: Routledge.

McGrath, J.E. & Rotchford, N. 1983. Time and behavior in organizations. *Research in Organizational Behavior*, 5, 57–101.

McTaggart, J.M.E. 1908. The unreality of time. *Mind*, 17, 457–474.

Mitchell, T. & James, L. 2001. Building better theory: Time and the specification of when things happen. *Academy of Management Review*, 26, 530–547.

Mol, A.P.J., Spaargaren, G. & Sonnenfeld, D.A. 2014. Ecological modernization theory: Taking stock, moving forward. *In:* Lockie, S., Sonnenfeld, D.A. & Fisher, D.A. (eds.) *Routledge International Handbook of Social and Environmental Change*. London and New York: Routledge.

Mosakowski, E. & Earley, P.C. 2000. A selective review of time assumptions in strategy research. *Academy of Management Review*, 25, 796–812.

Munn, N.D. 1992. The cultural anthropology of time: A critical essay. *Annual Review of Anthropology*, 21, 93–123.

Nowotny, H. 1992. Time and social theory: Towards a social theory of time. *Time & Society*, 1, 421–454.

Ofori-Dankwa, J. & Julian, S.D. 2001. Complexifying organizational theory: Illustrations using time research. *Academy of Management Review*, 26, 415–430.

Orlikowski, W.J. & Yates, J. 2002. It's about time: Temporal structuring in organizations. *Organization Science*, 13, 684–700.

Roe, R.A. 2008. Time in applied psychology: The study of "what happens" rather than "what is." *European Psychologist*, 13, 37–52.

Roe, R.A., Waller, M.J. & Clegg, S.R. (eds.) 2009. *Time in Organizational Research*. London: Routledge.

Roth, J.A. 1963. *Timetables: Structuring the Passage of Time in Hospital Treatment and Other Careers*. Indianapolis: Bobbs-Merrill.

Rousseau, D. & Fried, Y. 2001. Location, location, location: Contextualizing organizational research. *Journal of Organizational Behavior*, 22, 1–13.

Roy, D. 1960. Banana time: Job satisfaction and informal interaction. *Human Organization*, 18, 158–169.

Ryan, D. 2007. *Time and Social Theory.* djjr.net/papers/published/Ryan-Time-and-Social-Theory.pdf [Access 18 May 2009].

Schein, E.H. 1978. *Career Dynamics: Matching individual and Organizational needs.* Reading, MA: Addison-Wesley.

Schneer, J.A. & Reitman, F. 1995. The impact of gender as managerial careers Unfold. *Journal of Vocational Behavior,* 47, 290–315.

Schneidhofer, T.M., Schiffinger, M. & Mayrhofer, W. 2012. Still a man's world? The influence of gender and gender role type on income in two business school graduate cohorts over time. *Equality, Diversity and Inclusion: An International Journal,* 31, 65–82.

Schultz, M. & Hernes, T. 2013. A temporal perspective on organizational identity. *Organization Science,* 24, 1–21.

Shipp, A.J. & Fried, Y. (eds.) 2014a. *How Time Impacts Groups, Organizations, and Methodological Choices.* East Sussex, UK: Psychology Press.

Shipp, A.J. & Fried, Y. (eds.) 2014b. *Time and Work Volume 1: How Time Impacts Individuals.* East Sussex, UK: Psychology Press.

Simons, J., Vansteenkiste, M., Lens, W. & Lacante, M. 2004. Placing motivation and future time perspective theory in a temporal perspective. *Educational Psychology Review,* 16, 121–139.

Sofer, C. 1970. *Men in Mid-Career.* Cambridge: Cambridge University Press.

Sonnentag, S. 2012. Time in organizational research: Catching up on a long neglected topic in order to improve theory. *Organizational Psychology Review,* 2, 361–368.

Sorokin, P.A. & Merton, R.K. 1937. Social time: A methodological and functional analysis. *American Journal of Sociology,* 42, 615–629.

Sullivan, S.E. & Crocitto, M. 2007. The developmental theories: A critical examination of their continuing impact on careers research. *In:* Gunz, H. & Peiperl, M. (eds.) *Handbook of Career Studies.* Thousand Oaks, CA: Sage Publications.

Super, D.E. 1957. *The Psychology of Careers: An Introduction to Vocational Development.* New York: Harper.

Thrift, N.J. 2011. Space, place and time. *In:* Goodin, R.E. (ed.) *The Oxford Handbook of Contextual Political Analysis.* New York: Oxford University Press.

Weber, M. 2000 [Orig. 1904/05]. *Die protestantische Ethik und der "Geist" des Kapitalismus.* Weinheim: Beltz, Athenäum.

Whipp, R., Adam, B. & Sabelis, I. (eds.) 2002. *Making Time: Time and Management in Modern Organizations.* Oxford: Oxford University Press.

Yakura, E.L. 2002. Charting time: Timelines as temporal boundary objects. *Academy of Management Journal,* 45, 956–970.

Zaheer, S., Albert, S. & Zaheer, A. 1999. Time scales and organizational theory. *Academy of Management Review,* 24, 725–741.

Zerubavel, E. 1976. Timetables and scheduling: On the social organization of time. *Sociological Inquiry,* 46, 87–94.

Zerubavel, E. 1981. *Hidden Rhythms. Schedules and Calendars in Social Life.* Berkeley, CA: University of California Press.

Zerubavel, E. 1982. The standardization of time: A sociohistorical perspective. *American Journal of Sociology,* 88, 1–23.

9

From occupational choice to career crafting

Ans De Vos, Jos Akkermans, and Beatrice Van der Heijden

Introduction

A career is defined as the sequence of work experiences that evolve over the individual's life course (Arthur et al., 1989) and, obviously, is highly subjective and complex, unique to each individual, and dynamic over time (Khapova and Arthur, 2011). As outlined later in this book (see Chapter 15 on career patterns), research on career dynamics has often focused on career stages that were interpreted to occur in parallel with adult development or life stages (e.g., Dalton et al., 1977; Hall, 1976; Nicholson and West, 1989; Super, 1957). In this traditional view, occupational choice was almost exclusively concerned with the preparation stage of career development (Super, 1957) and was conceived as a single event usually occurring in adolescence or in one's early twenties, which was then enacted for the rest of one's career, assuming a linear career path and stable future performance.

Yet in the contemporary career context, it is generally acknowledged that there is no such thing as one idealized career path characterized by a set of predictable transitions all workers go through at specific points in their life. The increasingly pluriform working population requires us to move away from thinking in fixed categories regarding career peaks, career success, retirement age, and so forth. Employees may have totally different ideas on and answers to career-related questions such as: "What are my own criteria for a successful career? How can I achieve such career success?" (cf. Van der Heijden and De Vos, 2015). That is to say, the idea of "one-life-one-career" (Sarason, 1977) is changing towards a focus on adapting one's career identity and continuously acquiring new knowledge and skills throughout the lifespan, leading to much more complex and idiosyncratic career patterns, thereby making the individual employee the central actor.

In line with this development, the focus in the scholarly literature has shifted from the selection of an (occupational degree which would lead to an) occupation towards a broader and less fixed perspective on career choice, being a recurring issue throughout the lifespan. Moreover, the types of choices individuals need to make in the contemporary career context are not restricted to the *kind of occupation* they choose originally, but also to which *type of organization* to join, to the *type of employment* (e.g., independent contractor, employee, or temporary agency worker), the *form of employment* (working full-time or part-time), and the *continuity of employment* (e.g., temporarily interrupting one's career to take care for children or relatives).

Based on the above, we argue that there is a need for a broader view on career choices that does justice to the dynamics and complexity that individual employees encounter throughout their life course. In this chapter, we therefore broaden our focus on occupational choice and introduce the notion of career crafting which refers to an *individual's proactive behaviors aimed at optimizing career outcomes through improving person-career fit*. It entails individuals constantly reflecting on and being mindful about their career aspirations and motivation (Hall, 2002), and making choices that can impact both short-term (e.g., employability, work engagement, and performance) and long-term success (e.g., objective and subjective career success) (Hall, 2002). Hence, this perspective on career crafting recognizes that individual needs and contextual demands are dynamic and affect person-career fit at any given time and is more reflective of the reality of today's rapidly changing career context. Therefore, career crafting is a key individual behavior for safeguarding the sustainability of one's career over time. The latter may be defined as "the sequence of an individual's different career experiences, reflected through a variety of patterns of continuity over time, crossing several social spaces, and characterized by individual agency, herewith providing meaning to the individual" (Van der Heijden and De Vos, 2015: 7).

Inherent to the notion of sustainable careers is that individuals continuously affect their career potential (i.e., their employability; Van der Heijde and Van der Heijden, 2006; Van der Heijden et al., 2009) through the opportunities they encounter, the choices they make, and the learning cycles they go through. The individual's career potential, in turn, affects subsequent career opportunities and its sustainability over time. In other words, through career crafting "career-competent employees" who are weighing up carefully the pros and cons of certain choices, and who strive for fulfilling present career needs without compromising future ones, are expected to be better able to protect and foster the sustainability of their career (Akkermans and Tims, 2017).

We discern three factors that are closely associated with crafting sustainable careers across the life course, and which are prominent in contemporary views on careers, namely (1) employability, (2) adaptability, and (3) career competencies. First, *employability* is important for individuals in order to acquire and retain work that is in line with their career needs, and as such it determines the options that individuals have for realizing their desired career choices over time. This requires a broader set of knowledge and skills than only those related to keeping one's expertise up to date. Employees need to adjust their focus on "what are the right competencies?" on an ongoing basis, and should develop competencies that enable them to be proactive and flexible, to handle ambiguity, and to manage multiple tasks simultaneously. Second, *adaptability* is important for flexibly meeting changing demands in one's field of work or personal life throughout the career. Third, *career competencies* play a critical role for realizing workers' employability, as they reflect an attitude in which adaptability and continuous learning and development skills are key to successful career choices over time.

In the next section, we will describe how career research has evolved from a focus on the choice of an occupational field to the ongoing choice of a career that reflects a "contract with the self" (Hall, 2002). Subsequently, we will elaborate on the meaning of employability and its relevance for understanding career choice from the viewpoint of sustainable careers, followed by sections on career adaptability and on career competencies. In addition, we will address the role of organizations in affecting sustainability of career choices through their career management practices. We will conclude this chapter with implications and suggestions for future research on "career crafting" as the "new occupational choice."

From occupational choice to career crafting: a historical perspective

In the last decades, the concept of lifetime employment has been gradually replaced by the notion of lifelong employability (Forrier and Sels, 2003; Fugate et al., 2004; Hillage and Pollard, 1998; Rothwell and Arnold, 2007; Van der Heijden et al., 2009), thereby bringing lifelong learning and the career choices an employee has to make throughout the lifespan to the forefront. This means that workers need to be highly adaptable (Sullivan et al., 1998) and concerned with the continuity of their careers (Savickas, 2005). In this sense, the increasing emphasis on lifelong employability instead of employment security goes in parallel with the view of occupational choice as a recurring issue throughout one's career.

The evolution of occupational choice: 1960s through 1980s

The use of the term "employability" in both scientific and professional publications goes back to the 1950s, when employability was supposed to be an important determinant for securing a job, in particular, to make sure that one had paid work in the (near) future (Feintuch, 1955). This was consistent with the view on occupational choice as selecting an occupation – or a college major that would lead to an occupation – that provided prospects for long-term secure employment and a steady career path (Ginzberg, 1972). Consistent with this, scholars in the field of occupational choice were concerned with measuring individuals' vocational interests and matching these with suitable occupations, ultimately aiming to enhance the compatibility between the person and the occupation, such as the Strong Interest Inventory, initially published in 1943 (see Hall, 2002 for an elaborate discussion of how research on career choice has evolved over the past decades).

In the 1960s and 1970s, authors in the employability domain did not deal with the mobility of employees within the internal or external labor markets. Instead, they mainly dealt with the problems of unemployed persons and the difficulties they encountered in accessing the labor market, and with staying employed. Once on the payroll of a working organization, the opportunity to stay employed was rather high, given the dominant culture of lifetime employment (Magnum, 1976; Orr, 1973). In the literature on occupational choice, this is reflected in a focus on the factors affecting job choices and success in the 1970s (Hall, 1976; Schein, 1978), eventually followed by a focus on individual careers within the organizational system, and on matching individual and organizational needs in the 1980s (see for example Edgar Schein's career anchor model (Schein, 1978) and John Holland's vocational interest framework (Holland, 1985)). This development reflected the changing view that occupational choice implied the choice for a certain career path that could be pursued in a predictable and linear fashion, most often within the context of one single organization.

What united the views on employability and occupational choice until the 1980s was their concern with developing human capital – requiring the necessary skills and knowledge needed for a given occupational field, and hence for a career path – and guiding people towards a successful transition into employment. The latter was then subsequently presumed to result in employment security and, depending on the path taken, predictable and steady career progress. This was for instance reflected in employability measures that were aimed at full employment, with interventions at a national level (Feintuch, 1955; Forrier and Sels, 2003; Orr, 1973). The collective care of the government was primarily meant to help unemployed citizens to find a job and was largely focused at job market entry. As such, occupational choice concerned a relatively transparent and simple phenomenon (Ginzberg, 1972; Ginzberg et al., 1951; see also Thijssen et al., 2008: 170).

The evolution of occupational choice: 1980s through 2000s

Since the 1980s, organizations started to embrace the principles of the so-called flexible firm (Atkinson, 1984), making a distinction between core (permanent), periphery or temporary, and external workers (free agents). Core workers required relatively high wages to be retained, and management was more eager to invest in their future employability. On the contrary, the opportunities for training and development and other kinds of employment benefits were worse for the secondary segment (i.e., the periphery or so-called temporary workers who were 'just' needed for fluctuations in staffing demands; Barley and Kunda, 2006; O'Mahony and Bechky, 2006; see also Thijssen et al., 2008: 170). This implied that a growing group of workers was laid off, urging them to reconsider their initial occupational choice, and it also meant that some occupations provided more secure employment prospects than others. Practices such as outplacement, emerging in the 1990s, can be seen as an expressed concern of employers and the government to support the employability of laid-off workers. From a career perspective, these fit within a gradually shifting perspective on occupational choice, from a one-off decision occurring at the start of one's career to a dynamic process with multiple career choices in which not only workers' knowledge and skills (i.e., occupational expertise), but also their job search competencies became increasingly relevant. Moreover, in the career literature this gradually led to attention moving away from matching individual and organizational needs and organizationally driven career systems towards the individual as the central actor in careers, hereby building on Super's idea (1957, 1990) that a career is an ongoing, unfolding synthesis of the person's self-concept and the external realities of the work environment driven by the person through a series of choices and decisions. Already in 1976, Hall had speculated that the increasing number of changes in working organizations would lead to the dominance of another type of career (i.e., the so-called protean career), which is shaped more by the individual than by the organization and which may be redirected from time to time to meet personal needs (Hall, 1976).

In the same vein, the boundaryless career concept was introduced referring to the independence from traditional organizational principles (Arthur, 1994, 2014). What these so-called new career concepts have in common is their emphasis on flexibility, networking, marketable skills, and continuous learning (Sullivan and Arthur, 2006) as predictors of career success. Along with this development, we observe a growing field of research on employability and the importance of a broad set of employability-enhancing competencies (Forrier and Sels, 2003; Fugate et al., 2004; Van der Heijde and Van der Heijden, 2006).

The evolution of occupational choice: current careers as learning cycles

Contemporary career research elaborates on new career concepts in order to do justice to the evolution in competencies that are needed to stay employable. The combination of the ever-increasing speed in developments (e.g., new production concepts and new technology), expanded globalization, and increased demands for productivity, creativity, and flexibility urges employees to continuously update their knowledge and skills (Berntson et al., 2006; Nazar and Van der Heijden, 2012; Van der Heijde and Van der Heijden, 2006) after formal education and initial occupational choice. In addition, they need to be mindful of their (changing) career interests and needs. This requires more from them than only keeping their occupational expertise up to date. More and more, it is proclaimed that individuals need to be able and willing to adapt to continuously changing circumstances, which requires a broader set of career competencies and career behaviors (Akkermans et al., 2013b).

Indeed, in contrast to the traditional view of employability as an individual's chances for getting and staying employed (see Section 10.2.1), current definitions of employability refer to "the capacity of continuously fulfilling, acquiring or creating work through the optimal use of competences" (Van der Heijde and Van der Heijden, 2006: 453), "the chance for employment on the internal or external labor market" (Forrier and Sels, 2003: 106), or "a form of work-specific active adaptability that enables workers to identify and realize career opportunities" (Fugate et al., 2004). These definitions all imply a permanent acquisition and fulfillment of employment within or outside the current organization, and with regard to future prospects (Van der Heijde and Van der Heijden, 2006). Protecting one's lifelong employability requires individuals to manage the balance between their current performance in order to safeguard one's current position, and the need for learning and further career development, aimed at increasing one's future employability (Froehlich et al., 2014, 2015).

To conclude, the transition from the traditional perspective of occupational choice to the current emphasis on career crafting, wherein the individual has to proactively manage his/her person-career fit, is grounded in the principle of careers as continuous learning cycles rather than predictable and linear trajectories. Continuous learning and adaptation are at the core of the notion of careers as learning cycles (Hall, 1976, 2002), which reflect the idea that careers consist of continuous and conscious ways of exploring possible alternative ways of being. These learning cycles can take place within or across jobs, organizations, or occupations and they can be driven by (1) changes in the career context and (2) changes in the person.

Elaborating on this, first, careers will be increasingly driven by the changing skill demands of the specific fields in which a person works, as the life cycle of technologies and products has drastically shortened over the past decades. Obviously, this has implications for a person's learning cycle within a job (Gubler et al., 2014; Hall, 2002; Waters et al., 2015), which in turn affects the time it takes for individuals to grow and remain able to perform at the level of mastery in a job. Seen from this perspective, the key issue determining a learning cycle is not the employee's chronological age but his/her *career age*, where perhaps five years in a given occupational specialty may be midlife for that professional area or only the early career for another area (Hall, 2002). Think for instance of the time it requires a person to develop towards the level of mastery in performing a job as a call center agent, a management consultant, a specialized medical job (e.g., a heart surgeon) or a researcher doing clinical research on developing a new drug to fight a complex disease in a pharmaceutical company. These jobs all imply a different learning curve, where the time for reaching the level of mastery will be longer than for more complex jobs. Moreover, no matter what the typical length of a learning cycle for a job might be, when the competencies needed for successful performance change due to altered technologies, innovations, or new ways of working (e.g., Van der Heijden et al., 2015), the person will need to adapt and engage in a new learning cycle in order to develop and master the necessary competencies for staying employable within that job. When jobs or occupations disappear, individuals will need to reconsider their existing knowledge and skills to develop new competencies in view of sustained employment.

Second, individuals' personal career needs will be important in affecting their learning cycles. Given the dynamic nature of careers and the many interlinkages with individuals' broader life course, their personal needs, career ambitions and interests might change over the course of the career, as reflected by concepts such as the 'kaleidoscope career' (Mainiero and Sullivan, 2005).

This might trigger individuals to renew their competencies in order to gain sustained career engagement (Kim et al., 2014). Individual factors such as ambition and need for challenge but also a person's future work self are thereby important motivational forces for engaging in new learning cycles (e.g., Strauss et al., 2012; Taber and Blankemeyer, 2015).

As such, careers consist of a succession of mini-stages or short-cycle learning stages of exploration-trial-mastery-exit over the span of a person's work life (Mirvis and Hall, 1994), reflecting a view on occupational choice as recurring throughout the career. Many career patterns are possible, depending on the nature of the job or industry a person is working in, as well as on his/her personal needs and circumstances. For careers to remain sustainable over time, individuals will need the meta-skills of adaptability and identity (Hall, 2002; Savickas, 1997) in order to be aware of and to act upon the changing needs of their employment as well as their personal life context and changing personal needs. In this view, the notion of career maturity central in Super's (1990) lifespan, life-space approach to career development obtains a new meaning. Career maturity, or the person's readiness to make good career and private life-related decisions at a given point in his or her life, might imply changing occupations or making radically different career choices or developing new competencies in order to stay employable in one's current job. Persons grow in career maturity as they learn how to cope with changing demands stemming from the context or their personal needs, thereby developing their personal identity, which, in turn, may function as a form of personal competency facilitating subsequent career choices (Hall, 2002).

Based upon the historical overview of occupational choice given above, and our reasoning that the current era is characterized by continuous learning cycles, we argue that the key to having a successful career today lies in career crafting. Below, we will further elaborate on this notion.

Career crafting for career success

Managing one's employability in light of career sustainability, and engaging in career learning cycles imply that individuals need to take ownership of their career, and proactively manage their career success. Earlier research on career self-management (e.g., De Vos et al., 2009; King, 2004) has provided some clear direction in this regard, in terms of specific behaviors, such as networking, boundary management, and self-promotion, as hallmarks of managing one's career. In addition, recent research on *job crafting* (Tims et al., 2012; Wrzesniewski and Dutton, 2001) has clearly demonstrated that proactively adapting one's job to one's preferences is an effective way to enhance employee well-being (Tims et al., 2014) and performance (Tims et al., 2015). Besides enhancing work-related well-being and job performance, job crafting – in tandem with career competencies – is also related to subjective career success (Akkermans and Tims, 2017). Until now, however, the literatures on proactive work and career behaviors have mostly been developed in isolation (cf. Hall and Las Heras, 2010).

This isolation is surprising given that the concepts of proactive work and career behaviors share many common elements, as both (1) emphasize the importance of proactivity, (2) argue that the individual is the central actor in work and careers, and (3) have the underlying assumption that work and careers are becoming much more integrated in the sense that a career is basically enacted in the work one does on a daily basis, rather than being some future state. Indeed, being proactive and becoming an agent of one's own work (i.e., from a short-term perspective) and career (i.e., from a long-term perspective) is key to surviving in today's dynamic labor market. In essence, this implies that individuals are constantly managing the mini-careers as theorized in the learning cycles that we discussed earlier. Therefore, we would argue that – although it is evident that major career transitions such as the school-to-work transition (e.g., Akkermans et al., 2015b) are important hallmarks of one's career development – careers should no longer exclusively be defined in terms of a one-off transition into working life, or even as several major transition moments. Rather, individuals should employ a proactive attitude in which lifelong learning and employability are key pillars and in which both more minor activities in one's work and career and major transitions form part of the career development process. In sum, we argue that *career crafting* is 'the new occupational choice'.

As stated earlier in this chapter, career crafting can be considered as actual proactive behavior aimed to optimize career outcomes through improving person-career fit. It entails individuals actively crafting their careers over time by reflecting on and being mindful about their career aspirations and motivation and by making choices that can impact both short-term (e.g., work engagement and performance) and long-term success (e.g., objective and subjective career success). Hence, this perspective on career crafting recognizes that individual needs and contextual demands are dynamic and that they can affect person-career fit at any given time. An important distinction with related constructs such as career adaptability and career competencies (see the next section for more details) is that career crafting is about actual proactive behavior, whereas the other concepts are personal resources and competencies. We will argue below that being adaptable and career competent are key ingredients for crafting one's career, but that proactive behavior is an essential ingredient as well. As an example of proactive career crafting behavior, we refer to an individual taking the initiative to expand his/her professional network and to actively explore opportunities for further development.

Key ingredients for career crafting: adaptability and career competencies

The rise of career adaptability research

One important resource for taking responsibility and developing throughout one's career is the construct of career adaptability. In his seminal work, Savickas (1997: 254) defined career adaptability as "the readiness to cope with the predictable tasks of preparing for and participating in the work role and with the unpredictable adjustments prompted by the changes in work and work conditions." Following from this definition, Savickas and Porfeli (2012) characterized career adaptability resources as self-regulation capacities that individuals can draw on when facing unfamiliar and complex problems related to vocational tasks and occupational transitions. Accordingly, career adaptability is often considered as a personal resource that is closely related to psychological capital (Luthans et al., 2006).

Savickas and Porfeli (2012) argued that career adaptability consists of four different self-regulation strategies (or psychosocial resources), that can be helpful during various career transitions. First, *career concern* is about looking ahead and planning for one's future. Second, *career control* relates to using self-control, discipline, and persistence to become responsible for shaping one's career. Third, *career curiosity* refers to information-seeking activities that enable an individual to think about different possible selves. Finally, *career confidence* is about being confident enough to undertake activities that help to pursue career goals and overcome obstacles. Although they comprise different strategies, these four career adaptability resources are closely related and form the aggregate construct of career adaptability (Savickas and Porfeli, 2012).

Research thus far has clearly supported the relevance of career adaptability in contemporary career development and success. For example, Zacher (2014) performed an empirical study among 1,723 Australian employees and demonstrated that career adaptability predicted subjective career success, over and above the Big Five personality traits and core self-evaluations.

Furthermore, career adaptability has been shown to positively relate to academic achievement (Negru-Subtirica and Pop, 2016), career satisfaction (Chan and Mai, 2015), well-being (Hirschi, 2009), employment status (Guan et al., 2013), personality traits (e.g., Big Five), attitudes (e.g., commitment), behavior (e.g., career exploration), performance (Rudolph et al., 2017), and reemployment quality (Koen et al., 2010), and negatively to turnover intentions (Chan and Mai, 2015). In sum, when considering the need for individuals to proactively craft their career, career adaptability seems an important foundation for being a proactive agent of one's career and becoming employable.

The rise of career competency research

Over the past two decades, a wide array of empirical studies have been performed that focused on knowledge, skills, and abilities necessary to self-manage one's career and to remain employable throughout the life course. For example, based on the groundbreaking work on boundaryless careers by DeFillippi and Arthur (1994), several studies have examined *career capital* in the form of "knowing why," "knowing whom," and "knowing how" competencies (e.g., Eby et al., 2003; Fleisher et al., 2014), arguing that individuals need to learn what really matters to them, who can help them in their career, and how they can actually shape their career paths.

Similarly, research on the protean career and career orientation has, as mentioned above, focused on the *meta-competencies* of "adaptability" and "identity" (e.g., Hall and Mirvis, 1995; Waters et al., 2015), and centers around individuals shaping a career that gets the best out of themselves and that creates an optimal "person-career fit." This can be achieved by being adaptable (i.e., open to changes and being the active agent) and finding a clear career identity (i.e., knowing who you are and what you strive for). Both the boundaryless and protean career perspectives have been dominant in the scholarly literature on career development over the past two decades. The main takeaway messages from these two perspectives are that individuals need to (1) take responsibility for managing their own careers and (2) need to make sure that they continue to learn and develop throughout those careers.

An integrated framework of career competencies

Recently, Akkermans et al. (2013a) reviewed and integrated the literature on career-related competencies and presented an integrative framework of career competencies that individuals should master in order to realize their career needs, that is based upon the existing paradigms of the boundaryless career (i.e., career capital), protean career (i.e., career meta-competencies), career self-management, and the human capital perspective. They defined career competencies as "knowledge, skills, and abilities central to career development, which can be influenced and developed by the individual" (ibid.: 246), and their framework consists of three categories of career competencies, which each contain two specific competencies. *Reflective career competencies* refer to creating a long-term awareness of oneself and to matching these reflections on motivation and qualities to one's career development. First, reflection on motivation means reflecting on values, passions, and motivations with regard to one's career (e.g., "I know what is important to me in my career"). Second, reflection on qualities refers to reflecting on strengths, shortcomings, and skills, and about how to match those to one's career development (e.g., "I am aware of my talents in my work"). *Communicative career competencies* focus on being able to effectively communicate with significant others in order to achieve career success. First, networking is having a strong awareness of one's network as well as being able to expand it for career-related purposes (e.g., "I know how to ask for advice from people in my network"). Second, self-profiling means being able to present one's competencies to the internal and external labor market (e.g., "I can clearly show others what my strengths are in my work"). *Behavioral career competencies* are about being able to proactively take action regarding one's career development by exploration and control. First, work exploration refers to actively exploring career-related opportunities in the internal and external labor market (e.g., "I know how to search for development in my area of work") and second, career control is about being able to actively influence learning and work processes by setting goals and striving to fulfill those goals (e.g., "I can make clear career plans").

Akkermans and colleagues (2013a) provided preliminary evidence of the reliability and validity of their integrative framework by showing that it has good factorial, discriminant, and incremental validity. In addition, subsequent studies have shown that career competencies are positively related to perceived employability (Akkermans et al., 2015a), informal learning (Preenen et al., 2015), job resources and work engagement (Akkermans et al., 2013b; Tims and Akkermans, 2017), employee health and job satisfaction (Plomp et al., 2016), job crafting behaviors (i.e., changes that employees make to balance their job demands and job resources with their personal abilities and needs; Tims et al., 2012), and career success (Akkermans and Tims, 2017). The main conclusion is that mastering these career competencies will enable individuals to thrive both in their current job (e.g., becoming engaged and crafting one's job) and in their career as a whole (e.g., becoming employable and successful). Thus if we reflect on our statement that nowadays occupational choice is a series of continuous choices in which individuals need to maintain and enhance their career sustainability, career competencies would be a crucial way to achieve this goal in terms of finding one's career identity and becoming adaptable, as well as to provide the necessary knowledge and skills to make conscious career choices throughout one's lifespan.

What about the organization? (Re)contextualizing the new career

Although the focus of this chapter lies on the individual, the topic of career crafting cannot be considered whilst disregarding the context within which career crafting takes place. The trend towards individual agency has brought the organization somewhat to the background, with notions like the boundaryless career emphasizing more the unfolding of careers over different organizations rather than within an organization. However, the role of organizations for individual careers should not be underestimated, just like the role of individual careers for organizations should not be underestimated. A career that is sustainable implies a balance between individual and organizational needs, and hence enhances continuity not only for the individual but also for the organization (Valcour, 2015; Van der Heijden and De Vos, 2015).

After all, by the career choices they make, individuals impact organizations and these choices can have implications for important organizational challenges, such as attraction, performance, and retention (De Vos and Cambré, 2016). Yet at the same time, organizations affect the careers of individuals. That is, employees working in organizations that provide ample opportunities for learning, support employees in developing career competencies, stretch employees in staying employable, and engage in career conversations about employees' current position in the learning cycle of their job and their view on the future are just a few examples of how organizations can facilitate the career choices of employees in view of sustainable careers (e.g., Clarke, 2013; Lips-Wiersma and Hall, 2007; Segers and Inceoglu, 2012).

Moreover, the increasing awareness of the impact of the organizational context, the person's broader life context, and the societal context when studying careers highlight the role and interconnectedness of multiple actors (see also Baruch, 2015; De Lange et al., 2015). Otherwise stated, both employees' as well as employers' efforts and activities should be carefully aligned in order to come up with sustainable career management practices. To realize this, Valcour (2015) distinguished four important characteristics of contemporary organizational career management: (1) alignment of work with the individual's strengths, interests, and values; (2) ongoing learning and renewal; (3) security via employability; and (4) work-life fit over the life course. These practices can help organizations in realizing four core objectives: (1) maximum yield on human capital value; (2) continuous updating of organizational competencies; (3) stability via adaptability; and (4) organizational commitment and retention. Thus, the crafting of sustainable careers within organizations occurs at the *intersection between individuals and organizations*, and in case of a collaborative partnership has advantageous outcomes for both parties (De Vos and Cambré, 2016).

It also implies moving away from a focus on fixed career ladders, upward promotion and organizationally driven succession planning to more flexible career approaches, building on coaching and providing opportunities for employees to craft their own career path in line with organizational needs (Segers and Inceoglu, 2012).

What's next? From occupational choice to career crafting

The central idea brought forward in this chapter is that career choice has become more of a recurring issue throughout the career, requiring adaptability and career competencies, that is, career crafting, from the person, in view of their current and future employability and career sustainability. This implies a fresh perspective on the idea of occupational choice, thereby moving away our attention from how to enhance the quality of career choice as a once-in-a-lifetime type of decision, taken during the early career phase, to a focus on how to continuously facilitate individuals in going through different learning cycles and hence making occupational or career choices a serious point of attention in every stage of their career.

Further theory-building is needed in order to enhance our understanding of contemporary careers and the role of career crafting therein. For instance, what is the meaning of career crafting compared to related concepts such as job crafting, career competencies, and career self-management? What are its defining dimensions and how can it be measured? To what extent can we further build on models of occupational choice and career stages to understand career crafting throughout the career? How can we further integrate the idea of learning cycles in the notion of career crafting? What might be the relationship of career crafting with age?

The complexity of contemporary careers brings along new challenges for scholarly work on careers. More than ever, it urges us to incorporate the notion of time in the study of careers and to examine how careers unfold over the life course, thereby examining issues such as the characteristics of career crafting as well as antecedents and consequences of actively crafting one's career compared to taking a more reactive stance leading to career inaction. Possibly, new theoretical models and perspectives on occupational choice are needed.

In addition, as we have argued earlier, even though the emphasis of today's career success has changed to individual agency, career choices will always occur at the intersection of individuals and organizations. Although the traditional notion of lifetime job security within a single firm has mostly vanished, the vast majority of people are still working in organizations and, thus, have an interdependency with these. Yet, these interdependent relationships have significantly changed with the rise of short-term and flexible employment, and of entrepreneurs being hired for specific projects rather than receiving a longer-term contract (Cappelli and Keller, 2013), leading to an increase in non-standard career paths. All in all, these developments call for a reconsideration of the way in which both individual and organizational needs can be managed successfully in today's dynamic career landscape. In terms of career crafting, this leads to questions such as: "To what extent are organizations still responsible for investing in their employees' career development when they are often working part-time or on temporary contracts?" and "To what extent are individual career choices still dependent on organizational boundaries?" Following from this, future research should also not only address career choices from the perspective of the type of job, organization or occupation that individuals choose but also examine the factors affecting the sustainability of such choices throughout the career.

In addition, it will also be important to gain a better understanding of the learning cycles characterizing jobs and how the learning cycles individuals go through are affected by personal (e.g., experience, age, motivation to learn) as well as contextual (e.g., mentoring, supervisor support, development opportunities) characteristics. Thereby, elements such as job design, the complexity of a job, and the volatility versus stability of tasks characterizing a job might play an important role which needs to be further addressed as well. This also requires considering contextual elements such as technological evolutions characterizing a job, occupation, or sector.

Finally, labor markets, and the policies and regulations by which these are governed, are also likely to influence the extent to which individuals engage in career crafting. To fully understand career choices and their sustainability, multi-disciplinary research will be needed which incorporates the ways in which individuals are stimulated and supported in safeguarding their employability over time, for instance through access to lifelong learning or career guidance (De Vos et al., 2016).

Last but not least, it is interesting to investigate the meaning, antecedents, and outcomes of career crafting across countries in order to help individuals and organizations with evidence-based recommendations on how career crafting can protect individuals' career sustainability, taking into account cultural and contextual influences.

Conclusion

The objective of this chapter was to provide an overview of how the conceptualization of occupational choice has changed over the past decades, together with a changing perspective on employability and a growing emphasis on the importance of adaptability and career competencies. Given the many changes that are occurring simultaneously within the broader career context, we introduced the notion of "career crafting" to provide a fresh perspective on the current meaning of occupational choice, thereby emphasizing the dynamic, recurring nature of career choices, the central role of the individual career actor, and the importance of balancing individual needs with contextual demands.

References

Akkermans, J., Brenninkmeijer, V., Huibers, M. & Blonk, R.W.B. 2013a. Competencies for the contemporary career: Development and preliminary validation of the career competencies questionnaire. *Journal of Career Development*, 40, 245–267.

Akkermans, J., Brenninkmeijer, V., Schaufeli, W.B. & Blonk, R.W.B. 2015a. It's all about CareerSkills: Effectiveness of a career development intervention for young employees. *Human Resource Management*, 54, 533–551.

Akkermans, J., Nykänen, M. & Vuori, J. 2015b. Practice makes perfect? Antecedents and consequences of an adaptive school-to-work transition. *In:* Vuori, J. & Blonk, R.W.B. (eds.) *Sustainable Working Lives – Managing Work Transitions and Health Throughout the Life Course.* London: Springer Publishers.

Akkermans, J., Schaufeli, W.B., Brenninkmeijer, V. & Blonk, R.W.B. 2013b. The role of career competencies in the job demands – resources model. *Journal of Vocational Behavior*, 83, 356–366.

Akkermans, J. & Tims, M. 2017. Crafting your career: How career competencies relate to career success via job crafting. *Applied Psychology: An International Review*, 66, 168–195.

Arthur, M.B. 1994. The boundaryless career: A new perspective for organizational inquiry. *Journal of Organizational Behavior*, 15, 295–306.

Arthur, M.B. 2014. The boundaryless career at 20: Where do we stand, and where can we go? *Career Development International*, 19, 627–640.

Arthur, M.B., Hall, D.T. & Lawrence, B.S. 1989. Generating new directions in career theory: The case for a transdisciplinary approach. *In*: Arthur, M.B., Hall, D.T. & Lawrence, B.S. (eds.) *Handbook of Career Theory*. Cambridge, UK: Cambridge University Press.

Atkinson, J. 1984. The flexible firm and the shape of jobs to come. *Labour Market Issues*, 5, 26–29.

Barley, S.R. & Kunda, G. 2006. Contracting: A new form of professional practice. *Academy of Management Perspectives*, 20, 45–66.

Baruch, Y. 2015. 24 Organizational and labor markets as career ecosystem. *In*: De Vos, A. & Van der Heijden, B. (eds.) *Handbook of Research on Sustainable Careers*. Cheltenham, UK: Edward Elgar Publishing.

Berntson, E., Sverke, M. & Marklund, S. 2006. Predicting perceived employability: Human capital or labour market opportunities? *Economic and Industrial Democracy*, 27, 223–244.

Cappelli, P. & Keller, J.R. 2013. Classifying work in the new economy. *Academy of Management Review*, 38, 575–596.

Chan, S.H.J. & Mai, X. 2015. The relation of career adaptability to satisfaction and turnover intentions. *Journal of Vocational Behavior*, 89, 130–139.

Clarke, M. 2013. The organizational career: Not dead but in need of redefinition. *The International Journal of Human Resource Management*, 24, 684–703.

Dalton, G.W., Thompson, P.H. & Price, R.L. 1977. The four stages of professional careers – A new look at performance by professionals. *Organizational Dynamics*, 6, 19–42.

DeFillippi, R.J. & Arthur, M.B. 1994. The boundaryless career: A competency-based perspective. *Journal of Organizational Behavior*, 15, 307–324.

De Lange, A.H., Kooij, D.T.A.M. & Van der Heijden, B.I.J.M. 2015. Human resource management and sustainability at work across the lifespan: An integrative perspective. *In*: Finkelstein, L.M., Truxilio, D.M., Franccaroli, F. & Kanfer, R. (eds.) *Facing the Challenges of a Multi-Age Workforce: A Use-Inspired Approach*. New York and London: Psychology Press.

De Vos, A. & Cambré, B. 2016. Career management in high-performing organizations: A set-theoretic approach. *Human Resource Management*, 56, 501–518.

De Vos, A., de Clippeleer, I. & Dewilde, T. 2009. Proactive career behaviours and career success during the early career. *Journal of Occupational and Organizational Psychology*, 82, 761–777.

De Vos, A., Dujardin, J-M., Gielens, T. & Meyers, C. 2016. *Developing Sustainable Careers Across the Lifespan: European Social Fund Network on Career and AGE (Age, Generations, Experience)*. Dordrecht, The Netherlands: Springer.

Eby, L.T., Butts, M. & Lockwood, A. 2003. Predictors of success in the era of the boundaryless career. *Journal of Organizational Behavior*, 24, 689–708.

Feintuch, A. 1955. Improving the employability and attitudes of "difficult-to-place" persons. *Psychological Monographs: General and Applied*, 69, 1–20.

Fleisher, C., Khapova, S.N. & Jansen, P.G.W. 2014. Effects of employees' career competencies development on their organizations: Does satisfaction matter? *Career Development International*, 19, 700–717.

Forrier, A. & Sels, L. 2003. The concept employability: A complex mosaic. *International Journal of Human Resources Development and Management*, 3, 102–124.

Froehlich, D.E., Beausaert, S.A.J. & Segers, M.S.R. 2015. Age, employability and the role of learning activities and their motivational antecedents: A conceptual model. *The International Journal of Human Resource Management*, 26, 2087–2101.

Froehlich, D.E., Beausaert, S.A.J., Segers, M.S.R. & Gerken, M. 2014. Learning to stay employable. *Career Development International*, 19, 508–525.

Fugate, M., Kinicki, A.J. & Ashforth, B.E. 2004. Employability: A psycho-social construct, its dimensions, and applications. *Journal of Vocational Behavior*, 65, 14–38.

Ginzberg, E. 1972. Toward a theory of occupational choice: A restatement. *Vocational Guidance Quarterly*, 20, 2–9.

Ginzberg, E., Ginsburg, S.W., Axelrad, S. & Herma, J.L. 1951. *Occupational Choice: An Approach to a General Theory*. New York: Columbia University.

Guan, Y., Deng, H., Sun, J., Wang, Y., Cai, Z., Ye, L., Fu, R., Wang, Y., Zhang, S. & Li, Y. 2013. Career adaptability, job search self-efficacy and outcomes: A three-wave investigation among Chinese university graduates. *Journal of Vocational Behavior*, 83, 561–570.

Gubler, M., Arnold, J. & Coombs, C. 2014. Organizational boundaries and beyond: A new look at the components of a boundaryless career orientation. *Career Development International*, 19, 641–667.

Hall, D.T. 1976. *Careers in Organizations*. Pacific Palisades, CA: Goodyear Publishing.

Hall, D.T. 2002. *Careers in and Out of Organizations*. Thousand Oaks: Sage Publications.

Hall, D.T. & Las Heras, M. 2010. Reintegrating job design and career theory: Creating not just good jobs but smart jobs. *Journal of Organizational Behavior*, 31, 448–462.

Hall, D.T. & Mirvis, P.H. 1995. The new career contract: Developing the whole person at midlife and beyond. *Journal of Vocational Behavior*, 47, 269–289.

Hillage, J. & Pollard, E. 1998. *Employability: Developing a Framework for Policy Analysis*. London: DFEE.

Hirschi, A. 2009. Career adaptability development in adolescence: Multiple predictors and effect on sense of power and life satisfaction. *Journal of Vocational Behavior*, 74, 145–155.

Holland, J.L. 1985. *Making Vocational Choices: A Theory of Vocational Personalities and Work Environments*. Englewood Cliffs: Prentice-Hall.

Khapova, S.N. & Arthur, M.B. 2011. Interdisciplinary approaches to contemporary career studies. *Human Relations*, 64, 3–17.

Kim, B., Jang, S.H., Jung, S.H., Lee, B.H., Puig, A. & Lee, S.M. 2014. A moderated mediation model of planned happenstance skills, career engagement, career decision self-efficacy, and career decision certainty. *The Career Development Quarterly*, 62, 56–69.

King, Z. 2004. Career self-management: Its nature, causes and consequences. *Journal of Vocational Behavior*, 65, 112–133.

Koen, J., Klehe, U-C., Van Vianen, A.E.M., Zikic, J. & Nauta, A. 2010. Job-search strategies and reemployment quality: The impact of career adaptability. *Journal of Vocational Behavior*, 77, 126–139.

Lips-Wiersma, M. & Hall, D.T. 2007. Organizational career development is not dead: A case study on managing the new career during organizational change. *Journal of Organizational Behavior*, 28, 771–792.

Luthans, F., Avey, J.B., Avolio, B.J., Norman, S.M. & Combs, G.M. 2006. Psychological capital development: Toward a micro-intervention. *Journal of Organizational Behavior*, 27, 387–393.

Magnum, G.L. 1976. *Employability, Employment, and Income*. Salt Lake City, UT: Olympus.

Mainiero, L.A. & Sullivan, S.E. 2005. Kaleidoscope careers: An alternate explanation for the 'opt-out' revolution. *Academy of Management Executive*, 19, 106–123.

Mirvis, P.H. & Hall, D.T. 1994. Psychological success and the boundaryless career. *Journal of Organizational Behavior*, 15, 365–380.

Nazar, G. & Van der Heijden, B.I.J.M. 2012. Career identity and its impact upon self-perceived employability among Chilean male middle-aged managers. *Human Resource Development International*, 15, 141–156.

Negru-Subtirica, O. & Pop, E.I. 2016. Longitudinal links between career adaptability and academic achievement in adolescence. *Journal of Vocational Behavior*, 93, 163–170.

Nicholson, N. & West, M. 1989. Transitions, work histories, and careers. *In*: Arthur, M.B., Hall, D.T. & Lawrence, B.S. (eds.) *Handbook of Career Theory*. New York: Cambridge University Press.

O'Mahony, S. & Bechky, B.A. 2006. Stretchwork: Managing the career progression paradox in external labor markets. *Academy of Management Journal*, 49, 918–941.

Orr, D.B. 1973. *New Directions in Employability: Reducing Barriers to Full Employment*. New York: Praeger.

Plomp, J., Tims, M., Akkermans, J., Khapova, S.N., Jansen, P.G.W. & Bakker, A.B. 2016. Career competencies and job crafting: How proactive employees influence their well-being. *Career Development International*, 21, 587–602.

Preenen, P., Verbiest, S., Van Vianen, A. & Van Wijk, E. 2015. Informal learning of temporary agency workers in low-skill jobs: The role of self-profiling, career control, and job challenge. *Career Development International*, 20, 339–362.

Rothwell, A. & Arnold, J. 2007. Self-perceived employability: Development and validation of a scale. *Personnel Review*, 36, 23–41.

Rudolph, C.W., Lavigne, K.N. & Zacher, H. 2017. Career adaptability: A meta-analysis of relationships with measures of adaptivity, adapting responses, and adaptation results. *Journal of Vocational Behavior*, 98, 17–34.

Sarason, S.B. 1977. *Work, Aging, and Social Change: Professionals and the One Life-One Career Imperative*. New York: Free Press.

Savickas, M.L. 1997. Career adaptability: An integrative construct for life-span, life-space theory. *The Career Development Quarterly*, 45, 247–259.

Savickas, M.L. 2005. The theory and practice of career construction. *In:* Brown, S.D. & Lent, R.W. (eds.) *Career Development and Counseling: Putting Theory and Research to Work*. Hoboken, NJ: John Wiley & Sons.

Savickas, M.L. & Porfeli, E.J. 2012. Career adapt-abilities scale: Construction, reliability, and measurement equivalence across 13 countries. *Journal of Vocational Behavior*, 80, 661–673.

Schein, E.H. 1978. *Career Dynamics: Matching Individual and Organizational Needs*. Reading, MA: Addison-Wesley.

Segers, J. & Inceoglu, I. 2012. Exploring supportive and developmental career management through business strategies and coaching. *Human Resource Management*, 51, 99–120.

Strauss, K., Griffin, M.A. & Parker, S.K. 2012. Future work selves: How salient hoped-for identities motivate proactive career behaviors. *Journal of Applied Psychology*, 97, 580–598.

Sullivan, S.E. & Arthur, M.B. 2006. The evolution of the boundaryless career concept: Examining physical and psychological mobility. *Journal of Vocational Behavior*, 69, 19–29.

Sullivan, S.E., Carden, W.A. & Martin, D.F. 1998. Careers in the next millennium: Directions for future research. *Human Resource Management Review*, 8, 165–185.

Super, D.E. 1957. *The Psychology of Careers. An Introduction to Vocational Development*. Oxford, England: Harper & Bros.

Super, D.E. 1990. A life-span, life-space approach to career development. *In:* Brown, D. & Brooks, L. (eds.) *Career Choice and Development: Applying Contemporary Theories to Practice*. San Francisco, CA: Jossey-Bass.

Taber, B.J. & Blankemeyer, M. 2015. Future work self and career adaptability in the prediction of proactive career behaviors. *Journal of Vocational Behavior*, 86, 20–27.

Thijssen, J.G.L., Van der Heijden, B.I.J.M. & Rocco, T.S. 2008. Toward the employability-link model: Current employment transition to future employment perspectives. *Human Resource Development Review*, 7, 165–183.

Tims, M. & Akkermans, J. 2017. Core self-evaluations and work engagement: Testing a perception, action, and development path. *PLOS One*, 12, e0182745.

Tims, M., Bakker, A.B. & Derks, D. 2012. Development and validation of the job crafting scale. *Journal of Vocational Behavior*, 80, 173–186.

Tims, M., Bakker, A.B. & Derks, D. 2014. Daily job crafting and the self-efficacy – performance relationship. *Journal of Managerial Psychology*, 29, 490–507.

Tims, M., Bakker, A.B. & Derks, D. 2015. Job crafting and job performance: A longitudinal study. *European Journal of Work and Organizational Psychology*, 24, 914–928.

Valcour, M. 2015. Facilitating the crafting of sustainable careers in organizations. *In:* De Vos, A. & Van der Heijden, B.I.J.M. (eds.) *Handbook of Research on Sustainable Careers*. Cheltenham, UK: Edward Elgar Publishing.

Van der Heijde, C.M. & Van der Heijden, B.I.J.M. 2006. A competence-based and multidimensional operationalization and measurement of employability. *Human Resource Management*, 45, 449–476.

Van der Heijden, B.I.J.M., De Lange, A.H., Demerouti, E. & Van der Heijde, C.M. 2009. Age effects on the employability – career success relationship. *Journal of Vocational Behavior*, 74, 156–164.

Van der Heijden, B.I.J.M. & De Vos, A. 2015. Sustainable careers: Introductory chapter. *In:* De Vos, A. & Van der Heijden, B.I.J.M. (eds.) *Handbook of Research on Sustainable Careers*. Cheltenham, UK: Edward Elgar Publishing.

Van der Heijden, B.I.J.M., Peters, P. & Kelliher, C. 2015. New ways of working and employability: Towards an agenda for HRD. *In:* Poell, R.F., Rocco, T.S. & Roth, G.L. (eds.) *The Routledge Companion to Human Resource Development.* London: Routledge Taylor & Francis Group.

Waters, L., Hall, D.T., Wang, L. & Briscoe, J.P. 2015. Protean career orientation: A review of existing and emerging research. *In:* Burke, R.J., Page, K.M. & Cooper, C.L. (eds.) *Flourishing in Life, Work and Careers: Individual Wellbeing and Career Experiences.* Cheltenham, UK: Edward Elgar Publishing.

Wrzesniewski, A. & Dutton, J.E. 2001. Crafting a job: Revisioning employees as active crafters of their work. *Academy of Management Review,* 26, 179–201.

Zacher, H. 2014. Career adaptability predicts subjective career success above and beyond personality traits and core self-evaluations. *Journal of Vocational Behavior,* 84, 21–30.

10

Individual career outcomes

Conceptual and methodological concerns in the study of career success

Nicky Dries

What are the individual career outcomes that we, as career scholars and practitioners, should be focusing on in our research and career counseling or management practice? Traditionally, the focus has been on career *success* – the positive material and psychological outcomes resulting from a person's work-related activities and experiences (Seibert, 2006: 148). Research adopting career success as its main outcome of interest has typically studied how specific career strategies (e.g., frequent organizational moves, networking) can help people achieve success; how personal characteristics (e.g., personality traits, gender, race) relate to career success; and how planned or unplanned life events (e.g., becoming a parent) might hinder the road to success (Shockley et al., 2016).

Over the years, we have seen a shift in focus from studying only objective success as an outcome (measured primarily as salary; Dries et al., 2009; Heslin, 2003) to studying both objective and subjective career success (measured primarily as satisfaction; Seibert, 2006; e.g., Abele and Spurk, 2009). More recently still, there has been increasing acknowledgement of the need for more "subjectivist" approaches to studying and understanding career success – approaches that allow individuals to express, in their own words, what career success means to them and by which criteria they wish to evaluate their success for themselves (Dries et al., 2008). This trend towards subjectivist approaches has spurred multiple author teams to develop multidimensional measures of career success (Shockley et al., 2016; Briscoe et al., 2017), as an alternative to the widely used unidimensional Career Satisfaction Scale developed by Greenhaus et al. (1990). The cross-cultural generalizability of such measures (Benson et al., 2013; Mayrhofer et al., 2016) and the relationship between career outcomes and higher-order outcomes such as life satisfaction (e.g., Lounsbury et al., 2004) and work meaningfulness (e.g., Duffy and Sedlacek, 2010) are other "hot topics" in the field.

Building on the preceding observations, in this chapter we critically examine the range of individual career outcomes currently found in the literature and offer suggestions for making sense of the distinct yet often quite similar constructs encountered in this pursuit. Specifically, our analyses suggest a great degree of overlap between assumed "extrinsic" and "intrinsic" antecedents of career success on the one hand, and measures of objective and subjective career success on the other, and with assumed higher-order outcomes of career success. This observation is illustrated in Table 10.1 and is elaborated on in the subsequent sections of this chapter. There are two main points we want to make. First, individual career outcomes cannot be understood without understanding the related constructs of career norms, career drivers, career scripts, and higher-order career outcomes. And second, the overlap between these constructs potentially presents conceptual and methodological challenges in the empirical study of career outcomes.

In what follows, we first establish some basic definitions for the objective and the subjective career and subsequently, for objective and subjective career outcomes. Second, we make the case that understanding career outcomes also requires understanding (extrinsic) career norms, (intrinsic) career drivers, and career scripts, and explain how these constructs relate to each other (see Figure 10.1). Third, we provide a systematic overview of different career outcome constructs that can be classified as multidimensional, in so doing problematizing and discussing the surprising amount of overlap in their factor structures. Fourth, we examine some of the higher-order outcomes that have in recent years captured the attention of career scholars and discuss the nature of their relationship to career outcomes. Fifth, we investigate whether or not the conceptual overlap between different career constructs presents measurement and construct validity challenges in studying career outcomes. In the final section, we infer practical implications from all of the above for the further academic study and practice of individual career management.

The objective versus the subjective career

Before we can get to the issue of which individual career outcomes are most relevant for career researchers and practitioners to focus on, we first need to establish what we mean by a "career." A classical division relevant to providing a meaningful definition is that between the objective and the subjective career. While the former is defined as a *succession* of jobs or *roles*, arranged in a *hierarchy* of *prestige*, through which individuals move in an observable pattern or *sequence* over the course of their lives (Hall, 1976), the latter is framed in terms of *idiosyncratic experiences* and *self-perceptions* – "the evolving sequence of a person's work experiences over time" (Arthur et al., 1989: 8), or similarly, "the individually perceived sequence of attitudes and behaviors associated with work-related experiences and activities over the span of a person's life" (Hall, 1976: 4). Career outcomes, then, are the accumulated material and psychological achievements resulting from the act of movement through one's career, whichever shape or form that career may take (Altman, 1997; Seibert, 2006).

This distinction between the objective and the subjective career translates into the remarkably disparate definitions of objective versus subjective career success – raising the question of whether career success can even be understood as a singular construct. While objective career success is defined as directly *observable by others* and *measurable* in a *standardized* way (Shockley et al., 2016) – typically using criteria such as salary, job level, promotion history, or occupational prestige – subjective success is defined as a *sense of progress* towards *personally set goals* that are *perceived* as meaningful (Seibert, 2006). Some definitions of subjective career success make mention of comparisons between the present career situation and future prospects (Aryee et al., 1994), while others include *social comparison* to relevant others (i.e., "other-referent" career success; Heslin, 2003). Research describing "career success, personal failure" cases has clearly demonstrated that it is entirely possible to be objectively successful but *feel subjectively* unsuccessful and vice versa (Hall and Chandler, 2005). In fact, the correlation between both types of career success, according to meta-analytical reviews, is typically only around 0.18 to 0.30 (Ng et al., 2005).

As a final point, since both objective and subjective career success – especially over the course of the last decade – have come to include many different facets and meanings of careers, in this chapter we will treat "career success" and "career outcomes" as synonyms. Although the latter term may sound broader and more inclusive than the former, with the emergence of subjectivist, multidimensional measures of career success this nuance has all but vanished (Briscoe et al., 2017; Shockley et al., 2016; Mayrhofer et al., 2016).

Related constructs relevant to understanding career success

In order to establish what appropriate outcomes are to be considered in the scientific study of careers – as well as for organizational career management and career counseling practice – we first need to understand what career norms, career drivers, and career scripts are (we define these constructs below). Specifically, we propose that it is not possible to determine on which career outcomes we should focus as researchers and practitioners if we do not simultaneously consider which specific societal norms and individual preferences drive career decisions.

(Extrinsic) career norms

Norms are defined as "acceptable standards of behavior shared by [i.e., agreed to and accepted by] group members that express what they ought and ought not do under certain circumstances, with a minimum need for external controls" (Robbins and Judge, 2015: 284). Applied to careers, norms such as successful careers being characterized by an upward progression through jobs at increasing levels of prestige and income are still pervasive, regardless of the postmodern turn in the careers literature. Although high-profile entrepreneurs such as Elon Musk and Mark Zuckerberg may have supplanted more traditional types of corporate CEOs as career success role models (Mayrhofer et al., 2016), the underlying ideology is still the same – success means fast-moving, upwardly mobile, and rich (Altman, 1997). Below, we discuss the four most pervasive extrinsic norms of what it means to have a successful career.

A first extrinsic norm is that career success is typically quantified by *salary*. As stated by Altman (1997: 7): "Money is not only the simplest measure of success, it is also the finest measure. There is nothing as measurable, quantifiable, perfectly comparable like money." Cross-cultural studies on career success have indeed found that most societies see money as an expression of success, both in terms of allowing a person to provide for their family and community and as an outward indicator of wealth and prestige (Mayrhofer et al., 2016). A second extrinsic norm is that being successful is reflected in your *job level*. Being a manager or a leader, specifically, is widely regarded as an indication of being successful – much more so than being in a subordinate position (Shockley et al., 2016). This norm of a higher job level signifying higher success is also reflected in common expressions referring to careers – "the way to the top," "climbing the ladder," and "the organizational hierarchy" (Dries, 2011). Related to job level but focusing more on the process of achieving a higher-up position is the third extrinsic norm, *promotion history*, which can refer to number of promotions achieved to date, speed of promotions, or both (for instance, the number of promotions achieved in the career divided by years of experience; Dries et al., 2009). Especially advancing faster than what is commonly expected for one's age, or faster than peers (i.e., "being on the fast track") is seen as an outward indicator of success (Altman, 1997). A fourth and final extrinsic career success norm relates to *occupational prestige*. Occupational prestige is a normative construct reflecting a society's appreciation for different types of professions – often coinciding with educational level, earning potential, social class, and the exclusivity of entry requirements for those professions. It is a variable more often used by sociologists than by organizational behavior or management scholars, with occupational prestige indices (as rated by panels of judges) being available online for many different countries (Treiman, 2013). Together, these four extrinsic career norms correspond to the measures typically used to quantify objective career success (Dries et al., 2009; Seibert, 2006).

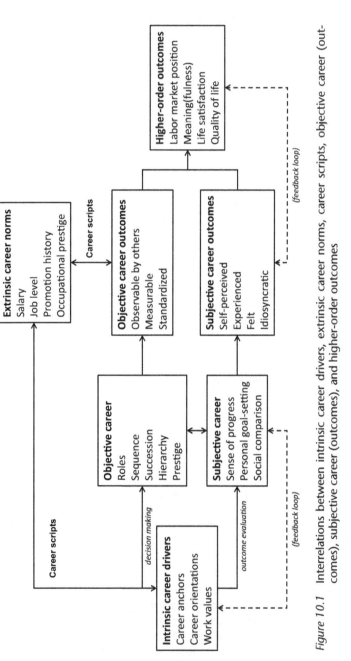

Figure 10.1 Interrelations between intrinsic career drivers, extrinsic career norms, career scripts, objective career (outcomes), subjective career (outcomes), and higher-order outcomes

(Intrinsic) career drivers

A career driver is an inner force that determines what a person wants and needs from their career. Career drivers originate from within an individual (hence the "intrinsic" qualifier between brackets) and stimulate action. They are not necessarily deliberately chosen – rather they tend to "reveal" themselves through choices and overt behavior – but follow logically from a person's personality, abilities, values, and self-image (Chia et al., 2008).

The notion of career drivers encompasses several different sub-constructs, most notably career anchors, career orientations, and work values. A first type of intrinsic career driver is the *career anchor* (Schein, 1974). A person's career anchor refers to his or her stable career self-concept and has three components: (1) self-perceived talents and abilities (based on actual successes in a variety of real-world work settings); (2) self-perceived motives and needs (based on actual experiences with a variety of job assignments); and (3) self-perceived attitudes and values (based on reactions to a variety of norms and values encountered in different work groups and organizations). The metaphor of the "anchor" refers to the fact that, although the career-related self-concept is formed over time and therefore susceptible to change in early career stage individuals, once it is more established it will serve as a stabilizing force in both career decision-making and career outcome evaluation (Schein, 1974). Schein originally identified five career anchors (technical/functional competence, managerial competence, security and stability, autonomy and independence, and entrepreneurial creativity), later adding three more (service and dedication to a cause, pure challenge, lifestyle). A ninth career anchor (geographic) was added by Burke (1983) and is also often included in empirical studies of career anchors (e.g., Cerdin and Pargneux, 2010). Although the idea is somewhat disputed by more recent research (Ramakrishna and Potosky, 2003; Rodrigues et al., 2013), Schein believed that each individual only truly has one dominant career anchor. Additionally, the notion of congruence was central to Schein's (1974) work on career anchors; he stated that satisfaction can only be achieved when a person's objective career matches their dominant anchor. Consequently, we can expect career outcomes that are more closely aligned with career norms and drivers to weigh more heavily in the evaluation of subjective career success. Having a highly successful career, then, would not necessarily require a high score on all possible facets of career – but rather, high scores specifically on those facets considered personally important. The idea of weighing career outcomes by the importance respondents attach to different facets of careers has so far been relatively unexplored in the career success literature – one exception being the Dual Aspect Importance and Achievement Career Success Scale recently developed by Briscoe et al. (2017), which asks respondents to indicate for each item both the importance they attach to it and the extent to which they have currently achieved it.

In addition to career anchors, we find literature on the construct of *career orientation*, defined as an individual's preferences regarding particular career-related opportunities, circumstances, and career types (Gerber et al., 2009: 304). Derr (1986) for example, building on the work of Schein (1974) developed a model consisting of five career orientations: getting ahead (leadership orientation), getting secure (job security orientation), getting free (entrepreneurial orientation), getting high (expertise orientation), and getting balanced (work-life balance orientation). Since career anchors and career orientations are quasi-identical constructs, we consider them here as one single type of intrinsic career driver.

A second distinct type of intrinsic career driver is the notion of *work values*, defined as generalized beliefs about the relative desirability of various aspects of work (e.g., pay, autonomy, working conditions), and work-related outcomes (e.g., accomplishment, fulfillment; Lyons et al., 2010: 971). Building on facet theory – which proposes that constructs are organized in theoretical patterns rather than just two-by-two correlations – Schwartz (1992) was the first to develop a multidimensional model comprising 10 basic human values (self-direction, stimulation, security, conformity, tradition, benevolence, universalism, power, achievement, and hedonism) organized in a circumplex factor structure. Building on his work, Lyons et al. (2010) developed a three-dimensional cylindrex model specifically for *work* values, at its most basic level consisting of four different types of work values: cognitive values, instrumental values, prestige values, and social-altruistic values.

Where career anchors and orientations refer to personal preferences and strengths, values are conceptualized primarily as normative, cognitive beliefs and/or manifestations of needs (Lyons et al., 2010). Together, these two distinct types of intrinsic career drivers serve as input to the objective career, in that they shape career decisions and choices, and to the subjective career, in that they shape outcome evaluation (i.e., career satisfaction).

Career scripts

The mutual relationship between norms and drivers is a central feature of "career scripts" – a construct that was coined in the 1980s by Barley (1989) but has received relatively little research attention in the careers literature, although some authors have spoken of a resurgence of interest in the topic (Valette and Culié, 2015). Career scripts are defined as

> interpretive schemas, resources, and norms [. . .] that specify the behaviors or event sequences that are appropriate for specific situations [. . .]; habitualized actions and taken-for-granted knowledge transmitted through socialization [. . .]. Career scripts mediate how actors actively enact the structures that constrain or enable their actions.
>
> *(Tams et al., 2012: 4–6)*

Career scripts result from the interactions between a context (which prescribes appropriate behaviors) and an individual (who conceives his or her career path according to personal preferences and aspirations). Put simply, a career script is a person's answer to the question: "In this given context, what are my possible and desirable career paths?" (Valette and Culié, 2015).

Some authors in the literature on career success explicitly state that subjective career success refers to the experience of reaching independently set, personally meaningful goals *rather than* goals imposed by parents, peers, organizations, or society (Seibert, 2006; Hall and Chandler, 2005). As with all social phenomena, it is of course unclear to what extent intrinsic career drivers could ever be fully "independently" formed. Older discussions of career success addressed this issue more explicitly than newer ones, for instance Betz and Fitzgerald (1987), who defined subjective career success as a combination of the internalized career success evaluations made by significant others and one's own evaluation of one's success, weighted against the careers of peers and certain age-related or personal expectations about career. This type of approach, acknowledging people's internalizations of extrinsic career norms, still rings as true today as it did 40 years ago; perhaps the present-day, postmodern definitions of subjective career success present all too rosy a picture of career actors' independence from extrinsic norms (Dries, 2011).

Figure 10.1 provides an illustration of the interrelations between intrinsic career drivers, extrinsic career norms, career scripts, objective career (outcomes), subjective career (outcomes), and higher-order outcomes. As we see in Figure 10.1, intrinsic career drivers inform objective career decisions as well as (concurrent and subsequent) subjective evaluations of career outcomes, the latter of which feed back into the former. In addition, through career scripts extrinsic career norms are internalized both into an individual's career drivers – putting into question whether career drivers can ever be "truly" intrinsic – and into socially shared understandings of what successful career outcomes should look like, both in objective and subjective terms. The career outcomes achieved and experienced by a person, at any given point in time, will also spill over into his or her other life domains as well as have more long-term consequences for his or her labor market position. In the figure, these are captured under the label "higher-order outcomes." Finally, the figure contains feedback loops as careers are cyclical by nature, with individuals continually re-evaluating their career decisions as their experiences change and their perspectives evolve (Hall and Chandler, 2005).

Individual career outcomes

As discussed earlier, the criteria typically used to evaluate people's objective career outcomes tend to be derived from extrinsic career norms, while the criteria typically used to evaluate people's subjective career outcomes tend to be derived from intrinsic career drivers. Interestingly, there is some – but not perfect – overlap between both types of criteria. It is thus possible to map correspondences between different objective and subjective career constructs found in the literature at the factor level, as we do in Table 10.1. (The table also includes a mapping to higher-order outcomes of career, which we will discuss in more detail in the next section of this chapter.) Specifically, we compare formal definitions and frequently used measures (both at the construct/scale and item level) for each of the constructs listed in Table 10.1 so as to come to a substantiated evaluation of their similarity. The procedure is similar to those of card-sorting (or 'Q-sort') studies described elsewhere in the careers literature (Briscoe et al., 2017; Dries et al., 2008) – similar constructs are grouped together, and dissimilar constructs are separated, until the full spectrum of constructs is mapped relative to one another. The mapping process suggests that, across all of these constructs, approximately 12 clearly separate factors or "regions of meaning" can be found, although no single source referenced in the table includes all 12. While this type of mapping, however systematic, is always to some extent subjective, we dare say that the overlap between the different constructs, at the very least, has high face validity (Ziegler et al., 2013).

Below, we summarize each of the 12 individual career outcomes found in the literature, attempting to assign an "umbrella" label to each. Incidentally, the table illustrates the value of considering subjective career success alongside its (more researched) objective counterpart, as the objective career success construct covers only 4 out of a possible 12 identified meanings of career success:

1 *Competence*: This type of individual career outcome refers to both performance outcomes and skill utilization outcomes, relating these to self-esteem. In other words, a successful career is a career that allows a person to use, and feel confident about, his or her abilities.
2 *Power and influence*: This type of individual career outcome refers to objective job level (i.e., being in a leadership versus a subordinate role), but also to the power, influence, and impact accompanying job level and the higher-quality working conditions associated with it. In other words, a successful career is a career consisting of (a sequence of, or progression towards) increasingly nonroutine and influential jobs.
3 *Upward advancement*: This type of individual career outcome refers to both objective promotion history and subjective perceptions of future career opportunities. In other words, a successful career is a career characterized by continuous advancement opportunities.
4 *Development*: This type of individual career outcome refers to learning and development, but also personal development ("becoming oneself") and the feeling of being challenged

through work. In other words, a successful career is a career that encourages lifelong growth and development.

5 *Financial well-being:* This type of individual career outcome refers to objective salary and wealth as opposed to the (more subjective) financial security that is also provided by money (see next factor). In other words, a successful career is a career that generates a solid level of income and material well-being.

6 *Security:* This type of individual career outcome refers to security and stability, both in terms of being able to provide for one's family financially and in terms of experiencing job security. In other words, a successful career is a career absent of financial or job loss worries.

7 *Satisfaction:* This type of individual career outcome refers to personal satisfaction with one's career (regardless of its objective features). In other words, a successful career is whatever type of career a given person is satisfied with.

8 *Balance:* This type of individual career outcome refers to both perceived work-life balance and some more objective features related to balance, like commute distance and working hours. In other words, a successful career is a career that allows a person to also have a satisfying life outside of work.

9 *Prestige:* This type of individual career outcome refers to both objective occupational prestige and more subjective feelings of recognition and labor market position. In other words, a successful career is a career that is appreciated by society.

10 *Relationships:* This type of individual career outcome refers to interpersonal relationships at work (e.g., with coworkers and supervisors), but also to the idea that "belonging" to a group to some extent requires "conforming" and respecting traditions. In other words, a successful career is a career that makes a person experience belongingness to a social group.

11 *Service:* This type of individual career outcome refers to the experience of doing work that is meaningful and impactful. In other words, a successful career is a career that contributes something valuable to society.

12 *Independence:* This type of individual career outcome refers to having autonomy and freedom in one's career. In other words, a successful career is a career characterized by a high level of personal agency.

It is important to note that these 12 factors cut across different career constructs, some of which are conceptualized as antecedents of careers (i.e., extrinsic norms, intrinsic drivers), some of which are conceptualized as career outcomes (i.e., objective and subjective career success), and some of which are conceptualized as higher-order outcomes of careers (i.e., labor market position, work meaningfulness, life satisfaction). While other authors in the past have conducted systematic reviews of different models of subjective career success, identifying overlapping factors – most recently, Shockley et al. (2016) – Table 10.1 reveals that factor structures are similar not only *within* different author's conceptions of objective and subjective career success (i.e., within the second and fourth columns in the table, respectively), but also *between* career success and constructs considered to be related to career success but not career success proper (i.e., between the different columns). The implications of this remarkable degree of overlap between career constructs will be discussed in a later section of this chapter.

Higher-order outcomes of career

Although it is clear from its definition that a career is an inherently longitudinal phenomenon, empirical career outcome measurements are treated by many scholars as "snapshots" of objective and subjective career-related states experienced by people "at any point in [their] work experiences over time" (Arthur et al., 2005: 179). Especially when measured subjectively, however, we can expect career outcomes to be highly volatile (Spurk and Abele, 2014), although there is also research implying the existence of some sort of "set point" of career satisfaction, with some individuals being more prone to dissatisfaction almost regardless of their objective career circumstances (Judge and Larsen, 2001). In addition, although there has been some discussion – both in review articles (e.g., Arthur et al., 2005) and in empirical studies (e.g., Abele and Spurk, 2009) – of the effects of objective career success on subjective career success and vice versa, empirical studies have only occasionally looked at higher-order outcomes of career (e.g., Abele et al., 2016). Theoretically, however, it has been argued that career success is not necessarily the "ultimate" outcome variable of careers but may also have important outcomes of its own (Hall and Chandler, 2005).

Higher-order outcomes of career, then, are defined as accumulated outcomes over time of an individual's objective career achievements and subjective career experiences – regardless of their relative volatility or stability – that are not *themselves* indicators (i.e., factors or facets) of career success (Spurk et al., 2018). As can be seen in Table 10.1, several higher-order outcomes of careers can be identified in the literature that that have in recent years captured the attention of career scholars and that demonstrate strong conceptual and empirical links both to norms and drivers and to objective and subjective career success – most notably labor market position, work meaningfulness, and life satisfaction. As Figure 10.1 shows, although we generally assume that these higher-order outcomes follow directly or indirectly from the accumulation of the aforementioned career outcomes over time, it is likely that 'feedback loops' exist, such that reverse-causal relationships between labor market position, work meaningfulness, life satisfaction, and objective and subjective career success can also be observed (Abele and Spurk, 2009).

Labor market position

First of all, *labor market position* – as an individual higher-order career outcome – can be understood as a function of a person's current employment quality and his or her employability, boundarylessness, and proteanism. *Employment quality* is typically defined and measured using lists of job characteristics such as nearness to home, working hours, working conditions, and opportunity to use skills (Wanberg et al., 2002; see Table 10.1). Discussions of employment quality are part of broader policy debates around "decent work" (cf. the work done on this topic by the International Labor Organization, 2018). In addition to currently having a decent job, a person's labor market position is also determined by his or her ability to find and keep work, a construct referred to as *employability* (De Cuyper and De Witte, 2011). In other words, if a person currently has a decent job but would be in trouble if he or she lost that job (due to low employability), we would evaluate that person's labor market position as precarious (Van Buren, 2003). The final indicators of being in a solid labor market position are boundaryless and protean career attitudes. Whereas *boundarylessness* is defined as perceiving and being open to career opportunities beyond the current employing organization's boundaries, *proteanism* refers to being strongly self-directed and values-driven in managing one's own career (Briscoe and Hall, 2006). Taken together, employability, boundarylessness, and proteanism are indicators of an individual's subjective confidence in his or her labor market position (above and beyond their more objective employment quality; Dries, 2011; Van Buren, 2003). All four variables together, we argue, represent the necessary and sufficient features needed to define and operationalize the aggregate construct of "labor market position." Whereas employment quality refers to a focal career actor's objective work situation, employability is most often operationalized as a state (which determines the extent to which an individual can escape or transcend their present situation if they so desire), while boundarylessness and proteanism have been conceptualized as more trait-like (Briscoe and Hall, 2006) – and thus only partly determined by a person's situation and state – in turn determining how situations and states are subjectively interpreted and evaluated (Gunz and Mayrhofer, 2018).

Meaning(fulness)

A second higher-order outcome of careers is the *meaning and/or meaningfulness of work* as attributed by a focal career actor. *Meaning* refers to "the output of having made sense of something, or what it signifies; as in an individual interpreting what her work means, or what role her work plays, in the context of her life" (Rosso et al., 2010). Rosso et al. (2010), based on their systematic review of the literature, developed a two-dimensional (self-other × agency-communion) model of work meanings, with four quadrants (individuation, self-connection, unification, and contribution) consisting of 13 different work meanings (control/autonomy, competence, self-esteem, self-concordance, identity affirmation, personal engagement, value systems, social identification, interpersonal connectedness, perceived impact, significance, interconnection, and self-abnegation; see Table 10.1). In contrast to career anchors, career orientations, and work values, the meanings attributed to work represent the *outcome* of a sensemaking process rather than a preference or a belief. It is also less normative in that meaning is in essence a neutral construct – however, it is true that in the meaningful work literature the use of the term "meaning" usually implies positive meaning. It is important not to confuse meaning with *meaningfulness*, however, which is defined as "the amount of significance something holds for an individual" (Rosso et al., 2010: 95). Whereas meaning refers to *type* of meaning, meaningfulness thus refers to the *amount* of significance attached to one's work more generally.

Satisfaction with life/quality of life

Finally, it is assumed that a given individual's objective and subjective career success will relate to his or her overall *satisfaction with life*. The exact degree to which a person's aggregated career outcomes predict their life satisfaction may depend, however, on his or her work role salience (i.e., the relative importance the work domain takes up in their life; Abele et al., 2016). Life satisfaction is defined as "a global assessment of a person's quality of life according to his chosen criteria [. . .] a hallmark of the subjective well-being area that centers on the person's own judgments, not upon some criterion which is judged to be important by the researcher" (Diener et al., 1985: 71). (Note the parallel with Hall and Chandler's (2005: 158) definition of subjective success as "the experience of reaching independently set, personally meaningful goals, rather than goals imposed by parents, peers, organizations, or society.") As has been the case in the subjective career success literature, the literature on life satisfaction – as well as the related literate stream on *quality of life* (QOL) – has seen a trend towards multidimensional and subjectivist measures, and for much of the same reasons (Felce and Perry, 1995). The major difference between the constructs of career satisfaction and life satisfaction is that the former only measures satisfaction within one life domain, whereas the latter measures satisfaction across all life domains – career being one of them (Lounsbury et al., 2004).

Although at face value, the higher-order outcome constructs may appear to be quite different from the other constructs in the table, at the level of construct definition and measurement they were, again, found to exhibit highly similar factors. As is illustrated by the last column of Table 10.1 – where we map the underlying factor structures of the most commonly used measures for each of these higher-order outcomes to our other constructs of interest – the literature

Table 10.1 The overlap between different multidimensional career constructs

Umbrella labels	Extrinsic career norms/ objective career success	Intrinsic career drivers	Subjective career success	Higher-order outcomes
	(Dries et al., 2009[1]; Heslin, 2003[2]; Seibert, 2006[3])	(Career anchors (Schein, 1974)[4], Career orientations (Derr, 1986)[5], Basic human values (Schwartz, 1992)[6], Work values (Lyons et al., 2010)[7]	(Dries et al., 2008[8]; Shockley et al., 2016[9]; Briscoe et al., 2017[10])	Work meanings (Rosso et al., 2010)[11], Employment quality (Wanberg et al., 2002)[12], Employability (De De Cuyper and De Witte, 2011)[13], Boundarylessness, Proteanism (Briscoe and Hall, 2006)[14,15], Quality of life (Felce and Perry, 1995)[16]
1. Competence		Technical/functional competence[4]	Performance[8] Quality work[9]	Competence[11] Work-based self-esteem[11] Opportunity to use skills[12]
2. Power and influence	Job level[1,2,3]	Managerial competence[4] Getting ahead[4] Power[6]	Influence[9]	Perceived impact[11] Type of work[12] Working conditions (comfortable vs. precarious)[12]
3. Upward advancement	Number of promotions[1,2,3] Speed of promotions[1,2,3]	Achievement[6]	Advancement[8]	Internal employability[13] Career opportunities[12]
4. Development		Pure challenge[4] Getting high[5] Stimulation[6] Cognitive values[7]	Self-development[8] Growth and development[9] Learning and development[10]	Development and activity[16] Learning oppportunities[12]
5. Financial well-being	Salary[1,2,3]	Instrumental values[7]	Financial success[10]	Material well-being[16] Wages[12] Fringe benefits[12]
6. Security		Security and stability[4] Getting secure[4] Security[6] Instrumental values[7]	Financial security[8,10] Job security[8]	Physical well-being[16] External employability[13] Job security[12]

(Continued)

Table 10.1 (Continued)

	Extrinsic career norms/ objective career success	Intrinsic career drivers	Subjective career success	Higher-order outcomes
7. Satisfaction		Hedonism[6]	Personal satisfaction[8] Satisfaction[9]	Self-esteem[11] Emotional well-being[16]
8. Balance		Lifestyle[4] Geographic[4] Getting balanced[5]	Personal life[9] Work-life balance[10]	Emotional well-being[16] Nearness to home[12] Working hours[12]
9. Prestige	Occupational prestige[1,2,3]	Prestige values[7]	Recognition[8,9]	External employability[13]
10. Relationships		Benevolence[6] Conformity[6] Tradition[6] Social-altruistic values[7]	Cooperation[8] Positive work relationships[10]	Social identification[11] Interpersonal connectedness[11] Social well-being[16] Supervision[12]
11. Service		Service and dedication to a cause[4] Universalism[6] Social-altruistic values[7]	Contribution[8] Meaningful work[9] Positive impact[10]	Perceived impact[11] Significance[11] Interconnection[11] Self-abnegation[11]
12. Independence		Entrepreneurial creativity[4] Autonomy and independence[4] Getting free[5] Self-direction[6]	Creativity[8] Authenticity[9] Entrepreneurial[10]	Control/autonomy[11] Self-concordance[11] Personal engagement[11] Boundarylessness[14,15] Proteanism[14,15] External employability[13]

Note: Superscript numbers attributed to constructs in the table refer back to the associated references listed in the second row of the table.

on each of these constructs has *also* seen a trend towards multidimensional scales, with factors strongly overlapping those of the other career constructs.

Is the overlap between different career constructs problematic?

This chapter was born out of the observation that much of the qualitative research into what careers mean to people (e.g., Dries et al., 2008) as well as much of the quantitative research seeking to develop multidimensional, subjectivist measures of career success (e.g., Briscoe et al., 2017; Shockley et al., 2016) keeps finding a similar factor structure across time periods, samples, and geographical locations. In addition, this factor structure also cuts across constructs typically considered antecedents, outcomes, and higher-order outcomes of careers (see Table 10.1). The most recently developed multidimensional measures of career success (Briscoe et al., 2017; Shockley et al., 2016), for instance, carry a very high degree of resemblance to Schein's 40-year old model of career anchors (1974), not least because in developing their item pool they adopted a similar, inductive method to the one originally used by Schein (i.e., asking people to describe what they see as desired career outcomes for themselves, in their own words). Moreover, striking similarities in factor structures were not only found among career constructs, but also *between* career constructs and multidimensional constructs from other, related OB/HRM fields: basic human values (Schwartz, 1992), meaningfulness (Rosso et al., 2010), and life satisfaction (Diener et al., 1985).

Although our finding that there is a lot of conceptual overlap between the factor structures of career norms, career drivers, objective and subjective career success, and higher-order career outcomes (Table 10.1) fits with the logic behind Figure 10.1 (i.e., an individual career outcome is only relevant if it is salient in terms of social context norms, if a person attaches much value to it, or both), it does raise questions about conceptual and empirical confounding, as well as about semantic similarities among constructs claimed to be different. We discuss both potential issues in more detail below.

Confounding

Confounding refers to instances where the independent, dependent, moderating, and mediating variables of a theory are not fully independent but rather share conceptual and empirical overlap. While conceptual confounding occurs when (components of) the definitions of independent and dependent variables are not mutually exclusive, empirical confounding occurs when (part of) a scale used to measure an independent variable is duplicated or replicated in the measure of an independent variable (or a moderator or mediator variable; Martinko et al., 2014). A simplified example would be to test a model in which skill variety (as a job characteristic) is modeled to predict work engagement, mediated by job satisfaction. While skill variety is defined as "the degree to which a job requires a variety of different activities in carrying out the work, which involve the use of a number of different skills and talents of the employee" (Hackman and Oldham, 1974: 161), work engagement is defined as "a positive, fulfilling work-related state of mind that is characterized by vigor, dedication, and absorption" (Schaufeli et al., 2006: 702), and job satisfaction as "the overall evaluative judgment one has about one's job; the assessment of the favorability of a job, typically arrayed along a continuum from positive to negative" (Judge et al., 2017: 357). From these definitions, we can infer that conceptual confounding – especially between work engagement and job satisfaction – might be a potential issue in modeling these variables as antecedents to each other. To assess empirical confounding, we need to look at frequently used measures of these constructs at the item level. Consider, for instance, the following sample items: "The job requires me to use a number of complex or high-level skills" (skill variety; Idaszak and Drasgow, 1987), versus "To me, my job is challenging" (work engagement; Schaufeli et al., 2006), and "How satisfied or dissatisfied are you with the way you carry out your work activities?" (job satisfaction; Janssen, 2001). It is clear in this example that both causality and discriminant validity would be an issue if these variables were modeled as antecedents to each other – the only plausible solution being to test a longitudinal, cross-lagged panel model measuring all variables at all time points – as these constructs exhibit high overlap both in terms of their definition, and in terms of the items used to measure them (Martinko et al., 2014). (Incidentally, a cursory search in Google Scholar shows that job satisfaction and work engagement are in fact quite often modeled as antecedents to each other, so the preceding example is by no means unrealistic.)

The issue of scales carrying a similar name measuring different constructs at the item level, and scales with different names measuring highly similar constructs, has been dubbed the "jingle-jangle fallacy" in the organizational research methods literature – the tendency to believe that nearly identical constructs are distinct because they carry different labels (Ziegler et al., 2013). To further illustrate the "slippery slope" of confounding, let us consider the typical research process causing fragmentation between related literature streams, and its consequences (Ziegler et al., 2013). Again using a simplified example, let us say that over time four literature streams develop around the topic areas of mood, feeling, affect, and satisfaction, with minimal cross-referencing (i.e., each area consists of different authors, who publish in different, domain-specific journals). Over time, each stream – separately from the others – comes to the insight that their focal construct is multidimensional, and so conceptual and qualitative work ensues to uncover its underlying factor structure. Additionally, new constructs are discovered or developed (e.g., happiness) from which yet other literature streams emerge. After years of dedicated research in all of these streams, what remains is a set of constructs measured by highly similar items – derived from inductive research designs using highly similar, open-ended interview protocols – that would run into trouble with exploratory factor analysis if they were included in the same study and modeled as antecedents to each other. Moreover, as these literature streams developed in parallel, only limited transfers or gains have occurred in the sense of insights from one stream informing the other. This seems to be what has happened to some extent with the subjective career success literature compared to the "old" literature on career anchors, for instance (Briscoe et al., 2017; Shockley et al., 2016). More generally, within the careers field there is surprisingly little cross-referencing between (those in) the vocational/counseling psychology literature, and (those in) the so-called career management literature (Collin and Patton, 2009). The former group is found mostly in psychology departments and published in journals such as the *Journal of Career Assessment* and the *Journal of Vocational Psychology*; the latter group consists mostly of business school professors who publish in journals such as the *Journal of Organizational Behavior* or the *Journal of Applied Psychology*.

Semantic similarities

A more recent stream of the organizational research methods literature that is highly relevant for understanding the potential implications of the overlap between career constructs is that on the semantic similarity of items. Using language processing algorithms Arnulf et al. (2014) showed – and quite shockingly so – that 60 to 86 percent of variance in response patterns to a wide range of commonly used organizational behavior surveys could be predicted by computers *prior to the survey being administered to actual human respondents*. Specifically, the authors showed that survey response patterns are predictable a priori from the semantic properties of, and overlap between, their items. For example, semantically and looking at the item level, leadership style (of one's supervisor), intrinsic motivation, and turnover intention were all found to be highly similar constructs, at least from a layman respondent (i.e., non-researcher) point of view. Not only did semantic relationships between items predict the internal consistency (α) of the scales in the survey – which is not necessarily a problem since internal consistency is in part reliant on semantic similarity among a scale's items – it also predicted correlations and even mediating relationships between different variables, thus implying contamination of the data. In fact, the authors (jokingly) state that constructing a survey based on semantic similarities between variables would be the most surefire way for obtaining good fit indices in a confirmatory factor analysis and/or confirming all of the study's hypotheses.

It is clear from our Table 10.1 that the measurement of individual career outcomes, career norms and drivers, and higher-order career outcomes is potentially plagued by both conceptual and empirical confounding and high semantic similarity between constructs (if only because most of the constructs have "career" in their name). Based on all of the above we must thus conclude that the conceptual and empirical overlap between career norms, career drivers, objective and subjective career success, and higher-order career outcomes (see Table 10.1) can create methodological issues – especially when including, for instance, career anchors, subjective career success, and employability (or any other outcome identified in this chapter) in a single study.

Martinko et al. (2014) estimate that common method bias (i.e., variance attributable to the measurement method, rather than to the constructs the measures represent) explains up to 26 percent of variance in organizational behavior (OB) research and warn their readers that even moderate overlap between a predictor and an outcome variable can single-handedly account for most of the variance in an outcome variable. It is thus crucially important that careers researchers understand that semantic, conceptual, and/or empirical confounding between careers variables measured in the same study will likely account for much, if not all of the resultant variance they find in their dependent variable (Arnulf et al., 2014; Martinko et al., 2014).

Implications for future research

A first piece of advice – related specifically to the issue of conceptual confounding – might be for junior researchers to go back to the seminal literature, as far back as the 1950s, before they start developing "new" constructs or measures in the belief that "nothing is known about X yet," simply because X represents a new construct label (Martinko et al., 2014; Ziegler et al., 2013). Additionally, researchers are recommended to perform literature reviews based on keywords rather than staying within a delineated field (e.g., vocational psychology versus management) or set of journals.

Second, as a potential solution to the issue of empirical confounding, Martinko et al. (2014) propose using exploratory factor analysis (EFA), specifically looking for patterns in cross-loadings. The authors point out that confirmatory factor analysis (CFA) is often "abused" to demonstrate discriminant validity when in fact EFA is more suited for this purpose. In addition, they recommend running EFA with oblique rather than orthogonal rotation (the latter being appropriate for use only when factors are assumed to be uncorrelated and thus potentially producing artificial separation of factors that in fact demonstrate construct overlap; for more details, readers are referred to Martinko et al., 2014). After running EFA with oblique rotation, the authors advise researchers to test hypothesized causal relationships both with and without overlapping items (i.e., items with high cross-loadings). If the removal of such items from two or more scales in a model causes a substantial change in the strength or direction of their relationships, empirical confounding within the dataset is likely (i.e., due to the removal of shared variance; see Martinko et al., 2014). Finally, Martinko et al. (2014) propose that in order to establish a solid nomological network for a focal variable (for instance, subjective career success), discriminant validity is crucially important, although research in our field tends to be more concerned with convergent validity (i.e., positive relationships between related constructs). In other words, career variables that correlate too highly (Kenny, 2016, proposes 0.85 as a cutoff) should not be modeled as predictors to one another. In practical terms, correlation coefficients between two constructs can be projected prior to designing a new study based either on a thorough review of the literature and of existing meta-analyses or by running a smaller-scale pilot study prior to actual survey administration.

Third, the issue of semantic similarity deserves more attention in doctoral programs around the topic of careers (and many others at that) since it represents another potential methodological problem that should be considered prior to designing a study using a survey composed of multiple scales. What is fascinating (and perhaps somewhat worrying) about Arnulf et al.'s (2014) findings is that they find semantic overlap between constructs that would, conceptually or at the item level, not immediately be identified as similar – transformational leadership (of one's supervisor) and affective organizational commitment. (Again, keep in mind that the authors are *not* talking about construct intercorrelations here, but semantic similarities at the item level assessed by a non-human algorithm.) This raises the question of whether we, as academics, sometimes see "too much" nuance between related constructs due to our deep expertise – while to our survey respondents, items from different scales may look and feel highly similar (leading to possible contamination in the sense of common method variance and/or mood effects). Personally, we feel that the Arnulf et al. (2014) article – as well as the Martinko et al. (2014) article on confounding – should be required reading for all PhD candidates entering a field, as well as for all those considering developing a new scale.

Put very simply, it is imperative for careers researchers to properly distinguish career outcomes from predictors, moderators, and higher-order outcomes both semantically (i.e., in terms of layman-respondent perceived similarity of items), theoretically (i.e., in terms of causation), and empirically (i.e., in terms of correlation and factor structure). The issues of confounding and semantic similarities are, of course, not limited to the study of careers alone, nor is it our intention to take away agency from careers researchers in selecting variables and scales for their research projects. Rather, our goal is to help readers reflect on issues such as confounding *prior* to designing a study and collecting data, so as to avoid the potential conceptual and methodological issues associated with it. We hope these recommendations will be useful as the field of careers research ventures into more complex, methodologically rigorous quantitative study designs.

References

Abele, A.E., Hagmaier, T. & Spurk, D. 2016. Does career success make you happy? The mediating role of multiple subjective success evaluations. *Journal of Happiness Studies*, 17, 1615–1633.

Abele, A.E. & Spurk, D. 2009. How do objective and subjective career success interrelate over time? *Journal of Occupational and Organizational Psychology*, 82, 803–824.

Altman, Y. 1997. The high-potential fast-flying achiever: Themes from the English language literature 1976–1995. *Career Development International*, 2, 324–330.

Arnulf, J.K., Larsen, K.R., Martinsen, Ø.L. & Bong, C.H. 2014. Predicting survey responses: How and why semantics shape survey statistics on organizational behaviour. *PloS One*, 9, e106361.

Arthur, M.B., Hall, D.T. & Lawrence, B.S. 1989. *Handbook of Career Theory*. Cambridge, UK: Cambridge University Press.

Arthur, M.B., Khapova, S.N. & Wilderom, C.P. 2005. Career success in a boundaryless career world. *Journal of Organizational Behavior*, 26, 177–202.

Aryee, S., Chay, Y.W. & Tan, H.H. 1994. An examination of the antecedents of subjective career success among a managerial sample in Singapore. *Human Relations*, 47, 487–509.

Barley, S.R. 1989. Careers, identities and institutions: The legacy of the Chicago school of sociology. *In:* Arthur, M.B., Hall, D.T. & Lawrence, B.S. (eds.) *Handbook of Career Theory*. New York: Harper Collins.

Benson, G., Mcintosh, C.K., Salazar, M. & Vaziri, H. 2013. Defining career success: A cross-cultural comparison. *Academy of Management Proceedings*, Academy of Management Briarcliff Manor, New York 10510, 17161.

Betz, N.E. & Fitzgerald, L.F. 1987. *The Career Psychology of Women*. San Diego, CA: Academic Press.

Briscoe, J.P. & Hall, D.T. 2006. The interplay of boundaryless and protean careers: Combinations and implications. *Journal of Vocational Behavior*, 69, 4–18.

Briscoe, J.P., Kase, R., Dries, N., Dysvik, A. & Unite, J. 2017. Minding the gap(s): Development and validation of a cross-cultural measure of subjective career success. *3rd Global Conference on International Human Resource Management*, May, New York.

Burke, R.J. 1983. Career orientations of type A individuals. *Psychological Reports*, 53, 979–989.

Cerdin, J.L. & Pargneux, M.L. 2010. Career anchors: A comparison between organization-assigned and self-initiated expatriates. *Thunderbird International Business Review*, 52, 287–299.

Chia, Y.M., Koh, H.C. & Pragasam, J. 2008. An international study of career drivers of accounting students in Singapore, Australia and Hong Kong. *Journal of Education and Work*, 21, 41–60.

Collin, A. & Patton, W.A. 2009. *Vocational Psychological and Organisational Perspectives on Career: Towards a Multidisciplinary Dialogue*. Rotterdam: Sense Publishers.

de Cuyper, N. & de Witte, H. 2011. The management paradox: Self-rated employability and organizational commitment and performance. *Personnel Review*, 40, 152–172.

Derr, C.B. 1986. *Managing the New Careerists: The Diverse Career Success Orientations of Today's Workers*. San Francisco, CA: Jossey-Bass.

Diener, E., Emmons, R.A., Larsen, R.J. & Griffin, S. 1985. The satisfaction with life scale. *Journal of Personality Assessment*, 49, 71–75.

Dries, N. 2011. The meaning of career success: Avoiding reification through a closer inspection of historical, cultural, and ideological contexts. *Career Development International*, 16, 364–384.

Dries, N., Pepermans, R. & Carlier, O. 2008. Career success: Constructing a multidimensional model. *Journal of Vocational Behavior*, 73, 254–267.

Dries, N., Pepermans, R., Hofmans, J. & Rypens, L. 2009. Development and validation of an objective intra-organizational career success measure for managers. *Journal of Organizational Behavior*, 30, 543–560.

Duffy, R.D. & Sedlacek, W.E. 2010. The salience of a career calling among college students: Exploring group differences and links to religiousness, life meaning, and life satisfaction. *The Career Development Quarterly*, 59, 27–41.

Felce, D. & Perry, J. 1995. Quality of life: Its definition and measurement. *Research in Developmental Disabilities*, 16, 51–74.

Gerber, M., Wittekind, A., Grote, G. & Staffelbach, B. 2009. Exploring types of career orientation: A latent class analysis approach. *Journal of Vocational Behavior*, 75, 303–318.

Greenhaus, J.H., Parasuraman, S. & Wormley, W.M. 1990. Effects of race on organizational experiences, job performance evaluations, and career outcomes. *Academy of Management Journal*, 33, 64–86.

Gunz, H. & Mayrhofer, W. 2018. *Rethinking Career Studies: Facilitating Conversation across Boundaries with the Social Chronology Framework*. Cambridge, UK: Cambridge University Press.

Hackman, J.R. & Oldham, G.R. 1974. The job diagnostic survey: An instrument for the diagnosis of jobs and the evaluation of job redesign projects. *Yale University Department of Administrative Sciences Technical Report*, New Haven, CT.

Hall, D.T. 1976. *Careers in Organizations*. Pacific Palisades, LA: Goodyear.

Hall, D.T. & Chandler, D.E. 2005. Psychological success: When the career is a calling. *Journal of Organizational Behavior*, 26, 155–176.

Heslin, P.A. 2003. Self-and other-referent criteria of career success. *Journal of Career Assessment*, 11, 262–286.

Idaszak, J.R. & Drasgow, F. 1987. A revision of the job diagnostic survey: Elimination of a measurement artifact. *Journal of Applied Psychology*, 72, 69–74.

International Labor Organization. 2018. *Decent Work*. Available: https://www.ilo.org/global/topics/decent-work/lang-en/index.htm [Accessed 17 July 2018].

Janssen, O. 2001. Fairness perceptions as a moderator in the curvilinear relationships between job demands, and job performance and job satisfaction. *Academy of Management Journal*, 44, 1039–1050.

Judge, T.A. & Larsen, R.J. 2001. Dispositional affect and job satisfaction: A review and theoretical extension. *Organizational Behavior and Human Decision Processes*, 86, 67–98.

Judge, T.A., Weiss, H.M., Kammeyer-Mueller, J.D. & Hulin, C.L. 2017. Job attitudes, job satisfaction, and job affect: A century of continuity and of change. *Journal of Applied Psychology*, 102, 356–374.

Kenny, D.A. 2016. *Discriminant Validity* [Online]. Available: http://davidakenny.net/cm/mfactor.htm#Dv [Accessed 20 March 2017].

Lounsbury, J.W., Park, S-H., Sundstrom, E., Williamson, J.M. & Pemberton, A.E. 2004. Personality, career satisfaction, and life satisfaction: Test of a directional model. *Journal of Career Assessment*, 12, 395–406.

Lyons, S.T., Higgins, C.A. & Duxbury, L. 2010. Work values: Development of a new three-dimensional structure based on confirmatory smallest space analysis. *Journal of Organizational Behavior*, 31, 969–1002.

Martinko, M.J., Harvey, P. & Mackey, J.D. 2014. Conceptual and empirical confounds in the organizational sciences: An explication and discussion. *Journal of Organizational Behavior*, 35, 1052–1063.

Mayrhofer, W., Briscoe, J.P., Hall, D.T., Dickmann, M., Dries, N., Dysvik, A., Kase, R., Parry, E. & Unite, J. 2016. Career success across the globe: Insights from the 5C project. *Organizational Dynamics*, 45, 197–205.

Ng, T.W.H., Eby, L.T., Sorensen, K.L. & Feldman, D.C. 2005. Predictors of objective and subjective career success: A meta-analysis. *Personnel Psychology*, 58, 367–408.

Ramakrishna, H.V. & Potosky, D. 2003. Conceptualization and exploration of composite career anchors: An analysis of information systems personnel. *Human Resource Development Quarterly*, 14, 199–214.

Robbins, S.P. & Judge, T.A. 2015. *Organizational Behavior*. Essex, UK: Pearson.

Rodrigues, R., Guest, D. & Budjanovcanin, A. 2013. From anchors to orientations: Towards a contemporary theory of career preferences. *Journal of Vocational Behavior*, 83, 142–152.

Rosso, B.D., Dekas, K.H. & Wrzesniewski, A. 2010. On the meaning of work: A theoretical integration and review. *Research in Organizational Behavior*, 30, 91–127.

Schaufeli, W.B., Bakker, A.B. & Salanova, M. 2006. The measurement of work engagement with a short questionnaire: A cross-national study. *Educational and Psychological Measurement*, 66, 701–716.

Schein, E.H. 1974. *Career Anchors and Career Paths: A Panel Study of Management School Graduates*. Technical report No.1, Cambridge, MA.

Schwartz, S.H. 1992. Universals in the content and structure of values: Theoretical advances and empirical tests in 20 countries. *Advances in Experimental Social Psychology*, 25, 1–65.

Seibert, S.E. 2006. Career success. *In*: Greenhaus, J.H. & Callanan, G.A. (eds.) *Encyclopedia of Career Development*. San Francisco, CA: Sage Publications.

Shockley, K.M., Ureksoy, H., Rodopman, O.B., Poteat, L.F. & Dullaghan, T.R. 2016. Development of a new scale to measure subjective career success: A mixed-methods study. *Journal of Organizational Behavior*, 37, 128–153.

Spurk, D. & Abele, A.E. 2014. Synchronous and time-lagged effects between occupational self-efficacy and objective and subjective career success: Findings from a four-wave and 9-year longitudinal study. *Journal of Vocational Behavior*, 84, 119–132.

Spurk, D., Hirschi, A. & Dries, N. 2018. Antecedents and outcomes of objective versus subjective career success: Competing perspectives and future directions. *Journal of Management*, 2246–2273.

Tams, S., Chudzikowski, K. & Gustafsson, S. 2012. Multiple perspectives on career scripts: Theoretical and empirical insights: Annual academy of management meeting. *Academy of Management Conference*, Boston, MA.

Treiman, D.J. 2013. *Occupational Prestige in Comparative Perspective*. New York: Academic Press.

Valette, A. & Culié, J.-D. 2015. Career scripts in clusters: A social position approach. *Human Relations*, 68, 1745–1767.

van Buren, H.J. 2003. Boundaryless careers and employability obligations. *Business Ethics Quarterly*, 13, 131–149.

Wanberg, C.R., Hough, L.M. & Song, Z. 2002. Predictive validity of a multidisciplinary model of reemployment success. *Journal of Applied Psychology*, 87, 1100–1120.

Ziegler, M., Booth, T. & Bensch, D. 2013. Getting entangled in the nomological net. *European Journal of Psychological Assessment*, 29, 157–161.

11

Individual difference antecedents of career outcomes

Peter A. Heslin and Markus Latzke

Ever since Aristotle's *Eudemian Ethics* lectures on the role of virtues in enabling a worthwhile, flourishing, and happy life (Kenny, 2011), philosophers and scholars have theorized about what leads some individuals to be more fulfilled and successful than others. In contrast to Aristotle's focus on the moral virtues of courage, generosity, justice, friendship, and citizenship, contemporary careers research has focused more on the role of psychometrically derived and assessed dispositions, along with intellectual ability, in predicting objective and subjective career outcomes. A review of such empirical developments by Judge and Kammeyer-Mueller (2007) highlighted the role of the Big Five personality traits and other personality dispositions (i.e., proactive personality) in career success, via mediated pathways including people's social behavior (i.e., relationship building), attractiveness to employers, perceptions of their job characteristics, and their job performance.

This chapter provides an updated review and commentary on the empirical literature on individual difference antecedents of careers outcomes, before suggesting areas for future research. We focus primarily on the research conducted since Judge and Kammeyer-Mueller's (2007) review of the Big Five, proactive personality, and core self-evaluations (CSE) predictors of career outcomes,[1] as well as recent research developments on the following predictors that have garnered relatively intense research attention over the last decade: the Dark Triad traits, self-monitoring, and general mental ability (GMA). Before proceeding with that discussion, we briefly consider the nature of career success and underscore that individual differences represent a mere component of the constellation of factors that affect the career outcomes people experience.

Career success

Career success is commonly defined as either the real or perceived achievements individuals have accumulated as a result of their work experiences (Judge et al., 1995), or the accumulated positive work and psychological outcomes resulting from one's work experiences (Seibert et al., 1999). The real achievements and positive work outcomes in these definitions reflect Hughes's (1937) concept of objective career success, as signified by career outcomes (i.e., pay, rank, and promotions) that are independently identifiable by a third party. Such outcomes may be career context specific (Heslin, 2005a), such as the letters of appreciation received by a teacher or a nurse, the publication citations of a scholar, or the angel funding garnered by an entrepreneur. The empirical literature on career success antecedents over the last decade has unfortunately still focused almost entirely on the traditional, generic objective career outcomes of pay and promotions.

Subjective career success involves people's reactions to both the objective career outcomes *and* the more inherently subjective facets of their career. The latter may include how engaged people feel with their work (Heslin, 2010), their satisfaction with their boss, colleagues and, work environment (Ballout, 2007), as well as their broader work-life balance, relationships, positive impact on other people (Mayrhofer et al., 2016), and the emergent unfolding of their career (Heslin and Turban, 2016). Such variation in the factors people consider in evaluating their careers, the differential weightings they accord to those factors, and the fact that careers are evaluated across a time frame that encompasses their satisfaction with their prior and anticipated as well as current jobs (Gunz and Mayrhofer, 2018), is captured when subjective career success is assessed using the single item: "Everything considered, how successful do you consider your career to date?" (Heslin, 2003: 271). Our review of the literature reveals, however, that the traditional indicators of job satisfaction and career satisfaction (Greenhaus et al., 1990) remain the most widely – indeed almost universally – used measures of subjective career success. Despite their deficiency by virtue of not tapping much of what often consider when they evaluate their career success (Heslin, 2005b), job and career satisfaction are thus the focal subjective career outcomes addressed in this review of the career success literature.

The bigger picture

The career success people experience is a function of far more than their personality and other individual differences, such as their GMA. Other ingredients of success examined by Ng et al.'s (2005) meta-analysis of career success predictors that are beyond the focus of this chapter include people's socio-demographic characteristics and sponsored mobility.[2] Ng et al. (2005) also observed that objective and subjective career outcomes have different antecedents. Specifically, they reported that human capital and socio-demographics generally displayed stronger relationships with objective than subjective career outcomes. On the other hand, organizational sponsorship and stable individual differences (i.e., the Big Five and proactivity) are generally more strongly related to subjective than objective career success.[3] In this chapter, we thus review the evidence regarding how individual differences differentially predict objective and subjective career outcomes, via the pathways depicted in Figure 11.1 and discussed below.

Overview and conceptual model

Before we provide a detailed review of the individual differences relevant to career success, we first delineate the range of variables that are likely to intervene between individual differences and career outcomes. To synthesize this voluminous literature, we therefore homed in on the *career-enabling behavior* and resultant *career capital* that our review led us to believe are the central mechanisms whereby individual differences manifest in objective career outcomes.

Career-enabling behavior

Potentially career enhancing dispositions (e.g., conscientiousness) are unlikely to result in objective career outcomes unless they lead people to act and perform in ways that (a) are valued by organizations or other gatekeepers of objective career outcomes and/or that (b) build

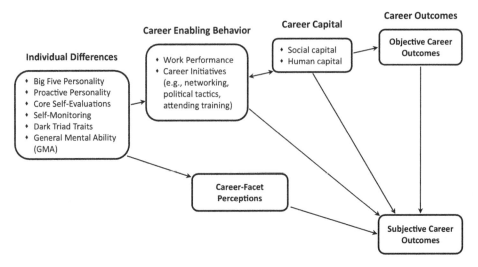

Figure 11.1 Intrapersonal antecedents of career outcomes*

* Career success is also a function of factors such as socio-demographics, career context, and serendipity, which lie beyond the scope of this chapter. Evidence regarding the role of career context is presented in Chapters 12 and 17 in this volume. Fully mediated relationships are depicted simply for parsimony. Owing to the evidence of direct relationships between individual differences and career outcomes, these relationships are likely partially mediated. Finally, career-facet perceptions are the career elements that are highly salient in evaluating one's career, given one's individual differences. The subjective career outcomes that result from these perceptions will be a function of both the nature of the salient career facets and how satisfied one is in these areas.

career-enhancing opportunities and resources, such as a network of supportive colleagues. We thus model career enabling behaviors as including both work performance (job and extra-role performance) and career initiatives (e.g., networking and attending training) that enable the accumulation of career capital.

Career capital

Career capital involves resources embedded within individuals and their relationships that influence career outcomes, by providing greater access to information, resources, and sponsorship (Seibert et al., 2001b). Although there are several conceptualizations of career capital (for an overview, see Latzke et al., 2015), common themes in most of them are human capital and social capital. *Human capital* refers to career-useful attributes and assets including an individual's education, qualifications, and record of training, development, publications, and work experience (Singh et al., 2009). *Social capital* encompasses both "the different network structures that facilitate (or impede) access to social resources *and* the nature of the social resources embedded in the network" (Seibert et al., 2001b: 221, italics in original).

As shown in Figure 11.1, we will discuss how individual differences prime career enabling behaviors, which in turn lead to objective career success via the accumulation of career capital. Given that career capital can enable work performance and provide access to career development opportunities, we posit a reciprocal relationship between career capital and career-enabling behavior. We supplement the extensive literature of bivariate relationships between individual differences and subjective career outcomes by reviewing evidence that subjective career success may also flow from career-enabling behavior, career capital, and objective career outcomes. We also depict career-facet perceptions as a prime mechanism through which individual differences influence subjective career outcomes.[4]

Career-facet perceptions

Beyond their satisfaction with different facets of their jobs (i.e., the work itself, pay, opportunities for promotion, supervision, and co-workers; Gillet and Schwab, 1975), people also vary in their satisfaction with broader facets of their careers, such as their financial status, learning and development, work-life balance, relationships, positive impact, entrepreneurship (Mayrhofer et al., 2016), and employability (Wille et al., 2013b). Indeed, individual differences shape the facets of people's careers they are most concerned with, that in turn shape how they evaluate their subjective career success. When people have an *enterprising* occupational personality, for instance, the extent to which their job provides scope for them to sell, manage, and persuade is highly salient and determinative of their subjective career success (Holland, 1997). Similarly, given that being extraverted increases concern with social interactions (Costa and McCrae, 1992), extraverts' satisfaction with the volume and quality of their work-related social interactions are liable to figure prominently in how they evaluate their subjective career success. Even though both facet salience and facet evaluations affect the career-facet perceptions that shape subjective career outcomes, most of the studies discussed below deal primarily with career-facet evaluation.

Next we review the literature on how the six most commonly investigated types of individual differences predict objective and subjective career outcomes, both directly and via relevant mediators. For objective career outcomes, these are the career-enabling behavior and the forms of career capital depicted in our conceptual model (see Figure 11.1). For subjective career outcomes, the mediators we discuss are career-facet perceptions. In each section, we generally discuss the nature of the focal individual difference before reviewing the evidence regarding its direct and then mediated prediction of objective career outcomes, followed by direct and indirect relationships with subjective career outcomes.

The Big Five

The Big Five personality traits are perhaps the most widely studied individual difference predictors of career outcomes. *Conscientiousness* entails being organized, persistent, dependable, deliberate, and ordered. *Extraversion* is the tendency to seek stimulation from the company of others and to enjoy being the centre of attention. Extraverted individuals are sociable, optimistic, enthusiastic, assertive, energetic, and highly sensitive to rewards. *Agreeableness* refers to the extent to which people exhibit a trusting, compliant, caring, gentle, and tender-minded approach. *Openness to experience* describes people who are imaginative, nonconforming, unconventional, curious, and enjoy reflecting on things and not having a strict routine. *Neuroticism* is the tendency to experience negative emotions such as anxiety, insecurity, anger, and guilt, to have a low tolerance for stress, and to be inclined to interpret situations as threatening. The inverse of neuroticism is emotional stability, indicated by people being generally calm, even-tempered, relaxed, and resilient in stressful situations (Costa and McCrae, 1992).

Objective career outcomes

People's status on these Big Five personality dimensions predict many important life outcomes, including mortality, divorce, and occupational attainment (Roberts et al., 2007). However, the relationships between the Big Five and salary attainment are weak (Ng and Feldman, 2014a, Ng et al., 2005). Specifically, although salary is predicted negatively by neuroticism, and positively by extraversion and conscientiousness, these personality traits account for only about 1 percent of variance in salary. Next we review the role of the Big Five in the career-enabling behavior of work performance, networking, political tactics, and setting career-advancement goals.

Career enabling behavior

Conscientiousness and emotional stability predict performance more strongly in high- than low-complexity jobs (Le et al., 2011). Li et al. (2014) observed that conscientiousness plays a role in task, contextual, and proactive work performance. Although emotional stability and agreeableness only weakly related to work performance, they had a much stronger influence on reducing the withdrawal behaviours of absenteeism, turnover, and counterproductive work behaviour. Conscientious people are less likely to exhibit these withdrawal behaviors.

The prediction of job performance is increased when the two higher-order and six lower-order facets of each Big Five dimension are also considered (Judge et al., 2013). With regard to conscientiousness, for instance, this approach entails using the higher- and lower-order facets of industriousness (achievement striving, competence, and self-discipline) and orderliness (deliberation, dutifulness, and order) to predict conceptually aligned aspects of job performance.

Networking is important for career success because it creates opportunities and aids in identifying the next career move within or beyond the organization (Bozionelos, 2008). The inclination of extraverted people to initiate social encounters results in networking behavior. Openness is also related to building, maintaining and using external contacts. With regard to internal contacts, agreeableness is similarly associated with these three types of networking (Wolff and Kim, 2012).

Individual differences shape the upward influence tactics that people adopt. For instance, extraverts tend to use inspirational appeals, while conscientiousness primes using the rational persuasion tactic of presenting evidence along with logical arguments. The calm and secure nature of those with high emotional stability manifests in a preference for using rational appeal rather than personal appeal influence tactics. Finally, agreeableness is associated with avoiding potentially coercive tactics like legitimizing and pressure influence tactics (Cable and Judge, 2003).

Conscientiousness and extraversion lead to higher salary via setting career-advancement goals, while a reluctance of highly agreeable individuals to set career-advancement goals helps explain why they earn less than people who are not so agreeable (Spurk and Abele, 2011). Although conceptually intuitive and statistically significant, again the size of these relationships is quite small.

Career capital

Conscientiousness and neuroticism respectively influence salary positively and negatively, via their influence on the occupational self-efficacy facet of human capital (Spurk and Abele, 2011). A meta-analysis of the relationship between personality and a person's position in networks (Fang et al., 2015) found that extraversion is positively related – in contrast to neuroticism and openness which are negatively related – to network size. Being highly conscientious and agreeable predicted network size. Being in brokerage positions, defined by being connected to people or clusters of people who are not connected (alternatively labeled "structural holes"; Burt, 1992), is also a positive function of being high in conscientiousness, extraversion, and openness as well as being low in agreeableness. Finally, network size predicts job performance and objective career outcomes more strongly than brokerage (Fang et al., 2015).

Subjective career outcomes

According to two meta-analyses (Ng et al., 2005; Ng and Feldman, 2014b), neuroticism primes moderately negative evaluations of one's career, though extraversion positively predicts subjective career success to a moderate extent. Conscientiousness, openness to experience, and agreeableness are each more modestly positively related to subjective career outcomes.

The association between personality and job satisfaction is often understood as an affective one (Heller et al., 2002), whereby people may perceive their job more positively as a function of being, for instance, high in extraversion (being optimistic and enthusiastic) and low in neuroticism (being relatively relaxed, resilient, and relatively free of anxiety). Neuroticism also predicts a negative perception of career facets such as employability (Wille et al., 2013b). This dynamic is reflected in the path in Figure 11.1 from the Big Five to subjective career outcomes, via career-facet perceptions. On the other hand, career-enabling traits may also lead to career satisfaction via enabling people to be promoted or otherwise hired into more fulfilling jobs (Woods et al., 2013), as reflected by the vertical line in Figure 11.1 leading from objective career outcomes to subjective career outcomes.

To summarize, the literature has fairly consistently supported the notion that Big Five personality attributes – especially neuroticism and extraversion – are moderately related to subjective career outcomes. We suspect that the relationship between personality and objective outcomes is relatively weak because it is partially mediated by a range of career-enabling behaviors and facets of career capital acquisition (Heslin, Keating, and Minbashian, 2019).

Proactive personality

Especially given trends such as increasing virtual work, self-managed teams, and self-employment, being proactive in one's career may be an important ingredient for career success. Bateman and Crant (1993: 105) conceptualized proactive personality as a relative stable tendency to exhibit proactive behavior aimed at effecting environmental change, illustrated by people who:

> scan for opportunities, show initiative, take action, and persevere until they reach closure by bringing about change. They are pathfinders . . . who change their organization's mission or find and solve problems.

Proactive personality is somewhat predictive of objective career outcomes, though is more strongly related to subjective career outcomes (Fuller and Marler, 2009). Indeed, Maurer and Chapman (2013) found that proactive personality was positively related to job satisfaction, career satisfaction, and promotions, but not pay, beyond the effects of the Big Five, goal orientation, and a host of other socio-demographic and human capital variables.

Career enabling behavior

A longitudinal study (Seibert et al., 2001a) revealed a proactive personality predicts several types of career enabling behavior, which in turn had positive relationships with salary growth, number of promotions, and career satisfaction. These include innovation (e.g., identifying problems or opportunities and generation of novel ideas to address them), political knowledge (e.g., gaining information regarding formal and informal work relationships and power structures within the organization[5]), and career initiatives, such as taking responsibility for one's career, career planning, skill development, and consultation with more senior personnel. Indeed, proactive personality affects work performance both directly and indirectly, via its prediction of all three aspects of work engagement: vigor, dedication, and absorption (Bakker et al., 2012).

A proactive personality leads to having high career self-efficacy, job search self-efficacy, a learning goal orientation, and entrepreneurial cognitions (Fuller and Marler, 2009). Besides mediating between proactive personality and proactive career behavior, these cognitions may also become embedded as forms of human capital that have a bidirectional causal relationship with proactive career behaviors. For instance, high career self-efficacy may prime taking career initiatives, which in turn may further bolster career self-efficacy, as long as those initiatives are successful. Future research might fruitfully explore such reciprocal, causal relationships between career-enabling behaviors and elements of career capital.

Core self-evaluations

Core self-evaluations (CSE) encompass some fundamental evaluations people make about themselves and their environment. They are comprised of self-esteem, generalized self-efficacy, emotional stability, and locus of control. These four traits are so interrelated that they are combined into a single scale (Judge and Bono, 2001). The concept of CSEs was introduced as an integrative framework to explain dispositional influences on job satisfaction (Judge et al., 1997), though it has since been associated with objective career outcomes.

Objective career outcomes

In terms of salary, individuals high in CSEs receive higher pay (Chang et al., 2012; Ng and Feldman, 2014a). Judge and Hurst (2008) found that individuals with high CSEs not only start their careers at significantly higher levels of pay and occupational status, but these markers of success also increase at a faster rate than their counterparts with low CSEs. These effects are partially mediated by education and health, such that people with high CSEs acquire education more rapidly. Education in turn affects growth in pay, occupational status, and job satisfaction. They also have fewer health problems that could interfere with their work and thereby undermine their pay and job satisfaction. CSEs also act as a moderator, such that those with high CSEs are better able to convert their early advantageous life circumstances (i.e., high socioeconomic status and educational attainment) into later financial success (Judge and Hurst, 2007).

The positive impact of CSEs on salary may be a function of how CSEs manifest in various forms of career enabling behaviors, such as greater job search intensity when unemployed (Wanberg et al., 2005) as well as generally more organizational citizenship behavior (OCB; Chang et al., 2012) and career adaptability (Zacher, 2014), with the latter two being mediated by job engagement (Rich et al., 2010).

Subjective career outcomes

CSEs strongly predict job, career, and life satisfaction (Chang et al., 2012; Ng and Feldman, 2014b) as well as growth in job satisfaction (Wu and Griffin, 2012). This can be attributed to the perception of career facets (see Figure 11.1). Individuals with high CSEs focus on the positive aspects of their environments, are more likely to regard their jobs and workplaces as attractive (Chang et al., 2012), and perceive less stressors and strains. CSEs also predict seeking more complex work, which in turn increases perceptions of desired job characteristics that flow through to higher work satisfaction (Srivastava et al., 2010).

People with high CSEs tend be more intrinsically motivated and committed to ambitious goals that they truly value, which fully mediates how CSEs enhance job satisfaction (Chang et al., 2012). Career commitment – defined as a person's motivation to work in a chosen vocation – also partially mediates the effect of CSEs on the job satisfaction (Zhang et al., 2014).

Self-monitoring

High self-monitors are sensitive to situational cues about what actions or self-presentations are appropriate (Snyder, 1974). They pay close attention to others' behavior and behave differently in various situations in order to win others' approval so as to maximize their self-interest – an approach typically rooted in a status enhancement motive (Day and Schleicher, 2006). Low self-monitors tend to show their true attitudes and disposition in most situations. They put more focus on self-validation than a positive image, displaying a high behavioral consistency between what they do and who they are. High self-monitoring predicts advancement but not job satisfaction (Day et al., 2002).

Career enabling behavior

Self-monitoring is positively related to job performance (Day et al., 2002), changing employers, moving locations, and receiving cross-company promotions (Kilduff and Day, 1994). High self-monitors achieve status through their precision at perceiving existing status dynamics and by establishing a reputation as a generous exchange partner (Flynn et al., 2006). They also use more self-promotion (Higgins and Judge, 2004), ingratiation and exemplification[6] (Turnley and Bolino, 2001) and are more likely to initiate promising mentoring relationships (Turban and Dougherty, 1994).

Career capital

High self-monitors are prone to reach favorable network positions. Even after controlling for network size, high self-monitors occupy more brokerage positions over time as they attract new friends who are unconnected with their existing friends (Sasovova et al., 2010). Self-monitoring increases these structural holes and ultimately job performance by having a more diverse network and by increasing leader-member exchange quality (Wang et al., 2015). Building up high-quality exchange relationships with their supervisor provides with actual and reputational advantages.

In contrast to the relatively long-studied individual differences we have reviewed so far, next we consider the bourgeoning literature on the role of the Dark Triad traits in career outcomes.

Dark Triad traits

Paulhus and Williams (2002) coined the term *Dark Triad* to refer to subclinical narcissism and psychopathy, as well as Machiavellianism. These traits reflect a tendency to be callous, selfish, and malevolent in their interpersonal dealings (Paulhus and Williams, 2002). Narcissism refers to a person with a grandiose sense of self-importance and entitlement, together with a lack of empathy and strong desire for admiration. Psychopathy is the tendency to lack concern for other people and social conventions, impulsivity, a desire for immediate gratification of needs, risk-taking, and a lack of guilt or remorse when actions cause harm to other people. Individuals with high levels of Machiavellianism are manipulative, pragmatic, emotionally distant, focus exclusively on their own goals, and inclined to believe that personally desired ends can justify ruthless means.

Objective career outcomes

Evidence concerning the relationship between narcissism and objective success indicators such as position and salary is inconsistent, showing either a positive (Spurk et al., 2016) or no direct relationship (Wille et al., 2013a). Similarly, some find that psychopathy predicts management level and number of subordinates (Wille et al., 2013a), while others (Spurk et al., 2016) question the often-stated overrepresentation of psychopathy in higher hierarchical echelons (Smith and Lilienfeld, 2013). Few studies investigated the effect of Machiavellianism; however, one study found it to be positively related to leadership position (Spurk et al., 2016).

Career enabling behavior

The Dark Triad traits are positively related to counterproductive work behavior, with narcissism having the strongest impact followed by Machiavellianism and psychopathy (O'Boyle et al., 2012). A subsequent meta-analysis Grijalva and Newman (2015) reported a more modest correlation between narcissism and counterproductive work behavior. Psychopathy also predicts bullying and unfair supervision (Boddy, 2011). The Dark Triad traits have only minor and mostly negative relationships with job performance. Individuals high in psychopathy, as well as those with strong Machiavellian tendencies, have lower performance levels, whereas narcissism is unrelated to job performance (O'Boyle et al., 2012).

Concerning influence tactics, Jonason et al. (2012) found that psychopathy predicted using hard tactics such as threats and direct manipulations, while narcissism is related to using soft tactics like ingratiation and favor exchange. Machiavellianism even more strongly predicts using both soft and hard influence tactics.

The most researched Dark Triad trait is narcissism. Narcissists are effective at creating positive first impressions. When applying for a job, their employability is increased by their self-promotion and talkativeness (Paulhus et al., 2013). The positive relationship of narcissism with leadership emergence decreases with the length of acquaintance, such that the better they are known, the less narcissists are perceived as leader-like and the more they are seen as hostile and arrogant. Indeed the effect of narcissism on leadership emergence disappears entirely when extraversion is held constant. This implies that the positive effect of narcissism on leadership emergence is largely explained by narcissists' extraversion (Grijalva et al., 2015).

Narcissism is unsurprisingly positively related to self-reported leadership effectiveness ratings, but not to supervisor or peer-reported effectiveness. Leaders with moderate levels of narcissism are rated by others as more effective than those with particularly high or low levels (Grijalva et al., 2015). Organizations with narcissistic CEOs tend to perform in an extreme and fluctuating way (Chatterjee and Hambrick, 2007), as these CEOs take actions that grab attention and have strong positive or negative consequences (Gerstner et al., 2013).

Subjective career outcomes

Individuals high in psychopathy generally report lower levels of job and career satisfaction. Machiavellianism is negatively related to job satisfaction but unrelated to career satisfaction (Bruk-Lee et al., 2009; Spurk et al., 2016). There is no direct effect of narcissism on job satisfaction (Bruk-Lee et al., 2009) and career satisfaction (Spurk et al., 2016), though narcissism does enhance career satisfaction by increasing self-efficacy and career engagement (Hirschi and Jaensch, 2015).

Career-facet perceptions

Dark Triad traits seem to affect job satisfaction via career-facet perceptions. For instance, narcissists imagine themselves as having or deserving high status so are prone to perceive themselves as underemployed, even when objectively they are not, and thus experience job dissatisfaction (Maynard et al., 2015). The yearning of individuals high in Machiavellianism for greater personal influence could account for them reporting low levels of job satisfaction and high levels of work-related stress (Dahling et al., 2009). This may be because they are under self-imposed pressure to augment their impressions at work and distrust their coworkers, which is likely to undermine the quality of their workplace relationships and their relational learning opportunities.

The Dark Triad also guide perceptions of work climate. Specifically, individuals high in psychopathy perceive their workplaces as competitive and not prestigious. Narcissists see their jobs as prestigious. Individuals high in Machiavellianism see their jobs as competitive. In turn, job satisfaction generally decreases to the extent that a workplace is perceived as competitive, whereas it increases with perceived prestige of their job and organization. The interaction of narcissism and perceptions of workplace prestige positively predict job satisfaction (Jonason et al., 2015).

General mental ability

General mental ability (GMA) is a highly general information-processing capacity that facilitates reasoning, problem solving, decision-making, and other higher-order thinking skills. Based on an extensive review of the literature, 52 prominent social science researchers concluded that GMA is "strongly related, probably more so than any other single measurable human trait, to many important educational, occupational, economic, and social outcomes" (Gottfredson, 1997: 14). A steady flow of studies has shown that GMA is a robust predictor of both objective career outcomes, and to a lesser extent, subjective career outcomes. GMA measured at around 12 years of age predicts these outcomes up to 50 years later (Judge et al., 1999).

Career enabling behavior and career capital

Regarding the GMA-work performance linkage in Figure 11.1, Schmidt and Hunter (2004) theorized and provided evidence that high GMA enables people to perform better as a function of high job knowledge, resulting from a capacity to learn more and faster than those with lower GMA. Byington and Felps (2010) offer the alternative explanation that social stratification and self-fulfilling dynamics enable individuals with high GMA to gain greater access to developmental resources, enabling them to acquire additional human capital over time and ultimately perform their jobs better than those with lower GMA (Byington and Felps, 2010).

The income and occupational prestige of individuals with high GMA ascends more steeply over time than those of low GMA (Judge et al., 2010): Intelligent people spend more years engaged in formal education, complete more job training, and gravitate towards more complex jobs. Additional education and perceived job complexity are in turn much more likely to translate into objective career success for those who are higher in intelligence (Judge et al., 2010). High performance and salary particularly result from the combination of high GMA and high social skills, though objective careers are eroded by being richly endowed with one of these attributes though lacking in the other (Ferris et al., 2001).

Subjective career success

The gravitational hypothesis (Wilk et al., 1995) assumes that over the course of their career, people sort themselves into jobs that are broadly compatible with their intellectual abilities,[7] such that highly intelligent people move into jobs that require more cognitive ability and those with lower GMA move into jobs that require less cognitive ability. Consequently, variability in GMA is less among highly experienced job role incumbents than among less experienced incumbents (Wilk et al., 1995).

In a study examining the implications of the gravitational hypothesis for subjective career outcomes, Ganzach (1998) observed a small negative direct relationship between intelligence and job satisfaction, yet a much larger and positive, indirect relationship between GMA and job satisfaction, via perceived job complexity. Highly intelligent people tend to have more complex jobs. This is fortunate given that adequate job complexity plays a particularly important role in their job satisfaction. This means that GMA is positively, albeit indirectly associated with job satisfaction because more intelligent people tend to get better, more interesting, and challenging jobs. Given their desire for intellectual stimulation, people with high GMA tend to be particularly dissatisfied by roles with low complexity.

Discussion

Given that the career success literature has continued to focus on the often most readily accessible, traditional indicators of objective (i.e., pay and promotions) and subjective (i.e., job satisfaction and career satisfaction) career outcomes, our review of this literature has also done so. In light of space limitations, we focused on a selection of studies conducted mostly over the last decade and pertaining to the relationships depicted in our conceptual model (Figure 11.1). Next we briefly summarize our findings and offer some comments on what may be inferred from them, before making a few suggestions regarding directions for future research.

Predicting objective career outcomes

Salary attainment and advancement are only weakly predicted by extraversion, conscientiousness, neuroticism, proactive personality, and self-monitoring. As depicted in Figure 11.1, most of these small direct relationships are mediated by career-enabling behavior and resulting career capital in ways we have discussed, as is the moderate relationship between high core self-evaluations and pay. The relationships between the Dark Triad traits and objective outcomes are generally inconsistent and mostly weak, probably owing to how they prime counterproductive work behavior that diminishes work and organizational performance, as well as the fact that moderate rather than high levels of Dark Triad traits are optimal for effective leadership.

GMA is the strongest predictor of pay and promotions, probably as a function of the capacity of those with high GMA to learn more and faster, as well as their tendency to spend greater time engaged in formal education, completing more job training, and gravitating towards more complex and highly paid jobs. The objective career yields from high GMA are increased by having high social skill, and undermined by not being socially skilled.

Predicting subjective career outcomes

Subjective career success is moderately undermined by neuroticism, though positively and more modestly associated with extraversion and proactive personality, and weakly, positively predicted by conscientiousness, openness to experience, agreeableness, and the Dark Triad traits. CSEs strongly predict subjective career success, probably as a function of CSEs leading people to engage in the career-enabling behavior of seeking out more challenging roles they enjoy and setting challenging goals that they are committed to attaining, as well as having of intrinsic motivation to perform their work roles and being prone to positively evaluate their career and life experiences. The moderate relationship between GMA and subjective career outcomes is increased when those with high GMA secure the more complex jobs that they find most satisfying. What are some implications for those engaged in their career?

Doomed to mediocrity?

Are the careers of those with low(er) levels of the career facilitating individual differences we have discussed doomed to be "losers . . . in the game of career success," as implied by the Neo-Darwinian perspective on careers (Nicholson and de Waal-Andrews, 2005: 37)? There are three reasons why typically career enabling dispositions are not necessarily critical for desirable career outcomes.

First is the typically small to moderate variance in career outcomes explained by individual differences. The remaining variance may be accounted for by contextual factors including social demographics, sponsorship, and serendipity, as well as *individual dynamics* such as personality change across the lifespan (Roberts et al., 2006) and/or people being socialized, mentored, educated, or otherwise inspired to act and perceive their careers in ways that differ from the prototypical behavioral and perceptual tendencies associated with how they completed a personality trait assessment questionnaire at an earlier point in time (Heslin et al., 2019).

Second, as statisticians like to remind us, averages tell you nothing about the dynamics of particular instances. For instance, being high in GMA and conscientiousness, as well as career capital (i.e., high educational level), does not necessarily result in higher objective or subjective career outcomes (cf. many scholars) relative to other people with lower levels of these generally career enabling attributes. Thus, although the individual differences we have discussed *generally* enable or impede desirable career outcomes across particular sample populations to a weak to moderate extent, they are far from determinative of any *particular* individual's career outcomes. This illustrates the idiosyncratic nature of career success. A career self-management implication is to follow Shakespeare's dictum in *As You Like It* (Act III, Scene v): "Sell when you can, you are not for all markets."

Third, most career success studies have been conducted on relatively homogenous samples of university students or alumni, a small minority of the working population in most societies. This is an issue because, for instance, GMA is much more predictive of performance on highly complex jobs than on less complex jobs (Schmidt and Hunter, 2004). Thus, the relationships between individual differences and career outcomes reported in the primary and meta-analytic studies reviewed here may not necessarily generalize to those performing the roughly 65 percent of work roles (Carnevale et al., 2013) that do not require a university education and have been substantially under-represented in the career success literature.

Future research directions

Future career success research focused on samples beyond managers, professionals, and other "WEIRD" (*W*estern, *e*ducated, *i*ndustrialized, *r*ich, and *d*emocratic countries; Mayrhofer et al.,

2016: 197) career contexts is needed to examine the generalizability of the results reported here, as well as begin to illuminate more contextually contingent intra-individual determinants of career outcomes. In light of the weak empirical relationships typically observed between objective and subjective career outcomes (Judge et al., 2010; Ng et al., 2005), numerous scholars (e.g., Arthur et al., 2005; Heslin, 2005a; Nicholson and de Waal-Andrews, 2005) have theorized about when objective career outcomes will be experienced as subjective success. We suggest that research may fruitfully examine the role of individual differences in moderating the relation-ship between objective and subjective career outcomes (a possibility beyond the relationships depicted in Figure 11.1), such as the extent to which neuroticism diminishes the extent to which objective attainments are subjectively experienced as career success. The role in these dynamics of individuals' being *in learning mode* (Heslin & Keating, 2017), as a partial function of the mindset cues in their career context (Heslin et al., 2019), is another promising area for future research.

Given the substantial accumulation of research on the generally modest role of the Big Five in work performance and objective career outcomes, we see little value in further research on bivariate relationships in this regard. On the other hand, the alternative approach of follow-ing the advice of Judge et al. (2013) to assess the 30 facets of the Big Five (Costa and McCrae, 1992), or at least the 10 facets using the scale developed by DeYoung et al. (2007), might enable fruitful lines of research regarding the role of personality in career outcomes within particular combinations of work roles, career stages, industries, national cultures, and other career contexts. Research may also usefully examine which individual differences, career initiatives, and types of human capital are most predictive of relevant objective (e.g., tenure and level of sustained income) and subjective outcomes (e.g., meaningfulness and low stress) of a career enacted in the particular segments of the burgeoning *gig economy* (i.e., a labour market characterized by the prevalence of short-term contracts or freelance work, such as that performed by *Uber* drivers). Such conceptually bounded research may enable substantial advances in understanding when, where, and how, and why some people thrive more than others in particular career contexts.

Beyond such contextually targeted studies, another potentially promising line of research is with regard to how career experiences and interventions influence personality trait activa-tion (Tett and Burnett, 2003) and development (Roberts et al., 2006). What career develop-ment interventions, such as training or guidance in job crafting (Tims et al., 2013), mindfulness (Hülsheger et al., 2013), or being *in learning mode* (Heslin and Keating, 2017), most foster the enactment or even cultivation of career enabling individual differences? We strongly encourage research aimed at discovering and rigorously testing fresh avenues for predicting and ultimately enabling positive sustainable career outcomes (i.e., happiness, health, and productivity) across the career lifespan (Heslin, Keating, and Ashford, in press).

Another avenue is to investigate boundary conditions on the utility of generally career-enabling individual differences. Given that proactivity involves challenging the status quo and bringing about change that may be seen as *rocking the boat*, for instance, being highly proactive will not necessarily lead to positive career outcomes if doing so leads people into a problematic level of misalignment and conflict with their superiors, colleagues, or other career stakeholders. Parker and Liao (2016) thus proposed that *wise proactivity* involves proactive changes that consider the interests of the broader organizational system (contextually sound) and those of other people affected by them (other-focused), as well as reflecting one's career agenda. Research is needed to empirically investigate this promising potential boundary condition on the positive direct and indirect impacts of a proactive personality and subsequent proactive behaviors on career outcomes depicted in Figure 11.1. Research is more generally needed on the career utility of various levels of individual differences. As has been shown for narcissism (Grijalva et al., 2015), such research might fruitfully explore curvilinear relationships between other individual differences and career outcomes – ideally in particular, contextually circumscribed career contexts.

Conclusion

Judge and Kammeyer-Mueller (2007: 74) concluded their chapter on personality and career success by noting that "there is a need to investigate factors that explain the relatively modest and apparently inconsistent results." We conclude that a decade later, this need remains and we hope that our conceptual model and discussion of avenues for more psychometrically nuanced and contextually-focused future research serve as a heuristically useful guide for conducting such investigations.

Notes

1 We do not discuss agentic and communal orientations (Judge and Kammeyer-Mueller (2007), or other potentially relevant individual difference predictors of career outcomes such as protean (Briscoe and Hall, 2006) and boundaryless (Sullivan and Arthur, 2006) career orientation, owing to the relatively few studies that have empirically investigated them over the last decade.
2 For an updated review of such factors, see Chapters 12 and 17 in this volume.
3 A notable exception is Ng et al.'s (2005) observation that GMA was more predictive of objective career success than the personality dimensions they examined. There was insufficient data, however, for them to report on the prediction of subjective career success by GMA.
4 Cf. Heslin et al. (in press), for theorizing about alternative cognitive and affective mediating mechanisms that are beyond the scope of this chapter.
5 For a discussion on careers as sites of power, see Schneidhofer et al. (2015).
6 That is, going above and beyond the call of duty to appear dedicated, like staying late at work or appearing busy.
7 The gravitational hypothesis also addresses compatibility in terms of interests and values, though these dimensions are beyond the scope of the present discussion.

References

Arthur, M.B., Khapova, S.N. & Wilderom, C.P.M. 2005. Career success in a boundaryless career world. *Journal of Organizational Behavior*, 26, 177–202.

Bakker, A.B., Tims, M. & Derks, D. 2012. Proactive personality and job performance: The role of job crafting and work engagement. *Human Relations*, 65, 1359–1378.

Ballout, H.I. 2007. Career success: The effects of human capital, person-environment fit and organizational support. *Journal of Managerial Psychology*, 22, 741–765.

Bateman, T.S. & Crant, J.M. 1993. The proactive component of organizational behavior: A measure and correlates. *Journal of Organizational Behavior*, 14, 103–118.

Boddy, C.R. 2011. The corporate psychopaths theory of the global financial crisis. *Journal of Business Ethics*, 102, 255–259.

Bozionelos, N. 2008. Intra-organizational network resources: How they relate to career success and organizational commitment. *Personnel Review*, 37, 249–263.

Briscoe, J.P. & Hall, D.T. 2006. The interplay of boundaryless and protean careers: Combinations and implications. *Journal of Vocational Behavior*, 69, 4–18.

Bruk-Lee, V., Khoury, H.A., Nixon, A.E., Goh, A. & Spector, P.E. 2009. Replicating and extending past personality/job satisfaction meta-analyses. *Human Performance*, 22, 156–189.

Burt, R.S. 1992. *Structural Holes: The Social Structure of Competition*. Cambridge, MA: Harvard University Press.

Byington, E. & Felps, W. 2010. Why do IQ scores predict job performance? An alternative, sociological explanation. *Research in Organizational Behavior*, 30, 175–202.

Cable, D.M. & Judge, T.A. 2003. Managers' upward influence tactic strategies: The role of manager personality and supervisor leadership style. *Journal of Organizational Behavior*, 24, 197–214.

Carnevale, A.P., Smith, N. & Strohl, J. 2013. *Recovery: Job Growth and Education Requirements Through 2020*. www.cew.georgetown.edu/recovery2020 [Online]. Georgetown Public Policy Institute. [Accessed 27 July 2017].

Chang, C-H., Ferris, D.L., Johnson, R.E., Rosen, C.C. & Tan, J.A. 2012. Core self-evaluations: A review and evaluation of the literature. *Journal of Management*, 38, 81–128.

Chatterjee, A. & Hambrick, D.C. 2007. It's all about me: Narcissistic chief executive officers and their effects on company strategy and performance. *Administrative Science Quarterly*, 52, 351–386.

Costa, P. & Mccrae, R. 1992. *Professional Manual for the NEO PI-R and NEO-Ffi*. Odessa, FL: Psychological Assessment Resources.

Dahling, J.J., Whitaker, B.G. & Levy, P.E. 2009. The development and validation of a new Machiavellianism scale. *Journal of Management*, 35, 219–257.

Day, D.V. & Schleicher, D.J. 2006. Self-monitoring at work: A motive-based perspective. *Journal of Personality*, 74, 685–714.

Day, D.V., Shleicher, D.J., Unckless, A.L. & Hiller, N.J. 2002. Self-monitoring personality at work: A meta-analytic investigation of construct validity. *Journal of Applied Psychology*, 87, 390–401.

Deyoung, C.G., Quilty, L.C. & Peterson, J.B. 2007. Between facets and domains: 10 aspects of the Big Five. *Journal of Personality and Social Psychology*, 93, 880–896.

Fang, R.L., Landis, B., Zhang, Z., Anderson, M.H., Shaw, J.D. & Kilduff, M. 2015. Integrating personality and social networks: A meta-analysis of personality, network position, and work outcomes in organizations. *Organization Science*, 26, 1243–1260.

Ferris, G.R., Witt, L.A. & Hochwarter, W.A. 2001. Interaction of social skill and general mental ability on job performance and salary. *Journal of Applied Psychology*, 86, 1075–1082.

Flynn, F.J., Reagans, R.E., Amanatullah, E.T. & Ames, D.R. 2006. Helping one's way to the top: Self-monitors achieve status by helping others and knowing who helps whom. *Journal of Personality and Social Psychology*, 91, 1123–1137.

Fuller, B., Jr. & Marler, L.E. 2009. Change driven by nature: A meta-analytic review of the proactive personality literature. *Journal of Vocational Behavior*, 75, 329–345.

Ganzach, Y. 1998. Intelligence and job satisfaction. *Academy of Management Journal*, 41, 526–539.

Gerstner, W-C., König, A., Enders, A. & Hambrick, D.C. 2013. CEO narcissism, audience engagement, and organizational adoption of technological discontinuities. *Administrative Science Quarterly*, 58, 257–291.

Gillet, B. & Schwab, D.P. 1975. Convergent and discriminant validities of corresponding job descriptive index and Minnesota satisfaction questionnaire scales. *Journal of Applied Psychology*, 60, 313–317.

Gottfredson, L.S. 1997. Mainstream science on intelligence: An editorial with 52 signatories, history, and bibliography. *Intelligence*, 24, 13–23.

Greenhaus, J.H., Parasuraman, S. & Wormley, W.M. 1990. Effects of race on organizational experiences, job performance evaluations, and career outcomes. *Academy of Management Journal*, 33, 64–86.

Grijalva, E., Harms, P.D., Newman, D.A., Gaddis, B.H. & Fraley, R.C. 2015. Narcissism and leadership: A meta-analytic review of linear and nonlinear relationships. *Personnel Psychology*, 68, 1–47.

Grijalva, E. & Newman, D.A. 2015. Narcissism and counterproductive work behavior (CWB): Meta-analysis and consideration of collectivist culture, Big Five personality, and narcissism's facet structure. *Applied Psychology: An International Review*, 64, 93–126.

Gunz, H. & Mayrhofer, W. 2018. *Rethinking Career Studies: Facilitating Conversation Across Boundaries with the Social Chronology Framework*. Cambridge, UK: Cambridge University Press.

Heller, D., Judge, T.A. & Watson, D. 2002. The confounding role of personality and trait affectivity in the relationship between job and life satisfaction. *Journal of Organizational Behavior*, 23, 815–835.

Heslin, P.A. 2003. Self- and other-referent criteria of career success. *Journal of Career Assessment*, 11, 262–286.

Heslin, P.A. 2005a. Experiencing career success. *Organizational Dynamics*, 34, 376–390.

Heslin, P.A. 2005b. Conceptualizing and evaluating career success. *Journal of Organizational Behavior*, 26, 113–136.

Heslin, P.A. 2010. 18 Mindsets and employee engagement: Theoretical linkages and practical interventions. *In:* Albrecht, S. (ed.) *Handbook of Employee Engagement: Perspectives, Issues, Research and Practice.* Cheltenham, UK: Edwin Elgar.

Heslin, P.A. & Keating, L.A. 2017. In learning mode? The role of mindsets in derailing and enabling experiential leadership development. *The Leadership Quarterly,* 28, 367–384.

Heslin, P. A., Keating, L. A., & Ashford, S. J. (in press, 2019). How being in learning mode may enable a sustainable career. *Journal of Vocational Behavior.* https://doi.org/10.1016/j.jvb.2019.103324

Heslin, P.A., Keating, L.A. & Minbashian, A. 2019. How situational cues and mindset dynamics shape personality effects on career outcomes. *Journal of Management,* 45, 2101–2131

Heslin, P.A. & Turban, D.B. 2016. Enabling career success as an emergent process. *Organizational Dynamics,* 45, 155–164.

Higgins, C.A. & Judge, T.A. 2004. The effect of applicant influence tactics on recruiter perceptions of fit and hiring recommendations: A field study. *Journal of Applied Psychology,* 89, 622–632.

Hirschi, A. & Jaensch, V.K. 2015. Narcissism and career success: Occupational self-efficacy and career engagement as mediators. *Personality and Individual Differences,* 77, 205–208.

Holland, J.L. 1997. *Making Vocational Choices: A Theory of Vocational Personalities and Work Environments.* Odessa, FL: Psychological Assessment Resources.

Hughes, E.C. 1937. Institutional office and the person. *American Journal of Sociology,* 43, 404–413.

Hülsheger, U.R., Alberts, H.J., Feinholdt, A. & Lang, J.W. 2013. Benefits of mindfulness at work: The role of mindfulness in emotion regulation, emotional exhaustion, and job satisfaction. *Journal of Applied Psychology,* 98, 310–325.

Jonason, P.K., Slomski, S. & Partyka, J. 2012. The Dark Triad at work: How toxic employees get their way. *Personality and Individual Differences,* 52, 449–453.

Jonason, P.K., Wee, S. & Li, N.P. 2015. Competition, autonomy, and prestige: Mechanisms through which the Dark Triad predict job satisfaction. *Personality and Individual Differences,* 72, 112–116.

Judge, T.A. & Bono, J.E. 2001. Relationship of core self-evaluations traits-self-esteem, generalized self-efficacy, locus of control, and emotional stability-with job satisfaction and job performance: A meta-analysis. *Journal of Applied Psychology,* 86, 80–92.

Judge, T.A., Cable, D.M., Boudreau, J.W. & Bretz, R.D. 1995. An empirical investigation of the predictors of executive career success. *Personnel Psychology,* 48, 485–519.

Judge, T.A., Higgins, C.A., Thoresen, C.J. & Barrick, M.R. 1999. The Big Five personality traits, general mental ability, and career success across the life span. *Personnel Psychology,* 52, 621–625.

Judge, T.A. & Hurst, C. 2007. Capitalizing on one's advantages: Role of core self-evaluations. *Journal of Applied Psychology,* 92, 1212–1227.

Judge, T.A. & Hurst, C. 2008. How the rich (and happy) get richer (and happier): Relationship of core self-evaluations to trajectories in attaining work success. *Journal of Applied Psychology,* 93, 849–863.

Judge, T.A. & Kammeyer-Mueller, J.D. 2007. Personality and career success. *In:* Gunz, H.P. & Peiperl, M. (eds.) *Handbook of Career Studies.* Thousand Oaks: Sage Publications.

Judge, T.A., Klinger, R.L. & Simon, L.S. 2010. Time is on my side: Time, general mental ability, human capital, and extrinsic career success. *Journal of Applied Psychology,* 95, 92–107.

Judge, T.A., Locke, E.A. & Durham, C.C. 1997. The dispositional causes of job satisfaction: A core evaluations approach. *Research in Organizational Behavior,* 19, 151–188.

Judge, T.A., Rodell, J.B., Klinger, R.L., Simon, L.S. & Crawford, E.R. 2013. Hierarchical representations of the five-factor model of personality in predicting job performance: Integrating three organizing frameworks with two theoretical perspectives. *Journal of Applied Psychology,* 98, 875–925.

Kenny, A. 2011. *The Eudemian Ethics.* Oxford, UK: Oxford University Press.

Kilduff, M. & Day, D.V. 1994. Do chameleons get ahead? The effects of self-monitoring on managerial careers. *Academy of Management Journal,* 37, 1047–1060.

Latzke, M., Schneidhofer, T., Pernkopf, K., Rohr, C. & Mayrhofer, W. 2015. Relational career capital: Towards a sustainable perspective. *In:* de Vos, A. & van der Heijden, B.I.J.M. (eds.) *Handbook of Research on Sustainable Careers.* Cheltenham, UK: Edward Elgar.

Le, H., Oh, I-S., Robbins, S.B., Ilies, R., Holland, E. & Westrick, P. 2011. Too much of a good thing: Curvilinear relationships between personality traits and job performance. *Journal of Applied Psychology*, 96, 113–133.

Li, N., Barrick, M.R., Zimmerman, R.D. & Chiaburu, D.S. 2014. Retaining the productive employee: The role of personality. *The Academy of Management Annals*, 8, 347–395.

Maurer, T.J. & Chapman, E.F. 2013. Ten years of career success in relation to individual and situational variables from the employee development literature. *Journal of Vocational Behavior*, 83, 450–465.

Maynard, D.C., Brondolo, E.M., Connelly, C.E. & Sauer, C.E. 2015. I'm too good for this job: Narcissism's role in the experience of overqualification. *Applied Psychology*, 64, 208–232.

Mayrhofer, W., Briscoe, J.P., Hall, D.T., Dickmann, M., Dries, N., Dysvik, A., Kase, R., Parry, E. & Unite, J. 2016. Career success across the globe: Insights from the 5C project. *Organizational Dynamics*, 45, 197–205.

Ng, T.W.H. & Feldman, D.C. 2014a. A conservation of resources perspective on career hurdles and salary attainment. *Journal of Vocational Behavior*, 85, 156–168.

Ng, T.W.H. & Feldman, D.C. 2014b. Subjective career success: A meta-analytic review. *Journal of Vocational Behavior*, 85, 169–179.

Ng, T.W.H., Eby, L.T., Sorensen, K.L. & Feldman, D.C. 2005. Predictors of objective and subjective career success: A meta-analysis. *Personnel Psychology*, 58, 367–408.

Nicholson, N. & de Waal-Andrews, W. 2005. Playing to win: Biological imperatives, self-regulation, and trade-offs in the game of career success. *Journal of Organizational behavior*, 26, 137–154.

O'Boyle, E.H., Forsyth, D.R., Banks, G.C. & Mcdaniel, M.A. 2012. A meta-analysis of the Dark Triad and work behavior: A social exchange perspective. *Journal of Applied Psychology*, 97, 557579.

Parker, S.K. & Liao, J. 2016. Wise proactivity: How to be proactive and wise in building your career. *Organizational Dynamics*, 45, 217–227.

Paulhus, D.L., Westlake, B.G., Calvez, S.S. & Harms, P.D. 2013. Self-presentation style in job interviews: The role of personality and culture. *Journal of Applied Social Psychology*, 43, 2042–2059.

Paulhus, D.L. & Williams, K.M. 2002. The dark triad of personality: Narcissism, machiavellianism, and psychopathy. *Journal of Research in Personality*, 36, 556–563.

Rich, B.L., Lepine, J.A. & Crawford, E.R. 2010. Job engagement: Antecedents and effects on job performance. *Academy of Management Journal*, 53, 617–635.

Roberts, B.W., Kuncel, N.R., Shiner, R., Caspi, A. & Goldberg, L.R. 2007. The power of personality: The comparative validity of personality traits, socioeconomic status, and cognitive ability for predicting important life outcomes. *Perspectives on Psychological Science*, 2, 313–345.

Roberts, B.W., Walton, K.E. & Viechtbauer, W. 2006. Patterns of mean-level change in personality traits across the life course: A meta-analysis of longitudinal studies. *Psychological Bulletin*, 132, 1–25.

Sasovova, Z., Mehra, A., Borgatti, S.P. & Schippers, M.C. 2010. Network churn: The effects of self-monitoring personality on brokerage dynamics. *Administrative Science Quarterly*, 55, 639–670.

Schmidt, F.L. & Hunter, J. 2004. General mental ability in the world of work: Occupational attainment and job performance. *Journal of Personality and Social Psychology*, 86, 162–173.

Schneidhofer, T.M., Latzke, M. & Mayrhofer, W. 2015. Careers as sites of power: A relational understanding of careers based on Bourdieu's cornerstones. *In:* Tatli, A., Özbilgin, M. & Karatas-Özkan, M. (eds.) *Pierre Bourdieu, Organization, and Management.* New York and London: Routledge.

Seibert, S.E., Crant, J.M. & Kraimer, M.L. 1999. Proactive personality and career success. *Journal of Applied Psychology*, 84, 416–427.

Seibert, S.E., Kraimer, M.L. & Crant, J.M. 2001a. What do proactive people do? A longitudinal model linking proactive personality and career success. *Personnel Psychology*, 54, 845–874.

Seibert, S.E., Kraimer, M.L. & Liden, R.C. 2001b. A social capital theory of career success. *Academy of Management Journal*, 44, 219–237.

Shakespeare, W. *As You Like It* [Online]. Available: http://www.shakespeare-online.com/plays/? [Accessed 24 September 2018].

Singh, R., Ragins, B.R. & Tharenou, P. 2009. What matters most? The relative role of mentoring and career capital in career success. *Journal of Vocational Behavior*, 75, 56–67.

Smith, S.F. & Lilienfeld, S.O. 2013. Psychopathy in the workplace: The knowns and unknowns. *Aggression and Violent Behavior*, 18, 204–218.

Snyder, M. 1974. Self-monitoring of expressive behavior. *Journal of Personality and Social Psychology*, 30, 526–537.

Spurk, D. & Abele, A.E. 2011. Who earns more and why? A multiple mediation model from personality to salary. *Journal of Business and Psychology*, 26, 87–103.

Spurk, D., Keller, A.C. & Hirschi, A. 2016. Do bad guys get ahead or fall behind? Relationships of the dark triad of personality with objective and subjective career success. *Social Psychological and Personality Science*, 7, 113–121.

Srivastava, A., Locke, E.A., Judge, T.A. & Adams, J.W. 2010. Core self-evaluations as causes of satisfaction: The mediating role of seeking task complexity. *Journal of Vocational Behavior*, 77, 255–265.

Sullivan, S.E. & Arthur, M.B. 2006. The evolution of the boundaryless career concept: Examining physical and psychological mobility. *Journal of Vocational Behavior*, 69, 19–29.

Tett, R.P. & Burnett, D.D. 2003. A personality trait-based interactionist model of job performance. *Journal of Applied Psychology*, 88, 500–517.

Tims, M., Bakker, A.B. & Derks, D. 2013. The impact of job crafting on job demands, job resources, and well-being. *Journal of Occupational Health Psychology*, 18, 230–240.

Turban, D.B. & Dougherty, T.W. 1994. Role of protégé personality in receipt of mentoring and career success. *Academy of Management Journal*, 37, 688–702.

Turnley, W.H. & Bolino, M.C. 2001. Achieving desired images while avoiding undesired images: Exploring the role of self-monitoring in impression management. *Journal of Applied Psychology*, 86, 351–360.

Wanberg, C.R., Glomb, T.M., Song, Z. & Sorenson, S. 2005. Job-search persistence during unemployment: A 10-wave longitudinal study. *Journal of Applied Psychology*, 90, 411–430.

Wang, S., Hu, Q. & Dong, B. 2015. Managing personal networks: An examination of how high self-monitors achieve better job performance. *Journal of Vocational Behavior*, 91, 180–188.

Wilk, S.L., Desmarais, L.B. & Sackett, P.R. 1995. Gravitation to jobs commensurate with ability: Longitudinal and cross-sectional tests. *Journal of Applied Psychology*, 80, 79–85.

Wille, B., de Fruyt, F. & de Clercq, B. 2013a. Expanding and reconceptualizing aberrant personality at work: Validity of five-factor model aberrant personality tendencies to predict career outcomes. *Personnel Psychology*, 66, 173–223.

Wille, B., de Fruyt, F. & Feys, M. 2013b. Big Five traits and intrinsic success in the new career era: A 15-year longitudinal study on employability and work – family conflict. *Applied Psychology*, 62, 124–156.

Wolff, H-G. & Kim, S. 2012. The relationship between networking behaviors and the big five personality dimensions. *Career Development International*, 17, 43–66.

Woods, S.A., Lievens, F., de Fruyt, F. & Wille, B. 2013. Personality across working life: The longitudinal and reciprocal influences of personality on work. *Journal of Organizational Behavior*, 34, 7–25.

Wu, C-H. & Griffin, M.A. 2012. Longitudinal relationships between core self-evaluations and job satisfaction. *Journal of Applied Psychology*, 97, 331–342.

Zacher, H. 2014. Individual difference predictors of change in career adaptability over time. *Journal of Vocational Behavior*, 84, 188–198.

Zhang, J., Wu, Q., Miao, D., Yan, X. & Peng, J. 2014. The impact of core self-evaluations on job satisfaction: The mediator role of career commitment. *Social Indicators Research*, 116, 809–822.

12

External factors shaping careers

Tracy Anderson, Matthew Bidwell, and Forrest Briscoe

Although people make choices about their careers, those choices are greatly shaped and constrained by the prevailing social structure – that is, the social, organizational, and institutional factors surrounding the individual. Such factors limit the set of career opportunities that individual workers have to choose from, and they also influence workers' perceptions about which choices are most appealing.

This chapter reviews recent research on the nature and operation of these "external" factors shaping careers, building upon earlier reviews that considered contextual factors in career research (Mayrhofer et al., 2007; see also Chapter 17, this volume). In doing this review, our goal is to outline and organize the many diverse external influences shaping careers, highlighting similarities and differences in these influences, and suggesting a framework for organizing and cumulating research in this broad domain. Research on external factors shaping careers takes place in several disciplines, including economics, industrial relations, management, psychology, and sociology. This disciplinary breadth ensures a rich set of theories, constructs, and mechanisms in use to describe external factors shaping careers – but at the same time, this diversity can also impede sharing and progression of research. Within this context, we hope that our review can help cross-fertilize research among the different perspectives present in this heterogeneous field of scholarship, and even serve as a springboard for future work in the area.

Because careers research is so multidisciplinary, and careers are themselves so ubiquitous, one finds a wide variety of terms and meanings being used in this area of research. Hence to bring a measure of simplicity and clarity to our review, we have tried to use the following common nomenclature. First off, we define a career as a sequence of work experiences (Wilensky, 1961; Arthur et al., 1989), with each work experience involving a *position* situated in a particular *setting*. A *position* involves a set of formal job responsibilities and informal role expectations, often including expectations about work relationships. The *setting* for a given position features the organization in which the position is located (including a specific unit in that organization), as well as the larger context – industry, sector, field, and/or society – within which that organization is embedded. In addition, because each position is associated with particular material and social rewards for the worker who occupies it, the sequence of positions that makes up a career is an important determinant of a worker's eventual socioeconomic attainment (Featherman and Hauser, 1978).

To organize the research literature, we offer a simple framework for thinking about external influences on careers. In the spirit of earlier career theories that featured external structural forces shaping careers (e.g., Jones and Dunn, 2007; Nystrom and McArthur, 1989; Rosenbaum, 1989; Sonnenfeld, 1989), we start from an understanding of careers as movement along a particular path of positions, with attendant rewards. We break down that career movement into two broad components. First, there is the shape of that pathway, or what we call the "nature of the sequence" of positions that define a career. Which sequence a worker follows will reflect both the general sets of sequences that are possible in a given setting, and the sequence that they themselves choose. Second, there is the rate of mobility through that sequence of positions, which can be a feature both of the setting and the individual worker. Together, these two components – the nature of the sequence and the rate of mobility – can be used to characterize and distinguish different careers, and hence to organize the effects of external influences on careers.

We begin our chapter by elaborating on this external careers framework. Then we organize our summaries of recent research according to three broad sets of external influences – institutional, ecological, and social – that affect careers. In each section, we briefly set the stage for thinking about influences on careers based on wider social theory and then delve into our review of recent papers. Broadly speaking, our review centers on articles published in the last 15 years in the major generalist journals for the disciplines listed above, as well as selected specialist journals that are especially relevant to careers. We also connect work in each of the three areas to the broad mechanisms of our career influences framework. We then conclude with a brief discussion and suggestions for future work.

An external careers framework

In outlining the myriad different ways that external pressures can influence careers, we create a simple framework to organize our thinking. This framework seeks to characterize the effects of pressures along two dimensions: the first dimension represents the different ways in which careers can vary in the face of pressures; the second dimension then categorizes the different kinds of pressures that the careers face.

The nature of variation across careers

As we note above, the definition of careers as a sequence of work experiences over time suggests two important dimensions along which the careers of different workers might vary. First, one worker might follow a different sequence of experiences than another, effectively moving into and through a different list of positions and/or settings. Second, even when workers follow the same sequence, they may do so at very different rates, with one worker being promoted through positions or moving across settings more rapidly than another worker. Where that mobility is upwards, into higher status or more rewarding jobs, then higher rates of mobility are associated with more rapid increases in rewards (Baker et al., 1994; Spilerman and Lunde, 1991), making this an important career dimension for understanding career outcomes.

Existing research also depicts careers as the outcome of a complex interplay between a common external social structure and individual-level differences (Barley, 1989; White, 1970). From the perspective of an individual worker, the social structure can be viewed as a largely external (i.e., exogenous) context, shaping and constraining behavior. For purposes of conceptualizing careers, the social structure defines the set of positions that workers move through as they develop their careers, and the kinds of moves that are possible within that structure. For workers facing a given social structure, the specific career moves that each makes, and the rate at which

Tracy Anderson et al.

Table 12.1 A framework for organizing external influences on careers

	Components of a career	
	Nature of the sequence	Rate of mobility
General effect of social structure on workforce	**1** Extent of variation in career sequences open to workers	**3** Structural ease of mobility for workers in general
Differential effect on individuals or sub-groups within workforce	**2** Individual worker's specific choice of sequence, from among those open to her	**4** Individual worker's rate of mobility, relative to other workers

they make those moves, will then vary further according to individual differences among the workers.

Putting these perspectives together identifies four broad sets of effects that external influences might have on the individual careers, as depicted in Table 12.1. Below, we briefly expand on each cell in this table.

Extent of variation in careers sequences (Cell 1)

Social structure shapes workers' careers by defining the range of variation of sequences within a given occupation or field. Although there is wide variation in the specific sequences of jobs that make up workers' careers, not all of those sequences are equally likely. Early work on careers highlighted the way that many occupations were characterized by a small set of traditional pathways along which most careers took place (Abbott and Hrycak, 1990; Barley, 1989; Spilerman, 1977). One of the most important questions in studying careers within a given occupation or field of activity is, therefore, whether those careers are made up of a small number of sequences which workers must traverse, or whether instead there are large numbers of possible transitions that workers are free to choose between. For example, the career pathways for corporate legal services in Europe and North America are narrow and highly prescribed, while those for managers are much more varied and fluid. Although work on the boundaryless career highlighted increases in the range of possible career patterns in many fields (Arthur and Rousseau, 1996), some sequences remain a lot more common than others. By shaping the degree of variety versus regularity that we see in career sequences within a given occupation or field of work, external influences can powerfully affect workers' careers.

Individual choice of sequence (Cell 2)

Although the social structure can strongly favor some career sequences over others, almost every career provides workers some measure of choice in the specific positions that they end up taking. Those choices have often been the focus of work that explores individual orientations, personality, and so on. At the same time, though, those choices can also be strongly influenced by external influences (such as social networks) which will direct people towards one role rather than another.

Structural ease of mobility (Cell 3)

We use the phrase "structural ease of mobility" to describe the extent to which workers within a setting find it easy to move from one job to the next along the sequence that defines careers in that setting. Some settings are characterized by relatively rapid progress from one role to the next, be that through promotions, moves across organizations or into new occupations. For example, workers in the information-technology industry with relevant computer programming skills may enjoy great ease of mobility across organizations, while tenure-track history professors likely face much greater constraints on their inter-organizational mobility.

Individual rate of mobility (Cell 4)

Although the social structure helps to determine the rate at which whole groups of people will move along career sequences, some will inevitably move faster than others. This important question of "who gets ahead" is partly shaped by individual qualities but also reflects external influences which favor one person over another or one group of people over another (such as settings that favor men over women).

Classifying external pressures

The literature on careers has identified a very broad range of external factors that can shape how careers unfold. The breadth of those influences requires a high-level classification to organize them effectively. Specifically, we draw on three general mechanisms through which people's behavior is susceptible to the influence of others.

The first of these mechanisms is based on institutional forces which induce regularity in individual behavior. Institutional pressures include formal codified rules governing career behaviors, as well as informal norms and expectations that have acquired "rule-like status" in a given setting and which affect career behaviors (Scott, 1995). Institutional forces can emanate from multiple aspects of an individual worker's setting.

Second, our behavior often responds to the ecological pressures that stem from competition for scarce resources. The effects of such pressures are well documented in the biological sphere, and have also been applied to our understanding of organizations, whose success is shaped by their ability to occupy niches with more resources and fewer competitors (Hannan and Freeman, 1977). Similar dynamics at the individual level also affect how careers unfold.

Third, people's behavior is heavily influenced by social influence, through their relationships with specific other individuals. Work on social networks highlights two broad mechanisms through which relationships shape behavior (Podolny, 2001). First, relationships are often a source of important resources such as information and support; second, our relationships shape how others see us, with our affiliations providing a strong signal of our qualities to others.

We explore how these institutionalization, ecological, and social influence pressures affect careers below. For each type of external pressure, we first review its basic nature as it has been theorized in the wider social science literature, and then we summarize recent research on how that external pressure has been applied to understand careers. In doing so, we consider how these pressures shape the four broad sets of career effects identified in Table 12.1 (i.e., effects on variation in career sequences open to workers; effects on the individual worker's specific choice of sequence, from among those open to her; effects on the structural ease of mobility for workers in general; and effects on an individual worker's rate of mobility, relative to other workers). In the recent careers literature, we find that each external pressure has been tied to certain of these four effects (and not others). Hence we also provide a summary of representative research in Table 12.2, organized by external pressure and career effect. In Table 12.2, empty spaces represent areas where we did not identify recent research. The reasons for those absences may vary; in some cases, they may arise because it does not appear logical for a given external pressure to influence a given career effect; in other cases, they may represent future research opportunities.

Table 12.2 Examples of representative external careers literature

Effect on career

	Nature of the sequence		Rate of mobility	
	1. Extent of variation in career sequences	**2.** Specific choice of sequence	**3.** Structural ease of mobility	**4.** Individual rate of mobility
A. Institutional forces	Kleiner and Krueger (2010); Von Nordenflycht (2010); Galanter and Palay (1991)			Leicht and Fennell (2001); Tomlinson et al. (2013); Baron et al. (1986); Barnett et al. (2000); Hultin (2003)
B. Ecological pressures		Pais (2013); Oyer (2008); Haveman and Cohen (1994); Greve (1994); Bidwell and Briscoe (2010)	Kahn (2010); Oyer (2006, 2008); Tilcsik (2014); Von Wachter and Bender (2006); Jacobson et al. (1993); DiPrete (1993); Haveman and Cohen (1994); Phillips (2001); White (1970); Stewman and Konda (1983)	
C. Social influence pressures		Granovetter (1973); Yakubovich (2005); Barbulescu (2015); Higgins (2001); Rivera (2011); Rivera and Tilcsik (2016)		Podolny and Baron (1997); Seibert et al. (2001); Cross and Cummings (2004)

Type of external pressure

Institutional pressures

Many social-structural influences on a worker's career can be traced to institutional pressures emanating from the setting in which that worker is situated. According to Scott (1995: 33), "Institutions consist of cognitive, normative and regulative structures that provide stability and meaning to social behavior. Institutions are transported by various carriers – cultures, structures, and routines – and they operate at multiple levels of jurisdiction." For purposes of this chapter, we will particularly distinguish between institutional pressures associated with *regulatory* structures on the one hand and *cognitive and normative* forces on the other.

Regulatory institutional structures include a variety of formal rules, especially those enacted by governmental agencies and occupational associations empowered with enforcement capabilities. These rule structures may exist and operate at various jurisdictional levels, including occupations, industries, regions, or nation states. For example, according to one recent study, a patchwork of state and federal laws now requires 29 percent of all American workers, across a wide range of occupations, to obtain government-issued licenses in order to do their jobs (Kleiner and Krueger, 2010). Classical internal labor market (ILM) theory also highlighted the presence of regulatory institutions such as job ladders and seniority rules within large bureaucracies in both the private and public sectors (Doeringer and Piore, 1971; Jacoby, 1985; Slichter, 1960; Slichter et al., 1960). Overall, these regulatory structures can greatly influence careers, for example by limiting who is able to begin a career in the occupation, and determining which positions are available for initial career entry.

Cognitive and normative institutional pressures also influence careers. When cognitive expectations and normative beliefs are widely shared by members of an organization, occupational field, or society – reflecting a high degree of institutionalization – this leads to a consistent interpretation of which behaviors (including career behaviors) are appropriate and which are inappropriate. In addition to implying that appropriate behaviors will be rewarded, these shared understandings also suggest that individuals in an institutional setting may voluntarily conform to institutional expectations through their career choices, because they have internalized norms and practices or because they see practical benefits to conformity.

Following our external influences framework, these institutional forces affect careers in two general ways. First, they serve to constrain the extent of variation in career sequences for all workers (Cell 1 in Table 12.1) by directly allowing or disallowing certain career sequences, or by instilling values that make some career sequences more acceptable than others. Second, institutional forces can also have a differentiating effect on careers, as many institutions have the effect of constraining certain workers more than others, or dictating different career paths as appropriate for different types of workers (Cell 4 in Table 12.1). Institutional forces may also influence the structural ease of mobility, through macro institutional shaping of occupation and industry career structures; however, recent research does not appear focused on this.

The importance of studying institutions as external factors shaping careers and worker outcomes was long recognized by social theorists such as Thorstein Veblen (1934) and John Commons (1934), who viewed both regulatory and normative influences as important forces determining behavior in firms and labor markets. Perhaps the most coherent attempt at a general theory of careers inside organizations, ILM theory (Doeringer and Piore, 1971) also strongly features institutional forces. ILM theory sought to explain the presence of a relatively stable, structured, and uniform career system found inside large American firms in the 1950s and 1960s, in part by directing attention toward the effects of common regulatory institutions, including labor and employment laws, as well as the effects of informal norms and behavioral conventions that had developed within firms and industries. In turn, later research seeking to explain the subsequent decline of ILMs in the 1980s and 1990s focuses on the weakening of regulatory institutions (including federal deregulation of many industries), the decline of unions, and the changing and fragmenting of societal norms (Bidwell, 2013; Bidwell et al., 2013; Cappelli, 1999; Osterman, 1999).

Institutional pressures on careers are notably stronger and more salient in certain organizations, occupations, industries, and societies. In some instances, the pressure is in fact exerted in the opposite direction, with institutions being shaped by careers (Jones and Dunn, 2007). Below, we highlight recent research on institutional pressures at the occupation/industry level, and at the society/nation state level.

Occupation/industry institutional pressures shaping career sequences

Strong institutional forces have been identified in professional occupations such as law, medicine, and education (Becker, 1952; Barley, 1989). In those settings, where institutional pressures are strong, a finite set of relatively well-defined career pathways are viewed as legitimate or acceptable. Rules exist for each aspect of the career, including career entry and early training, career progression and specialization, job promotion, inter-organizational mobility, and retirement. Career conformity is ensured through formal regulatory institutions, including occupational associations and governmental agencies, and reinforced through shared beliefs and expectations among members of the field. For example, in an early study from what came to be known as the Chicago School of institutional studies of careers, Becker (1952) showed how the regulatory and normative structures of public schools shaped teacher careers, limiting vertical mobility and shifting competition for horizontal moves to schools in certain neighborhoods. Galanter and Palay (1991) documented the career structures within American large law firms over several decades, showing how up-or-out "tournament competition" rules in firms greatly constrained career sequences for those working in the industry.

Importantly, at the other end of the spectrum, some occupation/industry settings appear to be associated with minimal institutional pressure and therefore do not appear to constrain or shape careers as much. Arthur and Rousseau (1996) argued that more occupations and industries, and more of the workforce overall, were shifting in this direction during the 1980s and 1990s, creating conditions with more choices in terms of the sequence of positions available to workers. Clearly, at a minimum, the importance of institutional pressures for workers' careers varies greatly across settings. Adding further complexity, a worker can simultaneously face multiple institutional forces emanating from distinct parts of her current setting, suggesting reinforcing or possibly contradictory forces operating on her career.

It is difficult to identify regularities in these institutional forces across the entire economy; instead, much of a given setting's institutional character, and therefore its influence on careers, appears to be idiosyncratic. Nonetheless, some work has sought to identify general patterns through which institutional pressures shape careers, regardless of the details of the institutional content. In particular, Zuckerman et al. (2003) offer a model of careers based on the extent to which an individual moves across institutionally defined categories (irrespective of their content). Within any given occupation or industry, there are categories of specialties, often related to the nature of the work and which over time become enshrined in historical tradition and enmeshed in a web of inertial rules, structures, and traditions. The core proposition offered by Zuckerman and colleagues is that audiences can better understand and better reward careers that conform to categories. Using data on the profession of feature film acting, they show the benefits of category-conforming career moves, especially early in an actor's career. Subsequent studies have extended this line of thinking. For example, Leung (2014) argues that shared expectations about the appropriateness of mobility itself creates a situation where the level of eccentricity in career moves is rewarded.

Occupation/industry institutional pressures shaping differential mobility

With rising demographic diversity in the professional workforce, an increasing body of research examines how institutional forces are influencing the careers of professional men and women, and of professionals of different race/ethnicity/nationality backgrounds (Epstein et al., 1999; Leicht and Fennell, 2001). These studies reveal how regulations, norms, and expectations lead to stratification within the professions, through different rates of mobility (Cell 4 in Table 12.1).

For example, in their study of the changing American health care system, Boulis and Jacobs (2008) documented shifts in occupational and organizational sorting of physicians stemming from both changes in the demographics of the medical profession (especially an increase in female doctors) and concurrent changes in the structure of the industry. They document how conventions related to working hours, conditions, and personal flexibility led female and male physicians to sort into careers in different medical specialties (with women often sorting into specialties with lower rewards). Briscoe (2006, 2007) showed that female physicians, and physicians with greater family caregiving responsibilities, were also sorting into different organizations and careers than male and single physicians. In particular, female and family-responsible physicians were entering salaried careers in larger medical bureaucracies, compared with male and single physicians who were apt to work in traditional private practice (with greater attendant rewards).

In the United Kingdom legal profession, Tomlinson et al. (2013) found that despite apparently broad institutional changes, traditional career structures – and the gender and racial stratification that attends them – were being reproduced rather than altered. They also identified different strategies that individuals were pursuing at key points in their careers in response to these enduring structures. McBrier (2003) studied the rapid growth of non-tenure-track positions in academia, finding a gender gap in career moves to/from the latter positions that was explained through a mixture of occupational structural constraints and workers' own personal family/geographic needs. In general, these studies of careers in the professions seem consistent with Leicht and Fennell's (2001) prediction that increasing diversity in professional settings would not reduce inequality in careers, but instead shift stratification from a "between occupations" pattern to a "within occupations" pattern (e.g., white men disproportionately occupying upper positions within each professional occupation).

A stream of related research has considered how (institutionalized) norms and expectations about the demographic profile of workers in a particular industry, occupation, or job may affect the careers of workers in that industry, occupation, or job setting (Baron et al., 1986; DiPrete and Soule, 1988). Much of this work builds off the observation that the most rewarding professional occupations have tended to be male-typed (i.e., dominated by men), creating barriers for female workers who do not fit the expected gender profile – and conversely, many female-typed occupations tend to hold poorer career prospects for workers. Exploring the impact of this gender-typing of jobs for worker careers, Barnett et al. (2000) used data on California state government employees to show associations between the sex (and race) composition of an occupation/job and different "avenues of attainment" (i.e., job transitions within and across organizations) and the pay consequences of those transitions.

More recent work in this area has probed the specific mechanisms operating to enable or curb the influence of such occupational gender-typing on careers. For example, looking within the legal profession (broadly, a historically male-typed occupation), Gorman (2006) showed that women were less likely to be promoted than men when working in specialties that have more inherent work uncertainty – leaving open the door for the expression of gender bias. Beckman and Phillips (2005) found that such a gender gap in promotions was reduced when lawyers were working in firms whose clients included more women. Looking across a set of occupations, Hultin (2003) found that men in typically female occupations had higher rates of promotion than their female counterparts. In another interesting study, Goldberg et al. (2004) examined the career progression and salaries of managerial workers in both masculine-typed and feminine-typed industries/jobs, finding career advantages for workers whose gender departed from the expected gender for their setting. They also explored effects related to young-typed and old-typed industries on the same career outcomes.

Societal institutional pressures shaping career sequences and mobility rates

Research has also extensively investigated how institutions at the nation state level shape the availability of different career sequences. Some of this research uses comparisons across countries in order to identify the effect of differing rules and norms on career patterns and career outcomes; other research examines institutional changes taking place within countries over time.

Some of these studies examine the overall effects of national institutional forces on the career sequences available to workers. For example, a study by Manzoni et al. (2014) uses a life course analysis approach to show how the stratified German educational and occupational training system greatly constrains career options available to individuals. In a rare paper on careers in the African context, Ituma and Simpson (2009) found that among highly skilled Nigerian information-technology workers, ethnic allegiances and work biographies significantly constrained careers, limiting the applicability of "boundaryless careers" concepts that appeared to apply to similarly skilled information technology workers in the United States.

Several recent studies have examined the effects of national institutional contexts on the determinants of individual career mobility. Major changes in the institutional setting can imply a rewriting of the rules of mobility. For example, Cao (2001) studied how the transition from state socialism to a market-based economy affected career mobility. Using data from two Chinese cities, Cao showed that an increase in market orientation was associated with less importance of political connections for promotion, and more importance of human capital criteria.

Looking across countries, an interesting collection of studies has begun to explore the diverse ways that societal differences in cultural values can influence careers. For example, in countries and regions typified by "hierarchical" culture (where people perceive more "power distance" between individuals at different levels) career progression may be guided by different factors when compared with more "egalitarian" locales. Ramaswami et al. (2014) found that the career benefits of mentoring depended on the extent to which workers conformed to the hierarchy/equality expectations of their societal context. In Taiwan (a hierarchical setting), mentoring benefited those who conformed to the setting's high "power distance" expectations, while the inverse was true in the United States (an egalitarian setting). In another example, Chudzikowski and colleagues (2009) explored how individualistic versus collectivistic cultures affect perceptions of careers. They found that attributions of career transitions tended to be more external (i.e., the career transitions were assumed to be caused by forces outside the individual) in collectivistic China, more internal (i.e., caused by the person's own agency or capabilities) in individualistic United States, and a mixture of the two in Europe.

As women have entered the workforce in large numbers across many countries, a growing body of research has sought to document the ways state-level institutional rules affect career mobility for women (Mandel and Semyonov, 2006). For example, using a matched sample of Swiss and American female workers, Charles and colleagues (2001) found that the effects of individual and family-structure factors on women's careers were much stronger in Switzerland compared with the United States. These differences, consistent with their predictions, led the authors to conclude that the "explanatory power of conventional individual-level models of female market behavior varies depending on the structural and normative conditions under which women make life choices" (Charles et al., 2001: 371). Aisenbrey et al. (2009) examined how national institutions in the United States, Germany and Sweden affected the career consequences of time out of paid work for mothers. Although longer time out of work was detrimental for women's careers across all settings, the risk of downward mobility varied greatly between countries.

Ecological pressures

A second set of external influences on careers come from ecological pressures. For the purposes of this chapter, we use the term "ecological pressures" to describe forces stemming from the abundance of and competition over resources. Success in any career is, at least in part, dependent on being able to attract resources from others, be those resources a job, pay, funding, customers, or even just the recognition of others. Those resources are often scarce, so that competition from others directly impacts people's ability to secure the resources that will advance their careers.

In reviewing this literature, we highlight the two ways in which ecological pressures affect careers. Most attention has been paid to the way that these pressures either accelerate or retard the rate of mobility along job sequences (cell 3 in Table 12.1). Some work, though, highlights how these pressures also shape people's choice of career sequence (cell 4), directing them towards career paths with more resources and less competition.

Economy-wide influences

One of the strongest and most frequently studied external influences on careers is the state of the macro-economy. When the economy is doing well, employers are hiring and jobs are abundant. In recessions, by contrast, people struggle to find work, with potentially long-lasting effects on their careers.

Research has tended to focus on two groups who are particularly affected by the state of the economy. The first group is those workers entering the labor market during a recession. Much work points to the early years of the career as a particularly important, formative period (Van Maanen, 1976; Marquis and Tilcsik, 2013). When those years are also a period of scarcity, the consequences for workers can be long-lasting. Lack of better opportunities means that people begin their careers in lower-paying and less prestigious positions from which they then struggle to escape.

Some studies have documented such effects using economy-wide data. Kahn (2010) and Oreopoulos et al. (2012) studied earnings among US and Canadian graduates, respectively. In both cases, people who graduated from college during periods of high unemployment earned lower wages subsequently. In Kahn's study, the effects lasted for at least the next 15 years, while Oreopoulos et al. found that the effects disappeared after 10 years. Both studies also found evidence that this penalty reflected the kinds of jobs that the graduates went into. Kahn found that being hired during a recession was associated with ending up in a less prestigious occupation. Oreopoulos et al. showed that during recessions, people were more likely to begin their careers at smaller and lower paying firms, leading to persistent declines in earnings, and that mobility into better paying organizations was key to their recovery.

Similar effects have also been documented within specific occupational groups, notably academic economists (Oyer, 2006) and MBA graduates (Oyer, 2008). In both cases, those graduating into stronger job markets found more rewarding first jobs (better ranked schools for the economists; investment banking jobs for the MBAs) and enjoyed better career outcomes throughout subsequent periods. Baker et al. (1994) demonstrated similar effects within a large corporation, showing that employees' wages continued to be influenced for many years by the year in which they joined the firm, with those who entered during tighter labor markets enjoying enduring gains.

Tilcsik (2014) adds a nice twist to these arguments, suggesting that economic conditions when employees enter organizations may also affect the kinds of skills that they develop. In his study of a consulting firm, he shows that consultants hired during recessions subsequently perform better when the economy is also struggling, while those that are hired in boom times perform better in times of plenty.

The second group that is most affected by recessions comprises those who suffer layoffs. Much research has shown that such layoffs lead to both short-term and long-term earnings declines (Bidwell and Mollick, 2015; Gibbons and Katz, 1991; Von Wachter and Bender, 2006). In a study of younger Germans, von Wachter and Bender (2006) found that layoffs led to a 15 percent decline in pay, but that the effects had largely disappeared after five years. Where employees are more strongly invested in their job, the effects can be much worse. Jacobson et al. (1993) found that high tenure employees who were laid off in Pennsylvania during the early 1980s were still suffering from a 25 percent decline in their earnings six years later. For those people who are well established in a particular career track, it appears that layoffs represent a profound disruption from which it can be almost impossible to recover.

While this research on economic cycles demonstrates the critical way in which the availability of resources affects careers, other research has begun to explore the equally important effects of competition for jobs. One driver of such competition is immigration, which helps to determine the supply of people looking for jobs. Studies of both Americans (Pais, 2013) and Europeans (Cattaneo et al., 2015) show that when labor markets contain larger numbers of immigrants, people who are native-born tend to enter occupations that are better paid and more prestigious. They suggest that immigrant competition may make lower paid jobs substantially less attractive while also expanding opportunities in better-paid work, encouraging workers to pursue higher-paid careers.

Related work has also explored the effects of globalization, which ultimately brings workers into increasing competition with those in many other countries. A variety of scholars have suggested that increased globalization may have played a role in increasing career complexity, as increased economic turbulence made stable careers harder to fashion (Cappelli, 1999; Osterman, 1999). Unlike research on immigration though, studies of globalization have so far found little evidence that mobility or career complexity has increased more in those industries most exposed to foreign competition (Bidwell, 2013; Biemann et al., 2011).

Effects of industry structures

Below the level of the macro-economy, careers are also powerfully shaped by the availability of different opportunities in different kinds of industries. It is very hard to pursue a career in a field that is in terminal decline, while the growth of new industries and occupations generates new opportunities to pursue new careers. People therefore end up being channeled into different kinds of jobs and different kinds of careers as opportunities decline in some areas and grow in others.

Thomas DiPrete (1993), for example, explored how the restructuring of the US economy away from manufacturing and towards services during the 1970s and 1980s shaped mobility between jobs, showing how industry expansion was associated with mobility into the industry, while decline was associated with mobility out of the industry. Haveman and Cohen (1994) explored similar dynamics within the California savings and loan industry. They showed that the births and deaths of companies directly accounted for a substantial proportion of managerial mobility, as managers moved to take roles in the new firms and were forced to quit dying ones. Less directly, they also found that the deaths of companies had a chilling effect on mobility of those who were not working there, as they removed potential jobs from the labor market and increased competition for available vacancies. Conversely, the growth of new firms increased internal mobility within other organizations, as the departure of managers for those new firms created vacancies that other managers were able to move up into.

Other research has examined how the distribution of opportunities within industries might matter. A series of papers by Greve and co-authors (Fujiwara-Greve and Greve, 2000; Greve, 1994; Greve and Fujiwara-Greve, 2003) drew on the idea that a more diverse population of organizations provides a wider variety of possible settings that people might explore as they search for the one that provides the best fit. Accordingly, they found that when industries have a greater diversity of organizational size, careers within the industry involve more mobility across firms within the industry and less mobility out of the industry (Fujiwara-Greve and Greve, 2000; Greve, 1994). Bidwell and Briscoe (2010) suggest that particular combinations of opportunities within a labor market also shape careers. Looking at young technology workers, they showed that mobility across organizations is higher when workers begin their careers in large organizations where they can build skills, but are working in regions with large numbers of technologically intensive organizations, which have high demands for those skills.

Phillips (2001) also explored ecological linkages between industries and careers by showing how an organization's success and fitness within the industry could influence a worker's chances of promotion in that organization. In particular, he argued that organizations with weaker fitness (and a correspondingly greater chance of failing) were in a weaker bargaining position with respect to employees, and therefore were likely to grant more of their workers promotions.

Opportunity structures within organizations

As well as the economy and the industry, ecological pressures also operate at the level of the organization. Moves across jobs within organizations remain a central building block of many careers (e.g., Bidwell and Mollick, 2015; Le Grand and Tåhlin, 2002; Valcour and Tolbert, 2003), and the relative balance of opportunities for mobility versus competition from other workers play an important role in shaping how those moves take place.

The way that opportunities within organizations shape careers has been most clearly articulated in work on vacancy chains (White, 1970) which highlights the critical role of vacancies in allowing workers to move between jobs: the more vacancies that there are in a given set of jobs, the easier it will be for workers to move into them.

White's original work emphasized the interdependence that these vacancy chains create among different individual's careers, as the mobility of one person out of a role creates a vacancy that allows another person to move into it. Subsequent research by Stewman and Konda (Konda and Stewman, 1980; Stewman, 1986; Stewman and Konda, 1983) extended these ideas to highlight how different organizational structures and processes would affect job mobility. In particular, they showed how employees were more rapidly promoted when organizations had more senior level jobs relative to junior ones, were growing faster, and had more turnover out of higher organizational levels.

These opportunity structures can also be linked to other forms of mobility, such as decisions to enter entrepreneurship. Many people only enter entrepreneurship after first working in regular employment, often in smaller organizations (Elfenbein et al., 2010; Sørensen, 2007). Sørensen and Sharkey (2014) suggest that these decisions ought in part to reflect opportunities within the organizations that the entrepreneurs are leaving, finding evidence that people are more likely to enter entrepreneurship when they face limited prospects for advancement in their current organization and have skills that are less easily transferable to other employers.

Other research has further refined these perspectives by highlighting further contingencies that shape careers. Work by Gunz (Gunz, 1989; Gunz and Jalland, 1996), for example, highlights how firms' histories and strategies shape career patterns within firms by helping to shape who gets hired and what kinds of opportunities the firms offer. Barnett and Miner (1992) noted that contingent workers' ineligibility for promotion reduced the competition faced by regular employees, increasing their rates of upward mobility. Bidwell and Keller (2014) examined some of the factors that drive organizations' decisions to fill jobs by promotion versus hiring, helping to illuminate the job- and organization-level factors that make internal careers more likely than external. Among other things, they show that a greater supply of workers eligible for promotion crowds out hiring, rendering external careers more difficult into organizations that train more junior workers. Hassard et al. (2012) explore how recent changes in organization structure have affected the opportunities facing workers, as delayering efforts have eliminated many of the positions that workers would previously be hired into, disrupting previous career patterns and limiting managerial mobility.

Social influence pressures

Social influence pressures describe the career influences that stem from the relationships that workers have with other actors. Relationships, or social networks, locate workers within the larger social setting, and can facilitate or constrain workers' careers. The existing literature points to two main mechanisms through which this occurs: through access to information and other resources (or lack thereof), and through signaling something about the worker.

Social network scholars have discussed networks as both "pipes" through which information and resources flow and "prisms" through which an actor is viewed and inferences formed (Podolny, 2001). In relation to the former, an actor is argued to benefit from "structural holes," where an actor is linked to other actors who are otherwise unconnected (Burt, 1992), and can benefit from the diversity of resources that these varied others have at their disposal. Such connections are often weak in terms of the degree of intimacy, reciprocity, and frequency of interaction (Granovetter, 1973), but not necessarily so (Granovetter, 1983; Burt, 1992). In relation to the "prism" perspective, an actor can benefit from being connected to high status or well-respected others, as the presence of such connections can serve as an indicator of the actor's own quality to others in the absence of an existing connection (Podolny, 2001). This is related to the strong ties and interconnections between actors that facilitate the establishment of trust and norms of conduct (Coleman, 1988).

Through these mechanisms the networks of individual workers help to determine the career opportunities that workers hear about, workers' ability to access those opportunities, and worker performance. This has implications for workers' choice of career sequence (Cell 2 in Table 12.1) and their rate of mobility (Cell 4). Furthermore, through shaping early opportunities and reputations, the impact of social influence pressures can be long-lasting and dynamic as workers accrue cumulative advantages (or disadvantage) over time (see DiPrete and Eirich, 2006 for a discussion and review).

Interpersonal relations and individual career paths

Worker relationships and social location shape the individual's career sequence via their influence on opportunities and preferences. Studies have explored the role of social networks in getting jobs or positions, which is of particular importance as employers make use of their employees' connections to recruit new employees. This body of work shows that interpersonal relationships can act as a source of information and influence when seeking and securing jobs (Barbulescu, 2015; Bian, 1997; Granovetter, 1973; Han and Han, 2009; Yakubovich, 2005). However, not all relationships are of similar benefit in this regard. The classic work of Granovetter (Granovetter, 1973; 1974) and the work of others (Barbulescu, 2015; Yakubovich, 2005) have highlighted the role of weak ties as a fruitful source of opportunities when searching for a job, as such connections are more likely to have access to job information that is not already available to the job-seeking worker and hold sway with others outside of the workers' realms of influence. Yet strong ties also provide benefits in contexts where trust and reciprocal obligation feature (Bian, 1997; Han and Han, 2009) or where a referral is required (Yakubovich, 2005), and at stages of the hiring process when the job-seeker will benefit from access to more sensitive information and frequent contact (Barbulescu, 2015). Thus workers' networks shape access to jobs and, hence, career paths. They also shape the moves made along the way, with network diversity being associated with an increased likelihood of changing career (Higgins, 2001).

Networks not only provide access to information and influence but also provide a route to other resources that shape the career path pursued. Workers' familial connections are of particular relevance in relation to access to careers. The resources and social standing of a worker's family, that is their social class, very often determine the education with which workers enter the labor market and their point of entry. Existing literature on social stratification has demonstrated the role of social class in determining educational access and outcomes (e.g., Alon, 2009; Lareau and Weininger, 2003; Mettler, 2014; Sacks, 2009; Stephens et al., 2012). Given the use of educational achievements to screen job applicants, and the predilection of some organizations and professions to strongly favor recruiting those who attended more elite educational institutions (Rivera, 2011), this has obvious implications for individual career paths taken.

However, recent work has examined the impact of social class beyond the educational resources that familial connections bring, exploring social class as a signal of worker quality (Rivera, 2015; Rivera and Tilcsik, 2016). Using an audit study methodology, Rivera and Tilcsik (2016) have shown that holding education constant applicants from higher social classes (as indicated by differing family names, activities, and awards) were more likely to be invited to interview for a legal internship than those from lower social class. However, such signals are not universal. Interestingly, Rivera and Tilcsik (2016) found that this advantage was only experienced by male applicants, as high social class women are viewed has being less committed to their employment.

While much existing work has focused upon the role of relationships in shaping the employment opportunities open to workers, other work has explored their role in shaping career preferences. Scholars have recognized the impact of a variety of relationships on career aspirations and choices, including friends and family, colleagues, mentors, and career advisers (Bosley et al., 2009). Other people may provide insights into different occupations and career patterns, act as role models, or shape individuals' self-perceptions and work-related values in such a way that they play a role in determining individuals' career preferences. Perhaps the most widely explored relational influence in this realm is the role of parents in the formation of the career aspirations of their children. In particular, parental social class has been shown to influence not only access to jobs, as discussed above, but also work-related aspirations among teenagers, which in turn predict adult career outcomes (e.g., Ashby and Schoon, 2010; Croll, 2008; Mello, 2008; Schoon et al., 2007; Schoon and Parsons, 2002). This occurs both through the material resources associated with social class which allow for a greater pool of careers to be considered, but also the class-related values and expectations (Ashby and Schoon, 2010; Schoon and Parsons, 2002). This highlights the psychosocial role of networks in determining careers through socialization and identity formation, which has been discussed in elsewhere (Ibarra and Deshpande, 2007).

Social networks as mobility facilitators or constraints

Just as networks affect the choice of career sequences through their impact on access to jobs and preferences, they also impact the rate of worker progression. Work exploring the impact of networks on promotion has found that large sparse networks and weak ties can offer informational advantages that facilitate progression (Burt, 1997; Podolny and Baron, 1997; Seibert et al., 2001). However, dense networks can be beneficial among those whom a worker needs to gain buy-in (Podolny and Baron, 1997). In such networks, a lack of connection may mean that performance expectations are not shared.

Existing work also suggests that the power and status of workers' connections may be important in relation to progression. Briscoe and Kellogg (2011) found that assignment to a powerful supervisor upon entry to an organization had a lasting impact among law firm associates, with those initially assigned to the highest billing partners benefiting in terms of performance pay and retention on their career track. This effect was driven by access to reputation enhancing work. Similarly, among university alumni Seibert et al. (2001) found that the number of contacts at higher levels was positively associated with greater promotion via increased access to information and greater career sponsorship (such as increased visibility and the opportunity to undertake challenging assignments). This echoes findings in the mentoring literature, which is considered in Chapter 13 of this volume.

One way in which networks may facilitate progression is through a direct impact on performance, with workers benefiting from information, advice, and support that their networks offer. Cross and Cummings (2004) found that ties that crossed internal boundaries and the centrality of the worker in the network of relationships within the firm had a positive association with supervisor performance ratings. However, evidence of an objective performance effect is largely lacking. Some work has explored the relationship between being a referral and subsequent job performance. While it has been posited that being referred for a job by an existing employee should enhance worker performance and thus aid progression courtesy of better information and support on the job (see, e.g., Castilla, 2005; Fernandez et al., 2000; Simon and Warner, 1992), no effects have been found in terms of the improved long-term productivity of employee referrals compared with that of non-referrals (Castilla, 2005; Shwed and Kalev, 2014). Nor have differential effects been found between these two groups in terms of wage growth (Fernandez et al., 2000; Simon and Warner, 1992). However, some short-term advantages have been detected, with referrals having higher initial productivity (Castilla, 2005).

While relationships may facilitate progression, they may also act as constraints. Scholars have noted that careers research typically conceptualizes a career as an individual pursuit, yet an individual's career can be shaped by the careers of others to whom they are connected (Svejenova et al., 2010). These others can include professional partners, mentors, and spouses/partners. Outside of mentors (covered elsewhere), the empirical work on this topic is limited and appears to be confined to dual-career couples. and career-prioritizing decisions such as relocation (Eby, 2001; Pixley, 2008) tend to have negative career consequences for the other partner.

Conclusion

The clearest conclusion from our review of the literature is that careers are subject to an almost overwhelmingly wide array of extra-personal influences which help to determine the sequences of jobs that people move through and the rate at which they do so. Although we undoubtedly exercise agency in how we each build our careers, our external environment shapes the choices that we get to make, and the obstacles that we must overcome to build a rewarding career.

The influences of that environment are myriad and complex, as our review has outlined. We do suggest, though, that they can be broadly grouped into three broad sets of processes that reflect institutional forces, ecological pressures, and social influence. Research on careers is famously eclectic, drawing on multiple different disciplines and perspectives. Nonetheless, we hope that grouping external influences into these simple categories helps to add a measure of structure to our understanding of those different influences, highlighting the reasonably small number of basic mechanisms that end up shaping the kinds of paths that people pursue and how quickly they move along those paths. We suspect that there is little value in trying to develop some grand unified theory of careers; it is possible, though, that clarifying how the different streams of research fit together and relate to one another can help us to develop more sophisticated lenses for examining different settings.

The sheer breadth of this topic makes it difficult to crystallize a few clear pieces of advice either for researchers or practitioners. We are left, rather, with very broad comments. It is clearly important for researchers to account for context in their research as the opportunities available in one setting are likely very different from those elsewhere. Generalizing across contexts requires a clear appreciation of the different effects of the processes we have highlighted in this chapter. For those who are thinking about how to build the most rewarding careers for themselves, it is important to be aware of the possible different effects of the setting, both to help choose the setting that will best suit their goals, and then make sure that they are exploiting the resources that it provides, bringing agency to our choice of structure.

References

Abbott, A. & Hrycak, A. 1990. Measuring resemblance in sequence data: An optimal matching analysis of musicians' careers. *American Journal of Sociology*, 96, 144–185.

Aisenbrey, S., Evertsson, M. & Grunow, D. 2009. Is there a career penalty for mothers' time out? A comparison of Germany, Sweden and the United States. *Social Forces*, 88, 573–605.

Alon, S. 2009. The evolution of class inequality in higher education: Competition, exclusion, and adaptation. *American Sociological Review*, 74, 731–755.

Arthur, M.B., Hall, D.T. & Lawrence, B.S. 1989. *Handbook of Career Theory*. New York: Harper Collins.

Arthur, M.B. & Rousseau, D.M. 1996. *The Boundaryless Career: A New Employment Principle for a New Organizational Era*. New York: Oxford University Press.

Ashby, J.S. & Schoon, I. 2010. Career success: The role of teenage career aspirations, ambition value and gender in predicting adult social status and earnings. *Journal of Vocational Behavior*, 77, 350–360.

Baker, G., Gibbs, M. & Holmstrom, B. 1994. The wage policy of a firm. *The Quarterly Journal of Economics*, 109, 921–955.

Barbulescu, R. 2015. The strength of many kinds of ties: Unpacking the role of social contacts across stages of the job search process. *Organization Science*, 26, 1040–1058.

Barley, S.R. 1989. Careers, identities and institutions: The legacy of the Chicago school of sociology. *In:* Arthur, M.B., Hall, D.T. & Lawrence, B.S. (eds.) *Handbook of Career Theory*. New York: Harper Collins.

Barnett, W.P., Baron, J.N. & Stuart, T.E. 2000. Avenues of attainment: Occupational demography and organizational careers in the California civil service. *American Journal of Sociology*, 106, 88–144.

Barnett, W.P. & Miner, A.S. 1992. Standing on the shoulders of others: Career interdependence in job mobility. *Administrative Science Quarterly*, 37, 262–281.

Baron, J.N., Davis-Blake, A. & Bielby, W.T. 1986. The structure of opportunity: How promotion ladders vary within and among organizations. *Administrative Science Quarterly*, 248–273.

Becker, H.S. 1952. The career of the Chicago public schoolteacher. *American Journal of Sociology*, 57, 470–477.

Beckman, C.M. & Phillips, D.J. 2005. Interorganizational determinants of promotion: Client leadership and the attainment of women attorneys. *American Sociological Review*, 70, 678–701.

Bian, Y. 1997. Bringing strong ties back in: Indirect ties, network bridges, and job searches in China. *American Sociological Review*, 62, 366–385.

Bidwell, M. 2013. What happened to long-term employment? The role of worker power and environmental turbulence in explaining declines in worker tenure. *Organization Science*, 24, 1061–1082.

Bidwell, M. & Briscoe, F. 2010. The dynamics of interorganizational careers. *Organization Science*, 21, 1034–1053.

Bidwell, M., Briscoe, F., Fernandez-Mateo, I. & Sterling, A. 2013. The employment relationship and inequality: How and why changes in employment practices are reshaping rewards in organizations. *Academy of Management Annals*, 7, 61–121.

Bidwell, M. & Keller, J. 2014. Within or without? How firms combine internal and external labor markets to fill jobs. *Academy of Management Journal*, 57, 1035–1055.

Bidwell, M. & Mollick, E. 2015. Shifts and ladders: Comparing the role of internal and external mobility in managerial careers. *Organization Science*, 26, 1629–1645.

Biemann, T., Fasang, A.E. & Grunow, D. 2011. Do economic globalization and industry growth destabilize careers? An analysis of career complexity and career patterns over time. *Organization Studies*, 32, 1639–1663.

Bosley, S.L., Arnold, J. & Cohen, L. 2009. How other people shape our careers: A typology drawn from career narratives. *Human Relations*, 62, 1487–1520.

Boulis, A.K. & Jacobs, J.A. 2008. *The Changing Face of Medicine: Women Doctors and the Evolution of Health Care in America*. Ithaca, NY: Cornell University Press.

Briscoe, F. 2006. Temporal flexibility and careers: The role of large-scale organizations for physicians. *Industrial and Labor Relations Review*, 60, 88–104.

Briscoe, F. 2007. From iron cage to iron shield? How bureaucracy enables temporal flexibility for professional service workers. *Organization Science*, 18, 297–314.

Briscoe, F. & Kellogg, K.C. 2011. The initial assignment effect: Local employer practices and positive career outcomes for work-family program users. *American Sociological Review*, 76, 291–319.

Burt, R.S. 1992. *Structural Holes: The Social Structure of Competition*. Cambridge, MA: Harvard University Press.

Burt, R.S. 1997. The contingent value of social capital. *Administrative Science Quarterly*, 42, 339–365.

Cao, Y. 2001. Careers inside organizations: A comparative study of promotion determination in reforming China. *Social Forces*, 80, 683–711.

Cappelli, P. 1999. *The New Deal at Work: Managing the Market-Driven Workforce*. Boston: Harvard Business School Press.

Castilla, E.J. 2005. Social networks and employee performance in a call center. *American Journal of Sociology*, 110, 1243–1283.

Cattaneo, C., Fiorio, C.V. & Peri, G. 2015. What happens to the careers of European workers when immigrants "Take their jobs"? *Journal of Human Resources*, 50, 655–693.

Charles, M., Buchmann, M., Halebsky, S., Powers, J.M. & Smith, M.M. 2001. The context of women's market careers: A cross-national study. *Work and Occupations*, 28, 371–396.

Chudzikowski, K., Demel, B., Mayrhofer, W., Briscoe, J.P., Unite, J., Bogićević Milikić, B., Hall, D.T.T., Heras, M.L., Shen, Y. & Zikic, J. 2009. Career transitions and their causes: A country-comparative perspective. *Journal of Occupational and Organizational Psychology*, 82, 825–849.

Coleman, J.S. 1988. Social capital in the creation of human capital. *American Journal of Sociology*, 94, 95–120.

Commons, J.R. 1934. *Institutional Economics: Its Place in Political Economy*. New York: Palgrave Macmillan.

Croll, P. 2008. Occupational choice, socio-economic status and educational attainment: A study of the occupational choices and destinations of young people in the British Household Panel Survey. *Research Papers in Education*, 23, 243–268.

Cross, R. & Cummings, J.N. 2004. Tie and network correlates of individual performance in knowledge-intensive work. *Academy of Management Journal*, 47, 928–937.

Diprete, T.A. 1993. Industrial restructuring and the mobility response of American workers in the 1980s. *American Sociological Review*, 74–96.

Diprete, T.A. & Eirich, G.M. 2006. Cumulative advantage as a mechanism for inequality: A review of theoretical and empirical developments. *Annual Review Sociology*, 32, 271–297.

Diprete, T.A. & Soule, W.T. 1988. Gender and promotion in segmented job ladder systems. *American Sociological Review*, 53, 26–40.

Doeringer, P. & Piore, M.J. 1971. *Internal Labor Markets and Manpower Analysis*. Lexington, MA: Heath.

Eby, L.T. 2001. The boundaryless career experiences of mobile spouses in dual-earner marriages. *Group & Organization Management*, 26, 343–368.

Elfenbein, D.W., Hamilton, B.H. & Zenger, T.R. 2010. The small firm effect and the entrepreneurial spawning of scientists and engineers. *Management Science*, 56, 659–681.

Epstein, C.F., Seron, C., Oglensky, B. & Saute, R. 1999. *The Part-Time Paradox: Time Norms, Professional Lives, Family, and Gender*. New York: Routledge.

Featherman, D.L. & Hauser, R.M. 1978. *Opportunity and Change: Studies in Population*. New York: Academic Press.

Fernandez, R.M., Castilla, E.J. & Moore, P. 2000. Social capital at work: Networks and employment at a phone center. *American Journal of Sociology*, 105, 1288–1356.

Fujiwara-Greve, T. & Greve, H.R. 2000. Organizational ecology and job mobility. *Social Forces*, 79, 547–585.

Galanter, M. & Palay, T. 1991. *Exponential Misunderstandings: A Response to Professor Johnson's Review of Tournament of Lawyers*. Chicago: University of Chicago.

Gibbons, R. & Katz, L.F. 1991. Layoffs and lemons. *Journal of Labor Economics*, 9, 351–380.

Goldberg, C.B., Finkelstein, L.M., Perry, E.L. & Konrad, A.M. 2004. Job and industry fit: The effects of age and gender matches on career progress outcomes. *Journal of Organizational Behavior*, 25, 807–829.

Gorman, E.H. 2006. Work uncertainty and the promotion of professional women: The case of law firm partnership. *Social Forces*, 85, 865–890.

Granovetter, M. 1973. The strength of weak ties. *American Journal of Sociology*, 78, 1360–1380.

Granovetter, M. 1983. The strength of weak ties: A network theory revisited. *Sociological Theory*, 201–233.

Granovetter, M. 1974. *Getting a Job: A study of Contacts and Careers*. Cambridge, MA: Harvard University Press.

Greve, H.R. 1994. Industry diversity effects on job mobility. *Acta Sociologica*, 37, 119–139.

Greve, H.R. & Fujiwara-Greve, T. 2003. Job search with organizational size as a signal. *Social Forces*, 82, 643–669.

Gunz, H.P. 1989. *Careers and Corporate Cultures: Managerial Mobility in Large Corporations*. Oxford: Blackwell.

Gunz, H.P. & Jalland, R.M. 1996. Managerial careers and business strategies. *Academy of Management Review*, 21, 718–756.

Han, J. & Han, J. 2009. Network-based recruiting and applicant attraction in China: Insights from both organizational and individual perspectives. *The International Journal of Human Resource Management*, 20, 2228–2249.

Hannan, M.T. & Freeman, J. 1977. The population ecology of organizations. *American Journal of Sociology*, 82, 929–964.

Hassard, J., Morris, J. & Mccann, L. 2012. My brilliant career'? New organizational forms and changing managerial careers in Japan, the UK, and USA. *Journal of Management Studies*, 49, 571–599.

Haveman, H.A. & Cohen, L.E. 1994. The ecological dynamics of careers: The impact of organizational founding, dissolution, and merger on job mobility. *American Journal of Sociology*, 100, 104–152.

Higgins, M.C. 2001. Changing careers: The effects of social context. *Journal of Organizational Behavior*, 22, 595–618.

Hultin, M. 2003. Some take the glass escalator, some hit the glass ceiling? Career consequences of occupational sex segregation. *Work and Occupations*, 30, 30–61.

Ibarra, H. & Deshpande, P.H. 2007. Networks and identities: Reciprocal influences on career processes and outcomes. *In:* Gunz, H.P. & Peiperl, M. (eds.) *Handbook of Career Studies*. Los Angeles: Sage Publications.

Ituma, A. & Simpson, R. 2009. The boundaryless' career and career boundaries: Applying an institutionalist perspective to ICT workers in the context of Nigeria. *Human Relations*, 62, 727–761.

Jacobson, L.S., Lalonde, R.J. & Sullivan, D.G. 1993. Earnings losses of displaced workers. *The American Economic Review*, 83, 685–709.

Jacoby, S.M. 1985. *Employing Bureaucracy: Managers, Unions, and the Transformation of Work in American Industry, 1900–1945*. New York: Columbia University Press.

Jones, C. & Dunn, M.B. 2007. Careers and institutions: The centrality of careers to organizational studies. *In: Handbook of Career Studies*. Los Angeles: Sage Publications.

Kahn, L.B. 2010. The long-term labor market consequences of graduating from college in a bad economy. *Labour Economics*, 17, 303–316.

Kleiner, M.M. & Krueger, A.B. 2010. The prevalence and effects of occupational licensing. *British Journal of Industrial Relations*, 48, 676–687.

Konda, S.L. & Stewman, S. 1980. An opportunity labor demand model and Markovian labor supply models: Comparative tests in an organization. *American Sociological Review*, 45, 276–301.

Lareau, A. & Weininger, E.B. 2003. Cultural capital in educational research: A critical assessment. *Theory and Society*, 32, 567–606.

Le Grand, C. & Tåhlin, M. 2002. Job mobility and earnings growth. *European Sociological Review*, 18, 381–400.

Leicht, K.T. & Fennell, M.L. 2001. *Professional Work: A Sociological Approach*. Oxford: Wiley–Blackwell.

Leung, M.D. 2014. Dilettante or renaissance person? How the order of job experiences affects hiring in an external labor market. *American Sociological Review*, 79, 136–158.

Mandel, H. & Semyonov, M. 2006. A welfare state paradox: State interventions and women's employment opportunities in 22 countries. *American Journal of Sociology*, 111, 1910–1949.

Manzoni, A., Härkönen, J. & Mayer, K.U. 2014. Moving on? A growth-curve analysis of occupational attainment and career progression patterns in West Germany. *Social Forces*, 92, 1285–1312.

Marquis, C. & Tilcsik, A. 2013. Imprinting: Toward a multilevel theory. *Academy of Management Annals*, 7, 195–245.

Mayrhofer, W., Meyer, M. & Steyrer, J. 2007. Contextual issues in the study of careers. *In:* Mayrhofer, W., Meyer, M. & Steyrer, J. (eds.) *Handbook of Career Studies*. Los Angeles: Sage Publications.

Mcbrier, D.B. 2003. Gender and career dynamics within a segmented professional labor market: The case of law academia. *Social Forces*, 81, 1201–1266.

Mello, Z.R. 2008. Gender variation in developmental trajectories of educational and occupational expectations and attainment from adolescence to adulthood. *Developmental Psychology*, 44, 1069–1080.

Mettler, S. 2014. *Degrees of Inequality: How the Politics of Higher Education Sabotaged the American Dream*. New York: Basic Books (AZ).

Nystrom, P.C. & Mcarthur, A.W. 1989. Propositions linking organizations and careers. *In:* Arthur, M.B., Hall, D.T. & Lawrence, B.S. (eds.) *Handbook of Career Theory*. Cambridge, UK: Cambridge University Press.

Oreopoulos, P., von Wachter, T. & Heisz, A. 2012. The short-and long-term career effects of graduating in a recession. *American Economic Journal: Applied Economics*, 4, 1–29.

Osterman, P. 1999. *Securing Prosperity*. Princeton, NJ: Princeton University Press.

Oyer, P. 2006. Initial labor market conditions and long-term outcomes for economists. *Journal of Economic Perspectives*, 20, 143–160.

Oyer, P. 2008. The making of an investment banker: Stock market shocks, career choice, and lifetime income. *The Journal of Finance*, 63, 2601–2628.

Pais, J. 2013. The Effects of US immigration on the career trajectories of native workers, 1979–2004. *American Journal of Sociology*, 119, 35–74.

Phillips, D.J. 2001. The promotion paradox: Organizational mortality and employee promotion chances in Silicon Valley law firms, 1946–1996. *American Journal of Sociology*, 106, 1058–1098.

Pixley, J.E. 2008. Life course patterns of career-prioritizing decisions and occupational attainment in dual-earner couples. *Work and Occupations*, 35, 127–163.

Podolny, J.M. 2001. Networks as the pipes and prisms of the market. *American Journal of Sociology*, 107, 33–60.

Podolny, J.M. & Baron, J.N. 1997. Resources and relationships: Social networks and mobility in the workplace. *American Sociological Review*, 62, 673–693.

Ramaswami, A., Huang, J-C. & Dreher, G.F. 2014. Mentoring across cultures: The role of gender and marital status in Taiwan and the US. *Journal of Business Research*, 67, 2542–2549.

Rivera, L.A. 2011. Ivies, extracurriculars, and exclusion: Elite employers' use of educational credentials. *Research in Social Stratification and Mobility*, 29, 71–90.

Rivera, L.A. 2015. *Pedigree: How Elite Students get Elite Jobs*. Princeton, NJ: Princeton University Press.

Rivera, L.A. & Tilcsik, A. 2016. Class advantage, commitment penalty: The gendered effect of social class signals in an elite labor market. *American Sociological Review*, 81, 1097–1131.

Rosenbaum, J.E. 1989. Organization career systems and employee misperceptions. *In:* Arthur, M.B., Hall, D.T. & Lawrence, B.S. (eds.) *Handbook of Career Theory*. Cambridge, UK: Cambridge University Press.

Sacks, P. 2009. *Tearing Down the Gates: Confronting the Class Divide in American Education*. Berkeley, CA: University of California Press.

Schoon, I., Martin, P. & Ross, A. 2007. Career transitions in times of social change. His and her story. *Journal of Vocational Behavior*, 70, 78–96.

Schoon, I. & Parsons, S. 2002. Teenage aspirations for future careers and occupational outcomes. *Journal of Vocational Behavior*, 60, 262–288.

Scott, W.R. 1995. *Institutions and Organizations. Foundations for Organizational Science*. London: Sage Publications.

Seibert, S.E., Kraimer, M.L. & Liden, R.C. 2001. A social capital theory of career success. *Academy of Management Journal*, 44, 219–237.

Shwed, U. & Kalev, A. 2014. Are referrals more productive or more likeable? Social networks and the evaluation of merit. *American Behavioral Scientist*, 58, 288–308.

Simon, C.J. & Warner, J.T. 1992. Matchmaker, matchmaker: The effect of old boy networks on job match quality, earnings, and tenure. *Journal of Labor Economics*, 10, 306–330.

Slichter, S.H. 1960. *The Impact of Collective Bargaining on Management*. Washington, DC: The Brookings Institution.

Slichter, S.H., Healy, J. & Livernash, E.R. 1960. *The Impact of Collective Bargaining on Management*. Washington, DC: Brookings Institution.

Sonnenfeld, J.A. 1989. Career system profiles and strategic staffing. *In:* Arthur, M.B. & Hall, D.T. (eds.) *Handbook of Career Theory*. Cambridge, UK: Cambridge University Press.

Sørensen, J.B. 2007. Bureaucracy and entrepreneurship: Workplace effects on entrepreneurial entry. *Administrative Science Quarterly*, 52, 387–412.

Sørensen, J.B. & Sharkey, A.J. 2014. Entrepreneurship as a mobility process. *American Sociological Review*, 79, 328–349.

Spilerman, S. 1977. Careers, labor market structure, and socioeconomic achievement. *American Journal of Sociology*, 83, 551–593.

Spilerman, S. & Lunde, T. 1991. Features of educational attainment and job promotion prospects. *American Journal of Sociology*, 97, 689–720.

Stephens, N.M., Markus, H.R. & Fryberg, S.A. 2012. Social class disparities in health and education: Reducing inequality by applying a sociocultural self model of behavior. *Psychological Review*, 119, 723–144.

Stewman, S. 1986. Demographic models of internal labor markets. *Administrative Science Quarterly*, 31, 212–247.

Stewman, S. & Konda, S.L. 1983. Careers and organizational labor markets: Demographic models of organizational behavior. *American Journal of Sociology*, 88, 637–685.

Svejenova, S., Vives, L. & Alvarez, J.L. 2010. At the crossroads of agency and communion: Defining the shared career. *Journal of Organizational Behavior*, 31, 707–725.

Tilcsik, A. 2014. Imprint – environment fit and performance: How organizational munificence at the time of hire affects subsequent job performance. *Administrative Science Quarterly*, 59, 639–668.

Tomlinson, J., Muzio, D., Sommerlad, H., Webley, L. & Duff, L. 2013. Structure, agency and career strategies of white women and black and minority ethnic individuals in the legal profession. *Human Relations*, 66, 245–269.

Valcour, P.M. & Tolbert, P. 2003. Gender, family and career in the era of boundarylessness: Determinants and effects of intra-and inter-organizational mobility. *International Journal of Human Resource Management*, 14, 768–787.

van Maanen, J. 1976. Breaking in: Socialization to work. *In:* Dubin, R. (ed.) *Handbook of Work, Organization, and Society*. Chicago: Rand McNally College Pub. Co.

Veblen, T. 1934. *The Theory of the Leisure Class*. New York: Modern Library.

von Nordenflycht, A. 2010. What is a professional service firm? Toward a theory and taxonomy of knowledge-intensive firms. *Academy of Management Review*, 35, 155–174.

von Wachter, T. & Bender, S. 2006. In the right place at the wrong time: The role of firms and luck in young workers' careers. *American Economic Review*, 96, 1679–1705.

White, H.C. 1970. *Chains of Opportunity: System Models of Mobility in Organizations*. Cambridge, MA: Harvard University Press.

Wilensky, H.L. 1961. Orderly careers and social participation: The impact of work history on social integration in the middle mass. *American Sociological Review*, 26, 521–539.

Yakubovich, V. 2005. Weak ties, information, and influence: How workers find jobs in a local Russian labor market. *American Sociological Review*, 70, 408–421.

Zuckerman, E.W., Kim, T-Y., Ukanwa, K. & von Rittmann, J. 2003. Robust identities or nonentities? Typecasting in the feature-film labor market. *American Journal of Sociology*, 108, 1018–1074.

13

Mentorship and developmental networks

Nikos Bozionelos

Introduction

This chapter focuses on mentorship and developmental networks within the context of careers. The various forms of mentoring are considered, along with the reasons that developmental networks have received attention as a supplement to rather than a replacement of traditional mentoring. The chapter reviews empirical evidence demonstrating that mentoring and developmental networks are linked with career outcomes and discusses the relative contribution of traditional mentoring relationships and the rest of developmental ties on career success. The two candidate mechanisms for the link between mentoring and career success, the performance and the political route, are presented and evidence for each is reviewed. Furthermore, factors that increase the probabilities of individuals' involvement in mentoring relationships and of participation in developmental networks are discussed. Though the literature has paid nearly exclusive attention to their positive aspects, the chapter also looks at the darker sides of mentorship and developmental networks. These are not limited to negative mentoring experiences, but they extend to evidence in favour of the political route for the link of mentoring with career success along with the possibility that mentoring may serve as a means of transmitting and perpetuating unethical mentalities. The chapter ends with suggestions for future research.

Definition and functions of mentoring

The notion of mentorship has been in existence for a long time, the term "mentor" being found first in Homer's *Odyssey*. Mentoring with specific reference to the work or organizational environment appeared in the early 1970s (Jennings, 1971). However, it was after the seminal work of Kram (1983, 1985) that it received systematic attention. Mentoring in the form it was initially conceived and described, referred to as "classical" or "traditional" mentoring, connotes an intense and largely exclusive relationship between two individuals of unequal status and experience, the mentor and the protégé, who work within the same organizational context (Burke, 1984; Kram, 1983; 1985). Within that relationship the protégé (or mentee) receives a variety of career-enhancing and socio-emotional functions. Kram (1985) identified five career-enhancing functions (challenging assignments, exposure and visibility, coaching, protection, and direct forms of sponsorship for the protégé) and four socio-emotional functions (friendship, counseling, acceptance and confirmation, and role modeling). New functions have been added since, including "freedom and opportunity for skill development" within the career-enhancing category, and "inspiration and motivation" within the socio-emotional category (Cotton et al., 2011). Most theoretical and empirical research, including all major meta-analyses, has treated role modeling as a socio-emotional function. However, recent thinking and empirical evidence suggests that it has substantive usefulness to consider role modeling as an independent third function (Bailey et al., 2016; Dickson et al., 2014; Haggard et al., 2011; Pellegrini and Scandura, 2005).

Mentoring has been mostly associated and researched within while-collar managerial and professional occupations that have traditionally been linked with the archetypal notion of career as involving generally planned upward moves (Baruch and Bozionelos, 2011). However, workplace mentoring should be seen as a social function that occurs in every context where work takes place and that must include technical, service, and blue-collar work (Bozionelos et al., 2016).

Mentoring on a continuum: from dysfunctional to relational

Kram (1985) noted and empirical research (Ensher et al., 2001; Ragins et al., 2000) has confirmed two important facts: first, not all mentoring functions are necessarily present in every relationship. In fact, mentoring relationships where all identified functions are present must represent only a tiny minority. Second, the intensity of particular functions differs across relationships.

Mentoring relationships, therefore, fall into a continuum with fully dysfunctional mentorship on the one end, "average" relationships around the middle, and relational mentoring near the other end (Ragins, 2012). Indeed, mentoring is not at all devoid of negative experiences (Scandura, 1998). Such experiences involve personality and values mismatch in the dyad, manipulative or distancing behavior from the part of the mentor or the protégé, inability of the mentor to deliver according to the protégé's expectations, or competition between the mentor and the protégé (Eby et al., 2000; Gunz and Mayrhofer, 2018). The relational end of the continuum reflects relationships of exceptional quality that are "interdependent and generative" and promote "mutual growth, learning, and development within the career context" (Ragins, 2012: 519). Such relationships differ not (only) quantitatively (e.g., amount of mentoring provided) but also qualitatively from "average" mentorship (Fletcher and Ragins, 2007; Ragins, 2012; Ragins and Verbos, 2007).

Variants of mentoring

Variants of mentoring that go beyond its traditional form include lateral or peer mentoring (McDaugall and Beattie, 1997), where there is no hierarchical difference between the two parties, and reverse mentoring (Murphy, 2012), where it is the junior member who assumes the role of mentor. The prevalence of these forms has increased substantially in the past three decades as a result of changes in organizational structures along with the acceleration in the pace with which new knowledge emerges and is incorporated into work and business practices (Baruch and Bozionelos, 2011). For example, rapid technological and societal change may render the technical knowledge of established organizational members obsolete, thus creating the need to be mentored by juniors who are more knowledgeable and experienced in particular domains (Morris, 2017; Murphy, 2012). Notwithstanding the substantial incidence of other forms of mentoring, however, traditional mentoring still corresponds to the archetypal notion of the concept.

Mentoring across boundaries

In traditional considerations of mentoring, both members of the dyad find themselves within the same organization (e.g., Higgins and Kram, 2001). However, mentoring may also take place across organizational or physical boundaries as epitomized in external mentoring (Baugh and Fagenson-Eland, 2005). This form also assumes contemporary importance in light of the increased inter-organizational mobility of workers we have witnessed over the recent decades.

Finally, the omnipresence of electronic communication has given rise to virtual or electronic mentoring, conventionally referred to as e-mentoring (Ensher et al., 2003), where most or all of the interpersonal exchange takes place through information communication technologies (e.g., Tanis and Barker, 2017). A potential caveat with e-mentoring is that the medium may constrain the intensity and quality of functions provided. Indeed, empirical evidence finds exclusive e-mentoring less effective than blended mentoring (where electronic means are supplemented with face-to-face or even voice-to-voice communication) (Murphy, 2011). In addition, there are questions over whether functions such as role modeling can be exercised effectively in e-mentoring (de Janasz and Godshalk, 2013; but see also Cotton et al., 2011).

Informal and formal mentoring

As initially identified, the mentoring relationship is initiated and evolves naturally as result of personal attraction and mutual identification (e.g., Kram, 1983; and also Humberd and Rouse, 2016). This is referred to as informal mentoring. Findings from early empirical research, and especially enthusiastic reports in practitioners' literature, incentivized firms and communities to establish formal mentoring programs (e.g., DuBois et al., 2011). As will be seen below, formal mentoring, though clearly inferior to informal, still contains benefits.

Constellations of relationships and developmental networks

The idea of simultaneously drawing upon different developmental ties was presented in detail and unambiguously in the work of Kram (1985), where she discussed "relationship constellations" as "[traditional] mentoring alternatives." The reasoning was that multiple ties can provide a flexible basis for support as individuals move through different career stages and phases in their organizational lives (Kram, 1985). However, the idea of multiple developmental relationships, referred to here as "developmental networks," drew systematic attention only towards the end of the previous millennium. Higgins and Kram (2001: 268) defined the developmental network as "the set of people a protégé names as taking an active interest in and action to advance the protégé's career by providing developmental assistance." The developmental network draws from every social sphere, intra-organizational, inter-organizational, non-work and family of the individual (Dobrow et al., 2012), and includes of course any primary mentoring relationships the individual may have. According to the notion of the developmental network, all developmental relationships fall within the mentoring framework, being "simply different types of mentoring" Higgins and Kram, 2001: 266).

Reasons behind the rise of the notion of the developmental network pertain mostly to changes in organizational structures and mentalities over recent decades. Because of these, (1) organizational structures have become much flatter while organizations have become generally "leaner," meaning simultaneous increase in managerial span of control along with work intensification (Cleveland, 2012; Wulf, 2012). This means availability of fewer and much more pressurized senior people to serve as traditional mentors. (2) The employment relationship contains less assurance and trust (Newman, 2008), which has rendered potential mentors less motivated to provide mentoring because of lower commitment and less certainty about their future in the organization (Eby et al., 2006). (3) Increasing globalization means that traditional mentors often find themselves in different countries from their protégés, hence, they are able to provide only limited or no support (Shen and Kram, 2011). (4) Increased diversity has created minorities who may have difficulties in establishing traditional mentoring relationships, hence, they need to draw from multiple, less exclusive relationships (Molloy, 2005). (5) Partly because of startling changes in technology that trigger ongoing increases in job complexity and partly because of changes in organizational structures and mentalities, modern organizational and professional life has become too complex and challenging for a single mentor to cover all developmental needs (e.g., DeCastro et al., 2013).

It ensues from the definition of developmental networks and relevant discourse (Dobrow et al., 2012; Higgins and Kram, 2001; Higgins and Thomas, 2001) that a developmental network (1) contains only people who the individual consciously views as being of assistance to his/her career; (2) includes only direct ties of the individual (i.e., it excludes ties of ties, who could be also of help); (3) excludes any ties the focal individual does not perceive (or recall) as career instrumental (but may in fact be); and (4) excludes ties with people who are not seen as consciously taking an active interest in developing him/her. For example, people whom the individual distantly models but they are not consciously aware of it are instrumental in career development (Cotton et al., 2011; Parker et al., 2004), but according to the definition they are not part of the individual's developmental network.

An interlude: from developmental networks to social capital

Developmental networks are critical in the sense that, by definition, they foster personal growth. However, arguably they do not capture the total impact of relationship ties on a person's career. Here, we will go one step further to expand career developmental ties to the entire network within which the individual finds itself, and we will consider it via the lens of social capital.

Social capital signifies the resources a person has at one's disposal by means of one's relationship ties with others within a particular social arena (Bourdieu, 1986; Portes, 1998). Social capital provides to the focal person the key career resources of information, influence, and solidarity (Adler and Kwon, 2002; Bourdieu, 1986). Consistent with theory of developmental networks that developmental ties come from every social arena (Higgins and Kram, 2001), social capital is created by means of ties found in every social domain (spanning from family to an alumni member on the other side of the globe to an occasional acquaintance). Social capital, therefore, encompasses the benefits of relationship ties in the sense that developmental networks do. However, it also contains ties with individuals who do not have conscious intention to assist our focal person, but who nevertheless have the potential and may do so, such as alumni members whom the person has never met or simple acquaintances who happen to know a key person or to have a helpful piece of information (Bozionelos, 2015; Granovetter, 1973; see also Cotton et al., 2011). Though in this work we will confine ourselves to traditional mentoring and developmental networks, it is important to keep in mind that these do not reveal the whole effect of relationship ties on an individual's career.

Empirical research on mentoring and developmental networks

Enough empirical studies on mentoring have been conducted so far to serve nine meta-analyses in the mainstream management and organizational psychology literature (Allen et al., 2004;

Dickson et al., 2014; Eby et al., 2008, 2013; Ghosh, 2014; Ghosh and Reio, 2013; Kammeyer-Mueller and Judge, 2008; O'Brien et al., 2010; Underhill, 2006), and around 20 meta-analyses that appeared in journals or edited books that examined mentoring in contexts other than the workplace (e.g., medicine, education, community and youth). Furthermore, workplace mentoring has been included in meta-analytic work on antecedents of career success (Ng and Feldman, 2014). Much of that work focused on two key issues: individual characteristics that are associated with involvement in developmental relationships, and the relationship of mentoring and other developmental ties with career-related outcomes.

Acquisition of mentors and developmental networks

A first question is what accounts for differences between individuals in acquiring mentors and other developmental ties. Here we will consider two sets of antecedents.

Dispositional traits and related behaviors

This stream of research considers dispositional traits, such as personality, as antecedents and suggests that certain behaviors attached to particular traits increase the probabilities of obtaining a mentor and of accumulating developmental ties. Such behaviors include proactively seeking advice, genuinely demanding performance feedback, demonstrating motivation in improving current affairs, displaying confidence in oneself, attending professional and social functions, showing interest in novelty and in disparate points of view, and being cooperative and helpful (e.g., Bozionelos, 2003; Bozionelos and Bozionelos, 2010; Forret and Dougherty, 2001; Ghosh, 2014; Liang and Gong, 2013; Wolff and Kim, 2012; Turban and Dougherty, 1994).

Recent evidence also suggests that the effect of at least some dispositional traits follows non-linear patterns. To illustrate, though the personality trait of openness is generally beneficial for involvement with traditional mentors and for building developmental networks (e.g., Bozionelos, 2003; Bozionelos and Bozionelos, 2010), at very strong levels it may turn detrimental (i.e., relationship of inverted U-shape) because it may make the individual appear unfocused, unreliable, and lacking perseverance (Bozionelos, 2017; Bozionelos et al., 2014). From the reverse viewpoint, it may also be that finding oneself at the low poles of certain traits, like trait emotional intelligence, may at certain occasions be advantageous for the establishment of network ties (Bozionelos and Bozionelos, 2018). In addition, the effects of some traits may differ for obtaining a mentor and for accumulating other developmental ties. For example, conscientiousness appears instrumental in obtaining a mentor (Bozionelos et al., 2014), but it may be detrimental in building ties with peers or outsiders (Bozionelos, 2003; Bozionelos, 2017).

Demographic factors

The demographic factors that have received most attention are gender and race or ethnic background. The general idea is that because racial minorities and women are under-represented in upper organizational echelons and other powerful positions they face more obstacles in obtaining mentors or other developmental ties or in finding protégés (e.g., O'Neill and Blake-Beard, 2002; Ragins, 1997a, 1997b).

Empirical findings, however, do not concur with the theoretical discourse. A recent exhaustive meta-analysis by Eby et al. (2013) found no difference between men and women in career-related or socio-emotional mentoring received or provided. A similar conclusion was reached by O'Brien et al.'s (2010) meta-analysis that focused exclusively on gender differences in workplace mentoring where, in fact, they found a very small advantage for women in socio-emotional mentoring receipt. Men were only somewhat more likely to have served as mentors, but the effect was so weak ($\rho = -.07$, Cohen's $d = -.14$) that its meaningfulness is questionable (O'Brien et al., 2010). Similarly, Eby et al. (2013) found no evidence for a race effect in mentoring receipt. The only significant relationships they obtained showed that racial minority members received slightly more career-related mentoring ($\rho = -.06$, $d = -.12$) and provided somewhat less career-related ($\rho = .09$, $d = .18$) and psycho-social mentoring ($\rho = .09$, $d = .18$) (Eby et al., 2013).

It is conceivable, however, that women and racial minorities form developmental relationships with less powerful individuals that compromises their career benefits. The idea of homophily in networks suggests that women and racial minorities form developmental networks that include mostly or exclusively other women or other racial minorities. Such networks contain less power, hence they can do less for the careers of their members (Ibarra, 1993; Ragins and Sundstrom, 1989). This argument finds distant support in the meta-analysis of Underhill (2006) who found a stronger general career benefit of mentoring receipt for men ($\rho = .55$, $d = 1.32$) than for women ($\rho = .39$, $d = .85$).

Demographic characteristics, such as gender and racial or ethnic background, represent surface-level similarity (Harrison et al., 1998). It must be stressed that it is deep-level similarity (that is perceived similarity in values, beliefs, attitudes, experiences, skills, and knowledge), which is by far the best predictor of mentoring quality. To illustrate, Ghosh (2014) found very strong relationships between perceived deep-level similarity with overall ($\rho = .42$, $d = .93$), career-related ($\rho = .60$, $d = 1.50$) and socio-emotional support ($\rho = .41$, $d = .90$) within the mentoring relationship. On the other hand, the effect sizes for surface-level similarity ranged from practically zero ($\rho = -.02$, $d = -.04$) to weak ($\rho = .14$, $d = .28$). This invites the possibility that, unless there are other factors or processes we are yet to discover, the impact of surface-level similarity epitomized in gender and race/ethnicity may have received attention disproportional to its actual significance.

How mentoring and developmental networks relate to career outcomes

Mentoring and career outcomes

Career outcomes for the protégé

In the first published meta-analysis, which remains the most influential, Allen et al. (2004) found that traditional mentoring receipt (as opposed to not receiving mentoring) was related to objective career success, including number of promotions achieved ($\rho =. 31$, $d = .65$) and financial success ($\rho = .12$, $d = .24$). In addition, receipt of traditional mentoring was related to a range of subjective success outcomes, including career satisfaction ($\rho = .21$, $d = .43$), job satisfaction ($\rho = .23$, $r = .47$), and expectations for advancement ($\rho = .27$, $d = .56$).

Eby et al. (2008) extended the context where mentoring takes place by considering studies in youth and academic mentoring in addition to workplace mentoring. With respect to subjective career success ("career attitudes") Eby et al.'s findings were close to Allen et al.'s. However, with respect to objective success ("career recognition and success"), their findings were somewhat less complimentary, finding a weak albeit significant ($\rho = .09$, $d = .18$) relationship. Similar relationship patterns were yielded in two other quantitative reviews (Kammeyer-Mueller and Judge, 2008; Underhill, 2006) of the same period.

These results cast some doubt upon how compelling the case for mentoring for objective career success is (Eby et al., 2008; Kammeyer-Mueller and Judge, 2008). This issue was partly resolved when Kammeyer-Mueller and Judge (2008: 277) found that mentoring receipt offered significant career benefits over and above the benefits of other established predictors of success, such as personality and education, which forced them to note that "this strengthens our appreciation of mentoring." Finally, in a meta-analysis on hurdles in financial attainment, an index of objective career success, Ng and Feldman (2014) identified lack of a mentor and mentoring relationships of short duration as such hurdles. Overall, therefore, there is solid empirical evidence that receiving mentoring is instrumental to career success.

Career benefits for the mentor

The idea behind expecting that mentoring is helpful for mentors' careers is founded upon the principles of mutuality (see, for example, Ragins and Verbos, 2007; Ragins, 2012; and also Bozionelos, 2004), meaning that both parties are able to benefit from and grow within the relationship. Empirical research on career outcomes of mentors is still relatively sparse. Nevertheless, individual studies show a relationship between providing mentoring and objective career success, such as promotions and financial attainment (Allen et al., 2006; Bozionelos, 2004; Bozionelos et al., 2011). Furthermore, a recent meta-analysis (Ghosh and Reio, 2013) revealed a relationship between providing mentoring and job satisfaction ($\rho = .12$, $d = .24$). Overall, therefore, it appears that mentoring entails career advantages for mentors as well, making the case for it ever stronger.

Mentoring functions and career outcomes

Career-related mentoring appears a stronger and more reliable contributor to career success than socio-emotional mentoring. Allen et al. (2004) found that career-related mentoring was associated with all their objective and subjective career indices, while socio-emotional mentoring was associated only with subjective ones. In the largest meta-analytic study so far, Eby et al. (2013) collapsed together studies from all three major mentoring contexts, workplace, academia and community/youth, and obtained results with the same pattern: career-related mentoring was associated with both objective and subjective career success, while socio-emotional mentoring was related only, and less strongly, to subjective success. The findings of Ghosh and Reio (2013) from the mentors' perspective largely echoed those from the perspective of protégés.

Evidence, therefore, is quite definite that nearly all benefits for objective career success and the largest part of the benefits for subjective career success are brought by the career-related functions of mentoring. Nevertheless, one should not be quick to dismiss the importance of socio-emotional mentoring. Allen et al.'s (2004) meta-analysis suggested that socio-emotional mentoring plays a potent role in a protégé's satisfaction with the mentor, which is an index of the quality of the relationship (Eby et al., 2013; Ragins, 2012).

As previously discussed, meta-analytic work has traditionally considered role modelling within the socio-emotional functions. Nevertheless, summative studies have recently started to treat it independently. It is, therefore, noteworthy that Dickson et al. (2014) found that role modelling ($\rho = .30$, $d = .63$) was related slightly more strongly with overall career success than career-related ($\rho = .27$, $d = .56$) or socio-emotional mentoring ($\rho = .25$, $d = .52$). Ghosh and Reio (2013) also found that only role modeling was related to mentors' job satisfaction ($\rho = .09$, $d = .18$). These finding, however piecemeal, make an empirical case for considering role modeling independently.

Informal versus formal mentoring and career outcomes

Informal mentoring appears to provide substantially more career benefits than formal mentoring. To illustrate, Underhill (2006) found no advantage for mentored over non-mentored individuals in objective success. However, when she categorized the studies according to whether mentoring was formal or informal it emerged that protégés in informal mentoring relationships did enjoy clear advantages over non-protégés (ρ = .26, d = .54), while in formal mentoring there was no such advantage. This is in line with the finding of Eby et al. (2013) that protégés in informal relationships report more career-instrumental and socio-emotional support than their counterparts in formal mentoring relationships. It makes sense that formal mentoring delivers fewer career benefits because formal relationships are "artificial" while participation in these is part of one's prescribed work duties that in many cases may not be even welcomed (e.g., Mallon, 2014). This means that if it were only informal mentoring – which is how mentoring was originally conceptualized – the benefits for careers would not be simply "modest" (Kammeyer-Mueller and Judge, 2008: 277) but rather "strong" instead.

Nevertheless, formal mentoring probably helps objective career success indirectly. For example, Srivastava (2015) found that formal mentoring facilitated access to career-enhancing workplace networks that resulted in greater network resources. Workplace network resources enhance career prospects (Bozionelos, 2003, 2008). Furthermore, much of the effectiveness in formal mentoring lies in proper matching between mentors and protégés. While matching has been traditionally considered against surface-level characteristics, such as gender and race, recent thinking extends matching to deep-level features that, as seen, bear a strong relationship with the quality of the mentoring relationship (Eby et al., 2013; Menges, 2016).

Developmental networks and career outcomes

Empirical research on developmental networks, in the sense these are defined in the literature (i.e., Higgins and Kram, 2001; Higgins and Thomas, 2001), and career outcomes is still limited. One reason may be that the notion is more recent than traditional mentoring. However, another plausible reason is that operationalization of developmental networks is more complex. Networks have a number of properties (for example, Higgins and Thomas, 2001, propose diversity and strength, but other properties can be added following network theory, e.g., Scott, 2012). To these one must add the amounts of career-related and socio-emotional support provided by the developmental ties (Murphy and Kram, 2010). These properties may relate differently and in various degrees of consistency with career outcomes, which perplexes and prevents the formation of a clear and unequivocal image.

Empirical evidence generally suggests that the greater the range (ties coming from different social spheres) and the lower the density (meaning that the ties are not connected to each other, so developmental efforts are less likely to be redundant) of the developmental network, the more able the individual is to achieve favorable career change (Higgins, 2001) and eventual career success (Seibert et al., 2001). In addition, studies find links between various aspects of developmental networks, including the amount of career-related and socio-emotional support flowing within them, with objective (Cotton et al., 2011; Higgins and Thomas, 2001; Murphy and Kram, 2010) and especially subjective career success (Dobrow and Higgins, 2005; Higgins et al., 2008, 2010; Murphy and Kram, 2010; van Emmerik, 2004). On the other hand, there are also many unsupportive results. To illustrate, neither Murphy and Kram (2010) nor Higgins and Thomas (2001) found relationships between developmental network size and salary or career satisfaction or subsequent promotion. And yet in a recent study Cheung et al. (2016) found that network size was negatively related to salary. Such findings arguably contradict the very idea behind developmental networks (i.e., more ties offer more sources and alternatives of support than a traditional mentoring relationship, and hence, greater career prospects). It is also important to note that non-significant next to significant results are present in the majority of studies.

A conclusion that ensues from extant research is that it is the status of the ties that carries most weight. Studies are generally consistent in finding that networks composed primarily of ties of greater hierarchical status than the focal individual are associated with objective career benefits (Seibert et al., 2001; Cheung et al., 2016). For example, Higgins and Thomas (2001) found that it was the status of the ties rather than the extensiveness of the network or the amount of career and socio-emotional support provided that predicted whether lawyers were promoted to partners in their firms seven years later. This, however, is again compatible with the idea behind traditional mentoring.

Traditional mentor(s) or a developmental network?

Acquisition and maintenance of social ties require energy and time, which are limited and hence they should be channeled with efficiency. Empirical evidence to inform the choice between investing in traditional mentors or multiple developmental ties may be leaning more toward the former. Singh et al. (2009a) conducted a sound longitudinal study and found that acquisition of a traditional informal mentor was associated with increased future probabilities of promotion, while the developmental network was not. Furthermore, presence of a traditional informal mentor was able to explain additional variance in advancement expectations, a subjective success index, beyond developmental networks but not the other way around.

As a potential reconciliation, it may be that the relative importance of traditional mentors versus developmental networks varies according to career stage or stage of personal development: traditional mentoring relationships may be most useful in early career stages or for tactical career plans while developmental networks may become gradually important as one moves towards middle and later career stages or for meeting longer-term career goals (Baruch and Bozionelos, 2011; Chandler and Kram, 2005; Higgins and Thomas, 2001). Furthermore, it must always be borne in mind that traditional mentors and developmental networks reinforce each other. For example, a traditional mentor may enlarge the protégé's developmental network (e.g., Blickle et al., 2009).

Second interlude: entire networks of relationship ties and social capital

As noted earlier, we can go one step further from developmental networks and consider the totality of the individual's ties as represented by the individual's social capital. A comprehensive, albeit somewhat simplistic, way to conceptualize social capital is as being composed of any primary mentoring relationships(s) along with the rest of the individual's ties (Bozionelos, 2003, 2008, 2015; and also Seibert et al., 2001). Ties in this case are not restricted to links with physical persons but also include links with social entities, such as institutions and associations (Bozionelos, 2015). It follows then that an individual's social capital is reflected on (a) any traditional mentor(s), (b) the developmental network of the individual, excluding traditional mentor(s), and (c) all other ties beyond (a) and (b). Though accurate operationalization of social capital under that definition must be challenging (nevertheless contemporary technology utilizing electronic social networking and big data may make it feasible), it has the advantage of allowing us to consider the effects of all social ties on the focal individual's career, hence allowing us to account for cases that ties offer unintentional or unconscious career assistance as well as for cases where individuals are assisted in their careers without being cognizant of it.

Furthermore, unlike the developmental network approach, the social capital approach to career progression does not assume, implicitly or explicitly, an effect attached to some kind of "betterment" of the individual (see also Bozionelos, 2014, 2015). To illustrate, graduate school alumni indicated that it was the social capital rather than the knowledge and skills they acquired during their studies that helped in their subsequent career progression (Cocchiara et al., 2010), while evidence shows that social capital can substitute for deficits in abilities, skills, and credentials in the job market (Combes et al., 2008; Godechot, 2016). Though we have restricted our discussion to the perspective of mentoring and developmental networks, it is worth remembering that these reflect only part of the picture.

Developmental relationships: are they all good?

Mentoring and developmental relationships have so far been embraced with pretty much unconstrained enthusiasm. Are they, however, as they are depicted, "all good"? As seen, developmental relationships are part of social capital on which there are recent calls for caution on its "dark side" (Bozionelos, 2014; Van Deth and Zmerli, 2010; also Gunz and Mayrhofer, 2018). Looking carefully at the literature on mentoring and considering the dynamics of developmental relationships one faces three issues that may be cause for alert:

(1) Evidence that mentoring leads to actual or meaningful performance improvements for protégés is still tenuous. In their meta-analysis Eby et al. (2008) found a very weak ($\rho = .07$, $d = .14$) relationship between workplace mentoring and protégé performance. Though mentoring is a career enhancer, career success is clearly distinct from job performance. Job performance signifies whether the individual meets or exceeds the requirements of one's work role (e.g., Christen et al., 2006). However, whether job performance will translate into objective career success (e.g., promotion, higher earnings, a favorable job move) depends on a host of factors, such as organizational reward systems, individual career choices, the profession or occupation, and the state of the economy (Baruch and Bozionelos, 2011). Hence, the fact that mentoring enhances career prospects is not tantamount to enhancing actual work output.

Maybe more important, however, is that it is most likely that it is job performance that leads to mentoring receipt and not vice versa. Experimental and longitudinal research shows that better job performers are more likely to attract mentors and receive mentoring (Olian et al., 1993; Singh et al., 2009b). On the other hand, unequivocal evidence that mentoring improves protégé performance is yet to emerge. Though Bozionelos et al. (2016) recently tested and confirmed a model posing that mentoring receipt improves job performance in prescribed roles, the cross-sectional design of that study does not allow certainty on causality. In another relatively recent study, Pan et al. (2011) found no relationship between amount of mentoring protégés received from their line mangers and protégés' job performance.

(2) In light of the absence of evidence that mentoring is connected with performance improvements, there is a strong case that organizational politics is mostly responsible for the beneficial effects of mentoring on protégé career success. For example, by means of mentoring functions such as protection, direct sponsorship and exposure and visibility, mentors may use their power to directly influence decisions in favor of the protégé, or expose the protégé to key decision makers (e.g., see Ragins, 1997b). Furthermore, what protégés mostly learn through mentoring and other developmental relationships is apparently political skills in the form of relational job learning and personal skill development (Hirschfeld et al., 2006; Kwan et al., 2010; Lankau and Scandura, 2002; Vatan and Temel, 2016). The former means ability to map the

network of relationships surrounding the focal individual's position (Kagan, 1994), while the latter essentially means acquisition of social, communication, and networking skills (Kram, 1996).

Though these skills may be useful in increasing one's work output, they also certainly help in devising and implementing political tactics (e.g., by understanding who the powerful individuals are, establishing ties with them, and then exploiting these ties to advance one's interests). In an important study, Kirchmeyer (2005) found that political processes rather than protégé performance were responsible for the positive effects of mentoring and developmental relationships on protégé objective career success. Similar conclusions were reached in more recent research (Godechot, 2016), and earlier research had found that the positive effect of mentoring on protégés' career success was fully explained by protégés' political networking behaviors (Blickle et al., 2009). This is essentially the idea behind the "dark side" of social capital: that the resources provided by interpersonal ties bypass or replace merit considerations in allocation of rewards such as promotions, salary increases, and favorable assignments, which gives unfair advantages to those involved (e.g., the protégé) while at the same time harms the collective (e.g., Bozionelos, 2015; Numerato and Baglioni, 2012).

(3) Finally, equally important to work output is the ethos and virtue of the individual, given the importance attached to ethical corporate and business behavior nowadays. Hence, we should also consider whether mentoring and other developmental relationships improve protégés' ethos and moral standards. Directly relevant research is not available, but we can engage in some contemplation based on (a) the nature of mentoring and (b) the ethical or moral qualities of those who find themselves in positions that allow mentoring others.

(a) The mentor's moral conduct undoubtedly affects the protégé's moral stance (Thomson et al., 2014). For example, via role modelling protégés copy the ways of the mentor, and that should include the mentor's moral and ethical standards and attached behaviors. Other functions, such as counseling, friendship, and coaching must also have similar effects.

(b) The above renders the issue of "who" is likely to provide mentoring critical. Though certainly people with sound ethos ascend corporate hierarchies, it is equally certain that individuals with impaired ethos and low moral standards also find themselves in powerful positions that allow them to mentor others. In fact, according to some experts (e.g., Babiak et al., 2010) such people may compose a sizable proportion, if not the majority, of those who occupy middle and especially senior positions. Evidence comes, amongst others, from the domain of personality and specifically the "dark triad," which is composed of the traits of Machiavellianism, narcissism, and psychopathy (Paulhus and Williams, 2002; see also Chapter 11 this volume). Common to these traits are beliefs of superiority and entitlement, self-promotion, manipulative behavior, deceitfulness, and a strong desire to acquire power by any means possible that are underlined by lack of compassion, remorse, or empathy (Paulhus and Williams, 2002; Spain et al., 2014). Naturally, the "dark triad" is associated with unethical conduct (e.g., Spain et al., 2014).

However, albeit arguably harmful to the wider social system (Boddy, 2011; Paulhus and Williams, 2002), the "dark triad" has career enhancing properties, as it is positively associated with objective career success, including promotions and ascendance to leadership positions (Babiak et al., 2010; Hirschi and Jaensch, 2015; Spurk et al., 2016; Chapter 11 this volume). This is because features like self-promotion and deceitfulness can help career advancement (e.g., Boddy, 2015; Hirschi and Jaensch, 2015). Therefore, people strong in the elements of the "dark triad" are likely to mentor others because: successful individuals are sought after as mentors; psychopathy is underlined by superficial charm that renders the person attractive to associate with (Hare, 1985); narcissism and psychopathy are characterized by strong need for admiration (Ames et al., 2006; Hare, 1985) that protégés would satisfy.

Assuming that a large proportion of mentors are strong in the "dark triad" then a significant number of protégés must "learn" and adopt morally unsound, albeit often career enhancing, ways of thinking and behaving. For example, studies from the medical context show that mentors regularly display unethical conduct (i.e., behaviors that contravene the ethical guidelines of the profession but also humanitarian values) to which, however, their mentees become habituated over time (Hilliard et al., 2007; Rees et al., 2015). Such conduct may also include political behaviors, given that those who score strong on traits of the "dark triad" also tend to be politically skilled (e.g., Smith and Webster, 2017). As seen earlier, most evidence suggests that it is via organizational politics rather than job performance that mentoring enhances career success.

The intention of this section was not to negate the benefits of mentoring and developmental networks, but instead to invite some skepticism. Developmental relationships may not necessarily lead to a "better" individual as far as actual work output, morality, and ethos are concerned despite producing a "career successful" individual.

Conclusions and directions for future research

Though substantial knowledge on the domain of mentoring and developmental networks in the context of careers has already been accumulated, further research is needed in a number of directions, including:

- Cross-cultural differences in mentoring antecedents, processes, and career outcomes. Mentoring has been documented in most parts of the globe, demonstrating beneficial relationships with career outcomes in most cases (e.g., Gentry et al., 2008; Hu et al., 2011). However, there is need for more nuanced accounts. For example, the relative weight of mentoring functions for career development may differ according to the national culture (Bozionelos, 2015; Bozionelos et al., 2016). National cultural factors may also impact the way demographic characteristics, such as gender and race/ethnicity, relate to access to mentors and participation in developmental networks (e.g., Ramaswami et al., 2014). In addition, the prevalence of mentoring may differ across cultures (Bozionelos, 2007), which means that optimal configurations of relationship ties may also vary. This has implications for career tactics and strategies in an era of intense international mobility of workers.
- The mechanism via which mentoring and developmental networks relate to career outcomes needs further exploration. As seen, evidence leans more towards the political than the job performance route – despite that the interests of most, including organizations and the society, are more compatible with the latter. In this case the argument for mentoring weakens. However, empirical research is still relatively sparse to allow a verdict. Given the critical importance of the issue, further research is imperative.
- Following from the above, it is also vital to focus more on the "darker" side. Though this may again seem "harmful" for the image of mentoring and developmental networks, knowledge gained from systematic research will in fact allow us to develop advice and policies that can limit the impact of the "dark side."
- Traditionally, mentoring has been explicitly or implicitly linked with the large corporate environment (Bozionelos et al., 2016). However, most people conduct their careers outside large corporations (e.g., Eurostat, 2015). It is, therefore, essential to study mentoring and developmental networks within the environment of small and medium-sized enterprises (SMEs), as the dynamics may differ (e.g., the influence of a strong mentor in a small company may be proportionally greater while functions like exposure and visibility may be

of less importance in SMEs than in large organizations) (Bozionelos et al., 2016; Haggard et al., 2011).

- Considering the pervasiveness of electronic communication and social media, it is important to conduct further research on e-mentoring. Such research should not only look at career benefits of e-mentoring, but also at whether there are mentoring functions that are unique to it.

- The idea of developmental networks has advanced our theoretical, empirical and practice horizons. Nevertheless, as seen, the construct is by no means inclusive of the total effect of social ties on individual careers. Though from a research design and execution viewpoint this may be more challenging, the totality of one's social network – regardless of whether the person realizes or not the value of particular ties – could be a subsequent step. The notion of career communities (Parker et al., 2004), which amongst others takes into account the career-instrumentality of people who may not be intentionally assisting the focal individual, could be helpful in this direction.

- Over the past few years, there has been substantial increase in utilization of methodologies with multiple time-point measurements, which constitutes a substantial improvement over cross-sectional methodologies that had dominated mentoring research until relatively recently (Allen et al., 2008). This trend must continue. Diary studies may also be of value, as these can provide insights into how relationships are initiated and unfold (for example, they can identify and monitor "mentoring episodes," Fletcher and Ragins, 2007, and how these may lead to a full-blown relationship) along with the timing of the processes that impact career outcomes.

- Finally, in social sciences we typically utilize the "average," and mentoring research has not been an exception. However, it may be worth focusing more on those rarer cases of developmental relationships that are characterized by exceptional quality and growth (Gunz and Mayrhofer, 2018), seen under the umbrella of relational mentoring (Ragins, 2012; also Cotton et al., 2011). Study of such cases may provide insights (for example, individual characteristics or circumstances that make them so mutually beneficial) that can assist in devising best practices.

References

Adler, P.S. & Kwon, S-W. 2002. Social capital: Prospects for a new concept. *Academy of Management Review*, 27, 17–40.

Allen, T.D., Eby, L.T., O'Brien, K.E. & Lentz, E. 2008. The state of mentoring research: A qualitative review of current research methods and future research implications. *Journal of Vocational Behavior*, 73, 343–357.

Allen, T.D., Eby, L.T., Poteet, M.L., Lentz, E. & Lima, L. 2004. Career benefits associated with mentoring for protégés: A meta-analysis. *Journal of Applied Psychology*, 89, 127.

Allen, T.D., Lentz, E. & Day, R. 2006. Career success outcomes associated with mentoring others: A comparison of mentors and nonmentors. *Journal of Career Development*, 32, 272–285.

Ames, D.R., Rose, P. & Anderson, C.P. 2006. The NPI-16 as a short measure of narcissism. *Journal of Research in Personality*, 40, 440–450.

Babiak, P., Neumann, C.S. & Hare, R.D. 2010. Corporate psychopathy: Talking the walk. *Behavioral Sciences and the Law*, 28, 174–193.

Bailey, S.F., Voyles, E.C., Finkelstein, L. & Matarazzo, K. 2016. Who is your ideal mentor? An exploratory study of mentor prototypes. *Career Development International*, 21, 160–175.

Baruch, Y. & Bozionelos, N. 2011. Career issues. *In:* Zedeck, S. (ed.) *APA Handbook of Industrial and Organizational Psychology, Volume 2: Selecting & Developing Members of the Organization.* Washington, DC: American Psychological Association.

Baugh, S.G. & Fagenson-Eland, E.A. 2005. Boundaryless mentoring: An exploratory study of the functions provided by internal versus external organizational mentors. *Journal of Applied Social Psychology*, 35, 939–955.

Blickle, G., Witzki, A.H. & Schneider, P.B. 2009. Mentoring support and power: A three year predictive field study on protégé networking and career success. *Journal of Vocational Behavior*, 74, 181–189.

Boddy, C.R. 2011. The corporate psychopaths theory of the global financial crisis. *Journal of Business Ethics*, 102, 255–259.

Boddy, C.R. 2015. Organisational psychopaths: A ten year update. *Management Decision*, 53, 2407–2432.

Bourdieu, P. 1986. The form of capital. *In:* Richardson, J.G. (ed.) *Handbook of Theory for Research in the Sociology of Education.* New York: Greenwood Press.

Bozionelos, G. 2017. The relationship of the big-five with workplace network resources: More quadratic than linear. *Personality and Individual Differences*, 104, 374–378.

Bozionelos, G. & Bozionelos, N. 2018. Trait emotional intelligence and social capital: The emotionally unintelligent may occasionally be better off. *Personality and Individual Differences*, 134, 348–351.

Bozionelos, N. 2003. Intra-organizational network resources: Relation to career success and personality. *The International Journal of Organizational Analysis*, 11, 41–66.

Bozionelos, N. 2004. Mentoring provided: Relation to mentor's career success, personality, and mentoring received. *Journal of Vocational Behavior*, 64, 24–46.

Bozionelos, N. 2007. A comparative study on mentoring in four European countries. *In:* Eby, L.T. & Evans, S.C. (Chairs.) *Cross-Cultural Perspectives on Mentoring Research.* Meeting of the Society for Industrial and Organizational Psychology, New York, April 26–29.

Bozionelos, N. 2008. Intra-organizational network resources: How they relate to career success and organizational commitment. *Personnel Review*, 37, 249–263.

Bozionelos, N. 2014. Careers patterns in Greek academia: Social capital and intelligent careers, but for whom? *Career Development International*, 19, 264–294.

Bozionelos, N. 2015. Social capital and careers: Indisputable evidence and note for caution. *In:* Vos, A. & van der Heijden, B.I.J.M. (eds.) *Handbook of Research on Sustainable Careers.* Northampton, MA: Edward Elgar Publishing.

Bozionelos, N. & Bozionelos, G. 2010. Mentoring received by protégés: Its relation to personality and mental ability in the Anglo-Saxon organizational environment. *The International Journal of Human Resource Management*, 21, 509–529.

Bozionelos, N., Bozionelos, G., Kostopoulos, K. & Polychroniou, P. 2011. How providing mentoring relates to career success and organizational commitment: A study in the general managerial population. *Career Development International*, 16, 446–468.

Bozionelos, N., Bozionelos, G., Polychroniou, P. & Kostopoulos, K. 2014. Mentoring receipt and personality: Evidence for non-linear relationships. *Journal of Business Research*, 67, 171–181.

Bozionelos, N., Kostopoulos, K., van der Heijden, B., Rousseau, D.M., Bozionelos, G., Hoyland, T., Miao, R., Marzec, I., Jędrzejowicz, P. & Epitropaki, O. 2016. Employability and job performance as links in the relationship between mentoring receipt and career success: A study in SMEs. *Group & Organization Management*, 41, 135–171.

Burke, R.J. 1984. Mentors in organizations. *Group & Organization Studies*, 9, 353–372.

Chandler, D.E. & Kram, K.E. 2005. Applying an adult development perspective to developmental networks. *Career Development International*, 10, 548–566.

Cheung, Y.H., Herndon, N.C. & Dougherty, T.W. 2016. Core self-evaluations and salary attainment: The moderating role of the developmental network. *The International Journal of Human Resource Management*, 27, 67–87.

Christen, M., Iyer, G. & Soberman, D. 2006. Job satisfaction, job performance, and effort: A reexamination using agency theory. *Journal of Marketing*, 70, 137–150.

Cleveland, B. 2012. *Staff to Supervisor Ratio: ICMI* [Online]. Available: http://www.icmi.com/Resources/Workforce-Management/2012/06/Staff-to-Supervisor-Ratio [Accessed 24 April 2018].

Cocchiara, F.K., Kwesiga, E., Bell, M.P. & Baruch, Y. 2010. Influences on perceived career success: Findings from US graduate business degree alumni. *Career Development International*, 15, 39–58.

Combes, P.-P., Linnemer, L. & Visser, M. 2008. Publish or peer-rich? The role of skills and networks in hiring economics professors. *Labour Economics*, 15, 423–441.

Cotton, R.D., Shen, Y. & Livne-Tarandach, R. 2011. On becoming extraordinary: The content and structure of the developmental networks of major league baseball hall of famers. *Academy of Management Journal*, 54, 15–46.

Decastro, R., Sambuco, D., Ubel, P.A., Stewart, A. & Jagsi, R. 2013. Mentor networks in academic medicine: Moving beyond a dyadic conception of mentoring for junior faculty researchers. *Academic Medicine: Journal of the Association of American Medical Colleges*, 88, 488–496.

de Janasz, S.C. & Godshalk, V.M. 2013. The role of e-mentoring in protégés' learning and satisfaction. *Group & Organization Management*, 38, 743–774.

Dickson, J., Kirkpatrick-Husk, K., Kendall, D., Longabaugh, J., Patel, A. & Scielzo, S. 2014. Untangling protégé self-reports of mentoring functions: Further meta-analytic understanding. *Journal of Career Development*, 41, 263–281.

Dobrow, S.R., Chandler, D.E., Murphy, W.M. & Kram, K.E. 2012. A review of developmental networks: Incorporating a mutuality perspective. *Journal of Management*, 38, 210–242.

Dobrow, S.R. & Higgins, M.C. 2005. Developmental networks and professional identity: A longitudinal study. *Career Development International*, 10, 567–583.

Dubois, D.L., Portillo, N., Rhodes, J.E., Silverthorn, N. & Valentine, J.C. 2011. How effective are mentoring programs for youth? A systematic assessment of the evidence. *Psychological Science in the Public Interest*, 12, 57–91.

Eby, L.T., Allen, T.D., Evans, S.C., Ng, T. & Dubois, D.L. 2008. Does mentoring matter? A multidisciplinary meta-analysis comparing mentored and non-mentored individuals. *Journal of Vocational Behavior*, 72, 254–267.

Eby, L.T., Allen, T.D., Hoffman, B.J., Baranik, L.E., Sauer, J.B., Baldwin, S., Morrison, M.A., Kinkade, K.M., Maher, C.P. & Curtis, S. 2013. An interdisciplinary meta-analysis of the potential antecedents, correlates, and consequences of protégé perceptions of mentoring. *Psychological Bulletin*, 139, 441–476.

Eby, L.T., Lockwood, A.L. & Butts, M. 2006. Perceived support for mentoring: A multiple perspectives approach. *Journal of Vocational Behavior*, 68, 267–291.

Eby, L.T., Mcmanus, S.E., Simon, S.A. & Russell, J.E. 2000. The protege's perspective regarding negative mentoring experiences: The development of a taxonomy. *Journal of Vocational Behavior*, 57, 1–21.

Ensher, E.A., Heun, C. & Blanchard, A. 2003. Online mentoring and computer-mediated communication: New directions in research. *Journal of Vocational Behavior*, 63, 264–288.

Ensher, E.A., Thomas, C. & Murphy, S.E. 2001. Comparison of traditional, step-ahead, and peer mentoring on protégés' support, satisfaction, and perceptions of career success: A social exchange perspective. *Journal of Business and Psychology*, 15, 419–438.

Eurostat. 2015. *Statistics on Small and Medium-Sized Enterprises* [Online]. Brussels: European Community. [Accessed 24 April 2018].

Fletcher, J.K. & Ragins, B.R. 2007. Stone center relational cultural theory. *In:* Ragins, B.R. & Kram, K.E. (eds.) *The Handbook of Mentoring at Work: Theory, Research, and Practice.* Thousand Oaks, CA: Sage Publications.

Forret, M.L. & Dougherty, T.W. 2001. Correlates of networking behavior for managerial and professional employees. *Group & Organization Management*, 26, 283–311.

Gentry, W.A., Weber, T.J. & Sadri, G. 2008. Examining career-related mentoring and managerial performance across cultures: A multilevel analysis. *Journal of Vocational Behavior*, 72, 241–253.

Ghosh, R. 2014. Antecedents of mentoring support: A meta-analysis of individual, relational, and structural or organizational factors. *Journal of Vocational Behavior*, 84, 367–384.

Ghosh, R. & Reio, T.G., Jr. 2013. Career benefits associated with mentoring for mentors: A meta-analysis. *Journal of Vocational Behavior*, 83, 106–116.

Godechot, O. 2016. The chance of influence: A natural experiment on the role of social capital in faculty recruitment. *Social Networks*, 46, 60–75.

Granovetter, M. 1973. The strength of weak ties. *American Journal of Sociology*, 78, 1360–1380.

Gunz, H. & Mayrhofer, W. 2018. *Rethinking Career Studies: Facilitating Conversation across Boundaries with the Social Chronology Framework.* Cambridge, UK: Cambridge University Press.

Haggard, D.L., Dougherty, T.W., Turban, D.B. & Wilbanks, J.E. 2011. Who is a mentor? A review of evolving definitions and implications for research. *Journal of Management*, 37, 280–304.

Hare, R.D. 1985. Comparison of procedures for the assessment of psychopathy. *Journal of Consulting and Clinical Psychology*, 53, 7–16.

Harrison, D.A., Price, K.H. & Bell, M.P. 1998. Beyond relational demography: Time and the effects of surface-and deep-level diversity on work group cohesion. *Academy of Management Journal*, 41, 96–107.

Higgins, M.C. 2001. Changing careers: The effects of social context. *Journal of Organizational Behavior*, 22, 595–618.

Higgins, M.C., Dobrow, S.R. & Chandler, D. 2008. Never quite good enough: The paradox of sticky developmental relationships for elite university graduates. *Journal of Vocational Behavior*, 72, 207–224.

Higgins, M.C., Dobrow, S.R. & Roloff, K.S. 2010. Optimism and the boundaryless career: The role of developmental relationships. *Journal of Organizational Behavior*, 31, 749–769.

Higgins, M.C. & Kram, K.E. 2001. Reconceptualizing mentoring at work: A developmental network perspective. *Academy of Management Review*, 26, 264–288.

Higgins, M.C. & Thomas, D.A. 2001. Constellations and careers: Toward understanding the effects of multiple developmental relationships. *Journal of Organizational Behavior*, 22, 223–247.

Hilliard, R., Harrison, C. & Madden, S. 2007. Ethical conflicts and moral distress experienced by paediatric residents during their training. *Paediatrics & Child Health*, 12, 29–35.

Hirschfeld, R.R., Thomas, C.H. & Lankau, M.J. 2006. Achievement and avoidance motivational orientations in the domain of mentoring. *Journal of Vocational Behavior*, 68, 524–537.

Hirschi, A. & Jaensch, V.K. 2015. Narcissism and career success: Occupational self-efficacy and career engagement as mediators. *Personality and Individual Differences*, 77, 205–208.

Hu, C., Pellegrini, E.K. & Scandura, T.A. 2011. Measurement invariance in mentoring research: A cross-cultural examination across Taiwan and the US. *Journal of Vocational Behavior*, 78, 274–282.

Humberd, B.K. & Rouse, E.D. 2016. Seeing you in me and me in you: Personal identification in the phases of mentoring relationships. *Academy of Management Review*, 41, 435–455.

Ibarra, H. 1993. Personal networks of women and minorities in management: A conceptual framework. *Academy of Management Review*, 18, 56–87.

Jennings, E.E. 1971. *Routes to the Executive Suite*. New York: McGraw-Hill.

Kagan, S. 1994. *Cooperative Learning*. San Clemente, CA: Kagan Cooperative Learning.

Kammeyer-Mueller, J.D. & Judge, T.A. 2008. A quantitative review of mentoring research: Test of a model. *Journal of Vocational Behavior*, 72, 269–283.

Kirchmeyer, C. 2005. The effects of mentoring on academic careers over time: Testing performance and political perspectives. *Human Relations*, 58, 637–660.

Kram, K.E. 1983. Phases of the mentor relationship. *Academy of Management Journal*, 26, 608–625.

Kram, K.E. 1985. *Mentoring in the Workplace: Development Relationships in Organizational Life*. Glenview, IL: Scott, Forseman.

Kram, K.E. 1996. A relational approach to career development. *In:* Hall, D.T. (ed.) *The Career Is Dead – Long Live the Career. A Relational Approach to Careers*. San Francisco: Jossey-Bass.

Kwan, H.K., Mao, Y. & Zhang, H. 2010. The impact of role modeling on protégés' personal learning and work-to-family enrichment. *Journal of Vocational Behavior*, 77, 313–322.

Lankau, M.J. & Scandura, T.A. 2002. An investigation of personal learning in mentoring relationships: Content, antecedents, and consequences. *Academy of Management Journal*, 45, 779–790.

Liang, J. & Gong, Y. 2013. Capitalizing on proactivity for informal mentoring received during early career: The moderating role of core self-evaluations. *Journal of Organizational Behavior*, 34, 1182–1201.

Mallon, M.N. 2014. Stealing the limelight? Examining the relationship between new librarians and their supervisors. *The Journal of Academic Librarianship*, 40, 597–603.

Mcdaugall, M. & Beattie, R.S. 1997. Peer mentoring at work: The nature and outcomes of non-hierarchical developmental relationships. *Management Learning*, 28, 423–437.

Menges, C. 2016. Toward improving the effectiveness of formal mentoring programs: Matching by personality matters. *Group & Organization Management*, 41, 98–129.

Molloy, J.C. 2005. Development networks: Literature review and future research. *Career Development International*, 10, 536–547.

Morris, L.V. 2017. Reverse mentoring: Untapped resource in the academy? *Innovative Higher Education*, 42, 285–287.

Murphy, W.M. 2011. From e-mentoring to blended mentoring: Increasing students' developmental initiation and mentors' satisfaction. *Academy of Management Learning & Education*, 10, 606–622.

Murphy, W.M. 2012. Reverse mentoring at work: Fostering cross-generational learning and developing millennial leaders. *Human Resource Management*, 51, 549–573.

Murphy, W. M, Marcinkus & Kram, K.E. 2010. Understanding non-work relationships in developmental networks. *Career Development International*, 15, 637–663.

Newman, K.S. 2008. *Laid Off, Laid Low: Political and Economic Consequences of Employment Insecurity*. New York: Columbia University Press.

Ng, T.W. & Feldman, D.C. 2014. A conservation of resources perspective on career hurdles and salary attainment. *Journal of Vocational Behavior*, 85, 156–168.

Numerato, D. & Baglioni, S. 2012. The dark side of social capital: An ethnography of sport governance. *International Review for the Sociology of Sport*, 47, 594–611.

O'Brien, K.E., Biga, A., Kessler, S.R. & Allen, T.D. 2010. A meta-analytic investigation of gender differences in mentoring. *Journal of Management*, 36, 537–554.

Olian, J.D., Carroll, S.J. & Giannantonio, C.M. 1993. Mentor reactions to protégés: An experiment with managers. *Journal of Vocational Behavior*, 43, 266–278.

O'Neill, R.M. & Blake-Beard, S.D. 2002. Gender barriers to the female mentor – male protégé relationship. *Journal of Business Ethics*, 37, 51–63.

Pan, W., Sun, L-Y. & Chow, I.H.S. 2011. The impact of supervisory mentoring on personal learning and career outcomes: The dual moderating effect of self-efficacy. *Journal of Vocational Behavior*, 78, 264–273.

Parker, P., Arthur, M.B. & Inkson, K. 2004. Career communities: A preliminary exploration of member-defined career support structures. *Journal of Organizational Behavior*, 25, 489–514.

Paulhus, D.L. & Williams, K.M. 2002. The dark triad of personality: Narcissism, machiavellianism, and psychopathy. *Journal of Research in Personality*, 36, 556–563.

Pellegrini, E.K. & Scandura, T.A. 2005. Construct equivalence across groups: An unexplored issue in mentoring research. *Educational and Psychological Measurement*, 65, 323–335.

Portes, A. 1998. Social capital: Its origins and applications in modern sociology. *Annual Review of Sociology*, 24, 1–24.

Ragins, B.R. 1997a. Antecedents of diversified mentoring relationships. *Journal of Vocational Behavior*, 51, 90–109.

Ragins, B.R. 1997b. Diversified mentoring relationships in organizations: A power perspective. *Academy of Management Review*, 22, 482–521.

Ragins, B.R. 2012. Relational mentoring: A positive approach to mentoring at work. *In:* Cameron, K.S. & Spreitzer, G.M. (eds.) *The Oxford Handbook of Positive Organizational Scholarship*. New York: Oxford University Press.

Ragins, B.R., Cotton, J.L. & Miller, J.S. 2000. Marginal mentoring: The effects of type of mentor, quality of relationship, and program design on work and career attitudes. *Academy of Management Journal*, 43, 1177–1194.

Ragins, B.R. & Sundstrom, E. 1989. Gender and power in organizations: A longitudinal perspective. *Psychological Bulletin*, 105, 51–88.

Ragins, B.R. & Verbos, A.K. 2007. Positive relationships in action: Relational mentoring and mentoring schemas in the workplace. *In:* Dutton, J. & Ragins, B.R. (eds.) *Exploring Positive Relationships at Work: Building a Theoretical and Research Foundation*. Mahwah, NJ: Lawrence Erlbaum and Associates.

Ramaswami, A., Huang, J-C. & Dreher, G.F. 2014. Mentoring across cultures: The role of gender and marital status in Taiwan and the US. *Journal of Business Research*, 67, 2542–2549.

Rees, C.E., Monrouxe, L.V. & Mcdonald, L.A. 2015. 'My mentor kicked a dying woman's bed. . .' Analysing UK nursing students' 'most memorable' professionalism dilemmas. *Journal of Advanced Nursing*, 71, 169–180.

Scandura, T.A. 1998. Dysfunctional mentoring relationships and outcomes. *Journal of Management*, 24, 449–467.

Scott, J. 2012. *Social Network Analysis*. London: Sage Publications.

Seibert, S.E., Kraimer, M.L. & Liden, R.C. 2001. A social capital theory of career success. *Academy of Management Journal*, 44, 219–237.

Shen, Y. & Kram, K.E. 2011. Expatriates' developmental networks: Network diversity, base, and support functions. *Career Development International*, 16, 528–552.

Singh, R., Ragins, B.R. & Tharenou, P. 2009a. What matters most? The relative role of mentoring and career capital in career success. *Journal of Vocational Behavior*, 75, 56–67.

Singh, R., Ragins, B.R. & Tharenou, P. 2009b. Who gets a mentor? A longitudinal assessment of the rising star hypothesis. *Journal of Vocational Behavior*, 74, 11–17.

Smith, M.B. & Webster, B.D. 2017. A moderated mediation model of machiavellianism, social undermining, political skill, and supervisor-rated job performance. *Personality and Individual Differences*, 104, 453–459.

Spain, S.M., Harms, P. & Lebreton, J.M. 2014. The dark side of personality at work. *Journal of Organizational Behavior*, 35, 41–60.

Spurk, D., Keller, A.C. & Hirschi, A. 2016. Do bad guys get ahead or fall behind? Relationships of the dark triad of personality with objective and subjective career success. *Social Psychological and Personality Science*, 7, 113–121.

Srivastava, S.B. 2015. Network intervention: Assessing the effects of formal mentoring on workplace networks. *Social Forces*, 94, 427–452.

Tanis, H. & Barker, I. 2017. E-Mentoring at a distance: An approach to support professional development in workplaces. *Turkish Online Journal of Distance Education*, 18, 135–155.

Thomson, A.L., Nakamura, J., Siegel, J.T. & Csikszentmihalyi, M. 2014. Elevation and mentoring: An experimental assessment of causal relations. *The Journal of Positive Psychology*, 9, 402–413.

Turban, D.B. & Dougherty, T.W. 1994. Role of protégé personality in receipt of mentoring and career success. *Academy of Management Journal*, 37, 688–702.

Underhill, C.M. 2006. The effectiveness of mentoring programs in corporate settings: A meta-analytical review of the literature. *Journal of Vocational Behavior*, 68, 292–307.

van Deth, J.W. & Zmerli, S. 2010. Introduction: Civicness, equality, and democracy – A "dark side" of social capital? *American Behavioral Scientist*, 53, 631–639.

van Emmerik, H.I. 2004. The more you can get the better: Mentoring constellations and intrinsic career success. *Career Development International*, 9, 578–594.

Vatan, F. & Temel, A.B. 2016. A leadership development program through mentorship for clinical nurses in Turkey. *Nursing Economics*, 34, 242–250.

Wolff, H-G. & Kim, S. 2012. The relationship between networking behaviors and the Big Five personality dimensions. *Career Development International*, 17, 43–66.

Wulf, J. 2012. The flattened firm: Not as advertised. *California Management Review*, 55, 5–23.

14

Organizational career management outcomes

Maike Andresen

Introduction

Careers are "an individual's work-related and other relevant experiences, both inside and outside of organizations, that form a unique pattern over the individual's life span" (Sullivan and Baruch, 2009: 1543). Most work careers take place within and between organizations. Correspondingly, organizations deal with careers as part of their efforts to manage human resources (e.g., Baruch, 2003; Gutteridge et al., 1993b). Organizational career management (OCM) has to take into account its effects both on the individual and the organization. However, career theory today almost always takes the perspective of the individual career actor (as an exception see Schein, 1978). In doing so, it largely fails to acknowledge careers as an organizational concern and ignores the strategic function careers serve for organizations (Dries et al., 2012). In this chapter, the focus is on the organizational perspective.

OCM implies an investment by an organization into its employees' human capital (De Vos and Cambré, 2017) with a view to building a pool of qualified workers to meet future organizational needs. The OCM activities carried out contribute to the career development of its employees (Baruch and Peiperl, 2000). As such, OCM is an important part of the management of human resources in organizations and relevant to all employees. Intended organizational outcomes of OCM efforts include, for example, attracting and keeping employees and contributing to the strategic flexibility of the organization and to organizational performance. The type and relative importance of different OCM outcomes depend on the world of work and the related employment relationship as reflected in the psychological contract and career contract between employers and employees. Some outcomes might be varyingly difficult to reach depending on the work conditions.

For example, computerization is likely to influence the nature of work across industries and occupations in that single job tasks or even whole occupations are automated by technology (Arntz and Zierahn, 2016; Frey and Osborne, 2013). Job areas particularly susceptible to automation include transportation and logistics, office and administrative support, and industrial production (Frey and Osborne, 2013). Most likely, the jobs that arise will require a more complex skill set than those being lost. A resulting mismatch risks putting organizations into a position in which they cannot find appropriately skilled employees. Already today, 45 percent of employers report difficulty in filling key job openings, according to a 2018 global survey (ManpowerGroup, 2018). These difficulties are likely to intensify as technology continues to transform jobs and increase skill levels needed and might cause a talent mismatch. Moreover, in order to cope with the challenges related to automation, both organizations and the employees need to be agile, to develop, and to learn continuously. As a consequence, employees' ability to adapt and acquire new skills becomes a prerequisite to their job security, while organizations have a critical role in supporting employees' continuous learning. Thus, under these conditions, OCM outcomes such as employee attraction or lifelong learning and development are highly relevant. A strategic OCM increases in importance, but at the same time it is also becoming more demanding in view of the changes in the nature of work and in work behavior.

This chapter will deal with the following questions:

1   What are the intended OCM outcomes of OCM efforts?
2   In what way do outcomes of OCM differ in the traditional versus the contemporary career environment?

This chapter is structured as follows. First, the concept of the psychological contract is presented and the traditional and contemporary social exchange relationship as reflecting environmental and organizational conditions are contrasted. This differentiation of the psychological contract is reflected in a traditional versus contemporary career and in the underlying career contract (i.e., the promises, expectations and experiences regarding careers; Sturges et al., 2005). Second, it is explained how the career contract affects the steps that organizations take towards OCM. Based on this background, we define several OCM outcomes and discuss how much their importance differs between traditional and contemporary careers. We illustrate important insights with practical examples from the world of organizations.

Traditional versus contemporary psychological contracts and career contracts

Career management encompasses all activities undertaken by the organization and the individual aimed at planning and managing the employees' careers to meet future (organizational and individual) needs (Sturges et al., 2002). As such, OCM is characterized by a long-term perspective (see Chapter 22 in this book for a definition of OCM).

A review of the literature suggests that differences in OCM exist that reflect the employment relationship and the content of the psychological contract between the employer and the employee (Arthur and Rousseau, 1996; Baruch, 2004; De Vos et al., 2008). The psychological contract is defined as an individual's beliefs, shaped by the organization, regarding the terms of an agreement between the individual and the organization. The psychological contract reflects the employee expectations about one's own and one's organization's promises and obligations leading to a voluntary social exchange relationship (Rousseau, 1995).

Part of the psychological contract reflects the career-related promises, expectations, and experiences, such as the provision of career management help by employers (Cavanaugh and Noe, 1999; Herriot and Pemberton, 1997). The employee's beliefs regarding the terms of the career-related agreement between the individual and the employer shapes the career contract. The career contract describes the kind of OCM that organizations provide and the OCM outcomes striven for by organizations (see Figure 14.1).

Several researchers argue that both the traditional organizational career and the contemporary career are relevant and alternative career forms, and existing evidence suggests that the

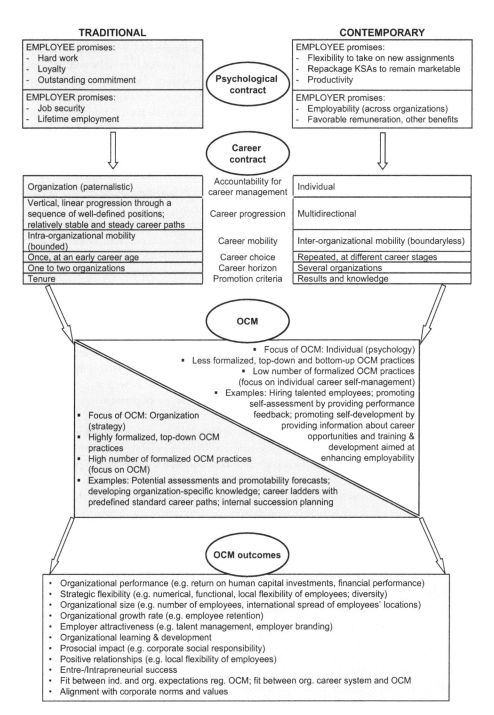

Figure 14.1 Influence of the psychological and career contract on OCM and career outcomes

boundaryless careers are not predominant (Inkson et al., 2012). Additional career forms coexist in practice that combine characteristics of the traditional and contemporary career as described earlier (Baruch, 2004; Clarke, 2013; Lips-Wiersema and Hall, 2007). As such, the traditional and contemporary career with their OCM logics as outlined in Figure 14.1 are to be understood as two poles of a continuum, with some if not most OCM being somewhere in between in reality. This simplification in terms of two poles was chosen for reasons of clarity and comparability. At the outcome level, a range of OCM outcomes can be found in practice that can be related to the different OCM logics. While some OCM outcomes are likely to be typical for *one* of the poles only, other outcomes are likely to be found on *both* ends of this continuum but are expected to differ regarding the importance that is assigned to them by organizations. And some OCM outcomes belong to the spectrum of OCM logics that are clearly situated *between* the two poles. To visualize this overlap, we used stripes in Figure 14.1.

According to the traditional, relational psychological contract, individuals are promised job security and lifetime employment by their employers in return for hard work, loyalty, and outstanding commitment (Rousseau, 1989, 1990). The conditions of the traditional career contract are reflected in a linear progression up the ladder through a sequence of well-defined positions in the organization's hierarchy, leading to relatively stable and steady career paths taking place within the boundaries of one organization (Arnold and Cohen, 2008; Clarke, 2013). Tenure is an important consideration in promotion decisions. Organizations take over the primary accountability for employees' career management and provide opportunities for intraorganizational career development (Clarke, 2013).

However, organizational changes such as downsizing, delayering, and redundancy including reduced job security have induced an alternative approach how individuals enact their career (Sullivan and Baruch, 2009). In order to be able to react to the decreased stability and the increased uncertainty resulting from general economic conditions, as well as changes within companies, individuals must have the ability to be adaptive in terms of performance and learning demands (Briscoe and Hall, 2006).

In consequence, in contrast to the traditional notion of job security in exchange for job performance the contemporary psychological contract between employer and employee is built around learning and development. This contemporary contract includes the expectation that employees can flexibly take on new work assignments and develop new skills according to changing organizational needs (Hall, 2002). In return, employers are concerned about securing employees' employability (although not necessarily in the current organization) by providing opportunities for continuous professional development. Thus, employees need to seek employment security within themselves, not the organization. Nevertheless, mutuality is still important in the contemporary psychological contract; employees are expected to show high productivity and engagement in exchange for employability. To conclude, this contemporary transactional psychological contract is rather short-term and economic, and provides for a simple withdrawal from the contract (Rousseau, 1990).

The contemporary career contract related to it expects individuals to take personal accountability for career management by seeking out opportunities for growth and professional development within the organization (Sargent and Domberger, 2007) and by taking responsibility for their own employability (Briscoe and Hall, 2006; Hall, 2004; Rousseau, 1989; and the related literature on "protean" and "boundaryless" careers). Individual career management refers to the process by which employees become aware of their interests, values, strengths, and weaknesses; receive information about job opportunities within the company; identify their own career goals; and develop action plans in order to reach their career goals. This means that employers are not job providers, as is typical for the traditional career, but career enablers that attract and retain high-value employees and make provision for their supply (Baruch and Peiperl, 2003). Organizations base the decision to promote employees in the internal career system on employees' competences and work results. With contemporary career paths being less structured and predictable than traditional career paths (Baruch, 2004), individuals are driven more by their own desires in their career-related decisions than by formalized OCM practices offered by their employer (De Vos et al., 2008; Hall, 2002) and act independently of traditional organizational career arrangements (Arthur and Rousseau, 1996). As a result of their life and work experience, individuals develop a career identity that can be defined as "a structure of meanings in which the individual links his own motivation, interests and competencies with acceptable work roles" (Meijers, 1998: 191). Moreover, contemporary careers are expected to involve inter-organizational mobility and/or regular transitions across job boundaries within one organization (Clarke, 2013; DeFillippi and Arthur, 1996; Verbruggen, 2012; and literature on the "boundaryless career") and varied experiences across jobs, industries and organizations (Goffee and Jones, 2000; Peiperl et al., 2000). This is why the contemporary career is associated with "less loyalty, greater mobility, and less certainty" (Briscoe and Hall, 2006: 5) (see Figure 14.1).

Traditional versus contemporary OCM

While over time OCM has all but disappeared from textbooks of human resource management (e.g., Boxall et al., 2008; Noe et al., 2016), much of the careers literature today focuses on how individuals manage their careers. Although many scholars recognize the importance of OCM (e.g., Baruch, 2003), the theoretical base of OCM is insufficient. OCM is the process by which companies select employees, assess employees' skills and potentials, develop their competencies, and assign tasks to them with a view to building a pool of qualified employees to meet future (organizational and individual) needs (De Vos et al., 2008; Eby et al., 2005; Chapter 22 in this volume). As such, OCM is characterized by a long-term perspective and aims to fit with the strategy of the firm (Baruch and Peiperl, 2003; Sonnenfeld and Peiperl, 1988).

Employee selection serves to identify a pool of employees that is or will be able to solve the organization's current and future needs for human capital at different layers of the hierarchy. In the context of strategic personnel development planning, the staff is subject to a regular assessment of their current competences, performance, and potential for advancement within the organizational career system. In order to close qualification gaps and to exploit the development potential of employees, employee development is used to adjust employee knowledge, skills, abilities, and other characteristics (KSAOs) through job-related learning experiences. Tasks are assigned to employees by matching their competencies and potential with the jobs that are or might become available on the internal labor market.

With changes in the organizations' needs and in the employer-employee relationship, as described earlier, the unpredictability of careers grows. Thus, a different organizational approach to careers is required. In the following, we distinguish two poles of OCM: traditional and contemporary OCM (De Vos et al., 2008). However, as noted earlier, in practice, much of OCM is situated between these extremes (see, e.g., Baruch, 2004; Clarke, 2013).

Traditional OCM is largely planned, controlled, and managed by the organization and serves to fulfill organizational needs (De Vos and Dries, 2013). The organization addresses their employees' careers from a paternalistic, centralized, and top-down perspective (Baruch, 2006; Nicholson, 1996; Segers and Inceoglu, 2012). The employer offers a large number of highly formalized OCM practices (Dries and Pepermans, 2008) that are typically run by the HR department and only with limited involvement of employees and their managers, such as potential assessments and promotability forecasts, career ladders with predefined standard career paths for employees' promotions within the organization, and succession planning systems (cf. Hamori et al., 2011; Kanter, 1989). It mainly aims to select and develop a pool of qualified employees. The assessment serves to ensure the succession for key positions by filling in internal vacancies throughout the different levels of their organization's hierarchical layers with the right persons taken from the current group of employees and according to the organizational needs (cf. Gutteridge et al., 1993b). The development of organization-specific knowledge, which has value for the employing organization (and less for outside organizations; Lepak and Snell, 2002), allows organizations to optimize their return on human capital investments. OCM practices in the field of recruitment, socialization, and training focus especially on the lower ranks. The aim is to offer employees internal opportunities by promoting them through the hierarchy based on a combination of talent and tenure (Sullivan and Baruch, 2009).

Contemporary OCM is focused on the idea of the "contemporary career" that emphasizes the importance of lifelong learning and individual responsibility for career development (Hall, 2004). All this notwithstanding, as the organization still forms the context in which career development takes place, OCM activities continue to be relevant. However, due to inward and outward fluctuation of employees at different career stages and hierarchical levels (in line with the more transactional employer-employee relationship), recruitment, socialization, training, succession planning, and other processes become more varied and complex (Baruch, 2004). Given the contemporary nature of careers and an unpredictable and complex socioeconomic environment, De Vos and colleagues (2008) and De Vos and Dries (2013) contend that organizations show a more limited interest in formalized OCM practices and as a consequence the extent to which they are used in organizations is low. Instead, companies aim at flexible practices and processes to match organizational as well as individual needs (Clarke, 2013).

Taking a more supportive approach (Clarke, 2013), employees are assisted and enabled in their individual career development (Baruch, 2006; Segers and Inceoglu, 2012). Employers provide their employees with feedback about their performance and competencies on a regular basis and with information about existing or possible career opportunities in view to facilitate their future career development (De Vos et al., 2008). Moreover, they provide support for upgrading of qualifications and maintenance of professional expertise (Clarke, 2013), including career coaching, career planning workshops, or career self-assessments (De Vos and Cambré, 2017). This allows individuals to make a realistic self-assessment of their own talents and capabilities in view of career opportunities (Noe, 1996; Sturges et al., 2000, 2002) and enables them to further develop themselves and to navigate their own career within and beyond the current organization (Baruch, 2006; Segers and Inceoglu, 2012). This second, contemporary approach to OCM implies that employees exercise considerable, albeit not complete, control over their careers (see Figure 14.1).

Organizational career management outcomes related to traditional versus contemporary OCM

OCM outcomes are framed by an organization's strategic goals and result from goal-oriented behaviors in terms of OCM. Whereas individual career outcomes have been operationalized and analyzed frequently in academic studies, we lack a definition and insight into organizational outcomes of managing careers (De Vos and Cambré, 2017). While several studies include organization-related outcomes in their analysis of individuals' career behaviors (e.g., De Vos and Cambré, 2017), no study to date provides an empirically based and systematic survey of organizational OCM outcomes as defined by organizations. This missing focus on OCM outcomes by scholars may be a consequence of the new role of organizations in contemporary OCM.

The contemporary career contract between the employer and the employee, as described in the literature, focuses on the individual as the central actor in his or her career development (Baruch, 2006; Sullivan and Baruch, 2009), leaving only a limited role for the organization (De Vos and Cambré, 2017). To fill this gap in research a range of OCM outcomes is proposed in the following to be considered both by research and practice.

Table 14.1 provides an overview of OCM outcomes as well as example indicators that can in practice be measured objectively or subjectively in terms of the internal evaluation of an organization's OCM outcomes as perceived by top management or employees. The indicators are derived from the (conceptual or empirical) careers literature. As will be illustrated in the following, the OCM outcomes are related to traditional and contemporary OCM logics. While some of the OCM outcomes are characteristic for one career logic only, most are relevant across

Table 14.1 Organizational career management outcomes

OCM outcomes	Example indicators	Sources
Organizational performance: Steadily increasing individual productivity and organizational performance and making more profits related to OCM (return on OCM investments)	Financial performance, e.g. shareholder value, profit before taxes	(Baruch and Rosenstein, 1992; De Vos and Cambré, 2017)
	Economic success, e.g. growth in sales, sales per employee	(Baruch and Rosenstein, 1992)
	Organizational efficiency and productivity	(Zhou and Li, 2008)
	Cost savings, e.g. the higher the employee retention rate the lower the replacement costs	
Strategic flexibility: Being able to provide the basic organizational necessities via employees' careers	Numerical flexibility: Improved HR planning	(Gutteridge et al., 1993 a, 1993b)
	Functional flexibility: Improved HR management and selection; discipline change, job change	(Gutteridge et al., 1993 a)
	Spatial flexibility of employees: mobility of employees within the (international) organization; employees' relocation mobility willingness; international diversity of the workforce	
	Employability	(Gutteridge et al., 1993 a; Tzabbar et al., 2003)
	Knowing how, knowing whom, knowing why competencies	(Kong et al., 2012)
	Better strategic advantage	(Gutteridge et al., 1993 a, 1993b)

(Continued)

Table 14.1 (Continued)

OCM outcomes	Example indicators	Sources
Size of the workforce: Organizational business strength and power based on an organization's ability to rely on a sufficient number of employees at different competence and hierarchical levels	Number of qualified employees	
	Staffing quality	(Baruch and Rosenstein, 1992; Gutteridge et al., 1993a, 1993b)
	Employees' competence profile	(Gutteridge et al., 1993a, 1993b)
	Internal promotion	(Baruch and Rosenstein, 1992)
Organizational growth rate: Reaching organizational growth in terms of (an increasing) number of employees	Employee retention rate	(Granrose and Baccili, 2006; Granrose and Portwood, 1987; Gutteridge et al., 1993a, 1993b; Rehman, 2017; Sturges et al., 2002; Zhou and Li, 2008)
	Loyalty; low search activities for external alternatives	(Baruch, 2004; Baruch and Vardi, 2016; Granrose and Portwood, 1987; Zhou and Li, 2008); turnover intention (Guan et al., 2014, 2015); employee turnover (Baruch and Rosenstein, 1992; De Vos and Cambré, 2017)
	Organizational commitment	(Bambacas, 2010; Baruch, 2004; Baruch and Vardi, 2016; De Vos et al., 2009; Granrose and Portwood, 1987; Jayasingam and Yong, 2013; Portwood and Granrose, 1986; Rehman, 2017; Sturges et al., 2002)
	Job and career embeddedness	(Baruch and Vardi, 2016)
Employer attractiveness: Being an attractive employer	Employees' job satisfaction	(Baruch and Rosenstein, 1992; Kim, 2002)
	Organizations' reputation	(Baruch and Rosenstein, 1992)
	Organizations' ability to attract and retain talent	(Barnett and Bradley, 2007; Lewis and Arnold, 2012)
	Employment continuity	(Clarke, 2013)
	Low absenteeism	(De Vos and Cambré, 2017)
Organizational learning and development: Having the employees that allow the organization to learn, develop, adapt, and change	Enhanced employee skills	(Gutteridge et al., 1993a, 1993b)
	Employee development	(Portwood and Granrose, 1986; Schnake et al., 2007; Zhou and Li, 2008)
	Employee empowerment	(Gutteridge et al., 1993 a, 1993b)
	Employees' career effectiveness	(Pazy, 1988)
Prosocial impact: Helping others through the organization's work	Corporate social responsibility	

OCM outcomes	Example indicators	Sources
Positive relationships: Reaching integration and cooperation within the organization	Enhanced employee morale Spatial flexibility of employees increasing intraorganizational contact: mobility of employees within the (international) organization; employees' relocation mobility willingness	(Gutteridge et al., 1993a, 1993b)
Entrepreneurial/intrapreneurial success: Promoting employees in their entrepreneurial and intrapreneurial ambitions	Employees' satisfaction with opportunities provided for entrepreneurial and intrapreneurial activities	
Fit: Match between individual and organizational expectations regarding OCM and between the organizational career system and OCM (Baruch and Rosenstein, 1992; Tzabbar et al., 2003)	Employees' satisfaction with the organization	(Baruch and Rosenstein, 1992; Granrose and Portwood, 1987; Portwood and Granrose, 1986)
	Employees' career satisfaction	(Barnett and Bradley, 2007; Baruch and Rosenstein, 1992; Crawshaw, 2006; De Vos et al., 2009; Granrose and Portwood, 1987; Jung and Takeuchi, 2018; Kong et al., 2012)
	Organization's satisfaction with the achievement of important OCM outcomes	
	Employees' self-actualization	(Zhou and Li, 2008)
Alignment with corporate norms and values: Cultivating desired norms and values in the organization's members	Organizational commitment	(Bambacas, 2010; Baruch, 2004; Baruch and Rosenstein, 1992; Baruch and Vardi, 2016; De Vos et al., 2009; Granrose and Portwood, 1987; Gutteridge et al., 1993a, 1993b; Jayasingam and Yong, 2013; Portwood and Granrose, 1986; Rehman, 2017; Sturges et al., 2002)
	Job engagement	(Baruch and Vardi, 2016; De Vos and Cambré, 2017)
	Employees' job involvement	(Zhou and Li, 2008)

career logics (albeit often more important in one logic than the other). These differences in the relevance of different OCM outcomes result from the differences in career contracts. The traditional career contract implies a commitment by employers to invest into their employees' human capital with a focus on organization-specific KSAOs. As this human capital can only be "made" but not "bought," organizations strive to optimize the return on their career investment.

Under the contemporary career contract, by contrast, organizations are confronted with opposing goals causing tensions. On the one hand, investments into employees' human capital and careers can represent an essential contribution to the long-term continuity of the organization. On the other hand, the growing unpredictability of the organizational reality and the rise of career patterns across rather than within organizations, coupled with a weakened employment relationship for the sake of flexibility, has put the organizational investment into human capital and careers at risk (Cappelli and Keller, 2014; De Cuyper and De Witte, 2011; Hamori et al., 2011). In view of the importance of a return on human capital investments, this tension between long-term continuity and flexibility has caused some organizations to doubt the necessity of this type of investment into employees' careers and to reduce OCM (De Vos and Dries, 2013). The different OCM outcomes are explained in Table 14.1.

Organizational performance

OCM serves to improve employee productivity, which is linked directly to the organization's performance. At the same time, OCM implies an investment of time and money for organizations (Baruch, 2006), which impacts firm-level financial results. Thus, organizations in general – independent of the underlying career contract – will have an interest to quantify in how far their OCM investments are beneficial to the organizational performance in terms of, for example, financial performance such as shareholder value or profit, economic success resulting inter alia from market penetration, organizational efficiency, and productivity or cost savings.

However, not much is known about factual effects of OCM on organizational performance. While empirical evidence shows that investing in the development and retention of firm-specific human capital (what an organization would typically do in the case of the traditional career contract) is beneficial for organizational performance (Crook et al., 2011) and for saving costs related to replacements, the relationship in the case of a contemporary career contract is less clear. Baruch and Vardi (2016) argue that contemporary careers may include a number of undesired consequences such as stress or burnout, career-related forms of misconduct (e.g., deception, undermining, fraud, abuse), and a lower level of engagement that are likely to decrease individual productivity and thus harm the OCM outcome organizational performance. De Vos and Cambré (2017), by contrast, show that under the contemporary career contract, investing in OCM is beneficial for organizational performance in terms of profit before taxes, provided that OCM practices are supportive and developmental and, thus, not characterized by an organization-driven "one size fits all" approach.

Strategic flexibility

OCM contributes to an organization's strategic flexibility by managing its employees' careers in a way that ensures the inherent flexibility of the human resources available to the company (resource flexibility) and that increases the company's flexibility in applying those human resources to alternative courses of action (coordination flexibility) (cf. Sanchez, 1995). This strategic flexibility can, for example, be reached by numerical flexibility (adjustment of the number of workers), functional flexibility (adjustment of the qualification of workers allowing for their transferability to different activities and tasks within the firm), and spatial flexibility (transferability of personnel between different sites within the firm). OCM is expected to be associated with improved HR planning, which positively relates to numerical flexibility, and to improved HR selection as well as functional and job change, which leads to functional flexibility (Gutteridge et al., 1993a, 1993b). Thus, employees' employability and career capital represent resources that play a part in *generating* competitive advantage (Gutteridge et al., 1993a, 1993b; Kong et al., 2012; Tzabbar et al., 2003).

Traditional and contemporary careers are characterized by different sets of rules in regard to hiring, firing, and career development. Operating in stable environments involving few organizational changes, organizations with traditional career contracts can offer lifelong employment and numerical and spatial flexibility are likely to be of lower importance. Functional flexibility is reached via internal training and development activities that serve to adapt existing kinds and levels of qualifications and to fill in internal vacancies (Baruch, 2004).

Transactional employment relationships underlying contemporary career contracts allow organizations to respond more easily to instability and rapid changes in the environment (Clarke, 2013) and employees with contemporary careers take advantage of their career capital to get access to and keep jobs (Kovalenko and Mortelmans, 2014). Being organized through external labor markets (Tolbert, 1996), organizations with contemporary career contracts become more flexible and thus more competitive as they can adapt their staff in terms of number, qualification, and location by hiring and laying off employees via the external, local, and also global employment system (Baruch, 2004). One important means to increase functional flexibility is the acquisition of talent. By establishing and managing high-quality relationships with suppliers, such as universities, training institutions, or agencies, companies not only get access to talent but can also collaborate to ensure that the potential employees have the required skills (Dyer and Ericksen, 2006; Nijssen and Paauwe, 2012). OCM practices conducive to this functional flexibility include practices such as training and development aimed at competencies instead of jobs and horizontal career paths (e.g., cross-training, job rotation) that allow employees to perform a flexible range of tasks (Nijssen and Paauwe, 2012). Functional flexibility can also contribute to workforce scalability (i.e., the organizational ability to reconfigure and transform its human resources quickly and easily, ad infinitum; Dyer and Ericksen, 2006). Apart from internal transitions of labor, external mobility also plays a role because continuous renewals and restructurations are likely to be needed in organizational life due to internal and external pressures. To reach numerical flexibility, the outflow of human resources needs to be managed (e.g., by integrated outplacement processes in collaboration with possible alternative employers for the workforce or other mobility concepts like mobility centers; Nijssen and Paauwe, 2012). The specific OCM outcome is determined by the speed and ease with which these transitions are made. Further, diversity management has been shown to contribute to applicant attraction among women and minority groups who interpret this this commitment to diversity as providing strong opportunities for career growth and development, and thus can serve to satisfy the rapid growth in the organizational demand for highly skilled workers (Ng and Burke, 2005; Rynes and Cable, 2003), and also to tap diverse markets and customers (Dass and Parker, 1999). In consequence, especially companies with contemporary career contracts that are more strongly organized through external labor markets are likely to strive for diversity that contributes to their functional and numerical flexibility. In sum, we expect the OCM outcomes functional and numerical flexibility to be more important for companies with a contemporary rather than with a traditional career contract. Spatial flexibility can be reached by OCM practices contributing to employees' geographic organizational mobility and by an international dispersion of the workforce.

Thus, commitment to diversity as an OCM approach plays an important role in order to achieve functional, numerical, and spatial strategic flexibility. Evidence shows that organizations value international diversity of their workforce to enhance organizational effectiveness and to create a competitive advantage in cost structures, creativity, problem solving, and flexible adaptation to change (Cox and Blake, 1991; Horwitz and Horwitz, 2007; Stahl et al., 2010). Thus, any organization that depends on innovation and adaptability, independent of whether it adopts a traditional versus contemporary career contract, is likely to value diversity as a means to learn from employees' different perspective and as an OCM outcome.

Organizational size and growth rate

A core function of OCM is to ensure that the organization has the right number of motivated employees with the right knowledge and skills in the right place and the right time to meet its current and anticipated future needs and reach the strategic goals of the organization (Wright and Snell, 1998). Thus, a central OCM outcome is organizational size indicating organizational business strength and (market) power (Haveman, 1993; Oliver, 1990), and that is correlated to differentiation, specialization of personnel, and slack resources (Aiken and Hage, 1971; Moch and Morse, 1977).

Especially in developed countries, new patterns of production emerge in combination with a continuous technological progress that imply a strong growth of high skilled jobs and need for employees. Many organizations need to rationalize, downsize, and lay off their employees on a large scale to gain competitiveness or improve market value (Baruch, 2004). Thus having an economically reasonable number of the right employees is expected to represent an important OCM outcome under the contemporary career contract, whereas the traditional career contract is more likely to be connected to a high number of employees as a means of organizational success and power. Moreover, we expect to find higher rates of internal promotions in companies with a traditional career contract (Baruch and Rosenstein, 1992).

Reaching organizational growth in terms of (an increasing) number of employees in the presence of growth of the business is another OCM outcome. One means to achieve this is employee retention. The loyalty-based traditional psychological contract between employers and employees is institutionalized in the form of internal labor markets (Fuller, 2008; Mirvis and Hall, 1994). In order to avoid qualitative and quantitative human capital shortages, continuity in employment constitutes a key deliverable of traditional OCM policies. Voluntary employee turnover has been shown to be lower among employees with higher levels of organizational commitment (e.g., De Vos et al., 2008) and job and career embeddedness (Baruch and Vardi, 2016), career satisfaction (Guan et al., 2014, 2015), and perceived security that can be increased by organization career support (Granrose and Baccili, 2006; Sturges et al., 2010).

In the contemporary career model, by contrast, interorganizational career mobility is seen positively and as instrumental to career development in contemporary transitional labor markets (DeFillippi and Arthur, 1996; Gerber et al., 2009; Hall, 1996; Inkson et al., 2012). Employees are expected to be willing and able to make the transition to alternate employment as the need arises (Clarke, 2013). At the same time, organizations might fear the loss of valuable employees and will invest in OCM to motivate individuals to pursue their careers inside the organization. However, overall employee retention as an OCM outcome is of lower importance under the contemporary as compared to the traditional career contract.

Employer attractiveness

Tight labor markets challenge organizations in attracting and retaining employees (Barnett and Bradley, 2007). Low unemployment rates in combination with labor shortages result in a competitive environment, where it is increasingly difficult and costly to attract employees with the necessary skills. In order to be judged as an attractive employer by employees, organizations need to provide better working conditions than their competitors do. This aim can be particularly challenging for companies that implement a traditional psychological and career contract characterized by structured career paths and job stability. Baruch and Rosenstein (1992) provide empirical support for a positive relationship between the quality of the organizational career planning and managing with reputation in the area of HRM. However, structured career paths and employment continuity are becoming more difficult to provide by organizations that operate in a dynamic environment. Thus, Barnett and Bradley (2007) propose that organizations may meet this challenge by implementing a contemporary career contract that aims at supporting employees in career self-management and increasing their job and career satisfaction. Empirical studies were able to show that OCM is positively associated not only with high levels of job satisfaction (Baruch and Rosenstein, 1992; Kim, 2002) and career satisfaction (Barnett and Bradley, 2007; De Vos et al., 2008; Jung and Takeuchi, 2018) but also with organizational commitment (De Vos et al., 2008). Employer attractiveness is likely to be reflected in low absenteeism (De Vos and Cambré, 2017).

Organizational learning and development

Under the conditions of the contemporary employment relationship, the ability to develop employees who are able to adapt to and cope with the instability and continuous change becomes an important OCM outcome (Hall, 2002). The highly dynamic environment requires organizations to go through processes of organizational transformation and adaption, which involves a shift in competences and required knowledge as a continuous process (Dyer and Shafer, 2003). Thus organizations need to adopt a continuous learning perspective and make sure that throughout their careers, all relevant employees in the organization understand what is going on in their environment, are aware of the organizational developments, and change their knowledge, behavior, and activities accordingly. By processing information efficiently and creating information and knowledge, organizations create appropriate organizational knowledge. This dynamic capability leads to organizational agility (Nijssen and Paauwe, 2012). However, Baruch and Vardi (2016) warn that contemporary careers may result in a loss of some of the best employees and to damage organizations' institutional memory and organizational learning.

Prosocial impact

Prosocial impact describes the extent to which others are helped through the organization's work. Pressures to devote resources to corporate social responsibility (CSR) emerge from multiple stakeholder groups, such as employees. CSR is defined as "actions that appear to further some social good, beyond the interests of the firm and that which is required by law" (McWilliams and Siegel, 2001: 117). Alongside eliminating pollution or embodying products with social attributes or characteristics, adopting progressive OCM programs are examples of CSR actions (McWilliams and Siegel, 2001). Evidence shows that organizations that invest into CSR are more attractive to potential employees and may profit from increased worker retention, organizational commitment, organizational identification, and knowledge-sharing behavior (Brammer et al., 2007; Coldwell et al., 2008; Farooq et al., 2014; Greening and Turban, 2000). McWilliams and Siegel (2001) argue that the relevance of these effects is likely to increase with the tightness of the labor market. Simmons (2009) showed that employees seek functional, economic, psychological, and ethical benefits from their employer and see the provision of these benefits as indicative of a socially responsible employer. The contemporary contract implies that employees are values-driven in the sense that individuals want to act according to their own norms and values that provide the guidance and measure of career success (Briscoe and Hall, 2006). The significance of employee expectation of socially responsible behavior by their employer again is a main driver of CSR practice (Mont and Leire, 2009). Thus we expect CSR to be an especially important outcome of contemporary OCM. However, no study has so far defined prosocial impact as a potential OCM outcome and analyzed any effects.

Positive relationships

Increasing an organization's integration of processes, people, and technologies and cooperation within and across units of a firm requires significant implementation efforts and positive relationships between organizational actors and units. Organizational integration is defined as "the extent to which distinct and interdependent organizational components constitute a unified whole" and reflects "how harmoniously the different departments of an organization work together and how tightly coordinated their activities are" (Barki and Pinsonneault, 2005: 166). Achieving higher levels of integration requires the involvement and collaboration of many individuals and integrated processes require the close collaboration of individuals working in different organizational units who communicate and share their knowledge. To facilitate this collaboration, OCM practices such as training and (intra- and interorganizational) employee mobility are likely to be conducive by decreasing the borders that often exist between different units, departments, locations, or functional areas, especially in large organizations (Barki and Pinsonneault, 2005; De Vos et al., 2008). Lawrence and Lorsch (1967) state that integration is needed for organizations to be successful in turbulent environments, which is typically conducive to a change in the employment relationship. Since personal relationships develop over time, the comparably shorter employment relationship as typical for the contemporary psychological contract poses a challenge to contemporary OCM and underlines the importance of personal relationships as an OCM outcome. However, no study has so far defined positive relationships as a potential OCM outcome and provided empirical insights into its effects (e.g., on employee morale; Gutteridge et al., 1993a, 1993b).

Entrepreneurial/intrapreneurial success

We propose entre- and intrapreneurial success (i.e., an organization's ability to promote employees in their entre- and intrapreneurial ambitions through OCM) as another OCM outcome. Under the conditions of the contemporary career contract, organizations are no longer the manager of their employees' careers, but employees take over responsibility for career self-management (Hall, 1996). Organizations can take advantage of the transactional psychological contract in their OCM if they learn to find alternatives to laying people off. For example, organizations can enable employees or even entire teams, especially those with entrepreneurial capabilities, to form and lead a new satellite firm that may grow within the large corporation or buy out parts of the operation (Baruch, 2004; Peiperl and Baruch, 1997). To reach this step, different methods of selection are needed. Hence, the importance of entre-/intrapreneurial success is likely to be higher under the conditions of a contemporary career contract and to be reflected in employees' satisfaction with opportunities provided for entre- and intrapreneurial activities.

Fit of actors and the organizational career system

Gutteridge et al. (1993a: 71) argue that "new information and communications technologies, along with harsh global economic realities (e.g., downsizing), now require new ways of looking not only at career development but also at the appropriate balance between individual and organizational needs." The achievement of OCM outcomes presupposes two kinds of fit regarding actors and the environment: a fit between individual and organizational expectations regarding OCM and a fit between the organizational career system as determined by the environment and OCM (Baruch and Rosenstein, 1992; Tzabbar et al., 2003).

In the case of the traditional career contract, it is mainly the organization that controls OCM. If individuals perceive OCM to be too strongly controlled and, thus, experience a lack of fit, some employees might lose motivation, become alienated in case of a loss of choice options or take advantage of development possibilities offered to employees, such as a foreign assignment, with the intention of making use of the competencies acquired and the documented objective career success when changing employers.

Under the conditions of a contemporary career contract, both individuals and organizations still have preference for organizational careers according to most empirical studies (Cohen and Mallon, 1999; Dries, 2011; Granrose and Baccili, 2006; Lips-Wiersema and Hall, 2007). Moreover, individuals were found to expect to receive some kind of career management help from their employers (Sturges et al., 2000). In the same vein, De Vos and Dries (2013) were able to show in their study that – according to the more than 300 HR directors of companies located in Belgium who were surveyed – careers became more protean in terms of a focus on individual outcomes and individual accountability, but that a clear preference for intra-organizational career mobility and formalized career management practices prevailed. Hence, even under the conditions of a contemporary career contract involving a high personal responsibility of individuals for their careers, organizational career management and support is likely to be advantageous for organizations and individuals. Individuals can make use of OCM practices to manage their own career development and establish a fit between their career goals with the organization's future needs (De Vos et al., 2008). Organizational benefits include an increase in employer attractiveness to potential (highly qualified) applicants, an improved organizational image ("needs of the employees are taken into account by employer X"), and better employee retention (Torrington et al., 2008). As a consequence, organizations may project the image of a stable and predictable internal career structure to applicants and employees in order to signal a fit, because it is in their interest to do so, regardless of what reality is. However, if the image of a stable and predictable internal career structure is just an illusion, this strategy may fail and OCM outcomes may be low due to the lack of fit. Empirical research shows that individuals who perceive a match between their own and their employer's plans for their careers perceived higher satisfaction with their organization (Baruch and Rosenstein, 1992; Granrose and Portwood, 1987; Portwood and Granrose, 1986) and with their career (e.g., Barnett and Bradley, 2007; Crawshaw, 2006; Granrose and Portwood, 1987; Jung and Takeuchi, 2018). Additional indicators to be included in future research include employees' self-actualization (Zhou and Li, 2008) and the organization's satisfaction with the achievement of important OCM outcomes.

Companies are expected to develop different types of career systems that serve to cope with the specifics regarding the internal labor market structure, organizational size and structure, and technology that shape the employees' career development opportunities (Garavan and Coolahan, 1996; Hurley and Sonnenfeld, 1998; Sonnenfeld et al., 1988). Sonnenfeld and Peiperl (1988) distinguish between four organizational career systems depending on the supply flow (completely internal supply to largely external supply of managerial labor) and assignment flow (i.e., the degree to which assignment and promotion decisions are based on individual performance versus overall contribution to the group or organization). These career systems – named baseball, fortress, academy, and club – differ in terms of staffing, development, and exit practices. Innovative types of firms pursue the baseball team's career system. Companies with a baseball system focus on the recruitment of "stars" ("buy" approach to talent) that they train – also in skills that apply beyond their present job. As these organizations offer no employment security, employee turnover is comparably high. The fortress system is characteristic for organizations that fight for survival in highly competitive markets and who are at the mercy of their environments. Essentially reactive, employers hire and fire because of market conditions, or because of competition. Organizations with an academy system are both product innovators and competitors in long-run production roles. Thus they are committed to early career hiring, while some outsiders are hired to fill higher-level positions (combination of "make" and "buy" approach to human resources). Moreover, they emphasize long-term professional growth by investing into firm-specific skill development, offering lateral or dual career paths and tracking and retaining talent. Finally, the club system is found in firms that value cost control, predictability, and a short-term focus. With the aim to stabilize the old way, these companies "make" their own higher-level employees and retain them. Baruch and Peiperl (2003) who tested the model empirically showed that some though not all of the characteristics from the typology existed in practice.

The typology of career systems with their specific OCM suggests, first, that OCM outcomes in terms of, for example, attracting and keeping talent, becoming an attractive employer, or contributing to the strategic flexibility of the organization, differ content-wise depending on the organizational strategy pursued. Second, companies that fail to align their OCM efforts to their corporate strategy are likely to fail to generate meaningful outcomes. However, empirical studies that analyze these relationships are lacking so far.

Alignment with corporate norms and values

We propose that management does not only need to align the organization with the ever-changing context, but must also to cultivate desired norms and values in their members through socialization processes and development programs. In early career, employees and organizations compare and, ideally, adjust their definitions of career and career outcomes (Dries, 2011) and employees are tied to so-called appropriate identities (Pfeffer, 2010). Later in their careers, the anchoring of organizational norms and values serves to give employees a sense of direction, which is gaining in importance within a dynamic environment. For employees to be aligned and be able to make a contribution to the organization, it is important for them to know and understand the corporate norms and values. Moreover, the organization's career system with its typical career types needs to be anchored in employees' belief systems and career goals to reach an alignment. An alignment is likely to be reflected in employees' organizational commitment (e.g., Granrose and Portwood, 1987; Sturges et al., 2002) and job engagement (Baruch and Vardi, 2016; De Vos and Cambré, 2017). With the implementation of the contemporary career contract, however, employees are likely to experience different organizational cultures and career systems due to a necessity to change employers. In consequence, they need to adjust to different cultures and career systems throughout their career. Thus, at the same time, organizations need to help employees develop a clear sense of personal and work identity that can act as an internal compass (Hall, 2002). To conclude, employees' alignment with corporate norms and values as well as the organizational career system as an OCM outcome is likely to gain in importance under the conditions of a contemporary career contract.

Complementarity of individual and organizational career management outcomes

Organizations are social entities (i.e., they are part of society and encompass people with their diverse individual goals and needs). This means that implicitly or explicitly social and individual goals need to be taken into consideration in the corporate career goals. Typical individual career outcomes include salary, number and speed of promotions, hierarchical position, title/status, and kind of contract (e.g., Ng et al., 2005) but also learning and development, work-life balance, making a difference, and a social working environment (Mayrhofer et al., 2016; Shen et al., 2015). Social career outcomes have never been defined in the literature. They could comprise the length of the career (and its impact on the individuals' contribution to the social system) or the health-related aspects of careers (e.g., social costs related to sick days). The extent to which individual and social career outcomes are considered by organizations is likely to depend on various factors, such as legal grounds, employee participation, the personal attitude of the owner or the management group of the organization or the overall economic situation.

The aforementioned OCM outcomes suggest that they fulfill economic goals (e.g., organizational performance) as well as social goals (e.g., prosocial impact/corporate social responsibility) and individual goals (e.g., employer attractiveness). However, in view of the fact that individual career outcomes gain in importance under the condition of the contemporary career contract, research is needed with regards to the degree of compatibility between individual and OCM outcomes (i.e., competing, indifferent and/or complementary relationship). Moreover, the need to consider additional OCM outcomes that explicitly target individual goals in order to reach a good balance between organizational and individual expectations needs to be analyzed (see section 'Fit of actors and the organizational career system') as well as the factors that drive this need.

Summary

In this chapter, we responded to recent academic calls for bringing the organization back into the study of careers (Clarke, 2013; De Vos and Dries, 2013; Dries et al., 2012; Lee et al., 2014; Lips-Wiersema and Hall, 2007). The focus on OCM got lost over time with the claimed dominance of contemporary careers over traditional careers. However, Inkson et al. (2012) stress that the predominance of contemporary careers received only poor empirical support and that substantial groups of workers still follow traditional, organizational careers. Thus, the analysis of the continuum between traditional and contemporary career logics in terms of its implications for OCM is relevant. The contribution of this chapter to the literature is twofold: (1) we proposed a definition of OCM outcomes and presented a list of OCM outcomes including sample indicators relevant for all organizations; and (2) we argued that the importance of the different OCM outcomes and indicators may be different under traditional and contemporary OCM (interpreted as two poles of a continuum), in that some outcomes matter more for traditional and others more for contemporary OCM. Future studies can make use of this list of OCM outcomes and indicators by making a theoretically sound choice of which OCM outcome variables to include. While we find empirical support for the relationship between OCM and several of the outcomes and indicators presented, no study so far has systematically analyzed all outcomes and their relevance according to different career logics.

We argued that in the course of the change to the contemporary career, organizations' career outcomes are no longer nearly exclusively determined by factors such as organizational performance and efficiency, organizational size, and growth, but additional outcomes become more relevant, such as organizational learning and development, prosocial impact in terms of CSR, positive relationships leading to integration, and cooperation.

Contemporary OCM is likely to be conducive to organizational effectiveness by supporting individuals' career management activities and, thus, has a dual purpose in that it serves to establish a fit between the satisfaction of individual needs and the organization's requirements for productivity and effectiveness (Greenhaus et al., 2010). Yet the question of whether organizations with contemporary OCM that encourage career self-management perform better in terms of OCM outcomes than the ones with traditional OCM remains to be answered. First, empirical evidence suggests that this dual purpose can be reached on condition that contemporary OCM practices do not follow a "one-size-fits-all" approach, but are flexible (e.g., De Vos and Cambré, 2017). Another research area that needs to be worked on is the degree of compatibility of organizational and individual career outcomes and the need to consider additional individual career goals in OCM outcomes. Another question that remains is how much responsibility a company has to bear for the career management of their employees in order to reach their OCM outcomes in the traditional versus contemporary career environment. An additional field to investigate is whether an employer can take too much responsibility for career development and, if yes, to what extent this can have adverse effects on employees and reduce OCM outcomes (Baruch and Vardi, 2016). Finally, we see a clear need for research that aims at an inductive definition of OCM outcomes leading to the development of a comprehensive scale. This scale of OCM outcomes would allow researchers to measure OCM outcomes and to generate comparable empirical results about the relative importance of OCM outcomes and its determinants and influencing variables.

References

Aiken, M. & Hage, J. 1971. The organic organization and innovation. *Sociology and Social Research*, 5, 63–82.

Arnold, J. & Cohen, L. 2008. The psychology of careers in industrial and organizational settings: A critical but appreciative analysis. *In:* Hodgkinson, G.P. & Ford, J.K. (eds.) *International Review of Industrial and Organizational Psychology*. London: Wiley.

Arntz, G.T. & Zierahn, U. 2016. The risk of automation for jobs in OECD countries: A comparative analysis. *In: OECD Social, Employment and Migration Working Papers* #189. Paris: OECD Publishing. DOI: 10.1787/5jlz9h56dvq7-en.

Arthur, M.B. & Rousseau, D.M. (eds.) 1996. *The Boundaryless Career: A New Employment Principle for a New Organizational Era*. New York and Oxford: Oxford University Press.

Bambacas, M. 2010. Organizational handling of careers influences managers' organizational commitment. *Journal of Management Development*, 29, 807–827.

Barki, H. & Pinsonneault, A. 2005. A model of organizational integration, implementation effort, and performance. *Organization Science*, 16, 165–179.

Barnett, B.R. & Bradley, L. 2007. The impact of organisational support for career development on career satisfaction. *Career Development International*, 12, 617–636.

Baruch, Y. 2003. Career systems in transition: A normative model for career practices. *Personnel Review*, 32, 231–251.

Baruch, Y. 2004. Transforming careers: From linear to multidirectional career paths. *Career Development International*, 9, 58–73.

Baruch, Y. 2006. Career development in organizations and beyond: Balancing traditional and contemporary viewpoints. *Human Resource Management Review*, 16, 125–138.

Baruch, Y. & Peiperl, M.A. 2000. Career management practices: An empirical survey and implications. *Human Resource Management*, 39, 347–366.

Baruch, Y. & Peiperl, M.A. 2003. An empirical assessment of Sonnenfeld's career systems typology. *The International Journal of Human Resource Management*, 14, 1267–1283.

Baruch, Y. & Rosenstein, E. 1992. Human resource management in Israeli firms: Planning and managing careers in high-technology organizations. *The International Journal of Human Resource Management*, 3, 477–495.

Baruch, Y. & Vardi, Y. 2016. A fresh look at the dark side of contemporary careers: Toward a realistic discourse. *British Journal of Management*, 27, 355–372.

Boxall, P., Purcell, J. & Wright, P. (eds.) 2008. *The Oxford Handbook of Human Resource Management*. Oxford: Oxford University Press.

Brammer, S., Millington, A. & Rayton, B. 2007. The contribution of corporate social responsibility to organizational commitment. *International Journal of Human Resource Management*, 18, 1701–1719.

Briscoe, J.P. & Hall, D.T. 2006. The interplay of boundaryless and protean careers: Combinations and implications. *Journal of Vocational Behavior*, 69, 4–18.

Cappelli, P. & Keller, J.R. 2014. Talent management: Conceptual approaches and practical challenges. *Annual Review of Organizational Psychology and Organizational Behavior*, 1, 305–331.

Cavanaugh, M.A. & Noe, R.A. 1999. Antecedents and consequences of relational components of the new psychological contract. *Journal of Organizational Behavior*, 20, 323–340.

Clarke, M. 2013. The organizational career: Not dead but in need of redefinition. *International Journal of Human Resource Management*, 24, 684–703.

Cohen, L. & Mallon, M. 1999. The transition from organisational employment to portfolio working: Perceptions of 'boundarylessness'. *Work, Employment & Society*, 13, 329–352.

Coldwell, D.A., Billsberry, J., van Meurs, N. & Marsh, P.J.G. 2008. The effects of person-organization ethical fit on employee attraction and retention: Towards a testable explanatory model. *Journal of Business Ethics*, 78, 611–622.

Cox, T. & Blake, S. 1991. Managing cultural diversity: Implications for organizational competitiveness. *Executive*, 5, 45–56.

Crawshaw, J.R. 2006. Justice source and justice content: Evaluating the fairness of organisational career management practices. *Human Resource Management Journal*, 16, 98–120.

Crook, T.R., Todd, S.Y., Combs, J.G., Woehr, D.J. & Ketchen, D.J., Jr. 2011. Does human capital matter? A meta analysis of the relationship between human capital and firm performance. *Journal of Applied Psychology*, 96, 3.

Dass, P. & Parker, B. 1999. Strategies for managing human resource diversity: From resistance to learning. *Academy of Management Executive*, 13, 68–80.

DeFillippi, R.J. & Arthur, M.B. 1996. Boundaryless contexts and careers: A competency-based perspective. *In:* Arthur, M.B. & Rousseau, D.M. (eds.) *The Boundaryless Career: A New Employment Principle for a New Organizational Era*. Oxford: Oxford University Press.

de Cuyper, N. & de Witte, H. 2011. The management paradox: Self-rated employability and organizational commitment and performance. *Personnel Review*, 40, 152–172.

de Vos, A. & Cambré, B. 2017. Career management in high-performing organizations: A set-theoretic approach. *Human Resource Management*, 56, 501–518.

de Vos, A., Dewettinck, K. & Buyens, D. 2008. To move or not to move? *Employee Relations*, 30, 156–175.

de Vos, A., Dewettinck, K. & Buyens, D. 2009. The professional career on the right track: A study on the interaction between career self-management and organizational career management in explaining employee outcomes. *European Journal of Work and Organizational Psychology*, 18, 55–80.

de Vos, A. & Dries, N. 2013. Applying a talent management lens to career management: The role of human capital composition and continuity. *International Journal of Human Resource Management*, 24, 1816–1831.

Dries, N. 2011. The meaning of career success: Avoiding reification through a closer inspection of historical, cultural and ideological contexts. *Career Development International*, 16, 364–384.

Dries, N. & Pepermans, R. 2008. 'Real' high potential careers: An empirical study into the perspectives of organizations and high potentials. *Personnel Review*, 37, 85–108.

Dries, N., van Acker, F. & Verbruggen, M. 2012. How 'boundaryless' are the careers of high potentials, key experts and average performers? *Journal of Vocational Behavior*, 81, 271–279.

Dyer, L. & Ericksen, J. 2006. Dynamic organizations: Achieving marketplace agility through workforce scalability. *CAHRS Working Paper* #06–12.

Dyer, L. & Shafer, R. 2003. Dynamic organizations: Achieving marketplace and organizational agility with people. *In:* Peterson, R.S. & Mannix, E.A. (eds.) *Leading and Managing People in the Dynamic Organization*. Mahwah, NJ: Lawrence Erlbaum.

Eby, L.T., Allen, T.D. & Brinley, A. 2005. A cross-level investigation of the relationship between career management practices and career-related attitudes. *Group and Organization Management*, 30, 565–596.

Farooq, M., Farooq, O. & Jasimuddin, S.M. 2014. Employees' response to corporate social responsibility: Exploring the role of employees' collectivist orientation. *European Management Journal*, 32, 916–927.

Frey, C.B. & Osborne, M.A. 2013. *The Future of Employment: How Susceptible Are Jobs to Computerization?* [Online]. Available: http://www.oxfordmartin.ox.ac.uk/downloads/academic/The_Future_of_Employment.pdf [Accessed 13 August 2017].

Fuller, S. 2008. Job mobility and wage trajectories for men and women in the United States. *American Sociological Review*, 73, 158–183.

Garavan, T.N. & Coolahan, M. 1996. Career mobility in organizations: Implications for career development – Part 1. *Journal of European Industrial Training*, 20, 30–40.

Gerber, M., Wittekind, A., Grote, G. & Staffelbach, B. 2009. Exploring types of career orientation: A latent class analysis approach. *Journal of Vocational Behavior*, 75, 303–318.

Goffee, R. & Jones, G.P. 2000. Career, community, and social architecture: An exploration of concepts. *In:* Peiperl, M.A., Arthur, M.B., Goffee, R. & Morris, T. (eds.) *Career Frontiers: New Conceptions of Working Lives.* Oxford: Oxford University Press.

Granrose, C.S. & Baccili, P.A. 2006. Do psychological contracts include boundaryless or protean careers? *Career Development International*, 11, 163–182.

Granrose, C.S. & Portwood, J.D. 1987. Matching individual career plans and organizational career management. *Academy of Management Journal*, 30, 699–720.

Greenhaus, J.S., Callanan, G.A. & Godschalk, V.M. 2010. *Career Management.* Thousand Oaks, CA: Sage Publications.

Greening, D.W. & Turban, D.B. 2000. Corporate social performance as a competitive advantage in attracting a quality work force. *Business and Society*, 39, 254–280.

Guan, Y., Wen, Y., Chen, S.X., Liu, H., Si, W., Liu, Y., Wang, Y., Fu, R., Zhang, Y. & Dong, Z. 2014. When do salary and job level predict career satisfaction and turnover intention among Chinese managers? The role of perceived organizational career management and career anchor. *European Journal of Work and Organizational Psychology*, 23, 596–607.

Guan, Y., Zhou, W., Ye, L., Jiang, P. & Zhou, Y. 2015. Perceived organizational career management and career adaptability as predictors of success and turnover intention among Chinese employees. *Journal of Vocational Behavior*, 88, 230–237.

Gutteridge, J.H., Leibowitz, Z.B. & Shore, J.E. 1993a. A new look at organizational career development. *Human Resource Planning*, 16, 71–84.

Gutteridge, J.H., Leibowitz, Z.B. & Shore, J.E. 1993b. *Organizational Career Development: Benchmarks for Building a World-Class Workforce.* San Francisco: Jossey Bass.

Hall, D.T. 1996. Protean careers of the 21st century. *The Academy of Management Executive*, 10, 8–16.

Hall, D.T. 2002. *Careers in and Out of organizations.* Thousand Oaks, CA: Sage Publications.

Hall, D.T. 2004. The protean career: A quarter-century journey. *Journal of Vocational Behavior*, 65, 1–13.

Hamori, M., Bonet, R. & Cappelli, P. 2011. How organizations obtain the human capital they need. *In:* Burton-Jones, A. & Spender, J-C. (eds.) *The Oxford Handbook of Human Capital.* Oxford: Oxford University Press.

Haveman, H.A. 1993. Organizational size and change: Diversification in the savings and loan industry deregulation. *Administrative Science Quarterly*, 38, 20–50.

Herriot, P. & Pemberton, C. 1997. Facilitating new deals. *Human Resource Management Journal*, 7, 45–56.

Horwitz, S.K. & Horwitz, I.B. 2007. The effects of team diversity on team outcomes: A meta-analytic review of team demography. *Journal of Management*, 33, 987–1015.

Hurley, A.E. & Sonnenfeld, J.A. 1998. The effect of organizational experience on managerial career attainment in an internal labor market. *The Journal of Vocational Behavior*, 52, 172–190.

Inkson, K., Gunz, H., Ganesh, S. & Roper, J. 2012. Boundaryless careers: Bringing back boundaries. *Organization Studies*, 33, 323–340.

Jayasingam, S. & Yong, J. R. (2013). Affective commitment among knowledge workers: The role of pay satisfaction and organization career management. *The International Journal of Human Resource Management*, 24, 3903–3920.

Jung, Y. & Takeuchi, N. 2018. A lifespan perspective for understanding career self-management and satisfaction: The role of developmental human resource practices and organizational support. *Human Relations*, 71, 73–102.

Kanter, R.M. 1989. *When Giants Learn to Dance: Mastering the Challenges of Strategy, Management, and Careers in the 1990s*. New York: Simon and Schuster.

Kim, S. 2002. Organizational support of career development and job satisfaction. *Review of Public Personnel Administration*, 22, 276–294.

Kong, H., Cheung, C. & Song, H. 2012. Determinants and outcome of career competencies: Perspectives of hotel managers in China. *International Journal of Hospitality Management*, 31, 712–719.

Kovalenko, M. & Mortelmans, D. 2014. Does career type matter? Outcomes in traditional and transitional career patterns. *Journal of Vocational Behavior*, 85, 238–249.

Lawrence, P.R. & Lorsch, J.W. 1967. *Organization and Environment: Managing Differentiation and Integration*. Boston: Harvard University Press.

Lee, C.I.S.G., Felps, W. & Baruch, Y. 2014. Toward a taxonomy of career studies through bibliometric visualization. *Journal of Vocational Behavior*, 85, 339–352.

Lepak, D.P. & Snell, S.A. 2002. Examining the human resource architecture: The relationships among human capital, employment, and human resource configurations. *Journal of Management*, 28, 517–543.

Lewis, S. & Arnold, J. 2012. Organisational career management in the UK retail buying and merchandising community. *International Journal of Retail & Distribution Management*, 40, 451–470.

Lips-Wiersema, M. & Hall, D.T. 2007. Organizational career development is not dead: A case study on managing the new career during organizational change. *Journal of Organizational Behavior*, 28, 771–792.

Manpowergroup. 2018. *Talent Shortage Survey* [Online]. Available: https://go.manpowergroup.com/talent-shortage-2018#thereport [Accessed 1 September 2018].

Mayrhofer, W., Briscoe, J.P., Hall, D.T., Dickmann, M., Dries, N., Kaše, R., Parry, E. & Unite, J. 2016. Career success across the globe – Insights from the 5C project. *Organizational Dynamics*, 45, 197–205.

Mcwilliams, A. & Siegel, D. 2001. Corporate social responsibility: A theory of the firm perspective. *Academy of Management Review*, 26, 117–127.

Meijers, F. 1998. The development of a career identity. *International Journal for the Advancement of Counselling*, 20, 191–207.

Mirvis, P.H. & Hall, D.T. 1994. Psychological success and the boundaryless career. *Journal of Organizational Behavior*, 15, 365–380.

Moch, M.K. & Morse, E.V. 1977. Size, centralization and organizational adoption of innovation. *American Sociological Review*, 42, 716–725.

Mont, O. & Leire, C. 2009. Socially responsible purchasing in supply chains: Drivers and barriers in Sweden. *Social Responsibility Journal*, 5, 389–407.

Ng, E. & Burke, R.J. 2005. Person-organization fit and the war for talent: Does diversity management make a difference? *International Journal of Human Resource Management*, 16, 1195–1210.

Ng, T.W.H., Eby, L.T., Sorensen, K.L. & Feldman, D.C. 2005. Predictors of objective and subjective career success: A meta-analysis. *Personnel Psychology*, 58, 367–408.

Nicholson, N. 1996. Career systems in crisis: Change and opportunity in the information age. *Academy of Management Executive*, 10, 40–51.

Nijssen, M. & Paauwe, J. 2012. HRM in turbulent times: How to achieve organizational agility? *The International Journal of Human Resource Management*, 23, 3315–3335.

Noe, R.A. 1996. Is career management related to employee development and performance? *Journal of Organizational Behavior*, 17, 119–133.

Noe, R.A., Hollenbeck, J.R., Gerhart, B. & Wright, P.M. 2016. *Human Resource Management*. New York, McGraw-Hill.

Oliver, C. 1990. Determinants of interorganizational relationships: Integration and future directions. *Academy of Management Review*, 15, 241–265.

Pazy, A. (1988). Joint responsibility: The relationships between organizational and individual career management and the effectiveness of careers. *Group & Organization Studies*, 13, 311–331.

Peiperl, M.A., Arthur, M.B., Goffee, R. & Morris, T. (eds.) 2000. *Career Frontiers: New Conceptions of Working Lives*. Oxford: Oxford University Press.

Peiperl, M.A. & Baruch, Y. 1997. Back to square zero: The post-corporate career. *Organizational Dynamics*, 25, 7–22.

Pfeffer, J. 2010. Management practices that sustain values. *In:* Giacalone, R.A. & Jurkiewicz, C.L. (eds.) *Handbook of Workplace Spirituality and Organizational Performance.* Armonk, NY: M.E. Sharpe.

Portwood, J.D. & Granrose, C.S. 1986. Organizational career management programs: What's available? What's effective? *Human Resource Planning,* 9, 107–119.

Rehman, S. 2017. Impact of career development on organizational commitment. *International Journal of Business and Administrative Studies,* 3, 100–111.

Rousseau, D.M. 1989. Psychological and implied contracts in organizations. *Employee Responsibilities and Rights Journal,* 2, 121–139.

Rousseau, D.M. 1990. New hire perceptions of their own and their employer's obligations: A study of psychological contracts. *Journal of Organizational Behavior,* 11, 389–400.

Rousseau, D.M. 1995. *Psychological Contracts in Organizations: Understanding Written and Unwritten Agreements.* Thousand Oaks, CA: Sage Publications.

Rynes, S.L. & Cable, D.M. 2003. Recruiting research in the 21st century: Moving to a higher level. *In:* Borman, W., Ilgen, D. & Klimoski, R. (eds.) *The Complete Handbook of Psychology, Industrial and Organizational Psychology.* New York: Wiley.

Sanchez, R. 1995. Strategic flexibility in product competition. *Strategic Management Journal,* 16, 135–159.

Sargent, L.D. & Domberger, S.R. 2007. Exploring the development of a protean career orientation: Values and image violations. *Career Development International,* 12, 545–564.

Schein, E.H. 1978. *Career Dynamics: Matching individual and Organizational needs.* Reading, MA: Addison-Wesley.

Schnake, M.E., Williams, R.J. & Fredenberger, W. 2007. Relationships between frequency of use of career management practices and employee attitudes, intention to turnover, and job search behavior. *Journal of Organizational Culture, Communications and Conflict,* 11, 53–63.

Segers, J. & Inceoglu, I. 2012. Exploring supportive and developmental career management through business strategies and coaching. *Human Resource Management,* 51, 99–120.

Shen, Y., Demel, B., Unite, J., Briscoe, J.P., Hall, D.T., Chudzikowski, K., Mayrhofer, W., Abdul-Ghani, R., Bogicevic Milikic, B., Colorado, O., Fei, Z., Heras, M.L., Ogliastri, E., Pazy, A., Poon, J.M.L., Shefer, D., Taniguchi, M. & Zikic, J. 2015. Career success across 11 countries: Implications for international human resource management. *International Journal of Human Resource Management,* 26, 1753–1778.

Simmons, J.A. 2009. Both sides now: Aligning external and internal branding for a socially responsible era. *Marketing Intelligence and Planning,* 27, 681–697.

Sonnenfeld, J.A. & Peiperl, M.A. 1988. Staffing policy as a strategic response: A typology of career systems. *Academy of Management Review,* 13, 588–600.

Sonnenfeld, J.A., Peiperl, M.A. & Kotter, J.P. 1988. Strategic determinants of managerial labor markets: A career systems view. *Human Resource Management,* 27, 369–388.

Stahl, G.K., Maznevski, M.L., Voigt, A. & Jonsen, K. 2010. Unraveling the effects of cultural diversity in teams: A meta-analysis of research on multicultural work groups. *Journal of International Business Studies,* 41, 690–709.

Sturges, J., Conway, N., Guest, D. & Liefooghe, A. 2005. Managing the career deal: The psychological contract as a framework for understanding career management, organizational commitment and work behavior. *Journal of Organizational Behavior,* 26, 821–838.

Sturges, J., Conway, N. & Liefooghe, A. 2010. Organizational support, individual attributes and the practice of career-self management behavior. *Group and Organization Management,* 35, 108–141.

Sturges, J., Guest, D., Conway, N. & Mackenzie Davey, K. 2002. A longitudinal study of the relationship between career management and organizational commitment among graduates in the first ten years at work. *Journal of Organizational Behavior,* 23, 731–748.

Sturges, J., Guest, D. & Mackenzie Davey, K. 2000. Who's in charge? Graduates attitudes to and experiences of career management and their relationship with organizational commitment. *European Journal of Work & Organizational Psychology,* 9, 351–370.

Sullivan, S.E. & Baruch, Y. 2009. Advances in career theory and research: A critical review and agenda for further exploration. *Journal of Management,* 35, 1542–1571.

Tolbert, P.S. 1996. Occupations, organizations and boundaryless careers. *In:* Arthur, M.B. & Rousseau, D.M. (eds.) *The boundaryless career: A new employment principle for a new organizational era.* New York: Oxford University Press.

Torrington, D., Hall, L. & Taylor, S. 2008. *Human Resource Management*. Harlow, Essex: Pearson Education.

Tzabbar, D., Vardi, Y. & Baruch, Y. 2003. Organizational career management in Israel. *Career Development International*, 8, 88–96.

Verbruggen, M. 2012. Psychological mobility and career success in the "new" career climate. *Journal of Vocational Behavior*, 81, 289–297.

Wright, P.M. & Snell, S.A. 1998. Toward a unifying framework for exploring fit and flexibility in strategic human resource management. *Academy of Management Review*, 23, 756–772.

Zhou, W. & Li, B. 2008. Study on the relationship between organizational career management and job involvement. *Frontiers of Business Research in China*, 2, 116–136.

15

Career patterns

Katja Dlouhy, Claartje J. Vinkenburg, and Torsten Biemann

Introducing the concept of career patterns

The origins of the construct of career patterns stem from industrial sociology. It was initially described as the number, duration, and sequence of jobs in the work history of individuals (Savickas, 2001). Early examples of research on career patterns include Wilensky (1961), who identified orderly, borderline, disorderly, and one job only careers; and Kalleberg and Hudis (1979), who distinguished between stayers, occupation-only-movers, firm-only-movers, and both-movers. Although the existence of career patterns is largely undisputed in careers research, there is still no widely accepted definition and a lack of conceptual clarity. In this chapter, we thus first offer a working definition of career patterns. We then give a brief overview of methods that can be used to analyze career patterns before reviewing the existing literature on career patterns through different lenses. In this effort, we answer three related questions: what is the extent of empirical evidence about career patterns, what do career patterns "objectively" look like, and how are patterns typically measured and analyzed?

We define career patterns as clusters of similar careers. Following Arthur et al. (1989), a career can be described as "the evolving sequence of a person's work experiences over time" (ibid.: 8). Thus, work experiences form the building blocks of individuals' careers. While content, order, and length of work experiences vary among individuals, we might find some sequences of work experiences that occur in the data more frequently than others do. These accumulations of similar sequences of work experiences form career patterns. It is important to note that the careers that together form a career pattern do not have to be identical. For example, individuals that follow a "full-time mobile career" pattern (e.g., Biemann et al., 2012) are characterized by full-time employment in various organizations, while the timing of the change from one organization to another might differ among individuals within this pattern. As this example indicates, career patterns are also not bounded by organizations or organizations' career planning.

It is not sufficient for a career pattern to emerge if an organization develops desired career pathways, but employees choose other ways (Gunz, 1989). Career patterns emerge only if the data show actual clusters of similar careers. Consequently, career patterns are an empirical classification concept rather than a typology (Doty and Glick, 1994). This means that career patterns are usually based on observable clusters of careers. While this approach to define career patterns has some advantages, it is difficult to determine the minimum degree of similarity and the frequency that is necessary for a career pattern to emerge. However, we will use this working definition in the remainder of this chapter and try to refine it with examples. Our understanding of career patterns is also shaped by the methodology used and by the lens we apply when trying to capture different patterns – including an individual, occupational, and contextual lens.

Methods for "capturing" career patterns

Research on career patterns requires methods that allow for measuring and analyzing whole career trajectories over the life course, not just occupational states or career outcomes at specific points in time. There have been frequent calls for the use of longitudinal data in numerous fields of research, as many research questions cannot be fully answered by studies using cross-sectional data. However, when conducting research on career patterns, the use of longitudinal data is especially important, because careers should be measured "as they are" (Vinkenburg and Weber, 2012). When searching for general patterns in careers (e.g., in Biemann et al., 2012; Joseph et al., 2012), data should cover a significantly large amount of career histories. Still, for specific research questions, only periods with critical work experience or life role transitions may be important, for example transitions from education to work (Anyadike-Danes and McVicar, 2010; Brzinsky-Fay, 2007) or transitions from work to retirement (Cahill et al., 2006; Han and Moen, 1999).

Information on occupational positions, promotions, and employer changes can often be derived from panel studies. Several large national household panels exist that offer easily accessible data not only on careers but also on personality values, health, and industry characteristics; examples include the German Socio-Economic Panel, the United Kingdom Household Longitudinal Study, and the Swiss Household Panel. Retrospective questionnaires and interviews are another possible source for career data. Information on occupational positions, promotions, or employer changes is usually well remembered and easily recalled even after years or decades. An interview method that can help overcome potential memory gaps is the event calendar method (Axinn et al., 1999; Kovalenko and Mortelmans, 2014), where life events are recalled as sequences. Another method that can help to assess data retrospectively is life grid interviews, which can improve recall (Berney and Blane, 2003) through structuring life events. A further possibility to retrieve career data is using information from individuals' CVs. Biemann and Wolf (2009), for example, collected publicly available data from CVs on company websites to study top managers' career patterns.

Interval-scaled or metric longitudinal data can be analyzed with statistical methods like regression analysis, multilevel analysis, or latent growth models. Career data, however, are frequently available only in categorical form, for example in the form of different states or categories for employment ("full-time employed"), hierarchical position ("middle manager level 2"), or upward career mobility ("promotion"). When categorical data have been collected for a certain period of time, single occupational states can be coded and appended to the preceding state such that career sequences are generated.

Those sequences can be analyzed with sequence analysis methods, for example with optimal matching analysis (for a more detailed description of optimal matching analysis and for recommendations on its use, see Abbott and Tsay (2000) or Biemann and Datta (2014). Career sequences are assessed as wholes, as the timing of events is important and should be preserved in the analysis. Career sequences or occupational trajectories can then be clustered according to similarity, with the resulting clusters containing sequences with similar underlying career patterns. One cluster could for example contain careers with stable, full-time employment career patterns, while another cluster would contain careers with upward mobility patterns (Biemann et al., 2012). A review of studies that deal with individuals' career patterns and apply sequence analysis can be found in Dlouhy and Biemann (2015).

Career patterns through the lens of individual differences

Most readily observable are individuals' objective career trajectories, specifically the observable sequences of positions they have occupied during their working life (Gunz and Jalland, 1996). They are shaped by individual differences, as personality variables affect entry into specific occupations and professional careers and also career mobility, such as promotions and employer changes. When looking at individual differences, the variables gender and age in particular as well as several personality variables have been shown to affect career patterns. In the following, we review studies that assess how individual factors are linked to career patterns.

Socio-demographic variables

Gender has a large impact on the evolvement of career patterns. Disparities between career patterns of men and women have been found in several studies: women frequently follow rather unstable, fragmented career patterns, and they also more often work part-time (Valcour and Tolbert, 2003; Vinkenburg and Weber, 2012). In a German sample that covered occupational and employment trajectories over 20 years, the majority of people with discontinuous and part-time careers were women (Biemann et al., 2012). In this study, interaction effects among gender and marital status as well as the number of children were shown to decrease the probability for women to follow a stable, full-time employment career pattern. Similar findings come from a study on gendered career patterns in Denmark in several birth cohorts (Ratniece and Nielson, 2016). Moreover, men have been shown to be more likely to change positions in one organization when pursuing their career, while women have been found to be more likely to move across employers (Valcour and Tolbert, 2003).

There exist several explanations for gender differences in career patterns. First, in most countries, women have a larger share in care responsibilities than men, including care for children, aging parents, and other dependents (Cabrera, 2007). The transition to parenthood has therefore an unequal impact on men's and women's occupational trajectories (Widmer and Ritschard, 2009). One reason here might be that it is easier and also more expected for individuals who have lower hierarchical positions and who are less commonly self-employed to switch from full-time to part-time employment, as it is more often the case for women (Biemann et al., 2012; Zacher et al., 2012). From their review of literature on women's careers, O'Neil et al. (2013) conclude that women are also facing several other obstacles when pursuing upward career patterns compared to men: they have fewer network ties and mentoring relationships than men, and are thus less likely to move to senior management positions (Ibarra, 1997). Furthermore, there are gender-specific occupational differences. Women work less often than men in the finance, mathematics, and consulting areas (Barbulescu and Bidwell, 2013; Reuben et al., 2014), and more often in caregiving and low-grade education professions (Ruggie, 2014). In these gender-typical occupations, women might have fewer opportunities for upward mobility than men.

Toning down claims of huge gender differences in career patterns, Brueckner and Mayer (2005) observed a homogenization of women's and men's life courses in Germany. Those converged in terms of education and labor force participation. That women's and men's work and life trajectories are becoming increasingly similar was also pointed out by McMunn and colleagues (2015); however, in their study too, careers involving part-time employment or unstable careers remained more common for women. In a small sample of female executives' career patterns, Blair-Loy (1999) found that their careers became more rigid and inflexible over time, resembling the career patterns of executive men.

Another individual variable that shapes career patterns is age. After having worked in a specific occupation for several years or decades, it gets more difficult to change the career path. Even though it would be theoretically possible for older employees to completely change their occupation, such a change often comes at the cost of making the previous education and career efforts at least partly futile. This is different when individuals stay in their occupation, but change their employment status to become self-employed. Older individuals have been found to be more often self-employed (Biemann et al., 2012). In a study of 24 years of career patterns in a German sample, being male and older increased the likeliness of following a continuous self-employment career pattern (Zacher et al., 2012). Younger individuals, on the other hand, have been found to be more flexible and to change their employers more often than older individuals (Ng and Feldman, 2009).

Personality variables

Before even starting a professional career, the choice of a vocational education or field of study is already a consequence of specific personality dispositions. These are often conceptualized using the Big Five model, interests, and self-efficacy (Rottinghaus et al., 2002). Rubinstein (2005), for example, found that law students were lower on agreeableness than students from other faculties like natural sciences. Educational aspirations have also been shown to shape the educational duration and thus the initial phase of women's careers. In a study of Swedish women's careers, career data for 27 years were analyzed with optimal matching analysis (Huang et al., 2007). Qualifying findings on the role of gender for career patterns, women were more career-oriented and less family-oriented; they were also more likely to have a continuous full-time working pattern.

Some individuals change their employers and their jobs more often than others (Ghiselli, 1974; Judge and Watanabe, 1995), irrespective of how satisfied they are with their work, pay, and with other aspects of working life that have been shown to influence turnover intentions. This behavior of frequent employer changes was termed as the "hobo syndrome" (Ghiselli, 1974). It seems to result from internal notions and to occur for seemingly instinctive reasons (Judge and Watanabe, 1995). In another study by Woo (2011) this urge to move, which shaped individuals career patterns, was related to higher levels of openness to experience. Woo (2011) differentiated between individuals who quit because they enjoyed leaving and starting over again in another job, and individuals who had to quit their job on a frequent basis but did not feel happy about doing so.

Other personality variables have an influence on whether individuals choose to be self-employed, be it in their old profession or starting in another occupation all over again. The intention to become and to stay self-employed has been shown to be stronger for individuals with more positive attitudes towards risk and independence (Nieß and Biemann, 2014; Douglas and Shepherd, 2002). A sample from the large German Socio-Economic panel study incorporated career sequences consisting of up to 24 annual employment states (Zacher et al., 2012). One specific personality variable that was positively related to pursuing a stable self-employment pattern was conscientiousness.

There exists vast evidence on how personality variables affect various career moves, for example changes in hierarchical position (Ng et al., 2005) or turnover (Griffeth et al., 2000). For example, personality characteristics like extraversion or openness to experience are positively correlated to career patterns with frequent job changes (Timmerman, 2006). Some variables that have been shown to be positively linked to upward career mobility and higher job status are a proactive personality (Seibert et al., 1999), extraversion and openness to experience (Gelissen and de Graaf, 2006; Seibert and Kraimer, 2001), and agentic orientation (Abele, 2003). As those personality variables affect single career stages, they consequently also affect career patterns.

Career patterns through an occupational lens

For some occupations, specific vocational education is needed, while others demand more generic study or an extensive further education. Transitions into the labor market and the career patterns that follow are thus often linked to specific forms of education. Also, in some occupations, types of employment, or industries, upward or flexible career patterns are easier to pursue than in others (e.g., in the public sector; Biemann et al., 2012; Ratniece and Nielson, 2016). In the following, we present evidence on how education and occupation shape career patterns, drawing on the literature on career patterns of employees with low-qualification jobs, and also the literature on career patterns of managers and science workers in academia.

Career patterns of individuals with low qualifications

Lower education and occupational qualification have been linked to lower promotion rates and job success (Ng et al., 2005) and to higher turnover (Griffeth et al., 2000). When studying career sequences covering the first 72 months of economic activity after leaving school, McVicar and Anyadike-Danes (2002) found that a poor education was linked to individuals' unsuccessful transitions from education to the labor market. Even at the beginning of their careers, which were yet to evolve, individuals without further education experienced pronounced phases of unemployment.

In a study on employment security in 13 European countries, Kovalenko and Mortelmans (2016) found that career patterns of low-educated individuals have become more precarious in several countries. Neither do they benefit from operating in flexible labor markets, nor are they qualified for external job mobility to boost their careers like highly educated individuals. Consequently, they are more likely to have careers with low job security and pay. In the management literature, there was not much emphasis on career patterns of individuals with low qualification; most findings here stem from the field of sociology. The management literature focuses more on individuals whose education and occupation allow for upward job mobility and diverse career patterns, as we will see in the following sections.

Scientists' career patterns

Career conventions in science entail normative descriptions of what careers in science should look like. The ideal of science likely translates into career conventions in terms of steady progress (Hewlett et al., 2008), path dependence (i.e., being predetermined for a career path early on; Gunz and Peiperl, 2007; Xie and Shauman, 2003), (inter)national mobility (Miller et al., 2005; Morano-Foadi, 2005), and gaining independence (Careers, 2017). These conventions have been surprisingly stable, despite the increasing diversity among those who do science, and the challenges to the conventional view of science careers associated with it (Long and Fox, 1995; Fumasoli et al., 2015). However, we lack insight into the appearance and frequency of "actual" career patterns in science across distinct institutional, disciplinary, and national contexts. The profound disconnect between this lack of insights and the often implicit but compelling notion of what a conventional career in science looks like, was the starting point of a literature review.

Our search of peer-reviewed published research on "career patterns in science" (the search strategy and criteria for which are available from the second author) resulted in a final selection of 23 unique articles. Strictly speaking only one of the reviewed studies empirically identifies and differentiates between distinct career patterns in academia (Wessel and Keim, 1994), for a sample of university presidents. In some of the studies career patterns are developed from literature reviews or theoretical considerations, for example in the analysis of careers with as opposed to careers without boundaries (Bilimoria et al., 2013; Martin Conley, 2005; Nerad and Cerny, 1999). Other studies compare careers in the fundamental sciences with careers in the applied sciences or careers in industry with careers in academia (e.g., Agarwal and Ohyama, 2013). Most studies classify individual research careers by looking at characteristics of the PhD program and early career progress on later career success, such as promotion, prestige, and income (Agarwal and Ohyama, 2013; Cable and Murray, 1999; Chubin et al., 1981; Hadani et al., 2012; Long et al., 1993; Rosenfeld and Jones, 1987). Research productivity in terms of publications, patents, and grants appears both as a predictor as well as an indicator of career success (Chubin et al., 1981; Dietz and Bozeman, 2005; Jagsi et al., 2011). Miller et al. (2005) find path dependence in terms of the impact of earlier success and productivity on later career stages. Subjective career experiences are discussed in studies based on interviews with scientists (Duberley and Cohen, 2010; Duberley et al., 2006; Fumasoli et al., 2015; Vázquez-Cupeiro and Elston, 2006), including accounts of promotion practices (Winchester et al., 2006).

Managerial career patterns

Vinkenburg and Weber (2012) in their review show the existing empirical evidence on managerial career patterns. From their literature review of 33 published empirical studies of managerial career patterns found in electronic bibliographic databases, it is clear that upward mobility is the norm against which careers are held. Upward mobility does not only mean promotion within organizations, but could also imply moving across organizations, industries, and occupations. In the studies reviewed, career patterns that deviate from the upward mobility norm are labeled negatively such as "deviant," "plodding," "flat," "plateaued," or "interrupted" (Vinkenburg and Weber, 2012: 603). Normative notions of upward mobility remain in place even in studies that contrast traditional or "old" career patterns (pre-1990) to contemporary or "new" career patterns (post-1990). The methodology used in the reviewed studies, as well as where and when the data were collected (i.e., empirical access), shapes the nature and number of the unique career patterns identified.

To illustrate the impact of empirical access, Vinkenburg and Weber (2012) show how the career patterns of cohorts of business school alumni tend to diverge, whereas career patterns of top management team members tend to converge over time. The organizational career evidently is not dead (Clarke, 2013) – organizations clearly still act as containing social structures for the patterning of managerial careers. In fact, contemporary managerial careers, despite some evidence of increasing inter-organizational mobility, appear to have new linearity-inducing boundaries set for example by executive searchers (Vinkenburg and Weber, 2012). A scan of the peer-reviewed literature on managerial career patterns that has appeared since 2012 shows a heightened interest in sequence analysis as a method (Andresen and Biemann, 2013), a renewed focus on elites (Davoine and Ravasi, 2013; Koch et al., 2017), and efforts to get a clearer grip on the incidence and consequences of inter-organizational mobility (Sammarra et al., 2013).

Career patterns through a contextual lens

Career patterns are shaped by the context in which they evolve. The environmental context includes regions or countries in which individuals live, and thus also the institutional context including laws, work policies and educational systems. The organizational context does also have an impact on the evolvement of careers; in our review, we focus on the influence of up-or-out systems on career patterns as an example. Finally, the temporal context has some influence on career patterns, and we assessed whether global changes have led to current career patterns being different from those in previous decades.

Environmental context

It was shown in a study with longitudinal data from a large sample of higher education graduates that the accessibility of jobs in a region negatively affects individuals' mobility patterns and positively affects early career success (Middeldorp et al., 2016). Not only the local job market, but also the institutional context is important. When analyzing school leavers' entry patterns to the labor market in 10 European countries, Brzinsky-Fay (2007) found that the highest volatility in careers exists in countries with well-established training systems. Also in a study on differences in early career patterns, Scherer (2001) found that those were mainly shaped by different education and training systems in West Germany and Great Britain. However, differences occurred mainly in the frequency of different patterns, but not so much in the pattern's characteristics. For example, more individuals followed a pattern that consisted only of positions in full-time employment in Germany, while in trajectories of British individuals, unemployment spells occurred more often.

Gender differences have been shown to vary across countries. An international comparative study of women's career patterns found that, over time, women were increasingly likely to combine motherhood and employment in many of the 18 OECD countries under research (Nieuwenhuis et al., 2012). Females with children were more likely to be employed in societies where it is easier to return from parental leave, and with limited family allowances. In a study by Scherer (2001) that focused on early career patterns during the first five years of employment after finishing education, the gender gap was more pronounced in Germany than in Great Britain. While fewer women in the German sample followed a stable, full-time career pattern, far more women in the sample from Great Britain had stable career trajectories (Scherer, 2001).

Up-or-out systems

As argued above, upward mobility is the norm against which careers are held, especially in science and in management occupations. The organizations in which these careers play out act as containing social structures for the patterning of careers (Vinkenburg and Weber, 2012). This is especially the case in so-called up-or-out career systems, which are common to academia, the military, and professional service firms. In corporate settings, high potential and talent development programs take on similar characteristics. Careers in such settings are subjected to a linear promotion process determined by elaborate performance measurements based on objective criteria and fixed time frames. In order to sustain the pyramidal shape of the hierarchy, those not advancing to the next career level according to the given parameters are "counseled to leave" (Ossenkop et al., 2015). Generally, an up-or-out system strongly suggests meritocracy through its reliance on formal procedures and transparent criteria. Indeed, in high-prestige settings such as academia and law, "performance criteria tend to be objective (e.g., billable hours or research productivity), yet reward allocation decision-making is highly subjective, opaque, and adversarial, and often involves high stakes" due to up-or-out promotion norms (Joshi et al., 2015: 1533).

If the systemic or structural conditions under which careers develop have such a large impact on the patterns that appear (namely up or out), it is interesting to explore why it appears to be easier for some compared to others to make it to the top of the hierarchy – and more likely for others than for some to leave the system. Clearly, gender, race or ethnicity, and social class sometimes outweigh pure merit when it comes to success in such systems (Vinkenburg, 2017). In addition, a system that was built on an increasingly obsolete male breadwinner/female caregiver model will no longer generate optimal results when faced with the realities of dual earners (or singles) who combine a career with care responsibilities throughout the life course (van Engen et al., 2012; Vinkenburg et al., 2015).

Temporal context

There are numerous studies that examine whether changes in career patterns have occurred and whether those are nowadays less stable than career patterns of people in previous decades. Individuals born around 1920 experienced heterogeneous life courses and work trajectories because of World War II. Evidence from West Germany shows that with rising prosperity, the cohorts born around 1955 and 1960 took a longer time to complete their education and training phase than any other cohort so far (Brückner and Mayer, 2005). Work and family trajectories achieved a high level of uniformity by the 1960s in most Western countries (Widmer and Ritschard, 2009).

In a qualitative study of career mobility patterns, Lyons et al. (2012) demonstrated that younger generations change jobs and employers at a greater rate than previous generations and that they are more willing to accept non-upward career moves. In their study on career achievement systems, Stovel et al. (1996) identified typical career patterns of employees in one company from 1890 to 1970. Over this extensive period of time, careers changed from being very stable – an employee could serve as a clerk for his whole occupational life – to getting more dynamic. In those dynamic and modern career patterns, mobility signaled achievement while stasis signaled poor performance and led to job changes (Stovel et al., 1996).

In a British sample, Malo and Muñoz-Bullón (2003) found that older cohorts have fewer changes in employment status (unemployment, second education, etc.), while younger cohorts show greater overall mobility and have rather homogeneous career patterns. In their study, they used optimal matching analysis for pattern detection, and included several cohorts that were born between 1906 and 1959 in their analysis. For younger cohorts, the probability of involuntary job changes was higher. Overall, mobility in employment status has increased during the 20th century (Malo and Muñoz-Bullón, 2003).

Martin et al. (2008) studied changes in career activity patterns of young British adults to see whether career sequences have become more diverse. Evidence from two cohorts born in 1958 and 1970, with career sequences that covered 14 years, suggests that they have changed to some degree, although not to a large extent. Using panel data from the Swiss Household Panel, Widmer and Ritschard (2009) also assessed whether a de-standardization of occupational patterns has taken place among cohorts. They found that while men in younger cohorts have maintained fairly stable and linear career trajectories, women nowadays more often switch between full-time employment, part-time employment, and family work. Rodrigues and Guest (2010) find that job tenure and turnover have remained relatively stable in Europe, Japan, and the United States. A growth of boundaryless careers, which is defined in terms of increasing mobility, thus cannot be fully supported by empirical evidence.

Discussion

When reviewing the existing literature, we used different lenses to uncover factors that influence the evolution of career patterns. Having presented different conceptualizations of career patterns, we proposed a new definition of career patterns that is more inclusive, no matter through which lens researchers look. We also collected evidence and gained insights from a number of disciplines. The studies that we reviewed were mainly conducted in the fields of management, sociology, and psychology, which all have an interest in describing and predicting the development of individuals' work histories and career patterns. Many studies that we presented here used longitudinal data which were oftentimes analyzed with sequence analysis methods.

As longitudinal career data have been mostly collected in large panels from the 1970s onwards, there exists some evidence on how career patterns have changed in the course of the last few decades (Martin et al., 2008; Malo and Muñoz-Bullón, 2003; Widmer and Ritschard, 2009). Other than various psychological constructs or performance indicators whose measures are nowadays often outworn, older data on careers and occupational trajectories can be analyzed using modern analysis techniques. In the literature on career patterns, there exist several studies that deal with gender differences – first, because gender has been assessed in all panel studies, no matter when they started, and second, because gender always has been and still is one of the great determinants of career pattern development. There are also many studies that deal with differences between individuals' career patterns in gender-homogeneous groups (Anyadike-Danes and McVicar, 2010; Huang and Sverke, 2007; Simonson et al., 2011).

Career patterns of different cohorts are relatively easily compared, and as there have been enormous changes in occupations, gender equality, and political systems in the last decades, the existing data cover much of the evolution in career patterns in Western countries. However, since sequence analysis methods in career research first emerged during the 1990s, previous studies frequently offered merely case descriptions when it came to assessing career trajectories. In many countries, changes in legislation, working environments, and occupational possibilities have led to changes in occupational trajectories and careers patterns. When reviewing available evidence on career patterns, it is apparent that multiple interacting factors influence the development of career patterns. However, given the existing evidence on career patterns, differences seem to have occurred mainly in the frequency of specific career patterns, but not so much in the career pattern's characteristics. This is an interesting finding, as the impression one might get from the existing career literature is that "new" careers are very much different from "traditional" careers.

The number of studies on career patterns has rapidly increased recently, but there are numerous areas that are clearly waiting for research. As large panel studies have been conducted mainly in Western countries, it would be interesting to see whether and to which degree changes in career patterns over time occur in countries where industrialization is only about to start, also given differences in culture, gender roles, and legislation. Additionally, despite a huge number of studies that focus on gender inequalities, there has been only sparse research on how other demographic and personality variables are linked to specific career patterns. Furthermore, acknowledging the fact that career decisions and career moves at most stages of individuals' education and professional careers are caused by specific personality variables, there should be more research on how broad personality variables affect career patterns. Another recommendation for further research would be to expand the scope of career pattern dimensions beyond time and direction (Vinkenburg and Weber, 2012). The very small number of existing peer reviewed empirical studies of career patterns in science are largely limited to the Anglo-Saxon context, often discipline-specific (e.g., academic medicine, engineering), and often dated well before 2000. We would also be interested to see if the response to the urgent call for more flexibility and customization in careers in academia, the military, and professional services, varying from "up or stay" to developing and supporting different routes to the top, will have consequences in the appearance and frequency of career patterns.

To sum up, judging from the number of studies that have been conducted lately, research on career patterns is gaining momentum. Even though changes in career patterns might not be as significant as one might assume, there are clearly many opportunities for further research.

References

Abbott, A. & Tsay, A. 2000. Sequence analysis and optimal matching methods in sociology: Review and prospect. *Sociological Methods & Research*, 29, 3–33.

Abele, A.E. 2003. The dynamics of masculine-agentic and feminine-communal traits: Findings from a prospective study. *Journal of Personality and Social Psychology*, 85, 768–776.

Agarwal, R. & Ohyama, A. 2013. Industry or academia, basic or applied? Career choices and earnings trajectories of scientists. *Management Science*, 59, 950–970.

Andresen, M. & Biemann, T. 2013. A taxonomy of internationally mobile managers. *The International Journal of Human Resource Management*, 24, 533–557.

Anyadike-Danes, M. & Mcvicar, D. 2010. My brilliant career: Characterizing the early labor market trajectories of British women from generation X. *Sociological Methods & Research*, 38, 482–512.

Arthur, M.B., Hall, D.T. & Lawrence, B.S. 1989. Generating new directions in career theory: The case for a transdisciplinary approach. *In:* Arthur, M.B., Hall, D.T. & Lawrence, B.S. (eds.) *Handbook of Career Theory*. Cambridge, UK: Cambridge University Press.

Axinn, W.G., Pearce, L.D. & Ghimire, D. 1999. Innovations in life history calendar applications. *Social Science Research*, 28, 243–264.

Barbulescu, R. & Bidwell, M. 2013. Do women choose different jobs from men? Mechanisms of application segregation in the market for managerial workers. *Organization Science*, 24, 737–756.

Berney, L. & Blane, D. 2003. The lifegrid method of collecting retrospective information from people at older ages. *Research, Policy and Planning*, 21, 13–22.

Biemann, T. & Datta, D.K. 2014. Analyzing sequence data: Optimal matching in management research. *Organizational Research Methods*, 17, 51–76.

Biemann, T. & Wolf, J. 2009. Career patterns of top management team members in five countries: An optimal matching analysis. *The International Journal of Human Resource Management*, 20, 975–991.

Biemann, T., Zacher, H. & Feldman, D.C. 2012. Career patterns: A twenty-year panel study. *Journal of Vocational Behavior*, 81, 159–170.

Bilimoria, D., Liang, X., Carter, S.D. & Turell, J.M. 2013. Gender differences in the academic work experiences of faculty at early, middle and late career stages. *In:* Burke, R.J., Vinnicombe, L.L. & BLAKE-Beard, S.D. (eds.) *Handbook of Research on Promoting Women's Careers*. Cheltenham, UK: Edward Elgar.

Blair-Loy, M. 1999. Career patterns of executive women in finance: An optimal matching analysis. *American Journal of Sociology*, 104, 1346–1397.

Brückner, H. & Mayer, K.U. 2005. De-standardization of the life course: What it might mean? And if it means anything, whether it actually took place? *In:* Macmillian, R. (ed.) *The Structure of the Life Course: Standardized? Individualized? Differentiated? Advances in Life Course Research*. Amsterdam: Elsevier.

Brzinsky-Fay, C. 2007. Lost in transition? Labour market entry sequences of school leavers in Europe. *European Sociological Review*, 23, 409–422.

Cable, D.M. & Murray, B. 1999. Tournaments versus sponsored mobility as determinants of job search success. *Academy of Management Journal*, 42, 439–449.

Cabrera, E.F. 2007. Opting out and opting in: Understanding the complexities of women's career transitions. *Career Development International*, 12, 218–237.

Cahill, K.E., Giandrea, M.D. & Quinn, J.F. 2006. Retirement patterns from career employment. *The Gerontologist*, 46, 514–523.

Careers, S. 2017. http://www.sciencemag.org/careers/2013/02/content-collection-gaining-independence [Online] [Accessed 14 May 2018].

Chubin, D.E., Porter, A.L. & Boeckmann, M.E. 1981. Career patterns of scientists: A case for complementary data. *American Sociological Review*, 46, 488–496.

Clarke, M. 2013. The organizational career: Not dead but in need of redefinition. *The International Journal of Human Resource Management*, 24, 684–703.

Davoine, E. & Ravasi, C. 2013. The relative stability of national career patterns in European top management careers in the age of globalisation: A comparative study in France/Germany/Great Britain and Switzerland. *European Management Journal*, 31, 152–163.

Dietz, J.S. & Bozeman, B. 2005. Academic careers, patents, and productivity: Industry experience as scientific and technical human capital. *Research Policy*, 34, 349–367.

Dlouhy, K. & Biemann, T. 2015. Optimal matching analysis in career research: A review and some best-practice recommendations. *Journal of Vocational Behavior*, 90, 163–173.

Doty, D.H. & Glick, W.H. 1994. Typologies as a unique form of theory building: Toward improved understanding and modeling. *Academy of Management Review*, 19, 230–251.

Douglas, E.J. & Shepherd, D.A. 2002. Self-employment as a career choice: Attitudes, entrepreneurial intentions, and utility maximization. *Entrepreneurship Theory and Practice*, 26, 81–90.

Duberley, J. & Cohen, L. 2010. Gendering career capital: An investigation of scientific careers. *Journal of Vocational Behavior*, 76, 187–197.

Duberley, J., Cohen, L. & Mallon, M. 2006. Constructing scientific careers: Change, continuity and context. *Organization Studies*, 27, 1131–1151.

Fumasoli, T., Goastellec, G. & Kehm, B.M. 2015. *Academic Work and Careers in Europe: Trends, Challenges, Perspectives*. Dordrecht, NL: Springer.

Gelissen, J. & de Graaf, P.M. 2006. Personality, social background, and occupational career success. *Social Science Research*, 35, 702–726.

Ghiselli, E.E. 1974. Some perspectives for industrial psychology. *American Psychologist*, 29, 80–87.

Griffeth, R.W., Hom, P.W. & Gaertner, S. 2000. A meta-analysis of antecedents and correlates of employee turnover: Update, moderator tests, and research implications for the next millennium. *Journal of Management*, 26, 463–488.

Gunz, H.P. 1989. The dual meaning of managerial careers – Organizational and individual levels of analysis. *Journal of Management Studies*, 26, 225–250.

Gunz, H.P. & Jalland, R.M. 1996. Managerial careers and business strategies. *Academy of Management Review*, 21, 718–756.

Gunz, H.P. & Peiperl, M. 2007. *Handbook of Career Studies*. Thousand Oaks, CA: Sage Publications.

Hadani, M., Coombes, S., Das, D. & Jalajas, D. 2012. Finding a good job: Academic network centrality and early occupational outcomes in management academia. *Journal of Organizational Behavior*, 33, 723–739.

Han, S-K. & Moen, P. 1999. Clocking out: Temporal patterning of retirement. *American Journal of Sociology*, 105, 191–236.

Hewlett, Luce, B. & Servon, L.J. 2008. Stopping the exodus of women in science reply. *Harvard Business Review*, 86, 22–24.

Huang, Q., El-Khouri, B.M., Johansson, G., Lindroth, S. & Sverke, M. 2007. Women's career patterns: A study of Swedish women born in the 1950s. *Journal of Occupational and Organizational Psychology*, 80, 387–412.

Huang, Q. & Sverke, M. 2007. Women's occupational career patterns over 27 years: Relations to family of origin, life careers, and wellness. *Journal of Vocational Behavior*, 70, 369–397.

Ibarra, H. 1997. Paving an alternative route: Gender differences in managerial networks. *Social Psychology Quarterly*, 60, 91–102.

Jagsi, R., Decastro, R., Griffith, K.A., Rangarajan, S., Churchill, C., Stewart, A. & Ubel, P.A. 2011. Similarities and differences in the career trajectories of male and female career development award recipients. *Academic Medicine*, 86, 1415–1421.

Joseph, D., Boh, W.F., Ang, S. & Slaughter, S.A. 2012. The career paths less (or more) trafeled: A sequence analysis of IT career histories, mobility patterns, and career success. *Mis Quarterly*, 36, 427–452.

Joshi, A., Son, J. & Roh, H. 2015. When can women close the gap? A meta-analytic test of sex differences in performance and rewards. *Academy of Management Journal*, 58, 1516–1545.

Judge, T.A. & Watanabe, S. 1995. Is the past prologue? A test of Ghiselli's hobo syndrome. *Journal of Management*, 21, 211–229.

Kalleberg, A.L. & Hudis, P.M. 1979. Wage change in the late career: A model for the outcomes of job sequences. *Social Science Research*, 8, 16–40.

Koch, M., Forgues, B. & Monties, V. 2017. The way to the top: Career patterns of Fortune 100 CEOs. *Human Resource Management*, 56, 267–285.

Kovalenko, M. & Mortelmans, D. 2014. Does career type matter? Outcomes in traditional and transitional career patterns. *Journal of Vocational Behavior*, 85, 238–249.

Kovalenko, M. & Mortelmans, D. 2016. Employment security in non-traditional careers: Exploring the dynamic of long-term work trajectories in thirteen European countries. *In:* Ritschard, G. & Studer, M. (eds.) *Proceedings of the International Conference on Sequence Analysis and Related Methods* (LaCOSA II), 105–128.

Long, J.S., Allison, P.D. & Mcginnis, R. 1993. Rank advancement in academic careers: Sex differences and the effects of productivity. *American Sociological Review*, 703–722.

Long, J.S. & Fox, M.F. 1995. Scientific careers: Universalism and particularism. *Annual Review of Sociology*, 21, 45–71.

Lyons, S.T., Schweitzer, L., Ng, E.S. & Kuron, L.K. 2012. Comparing apples to apples: A qualitative investigation of career mobility patterns across four generations. *Career Development International*, 17, 333–357.

Malo, M.A. & Muñoz-Bullón, F. 2003. Employment status mobility from a life-cycle perspective: A sequence analysis of work-histories in the BHPS. *Demographic Research*, 9, 119–162.

Martin Conley, V. 2005. Career paths for women faculty: Evidence from NSOPF: 99. *New Directions for Higher Education*, 25–39.

Martin, P., Schoon, I. & Ross, A. 2008. Beyond transitions: Applying optimal matching analysis to life course research. *International Journal of Social Research Methodology*, 11, 179–199.

Mcmunn, A., Lacey, R., Worts, D., Mcdonough, P., Stafford, M., Booker, C., Kumari, M. & Sacker, A. 2015. De-standardization and gender convergence in work – family life courses in Great Britain: A multi-channel sequence analysis. *Advances in Life Course Research*, 26, 60–75.

Mcvicar, D. & Anyadike-Danes, M. 2002. Predicting successful and unsuccessful transitions from school to work by using sequence methods. *Journal of the Royal Statistical Society: Series A (Statistics in Society)*, 165, 317–334.

Middeldorp, M.M., Edzes, A.A. & van Dijk, J. 2016. Job access and the spatial mobility trajectories of higher education graduates in the Netherlands. *In:* Ritschard, G. & Studer, M. (eds.) *International Conference on Sequence Analysis and Related Methods* (LaCOSA II). Lausanne, 607–630.

Miller, C.C., Glick, W.H. & Cardinal, L.B. 2005. The allocation of prestigious positions in organizational science: Accumulative advantage, sponsored mobility, and contest mobility. *Journal of Organizational Behavior*, 26, 489–516.

Morano-Foadi, S. 2005. Scientific mobility, career progression, and excellence in the European research area. *International Migration*, 43, 133–162.

Nerad, M. & Cerny, J. 1999. Postdoctoral patterns, career advancement, and problems. *Science*, 285, 1533–1535.

Ng, T.W. & Feldman, D.C. 2009. Re-examining the relationship between age and voluntary turnover. *Journal of Vocational Behavior*, 74, 283–294.

Ng, T.W., Eby, L.T., Sorensen, K.L. & Feldman, D.C. 2005. Predictors of objective and subjective career success: A meta-analysis. *Personnel Psychology*, 58, 367–408.

Nieß, C. & Biemann, T. 2014. The role of risk propensity in predicting self-employment. *Journal of Applied Psychology*, 99, 1000–1009.

Nieuwenhuis, R., Need, A. & van der Kolk, H. 2012. Institutional and demographic explanations of women's employment in 18 OECD countries, 1975–1999. *Journal of Marriage and Family*, 74, 614–630.

O'Neil, D.A., Hopkins, M.M. & Bilimoria, D. 2013. Patterns and paradoxes in women's careers. *In:* Patton, M.Q. (ed.) *Conceptualising Women's Working Lives: Moving the Boundaries of Discourse*. Rotterdam: Sense Publishers.

Ossenkop, C., Vinkenburg, C.J., Jansen, P.G. & Ghorashi, H. 2015. Ethnic diversity and social capital in upward mobility systems: Problematizing the permeability of intra-organizational career boundaries. *Career Development International*, 20, 539–558.

Ratniece, L. & Nielson, L.P. 2016. The cohorts of convergence? Danish women and the changing paradigm of women's labour market participation. *In:* Ritschard, G. & Studer, M. (eds.) *International Conference on Sequence Analysis and Related Methods*, Lausanne, 645–693.

Reuben, E., Sapienza, P. & Zingales, L. 2014. How stereotypes impair women's careers in science. *Proceedings of the National Academy of Sciences*, 111, 4403–4408.

Rodrigues, R.A. & Guest, D. 2010. Have careers become boundaryless? *Human Relations*, 63, 1157–1175.

Rosenfeld, R.A. & Jones, J.A. 1987. Patterns and effects of geographic mobility for academic women and men. *The Journal of Higher Education*, 58, 493–515.

Rottinghaus, P.J., Lindley, L.D., Green, M.A. & Borgen, F.H. 2002. Educational aspirations: The contribution of personality, self-efficacy, and interests. *Journal of Vocational Behavior*, 61, 1–19.

Rubinstein, G. 2005. The big five among male and female students of different faculties. *Personality and Individual Differences*, 38, 1495–1503.

Ruggie, M. 2014. *The State and Working Women: A Comparative Study of Britain and Sweden*. Princeton, NJ: Princeton University Press.

Sammarra, A., Profili, S. & Innocenti, L. 2013. Do external careers pay-off for both managers and professionals? The effect of inter-organizational mobility on objective career success. *The International Journal of Human Resource Management*, 24, 2490–2511.

Savickas, M.L. 2001. A developmental perspective on vocational behaviour: Career patterns, salience, and themes. *International Journal for Educational and Vocational Guidance*, 1, 49–57.

Scherer, S. 2001. Early career patterns: A comparison of Great Britain and West Germany. *European Sociological Review*, 17, 119–144.

Seibert, S.E., Crant, J.M. & Kraimer, M.L. 1999. Proactive personality and career success. *Journal of Applied Psychology*, 84, 416–427.

Seibert, S.E. & Kraimer, M.L. 2001. The five-factor model of personality and career success. *Journal of Vocational Behavior*, 58, 1–21.

Simonson, J., Gordo, L.R. & Titova, N. 2011. Changing employment patterns of women in Germany: How do baby boomers differ from older cohorts? A comparison using sequence analysis. *Advances in Life Course Research*, 16, 65–82.

Stovel, K., Savage, M. & Bearman, P. 1996. Ascription into achievement: Models of career systems at Lloyds Bank, 1890–1970. *American Journal of Sociology*, 102, 358–399.

Timmerman, T.A. 2006. Predicting turnover with broad and narrow personality traits. *International Journal of Selection and Assessment*, 14, 392–399.

Valcour, P.M. & Tolbert, P. 2003. Gender, family and career in the era of boundarylessness: Determinants and effects of intra-and inter-organizational mobility. *International Journal of Human Resource Management*, 14, 768–787.

van Engen, M.L., Vinkenburg, C.J. & Dikkers, J.S. 2012. Sustainability in combining career and care: Challenging normative beliefs about parenting. *Journal of Social Issues*, 68, 645–664.

Vázquez-Cupeiro, S. & Elston, M.A. 2006. Gender and academic career trajectories in Spain: From gendered passion to consecration in a Sistema Endogámico? *Employee Relations*, 28, 588–603.

Vinkenburg, C.J. 2017. Engaging gatekeepers, optimizing decision making, and mitigating bias: Design specifications for systemic diversity interventions. *The Journal of Applied Behavioral Science*, 53, 212–234.

Vinkenburg, C.J., van Engen, M.L. & Peters, P. 2015. Promoting new norms and true flexibility: Sustainability in combining career and care. *In:* de Vos, A. & van der Heijden, B.I.J.M. (eds.) *Handbook of Research on Sustainable Careers*. London: Edward Elgar.

Vinkenburg, C.J. & Weber, T. 2012. Managerial career patterns: A review of the empirical evidence. *Journal of Vocational Behavior*, 80, 592–607.

Wessel, R.D. & Keim, M.C. 1994. Career patterns of private four-year college and university presidents in the United States. *The Journal of Higher Education*, 65, 211–225.

Widmer, E.D. & Ritschard, G. 2009. The de-standardization of the life course: Are men and woman equal? *Advances in Life Course Research*, 14, 28–39.

Wilensky, H.L. 1961. Orderly careers and social participation: The impact of work history on social integration in the middle mass. *American Sociological Review*, 26, 521–539.

Winchester, H., Lorenzo, S., Browning, L. & Chesterman, C. 2006. Academic women's promotions in Australian universities. *Employee Relations*, 28, 505–522.

Woo, S.E. 2011. A study of Ghiselli's hobo syndrome. *Journal of Vocational Behavior*, 79, 461–469.

Xie, Y. & Shauman, K.A. 2003. *Women in Science: Career Processes and Outcomes*. Cambridge: Harvard University Press.

Zacher, H., Biemann, T., Gielnik, M.M. & Frese, M. 2012. Patterns of entrepreneurial career development: An optimal matching analysis approach. *International Journal of Developmental Science*, 6, 177–187.

16

The dark sides of organizational careers

Yoav Vardi and Itai Vardi

Introduction

That experiences and meanings of careers may differ significantly from one person to another, and in time and place, is embodied in the life trajectories of the authors of the present chapter – a father and son in academia. The senior author, upon completing his PhD in the late 1970s, immediately received job offers from several universities and had the luxury of choosing one that suited his needs at the time. He has pursued a conventional academic career with a secure and rewarding retirement, as well as the usual regret about missing opportunities and taking wrong paths. But the opportunities and paths were there all along. Such fortune seemed to be the case for many in his professional cohort. Indeed, partaking in decades of research in organizational behavior, he has observed how scholars in management and organizational studies upheld a simple causal view of careers. Just recently, at the Academy of Management's annual meeting, he sat through several sessions of the flourishing Careers Division dealing with "career success" as a socially promulgated "career outcome" and well-researched construct (e.g., Arthur et al., 2005; Heslin, 2005; Seibert et al., 2001). Surprisingly, only marginal discussion occurred over what really constitutes "success" in career, at what costs is success achieved, and why people still choose to pursue such unclear and at times dubious outcomes. The term "career failure" was scantly raised.

Indeed, career has meant something completely different for the junior author. Perhaps he can be termed as having a non-career career. By that we mean a sequence of jobs (mostly partial) unfolding non-linearly through temporary and sporadic engagements with different employers, and not necessarily within distinct professional boundaries and defined timetables. Having completed a PhD and postdoctorate a few years ago, and being fairly well published by that stage, he has yet to receive a mere reply to the hundreds of his academic job applications. With little to no prospects of a steady academic career, he has experienced a fragmented and precarious pathway, settling for a part-time college lecturer position and freelance investigative journalist. Since writing this chapter he has started a new full time non-academic job as a researcher on energy policy. Yet, the chance for a secure retirement seem bleak at the moment. Paradoxically though, his readership and public impact already far exceed those of the senior author. What, then, is a "successful career"?

As a social construct, there is no consensus as to what career actually means. Clearly, dominant culture in the industrialized world still socializes citizens to aspire for and work hard toward "a successful career." Moreover, organizations and occupations plan, offer and manage careers as a rewarding aspect of their social, functional and hierarchical arrangements by ostensibly matching individual and organizational needs (Schein, 1978). But what precisely are people asked to yearn for? Why do professions and organizations continuously promote and glorify it? Who ultimately benefits from careers? And, conversely, what are the darker sides of careers?

To probe these questions, this chapter delves into a critical analysis of career by investigating its more problematic or overlooked sides. Such an undertaking will follow the two central meanings associated with the "dark side" metaphor. One connotes aspects of a phenomenon that are negative, sinister, dysfunctional or counterproductive. Management studies have by and large eschewed an association of careers with its downfalls. Instead, dominant discourses in academia and beyond linked career with positive, rewarding, productive and functional processes of mobility and development. The second meaning pertains to aspects of a phenomenon we cannot see, fail to observe or choose to ignore. Here our challenge is to both look at careers from the myopic "other side" and explore those aspects that are indeed difficult to see. We will show that dark side attributes are actually quite integral to the career phenomenon, and that such elements should be acknowledged, further explored and better managed. We will argue that to do so requires a critical analysis of dominant definitions of career management in the literature, which typically provide misleading or partial statements about what careers and management mean. Such discourses are normatively tainted and unrealistic, amounting to formalized versions of social wishful thinking. Our chapter thus responds to recent calls to critically balance views of the career phenomenon, especially in regards to those career experiences that are work-organization-related (Baruch and Vardi, 2016; Vardi and Kim, 2007) and are not, naturally, unrelated to dark-side job behavior patterns that are considered forms of misbehavior (Vardi and Weitz, 2016), deviant (Robinson and Bennett, 1995), counterproductive (Sackett and DeVore, 2001), or insidious organizational behavior (Greenberg, 2010). To be clear: our purpose is neither to negate current career approaches nor to scare career pursuants, but rather advocate a more realistic view of careers where light and shadow naturally intertwine.

The chapter proceeds in three main stages. We first discuss career from a critical sociohistorical perspective, highlighting the contingent nature of the term and the multifarious ways in which it was deployed as a vehicle for power and domination. We then look at organizational careers from people management and human resource lenses. Finally, we suggest a critical approach by linking organizational careers with a temporal model of work-related misconduct. Our chapter will propose that work careers are not simply a promise with a defined direction, but complex cultural and ideological processes shaped by personal, organizational and structural forces. They are always replete with danger and adventure and involve not just competency and aspiration, but also the application of a wide repertoire of attitudes and behaviors ranging from good citizenship to cunning and misconduct.

Historicizing careers

Career, class and exploitation

Seminal works historicizing the rise of modern forms of labor in industrial society and capitalism have revealed the contingent nature of career and careerism. A quintessentially modernist idea, the term "career" can be traced to the medieval French word for road, *carrière*. In its inception, the term largely denoted the progression of lifelong labor in a certain field. Signifying linear movement on a steady path, career became culturally associated with professionalism and expert knowledge, in contradistinction to mere holders of "jobs" – literally, those who carry out lumps or pieces of labor (Williams, 1983). Historically, the notion of career as one's "calling" in work or "vocation" developed in tandem with the rise of large rational bureaucracies and the nation state (Weber, 2013). In Weber's seminal analysis, the purpose of the sequenced career avenue of the bureaucrat, to be traversed through a merit-based reward system, was to ensure organizational efficiency and the excise of pre-modern patrimonial decision-making processes. In his ideal type analysis, Weber situated the bureaucratic career as a central locus of the rationally designed hierarchic organization, which includes:

- Delineated lines of authority with fixed areas of activity;
- Action taken on the basis of, and recorded in, written rules;
- Bureaucratic officials with expert training;
- Rules implemented by neutral officials;
- Career advancement depending on technical qualifications judged by the organization, not individuals ("the office is the career").

Such long-term commitment to a single track of human activity did not, however, originate solely from structural socioeconomic changes and the institution of wage-labor; powerful cultural ethos propelled people into new forms of stringent dedication to work that were largely absent from earlier labor regimes (Thompson, 1967). In Weber's (1958) classic account, it was the "worldly ascetic" of early Protestantism – with its edicts of self-sacrifice, delay of gratification, and personalized commitment to labor in the name of increasing God's glory – that contributed to the development of a strong work ethic unique to Western societies.

Yet the new ethic did not merely evolve in response to the challenge of motivating laborers to enter the novel social relationship of wage employment. Weber also identified the way it was wielded as a tool by the powerful. For him, the individualizing work ethic of Protestantism operated as an ideological mechanism for rationalizing early capitalist exploitation by providing its devotees "the comforting assurance that the unequal distribution of the goods of this world was a special dispensation of Divine Providence" (Weber, 1958: 177). With the later transition to industrial capitalism, the work ethic, by now devoid of its religious core, continued to legitimize inequality by masking the structural causes of poverty and unemployment (Beder, 2000; Bourdieu and Nice, 1998; Ryan, 1971).

Crucially, the work ethic at the center of career operates ideologically through its individualizing properties. One cultivates a career as a personal project of the self, where success and failure are necessarily defined as private matters (Beck, 1992; Bauman, 2000; Giddens, 1991). Achievement – or lack thereof – are constituted by, and are a sign of, the moral fiber and character residing supposedly within the individual. Any collective responsibility for one's fate is elided in favor of a privatized form of career development, as the individual stands alone to face his or her shortcomings (Fraser and Gordon, 1994).

Such a narrow conceptualization of labor and identity may indeed benefit the (successful) career person materially, symbolically or emotionally. Structurally, however, it ultimately serves to augment the social dominance of the ruling classes by ensuring high levels of production and the accumulation of surplus capital (Harvey, 2007; Schor, 1991).

Career and disciplined subjectivities

Others have used Foucault's genealogical analysis to locate the rise of career within discursive systems of power/knowledge (Deetz, 1998; Grey, 1994; McKinlay and Starkey, 1998). Instead of interrogating the changing meanings of career as a social construct, they ask: when does it become possible to see oneself as "having a career"? What are the conditions under which subjects understand their lives as necessarily centering around a devoted pursuit of wage labor?

Dandeker (1990) traces the advent of career structures to the birth of the modern military, where new forms of surveillance were required to mold and control the body of the conscript into organized army discipline. But it is Savage's (1997) work on the utility of careers in the great railway companies of the 19th century that employs a more distinct Foucauldian analysis. As the significant spatial dispersion of workers on the railway network undermined the direct disciplinary gaze, by mid-century employers realized that controlling labor through traditional punitive measures was ineffective. Management thus devised the "career ladder" as a softer modality of power, one that "worked on the soul" of workers by incentivizing them to engage in self-control to align with the company's new individualized system of reward and status attainment. These technologies for cultivating self-surveillance were soon adopted by other large corporate entities such as banks (McKinlay, 2002).

In the 20th century, the pursuit of career continued to transform citizens into ostensibly willing participants in the labor market, from managers and professionals to pink- and blue-collar workers. Internalized discourses about individual achievement and rounded identities generated dedication to employment that could gloss over contradictions inherent in capitalism. Indeed, the work ethic's remarkable resilience in liberal democracies can be attributed to its ability to "get things done" for economic and political regimes predicated on constant growth: devotion to one's work operates not merely as a normative prescription but a *practical* discourse that creates consenting, docile bodies who are socialized into, and reproduce, the social order (Burawoy, 1979).

In the post-Fordist service and knowledge-based economy, the need to craft, release and manage subjectivities predicated on the creative and emotive faculties of the worker becomes all the more critical (Hochschild, 1983; Rose, 1998). In such environments, where workers are asked to flexibly adapt to rapidly changing circumstances and marshal their communicative and affective capacities – their "head and heart, not only their hands" (Weeks, 2011) – to carry out tasks, what is prized is not blind obedience but commitment; not fearful submission but the willing sense of obligation (Bunting, 2011).

In place of traditional authority relations and direct control, knowledge-based and networked organizations thus induce adherence to their goals through normative mechanisms. These include ingraining in workers a strong sense of shared culture through vision statements, codes of conduct, company imagery and branding and group loyalty (Alvesson, 1993; Kunda, 1992).

The new discipline at the core of career thus operationalizes a willingness to accept unexpected change, constant reinvention and adaptability (Arthur et al., 1995; Hall, 2004; Sennett, 1998). This is often ensured by the common injunction, now aimed at workers at all levels, to continuously learn and "be professional." Discourses linking professionalism to competence and flexible identity require workers to invest in, and identify with, their labor in terms of attitude, style and character (Weeks, 2011; Ross, 2003). Other fashionable managerial discourses play on the current cultural preoccupation with authenticity. When workers are persuaded to "just be yourself," new, softer forms of discipline are put into play (Fleming, 2009). Such managerial ethos, instantiated through mechanisms of teamwork, participation, malleability, playfulness and enrichment, is mustered to create productivity in the pursuit of profit by blurring the lines between work and non-work, compulsion and voluntarism, and authority and autonomy.

While managerial discourses laud such flexibility as a sign of worker autonomy and empowerment, not enough critical attention has been given to the ways such novel arrangements introduce new forms of control that center precisely on unstable worker identities. In a society where work and career are still paramount to one's social status, the difficulty to construct a solid professional identity within fluid labor arrangements – "Who and what am I?" – confounds this project of self (Sennett, 1998). As Deetz (1998) found in his study of knowledge-economy workers, sustaining such identity becomes a highly privatized and unanchored effort, where "a lingering sense of falseness and insecurity comes with [such] symbolic identity" (Deetz, 1998: 158). In order to re-acquire some sense of identity stability, workers succumb quietly to management ideology in a way that glosses over contradictions produced in their supposed autonomous and expert subjectivities. For instance, when a certain unit in the company was converted into an independent "profit making" consultancy, a crucial transformation ensued in employee identity. Whereas worker loyalty increased thanks to feeling it was now "their company," their self-worth changed from being based on product quality to being determined by how much money they were bringing into the company. Indeed, Deetz found that workers in the networked organization he studied are generally happy in their positions – just as they report their many sacrifices owing to changing work expectations, unit instabilities and long hours.

As discourses of flexibility, adaptability, and constant reinvention come to define new labor arrangements, constructing and sustaining non-work-related identities becomes an arduous undertaking. In his study of employees at a major US bank, Michel notes how the organization's transformation into a "lifestyle firm" entailed a radical erasure of boundaries between work and non-work. This included the collapsing of distinctions between work and leisure by providing administrative support 24 hours a day, seven days a week, encouraging leisure at work, and providing free amenities, including childcare, valets, car service and meals (Michel, 2011: 336).

Within this process, Michel closely documented the ways in which workers' identities became completely overtaken by work. The lack of spatial and mental boundaries between personal concerns and job matters led one employee to lament, "my work is my life" (Michel, 2011: 344).

Still, the more indirect forms of surveillance informing flexible careers have not done away completely with the older forms of disciplinary control characteristic of top-bottom hierarchies; instead, these emerge as reconfigured layers of bureaucracy replete with the catchword phraseology of a new managerialism. Grey (1994) found that appraisal ratings and professional examinations are construed among novice accountants not as disciplinary devices but as means to "maximize their career prospects" (Grey, 1994: 494). In actuality, these micro-techniques of control and surveillance operate as internalized "panoptic gazes" encouraging trainees to display enthusiasm and commitment to the organization at all times. Similar arguments have been made about the disciplinary effects of vocational psychology and psychometric exams prevalent among career development professionals (McIlveen and Patton, 2006). Indeed, at least one study found that, not infrequently, many workers nowadays employ the metaphors of imprisonment, army and surveillance when describing their own careers (El-Sawad, 2005).

Gender, race and career

Feminist and critical race scholars have noted the exclusionary nature of the Western work ethic, wherein those who don't live up to its idealized prescriptions are labeled as inadequate. While leading a career signifies independence as ostensible control over one's destination, the racialized discourse surrounding work and commitment stigmatizes abject others as hopelessly *dependent*. Ongoing political debates about such groups as "inner city residents," "welfare queens," "moochers" and "freeloaders" are rife with racist codes (Weeks, 2011).

The work ethic and wage labor are also historically gendered concepts. Myriad works have shown that the transition to industrial capitalism ushered a new division of labor based on sexual domination (Cockburn, 1993; Lorber, 1994). Compensated labor was to be the realm of masculinity, whereas femininity became associated with the unpaid work of domestic life (Boydston, 1990). In many senses, it was men who "had" careers, and the aggressive pursuit of career was an attribute of dominant masculinity.

While historical gains in women's rights transformed these ideologies so that both men and women are today expected to pursue – and enjoy – careered lives, subtler forms of gendering persist. Social expectations for better balancing between family and work roles, for bearing the brunt of the "second shift" at home (Hochschild and Machung, 2012), and for committing to new forms of "intensive" or "helicopter" parenting (Cotter et al., 2011) continue to be disproportionally leveled at women. And while the fluidity of the knowledge economy has disrupted historical patriarchal barriers in traditionally hierarchical organizations, the insecurity associated with fragmented careers and network economies has also introduced new forms of career precarity for women (Vardi and Smith-Doerr, 2014).

The ideal of career in a career-less world

A growing number of analysts observe that in a fundamental sense, we are living in a post-work society. That is, work as we knew it in the post-war years of high capitalism; professional or skilled work that lasted a lifetime; full-time, work with benefits and job security; and work that could serve as a steady plotline to craft one's identity and life narrative – all, for the most part, are a thing of the past (Aronowitz and DiFazio, 1994; Bauman, 2000; Beck, 1992; Strasser, 1999; Rifkin, 1995).

The coming of post-industrial society and its meteoric rise of service sector work, the dominance of the knowledge-economy and networked organizations, and widespread automation – have all rendered large swaths of the population as either chronically jobless, independently working, underemployed, casually or informally employed or eternally redundant. Recent analysis has found a substantial rise in the incidence of alternative work arrangements for US workers from 2005 to 2015, with a particularly sharp increase in the share of workers being hired through contract firms (Katz and Krueger, 2016) or working informally (Bracha et al., 2015). These include increases in temporary help agency workers, on-call workers, contract company workers and independent contractors or freelancers. The advent of fluid, "gig economy" employment characterized by short-term, part-time, episodic and project-based work joins material insecurity with existential instability to create the new class formation of the "precariat." Standing (2014) has traced the steady growth of this group throughout the industrialized world to the 1970s' ideology of labor market flexibility. While the term is somewhat nebulous and not entirely antithetical to people who are career-less, what links precariats in both blue-collar, deskilled and professionals and knowledge-based fields is a precarious existence (in terms of employment, job, work, income, skill reproduction and representation), a tenuous social status and an unstable work-based identity. And though many in the knowledge economy have reaped enormous benefits springing from continuous revolutions in technological innovation and entrepreneurship, the fluid and flatter organizations characteristic of this sector complement rather than negate this condition of perennial insecurity and short-termism: while networked workplaces are "lighter on their feet," they are also riskier in that they are "more readily decomposable or redefinable" (Powell and Smith-Doerr, 1994).

Yet despite this momentous structural economic and social shift, the core edicts of the work ethic have remained remarkably resilient: one still must devote oneself to work, work is the center of one's life and work is an end in itself (Weeks, 2011). Put differently, we are still, for the most part, expected and trained to develop and hold a career in a post-career world.

The expectation to pursue, attain and sustain a career when the institution of career is in shambles is perhaps one of the most powerful modes of domination in and around the world of labor. The persistence of such mechanisms as career coaching, teaching career competencies, career fairs and traditional professional career socialization processes encourage people to pursue what Ulrich Beck (2001) calls a "zombie category" – one that persists from historical inertia or ideological utility but in all practically has ceased to exist.

Not only is having a career a remote reality for many workers, but the powerful work ethic at its core is increasingly detaching from reality. With fewer and fewer signposts guiding people toward stable and fulfilling work, those signs that still exist are now constantly moving on coasters (Bauman, 2000). For example, workers often face the difficulty of making informed career moves in networked and flexible organizations. Since such organizations are in constant flux and a state of uncertainty, making decisions about one's future becomes increasingly risky (Lash and Urry, 1987). This capricious reality corrodes character and diminishes trust in others, as people fail to string a coherent identity and meaningful narrative of self and society. Those who succeed in this environment, in fact, "must have the confidence to dwell in disorder" and flourish "in the midst of dislocation" (Sennett, 1998: 62).

Such disorienting attitudes towards career engulf not only white-collar and knowledge economy employees but those workers outside of professional and expert circles as well. As Thompson (1963) had shown in his seminal works, the desire for a career was traditionally present not only in the professional classes, but also amongst manual and servant classes as well. Regularly yearning to be more than just "a pair of hands," laborers seek to attain a sense of long term purpose and pride in work as well as responsibility for one's conduct. With the ideal of career as stable, meaningful work disappearing, and as actual labor is fragmented into a patchwork of short-term and casual employment, how can such attributes be sustained?

Career management

Overlooking the negative

Career experiences, then, are relative phenomena. Like all other organizational phenomena, they are both "good" and "bad." Yet mainstream career theory has tended to reify career processes, typically loading them with favorable meanings. Baruch and Vardi (2016) have suggested that many core concepts in career discourse, such as protean careers, intelligent careers, kaleidoscopic careers and authentic careers, are underlined with positively skewed views. To cite one example, consider this quote concerning a career construction by adaptability theory:

> Viewing career construction as a series of attempts to implement a self-concept in work roles concentrates attention on adaptation to a series of transitions from school to work, from job to job, and from occupation to occupation. People construct careers by using adaptive strategies that implement their personalities in work roles. This adaptation is motivated and guided by the goal of bringing inner needs and outer opportunities into harmony, with the harmonics of a good fit amplifying in present activity the individual's past preoccupations and current aspirations. Adaptation, or goodness of fit, is indicated by success, satisfaction, and development.
>
> *(Savickas and Porfeli, 2012: 661)*

Only one item in the authors' career adaptability scale pertains to "Overcoming obstacles," while the other 23 consist of such items as "Planning how to achieve my goals," "Keeping upbeat," "Looking for opportunities to grow as a person" and "Working up to my ability" (Savickas and Porfeli, 2012: 667).

Generally speaking, the depiction and analysis of organizational life in management, career and organization studies literature has traditionally been positively and normatively biased (Ackroyd and Thompson, 1999; Vardi and Wiener, 1996; Vaughan, 1999). Careers in organizations have mostly been branded as enticing, developmental and growth enabling experiences (e.g., Hall, 1976; Schein, 1978) replete with images such as "ladder climbing" and "executive suites" (see review in Inkson et al., 2012). In their critical review of the *Handbook of Career Studies* (Gunz and Peiperl, 2007), Vardi and Kim (2007) affirmed that the majority of the contributions to the handbook conceived and portrayed careers as positive phenomena, both as personal and organizational experiences. Undoubtedly, the leading paradigm has been the congruence model (e.g., job-person fit, person-environment fit), which by definition emphasized matches over mismatches, averages over outliers, fit over misfit, success over failure and effective movement over stuckness.

Yet this paradigm is increasingly myopic, as it no longer reflects the complexity and volatility of labor markets and career structures in post-industrial economies. For instance, some see the new workplace as becoming employee-less because many jobs are being outsourced to external contractors, become modular and temporary, virtual and replaceable by automation (cf. Weber, 2017). Thus, the axiom that fit is always superior to misfit, and that job-person matching should always be pursued in managing human resources, becomes moot. As the nature of work and work organizations has changed in recent decades, so have those work-related experiences as organizational careers. These undoubtedly include not only the few orderly sequences of company promotions, which exist in most places of work, but the vast variety of transitions and adjustments that reflect the changed organizational arena. A related problem with the prevailing management literature is its tendency to highlight success stories and glorify corporate stars while paying much less attention to what Ference et al. (1977) characterize as the plateaued solid citizens who are committed to continued employment despite the lack of career advancement. Scholarship thereby neglects to properly investigate those who are both dysfunctional and stuck – the "deadwood." Overall, the discourse of career as promise focuses on how occupations and organizations offer aspirants continuity, advancement, reputation, predictability and marketability. For some, such promises eventually materialize into a series of both subjective and objective rewarding successes. But for many, these promises turn to a series of struggles, obstacles, frustrations, disillusionments and failures. Career failures and their antecedents and consequences, like many other darker aspects of careers, rarely capture the attention of researchers. Career management systems in organizations mostly operate under the assumption that their mission is to manage the optimal supply of talent for the organization (Baruch, 2004; Greenhaus et al., 2000). To that end, they engage in analyzing skill needs and plan the tools and means for individuals to acquire them and facilitate their allocation. Most person-job fit and match models (Schein, 1978) support such systems conceptually and ideologically. Yet in periods of rapid change, restructuring, downturns, mergers, acquisitions or sociopolitical shifts, career management is more about crisis management, whether dealing with personal calamities or downsizing accompanied by mass terminations or dismissals. This is when outplacement services (preferably outsourced) replace internal career and talent development.

The price of competition and competitiveness

Rosenbaum (1979) documented career mobility patterns in an organization that manages employee and managerial careers such that promotions up the hierarchical ladder are akin to a sports tournament where in each stage a new competition unfolds, as some "win" and many others "lose." What such an objective depiction of organizational careers misses are the complacency and apathy, the dashed hopes, the failed promises, the broken hearts and the covert reprisals by the losers. This study is typical of how the literature tends to praise winning while neglecting to evaluate the damages "career tournament" structures may cause to individuals and low-power groups.

While competitiveness as an organization culture value may be a noble message, it can also backfire. In academia, the "publish or perish" career culture has resulted in an increase of scientific fraud (e.g., Crocker and Cooper, 2011). Especially in the hard sciences, the institutional expectations to produce has alarmingly contributed to unscientific as well as unethical conduct both by organizations and by careerists, as evidenced by recent studies of paper retraction (e.g., Shuai et al., 2017).

In the business world, recently, regulators announced Wells Fargo is being fined $185 million for illegally opening millions of unauthorized accounts for their customers in order to meet aggressive sales goals. Wells Fargo agreed to pay the largest fine ever collected by the US federal government's new consumer protection agency after an investigation found its staff opened more than two million fake checking, credit card and other accounts for customers in order to meet sales targets and earn bonuses. The bank, one of the largest in the United States, said it has fired 5,300 workers over the last five years for the conduct. But the Wells Fargo scheme is striking because those accused included thousands of ordinary workers inside one of the country's largest banks (Merle, *Washington Post*, September 8, 2016).

What should career scholars make of the fate of these 5,300 careers tragically careening off the road? Thousands of employees, perhaps with the implicit consent of their bosses, willfully engaged in on the job misbehavior which, after being exposed and tried, in turn, terminated their Wells Fargo promising organizational careers, their individual plans, family well-being, and personal dreams smashed. Yet here is a research population that will not be investigated as an interesting case for career analysis. A framework linking career to misbehavior helps us to overcome this blind spot.

Misbehavior and careers

Without doubt, career systems and those managing such systems subsume a positive dependence between advancement and organizationally accepted and condoned behavior. We contend that both conceptually and practically one cannot separate careers and misconduct because various forms of organizational misbehavior are an integral part of most people's work experiences and are either detrimental or instrumental to their own career management and that of others within the organization.

The OMB framework

Organizational misbehavior (OMB) refers to those discretionary acts by members of organizations that violate core organizational and/or societal norms defined as proper conduct. This umbrella construct encompasses a full spectrum of phenomena of work-related misconduct present in every organization and experienced by most members throughout their careers. All such behaviors are considered prevalent workplace experiences. During their careers, employees experience them as witnesses, perpetrators, targets or victims. Moreover, we argue that they are inescapable and inevitable career-related experiences in work organizations. The OMB approach adopted here (Vardi and Wiener, 1996; Vardi and Weitz, 2016) views acts of misbehavior as career related because they either precede, are part of, or follow organizational career experiences such as entry, movement, plateau, change, transition or exit. Those acts (as well as positive ones) obviously are manifested in organizations in various ways, at different levels of intensity and frequencies, but their prevalence is undeniable.

Vardi and Weitz (2016) categorized OMB manifestations into five forms: intrapersonal, interpersonal, work-process-related, property-related and political. Abusive supervision, for example, will be interpersonal misbehavior; drug abuse and workaholic excess will be intrapersonal misbehavior; and theft, corruption and fraud will be regarded as property misbehavior. Our point here is that such acts are committed by the very individuals who experience organizational careers, and therefore studying careers while ignoring the reasons, circumstances and outcomes of such behaviors is unrealistic and shortsighted.

The OMB approach also searches for the motivational forces underlying such acts. OMB type S is thus motivated by mostly instrumental forces to benefit the self (such as the improper acquisition of (human, material) resources which are property of the corporation). In the US retail sector alone, stealth employee theft, for instance, seems to inflict humongous costs on employers, even exceeding damages from shoplifting by customers (Leinbach-Reyhle, 2015). OMB type O is mostly motivated by normative forces such as duty and loyalty and is intended to benefit the organization (such as whistleblowing, misleading customers, engaging in espionage, bribery, etc.). The overidentification with one's career may lead to the development of instrumental rationality that champions means at the expense of considering the merit of ends. Such is the banality of evil thesis: when harnessed to destructive social goals and ideologies, this technocratic attitude toward work fuses the career uncritically with the objectives of the hierarchal organization. OMB type D is motivated to inflict some kind of damage on others or on organization resources and equipment. Such conduct could be motivated by either instrumental or normative forces (Vardi and Wiener, 1996). Crucially, all such acts are career related. Take the case of the employee who because of high morality and conscientiousness decides to blow the whistle on her supervisor for gross unethical conduct. It is very likely that her career with the organization is in jeopardy because for most employers this would be considered an act of dissidence or subversion (e.g., Near and Miceli, 1985).

From a temporal and dynamic perspective of life within organizations, unfolding careers of organization members at all levels must influence, and be influenced by, many factors including prevalent "dark side" policies and activities (Baruch and Vardi, 2016). While unfolding careers are normally attributed to work behavior that conforms to prescribed performance rules and standards and evaluated by employers as such, certain discretionary misdeeds affect careers both positively and negatively. For example, OMB type O acts motivated by loyalty to organizational leadership, may result in positive exposure to career decision makers. But such acts of misconduct could also become a liability for upward-career aspirants. To date, these differential effects have not been looked at in a systematic way by career and organizational behavior researchers. Vardi (2011) found that past misconduct (both work-related and non-work-related) blocked leading candidates from being considered for top-echelon public positions. Interestingly, those same forms of misconduct at earlier career stages were either instrumental in their promotion or simply ignored as career criteria. We thus maintain that in principle, from a temporal perspective, career aspirations and choices must affect the intentions to both behave and misbehave, and the consequences of such choices and behaviors, must in turn, affect careers.

The OMB framework for career research

We deem our OMB approach (Vardi and Weitz, 2016) quite useful because of its breadth and basic refrain from prejudging the effects and costs of these career behaviors. The general

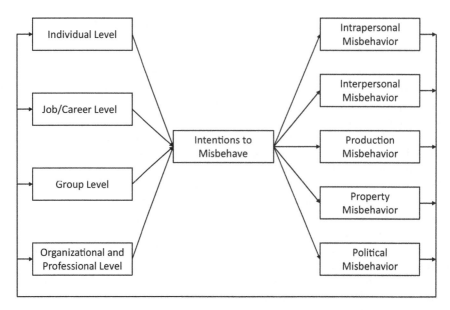

Figure 16.1 A temporal framework for the study of organizational misbehavior
Source: Vardi and Weitz, 2016: 49.

integrative framework we present in Figure 16.1 depicts the concept in terms of OMB mani-festations, antecedents and mediators (i.e., intentions to misbehave) and highlights the role of career as both an antecedent and consequence of misconduct. For example, at the individual level, experienced frustration of not being promoted as expected might affect the intention to misbehave and subsequently lead to "production misbehavior" in the form of intentional loaf-ing, rule-breaking or sabotaging. At the same time, we acknowledge that individual differences mean that certain people will be more vulnerable as compared with others, who may be more resilient. At the position level, we have some evidence from field and lab studies that autonomy may lead to unethical conduct (Lu et al., 2016) and we can now suggest that such conduct, in turn, should affect future career experiences.

By the same token, a strong organizational culture that "forces" career-minded employees to work long and hard may affect the intention to misbehave and lead to "political misbehavior," such as deception of management in which employees manipulate office technology to create the false impression that work is being done when actually it is not. Thus, as part of the career and organizational socialization process, employees must learn and internalize the rules of local deception (Shulman, 2007), and utilize impression management tactics (Goffman, 1959) and internal politics (Vigoda, 2000) to achieve long-term success.

Dark sides of new career concepts

To promote a more realistic discourse about contemporary careers, Baruch and Vardi, 2016 pro-posed that because of the present-day changing nature of organizations, labor markets and career patterns, and with the growing the realization that misconduct is inherent in organizations, a framework that connects careers and misbehavior should be used in future research. Such an approach will be instrumental for generating conceptual, empirical and practical thinking that may better account for learning about, and indeed, managing careers in modern work systems. In line with their work, in order to critically demonstrate the possible connection with OMB, we examine below two of the leading career constructs: the protean career and the boundary-less career.

Protean careers and OMB

The "protean career" (Hall, 2004) is a career form in which the individual, rather than the organization, takes on the responsibility for enacting career paths and develops himself or herself according to his or her emerging needs. The protean person's career choices and search for self-fulfilment are unifying and integrative elements in his or her life. This idea is insightful, but it overlooks the immense difficulty in developing such inner shifts of values and attitudes (Baruch and Quick, 2007; Nicholson, 1998). More importantly, not everyone has the practical ability to transform and follow his or her needs and values (Hall, 2004).

Like many metaphors, the protean career suffers from certain limitations. Even the Greek god Proteus changed his shape only when he faced with severe threat. While Proteus could initiate his own shape-changes, he apparently was not proactive in doing so, he did not engage in a planned and skilled manner but rather randomly and desperately when faced by a crisis and grave danger (Inkson, 2007). This would be fine if a person is willing and able to move (although the organization will incur loss in terms of human capital); however, it is not feasible if the person cannot move or has no will to do so, yet is forced to. Then the individual, for the sake of maintaining employability, is the one obliged to reinvent himself or herself despite inability or reluctance, which can lead to bitterness, inefficiency and even to misconduct. The protean idea fits well with moves across managerial roles, or from professional roles to managerial positions. In most instances, however, it does not fit well with a transition from managerial to professional careers (e.g., even a very talented manager will find it challenging to transition to working as a medical doctor or accountant or lawyer).

The main problem with the protean career mode is its narrow application to the labor market. The majority of change-adverse individuals might regard it as a risky or even career-destructive modus operandi. Furthermore, stress and ambiguity associated with frequent identity transformations could inadvertently produce inappropriate work-related impression management behaviors, such as deceiving, faking and politicking, which eventually will become career hindrances. Frequent transitions end in too many short-circled transitory career experiences, limiting the chances of reaching maturity and high-level achievements. For many individuals, excessive transformations may prohibit the crystallization of a solid and constructive career identity. Individuals who have gathered significant human capital might find it too hard and demanding to replace it and to capitalize on it in a new career; the costs attached to frequent career moves, whether voluntary or forced, may be significant indeed.

Thus, we propose that for organization members, the demanding experience of continually reinventing oneself may be related to increased intentions to engage in self-promoting and politicking forms of OMB, be they type S, type O or type D, either for mere survival, or for managing some change.

Boundaryless careers and misbehavior

The "boundaryless career" construct offers a positive perspective, depicting a transparent and open system that is free of rigidity and full of opportunities (Arthur and Rousseau, 1996). This concept has attracted wide attention in the career literature (Lee and Felps, 2013). In a boundaryless world, individuals can move across organizations and occupations to pursue the best opportunities for their personal and professional development without the negative stigma of failing in an organizational career. Career progress comes not only from intra-company hierarchical advancement but also, and even more often, from self-development. From this perspective, careers can be viewed as boundaryless as the borders between organizations and work environments become blurred (Ashkenas et al., 1995); yet the boundaryless career may also be accompanied by a loss of clarity and stability, growing ambiguity, job insecurity and the need to readjust on a continual basis (Adkins et al., 2001).

Boundaryless career suffers from several conceptual weaknesses. First, careers cannot really or fully be boundaryless (Inkson et al., 2012). Some boundaries have become blurred, but most remain intact and help shape and direct people's career attitudes and aspirations as well as maintain organizational career systems. Boundaries are an inherent attribute of organizational and professional systems, and crossing boundaries is an integral part of careers. Such crossings may entail both positive and negative experiences for both the individual and the organization. In addition, many are unable to cross boundaries; or are unwilling to do so. Thus, the boundaryless career may be more rhetoric than reality.

Second, while for some people, in particular managers and professionals, boundarylessness may be a refreshing and challenging source of optimism (Arthur et al., 1999), for many it may create confusion, anxiety and career despair. For such individuals, uncertain opportunities may actually enhance stress rather than increase motivation. Additionally, while for some organizations the boundaryless career notion offers new structural and systemic solutions, for others it leads to the loss of some of the best people and possibly of their institutional memory and organizational learning. Newer practices such as talent management can be effective in this respect because they enhance adjustment competencies and the ability to cope with uncertainty.

The climate of career boundarylessness may be interpreted by transient careerists as legitimizing low commitment to organizational norms of loyalty and proper conduct. Such an interpretation may be a precursor to engaging in career-related forms of OMB, such as deception, undermining, fraud and abuse. Thus, for organization members the experience of boundarylessness and career uncertainty may be also related to increased intentions to engage in self-benefitting forms of misbehavior (OMB type S).

Conclusion

Career is a historically contingent phenomenon closely associated with the rise of modernity and personalized contractual wage labor. The tendency for bright siding career obscures its origins within relations of domination and exploitation. Such normalization masks the continuing uses of career as a vehicle for disciplining workers through self-surveillance and identity building that operationalizes a strict work ethic. To make things worse, as a lingering ideal that is becoming increasingly unattainable in post-work societies, career primarily serves the interests of comfortable elites while disadvantaging great swaths of the population who would benefit from a redefinition of the term and its centrality in labor activities. Furthermore, as a gendered and racialized term, career must also be analyzed within the context of broader systems of oppression between groups.

Work careers in the 21st century thus cannot be fully understood if mainstream management and HRM literature continues to assume their positive and attractive attributes. There are, however, signs that tides may be turning. A more balanced (i.e., transparent) view of organizations has recently been advanced by a surge of interest in both prevalent macrolevel organizational dark sides such as corporate corruption (e.g., Ashforth et al., 2008; Vaughan, 1999), and microlevel forms of potentially harmful (unethical) work-related behavior (e.g., Treviño et al., 2006). Following Vardi and Weitz (2016) we believe that by relating organizational careers and organizational misbehavior, we contribute to a more balanced and more realistic view of organizations. Organizations, like individual players, are both "good" and "bad," and so are most career experiences.

The challenges for human resources practitioners in managing both careers and the many forms of OMB are many and varied (Benson et al., 2013). Those in charge must be well equipped to grasp the full spectrum of new careers' realities, including the opportunities as well as threats that come along with them, their commonalities and differences. Not only savvy employees, but practitioners as well, must expand their repertoire of skills and competencies as well as their perspectives to safely walk the darker and riskier career grounds. Many organizations indeed venture into OMB management by instilling codes of ethics and better monitoring employee and managerial conduct (e.g., Weitz and Vardi, 2008). At the practical level, organizational support (e.g., in the shape of coaching and mentoring) can be offered to individuals experiencing career difficulties. HR policies and practices need to be developed, adapted or discontinued in line with their anticipated fit for the new shape of careers (Baruch and Peiperl, 2000). An integrative model of OMB management offers a strategic tool and guidelines because it views careers as both antecedents of OMB and consequences of OMB. It has implications for employees and managers, it offers preventive and corrective interventions and it is dynamic and temporal to be able to address such unfolding and interconnected processes.

Scholars of organizations and careers should portray the career accurately and realistically, providing a fair and balanced depiction of working life. Are not negative traits, attitudes, emotions, intentions and behaviors important elements of people's career experiences? In our careers, we are both actors and spectators. A good drama (Nicholson, 2007) does not necessarily end happily, and yet it receives both applause and criticism. Without exploring the darker side of careers, even exposing intentional forms of related organizational misbehavior, a well-rounded, balanced and comprehensive understanding of careers cannot be successfully attained. By acknowledging the negative aspects of careers, and accepting the dark sides as significant and salient components of organizations, we encourage a balanced perspective in the study of careers, and the complex, temporal and dynamic interactions between person, work and organization.

References

Ackroyd, S. & Thompson, P. 1999. *Organizational Misbehaviour*. Thousand Oaks, CA: Sage Publications.

Adkins, C.L., Werbel, J.D. & Farh, J-L. 2001. A field study of job insecurity during a financial crisis. *Group & Organization Management*, 26, 463–483.

Alvesson, M. 1993. Organizations as rhetoric: Knowledge-intensive firms and the struggle with ambiguity. *Journal of Management Studies*, 30, 997–1015.

Aronowitz, S. & Difazio, W. 1994. *The Jobless Future: Sci-Tech and the Dogma of Work*. Minneapolis, MN: Univerity of Minnesota Press.

Arthur, M.B., Inkson, K. & Pringle, J. 1999. *The New Careers: Individual Action and Economic Change*. London: Sage Publications.

Arthur, M.B., Claman, P.H. & Defillippi, R.J. 1995. Intelligent enterprise, intelligent careers. *The Academy of Management Executive*, 9, 7–20.

Arthur, M.B., Khapova, S.N. & Wilderom, C.P. 2005. Career success in a boundaryless career world. *Journal of Organizational Behavior*, 26, 177–202.

Arthur, M.B. & Rousseau, D.M. 1996. *The Boundaryless Career: A New Employment Principle for a New Organizational Era*. New York: Oxford University Press.

Ashforth, B.E., Gioia, D.A., Robinson, S.L. & Trevino, L.K. 2008. Re-viewing organizational corruption. *Academy of Management Review*, 33, 670–684.

Ashkenas, R., Ulrich, D., Jick, T. & Kerr, S. 1995. *The Boundaryless Organization: Breaking the Chains of Organizational Structure*. San Francisco, CA: Jossey-Bass.

Baruch, Y. 2004. *Managing Careers: Theory and Practice*. Harlow, GB: Hall/Pearson.

Baruch, Y. & Peiperl, M. 2000. Career management practices: An empirical survey and implications. *Human Resource Management*, 39, 347–366.

Baruch, Y. & Quick, J.C. 2007. Understanding second careers: Lessons from a study of US navy admirals. *Human Resource Management*, 46, 471–491.

Baruch, Y. & Vardi, Y. 2016. A fresh look at the dark side of contemporary careers: Toward a realistic discourse. *British Journal of Management*, 27, 355–372.

Bauman, Z. 2000. *Liquid Modernity*. Cambridge: Polity Press.

Beck, U. 1992. *Risk Society: Towards a New Modernity*. London, UK: Sage Publications.

Beck, U. 2001. Interview with Ulrich Beck. *Journal of Consumer Culture*, 1, 261–277.

Beder, S. 2000. *Selling the Work Ethic: From Puritan Pulpit to Corporate Pr.* London, UK: Zed Books.

Benson, P., Hanley, G. & Scroggins, W. 2013. Human resource management and deviant/criminal behavior. *In*: Elias, S.M. (ed.) *Deviant and Criminal Behavior in the Workplace*. New York: University Press.

Bourdieu, P. & Nice, R. 1998. *Acts of Resistance: Against the Tyranny of the Market*. New York: New Press.

Boydston, J. 1990. *Home and Work: Housework, Wages, and the Ideology of Labor in the Early Republic*. New York: Oxford University Press.

Bracha, A., Burke, M.A. & Khachiyan, A. 2015. Changing patterns in informal work participation in the United States 2013–2015. *Federal Reserve Bank of Boston Research*, Paper Series Current Policy Perspectives Paper No. 15–10. Available SSRN: https://ssrn.com/abstract=2723814.

Bunting, M. 2011. *Willing Slaves: How the Overwork Culture is Ruling our Lives*. London, UK: HarperCollins.

Burawoy, M. 1979. *Manufacturing Consent: Changes in the Labor Process under Monopoly Capitalism*. Chicago, IL: University of Chicago Press.

Cockburn, C. 1993. *Brothers: Male Dominance and Technological Change*. London, UK: Pluto Press.

Cotter, D., Hermsen, J.M. & Vanneman, R. 2011. The end of the gender revolution? Gender role attitudes from 1977 to 2008. *American Journal of Sociology*, 117, 259–289.

Crocker, J. & Cooper, M.L. 2011. Addressing scientific fraud. *Science*, 334, 1182.

Dandeker, C. 1990. *Surveillance, Power and Modernity: Bureaucracy and Discipline from 1700 to the Present Day*. Cambridge, UK: Polity Press.

Deetz, S. 1998. Subordination and Self-Surveillance. *In*: Mckinlay, A. & Starkey, K. (eds.) *Foucault, Management and Organization Theory: From Panopticon to Technologies of Self*. London, UK: Sage Publications.

El-Sawad, A. 2005. Becoming a lifer? Unlocking career through metaphor. *Journal of Occupational and Organizational Psychology*, 78, 23–41.

Ference, T.P., Stoner, J.A. & Warren, E.K. 1977. Managing the career plateau. *Academy of Management Review*, 2, 602–612.

Fleming, P. 2009. *Authenticity and the Cultural Politics of Work: New Forms of Informal Control*. Oxford, UK: Oxford University Press.

Fraser, N. & Gordon, L. 1994. A genealogy of dependency: Tracing a keyword of the US welfare state. *Signs: Journal of Women in Culture and Society*, 19, 309–336.

Giddens, A. 1991. *Modernity and Self-Identity: Self and Society in the Late Modern Age*. Stanford, CA: Stanford University Press.

Goffman, E. 1959. *The Presentation of Self in Everyday Life*. Garden City, NY: Doubleday Anchor.

Greenberg, E. 2010. *Insidious Workplace Behavior*. New York: Routledge.

Greenhaus, J.H., Callanan, G.A. & Godshalk, V.M. 2000. *Career Management*. Orlando, FL: Dryden Press.

Grey, C. 1994. Career as a project of the self and labour process discipline. *Sociology*, 28, 479–497.

Gunz, H. & Peiperl, M. 2007. *Handbook of Career Studies*. Thousand Oaks, CA: Sage Publications.

Hall, D.T. 1976. *Careers in Organizations*. Pacific Palisades, LA: Goodyear.

Hall, D.T. 2004. The protean career: A quarter-century journey. *Journal of Vocational Behavior*, 65, 1–13.

Harvey, D. 2007. *A Brief History of Neoliberalism*. Oxford, UK: Oxford University Press.

Heslin, P. 2005. Experiencing career success. *Organizational Dynamics*, 34, 376–390.

Hochschild, A. 1983. *The Managed Heart: Commercialization of Human Feeling.* Berkeley, CA: University of California Press.

Hochschild, A. & Machung, A. 2012. *The Second Shift: Working Families and the Revolution at Home.* New York: Penguin.

Inkson, K. 2007. *Understanding careers: Metaphors of working lives.* Thousand Oaks, CA: Sage Publications.

Inkson, K., Gunz, H., Ganesh, S. & Roper, J. 2012. Boundaryless careers: Bringing back boundaries. *Organization Studies,* 33, 323–340.

Katz, L.F. & Krueger, A.B. 2016. The rise and nature of alternative work arrangements in the United States, 1995–2015. *The National Bureau of Economic Research,* Working Paper No. 22667, Cambridge, MA.

Kunda, G. 1992. *Engineering Culture: Control and Commitment in a High-Tech Corporation.* Philadelphia, PA: Temple University Press.

Lash, S. & Urry, J. 1987. *The End of Organized Capitalism.* Madison, WI: University of Wisconsin Press.

Lee, C.I. & Felps, W. 2013. Towards a Taxonomy of Career Studies. *EGOS Colloquium.* Montreal, Canada.

Leinbach-Reyhle, N. 2015. New report identifies US retailers lose $60 billion a year, employee theft top concern. *Forbes Magazine,* New York: Forbes, 7 October.

Lorber, J. 1994. *Paradoxes of Gender.* New Haven, CT: Yale University Press.

Lu, J.G., Brockner, J., Vardi, Y. & Weitz, E. 2016. The dark side of job autonomy: Unethical behavior. *Academy of Management Meetings, August,* Anaheim, CA.

Mcilveen, P. & Patton, W. 2006. A critical reflection on career development. *International Journal for Educational and Vocational Guidance,* 6, 15–27.

Mckinlay, A. 2002. Dead selves': The birth of the modern career. *Organization,* 9, 595–614.

Mckinlay, A. & Starkey, K. 1998. *Foucault, Management and Organization Theory: From Panopticon to Technologies of Self.* London, UK: Sage Publications.

Merle, R. 2016. Wells Fargo boots 5300 employees for creating accounts its customers didn't ask for. *Washington Post,* 8 September.

Michel, A. 2011. Transcending socialization: A nine-year ethnography of the body's role in organizational control and knowledge workers' transformation. *Administrative Science Quarterly,* 56, 325–368.

Near, J.P. & Miceli, M.P. 1985. Organizational dissidence: The case of whistle-blowing. *Journal of Business Ethics,* 4, 1–16.

Nicholson, N. 1998. How hardwired is human behavior? *Harvard Business Review,* 76, 134–147.

Nicholson, N. 2007. Destiny, drama, and deliberation. *In:* Gunz, H.P. & Peiperl, M.A. (eds.) *Handbook of Career Studies.* Los Angeles: Sage Publications.

Powell, W.W. & Smith-Doerr, L. 1994. Networks and economic life. *In:* Smelser, N. & Swedberg, R. (eds.) *The Handbook of Economic Sociology.* Princeton, NJ: Princeton University Press.

Rifkin, J. 1995. *The End of Work: Technology, Jobs, and Your Future.* New York: Putnam.

Robinson, S.L. & Bennett, R.J. 1995. A typology of deviant workplace behaviors: A multidimensional scaling study. *Academy of Management Journal,* 38, 555–572.

Rose, N. 1998. *Inventing Our Selves: Psychology, Power, and Personhood.* Cambridge, UK: Cambridge University Press.

Rosenbaum, J.E. 1979. Tournament mobility: Career patterns in a corporation. *Administrative Science Quarterly,* 24, 220–241.

Ross, A. 2003. *No-Collar: The Humane Workplace and Its Hidden Costs Basic Books.* New York: Basic.

Ryan, W. 1971. *Blaming the Victim.* New York: Pantheon.

Sackett, P.R. & Devore, C.J. 2001. Counterproductive behaviors at work. *In:* Anderson, N., Ones, D.S., Sinhangil, H.K. & Viswesvaran, C. (eds.) *Handbook of Industrial, Work and Organizational Psychology.* London, UK: Sage Publications.

Savage, M. 1997. Discipline, surveillance and the 'career': Employment on the great western railway 1833–1914. *In:* Mckinlay, A. & Starkey, K. (eds.) *Foucault, Management and Organization Theory: From Panopticon to Technologies of Self.* London, UK: Sage Publications.

Savickas, M.L. & Porfeli, E.J. 2012. Career adapt-abilities scale: Construction, reliability, and measurement equivalence across 13 countries. *Journal of Vocational Behavior,* 80, 661–673.

Schein, E.H. 1978. *Career Dynamics: Matching Individual and Organizational Needs*. Reading, MA: Addison Wesley Publishing Company.

Schor, J. 1991. *The Overworked American: The Unexpected Decline of Leisure*. New York: Basic books.

Seibert, S.E., Kraimer, M.L. & Liden, R.C. 2001. A social capital theory of career success. *Academy of Management Journal*, 44, 219–237.

Sennett, R. 1998. *The Corrosion of Character: The Transformation of Work in Modern Capitalism*. New York and London: Norton.

Shuai, X., Rollins, J., Moulinier, I., Custis, T., Edmunds, M. & Schilder, F. 2017. A multidimensional investigation of the effects of publication retraction on scholarly impact. *Journal of the Association for Information Science and Technology*, 68, 2225–2236.

Shulman, D. 2007. *From Hire to Liar: The Role of Deception in the Workplace*. Ithaca, NY: Cornell University Press.

Standing, G. 2014. *The Precariat: The New Dangerous Class*. London, UK: Bloomsbury Publishing.

Strasser, J. 1999. *Wenn der Arbeitsgesellschaft die Arbeit ausgeht*. Stanford: Pendo Press.

Thompson, E.P. 1963. *The Making of the English Working Class*. New York: Pantheon.

Thompson, E.P. 1967. Time, work-discipline, and industrial capitalism. *Past & Present*, 56–97.

Treviño, L.K., Weaver, G.R. & Reynolds, S.J. 2006. Behavioral ethics in organizations: A review. *Journal of Management*, 32, 951–990.

Vardi, I. & Smith-Doerr, L. 2014. Women in the knowledge economy: Understanding gender inequality through the lens of collaboration. *In:* Kleinman, D. & Moore, K. (eds.) *Handbook of Science, Technology, and Society*. London, UK: Routledge.

Vardi, Y. 2011. The pigheaded careerist: If you are climbing up a ladder, make sure your closets and conscience are spotless. *7th Critical Management Studies Conference*, Naples, Italy.

Vardi, Y. & Kim, S. 2007. Considering the darker side of careers: Toward a more balanced perspective. *In:* Gunz, H. & Peiperl, M. (eds.) *Handbook of Career Studies*. Los Angeles: Sage Publications.

Vardi, Y. & Weitz, E. 2016. *Misbehavior in Organizations: A Dynamic Approach*. New York: Routledge.

Vardi, Y. & Wiener, Y. 1996. Misbehavior in organizations: A motivational framework. *Organization Science*, 7, 151–165.

Vaughan, D. 1999. The dark side of organizations: Mistake, misconduct, and disaster. *Annual Review of Sociology*, 25, 271–305.

Vigoda, E. 2000. Organizational politics, job attitudes, and work outcomes: Exploration and implications for the public sector. *Journal of Vocational Behavior*, 57, 326–347.

Weber, L. 2017. The end of employees. *Wall Street Journal*, 2 February, https://www.wsj.com/articles/the-end-of-employees-1486050443.

Weber, M. 1958. *The Protestant Ethic and the Spirit of Capitalism, Translated by Talcott Parsons (New York, Charles Scribner's Sons)*. New York: Charles Scribner's Sons.

Weber, M. 2013. *From Max Weber: Essays in Sociology*. London, UK: Routledge.

Weeks, K. 2011. *The Problem with Work: Feminism, Marxism, Antiwork Politics, and Postwork Imaginaries*. Durham, NC: Duke University Press.

Weitz, E. & Vardi, Y. 2008. Understanding and managing misbehavior in organizations. *In:* Wankel, C. (ed.) *21st Century Management: A Reference Handbook*. Thousand Oaks: Sage Publications.

Williams, R. 1983. *Keywords: A Vocabulary of Culture and Society*. London, UK: Fontana.

Part III
Contextualizing careers

17

Multilevel career analysis in the film industry and professional service firms

Exploring the roles of relations and institutions in bounding careers

Frans Bévort and Iben Sandal Stjerne

"The career is dead – long live the career" was the statement Mirvis and Hall (1994) ascribed to, at the time, the new situation in which organizational careers seemed of less relevance as a result of the changes of employment relations in the new economy. Following that came the "boundaryless career," a concept that removed the organization as well as at its bureaucratic boundaries from the career debate, favoring agency and boundarylessness over structure, institutions and boundaries. Despite the popularity of the construct, boundaryless careers have also been criticized for oversimplifying the complexity of careers and for overlooking the fact that careers exist in a context with boundaries at multiple levels. We concur with the literature that there has been a transformation of careers as a result of short-term employments and flexible ways of organizing work. However, this chapter will challenge the unproductive simplification put forward by this view that states that organizational boundaries and other structures have no, or only have limited impact on career processes.

Within the career literature, "career boundaries" have been the focus of a long-standing scholarly debate that has been going on for 20 years. Recently, the study of career has been considered irrelevant by some management scholars and have been replaced by studying – using the more recent buzzword "talent management" (Cappelli, 2008). With the introduction of the concept of "boundaryless careers" (Arthur and Rousseau, 1996), in which the boundaries of the firm are no longer seen as limiting individuals in their career mobility, the role of the organization in our understanding of careers has become much too limited. Career holders are depicted as being fully able to manage their own careers beyond and between firms (Arthur and Rousseau, 1996). This argument, we think, has led to an overemphasis on agency in career studies. This is illustrated by the large number of agency-oriented concepts in career studies such as protean careers (Hall et al., 2002; Hall, 2004; De Vos and Soens, 2008), career self-management (King, 2004), kaleidoscope careers (Mainiero and Sullivan, 2005), authentic careers (Svejenova, 2005) and career crafting and entrepreneurship (De Bruin and Lewis, 2004). The role of the organization and to some extent the role of social boundaries such as gender, ethnicity and socioeconomic backgrounds are less likely to be considered in the career debate. This has led to calls to bring back boundaries to the career research stating, referring to "boundaryless career," that "the concept and its elaboration in the literature render it inadequate as a central concept in future theory-building" (Inkson et al., 2012: 314). Further, there have been increasing calls for the development of boundary-focused career studies (Gunz et al., 2007) and related papers on career boundaries (Mayrhofer et al., 2007; King et al., 2005; Gunz et al., 2000).

Careers are not unbound and free for the individual to define and create; they are in fact embedded in local as well as larger social systems that set boundaries that delimit individuals' opportunities. Despite the negative connotations boundaries have acquired, they can also be understood as structures which enable and delimit activities (Inkson et al., 2012) and hence also careers. Nevertheless, the concept "boundaryless career" is still of considerable relevance for understanding careers in the new economy wherein firms increasingly organize to be flexible and agile, most often using projects. This tendency has increased and has resulted in employment relationships and work tasks being organized outside the firms in social networks (Sydow, 2009; Haunschild, 2003, 2004; Jones, 1996; Blair, 2003) and in careers being developed outside and between organizations. The boundaries of the organization are, in this conceptualization, sometimes seen as being replaced by the boundaries in industry fields (Jones, 2001; Peterson and Anand, 2002), and the institutional resources seen as being conveyed through social networks and occupational groups and standards (Barley and Kunda, 2006; O'Mahony and Bechky, 2006).

The views expressed in the boundaryless career literature do not necessarily entail individuals getting more agency in determining their careers. Careers should be understood as a result of individuals' working history over time, the "unfolding sequence of a person's work experiences over time" (Arthur and Rousseau, 1996: 4). The very same institutions which enable people to perform work also constrain and create boundaries for acceptable behavior and thus influence careers (Inkson et al., 2012). Even in the most extreme cases of apparent absence of organizational boundaries (e.g. the creative industries and professional service firms (PSFs)), there are structures that both penetrate and transcend organizations that limit and enable individuals' careers (Starkey et al., 2000; Eikhof, 2014; Bechky, 2006). At the end of the day, individuals are bound – by the relations, structures and institutions in which work is embedded. Careers can hence not be understood as being detached from the social context and the boundaries inherent in which they are played out. This calls for multilevel analysis of careers that takes the institutional context of industry, organizational and occupational norms, structures and standards into account.

In this chapter we show how careers evolve as a result of boundaries which enable as well as constrain careers at multiple analytical levels: at the industry and field level, the career system applied in the organizations, and at the level of the individual career, careers remain bounded in a number of ways; and these boundaries define the possible trajectories and professional identities in specific organizational and institutional setting (Bévort, 2012; Stjerne, 2016). At the same time we show how boundaries are critical for the trajectories that individuals follow in these organizationally loosely coupled settings. We draw on two distinct cases that have been depicted in prior research as extreme cases that are described by a lack of organizational structures for careers and thus create settings that are ideally suited for the development of "boundaryless careers": professional service firms (PSFs; Jones et al., 1998; Greenwood et al., 1990) and the film industry (Jones, 1996). By drawing on these two distinct cases, the chapter shows how a multilevel analysis can enrich our understanding of careers by identifying the contextual boundaries which co-constitute careers. We show that careers in the cases of PSFs and the Danish film industry are always developed within, yet across and beyond, these structural frames. Despite the fact that the organizational boundaries play a relatively small role for careers in these settings, other boundaries remain important.

How do we understand the boundaries which enable and constrain careers?

Our theoretical point of departure rests on the view that human rationality is always bounded (March and Simon, 1958) by the institutions and social structures which make up the context of individuals and organizations. While individuals are not "cultural dopes" (Garfinkel, 1967), they are to a large extent molded from the social material in which they are situated. This relates to the total biography of each individual, the career in the form of experiences in the job market and specific occupation and/or organization within which the individual may end up anchoring her career and the broader institutional context in question. But we also think agency, understood as the individual's aspirations, knowledgeable choices and strategic action, is a necessary component in the analysis of career. Thus, as Inkson et al. (2012: 327) put it: "A fundamental question in career studies is whether careers are mainly the product of institutional frameworks or of individual agency." However, we will surmise, the really interesting point for research is where actors' agency intersects with institutional boundaries – the way actors cope with the boundaries they encounter in their careers. Therefore, it is a problem to underemphasize the role of boundaries as we think is the case in the "boundaryless career" literature. On the other hand, it is important to conceptualize the role of individual agency in responding to and coping with these boundaries in the career-making process.

Micro-foundations of institutions – the role of identity and subjectivity in careers

Many theoretical thinkers and schools have had more or less explicit formulations of this structure-agency dynamic (Giddens, 1984; Bourdieu, 1977; Schatzki et al., 2001; Meyer and Rowan, 1991(1977); Friedland and Alford, 1991; Barley and Tolbert, 1997). We draw from recent institutional theory which, from the now classical structural new-institutional starting point (Meyer and Rowan, 1991(1977); DiMaggio and Powell, 1983), seeks to understand the role of actors and individuals (called for by DiMaggio, 1988; Powell and Colyvas, 2008) in the creation, maintenance and disruption of institutions (Lawrence and Suddaby, 2006). For example, Lok (2010) shows how the creation of specific identities is critical to understanding institutional change by analyzing the way financial professionals and investment bankers incorporate conflicting institutional norms and values in the way they create their professional identity. Creed et al. (2010) show how LGBT ministers in the United States struggle with the clash between their sexual identity and their professional identities and roles in the church. Hallett (2010) discusses how a school superintendent embodied the recoupling of an accountability policy implementation when confronting the teacher group that had ignored it. What these new voices have in common is that they see actors and identity as key to understanding institutional structures and especially change. Hence individuals enact the boundaries which eventually bound their future actions.

Another relevant strand of literature combines the actor perspective with professions and occupational roles. Scott (2008) discusses the role of professionals as institutional agents, how they are, in a way, boundary creators by establishing legal, cultural and cognitive rules, norms and interpretations. Bévort and Suddaby (2016) describe how professionals (accountants) (co-) create new identity scripts enabling them to assume new managerial roles as part of a wider institutional change taking place in professional service firms (Bévort, 2012).

Drawing on these micro-sociological views, we accept a subjectivist position (Gunz et al., 2007) in which career boundaries exist in the minds of actors and are enacted and maintained in the interaction of groups of actors (Barley, 1986; Barley and Tolbert, 1997). While boundaries (and social structure more generally) are too complex a phenomenon to define in a simple way, it will for our purposes suffice to point out that it is organizational boundaries, hierarchical order, job ladders, role systems, delimitation of the organization and so forth which are usually referred to in the discussion of boundaryless careers. We add to this by including boundaries at various levels, for instance identity, professional and industry boundaries. These boundaries simultaneously bound and define the way individuals can craft their careers. Furthermore, we understand boundaries as holding other properties than just being constraints, which is implied in the alleged decay of organizational boundaries in the literature. Thus, in addition to organizational boundaries, which are still very much in place in organizations, individuals cope with and utilize boundaries at both the individual and the institutional level. When we speak of the institutional level we speak of transorganizational structures such as professions, industries or organizational fields. An organizational field, for instance, could be the field of filmmaking, which consists of artists, public agencies, film companies and several other commercial actors (Scott, 1991).

Analyzing career boundaries at the individual, organizational and institutional levels

Boundaries of careers can be seen as situational or local as well as trans-situational or global (Inkson et al., 2012; Mayrhofer et al., 2007). A boundary can be very individual, rooted in the biography and identity work of the individual, it can be organizationally based on policy choices or traditions in the field, or it can be institutional, like professional norms or country-specific regulations. Institutions permeate boundaries at all levels as practices, norms, values and knowledge (e.g., institutional logics; Friedland and Alford, 1991; Thornton et al., 2012) that bound actors and action at all levels.

Inkson et al. (2012) observe that boundaries in the career literature are often seen (e.g., Arthur and Rousseau, 1996) as objective and subjective – or maybe external and internal to the career-actor. While this is intuitively tempting, we think this isn't compatible with a fundamentally phenomenological (Bévort and Suddaby, 2016) and structuration (Barley and Tolbert, 1997; Giddens, 1984) position on structure and agency. The debate on boundaryless (agency) – bounded (structure) in career theories is strongly connected to the objective-subjective careers formulation. This debate centers on who gets to define career success – the subjective side is the implication that individuals are able to define career success by their own parameters, while the objective career is the factual happenings such as who got the job, where did they work, for how long and so on. Most scholars within the boundaryless career school of thinking take on a subjective understanding of career success (see, e.g., Mirvis and Hall, 1994), while the ones emphasizing the bounded sides of the career debate tend to focus on the structural and objective aspects of careers and career success (e.g., Inkson et al., 2012). By describing a boundary as "objective," it becomes reified and detached from the meaning the individuals ascribe to it (Bévort and Suddaby, 2016; Lok, 2010). Boundaries can be constructed as objective by the individual, but will nevertheless be socially constructed (in different degrees as, for instance, gender) and therefore can be modified, changed or discarded (Gunz et al., 2007). The boundary can be felt as no less real or objective, but it does not make it inevitable (Gunz et al., 2007: 478). Inkson et al. (2012: 327) point out that most writers on career boundaries still tend to emphasize organizational boundaries, which is not surprising as the notion of career was born with an organizational context as the taken-for-granted backdrop.

We will provide a more nuanced perspective that investigates boundaries at three levels; organizational, individual/relational and institutional. The organizational level is well-known and refers to the hierarchical structure and organizational roles and practices which bind careers. The individual/relational level refers to the boundaries which occur in the interaction orders (Goffman, 1983) between the career holder and the other actors in the work life. The institutional level refers to the boundaries that reach beyond the organization in time and space, as for instance an industry or a profession.

In the chapter, we will focus especially on boundaries at the individual/relational and institutional level boundaries, and on how they enable and constrain careers, because this is where the extant literature is least developed (Gunz et al., 2007; Inkson et al., 2012). However, the organizational level still holds important insights as to how boundaries constrain and especially enable careers in ways which is not often discussed in the literature. In the analysis of the two cases (a film company and a professional firm), we will use these three levels and look for boundaries which enable as well as constrain the careers which the career-holders can build.

Multilevel analyses of two extreme cases of careers in boundaryless organizations: a professional service firm and a film production company in the Danish film industry

The following analysis is based on two cases of organizations selected as 'least likely' cases of finding boundaries in careers, building on the case selection principle that if you can find it here then you can find it everywhere (Flyvbjerg, 2006). This analysis sheds light on two distinct organizational cases from (and of) the professional services field and the Danish film industry respectively. The two organizational cases are in many ways different but also similar in that they used to organize in ways which included very few of the traditional organizational boundaries. Organizations in both industries have undergone a gradual managerial bureaucratization that influences and changes the boundaries for how careers develop. Both industries are working with labor markets which structure careers independently from organizations. As a result, when we look at the Big 4 and Danish film (pseudonyms for the case companies), we find good instances "of finding boundaries where we might not expect it" and which can serve to contribute to bringing back a more nuanced view of boundaries to the study of careers (Inkson et al., 2012). The case-observations used in the illustrative analysis are drawn from a three-year ethnography in a local division of a "Big 4" accounting-based multidisciplinary advisory firm (professional service firm) employing 2,400 staff, published in Bévort (2012) and 60 interviews and six months of ethnography from a company in the Danish film industry, published in Mathieu and Stjerne (2012), Mathieu and Stjerne (2014), Stjerne (2016), and Stjerne and Svejenova (2016). We will address the two organizational cases as "Big 4" and "Danish Film" in the analyses below.

Case 1: Professional service firm – Big 4

Organizations dominated by professionals[1] are characterized as more or less devoid of the *organizational boundaries* that we know from more traditional bureaucratic organizations with well-defined managerial roles, career systems and talent management programs (Greenwood et al., 1990; Cooper et al., 1996; Bévort, 2012). This is maybe most extreme in the professional partnership model seen in PSFs such as law, accounting, architectural firms and so forth (Von Nordenflycht, 2010). The partnering model implies two levels in the organization: the professional and the partner. Between these two levels, the professionals move through several levels of (professional) seniority (e.g., junior, senior, manager) on the path to partnership but with little hierarchical consequence as the titles do not imply more managerial responsibility for employees at the firm. What may occur as a rather structured organizational hierarchy is in reality often a rather flat (few levels) informal meritocracy in which it is levels of competencies and task-responsibility that organize work rather than management and managerial roles. This may seem a very subtle distinction, which we will argue, with the PSF-literature, it is not.

Our case company, Big 4, had experienced a long period of growth and mergers, which is typical for the large global accounting based PSFs in the so-called big four group (KPMG, Deloitte, E&Y and PWC). Big 4 is the Danish division of one of these. An interesting aspect of this development, which is also well documented in the PSF literature, is that Big 4 has developed its organization and management in a way that introduces elements of traditional (bureaucratic) organization while retaining many of the characteristics of the profession-focused organization (Cooper et al., 1996). This means that some of the organizational boundaries not present in the classic professional partnership are introduced (for instance new managerial roles). In this way Big 4 provides two ways of observing how organizational boundaries enable and constrain careers; the relative absence of traditional managerial careers in the classic partnership model before the change, and how careers develop when boundaries are introduced where there were formerly very few.

To the observer who never experienced the everyday life of an accounting firm, it may be surprising that a professional firm, which delivers accounting work which is very structured and regulated compared to, for instance, law, is at the same time informally organized. Indeed, accounting and bookkeeping could be seen as central tenets of bureaucracy. Despite this, most accounting firms share the same "profession-based organization and management" character-istic of other professional service firms which is much different from traditional bureaucracies (Greenwood et al., 1990; Greenwood and Suddaby, 2006; Bévort and Poulfelt, 2015).

In the following we will show how a multilevel analysis can open up the role of boundaries in career studies, even in an atypical non-bureaucratic context.

Enablers and constraints at the field and social level

Following the institutionalist approach above, professions and the career systems integrated in the occupational system defined by them are from the outset very strong institutional bounda-ries, which define many aspects of the careers possible within the profession (Abbott, 1988). Put another way, professionals in accounting firms face strong institutional boundaries. The profes-sional service firm's way of organizing knowledge work has often been praised as a unique and future-oriented way of supporting independent and highly competent professionals in their career (e.g., Peters, 2004). This rests on the fact that the focus of these firms is on professional competence, and the biggest asset in these firms is their professional staff (Bévort and Poulfelt, 2015). The fact is that this may not seem to be the case when we apply a multilevel analysis on the careers in a typical professional service firm such as Big 4. It may be more the case in organizations that can be termed "Neo-PSFs" (Von Nordenflycht, 2010), for instance manage-ment consultancies in which the professional element, especially in the form of a dominating discipline, is less salient. A corollary of this is that these professional careers are indeed sometimes seen as "protean" (however debatable) and more or less detached from any organizational or other boundaries or long-term commitment. The professional knowledge worker's career may be regarded as the archetype of the "boundaryless career" (Arthur and Rousseau, 1996; 2001).

The literature investigating the special form of organization, "the professional partnership" (Greenwood et al., 1990; Cooper et al., 1996; Brock, 2008; Bévort, 2012), sees a strong and growing influence on this form of organization from more managerial or bureaucratic forms of management and organizing. We see Big 4 as showcasing how multilevel boundaries apply to the careers of the professionals and how these changes as a result of institutional changes taking place in the field and how the boundaries (and the change of boundaries) enable and constrain different career trajectories and choices in Big 4. The fact is that while professionals' careers are faintly bounded at the organizational level, they are bounded to a much higher extent at the institutional level, through the norms, values and associations of the profession. There is, however, an interesting twist on this, as we shall discuss in the next section.

Enablers and boundaries for careers at the organizational level

While the structures and practices at the organizational level are very different and more ambiguous compared to a bureaucratic organization (Bévort, 2012; Von Nordenflycht, 2010), there are specific aspects of professional organizations that structure part of a professional career path. Indeed, professional organizations are, as seen from a certain perspective, "career-factories" – they are what Larson (1977) called the professions "producer of producers." However, the enablers are not based on traditional divisions of labor, specialization of roles and formalized career progression and so forth. As mentioned before, the training and development is deeply embedded in the relations between less and more trained and senior professionals who are following an institutionalized set of professional norms, more than an organizational plan or a progressing hierarchy of organizational roles. The boundaries in the organization are created through professional norms and standards, which imply the tacit expectations of acting appropriately towards clients, rather than formalized organizational roles and rules. As such, the structures of the organizational level are not salient either as enablers or as boundaries for the professional career.

The profession and the professional practice community provide, to a much higher degree, the framework within which professional careers are structured. This is of course rather unsurprising. The organizational consequence of this was, in the "classic PSF," a structure wherein career success was equivalent to making it to becoming professional partner, which was supported by the development activities having the same goals and purpose. Indeed, if a professional employee's career goals were not aimed at partnership, the employee in question would soon be asked to leave ("up-or-out").

While being flat in terms of organizational levels, this is at the same time a rather authoritarian system in which the relative few who become partners hold considerable personal power. The governance is based on a collegial system in which the partnership elect managing partners and top-management group positions in which partners typically take turns. These board positions are seen as doing communal service rather than a career goal in itself. What is interesting, though, is the fact that the growing influence of "managerial" or "bureaucratic" logics in professional organizations re-introduces organizational boundaries in professional organizations like professional service firms (Cooper et al., 1996). In Big 4 (Bévort, 2012) the change in management practices created a number of boundaries, which in turn enabled and constrained career development of the professionals. For instance, new managerial roles were introduced and supported by training activities. This was a radical departure from the "single-track" career of the old organizational model. This legitimized "management" as a possible career option, and on the other hand it also paved the way for a formal specialization of the partner-role. Also, the strict adherence to the "up-or-out" model, mentioned above, was loosened up, making it possible for senior professionals to stay and tend to a portfolio of clients with a partner as his/her manager, but choosing to forgo partnership as a career goal. The point is that the profession-based single-path career is opened up with new career options as organizational boundaries are introduced in Big 4.

The fascinating thing is that the enabling part of this was the formalization and standardization of specialized roles and alternative career paths, which also opens up alternatives way of enacting the roles. Women have traditionally had great difficulty obtaining and holding roles as partners in PSFs, because the received practice of partners prescribed excessively long hours and a 100 percent dedication to clients' needs, beyond any reasonable limit. In the new "bureaucratic" organization, women and other less traditional profiles – for instance with other professional backgrounds such as HRM – conceivably have a greater likelihood for a successful career in this kind of organization (Bévort and Poulfelt, 2015; Briscoe, 2006). Thus (re-)introducing organizational boundaries creates leeway for a number of new career paths and makes a greater diversity of career-holders possible.

The above description takes its point of departure in the "traditional" professional partnership organization. In Big 4 there was a movement away from this model towards the introduction elements from a more traditional managerial/bureaucratic management (Bévort, 2012). This institutional change of organizational form changes the career game – the way careers are enabled and constrained at the individual and relational level – in a number of ways.

Enablers and constraints at the relational and individual level

The classic PSF's way of organizing is centered on the relationship between the professional and the professional partner (owner), both of which are organized in small groups. This resembles a master-apprentice model in a small workshop known from classical artisan production. The difference is, of course, that the work is 'knowledge expert work' and the clients range from small to very large organizations which typically nurture very long-lasting relationships with clients that are of vital importance for the partner and the professionals she/he employs. In Big 4, the total staff was more than 2,400 employees. The junior professional may become responsible for a project task team (for instance a small client) even in her/his second year, and while the partner is the formal relation-owner of the client, the professional gradually becomes the daily contact to the client. The aim of all professionals traditionally used to be to become partner; if this turns out not to be possible, most accountants choose to find jobs as management accountants in a regular organization (the Cravath system or the "up-or-out model"). As we saw above, this is gradually changing because the firms are changing towards a more traditional managerial system, introducing new role and divisions of labor (Empson et al., 2015), which was also visible in Big 4 (Bévort, 2012).

Even at this level we can see how boundaries in this kind of organization are different from traditional bureaucracies. First of all, there is just one primary career goal offered – the partnership role. There is not an employer-employee relationship, but rather a highly committed collegial relationship between a senior professional and a number of professionals at varying levels of seniority and competence. Also, the relationship to clients becomes even more important than relations to colleagues of managers elsewhere in the firm. The career constraints are obvious in this model. There is either the career goal of becoming partner – or finding a job elsewhere. There are no other roles possible to aim for. In other organizations there would be specialist roles, key account roles, manager roles, training or HR roles to aspire to.

The relation between the professional and the partner is even more important than the relation between an employee and her manager in a non-PSF. The partner is responsible for the continuous professional learning process, following up on performance, introducing the professional to clients, championing the professional in the partnership and eventually pitching the senior professional for partnership. It goes without saying that this relationship can leverage a professional's career prospects, but the relation can become a constraint and obstacle for the professional's career as well. The quality of the relationship to clients has similar ramifications: if the relations to partners and clients do not develop in a positive way, the prospects for the professional are bleak and the choices few. While there are always at least two to make a relationship, it is clear that the partner/client – professional relationship is highly asymmetrical, leaving the (junior) professional as the weaker party. If the partner and even important clients are in favor of you a person and a professional, your career prospects are much better. While the organizational boundaries are diffuse, the relational boundaries are very strong and the individual career choices limited. However, when organizational boundaries are reintroduced (Bévort, 2012), this changes the relations between partners and professionals. In Big 4 (Bévort, 2012), the introduction and maturing of a department manager role waters down the relationship between the partner and the professional. This disturbs the traditional mono-track career practice and as we saw above, makes for a more differentiated career practice. On the one hand, the constraining and enabling idiosyncratic relationship to the partner is substituted with a more formal manager-employee relationship, which may threaten the creation traditional skill-based professional identity and career, but on the other hand it may facilitate a greater range of career trajectories.

Case 2: The Danish film industry – Danish film

The film industry has often been depicted as a critical case for studying boundaryless careers (Jones, 1996; Blair, 2003; O'Mahony and Bechky, 2006). The film industry underwent a severe transformation from being a traditional production system with permanent employees to become organized on a project basis, which implied a high degree of project and freelance based employments (Storper and Christopherson, 1987). The project employments created the official career bounds to the production companies and instead of careers being performed in one firm, film workers' careers were performed across firms. These extreme ways of organizing an entire industry in project-based systems were often said to result in lack of formalized structures that organize work, employment and careers (Haunschild, 2003, 2004; Haunschild and Eikhof, 2009).

The Danish film industry underwent the same kind of changes a few decades after the American film industry. It initially implied that most film workers in an entire industry from one day to the next became freelancers and were free to choose between all the projects in the entire industry whereas previously they had often been limited in their options and got stuck in roles defined by the studio system (Christopherson and Storper, 1989). The transformation released careers from the strings of the long-term employment relationship and brought renewed challenges of finding work, steep competition and being unemployed for sometimes longer periods of time – however this is just one side of the story. In this process a larger institutionalization of informal "industry-level structures" initially grew stronger and became a new multilevel organizer of work and careers in these industries (Eikhof, 2014; Stjerne, 2016).

Enablers and constraints at the field and social level

Instead of having norms, rules and roles controlled and organized by the firm, these became institutionalized at an industry level (Eikhof, 2014). Role expectations such as enthusiasm, gratitude, polite reprimands and humor represent acceptable behavior, while anger and impoliteness are perceived as unacceptable and unprofessional (Bechky, 2006). These role expectations enable work to be performed in an efficient manner despite people having never worked together before, but at the same time they bind individuals in their daily work and set limitations for who can succeed career-wise and who cannot. Film workers who transgress these norms are mostly passed by for future projects as these stories become part of the person's industry reputation. Another example of this was the normative boundaries for freelance workers' ability to take on too many potential projects. Applications for funding film projects must have crew forecasts attached even though it is not yet known whether funding will be granted for the film. At this stage, film freelancers are often "optioned" for the movie, which implies that they make a verbal agreement to work on the film if it gets funding. However, this is a challenge as more than half of all film applications don't get funding and never get produced into a film. As a result, film workers need to risk, balance and prioritize "optioning". There are in these matters certain industry norms for who you can let down and for what reasons (e.g., semi-permanent work relations; Blair, 2003) must be mentioned to others and they always have first priority. However semi-permanent work relations can never be let down for the benefit of a more prestigious movie with another film team.

Although organizational long-term careers are as good as dead in the film industry, there are many structures that influence individual careers. In the film industry most careers are initiated with a traineeship, runner or gofer job. These positions are practical functions responsible for low-risk tasks and are expected to be filled by young people as the payment is often very low and the understanding of the function is associated with it being performed by a young person. The next level is taking on a job as an assistant or a grip, which requires more responsibility for the film making process yet without any responsibility for the film's aesthetics. More recently the next step from this is getting into film school. Film school is important as this is where many of the fundamental industry filmmaking practices are learned, such as the right way of giving feedback (Mathieu and Stjerne, 2014), building up a repertoire of movie references, experimenting with film crafting and, as well, finding one's own initial aesthetic expression. The people who did not go to the national film school have in several cases been described as difficult to work with due to lack of "common language." After film school, overcoming the boundary for getting the first feature film is a huge challenge that is described as a Catch-22: "you cannot make a feature film without having already made a feature film." At this stage the breaking point for survival or perishing is getting into a feature film and only a few make it that far. Later in the career the challenges are about staying on top of the film development and avoiding ending up as "old hat." This clearly shows that despite careers being performed in projects and choices being made by the individual, the agency in film making careers is limited. There are clear career paths and structures although these have also changed and some might find their own paths with "the heart" (Svejenova, 2005), that is following their passion and intuition and breaking with the already established career structures of an industry.

Enablers and boundaries for careers at the organizational level

The role of the organization is in project-based industries much smaller and more ambiguous than in bureaucratic organizations (Eikhof, 2014). Despite this fact, any film project is attached to a film production company, and therefore inherently also careers are carried out in and between projects. The production firm decides which film projects they support, and often they hire in people who seems to fit the values, vision and aesthetics of the film project, which are strongly interlinked with the firm's. This makes certain genres and aesthetics predominant in the film industry, which creates boundaries for individuals' career opportunities. Changing aesthetics is a natural result of the fact that there is an inherent striving for innovation in the film industry and 50 percent of the total granting goes to creative and innovative projects that push forward the local filmic language[2] (see also Mathieu and Stjerne, 2014).

These attempts often imply bridging genres and aesthetics as well as film production practices. When production companies initiate new innovative projects, they challenge the industry's practices and the people selected for these projects become the new "leading edge" within the new genre. Usually these firms seek out and hire upcoming talent as they are cheaper and more can be won. As a result of this talent hunting practice, inexperienced film workers who have just finished film school get a chance to produce their first movie and they become "someone's talent project", which is necessary to overcome the Catch-22 of not having produced a feature film. This also implies that people who get a chance are the ones aligning with the visions, values and aesthetics of the production firm and hence they create and recreate strong career boundaries for insiders and outsiders. As a result, the selection practices performed by the production firm both enable and create new boundaries for careers.

Enablers and constraints at the relational and individual level

In film research, careers have frequently been described as highly dependent on relations and social networks (Blair, 2001, 2003; Jones, 1996). Although every freelancer is hired in on a project anew there are some relational aspects that influence individuals' careers.

First of all, getting into the film industry depends on having the right connections that can support and guide the individual in getting the initial access. Getting into the entry level positions often requires being recommended by family or friends who work in the industry, which was stated clearly in an interview with a successful Danish film producer:

> and film, you just couldn't get anywhere near, and one needed to shoot a white arrow after working with film, because if your uncle wasn't director for Nordic Film or something like that, then you couldn't [get access]. . . . I have applied for everything there was . . . and have never gotten anything . . . and for five years I was searching.
>
> *(Interview, 2010-04-06)*

Relations to senior film workers were essential for enhancing the individuals' position further than the entrance level. It helps if the application has been supervised and edited by very experienced film workers who know the drill and can provide feedback to improve the quality of the application. Creating these important relations depends on showing an extraordinary interest in film and eagerness to learn as well as being a sociable and hard-working person in daily work collaborations. Hence what happens at the individual-relational level can either restrain or enable success at the field level.

However, the importance of managing relations and building the social network does not end at the entrance level of film workers' careers. After film school, as noted above, an important career boundary is making the first feature film. This requires getting a chance in a production company that will take the chance of producing a feature film with an unknown film worker who they perceive as a potential talent. Again in this situation recommendations from prior trusted partners of the production firm are essential. These recommendations are often based on more senior film workers getting acquainted with film school projects by being invited in to give feedback on film school projects or the alternative to the film school, a film education program called "Super 16". It's identifying and finding people with mutual taste who would see the person as a potential talent while at the same time enhancing this talent through giving feedback for school projects.

Secondly, for more established film workers film making is a social process wherein many people contribute to the final outcome of the movie, and the success of a movie can never be attributed to one individual (Becker, 1982) although at the same time success of a film does reflect back on the person and career opportunities: "you are only as good as your last production" (Blair, 2001). As a result of "career shadows" or "career coupling," terms that describe how an individual's career success is also influenced by prior collaboration partners' success or failure, as their image rubs off on the individual film worker and vice versa despite having ended the collaboration years ago (Wagner, 2012; Mathieu and Stjerne, 2012). As a result of these shared career practices, careers can be argued to be collective careers (Tams and Arthur, 2010; Svejenova et al., 2010). Often careers are developed in teams of people collaborating in "repeat collaborations" (Zuckerman, 2005) or "semi-permanent work relations" (Blair, 2003). People tend to prefer collaborating with the same team on more projects over time. This allows them to refine tastes and expressions and build on experience from prior movies wherein the entire team has a practical shared knowledge that functions as a common base for refining and experimenting with the status quo filmic "language" or expression (Mathieu and Stjerne, 2014). The relations between artists and learning in collaboration is all there is. Career making is all about staying on top of the development by collectively pushing forward the "filmic language" in the film industry or ensuring a large audience for the film. People need to find collaboration partners with whom they can "shine"; in collaboration they need to stay leading edge in a genre in the film industry in order to be perceived relevant. The foundation for successful careers hence requires having the right collaborations, which starts with finding people with whom they can build semi-permanent work relations that allow them to experiment, refine and challenge the current "filmic language". This requires building on top of existing practices, and hence it requires gathering a team of people who have been on the latest projects with leading edge practices. As a result, these people are in high demand and, in order to be considered a relevant partner, relations matter.

Often, leading edge film workers may agree to work on low budget movies (the majority in the Danish film industry) or less prestigious movies because they owe something to some of the project owners or they have good relations with people in the team. Semi-permanent work relations can however also at times imply following the same track and getting too grounded in "ways of doing things" which can hinder innovation. This is a boundary for staying at the leading edge and hence having many opportunities in careers. This, however, may imply getting stuck in too settled relations. In order for the individual film worker to develop, and hence stay on top of their career, they need to find the right balance between collaborating in semi-permanent relationships and getting new input from working with new people. These relations can both work as hindering and enabling boundaries for individuals' careers.

Discussion

We have examined two "extreme cases" of boundaryless careers in order to find career boundaries where we would not at first expect them. We identify boundaries at multiple levels: institutional, organizational and relational/individual level. The aim has been to provide insights into how boundaries enable and constrain individuals' careers at multiple levels (Inkson et al., 2012).

In the case of the professional service firm career paths (Big 4), the formal organizational boundaries are very loose and rudimentary. Nevertheless, the institutional boundaries of the professional norms and values create – especially in the classic PSFs (Von Nordenflycht, 2010) – a very strong set of boundaries which constrain the professional career to narrow career trajectories. At the same time these boundaries offer the privileged prospects of partnership in the firm. The introduction of organizational boundaries by the "bureaucratization" of the PSF organizations ironically enables a wider choice of career trajectories within the firm by facilitating differentiated roles. On the other hand, this undermines the professional relations between partners and professionals which used to bound the professional career, that again threatens the traditional skill-based career-model, which was based on the partner-professional relation.

The multilevel analysis of Big 4 shows that boundaries, even in cases where most organizational boundaries are absent, have great impact on career paths. And surprisingly, that organizational boundaries may turn out to set individuals free, in this case by changing the partner career structure that resulted in a binary "up or out" career path with a very poor work-life balance; this was a single-track career structure where non-partner professional careers and female partners were rare or non-existent career constructs. The PSF firms have in many cases (Cooper et al., 1996; Brock, 2008; Richter et al., 2008) changed their internal careers by introducing new managerial roles, legitimizing "management" as a possible career option, and on the other hand also paving the way for a formal specialization of the partner-role. These changes loosened up the "up-or-out" model (e.g., making it possible for senior professionals to stay and tend to a portfolio of clients with a partner at his/her side). This proves that even in the cases where institutions such as professions organize careers, the role of the organization matters. When the ways the PSFs are organized are changed by institutional influences, the changes in turn affect the relations and the structures that enable and constrain individuals' careers.

In the case of Danish film, the role of the firm was less prominent in comparison to Big 4 even though it is still clear that organizations play a central role for developing projects and not least selecting people into projects which makes person-project organization fit important. As a result, organizational values, visions and aesthetics are essential boundaries for individual's careers. On a relational level, Danish film shows how actors balance industry norms and requirements that set boundaries and define the wriggle room for actors to perform career self-management that allow them to define and direct their own careers. Even in the film industry in which "boundaryless careers" are predominant (Jones, 1996), there are more than gender and macro segmentation divides for who gets a career and who doesn't. Individuals, organizations and fields are at the same time bound by but also reconstruct and constantly change the boundaries that define the span between structures and agency in career self-management. In the career self-management literature the idea can be found of strategies or behaviors that lead to career success. King (2004) mentions three types of behavior: positioning in relation to ensuring skills, contacts and experience; influencing decisions of key gatekeepers; and boundary management between work and non-work. Even though boundaries are often mentioned as a result of gatekeepers in organizations and fields (Gunz et al., 2007), the two cases described in this chapter nuance this perspective as gatekeepers are informed by structures such as professional norms, values and aesthetics when making decisions.

Hence, we need to understand these structures in order to navigate within, or in some instances, to manage, the boundaries at various levels that permeate careers. These boundaries might be changed in the process of reenactment, however they are inert and most often people navigate (to steer, get around, move) rather than manage (to work upon or try to alter for a purpose) career boundaries, as careers are outcomes of people performing work and navigating the boundaries they encounter along the way rather than seeking to reach a final career goal (Lichtenstein and Mendenhall, 2002). Several examples have been seen of entrepreneurs changing these boundaries of an entire industry or field as they create their own style or genre; examples can be seen in film the work of the Danish director Lars von Trier (Mathieu and Stjerne, 2014) and in haute de cuisine, Ferran Adria, el Bulli chef and co-owner (Svejenova et al., 2010).

Despite several studies elaborating on the issues of individual entrepreneurs' ability to challenge and change structures, and on the other hand people arguing that structures are important for career outcomes, more empirical studies that bridge and seek to explain changes in careers from a multilevel perspective are needed. We have also seen in this chapter that boundaries at multiple levels can hinder and/or enable individual careers, and that "boundaryless careers" might be a misguiding concept. The two cases from this chapter provide a number of initial insights into the boundaries that careers engage with in so-called boundaryless settings. The two cases show how profession, role, aesthetics belonging to a certain group of professionals, and industry norms for relational collaboration are boundaries that careers cross. These findings build on the debate that was opened by Inkson et al. (2012) in their call for further research on these matters in order to understand what boundaries careers cross, if they are not boundaryless?

An important point is that applying a "multiple levels" analysis, as we have in this chapter, may in some ways be misleading. For instance, the institutional level may be claimed to penetrate all levels as with the "institutional logics" approach (Thornton et al., 2012), while the interaction level may be seen as where the meaning structures of careers are constituted and thus defines the results at the other levels. The former goes for "profession," "role" and "status" as institutions which permeate all levels, while the latter applies to "practice" as social (inter-)action.

Also, we are in peril of getting caught in the rhetoric of the "boundaryless career" by studying actors who are resourceful autonomous agents (professional advisors and film professionals), but who are arguably elite players compared to the labor market in general (Inkson et al., 2012). Our response to this is, of course, that this is exactly why the cases are compelling. Even when looking at these resourceful agents, supposedly equipped to revel in the "boundarylessness" of their organizational contexts, the importance of analyzing how boundaries affect their careers become particularly apparent. As the labor market theorist David Marsden (1999) wrote commenting on the state of film worker careers in Hollywood:

> Thus, systems of "boundaryless careers" appear analogous to OLMs [occupational labor markets, eds.] in many respects, and although less codified than those of blue-collar crafts and established white-collar professions, they are dependent upon institutional structures to cope with the many problems of opportunism that would otherwise beset them.
>
> *(Marsden, 1999, 2008: 241)*

At the end of the day, the scope of this chapter is not to make an exhaustive rendering of the significance of boundaries to the study of careers, not even in professional service firms and the film industry. Rather, the contribution of the chapter is to heed the call for more analyses of careers which take boundaries at all levels into account and by the concrete analyses, make the case that we can obtain important insights this way (Inkson et al., 2012; Gunz et al., 2007).

Concluding remarks

In this chapter we argue that contemporary career theories have until recently been overemphasizing the role of the individual in crafting careers. These perspectives have emphasized individual agency over structures (Inkson et al., 2012; Mathieu, 2012), though the notion of "boundaryless" was problematized to some extent by different authors as early as in the boundaryless career handbook (Arthur and Rousseau, 1996) looking into the bounded aspects of gender and challenges for non-proactive individuals as well as actors' ability to make sense of a fragmented career. We think the career literature tends to overlook important structural aspects of the boundaries that both enable and constrain careers. Although careers are built by and of competent individual actors, the structures of employment systems often qualify the scope for individuals to shape their own careers freely. Even when looking at the strong relative free agents who populate professional services and the film industry, we show how this can be said to be the case.

Looking at career boundaries from a multilevel perspective, we see the way actors and boundaries interact; how boundaries create the material careers are made of, but at the same time frame the scope for career-building in any specific context as well the institutional field, the organizational as the relational/individual level.

Notes

1 Here it is "professional" in the sociology of professions sense we refer to: e.g. lawyer, medical doctor, architect (Abbott, A. 1988. *The System of Professions,* Chicago, University of Chicago Press.).
2 Filmic language refers to the "visual aspects of a film that gives it a certain expression. In practice this refers to the way of using pictures, sound and editing to tell the story. More technically this implies the picture cropping and camera angle and the transitions between the two" (retrieved from Danish Film Federation Homepage. 2017. Available: www.dfi.dk [Accessed 27 November 2017], translated by the authors). For a further description of the kind of aesthetic techniques referred to with "filmic language": http://filmcentralen.dk/grundskolen/filmsprog/filmiske-virkemidler.

References

Abbott, A. 1988. *The System of Professions.* Chicago: University of Chicago Press.

Arthur, M.B. & Rousseau, D.M. 1996. *The Boundaryless Career: A New Employment Principle for a New Organizational Era.* New York: Oxford University Press.

Arthur, M.B. & Rousseau, D.M. 2001. *The Boundaryless Career: A New Employment Principle for a New Organizational Era.* Oxford: Oxford University Press.

Barley, S.R. 1986. Technology as an occasion for structuring: Evidence from observations of CT scanners and the social order of radiology departments. *Administrative Science Quarterly,* 78–108.

Barley, S.R. & Kunda, G. 2006. *Gurus, Hired Guns, and Warm Godies: Itinerant Experts in a Knowledge Economy.* Princeton: Princeton University Press.

Barley, S.R. & Tolbert, P.S. 1997. Institutionalization and structuration: Studying the links between action and institution. *Organization Studies,* 18, 93–117.

Bechky, B.A. 2006. Gaffers, gofers, and grips: Role-based coordination in temporary organizations. *Organization Science,* 17, 3–21.

Becker, H.S. 1982. *Art Worlds.* Berkeley, CA: University of California Press.

Bévort, F. 2012. *Making Sense of Management with Logics: An Ethnographic Study of Accountants Who Become Managers.* Denmark, Copenhagen: Business School [Phd].

Bévort, F. & Poulfelt, F. 2015. Human resource management in professional services firms: Too good to be true? Transcending conflicting institutional logics. *German Journal of Human Resource Management,* 29, 102–130.

Bévort, F. & Suddaby, R. 2016. Scripting professional identities: How individuals make sense of contradictory institutional logics. *Journal of Professions and Organization,* 3, 17–38.

Blair, H. 2001. 'You're only as good as your last job': The labour process and labour market in the British film industry. *Work, Employment and Society,* 15, 149–169.

Blair, H. 2003. Winning and losing in flexible labour markets: The formation and operation of networks of interdependence in the UK film industry. *Sociology,* 37, 677–694.

Bourdieu, P. 1977. *Outline of a Theory of Practice.* Cambridge: Cambridge University Press.

Briscoe, F. 2006. Temporal flexibility and careers: The role of large-scale organizations for physicians. *Industrial and Labor Relations Review,* 60, 88–104.

Brock, D.M. 2008. The reconstructed professional firm: A reappraisal of Ackroyd and Muzio (2007). *Organization Studies,* 29, 145–149.

Cappelli, P. 2008. Talent management for the twenty-first century. *Harvard Business Review,* 86, 74–81.

Christopherson, S. & Storper, M. 1989. The effects of flexible specialization on industrial politics and the labor market: The motion picture industry. *Industrial and Labor Relations Review,* 42, 331–347.

Cooper, D.J., Hinings, B., Greenwood, R. & Brown, J.L. 1996. Sedimentation and transformation in organizational change: The case of Canadian law firms. *Organization Studies*, 17, 623–647.

Creed, W.D., Dejordy, R. & Lok, J. 2010. Being the change: Resolving institutional contradiction through identity work. *Academy of Management Journal*, 53, 1336–1364.

Danish Film Federation Homepage. 2017. Available: www.dfi.dk [Accessed 27 November 2017].

de Bruin, A. & Lewis, K. 2004. Toward enriching united career theory: Familial entrepreneurship and copreneurship. *Career Development International*, 9, 638–646.

de Vos, A. & Soens, N. 2008. Protean attitude and career success: The mediating role of self-management. *Journal of Vocational Behavior*, 73, 449–456.

Dimaggio, P.J. 1988. Interest and agency in institutional theory: Institutional patterns and organizations. *In:* Zucker, L.G. (ed.) *Culture and Environment*. Cambridge, MA: Ballinger.

Dimaggio, P.J. & Powell, W.W. 1983. The iron cage revisited: Institutional isomorphism and collective rationality in organizational fields. *American Sociological Review*, 48, 147–160.

Eikhof, D.R. 2014. Transorganisational work and production in the creative industries. *In:* Bilton, C. & Cummings, S. (eds.) *Handbook of Management and Creativity*. Cheltenham, UK and Northampton, MA: Edward Elgar.

Empson, L., Muzio, D., Broschak, J. & Hinings, B. 2015. *The Oxford Handbook of Professional Service Firms*. New York: Oxford Handbooks.

Flyvbjerg, B. 2006. Five misunderstandings about case-study research. *Qualitative Inquiry*, 12, 219–245.

Friedland, R. & Alford, R.R. 1991. Bringing society back in: Symbols, practices and institutional contradictions. *In:* Powell, W.W. & Dimaggio, P.J. (eds.) *The Institutionalism in Organizational Analysis*. Chicago: University of Chicago Press.

Garfinkel, H. 1967. *Studies in Ethnomethology*. Englewood Cliffs, NJ: Prentice-Hall.

Giddens, A. 1984. *The Constitution of Society*. Berkeley and Los Angeles: University of California Press.

Goffman, E. 1983. The interaction order: American sociological association, 1982 presidential address. *American Sociological Review*, 48, 1–17.

Greenwood, R., Hinings, C.R. & Brown, J. 1990. 'P2-form' strategic management: Corporate practices in professional partnerships. *Academy of Management Journal*, 33, 725–755.

Greenwood, R. & Suddaby, R. 2006. Institutional entrepreneurship in mature fields: The big five accounting firms. *Academy of Management Journal*, 49, 27–48.

Gunz, H., Evans, M. & Jalland, M. 2000. Career boundaries in a 'boundaryless' world. *In:* Peiperl, M., Arthur, M., Goffee, R. & Morris, T. (eds.) *Career Frontiers: New Conceptions of Working Lives*. Oxford: Oxford University Press.

Gunz, H., Peiperl, M. & Tzabbar, D. 2007. Boundaries in the study of career. *In:* Gunz, H. & Peiperl, M. (eds.) *Handbook of Career Studies*. Thousand Oaks, CA: Sage Publications.

Hall, D.T. 2004. The protean career: A quarter-century journey. *Journal of Vocational Behavior*, 65, 1–13.

Hall, D.T., Zhu, G. & Yan, A. 2002. Career creativity as protean identity transformation. *In:* Peiperl, M., Arthur, M.B. & Anand, N. (eds.) *Career Creativity: Explorations in the Remaking of Work*. Oxford: Oxford University Press.

Hallett, T. 2010. The myth incarnate: Recoupling processes, turmoil, and inhabited institutions in an urban elementary school. *American Sociological Review*, 75, 52–74.

Haunschild, A. 2003. Managing employment relationships in flexible labour markets: The case of German repertory theatres. *Human Relations*, 56, 899–929.

Haunschild, A. 2004. Employment rules in German theatres: An application and evaluation of the theory of employment systems. *British Journal of Industrial Relations*, 42, 685–703.

Haunschild, A. & Eikhof, D.R. 2009. From HRM to employment rules and lifestyles: Theory development through qualitative case study research into the creative industries. *German Journal of Human Resource Management*, 23, 107–124.

Inkson, K., Gunz, H., Ganesh, S. & Roper, J. 2012. Boundaryless careers: Bringing back boundaries. *Organization Studies*, 33, 323–340.

Jones, C. 1996. Careers in project networks: The case of the film industry. *In: The Boundaryless Career: A New Employment Principle for a New Organizational Era*. New York: Oxford University Press.

Jones, C. 2001. Co-evolution of entrepreneurial careers, institutional rules and competitive dynamics in American film, 1895–1920. *Organization Studies*, 22, 911–944.

Jones, C., Hesterly, W.S., Fladmoe-Lindquist, K. & Borgatti, S.P. 1998. Professional service constellations: How strategies and capabilities influence collaborative stability and change. *Organization Science*, 9, 396–410.

King, Z. 2004. Career self-management: Its nature, causes and consequences. *Journal of Vocational Behavior*, 65, 112–133.

King, Z., Burke, S. & Pemberton, J. 2005. The 'bounded' career: An empirical study of human capital, career mobility and employment outcomes in a mediated labour market. *Human Relations*, 58, 981–1007.

Larson, M.S. 1977. *The Rise of Professionalism*. Berkeley, CA and London: California University Press.

Lawrence, T.B. & Suddaby, R. 2006. Institutions and institutional work. *In:* Clegg, S.R., Hardy, C., Lawrence, T.B. & Nord, W.R. (eds.) *Handbook of Organization Studies*, 2nd ed. London: Sage Publications.

Lichtenstein, B.M.B. & Mendenhall, M. 2002. Non-linearity and response-ability: Emergent order in 21st-century careers. *Human Relations*, 55, 5–32.

Lok, J. 2010. Institutional logics as identity projects. *Academy of Management Journal*, 53, 1305–1335.

Mainiero, L.A. & Sullivan, S.E. 2005. Kaleidoscope careers: An alternate explanation for the 'opt-out' revolution. *Academy of Management Executive*, 19, 106–123.

March, J. & Simon, H. 1958. *Organizations*. New York: John Wiley and Sons Inc.

Marsden, D. 1999. *A Theory of Employment Systems: Micro-Foundations of Societal Diversity*. Oxford: Oxford University Press.

Marsden, D. 2008. *A Theory of Employment Systems: Micro-Foundations of Societal Diversity*. Oxford: Oxford University Press.

Mathieu, C. 2012. *Careers in Creative Industries*. New York: Routledge.

Mathieu, C. & Stjerne, I.S. 2012. Central collaborative relationships in career-making. *In:* Mathieu, C. (ed.) *Careers in Creative Industries*. Abingdon and New York: Routledge.

Mathieu, C. & Stjerne, I.S. 2014. Artistic practices over careers in film. *In:* Zembylas, T. (ed.) *Artistic Practices: Social Interactions and Cultural Dynamics*. New York: Routledge.

Mayrhofer, W., Meyer, M. & Steyrer, J. 2007. Contextual issues in the study of careers. *In:* Mayrhofer, W., Meyer, M. & Steyrer, J. (eds.) *Handbook of Career Studies*. Los Angeles: Sage Publications.

Meyer, J.W. & Rowan, B. 1991(1977). Institutionalized organizations: Formal structure as myth and ceremony. *In:* Dimaggio, P.J. & Powell, W.W. (eds.) *The New Institutionalism in Organisational Analysis*. Chicago: University of Chicago Press.

Mirvis, P.H. & Hall, D.T. 1994. Psychological success and the boundaryless career. *Journal of Organizational Behavior*, 15, 365–380.

O'Mahony, S. & Bechky, B.A. 2006. Stretchwork: Managing the career progression paradox in external labor markets. *Academy of Management Journal*, 49, 918–941.

Peters, T. 2004. *The PSF is everything, or: Making the professional service firm a 'Lovemark' in an age of 'Managed asset reflation'* [Online].

Peterson, R.A. & Anand, N. 2002. How chaotic careers create orderly fields. *In:* Peiperl, M., Arthur, M.B. & Anand, N. (eds.) *Career Creativity: Explorations in the Remaking of Work*. Oxford: Oxford University Press.

Powell, W.W. & Colyvas, J.A. 2008. Microfoundations of institutional theory. *In:* Greenwood, R., Oliver, C., Sahlin, K. & Suddaby, R. (eds.) *The Sage Handbook of Organizational Institutionalism*. London: Sage Publications.

Richter, A., Dickmann, M. & Graubner, M. 2008. Patterns of human resource management in consulting firms. *Personnel Review*, 37, 184–202.

Schatzki, T.R., Cetina, K.K. & von Savigny, E. 2001. *The Practice Turn in Contemporary Theory*. London: Routledge.

Scott, W.R. 1991. Unpacking institutional arguments. *In:* Powell, W. & Dimaggio, P.J. (eds.) *The New Institutionalism in Organizational Analysis*. Chicago: University of Chicago Press.

Scott, W.R. 2008. Lords of the dance: Professionals as institutional agents. *Organization Studies*, 29, 219–238.

Starkey, K., Barnatt, C. & Tempest, S. 2000. Beyond networks and hierarchies: Latent organizations in the UK television industry. *Organization Science*, 11, 299–305.

Stjerne, I.S. 2016. *Transcending Organization in Temporary Systems: Aesthetics' Organizing Work and Employment in Creative Industries* [Online]. Available: http://hdl.handle.net/10398/9395.

Stjerne, I.S. & Svejenova, S. 2016. Connecting temporary and permanent organizing: Tensions and boundary work in sequential film projects. *Organization Studies*, 37, 1771–1792.

Storper, M. & Christopherson, S. 1987. Flexible specialization and regional industrial agglomerations: The case of the US motion picture industry. *Annals of the Association of American Geographers*, 77, 104–117.

Svejenova, S. 2005. 'The path with the heart': Creating the authentic career. *Journal of Management Studies*, 42, 947–974.

Svejenova, S., Vives, L. & Alvarez, J.L. 2010. At the crossroads of agency and communion: Defining the shared career. *Journal of Organizational Behavior*, 31, 707–725.

Sydow, J. 2009. Path dependencies in project-based organizing: Evidence from television production in Germany. *Journal of Media Business Studies*, 6, 123–139.

Tams, S. & Arthur, M.B. 2010. New directions for boundaryless careers: Agency and interdependence in a changing world. *Journal of Organizational Behavior*, 31, 629–646.

Thornton, P.H., Ocasio, W. & Lounsbury, M. 2012. *The Institutional Logics Perspective: A New Approach to Culture, Structure, and Process*. Oxford: Oxford University Press.

von Nordenflycht, A. 2010. What is a professional service firm? Toward a theory and taxonomy of knowledge-intensive firms. *Academy of Management Review*, 35, 155–174.

Wagner, I. 2012. Transnational careers in the virtuoso world. *In:* Mathieu, C. (ed.) *Careers in Creative Industries*. London and New York: Routledge.

Zuckerman, E.W. 2005. Typecasting and generalism in firm and market: Genre-based career concentration in the feature film industry, 1933–1995. *Research in the Sociology or Organizations*, 23, 171–214.

18

Careers across countries

Jon P. Briscoe, Michael Dickmann, and Emma Parry

Introduction

If you have ever met a carpenter, anywhere in the world, you know in general what their job entails in any other part of the world. The same goes for a nurse, a teacher and so forth. Right? Or maybe not? Hopefully your mind immediately challenged the first two sentences as you read them. Different occupations and the careers associated with them will vary across cultures. Despite the implicit assumptions about a strong universalist element in careers discussed in Chapter 4 of this book, we argue here that contextual settings linked with cultural or institutional specifics of a society play an important role in describing and explaining careers. Yet there is little systematic insight available about commonalities and differences of career patterns as well as the relative importance of career antecedents and career outcomes in different societies. Our text has both a conceptual and an empirical emphasis. Conceptually, it looks at major arguments for the importance of cultural and institutional factors for explaining careers. Empirically, it reviews available studies and suggests directions for future research.

Context matters (Mayrhofer et al., 2007) and the notion of "career" varies across contextual settings such as cultures, occupations, social classes and countries. On the one hand, take the carpenter from the start of the chapter. In Germanic cultures such as Austria, Germany and Switzerland, a carpenter is not simply a skilled journeyman or woman for hire. They will likely have to be certified by the state and work association and will have had a long incubation in formal training and socialization. Their careers are more regulated than a carpenter in the United States and have more professional status than a carpenter in, for example, Malaysia. On the other hand, in Malaysia or in the United States a carpenter is less likely to need formal certification to practice their craft as a sole proprietor. In both of these latter cases, there will be more informal networking as such an activity will enable a carpenter to establish new connections, new possibilities for collaboration, work, informal training and more.

Like other theories in organizational behaviour such as motivation (Hofstede, 1980), career theory has been intellectually constructed and researched primarily in the United States. The currently prominent protean (Hall, 1976, 2002) and boundaryless (Arthur, 1994) career theories, for example, were both incubated in the New England region of the United States. This region is famous for intellectual independence via such free thinkers as Emerson and Thoreau and the entire country is an outlier in terms of individualism. Is it accurate to use such theories as gestalts across the world? Are there other theories that might be more illustrative of career perspectives in other cultures? How might they be identified and tested? These are the sort of questions careers researchers face as they seek to understand careers across countries.

The study of careers in different countries, whether taking an emic (within cultures) or an etic (across cultures) approach (Harris, 1976) is extremely important. Careers represent a nexus of individual, familial, social, organizational, industrial and societal concerns and drivers as they play out in individuals' lives over time. While we are becoming more global day by day, we still belong to different societies with different pasts, different values and different futures. It is critical that we understand career differences both across as well as within cultures so that we can investigate countries' unique stories and, in the process, help them better fathom what works in sustaining fulfilment and productivity in juxtaposition to a changing world.

In the remainder of this chapter we will consider multiple theoretical perspectives (including organizational and cross-cultural) and related empirical studies, and we also introduce the "5C" research project (Cross-Cultural Collaboration on Contemporary Careers) which involved in-depth interviews and comparative analysis in 12 countries (Briscoe et al., 2012b). From these various sources, we will discuss the implications for future theory and research.

Existing cross-cultural theory and links to career scholarship

Clearly, careers are influenced by the context in which they unfold. It is certain that the great protagonists of careers are individuals (Hall, 2004; Briscoe and Hall, 2006). However, to pronounce organizational career management as "dead" is premature (Granrose and Portwood, 1987; Sturges et al., 2005), especially where organizations work with their "top" or "young" talent and/or in global career management (Farndale et al., 2010; Berger and Berger, 2011; Scullion and Collings, 2011). While the force field of agency and structure has had a long history of academic attention (Gunz and Peiperl, 2007; Forrier et al., 2009), the role of the cultural and institutional contexts and their impact upon careers and career success across different countries and national cultures remains underexplored (Khapova et al., 2012).

Institutional factors, such as legal systems and regulations (Alesina and Giuliano, 2014), particularly in the areas of labour law, or economic conditions (such as unemployment rates) that shape labour markets have an impact on careers. It is clear that institutional factors shape the way that individuals act within their careers, such as how they view their job security and employability with subsequent effects on employer continuance or job seeking behaviours (Chan and Huff Stevens, 2001; De Graaf-Zijl et al., 2015; Van Dam, 2004). Institutions vary substantially across different countries, but there are processes of "institutional transplantation" (Mamadouh et al., 2002; Couyoumdjian, 2012) that might, over time, lead to a convergence of influences on careers. There are some studies that investigate the impact of institutions on careers (Watt and Eccles, 2008; Dahling et al., 2013), but by and large this is an underexplored area (Cox, 2013; Kumlin and Rothstein, 2005; Gunz and Peiperl, 2007).

Although the literature lacks agreement even on the definition of institutions (Hodgson, 2007; Fleetwood, 2008), it is relatively uncontested that institutions, variously defined, govern behaviours and if an actor deviates from these there might be penalties (Jepperson, 1991). Some writers see institutions as bundles of accumulated understandings and beliefs that trigger group-conform behaviours (Lammers and Barbour, 2006; Searle, 2005). While these "wide" definitions of institutions would incorporate national culture, we prefer to discuss national culture as a somewhat distinct, yet interrelated, element that influences career attitudes and behaviours.

National culture can be defined as a system of values, attitudes, norms and behaviours that is shared amongst the members of one societal group and is formally or informally taught to subsequent generations, that is, it is learned by them (Thomas and Peterson, 2015). Given the huge effect on the values and behaviours of individuals, there are several authors who call for the inclusion of national cultural context in career studies (Schein, 1984; Tams and Arthur, 2007). Such an approach allows us to capture the rich context that leads to varying perceptions and the related diverse behaviours of careerists, resulting in a more nuanced understanding of career patterns in different nations, across cultural and institutional environments.

Career attitudes, values and behaviours are (partly) shaped by national culture (Kluckhohn and Strodtbeck, 1961; Trompenaars and Hampden-Turner, 2011) and institutional factors (Gunz and Peiperl, 2007). Given the substantial variation in national cultures (Hofstede, 1980; House et al., 2004) these values and behaviours are likely to differ substantially. It is therefore surprising that we have a relative dearth in studies that systematically explore cultural and institutional differences and their impact upon careers and career success (Arthur et al., 1989; Boudreau et al., 2001; Kats et al., 2010). It is important to understand and contrast systematically the influence that the cultural and institutional environments of individuals have on how they view and enact their careers (Hartung, 2002) and how they conceptualize career success (Heslin, 2005; Gunz and Heslin, 2005).

The influence of national context in careers research

The vast majority of cross-country research within the careers field focuses on national culture rather than institutions. In fact, as briefly noted above, the influence of institutions on careers has, to date, been largely ignored. We will now summarise the cultural perspective and empirical studies that use culture as an indicator of contextual effects on careers, before, more briefly (given the sparse research in this area) looking at institutional approaches.

Cultural approaches to careers research

Possibly the best-known cultural research in the field of management was developed by Geert Hofstede, originally based on a large-scale survey of IBM employees in the late 1960s and early 1970s. Over the decades that followed, Hofstede's research has been subject to much criticism (e.g., McSweeney, 2002) and other models of culture and cultural dimensions have emerged and been embraced by researchers (e.g., GLOBE, Schwartz's World Value Survey) but there are still debates with respect to both culture's conceptualization and measurement (Caprar et al., 2015). Nevertheless, the many articles that either directly or indirectly investigate the role of cultural differences for careers is testament to the enduring appeal and value of the concept.

Hofstede originally identified four cultural dimensions, but his latest model includes six (Hofstede et al., 2010). While the most recently introduced sixth dimension (indulgence – restraint) is less used, the other five are well known and widely employed by researchers. *Power distance* expresses the degree to which the less powerful members of a society accept (and expect) that power is distributed unequally. *Individualism* is the degree of preference for a loosely knit social framework in which people are expected to take care of themselves and their immediate families. *Masculinity* is a preference for achievement, assertiveness and monetary rewards. Society is highly competitive. In feminine societies there is a preference for modesty, cooperation, caring and quality of life which is often expressed through a high interest in work-life balance. The extent of *uncertainty avoidance* expresses the degree to which the members of a society feel comfortable with uncertainty and ambiguity. Lastly, cultures that show a *long-term orientation* prefer to maintain traditions and norms while viewing societal change with suspicion. Those cultures high on *restraint* work towards future rewards and encourage perseverance and thrift (Hofstede et al., 2010 and Hofstede's website[1]).

Myriad career studies have relied upon Hofstede's cultural framework. For example, studies have found that in individualistic cultures, career advancement as well as pay and status are more important than in collectivist societies (Agarwala, 2008). In addition, staff are less interested in tenure and report lower levels of affective and normative commitment (Ramamoorthy et al., 2007), both of which are likely to affect career progression and behaviour. More networking behaviours are reported in collectivist countries (Claes and Ruiz-Quintanilla, 1998). In turn, in individualistic countries, careers are seen as a personal, long-term project shaped by the individual's own agency (Thomas and Inkson, 2007). In masculine countries monetary rewards are indeed more important as stipulated by the Hofstede definition (Chiang and Birtch, 2007). Meanwhile, in more feminine societies women are more likely to be promoted to management positions (Hofstede, 2001). Low power distance cultures experience less pronounced gender wage differentials (Hofstede, 2001) and organizations are more likely to abstain from the use of performance-based rewards (Chiang, 2005). General, rather than specialized, skills are preferred as job mobility, flexibility and innovation are valued (Dickson et al., 2012). In countries that have high levels of uncertainty avoidance, employees are seen to be keen to enter mentoring relationships (Bozionelos and Wang, 2006) and prefer that their supervisors promote career stability, formal rules and planning (Dickson et al., 2003). Chang and Lu (2007) found that employees prefer longer job tenure. Lastly, in long-term oriented countries, short-term rewards are less valued than the development of skills and expertise (Zhang et al., 2006; Chay and Aryee, 1999).

Beyond those studies which rely upon Hofstede's framework, there are other conceptual and empirical studies which contribute to the knowledge base about careers across country contexts. However, at this point none of the studies centred around particular perspectives offer anything approaching the emphasis on Hofstede's framework.

For example, Derr and Laurent (1989) argued that Schein's theory of organizational culture using artifacts, values and basic assumptions could be used to understand country cultures. Using that baseline, they explored how internal and external careers could vary and found similarities across national cultures. Tams and Arthur (2007) primarily reviewed the existing empirical scholarship covering cross-cultural careers including expatriation, international HRM and self-initiated international careers (all of which are not covered in this chapter; see Chapter 19). They explored how cross-cultural careers might illustrate universal career concepts and globalization. Thomas and Inkson (2007) reviewed empirical cross-cultural research and concluded that most cross-cultural studies do not have a theoretical rationale behind their sampling. Furthermore, they explored the relevance of new career paradigms in disadvantaged or less developed countries of the world.

Considering empirical work beyond the widely used Hofstede paradigm, there are several good examples of *one*-culture examinations that look at newer career paradigms in context (Dany, 2003; Yi et al., 2010). A particularly good study was one of New Zealand that provided great depth into newer career forms' manifestation in that society (Arthur et al., 1999) by showing how networks and boundaryless careers are an emerging reality even in seemingly simple contexts. Some research has also looked at traditional career issues such as expatriate perspectives of student sojourners abroad (Guan et al., 2018), and tested applicability of instruments developed in other cultures (Aryee et al., 1999; Kim et al., 2016; Liñán and Chen, 2009).

A limited number of studies have extended the one-country model to a few countries or even a few cultural regions. These studies have investigated career issues related to women (Burke, 2001; Lirio et al., 2007; Rani Thanacoody et al., 2006), the nature of career development (Jiwen Song and Werbel, 2007), differences between college students (Mau, 2000), and work and family (Spector et al., 2004). Given that cultural influences into career attitudes and behaviours are important, studies that enable a more nuanced, context-sensitive view on careers are highly welcome. The above indicates that hitherto such research is often piecemeal and selective.

Institutional approaches to careers research

The continued survival and successful operations of organizations depends on their successful adaptation to their institutional and market environments (Bartlett and Ghoshal, 2002). Corporate legitimacy, partly derived from the abiding with the laws, regulations, norms and values associated with institutions, is crucial for organizational success – just as capital, knowledge, networks, material resources and human capital is (Palthe, 2014). If organizations have to adjust to markets and institutions so do individuals pursuing their careers (Arthur et al., 1995). The strong relationship between careers and institutions has already been outlined decades ago (Hughes, 1936) and researchers are still critically debating the influence of institutions on careers (Gunz and Mayrhofer, 2018). However, much of the work on this has focused on intra-organizational rather than national institutions and has examined issues such as how staff can be socialized into existing roles (Van Maanen and Schein, 1979), how organizational structures and strategies are perpetuated (Jones, 2001), or how members are meant to behave and what values and norms they are expected to hold – and what the career consequences of deviating from such norms may be (Johnson et al., 2008).

In contrast, national level institutions such as a country's educational systems, laws with respect to labour markets (including labour market protection and employment/development policies) or employment relation systems are discussed relatively infrequently. It has been suggested that educational systems – including vocational training – influence career patterns of individuals and the career management or organizations (Dickmann, 2003). For example, many countries have created increasing access to universities, sometimes with a corresponding decline in graduate status and average job opportunities (Brown and Scase, 2005). Among other macro indicators, unemployment is seen to reduce individuals' perceived employability and to increase their incentives to engage in training and developmental activities to avoid resource loss (Halbesleben et al., 2014; Hobfoll, 2002; Hobfoll et al., 2018). In contrast, where extensive labour market protection exists, people may be less eager to augment their knowledge, skills and abilities as they trade external with internal marketability and careers (Betcherman, 2012; Scherer, 2005). In addition, strong labour unions may create protection for existing workers to the detriment of unemployed individuals or persons who want to enter a particular occupation or profession where there are entry barriers such as licencing (Kleiner and Krueger, 2010).

In short, national institutions have been discussed as relevant to careers. However, existing research speaks of careers mostly indirectly, and most studies are rather restricted in that they either concentrate on one or a few institutional constraints and/or are conducted only in one or very few countries. Broad career studies that explore institutional factors using organizational and societal perspectives across several countries are lacking – but very necessary as they can advance our understanding of how careers develop across multiple societies. We describe below one such study, the 5C project, which aims to contribute to this complex research arena by specifically addressing the influence of institutional and cultural context (Briscoe et al., 2012b).

The 5C research

The remainder of this chapter will focus on an international research project design to examine careers, specifically career success and career transitions, in different countries – the "5C"

(Cross-Cultural Collaboration on Contemporary Careers) project.[2] The overall goal of 5C was to discover how careers are experienced in different contexts, using researchers familiar with these contexts.

The original objective of 5C was to examine new career approaches (e.g., protean) in different countries. Upon reflection, the research team realized that it was impossible to say with confidence what "career" meant within and across different cultures and the objectives of the project were revisited. The work that followed was driven by two primary questions: How do people define career success? How does management of career transitions occur across cultures? There have been two phases of the 5C project to date. The first involved qualitative interview research in 12 countries; the second, a survey across over 30 countries.

Informed by considerations of an emic or etic approach (Harris, 1976), this project attempted to combine the two approaches to a degree. The first phase was in line with the emic approach. This was achieved through an "N-Way" approach (Brett et al., 1997) which initially involved participants from 12 country teams (Austria, China, Costa Rica, Israel, Japan, Malaysia, Mexico, Serbia, South Africa, Spain, the United Kingdom and the United States) to inform the research questions, methodology, coding and theory generation from the first qualitative phase of the research (Briscoe et al., 2012b). The N-Way approach contrasts with an approach where the research is driven by a dominant central individual or team.

In the literature, some discuss the limitations of an emic approach in that it is more difficult to replicate findings or ensure the reliability of qualitative methods in particular (Berry, 2002). But the so noted limitations of the emic approach can be outweighed by this thick understanding of individual and multiple cultures. Such an understanding allowed the development of a nuanced perspective of how and why career meanings and behaviours might vary on individual and societal levels. After interview data were collected, the research team used across-countries coding that was closer to an etic approach. An etic approach also dominated the second phase of the project: integrating the findings from phase one, a standardized questionnaire was developed and (the same) data were collected from individuals in over 30 countries.

Research team selection

For researcher selection, the 5C group tried to attract colleagues with an interest and background in careers research to join them and attempted to find people who demonstrated attitudes of collegiality, developmental orientations, and values related to improving the lives of those studied more than professional ambition. This meant that the group elicited a fuller participation due to fewer status concerns and a dedication to the N-Way approach governed by common norms and goals.

Country sampling

The 5C team aimed for a comprehensive country representation and researchers opted to utilize the research of Shalom Schwartz. Schwartz's theory of cultural values (1994) started with a conceptual framework of values driven by the logic that must exist in any society. These values were organized into three polarities: *autonomy versus embeddedness, egalitarianism versus hierarchy*, and *harmony versus mastery*. He then used this organization of cultural values to develop instruments in local languages in over 70 countries and he tested the derived culture values, arguing that they play a similar role in societies (of cultural transmission). The fact that he used local language is one big advantage to Schwartz's research. Another considerable advantage is that unlike Hofstede's framework, which cannot be easily applied to create country clusters, Schwartz's research has developed seven distinct cultural regions (Schwartz, 1994): Africa and the Middle East (one region); Confucian (Asia); East Europe; English-speaking; Latin America; South Asia; West Europe. The 5C research used these regions to select country samples in the first phase of its qualitative research.

As the 5C project moved to its second phase of quantitative testing, more recent research conducted by the GLOBE research consortium became available (House et al., 2004). The GLOBE study is the most ambitious and highly regarded study of cultural differences, in relation to leadership, conducted in 62 different cultures (House et al., 2004). GLOBE too developed 10 distinct cultural regions, which largely overlapped and were consistent with Schwartz's scholarship (Anglo; Confucian Asia; Eastern Europe; Germanic Europe; Latin America; Latin Europe; Middle; East; Nordic Europe; Southern Asia; Sub-Sahara Africa). It is those clusters which were used in the second phase of the 5C project.

Methodological approach

A qualitative approach was used in order to capture and compare careers across country contexts. Interviews were undertaken in each of the 12 initial project countries (see above) in selected occupational groups based upon assumptions about how these might vary across countries. Nurses, business people and blue-collar workers were chosen. Nurses were thought to have similar motives but also have careers more shaped by regulatory influences, whereas it was thought that blue-collar workers in most countries (but not all, as it turns out) would depend upon more informal career networks to develop themselves and find new opportunities. Finally, business people across countries were included in part because they have career independence and mobility, including cross-country mobility, that is not typically demonstrated among blue-collar employees and nurses. The norms and organization of business typically allow more career transparency and opportunity as well. A total of 226 people were interviewed at this stage.

In relation to this qualitative data the 5C group developed initial coding schemes on a country level and then integrated these coding schemes via discussion within the research team. It was critical to use the N-Way approach in sharing and interpreting data just as it was in designing the research. This required careful attention to inviting participation, and de-emphasizing factors such as status and seniority in the combined research team. Eventually a coding guide was developed that was inclusive of country nuances. Then career success meanings and transition management were coded across the 12 countries. Below, we review some of the contextual factors that were identified as key (see also Briscoe et al., 2012a) from this qualitative research and that can inform the process of undertaking broader comparative research in careers across countries.

Key contextual factors identified from the 5C qualitative research

Various contextual factors were found in the qualitative research that had a strong impact upon how careers were experienced and enacted in various countries. We review some of the key areas of impact below.

Occupational and professional structures and systems

These vary in important ways across countries and have a huge impact on how careers are identified as options, learned, legitimized and so on. For example, in Germanic countries blue-collar work is very formalized, regulated and certified by official agencies. In Malaysia, it is quite informal. In the United States it is somewhere in between. Business people tended to have more in common as they were relatively less regulated or structured by professional norms (Briscoe et al., 2012b).

Class and socioeconomic status

Inkson (2006) and others have questioned if protean (Hall, 1976) and boundaryless (Arthur, 1994) careers are only for the elite. The 5C research would suggest that they are not only for the elite but that they are much easier for the elite. To see the more severe (formal and informal) career boundaries that the poor or the politically segregated face is to identify true career hindrances. For example, a black woman in South Africa was the first person in her bank who had been allowed to interact with a white customer. In another instance, a younger Latino business person in the United States decided to leave his family's blue-collar trade to pursue a degree in business (Briscoe et al., 2012b). In both cases barriers and opportunities of dramatically different degrees and class (and race) bounded the entry into new realms of career opportunity.

Education

Education plays a substantial role in how societies shape the careers of groups and individuals. In more highly developed economies where education is normally highly accessible, the career and ideas of career success can border more on the abstract or even esoteric. In parts of society where educational access is less available, careers can become much simpler, and when education is obtained, it is not often taken for granted. Eating, providing for family and shelter take precedence for the less privileged. The research also suggested that education allows a more causal logic to prevail in individuals, whereas those without sophisticated insights and systematic approaches borne of education may more often lack the basic ability to think through events and plan in effective, consequential ways (Briscoe et al., 2012b).

Race and ethnicity

Race and ethnicity need not impact careers, but often do. Due to prejudice and discrimination, past and/or present, many get opportunities or face barriers based solely or partly upon these factors. For example, one of our research participants was a black South African who was told that he would never receive a real opportunity for his education in (then) apartheid South Africa and that he must try to go to Britain or the United States, which he did. The 5C research indicated that Malay people in Malaysia seem to have a distinct advantage over Chinese and Indian citizens when it comes to political opportunities and access to professions.

Gender

Male and female roles vary by country based upon culture and power dynamics, impacting careers. In some societies women are less expected to have a full-time career so that they can devote themselves more to domestic roles. In others, full-time career and commensurate education is expected. Female careers can be supported by factors from government policy (e.g., in countries where maternal and paternal leave is an entitlement) to cheap domestic labour and can be undone by familial expectations or societal discrimination.

Age/generation

The qualitative research (Briscoe et al., 2012b) showed that age is a relevant factor shaping career attitudes and behaviours. However, it combines with the era in which a certain age cohort (or "generation") embarks on their working lives and moves through their career journeys. For example, in China the older generation had little say over their careers. This is not so much a result of age but a result of changes in government regulations. In the United States, the older generation had a greater tie to career scripts and bureaucracy, in part as a result of the post-World War II economic boom. Younger workers have been forced to be more independent due to changing psychological contracts that are partly driven by the ephemeral information economy. It is important to note that age differences were not systematically similar across the countries in the 5C sample as individuals were so strongly embedded in their country contexts.

Overall the first phase of the 5C project provided evidence that while individuals across countries shared some common understandings of careers (e.g., a general time orientation and an understanding that career involves learning and a sequence of work experiences), there were also important differences between national contexts including cultural, economic, political and social institutions within a particular country.

For example, the data suggested that individuals' preferences around the career success element of financial advancement are based strongly upon the economic situation within which they live and work. Within countries that have experienced economic uncertainty and change (e.g., China and Serbia), financial achievement is seen more as an end goal. In countries with a longer history of wealth, like Austria, financial advancement was more likely to be seen as a means to other ends (Briscoe et al., 2012b) amongst the interviewees.

The qualitative 5C data also show that national context affects the number and nature of the transitions that an individual makes during their career *as well as how they interpret these transitions causally*. For example, in highly individualized countries such as the United States and UK, the interviewees cited more individual reasons for their career changes, as opposed to external institutional factors such as the labour market. In countries which are undergoing economic transition, people are more likely to make career transitions due to educational opportunities or government initiatives. In relation to the nature of career transitions, planning and formal education strategies in managing transitions are more common in countries categorized by high rather than low mastery (e.g., US, China and Japan; Briscoe et al., 2012b).

5C quantitative research phase

The insights from the 5C qualitative study have recently been expanded to enable and utilize quantitative survey research focusing upon career success. Initially, our first step was to build a scale that was representative of subjective career success meanings across country contexts. We utilized the interview data from the qualitative research on meanings of career success to elucidate a list of 63 career success definitions. Meanings and redundancies across cultures were clarified via dialogue with country teams. We developed an online "card sort" technique which participants in 13 countries (i.e., Belgium, Brazil, China, France, Greece, India, Italy, Nigeria, Norway, South Korea, Slovenia, Turkey, and the United States) used to electronically sort meanings of career success into larger categories (364 people across a range of occupations participated). An island analysis technique (De Nooy et al., 2011) was used to determine final clusters of meaning within and across countries (this is detailed in Kaše et al., in press). Further stages of the scale development process spanned all GLOBE regions and established cross-national parsimony, discriminant and convergent validity, cross-cultural measurement invariance, and criterion validity (see Briscoe et al., 2018, for a detailed overview of the developed career success meaning scale). In the end, the scale development process involved 18,471 individual respondents from 30 countries. The eventual career success meanings that the scale development process produced were Learning and Development; Work-Life Balance; Positive Impact; Positive Work-Relationships; Financial Security; Financial Achievement; and Entrepreneurship.

Having the newly developed career success scale and measuring a variety of other constructs from individual to country levels (some using archival data, e.g. publicly available indices), allowed us to explore a number of research questions.

Initial analyses using this data have shown a relationship between various cultural indicators and individuals' conceptualizations of career success and career behavior. For example, one analysis found that proactive career behaviors were positively related to subjective financial success across 22 countries covering 9 out of 10 GLOBE cultural regions; this relationship with proactive career behaviors was not significant for work-life balance. Furthermore, career proactivity was relatively more important for subjective financial success in cultures with high in-group collectivism, high power distance and low uncertainty avoidance. For work-life balance, career proactivity was relatively more important in cultures characterized by high in-group collectivism and high humane orientation (Smale et al., 2019). The authors speculate that perhaps proactive career behavior is powerful enough to overcome the impact of country context whereas successful work-life balance may be more dependent upon it. If true, these speculations offer support both for and against a universalist view of how country contexts shape individual and subjective career success meanings.

Another study based on the 5C survey data showed that in countries with stronger institutional collectivism, Positive Impact was seen as a less important aspect of subjective career success. Alternatively, Financial Achievement was seen as a less important indicator of subjective career success in countries with a stronger performance orientation. In addition, the relationship between income inequality within a country and conceptualizations of career success was investigated, showing that in countries with higher income equality, (subjective) Financial Achievement was seen as a more important aspect of subjective career success (Mayrhofer et al., 2016). These early analyses suggest an important role of both culture and institutions in driving conceptualizations of career success.

A third 5C study (Andresen et al., 2016) took a structuration approach and used multilevel mediation modelling, with a survey of 13,096 respondents from 24 countries and national statistical data to examine how career actors' career goals and work engagement and career behaviour are affected by social context factors (career-opportunity structure). The study showed that society affects the importance individuals give to specific career goals that again mediate their proactive career behaviours.

The results clearly suggest that careers, in this case conceptualizations of career success and the factors driving and influencing career transitions, are at least partially contextually driven. Our discussion here suggests that national context in relation to both national culture and institutional aspects are important influences of the nature of careers.

Conclusions and recommendations

We have reviewed relevant theory and empirical evidence to careers research across country contexts with a particular focus upon the recent 5C research project. We will now step back and reflect upon our learning and make recommendations for future research.

Context matters

A clear principle that this chapter hopefully solidifies is that the definition and experience of "career" depends upon context. Social and even physical contexts shape how careers may represent different things to different people from an abstraction of status to basic sustenance. Nations at least regionally offer shared meaning via culture and shared opportunities and constraints via institutional factors, to create and sustain the objective and subjective realities of social and other micro contexts. We argue that career scholarship to date, as with much of HRM and organizational management, vastly under-considers context, especially as it varies across nations. While more cross-cultural research is needed, research within singular country contexts also needs to be more aware of its applicability and limitations. Research replicating theory or data from a certain given culture should take pains to explicate why and how cultural and institutional differences may explain differences and similarities.

Theory matters

If a single improvement were to be made to cross-country research, the most valuable would be to strategically center it upon theory. Too often studies seem to be based upon who some author met at a conference or where they happened to travel one summer rather than upon careful theoretical reasoning. A simple but important line of inquiry involves why a given phenomenon should vary between country contexts. If slight variations in a career dynamic of interest emerged in, say, two Western European countries, then by all means they could be pursued. But greater contrast of theoretical differences might suggest that a Western European versus Southeast Asian or North American culture(s), as one example, could yield more valuable information.

Even when empirical data is not easily obtained or even approached, the generation and critique of theory has the chance to move our conversation forward. Because of an over-reliance upon Western data in the social sciences and organizational studies in particular, theoretical innovation and the challenging of ideas is a highly needed contribution.

Constructs matter

Because attitudinal and behavioural constructs represent theory, which itself represents cultural and institutional contextual differences in the majority of cases, care must be taken in how constructs are developed, selected, used, and interpreted. Savickas and Porfeli (2012) explored how to adapt a scale to different country contexts through careful interaction with country representatives. Above, we discussed the 5C Project's building of a career success scale using qualitative data obtained from strategically representative samples. As much attention should be paid to the contextual sourcing and limits of a construct as to statistical and other methodological considerations.

Stories matter

While studies such as 5C, GLOBE, Hofstede and Schwartz have their place, they struggle more in their grand scale to tell the stories of individuals and their country contexts. We believe that stories are irreplaceable to understand cross-country differences on an affective and descriptive level. For example, in our own experience the stories of older Chinese research participants were remarkable in the lack of choice they felt in their careers and the resultant irrelevance of "career success" or proactivity as a dimension of their career experience. Going to another setting, in Malaysia, the country's history of racial strife and later bargaining meant that the stories of Malay, Chinese and Indian subcultures had more distinct and predictable variables. In Mexico, a lower standard of living amongst some classes made it easier to understand possible explanations for why they exhibited more spiritual insight as to why they worked, tying it more carefully to their whole life identities.

We view stories as an important place to start cross-national comparisons. In this respect, qualitative methods are irreplaceable and have an important place in cross-national research. Stories can be highly illuminating and will be more so to the extent that they are motivated and reliant upon theory-informed foundations. Even in studies of large country collections, stories can and should be used to accompany and give texture to the high-level patterns observed and documented.

Relationships matter

The relationships between research team members and between the researcher(s) and respondents/participants are very important. It is critical that research team members reflect the diversity of the contexts they are studying as much as is reasonably possible. They should at least have some representative "insiders" from the culture who can communicate with and identify local focal groups of interest. Because of the research skills required it will be difficult to match the studied groups many times due to educational, class and other differences. This highlights the importance of good communications skills and familiarity with local populations.

Within the research team itself communication, interpersonal skills and functional norms are critical. This can be challenging with diverse teams due to language skills and differences. In part because of this but also for other reasons, status and rank associated with country, tenure and reputation must be neutralized as much as possible so that team members are comfortable sharing and challenging ideas. This is perhaps more obvious in situations involving qualitative research where coding and the generation of shared meaning is critical; but it is also critical in quantitative research.

The common "language" of numbers is a double-edged sword. While the scientific method provides a certain comfort and routine, it also creates an illusion of "sameness" that can hide important differences. This extends to the use and creation of constructs that are or are not representative of the studied country contexts. In these settings it is critical that researchers feel empowered and supported in exchanging and challenging ideas.

A fringe benefit of working in a cross-cultural team is that you are exploring other cultures and intercultural dynamics in real time as you do your work. Where possible, it is helpful to have some cultural cross-over even on country teams as an outsider might notice what is different from another country. In our experience, the relationships created by a good research team and the process used to create meaningful research are inherently valuable and rewarding, at least as much as the actual outputs of the research itself.

As a concluding thought, we would suggest that imagination, daring and relevance be taken account of as researchers approach cross-national comparative research. Explore questions that go beyond obvious answers. Anticipate how culture, institutions, societal change and so forth might inform or warp the expected findings. Paucity of research about comparative careers across cultures truly demands that we expand our comfort zones so that our research can better inform the realities of careers for the benefit of workers, organizations, and their countries.

Notes

1 https://geert-hofstede.com/national-culture.html.
2 www.5C.careers.

References

Agarwala, T. 2008. Factors influencing career choice of management students in India. *Career Development International*, 13, 362–376.

Alesina, A. & Giuliano, P. 2014. Family ties. *In:* Aghion, P. & Durlauf, S.N. (eds.) *Handbook of Economic Growth.* Amsterdam: Elsevier.

Andresen, M., Naito, C., Apospori, E., Gunz, H., Taniguchi, M., Lysova, E., Lehmann, P. & Briscoe, J. 2016. Agency and structure in careers: An international empirical study. *32nd EGOS Colloquium 'Organizing in the Shadow of Power'.* Naples, Italy.

Arthur, M.B. 1994. The boundaryless career: A new perspective for organizational inquiry. *Journal of Organizational Behavior*, 15, 295–306.

Arthur, M.B., Claman, P.H. & Defillippi, R.J. 1995. Intelligent enterprise, intelligent careers. *Academy of Management Executive*, 9, 7–20.

Arthur, M.B., Hall, D.T. & Lawrence, B.S. 1989. Generating new directions in career theory: The case for a transdisciplinary approach. *In:* Arthur, M.B., Hall, D.T. & Lawrence, B.S. (eds.) *Handbook of Career Theory.* Cambridge, England: Cambridge University Press.

Arthur, M.B., Inkson, K. & Pringle, J.K. 1999. *The New Careers: Individual Action and Economic Change.* Thousand Oaks, CA: Sage Publications.

Aryee, S., Luk, V. & Fields, D. 1999. A cross-cultural test of a model of the work-family interface. *Journal of Management*, 25, 491–511.

Bartlett, C.A. & Ghoshal, S. 2002. *Managing Across Borders: The Transnational Solution.* Boston: Harvard Business Press.

Berger, L.A. & Berger, D.R. 2011. *The Talent Management Handbook: Creating a Sustainable Competitive Advantage by Selecting, Developing, and Promoting the Best People.* New York: McGraw-Hill.

Berry, J.W. 2002. *Cross-Cultural Psychology: Research and Applications.* Cambridge: Cambridge University Press.

Betcherman, G. 2012. *Labor Market Institutions: A Review of the Literature.* Washington, DC: The World Bank.

Boudreau, J.W., Boswell, W.R. & Judge, T.A. 2001. Effects of personality on executive career success in the United States and Europe. *Journal of Vocational Behavior*, 58, 53–81.

Bozionelos, N. & Wang, L. 2006. The relationship of mentoring and network resources with career success in the Chinese organizational environment. *The International Journal of Human Resource Management*, 17, 1531–1546.

Brett, J.M., Tinsley, C.H., Janssens, M., Barsness, Z.I. & Lytle, A.L. 1997. New approaches to the study of culture in I/O psychology. *In:* Earley, P.C. & Erez, M. (eds.) *New Perspective on International/Organizational Psychology.* San Francisco: Jossey-Bass.

Briscoe, J.P., Chudzikowski, K. & Unite, J. 2012a. Career transitions: Windows into the career experience in 11 country contexts. *In:* Briscoe, J.P., Hall, D.T. & Mayrhofer, W. (eds.) *Careers Around the World: Individual and Contextual Perspectives.* New York: Routledge.

Briscoe, J.P. & Hall, D.T. 2006. The interplay of boundaryless and protean careers: Combinations and implications. *Journal of Vocational Behavior*, 69, 4–18.

Briscoe, J.P., Hall, D.T. & Mayrhofer, W. (eds.) 2012b. *Careers Around the World: Individual and Contextual Perspectives.* New York: Routledge.

Briscoe, J.P., Kaše, R., Dries, N., Dysvik, A., Unite, J. & On Behalf of the 5C Research Collaborative. 2018. *Here, There, and Everywhere: Development and Validation of a Cross-Culturally Representative Measure of Subjective Career Success.* (Submitted for review.)

Brown, P. & Scase, R. 2005. *Higher Education and Corporate Realities: Class, Culture and the Decline of Graduate Careers.* London: Routledge.

Burke, R.J. 2001. Managerial women's career experiences, satisfaction and well-being: A five country study. *Cross Cultural Management: An International Journal*, 8, 117–133.

Caprar, D.V., Devinney, T.M., Kirkman, B.L. & Caligiuri, P. 2015. Conceptualizing and measuring culture in international business and management: From challenges to potential solutions. *Journal of International Business Studies*, 46, 1011–1027.

Chan, S. & Huff Stevens, A. 2001. Job loss and employment patterns of older workers. *Journal of Labor Economics*, 19, 484–521.

Chang, K. & Lu, L. 2007. Characteristics of organizational culture, stressors and wellbeing: The case of Taiwanese organizations. *Journal of Managerial Psychology*, 22, 549–568.

Chay, Y.W. & Aryee, S. 1999. Potential moderating influence of career growth opportunities on careerist orientation and work attitudes: Evidence of the protean career era in Singapore. *Journal of Organizational Behavior*, 20, 613–623.

Chiang, F.F. 2005. A critical examination of Hofstede's thesis and its application to international reward management. *The International Journal of Human Resource Management*, 16, 1545–1563.

Chiang, F.F. & Birtch, T. 2007. The transferability of management practices: Examining cross-national differences in reward preferences. *Human Relations*, 60, 1293–1330.

Claes, R. & Ruiz-Quintanilla, S.A. 1998. Influences of early career experiences, occupational group, and national culture on proactive career behavior. *Journal of Vocational Behavior*, 52, 357–378.

Couyoumdjian, J.P. 2012. Are institutional transplants viable? An examination in light of the proposals by Jeremy Bentham. *Journal of Institutional Economics*, 8, 489–509.

Cox, M.D. 2013. The impact of communities of practice in support of early-career academics. *International Journal for Academic Development*, 18, 18–30.

Dahling, J.J., Melloy, R. & Thompson, M.N. 2013. Financial strain and regional unemployment as barriers to job search self-efficacy: A test of social cognitive career theory. *Journal of Counseling Psychology*, 60, 210–218.

Dany, F. 2003. 'Free actors' and organizations: Critical remarks about the new career literature, based on French insights. *International Journal of Human Resource Management*, 15, 821–838.

de Graaf-Zijl, M., van der Horst, A., van Vuuren, D., Erken, H. & Luginbuhl, R. 2015. Long-term unemployment and the great recession in the Netherlands: Economic mechanisms and policy implications. *De Economist*, 163, 415–434.

de Nooy, W., Mrvar, A. & Batagelj, V. 2011. *Exploratory Social Network Analysis with Pajek*. Cambridge: Cambridge University Press.

Derr, C.B. & Laurent, A. 1989. The internal and external career: A theoretical and cross-cultural perspective. *In*: Arthur, M.B., Hall, D.T. & Lawrence, B.S. (eds.) *Handbook of Career Theory*. Cambridge: Cambridge University Press.

Dickmann, M.W. 2003. Implementing German HRM abroad: Desired, feasible, successful? *International Journal of Human Resource Management*, 14, 265–283.

Dickson, M.W., Castaño, N., Magomaeva, A. & Den Hartog, D.N. 2012. Conceptualizing leadership across cultures. *Journal of World Business*, 47, 483–492.

Dickson, M.W., Den Hartog, D.N. & Mitchelson, J.K. 2003. Research on leadership in a cross-cultural context: Making progress, and raising new questions. *The Leadership Quarterly*, 14, 729–768.

Farndale, E., Scullion, H. & Sparrow, P. 2010. The role of the corporate HR function in global talent management. *Journal of World Business*, 45, 161–168.

Fleetwood, S. 2008. Institutions and social structures 1. *Journal for the Theory of Social Behaviour*, 38, 241–265.

Forrier, A., Sels, L. & Stynen, D. 2009. Career mobility at the intersection between agent and structure: A conceptual model. *Journal of Occupational and Organizational Psychology*, 82, 739–759.

Granrose, C.S. & Portwood, J.D. 1987. Matching individual career plans and organizational career management. *Academy of Management Journal*, 30, 699–720.

Guan, Y., Liu, S., Guo, M.J., Li, M., Wu, M., Chen, S.X., Xu, S.L. & Tian, L. 2018. Acculturation orientations and Chinese student Sojourners' career adaptability: The roles of career exploration and cultural distance. *Journal of Vocational Behavior*, 104, 228–239.

Gunz, H.P. & Mayrhofer, W. 2018. *Rethinking Career Studies: Facilitating Conversation Across Boundaries with the Social Chronology Framework*. Cambridge: Cambridge University Press.

Gunz, H.P. & Peiperl, M. (eds.) 2007. *Handbook of Career Studies*. Thousand Oaks, CA: Sage Publications.

Gunz, H.P. & Heslin, P.A. 2005. Reconceptualizing career success: Introduction to a special issue of the journal of organizational behavior. *Journal of Organizational Behavior*, 26, 105–111.

Halbesleben, J.R., Neveu, J.P., Paustian-Underdahl, S.C. & Westman, M. 2014. Getting to the 'COR' understanding the role of resources in conservation of resources theory. *Journal of Management*, 40, 1334–1364.

Hall, D.T. 1976. *Careers in Organizations*. Pacific Palisades, CA: Goodyear Pub. Co.

Hall, D.T. 2002. *Careers in and Out of organizations*. Thousand Oaks, CA: Sage Publications.

Hall, D.T. 2004. The protean career: A quarter-century journey. *Journal of Vocational Behavior*, 65, 1–13.

Harris, M. 1976. History and significance of the emic/etic distinction. *Annual Review of Anthropology*, 5, 329–350.

Hartung, P.J. 2002. Cultural context in career theory and practice: Role salience and values. *Career Development Quarterly*, 51, 12–25.

Heslin, P.A. 2005. Conceptualizing and evaluating career success. *Journal of Organizational Behavior*, 26, 113–136.

Hobfoll, S.E. 2002. Social and psychological resources and adaptation. *Review of General Psychology*, 6, 307–324.

Hobfoll, S.E., Halbesleben, J., Neveu, J.P. & Westman, M. 2018. Conservation of resources in the organizational context: The reality of resources and their consequences. *Annual Review of Organizational Psychology and Organizational Behavior*, 5, 103–128.

Hodgson, G.M. 2007. Institutions and individuals: Interaction and evolution. *Organization Studies*, 28, 95–11.

Hofstede, G. 1980. Motivation, leadership, and organization: Do American theories apply abroad? *Organizational Dynamics*, 9, 42–63.

Hofstede, G. 2001. *Culture's Consequences: Comparing Values, Behaviors, Institutions and Organizations Across Nations*. Thousand Oaks, CA: Sage Publications.

Hofstede, G., Hofstede, G.J. & Minkov, M. 2010. *Cultures and Organizations: Software of the Mind. Revised and Expanded*. New York: McGraw-Hill.

House, R.J., Hanges, P.J., Javidan, M., Dorfman, P.W. & Gupta, V. (eds.) 2004. *Culture, Leadership, and Organizations: The Globe Study of 62 Societies*. London: Sage Publications.

Hughes, E.C. 1936. The ecological aspect of institutions. *American Sociological Review*, 1, 180–189.

Inkson, K. 2006. Protean and boundaryless careers as metaphors. *Journal of Vocational Behavior*, 69, 48–63.

Jepperson, R. 1991. Institutions, institutional effects, and institutionalism. *In*: Powell, W.W. & Dimaggio, P.J. (eds.) *The New Institutionalism in Organizational Analysis*. Chicago: University of Chicago Press.

Jiwen Song, L. & Werbel, J.D. 2007. Guanxi as impetus? Career exploration in China and the United States. *Career Development International*, 12, 51–67.

Johnson, G., Scholes, K. & Whittington, R. 2008. *Exploring Corporate Strategy: Text and Cases*. London, UK: Pearson Education.

Jones, C. 2001. Coevolution of entrepreneurial careers, institutional rules and competitive dynamics in American film, 1895–1920. *Organization Studies*, 22, 911–944.

Kaše, R., Dries, N., Briscoe, J.P., Cotton, R.D., Apospori, E., Bagdadli, S., Çakmak-Otluoğlu, O., Chudzikowski, K., Dysvik, A., Saxena, R., Shen, Y., Verbruggen, M., Adeleye, I., Babalola, O., Casado, T., Cerdin, J.-L., Kim, N., Kumar, M., Unite, J. & Fei, Z. In press. Career success schemas and their contextual embeddedness: A comparative configurational perspective. *Human Resource Management Journal*.

Kats, M.S., van Emmerik, H., Blenkinsopp, J. & Khapova, S.N. 2010. Exploring the associations of culture with careers and the mediating role of HR practices: A conceptual model. *Career Development International*, 15, 401–418.

Khapova, S.N., Briscoe, J.P. & Dickmann, M. 2012. Careers in cross-cultural perspective. *In*: Briscoe, J.P., Hall, D.T. & Mayrhofer, W. (eds.) *Careers Around the World: Individual and Contextual Perspectives*. New York: Routledge.

Kim, B., Rhee, E., Ha, G., Jung, S.H., Cho, D., Lee, H.K. & Lee, S.M. 2016. Cross-cultural validation of the career growth scale for Korean employees. *Journal of Career Development*, 43, 26–36.

Kleiner, M.M. & Krueger, A.B. 2010. The prevalence and effects of occupational licensing. *British Journal of Industrial Relations*, 48, 676–687.

Kluckhohn, F.R. & Strodtbeck, F.L. 1961. *Variations in Value Orientations*. Chicago: Row, Peterson and Company.

Kumlin, S. & Rothstein, B. 2005. Making and breaking social capital: The impact of welfare-state institutions. *Comparative Political Studies*, 38, 339–365.

Lammers, J.C. & Barbour, J.B. 2006. An institutional theory of organizational communication. *Communication Theory*, 16, 356–377.

Liñán, F. & Chen, Y.W. 2009. Development and cross-cultural application of a specific instrument to measure entrepreneurial intentions. *Entrepreneurship Theory and Practice*, 33, 593–617.

Lirio, P., Lituchy, T.R., Ines Monserrat, S., Olivas-Lujan, M.R., Duffy, J.A., Fox, S. & Punnett, B.J. 2007. Exploring career-life success and family social support of successful women in Canada, Argentina and Mexico. *Career Development International*, 12, 28–50.

Mamadouh, V., de Jong, M. & Lalenis, K. 2002. An introduction to institutional transplantation. *In:* de Jong, M., Lalenis, K. & Mamadouh, V. (eds.) *The Theory and Practice of Institutional Transplantation*. Dordrecht: Springer.

Mau, W.C. 2000. Cultural differences in career decision-making styles and self-efficacy. *Journal of Vocational Behavior*, 57, 365–378.

Mayrhofer, W., Apospori, E., Dickmann, M., Dries, N., Gubler, M., Kaše, R., Khapova, S., Bosak, J., Cerdin, J-L., Fei, Z., Ferencikova, S., Madero, S., Mandel, D., Mishra, S. & Saxena, R. 2016. *Views on Career Success Across the Globe*. Paper presented as part of symposium Career success around the world: New findings from the 5c project at the Academy of Management Annual Meeting, Anaheim, CA.

Mayrhofer, W., Meyer, M. & Steyrer, J. 2007. Contextual issues in the study of careers. *In:* Gunz, H. & Peiperl, M. (eds.) *Handbook of Career Studies*. Thousand Oaks, CA: Sage Publications.

Mcsweeney, B. 2002. Hofstede's model of national cultural differences and their consequences: A triumph of faith – a failure of analysis. *Human Relations*, 55, 89–118.

Palthe, J. 2014. Regulative, normative, and cognitive elements of organizations: Implications for managing change. *Management and Organizational Studies*, 1, 59–78.

Ramamoorthy, N., Kulkarni, S.P., Gupta, A. & Flood, P.C. 2007. Individualism –collectivism orientation and employee attitudes: A comparison of employees from the high-technology sector in India and Ireland. *Journal of International Management*, 13, 187–203.

Rani Thanacoody, P., Bartram, T., Barker, M. & Jacobs, K. 2006. Career progression among female academics: A comparative study of Australia and Mauritius. *Women in Management Review*, 21, 536–553.

Savickas, M.L. & Porfeli, E.J. 2012. Career adapt-abilities scale: Construction, reliability, and measurement equivalence across 13 countries. *Journal of Vocational Behavior*, 80, 661–673.

Schein, E.H. 1984. Culture as an environmental context for careers. *Journal of Organizational Behavior*, 5, 71–81.

Scherer, S. 2005. Patterns of labour market entry – long wait or career instability? An empirical comparison of Italy, Great Britain and West Germany. *European Sociological Review*, 21, 427–440.

Schwartz, S.H. 1994. Beyond individualism/collectivism: New dimensions of values. *In:* Kim, U., Triandis, H.C., Kagitçibasi, C., Choi, S.C. & Yoon, G. (eds.) *Individualism and Collectivism: Theory Application and Methods*. Newbury Park, CA: Sage Publications.

Scullion, H. & Collings, D. 2011. *Global Talent Management*. London: Routledge.

Searle, J.R. 2005. What is an institution? *Journal of Institutional Economics*, 1, 1–22.

Smale, A., Bagdadli, S., Cotton, R., Dello Russo, S., Dickmann, M., Dysvik, A., Gianecchini, M., Kaše, R., Lazarova, M., Reichel, A., Rozo, P., M., V. & On Behalf of the 5C Research Collaborative. 2019. Proactive career behaviors and subjective career success: The moderating role of national culture. *Journal of Organizational Behavior*, 49(1), 105–122.

Spector, P.E., Cooper, C.L., Poelmans, S., Allen, T.D., O'Driscoll, M., Sanchez, J.I., Siu, O.L., Dewe, P., Hart, P. & Lu, L. 2004. A cross-national comparative study of work-family stressors, working hours, and well-being: China and Latin America versus the Anglo world. *Personnel Psychology*, 57, 119–142.

Sturges, J., Conway, N., Guest, D. & Liefooghe, A. 2005. Managing the career deal: The psychological contract as a framework for understanding career management, organizational commitment and work behavior. *Journal of Organizational Behavior*, 26, 821–838.

Tams, S. & Arthur, M. 2007. Studying careers across cultures: Distinguishing international, cross-cultural and globalization perspectives. *Career Development International*, 12, 86–98.

Thomas, D.C. & Inkson, K. 2007. Careers across cultures. *In:* Gunz, H. & Peiperl, M. (eds.) *Handbook of Career Studies.* Thousand Oaks, CA: Sage Publications.

Thomas, D.C. & Peterson, M.B. 2015. *Cross-Cultural Management: Essential Concepts.* Thousand Oaks, CA: Sage Publications.

Trompenaars, F. & Hampden-Turner, C. 2011. *Riding the Waves of Culture: Understanding Diversity in Global Business.* London: Nicholas Brealey Publishing.

van Dam, K. 2004. Antecedents and consequences of employability orientation. *European Journal of Work and Organizational Psychology*, 13, 29–51.

van Maanen, J. & Schein, E.H. 1979. Toward a theory of organizational socialization. *In:* Staw, B. (ed.) *Research in Organizational Behavior.* Greenwich, CT: Jai Press.

Watt, H.M. & Eccles, J.S. 2008. *Gender and Occupational Outcomes: Longitudinal Assessments of Individual, Social, and Cultural Influences.* Washington, DC: American Psychological Association.

Yi, X., Ribbens, B. & Morgan, C.N. 2010. Generational differences in China: Career implications. *Career Development International*, 15, 601–620.

Zhang, K., Song, L.J., Hackett, R.D. & Bycio, P. 2006. Cultural boundary of expectancy theory-based performance management: A commentary on DeNisi and Pritchard's performance improvement model. *Management and Organization Review*, 2, 279–294.

19

From global work experiences to global careers

A review and future research agenda

Kevin McKouen, Margaret A. Shaffer, and B. Sebastian Reiche

Introduction

As businesses become increasingly global, so do the experiences of many of their employees. The escalation of globalization over the past few decades has led to the emergence of a growing variety of global work experiences while also exposing many of the limitations of traditional expatriation (Mayrhofer et al., 2004). The result has been an exponential growth in the types of work experiences and career paths available to global workers, defined as individuals whose work requires them to either live in a foreign country, travel internationally, and/or regularly interact with business partners living in or from a different country (Shaffer et al., 2016). In this chapter, we explore current research on global work experiences, global careers, and the relationships between the two.

Before delving into the research, it is first critical to draw a distinction between global careers and global work experiences. A career can be objectively defined as the succession of work positions held by individuals throughout their life (Hughes, 1958; London and Stumpf, 1982). However, given the increasingly dynamic nature of many work-related "positions", we have chosen the more subjective view of a career, which refers to a series of work experiences that individuals accrue over time (Cappellen and Janssens, 2010b; Greenhaus et al., 2010). For a work experience to be considered "global," it must include collaboration across national boundaries (Hinds et al., 2011). Therefore we define a global career as a series of work experiences accrued over time, in which one or more work experience includes collaboration across national boundaries. In the previous edition of the careers handbook, Peiperl and Jonson defined a global career as "a career that takes place in more than one region of the world, either sequentially or concurrently" (2007: 351), and they refer to the definition of "career" as "the evolving sequence of an individual's work experience over time" (2007: 367, note 4). Though neither definition specifies the amount of "global" experience required for a career to be considered global, our working definition more overtly signifies a need for more clarity in the types of global careers that exist by eliciting the questions: what are the differences between global careers that include one global work experience (GWE), and global careers that include many? And, what are the different ways in which different types of GWEs contribute to global careers?

Work experiences have been conceptualized as being composed of quantities (amount and duration), interactions (density and timing), and qualities (type, complexity, etc.) that exist at multiple levels (task, job, group, occupation, etc.) and that interact and accumulate over time (Tesluk and Jacobs, 1998). GWEs are work experiences that involve collaboration across national boundaries; they can vary greatly across these dimensions because they are comprised of a wide range of international travel requirements and cross-cultural interaction demands. Work experiences are tightly linked to careers because work experiences are the building blocks individuals and organizations use to co-create various career paths. Similar to building blocks, some work experiences connect more naturally with others, which means that an individual's career path is determined not only by the career management practices of the individual and organization, but also by the individual's current and previous work experiences. It is likely that this central role that work experiences play in shaping careers has led many authors to use the concepts of *global work experience* and *global career* interchangeably. However, the fact that GWEs are both central to yet distinct from global careers makes the differentiation of these two concepts crucial for future scholarship on global careers.

In this chapter, we review existing research to provide a picture of how different types of global career paths both emerge from and unlock the possibilities of various GWEs. We start with a description of how we conducted our article search, followed by a brief summary of the field and a description of the five major types of GWEs currently discussed in the literature. Next, we introduce a process model that is then used both to organize the literature review and to develop a framework for future research focused on understanding (1) how individuals discover GWE opportunities; (2) how they prepare for them; (3) the challenges and opportunities faced while on a GWE; (4) the career-related outcomes of GWEs; and (5) how these experiences relate to future work experiences as well as subjective and objective forms of career success.

Methodology

To review the literature on global careers, we searched academic databases (ABI/INFORM Complete and EBSCO Business Premier) for scholarly articles in which the abstract included "career" and any one of the following globally themed keywords: "global," "international," "overseas," "expatriat*," "inpatriat*," "repatriat*," "flexpatriat*," "flex-patriat*," "travel," "transnational," "multinational," "trans-national" or "multi-national," yielding a combined set of 3,831 articles (with duplicates). Of these, only 303 unique articles focused on global careers (others focused on careers or global issues, but not the combination). We downloaded these 303 articles, then filtered out articles that did not focus particularly on the *career-related* antecedents, challenges, strategies, or outcomes of international workers. We also removed articles focused purely on immigration and those in which the same sample was used to tell similar stories in different journals (one author used the same sample to publish overlapping analyses in at least 10 journals). In the end, we focused our analysis on 74 articles of which 26 were quantitative, 32 were qualitative and 16 were conceptual papers. In a pattern indicative of the fledgling state of research on newer forms of GWEs and global careers, newer forms of GWEs are mostly found in conceptual papers, with a few beginning to appear in qualitative studies.

Types of global work experiences

Several typologies have been developed both for global career types (Andresen and Biemann, 2013; Banai and Harry, 2004) and for GWEs (Baruch et al., 2013). Since global careers, by definition, include GWEs, we will begin with an examination of the most common GWEs, followed by a discussion of how these GWEs may connect to form various global careers. The most common GWEs include (1) corporate expatriates (CEs), defined as "employees working for business organizations. . . [who are] sent overseas on a temporary basis to complete a time-based task or accomplish an organizational goal" before returning to the home office (Shaffer et al., 2012: 1286); (2) self-initiated expatriates (SIEs), "who initiate and usually finance their own expatriation and are not transferred by organizations"; (3) short-term assignees (STAs), who temporarily relocate to an international location for their organization for a few months to a year; (4) flexpatriates (FLEXs), "who travel for brief assignments, away from their home base and across cultural or national borders"; and (5) international business travelers (IBTs), "who take multiple short international business trips to various locations" (Shaffer et al., 2012: 1286–1287). One major difference among these types of global workers is that, due to shorter assignment lengths, the families of STAs, FLEXs and IBTs typically do not travel with the employee, while families of CEs and SIEs do tend to relocate. The difference between FLEXs and IBTs is that FLEXs are typically on location for a month or two to complete a project or solve a problem, while IBTs tend to work in a global office, traveling to international locations for one to three weeks at a time, primarily focused on knowledge transfer, negotiations or business-related meetings.

An integrative global career model: cycling through (global) work experience phases

Regardless of the assignment type, all global workers follow a more or less similar process of experiencing global work. We conceptualize this process in terms of five GWE phases, depicted in Figure 19.1. Similar to Shen and Hall's (2009: 795) description of an expatriate assignment as a "career learning cycle," we contend that these five phases can be thought of as components of a GWE cycle, to be included in the larger set of cycles making up a global career.

The model begins with the discovery phase, in which individuals either passively become aware of or actively seek out the GWE opportunity, depending on circumstances and their individual agency. In the second phase, individuals prepare for the GWE, a process that may also have active and passive elements. The third GWE phase involves the execution of the global work experience; it is during this phase that global workers experience the myriad challenges and opportunities of engaging in global work. In the fourth phase, global workers leverage their GWEs to obtain career capital and job opportunities. In the fifth and final phase, the individuals build upon their career through the active or passive acquisition of their next work experience. This last phase opens the model to the examination of global careers, including how they are formed, what direction they may take, and what measures might be used to assess success.

Below, we explain each phase in more detail, discuss how each phase relates to other phases and suggest promising directions for future research.

Phase 1: Discovering GWE opportunities

Many individuals actively and intentionally seek GWEs, either for the perceived career advancement opportunities offered, such as the acquisition of global management skills and the development of international networks, or for the immediate experiences provided by international work, such as the opportunity to explore other countries and cultures or to escape one's home country (Myers and Pringle, 2005). Obviously, many individuals are motivated by both career advancement and international exploration, but it is important to recognize that these

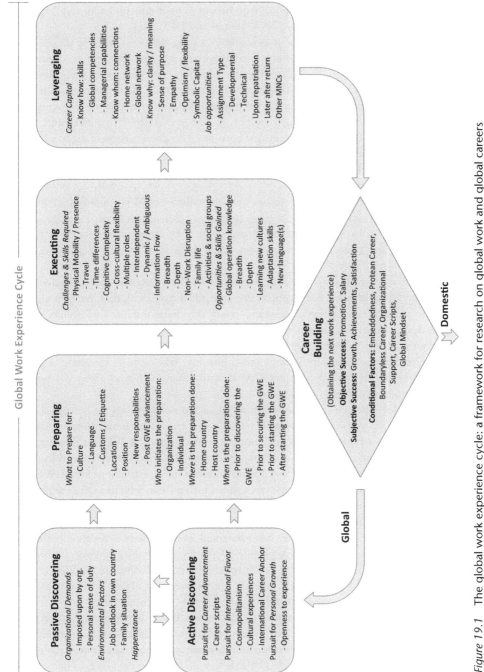

Global Work Experience Cycle

Passive Discovering

Organizational Demands
- Imposed upon by org.
- Personal sense of duty

Environmental Factors
- Job outlook in own country
- Family situation

Happenstance

Active Discovering

Pursuit for Career Advancement
- Career scripts

Pursuit for International Flavor
- Cosmopolitanism
- Cultural experiences
- International Career Anchor

Pursuit for Personal Growth
- Openness to experience

Preparing

What to Prepare for:
- Culture
  - Language
  - Customs / Etiquette
- Location
- Position
  - New responsibilities
- Post GWE advancement

Who initiates the preparation:
- Organization
- Individual

Where is the preparation done:
- Home country
- Host country

When is the preparation done:
- Prior to discovering the GWE
- Prior to securing the GWE
- Prior to starting the GWE
- After starting the GWE

Executing

Challenges & Skills Required
- Physical Mobility / Presence
  - Travel
  - Time differences
- Cognitive Complexity
  - Cross-cultural flexibility
  - Multiple roles
  - Interdependent
  - Dynamic / Ambiguous
  - Information Flow
  - Breadth
  - Depth
- Non-Work Disruption
  - Family life
  - Activities & social groups

Opportunities & Skills Gained
- Global operation knowledge
  - Breadth
  - Depth
- Learning new cultures
- Adaptation skills
- New language(s)

Leveraging

Career Capital
- Know how: skills
  - Global competencies
  - Managerial capabilities
- Know whom: connections
  - Home network
  - Global network
- Know why: clarity / meaning
  - Sense of purpose
  - Empathy
  - Optimism / flexibility
- Symbolic Capital

Job opportunities
- Assignment Type
  - Developmental
  - Technical
  - Upon repatriation
  - Later after return
  - Other MNCs

Career Building

(Obtaining the next work experience)
Objective Success: Promotion, Salary
Subjective Success: Growth, Achievements, Satisfaction

Conditional Factors: Embeddedness, Protean Career, Boundaryless Career, Organizational Support, Career Scripts, Global Mindset

Global

Domestic

Figure 19.1 The global work experience cycle: a framework for research on global work and global careers

motivational drivers are qualitatively different in terms of the expectations, hopes, desires and temporal focus placed on the experience. To gain a better understanding of what may be driving an individual to actively seek out a GWE, the Internationalism Career Anchor measure captures the extent to which one desires international experiences in their career (Cerdin and Pargneux, 2010; Lazarova et al., 2014; Mäkelä et al., 2015; Suutari and Taka, 2004).

On the passive side, a GWE may be imposed by one's organization (Pinto et al., 2012), or may come about after the search for other suitable opportunities in one's home country has been exhausted (Suutari, 2003). Though expatriates often feel they were given some choice in accepting an international assignment (Feldman and Thomas, 1992), Mayerhofer and colleagues (2004) found this was often not the case for flexpatriates. Since the demand for managers with global business skills has been outpacing the supply (Collings et al., 2007), it is likely that many IBTs and other types of GWEs will increasingly become compulsory aspects of many jobs. This illustrates the importance of conceptualizing a global career as a collection of experiences, as opposed to positions, as the global content of many careers has increased unaccompanied by any change in position or job title.

There are several other ways individuals may passively discover GWE opportunities, including chance encounters, learning about their organization's global operations, a change in job assignment or other forms of happenstance. In one study of expatriate academics, 26 of the 30 interviewees said their international assignment came about unexpectedly (Richardson and Mallon, 2005).

While the discovery of a GWE may happen *either* passively *or* actively, in reality the discovery process may be a mix of both. For example, one individual may think that living in another country sounds exciting, but never do anything about this desire until an opportunity comes across their desk. Similarly, another individual may have never thought about working overseas, but once their company acquires a subsidiary, that individual may be inspired to actively search for GWEs related to that subsidiary. Though individuals may take more or less active or passive roles in the discovery of these opportunities, what is important is that how they discover the global work opportunity is likely to influence how they prepare for it.

One pattern that emerged from the literature is that the more actively an individual seeks a GWE, the more likely that individual will enact independent preparation behaviors prior to securing the GWE. Such patterns were seen both for those pursuing GWEs for their international flavor (Vance, 2005) and for those seeking to advance their careers through GWEs (Cappellen and Janssens, 2010a). However, the nature of an individual's preparations for a GWE may change depending on that individual's objectives. Individuals primarily interested in the international and cultural aspects of a GWE may focus on more immediate concerns, such as living in a different culture, enabling them to get the most out of the experience itself. Those primarily interested in a GWE for its career-advancement potential are more likely to focus on both distal concerns, such as post-assignment career planning activities, and immediate concerns, such as the skills required to successfully fulfill new job responsibilities. Individuals who discover their GWE more passively, however, will likely have less time to prepare, and thus will be more likely to depend on pre-assignment or on-site training, if offered by the organization.

In general, the way in which an individual discovers a GWE opportunity can influence their preferences toward *what* they prepare for, *who* initiates the preparation (the individual or organization), *where* the preparations are made (home versus host country) and *when* the preparations are initiated (before discovering the GWE, before undertaking the GWE or upon GWE commencement), which we will discuss in more detail in the next section. Taken together, this highlights a need for research in at least two areas.

First, how do individuals tend to discover different GWE opportunities? As found in our literature review, it seems that individuals in some GWE types (SIEs in particular) are more likely to have actively sought out their position, while individuals in other GWE types (FLEXs, IBTs, and STAs) are more likely to have had GWEs thrust upon them. As both MNCs and workers become more global, how does this affect organizations and individuals with respect to filling or pursuing GWE positions? Are there more efficient ways to match open GWE opportunities in MNCs with individuals interested in filling such positions?

Second, how does the way one discovers their GWE relate to their preparation desires and expectations? Do employees who feel the GWE was thrust upon them have higher expectations of their organization's pre-departure programs? Will those actively pursuing a GWE for the international adventure want the organization to provide more cultural training? Or, will they prefer to develop their own training regimen? Research has shown that those actively pursuing a GWE for career advancement typically prefer to have a career management plan in place prior to embarking on their assignment (Riusala and Suutari, 2000). Do those who feel their GWE was imposed upon them have similar preferences? Given the disappointment in organization-led pre-departure preparations for GWEs (Cappellen and Janssens, 2010a; Feldman and Thomas, 1992; Mayerhofer et al., 2004; Riusala and Suutari, 2000; Stahl and Cerdin, 2004), understanding how the discovery of a GWE relates to an individual's desires for different forms of preparation could lead to valuable insights for global career and human resource management.

Phase 2: Preparing for GWEs

As discussed above, the differing expectations, hopes, desires and temporal foci of those pursuing global work are likely to lead to different preferences in terms of preparing for the GWE. For example, those looking for longer-term career advancement are more likely to prioritize their need for distant-future-focused pre-departure preparations, such as the career management support programs desired by participants in Riusala and Suutari's (2000) study. In line with this argument, Feldman and Thomas (1992) found that job satisfaction was related to the combination of the extent to which the expatriate's assignment is seen as part of their long-term career plans and the clarity of their repatriation plans.

Those pursuing GWEs to advance their careers can be seen as actors, guided by "career scripts" (institutionalized career norms and schemas) produced within their overarching organizational and economic settings (Cappellen and Janssens, 2010a). Illustrating the use of organizational career scripts, Point and Dickmann's study of 67 French and German corporate websites (2012) found that French websites tended to market GWEs as career advancement steps for high-potential managers, while German websites focused on the functional, skill-building opportunities provided by global work. However, formal organizational communications and policies are often distortions or incomplete pictures of reality, and thus individuals base their career actions on other signals, such as the experiences of others. Cappellen and Janssens (2010a) found that employees often develop and enact their own strategies, outside of their organization's career scripts in order to acquire the skills and visibility required to secure GWEs. In other words, counter to traditional expatriation career scripts, which concentrate on preparation after securing an assignment, many employees who actively seek GWEs prepare independently for their first GWE prior to securing or even often prior to discovering the assignment. This active, independent preparation may be even more prevalent for individuals seeking global work for the international experience itself (travel, culture, etc.). From his qualitative study of SIEs, Vance (2005) proposed that, for individuals interested in the international aspects of expatriation, the path to their first GWE tends to follow three stages. In the first stage, "foundation building," the individual gains initial exposure to other cultures or countries through previous travel experiences, such as tourism, international studies, relocation or humanitarian work, or through intercultural experiences, such as befriending foreigners or hosting students studying abroad. These experiences provide individuals an opportunity to gain an appreciation for other cultures and travel, often translating into a strong desire to incorporate these elements into their careers. The second stage for such individuals is preparation, which includes networking, studying foreign languages and cultures, and developing marketable skills. In the final stage, the individual attempts to secure a GWE, which can be done either by self-initiated expatriation or by securing a position within a multinational corporation (MNC), in which the individual would continue preparation for – and active pursuit of – a GWE (Vance, 2005).

However, not all global employees are actively involved in preparing for a GWE. In studies that inquired about pre-departure preparation, expatriates generally reported that they did not have a realistic preview of their upcoming assignment (Feldman and Thomas, 1992) and were highly dissatisfied with their pre-departure preparations (Riusala and Suutari, 2000; Stahl and Cerdin, 2004). Mayerhofer, Hartmann and Herbert's study of flexpatriates (2004) had similar findings. Although it has not been the subject of systematic study, this general dissatisfaction with provided pre-departure preparations leads us to wonder whether IBTs, STAs and those in other GWEs face the same issue. At the same time, however, Feldman and Thomas (1992) found that unrealistic job previews correlated with increased psychological stress and strain, but they also correlated with an increase in perceived intercultural management skills and had no association with job satisfaction.

Another, potentially much stronger, driver of *what* preparations are needed (or desired) is likely to be the expectations related to the specific type of GWE for which the individual is preparing. GWEs can vary significantly with regards to the demands they place on workers (discussed in more detail in the next section). Thus, to enhance their employees' performance, organizations should consider the specific needs related to each type of GWE when they design global work preparatory programs. For example, the leader of a global team will likely benefit more from preparations that focus on developing professional networks, communication skills and abilities for coordinating knowledge flows among team members, while a traditional CE would likely benefit more from training focused on language, culture and the difficulties related to international relocations. At the same time, one of the key skills gained during a GWE is the ability to adapt to and handle highly dynamic situations filled with uncertainty. Since learning how to learn and learning how to adapt quickly are both skills many claim to gain in GWEs, it is difficult to surmise whether the benefits of pre-GWE preparations (especially with regards to performance) will be visible in the long term.

With respect to this last point, research on global work should assess more than just an employee's satisfaction with pre-departure preparations; it should also evaluate the influence of pre-departure preparations on GWE performance and other GWE outcomes, such as job satisfaction and objective and subjective measures of career success. We have much to learn both in terms of what preparations may work best for which GWE types, and in terms of whether or not there is an optimal level of preparation. There is a popular story of a kid who helps a butterfly break through its chrysalis, only to discover that freeing the butterfly from its struggles kept it from building enough strength to fly. Similarly, is it possible to engage in too much preparation or receive too much support for a GWE? This may be the case with organizations that provide employees with so much support (e.g., cars and chauffeurs, fancy apartments, and club memberships) that they live in a bubble and never really have to interface with the local environment. In other words, can some types of preparation or support rob individuals of the struggles required to build their adaptation skills?

Phase 3: Executing GWEs

In their review of the literature, Shaffer and colleagues (2012) developed a taxonomy of the requirements of GWEs that included three aspects: *physical mobility* (also referred to as international travel), the intensity of international travel or relocation required; *cognitive flexibility*, the degree to which thought patterns and interaction behaviors must be adjusted to accommodate cross-cultural situations; and *non-work disruption*, the extent to which normal life activities and routines are interrupted or disturbed. At the same time these dimensions were being developed, Mendenhall et al. (2012) were conceptualizing the demands faced by "global leadership" as comprising three main elements: *complexity*, contextual elements that make global work particularly challenging (multiple interdependent roles, responsibilities, and knowledge structures that are often ambiguous, nonlinear, and continuously changing); *flow*, the richness (frequency, volume, and scope) and quantity (number and variety of channels) of information communicated; and *presence*, the intensity of travel or relocation required. Though both frameworks cover skills required and challenges faced during GWEs, there are some important differences with respect to each framework's focus. Shaffer et al. (2012) take a more holistic view of how the demands and challenges of GWEs can affect individuals both in their work and non-work lives. From a careers perspective, these elements may relate more to career desires, aspirations, and satisfaction. Mendenhall et al. (2012), on the other hand, focus more on teasing out the different skills required for or gained through exposure to different types of GWEs, which, from a careers perspective, are likely to be related more with career capital.

With respect to these taxonomies, both corporate expatriates (CEs) and self-initiated expatriates (SIEs) face many challenges and hurdles. Compared to other GWEs, CEs and SIEs require high levels of physical mobility (or presence), complexity, and cognitive flexibility, and moderate levels of both non-work disruption, since family members usually accompany the expatriate, and flow, since expatriates typically concentrate on a single region (Mendenhall et al., 2012; Shaffer et al., 2012). Adding to these challenges, many expatriates work in higher-level positions than they had prior to their assignment (Riusala and Suutari, 2000), while at the same time being away from the home office for much longer periods of time than IBTs, FLEXs or STAs. For CEs this combination of having more responsibility yet feeling farther away from home office support (out of sight, out of mind) can be quite stressful.

Adding to their stress, not only do CEs have to adjust to their new responsibilities, but they also have to adjust to their new environments. In their meta-analysis of expatriate adjustment research, Bhaskar-Shrinivas et al. (2005) found that cultural adjustment, interaction adjustment, and work adjustment all had significant relationships with expatriate performance and withdrawal cognitions. These three forms of adjustment were driven by a multitude of attitudinal, cognitive, and behavioral stressors, with spousal adjustment, cultural novelty, relational skills, role clarity and role discretion having the highest impact.

Expatriation also provides some unique opportunities, due in large part to the fact that expatriates stay in the same location for a long time. This gives them the opportunity not only to become more deeply ingrained in the culture, learn the language and go sightseeing (Tung, 1998), but also to learn the detailed nuances of the host office's operations. This is critical for transferring knowledge, improving communications between home and host offices and gaining country specific skills, all of which are often prime organizational objectives (Stahl and Cerdin,

2004) and can lead to career advancement opportunities. However, for global MNCs, with operations in many different regions, expatriates rarely gain the broad views of a firm's global operations that other GWEs offer.

International business travelers (IBTs), who travel internationally for brief business trips (1–3 weeks), numerous times per year, have more opportunity to gain a holistic view of the company's global operations. The title that often accompanies an IBT can signal one's flexibility, mobility and international problem-solving abilities. Many IBTs believe these signals attract future positions both within and outside of the organization, as work continues to become more global in nature (Demel and Mayrhofer, 2010). However, IBTs also come with their own set of challenges. They require high levels of continuous physical mobility, which is quite different from CEs and SIEs, who may or may not travel as much after relocation. The biggest stressors for IBTs relate to the fact that their "frequent flyer" status means they often have little time for family, friends or romantic partners and can find it difficult to commit to their associated social obligations (Demel and Mayrhofer, 2010). Summing up his many stressors, one IBT interviewed by Mayerhofer and colleagues (2004) stated "It is hard work. You don't sleep much because of time changes, you have to drink a lot of alcohol, and at the end of the day you feel lonely" (2004: 661). Despite these challenges, many IBTs enjoy the work. Mäkelä et al. (2015) found that more frequent travel actually lowered perceived work-life conflict and raised perceived work-life enrichment for individuals with a high internationalism career orientation.

While many studies in our review focused on the challenges and opportunities related to CEs and SIEs, few have focused specifically on the experiences of flexpatriates (FLEXs) (1–2-month project or problem-based assignments), short-term assignees (STAs) (3–12 month assignments) or other types of global workers. In the literature, any such workers were either subsumed into the category of expatriate, or were labeled as flexpatriates in studies predating the IBT versus FLEX versus STA distinctions. One potential issue related to FLEXs, STAs and IBTs is that these types of GWEs may take a heavier toll on one's personal life, as the short periods of time they spend in any place makes it difficult to maintain a stable support network, or even a circle of friends, either at home or abroad. At the same time, however, as Mäkelä et al. (2015) found with respect to IBTs, the work-life conflict felt by FLEXs and STAs may be influenced by how much internationalism is part of their career anchors, such that those who place more importance on internationalism in their career may feel less work-life conflict and more work-life enrichment with more frequent travel.

The fact that an "internationalism career anchor" has been developed brings up a number of questions for researchers. First, is there a set of core experiences, challenges, and opportunities that attract individuals to GWEs, regardless of the GWE type? If so, identifying these common-alities may provide insights into how various GWEs can link together to form different kinds of global careers. If not, this may call for a multi-dimensional form of the internationalism career anchor, such that the dimensions relate more or less to the different subsets of experiences provided by various GWEs. The frameworks provided by Mendenhall et al. (2012) and Shaffer et al. (2012) may prove useful for the challenge-related aspects of the internationalism anchor, but we are not aware of any research that provides a detailed analysis of the various opportunities (beyond having challenging work) afforded by each type of GWE. We know CEs and SIEs have more opportunity to become fully immersed in a culture, learning the language and traveling around the local area, while FLEXs, STAs and IBTs usually have the opportunity to gain a broader, yet shallower understanding of multiple cultures. However, there are likely many other opportunities uniquely afforded by each type of GWE. A more comprehensive understanding of these opportunities could lead to valuable insights into what draws individuals to pursue and/or accept different types of GWEs.

At the same time, we have much to learn about the organizational challenges and the organizational opportunities related to each type of GWE, both with respect to the home office and especially the host office. What are the most challenging and rewarding aspects of managing employees who undertake each kind of GWE? Do host country nationals prefer to work with CEs and SIEs, due to the longer commitment that allows them to become more immersed in the local culture? Or, does this longer commitment lead to more employment threat felt by host country nationals? Answers to these questions, and many others, may shed more light on why organizations implement one type of GWE instead of another, or when an organization *should* use one instead of the other. The GWE chosen by an organization may (or possibly should) depend on the types of knowledge and skills the organization wants to develop as well as the knowledge and skills required to perform specific functions.

Phase 4: Leveraging GWEs

The various challenges and opportunities employees experience during their GWE can influence both their career capital and their access to future job opportunities.

Career capital

One commonly studied career outcome of GWEs is career capital, which is often conceptualized in terms of "knowing why," "knowing how," and "knowing whom." According to DeFillippi and Arthur (1994), "knowing why" relates to clarity in one's career motivation, including career identification and personal meaning, "knowing how" covers job-relevant skills and knowledge, and "knowing whom" reflects one's career-related social networks. GWEs have generally positive impacts on "knowing why," including more openness, flexibility, optimism, extraversion, and empathy (Jokinen, 2010), improved self-image and self-awareness (Suutari and Mäkelä, 2007; Yao, 2014), and a higher sense of purpose (Haslberger, 2013). Finally, "symbolic capital" (the signals sent to future employers, managers, and coworkers about the skills and knowledge gained during an assignment) is created when hiring managers for potential future positions assume that a GWE has enabled a global worker to gain these different forms of "knowing" (Doherty and Dickmann, 2009).

"Knowing how" also has mostly positive gains for global workers, in the form of operational skills (Cappellen and Janssens, 2008), managerial capability, cultural awareness, inter-cultural competence, political sensitivity, communication skills (Dickmann and Doherty, 2008; 2010), leadership skills, global competencies (Suutari and Mäkelä, 2007), industry awareness, new ways of doing things and language skills (Yao, 2014). As they are exposed to many different cultures, IBTs were especially found to enhance cross-cultural and adjustment abilities (Mayerhofer et al., 2004).

GWEs seem to have a mixed impact on "knowing whom" career capital. Many global workers gain contacts that are advantageous to their global careers while simultaneously losing touch with important contacts at the home office (Dickmann and Doherty, 2008, 2010; Jokinen, 2010; Suutari and Mäkelä, 2007). In a Chinese context, this translates to expatriates often suffering significant losses of *guanxi* (Yao, 2014). In addition to career related contacts, when families accompany global workers, these workers tend to make more contacts in the local host communities, improving their cultural adjustment (Jokinen, 2010).

Career capital gained on a GWE is also likely to vary with the purpose of the GWE. For example, while developmental CE assignments are specifically designed to groom an individual for higher levels of management, in which network building is a key factor, functional CE assignments tend to focus on addressing problems for which specific skills are not locally available. Thus, it seems that developmental assignments would lead to a greater increase in 'knowing whom' than functional assignments. However, since many functional assignments require someone already equipped with knowledge for addressing a given issue, these assignments may or may not lead to an increase in "know-how." For example, Rodriguez and Scurry (2014) found that because of localization policies that prioritized career development for local workers, SIEs in Qatar typically do not receive training. Instead, they are hired to perform tasks for which they are already highly skilled, leading to less significant gains in "know-how."

The differences in the capital developed during different types of GWEs (e.g., CE vs. IBT) are likely to be even larger. Understanding these differences may provide crucial insights related to global careers, since "knowing how" relates to future positions an individual is qualified to take on; "knowing whom" can be a deciding factor as to whether an individual discovers, or is privy to potential opportunities; "knowing why" impacts the meaning an individual places on potential opportunities; and symbolic capital acts as a signal of the individual's capabilities, influencing the evaluations of hiring managers.

Job opportunities

Many global workers expect that the skills and qualifications they gain during their GWE will be valued, utilized, and lead to career advancement opportunities within or outside their organizations (Riusala and Suutari, 2000; Stahl and Cerdin, 2004; Tung, 1998). However, these high expectations often do not come to fruition; at least not immediately. Many find that they return to jobs similar to their old ones, that they are not able to utilize their newly acquired skills, that they have lost too much "knowing whom" capital (Jassawalla and Sashittal, 2009), and that they yearn for the challenges they experienced while on assignment (Myers and Pringle, 2005). Though these issues often cause repatriates to quit upon return, Doherty and Dickmann (2009) found that many of the repatriates who stayed with their organization through the pain of their first unsatisfactory post-assignment position saw their careers quickly advance in later post-assignment opportunities. Overall, unmet expectations upon repatriation are often attributed to ineffective or non-existent repatriation career support from the organization and are considered a major cause for consistently high repatriate turnover (Collings et al., 2007); an issue Lazarova and Cerdin (2007: 404) called "a major source of concern . . . invariably present in the literature for several decades."

Shen and Hall (2009) proposed that the form of a repatriate's career exploration would depend on the degree of their job embeddedness (leading to internal vs. external exploration) and their difficulty in adjusting back to the home office (leading to forced vs. self-initiated exploration). Similarly, Reiche et al. (2011) found that retention for returning inpatriates was indirectly predicted by trusting network ties with former colleagues at headquarters, and that this relationship operated through the mediating mechanisms of their felt "fit" with headquarters and their perceived career prospects. Taking a career agency perspective, Lazarova and Cerdin (2007) reported that repatriation support programs were positively related to repatriation retention, while career activism was positively related to turnover intentions.

Finally, the purpose of a GWE has a significant influence on the GWE's outcomes. For example, in comparison to technical assignments, developmental assignments tend to be related to higher levels of actual career advancement upon repatriation (Kraimer et al., 2009), as well as to perceived career opportunities (within and outside of the organization) and to turnover intentions (Stahl et al., 2009). This is likely because the purpose of a developmental assignment is to prepare an employee for career advancement and because developmental assignments tend to generate more "knowing whom" capital, building connections critical to finding future career advancement opportunities.

Phase 5: Career building

As Figure 19.1 suggests, upon completion of a GWE, individuals build upon their career through the decision to pursue another GWE or to pursue a domestic-based work experience. The work experience the individual secures is contingent on several factors, including the individual's career capital and career path preferences. With respect to career capital, simply measuring "knowing whom," "knowing how," or "knowing why" capital only tells part of the story. An individual's next work experience relies heavily on where these networks, skills, and understandings are relevant. For example, many studies found that "knowing whom" capital for expatriates often increased in host-country networks while significantly decreasing with respect to home-office networks. Many global workers will likely develop the intellectual, psychological, and social capital that Javidan and Bowen (2013) define as making up a "global mindset," which they purport as essential for global managers, and which we would extend as being important for any global worker. However, as global workers are developing their global mindset, their domestic counterparts may be developing other skill sets more relevant to domestic opportunities, making it potentially more difficult for global workers to compete for some domestic positions.

An individual's eventual pursuit of a subsequent work opportunity depends on the exploratory horizon of the individual. For example, what factors in a work experience (location, function, title, responsibilities, organization, etc.) will individuals view as both viable and contributing to their desired career path? This is where the interdependence between global work experiences and global careers becomes most clear, because an individual's subsequent work experience will likely be influenced greatly by their internalized career beliefs, goals, and attitudes, and these career beliefs, goals, and attitudes are likely to change based on their previous GWE.

With respect to career beliefs, goals and attitudes, many global workers still prioritize objective measures of success such as vertical promotions and increases in salary. However, subjective measures, such as personal growth, the feeling of accomplishment, learning of new cultures, and becoming a global citizen, are increasingly valued by global workers. Given the rise of these more subjective career goals, especially among global workers, scholars have argued that global careers follow paths similar to the boundaryless career (Cappellen and Janssens, 2005; Wittig-Berman and Beutell, 2009) or protean career (Cao et al., 2013) concepts. According to the boundaryless career concept, organizations are no longer seen as relevant boundaries for one's career progression (DeFillippi and Arthur, 1994), while in the protean career, careers are seen as self-managed and constantly changing to adapt to the external environment (Hall, 1976). These career concepts combine to allocate more agency and more available options to individuals as they consider their next work experience.

At the same time, there are many factors that may limit individuals' perceived options, such as their embeddedness within the organization or community, their perceived organizational support, and various portions of the career scripts to which they subscribe. Cappellen and Janssens' study of career triggers among global managers (2010a) shed light on a number of other factors that can influence individuals' subsequent work experience, including their time perspective (both short- and long-term career planning), desires for lateral or hierarchical moves, and desires to align oneself along personal, familial, or career growth objectives.

Global careers as chains of global (and domestic) work experiences

Considering a global career as a chain of experiences that include at least one GWE, the decision to pursue, accept, or acquiesce to one's next work experience acts as the link between one work experience and the next, allowing us to examine how global careers unfold over time. Viewing global careers through this framework leads to the question of how the experiences of one GWE cycle can inform an individual's career-related attitudes and definitions and how these changes can then influence the individual's experiences throughout the next GWE cycle. One interesting area for research is how career paths develop through sequences of different types of global experiences. For example, Riusala and Suutari (2000) found that 91 percent of the expatriates in their study reported interest in new foreign assignments and 59 percent were interested in more permanent expatriation. Since some global workers feel compelled by external factors to take on GWEs, while others actively seek GWEs, the question remains as to whether these individuals were originally interested in global work or whether their interest developed while on assignment. Suutari's (2003) qualitative study found many global managers that originally felt compelled by their organizations to take on GWEs ended up loving the related challenges and intrigue and seeking more GWEs upon completion of their initial global assignment. However, this was a study in which the entire sample consisted of global managers with extensive global experience. Those choosing to go back to domestic work would have been filtered out of the study's sample, making it impossible to generalize as to how an initial GWE influences the average individual's career. Longitudinal career studies would be helpful in determining how one GWE leads to pursuing (or accepting) a similar GWE, a different type of GWE, or a domestic work experience upon completion. Do some IBTs or FLEXs yearn for deeper cultural immersion, leading to more traditional CE or SIE GWEs? Do some CEs and SIEs feel too stagnant, leading to assignments with more frequent, yet shorter stints in the future?

To gain a better understanding of the potential career trajectories accessible upon completion of a GWE, we also need more research on what signals different types of GWEs send to employers. Demel and Mayrhofer (2010) found that IBTs thought their positions signaled their flexibility, mobility, and international problem-solving abilities to other employers, but is this how employers actually see them? In the studies that included individuals with longer global work histories, their careers often involved repeated sequences of the same global career type. This is most evident in the case of repeat expatriates, but it is difficult to ascertain whether or not this is simply due to the fact that until quite recently expatriation was the main mode of global work. Do employers tend to recruit for a specific GWE type by looking for others who have experience with that same type of GWE? Do individuals tend to look for the same kind of experiences? Gaining a better understanding of what different GWEs signal to employers could help answer some of these questions. In addition, teasing out which experiences are common among most global workers and which experiences are more specific to each type of GWE could help MNCs more accurately assess how individuals with certain global experiences may fit within their organization.

Career success

Career success, whether studied as an objective or subjective construct, is qualitatively different from job satisfaction or job success in that it reflects the progression both in one's career thus far and one's likely career trajectory, as well as the satisfaction with that progression. Job satisfaction and job success, on the other hand, focus more on momentary states of satisfaction and success, which emphasize attitudes toward current work experiences. Thus, to assess the influence of a

GWE (or GWEs) on one's career success requires that some time has passed between the end of the assignment and the measurement of success. This time lag was considered in only a few of the studies we reviewed. Measuring objective career success as hierarchical advancement (to the C-level position), Hamori and Koyuncu (2011) found that international assignments, especially longer assignments and higher frequencies of assignments, were related to slower rates of ascent to the CEO position for the CEOs of the 500 largest corporations in the United States and 500 largest in Europe. Using salary and promotions as measurements of objective career success, Benson and Pattie (2008) found that international assignments had no effect, yet Biemann and Braakmann (2013) found a significant increase in salary. Biemann and Braakmann (2013) also found positive relationships between international assignments and subjective career success, which was measured as satisfaction with one's current position, income, and training and promotion opportunities.

Studying repatriates up to two and a half years after repatriation, Ren et al. (2013) found several complex relationships leading to career satisfaction, an indicator of subjective career success. First, they found that pay-related psychological breach and career derailment (a lower-level position upon return) interacted with the repatriate's assessment of how valuable the assignment was to their career. When the assignment was considered valuable to their career, pay-related psychological breach had a weak negative relationship with career satisfaction and career derailment had a strong negative relationship with career satisfaction. When the assignment was not considered valuable, the negative impact of pay-related psychological breach on career satisfaction became much stronger while the relationship between career derailment and career satisfaction actually became slightly positive. In addition to these interactions, perceived underemployment interacted with the value the employee perceived the organization placed on their international assignment such that when the organization was perceived to value the assignment, repatriates expressed more career dissatisfaction as a result of being underemployed. This study highlights the complexity of the relationship between GWEs and subjective career success, as it is intertwined with one's perceptions, expectations, and sense of entitlement related to how the GWE *should* relate to different elements of one's career (pay, advancement, responsibilities, etc.). For example, as Ren et al. (2013) contend, it seems that those who considered their assignments as a valuable asset to their careers may have felt entitled to advancement when they repatriated. If advancement was not forthcoming, however, this may have increased their sense of feeling deprived, which in turn may have led to decreased job satisfaction.

As this study illustrates, for subjective forms of career success, individuals' expectations of their GWE are intricately woven together with their overall career expectations, making it difficult to tease them apart. The perceived success of a GWE can depend upon how the GWE was originally meant to fit (or not) within longer-term career plans. For instance, individuals pursuing adventure through an international assignment will prioritize different indicators of success for the GWE and its perceived influence on their career in general than individuals pursuing a GWE for career advancement. At the same time, GWEs can have significant influence on individuals' career plans through many mechanisms discussed earlier such as developing "knowing why" career capital and having an internationalism career anchor. Thus, GWEs are more than just building blocks that assemble together to create a global career. Instead, they are often active elements of a career that can significantly affect individuals' career options moving forward, as well as their fundamental notion of what a desirable career can – or should – look like.

Conclusion

Given the intricate links between GWEs and global careers, the framework developed in this chapter can aid in the research of global work and global careers in at least three ways. First, it can provide guidance for comparing different types of GWEs, leading to questions such as: Which types tend to be discovered and secured more actively or more passively? How do preparations vary for the different kinds of experiences? And, how *should* preparations be different? There are many ways, within each phase of the global career cycle, in which GWEs can differ, and it appears research is just beginning to scratch the surface in most areas.

Second, the model provides a map as to where future research can be most helpful. At this point, we know a decent amount about CEs and SIEs, but we have much less knowledge of other types of GWEs with respect to the various phases in this model. That said, global work is changing rapidly, both from the perspective of the individual and that of the organization, calling into question some of our historical knowledge of CEs and SIEs. Also, much of our knowledge is based on Western-based expatriates, so this model can also provide a framework for comparing the same types of GWEs across different cultures.

Third, our model can act as a framework to examine the dynamics of global careers. How do experiences in each phase contribute to career success, or the career scripts used to obtain this success? How and why does one global (or domestic) work experience shape future career choices and work experiences? Understanding how various GWE outcomes interact with other factors to determine the individual's next work experience could greatly enhance our understanding of how global careers are developed. Beyond a few global career taxonomies (Andresen and Biemann, 2013; Banai and Harry, 2004), we found very little empirical research that explored the notion of a long-term global career. Such research seems essential for organizations to develop more effective global talent management and development programs and to better serve the career planning needs of their employees.

Considering the fact that global careers started their rapid proliferation within the last two decades (less than half the length of an average career) it is not surprising we are just beginning to understand what current global career paths look like. Though we had to limit our discussion to the most common forms of corporate-related global work experiences of traditional workers, our review and framework sheds light on many promising areas in which scholars can contribute to our understanding of GWEs and global careers; areas with qualitative but no quantitative work; areas with theory, but no empirical work; and even areas in which theory has barely scratched the surface. It is our hope that the framework developed from our review is helpful in providing a guide for researchers, both informing us as to where we have been and mapping out some of the exciting directions in which we can go.

References

Andresen, M. & Biemann, T. 2013. A taxonomy of internationally mobile managers. *The International Journal of Human Resource Management*, 24, 533–557.

Banai, M. & Harry, W. 2004. Boundaryless global careers: The international itinerants. *International Studies of Management & Organization*, 34, 96–120.

Baruch, Y., Dickmann, M., Altman, Y. & Bournois, F. 2013. Exploring international work: Types and dimensions of global careers. *The International Journal of Human Resource Management*, 24, 2369–2393.

Benson, G.S. & Pattie, M. 2008. Is expatriation good for my career? The impact of expatriate assignments on perceived and actual career outcomes. *The International Journal of Human Resource Management*, 19, 1636–1653.

Bhaskar-Shrinivas, P., Harrison, D.A., Shaffer, M.A. & Luk, D.M. 2005. Input-based and time-based models of international adjustment: Meta-analytic evidence and theoretical extensions. *Academy of Management Journal*, 48, 257–281.

Biemann, T. & Braakmann, N. 2013. The impact of international experience on objective and subjective career success in early careers. *The International Journal of Human Resource Management*, 24, 3438–3456.

Cao, L., Hirschi, A. & Deller, J. 2013. The positive effects of a protean career attitude for self-initiated expatriates: Cultural adjustment as a mediator. *Career Development International*, 18, 56–77.

Cappellen, T. & Janssens, M. 2005. Career paths of global managers: Towards future research. *Journal of World Business*, 40, 348–360.

Cappellen, T. & Janssens, M. 2008. Global managers' career competencies. *Career Development International*, 13, 514–537.

Cappellen, T. & Janssens, M. 2010a. The career reality of global managers: An examination of career triggers. *The International Journal of Human Resource Management*, 21, 1884–1910.

Cappellen, T. & Janssens, M. 2010b. Enacting global careers: Organizational career scripts and the global economy as co-existing career referents. *Journal of Organizational Behavior*, 31, 687–706.

Cerdin, J.L. & Pargneux, M.L. 2010. Career anchors: A comparison between organization-assigned and self-initiated expatriates. *Thunderbird International Business Review*, 52, 287–299.

Collings, D.G., Scullion, H. & Morley, M.J. 2007. Changing patterns of global staffing in the multinational enterprise: Challenges to the conventional expatriate assignment and emerging alternatives. *Journal of World Business*, 42, 198–213.

Defillippi, R.J. & Arthur, M.B. 1994. The boundaryless career: A competency-based perspective. *Journal of Organizational Behavior*, 15, 307–324.

Demel, B. & Mayrhofer, W. 2010. Frequent business travelers across Europe: Career aspirations and implications. *Thunderbird International Business Review*, 52, 301–311.

Dickmann, M. & Doherty, N. 2008. Exploring the career capital impact of international assignments within distinct organizational contexts. *British Journal of Management*, 19, 145–161.

Dickmann, M. & Doherty, N. 2010. Exploring organizational and individual career goals, interactions, and outcomes of developmental international assignments. *Thunderbird International Business Review*, 52, 313–324.

Doherty, N. & Dickmann, M. 2009. Exposing the symbolic capital of international assignments. *The International Journal of Human Resource Management*, 20, 301–320.

Feldman, D.C. & Thomas, D.C. 1992. Career management issues facing expatriates. *Journal of International Business Studies*, 23, 271–293.

Greenhaus, J.H., Callanan, G.A. & Godshalk, V.M. 2010. *Career Management*. Los Angeles: Sage Publications.

Hall, D.T. 1976. *Careers in Organizations*. Pacific Palisades, LA: Goodyear.

Hamori, M. & Koyuncu, B. 2011. Career advancement in large organizations in Europe and the United States: Do international assignments add value? *The International Journal of Human Resource Management*, 22, 843–862.

Haslberger, A. 2013. Does cross-cultural adjustment coincide with career capital growth? Evidence from Vienna, Austria. *The International Journal of Human Resource Management*, 24, 791–805.

Hinds, P., Liu, L. & Lyon, J. 2011. Putting the global in global work: An intercultural lens on the practice of cross-national collaboration. *Academy of Management Annals*, 5, 135–188.

Hughes, E.C. 1958. *Men and Their Work*. Glencoe, IL: Free Press.

Jassawalla, A.R. & Sashittal, H.C. 2009. Thinking strategically about integrating repatriated managers in MNCs. *Human Resource Management*, 48, 769–792.

Javidan, M. & Bowen, D. 2013. 'Global mindset' of managers. What it is, why it matters, and how to develop it. *Organizational Dynamics*, 42, 145–155.

Jokinen, T. 2010. Development of career capital through international assignments and its transferability to new contexts. *Thunderbird International Business Review*, 52, 325–336.

Kraimer, M.L., Shaffer, M.A. & Bolino, M.C. 2009. The influence of expatriate and repatriate experiences on career advancement and repatriate retention. *Human Resource Management*, 48, 27–47.

Lazarova, M.B. & Cerdin, J-L. 2007. Revisiting repatriation concerns: Organizational support versus career and contextual influences. *Journal of International Business Studies*, 38, 404–429.

Lazarova, M.B., Cerdin, J-L. & Liao, Y. 2014. The internationalism career anchor: A validation study. *International Studies of Management & Organization*, 44, 9–33.

London, M. & Stumpf, S.A. 1982. *Managing Careers*. Reading, MA: Addison Wesley Publishing Company.

Mäkelä, L., Kinnunen, U. & Suutari, V. 2015. Work-to-life conflict and enrichment among international business travelers: The role of international career orientation. *Human Resource Management*, 54, 517–531.

Mayerhofer, H., Hartmann, L.C. & Herbert, A. 2004. Career management issues for flexpatriate international staff. *Thunderbird International Business Review*, 46, 647–666.

Mayrhofer, W., Iellatchitch, A., Meyer, M., Steyrer, J., Schiffinger, M. & Strunk, G. 2004. Going beyond the individual: Some potential contributions from a career field and habitus perspective for global career research and practice. *Journal of Management Development*, 23, 870–884.

Mendenhall, M.E., Reiche, B.S., Bird, A. & Osland, J.S. 2012. Defining the 'global' in global leadership. *Journal of World Business*, 47, 493–503.

Myers, B. & Pringle, J.K. 2005. Self-initiated foreign experience as accelerated development: Influences of gender. *Journal of World Business*, 40, 421–431.

Peiperl, M.A. & Jonson, K. 2007. Global careers. *In:* Gunz, H.P. & Peiperl, M. (eds.) *Handbook of Career Studies*. Los Angeles: Sage Publications.

Pinto, L.H., Cabral-Cardoso, C. & Werther, W.B., Jr. 2012. Compelled to go abroad? Motives and outcomes of international assignments. *The International Journal of Human Resource Management*, 23, 2295–2314.

Point, S. & Dickmann, M. 2012. Branding international careers: An analysis of multinational corporations' official wording. *European Management Journal*, 30, 18–31.

Reiche, B.S., Kraimer, M.L. & Harzing, A-W. 2011. Why do international assignees stay? An organizational embeddedness perspective. *Journal of International Business Studies*, 42, 521–544.

Ren, H., Bolino, M.C., Shaffer, M.A. & Kraimer, M.L. 2013. The influence of job demands and resources on repatriate career satisfaction: A relative deprivation perspective. *Journal of World Business*, 48, 149–159.

Richardson, J. & Mallon, M. 2005. Career interrupted? The case of the self-directed expatriate. *Journal of World Business*, 40, 409–420.

Riusala, K. & Suutari, V. 2000. Expatriation and careers: Perspectives of expatriates and spouses. *Career Development International*, 5, 81–90.

Rodriguez, J.K. & Scurry, T. 2014. Career capital development of self-initiated expatriates in Qatar: Cosmopolitan globetrotters, experts and outsiders. *The International Journal of Human Resource Management*, 25, 190–211.

Shaffer, M.A., Kraimer, M.L., Chen, Y-P. & Bolino, M.C. 2012. Choices, challenges, and career consequences of global work experiences: A review and future agenda. *Journal of Management*, 38, 1282–1327.

Shaffer, M.A., Reiche, B.S., Dimitrova, M., Lazarova, M., Chen, S., Westman, M. & Wurtz, O. 2016. Work- and family-role adjustment of different types of global professionals: Scale development and validation. *Journal of International Business Studies*, 47, 113–139.

Shen, Y. & Hall, D.T.T. 2009. When expatriates explore other options: Retaining talent through greater job embeddedness and repatriation adjustment. *Human Resource Management*, 48, 793–816.

Stahl, G.K. & Cerdin, J-L. 2004. Global careers in French and German multinational corporations. *Journal of Management Development*, 23, 885–902.

Stahl, G.K., Chua, C.H., Caligiuri, P., Cerdin, J.L. & Taniguchi, M. 2009. Predictors of turnover intentions in learning-driven and demand-driven international assignments: The role of repatriation concerns, satisfaction with company support, and perceived career advancement opportunities. *Human Resource Management*, 48, 89–109.

Suutari, V. 2003. Global managers: Career orientation, career tracks, life-style implications and career commitment. *Journal of Managerial Psychology*, 18, 185–207.

Suutari, V. & Mäkelä, K. 2007. The career capital of managers with global careers. *Journal of Managerial Psychology*, 22, 628–648.

Suutari, V. & Taka, M. 2004. Career anchors of managers with global careers. *Journal of Management Development*, 23, 833–847.

Tesluk, P.E. & Jacobs, R.R. 1998. Toward an integrated model of work experience. *Personnel Psychology*, 51, 321–355.

Tung, R.L. 1998. American expatriates abroad: From neophytes to cosmopolitans. *Journal of World Business*, 33, 125–144.

Vance, C.M. 2005. The personal quest for building global competence: A taxonomy of self-initiating career path strategies for gaining business experience abroad. *Journal of World Business*, 40, 374–385.

Wittig-Berman, U. & Beutell, N.J. 2009. International assignments and the career management of repatriates: The boundaryless career concept. *International Journal of Management*, 26, 77–88.

Yao, C. 2014. The impact of cultural dimensions on Chinese expatriates' career capital. *The International Journal of Human Resource Management*, 25, 609–630.

Part IV

Implementing career research; interventions

20

Career counseling

Andreas Hirschi and Ariane Froidevaux

Introduction

The career counseling profession is both large and highly influential in the sense that many individuals rely on counselors to guide them in their career decisions and help them find meaning and purpose in their careers. The need for career counseling is substantial. To take the United States as an example, 61 percent of the 18+ US population indicated that they would seek out career assistance, according to a representative survey conducted by the US National Career Development Association (2011). However, only 24 percent reported that they had already visited a trained career counselor, which indicates that although a substantial number of the US population has already benefited from career counseling there is also a clear potential for offering career assistance to even more people. According to the Bureau of Labor Statistics (2016), in the United States over 220,000 career counselors are employed in elementary and secondary schools, college, universities, and professional schools, junior colleges, vocational rehabilitation services, and individual and family services. Around the globe, countries have established a range of career counseling services and policies (Watts and Sultana, 2004) and the European Union has specifically identified career counseling as a critical component to manage human resources, to help individuals and organizations adapt to changes in the world of work, to support citizens in the development of professional skills, and to secure and enhance economic prosperity of its member states (Council of the European Union, 2008).

There are many distinct schools of thought within the profession, drawing on distinctive theoretical foundations. In a chapter on career counseling in a previous handbook on career studies, Kidd (2007) presented a variety of career development and career counseling theories, followed by a model of general steps in a career counseling process and a summary of research on effectiveness of career counseling. In the current chapter, we focus on the two main trends in contemporary thinking on career counseling: more traditional career guidance and counseling, and career counseling within the life design paradigm that is becoming increasingly important in career counseling (Savickas et al., 2009). Moreover, we provide an updated review on research on the effectiveness of more traditional and recent forms of career counseling.

We start by differentiating between different approaches to career counseling and career guidance. We then outline four characteristics that are typical among different approaches of career guidance and counseling. This will be followed by presenting a counseling process that is aligned with more traditional approaches in career guidance, focusing on helping clients to make better career decisions. Next, we will describe a more modern approach to career counseling based on the life design paradigm. Finally, we will review research investigating the effectiveness of career interventions to promote career development among diverse clients.

Career guidance, career counseling, and life design

Career counseling can be seen as a specific application of counseling psychology. At its core, counseling psychology is about supporting people to improve the assessment of themselves, their environment, and their current challenges as well as optimizing their experiences and their behavior (Gelso and Fretz, 2001). However, career counseling is often misconceived because the word "counseling" may imply providing someone with expertise and knowledge. The word "counseling" could be interpreted in the way that clients get to know which professions would fit them best through information and advice given by the counselors. According to this conception, the counselor would provide information about certain professions and the labor market in general, based on his or her expertise. The counselor would also suggest specific occupations or career directions that fit the client. Such a view of career counseling is, however, not in accordance with a modern understanding of career counseling as described in this chapter. Rather, it corresponds to what should be named vocational or career *guidance*. In guidance, the client is treated as an object that ought to be analyzed (e.g., in terms of abilities, interests, personality) and for whom corresponding work environments and occupations ought to be identified. Vocational guidance thus aims to match the client with work that resembles his or her objective traits and abilities. In such an approach, the career counselor acts as an expert for assessment and information about the world-of-work.

In contrast, more recent approaches speak of career counseling or *career construction* (Savickas, 2013) within the *life design* paradigm (Savickas et al., 2009; Nota and Rossier, 2015). According to these approaches, career counseling is about helping clients to construct a subjectively meaningful identity, to increase their self-reflection, and to help them create their career according to their personal identity and life story. This approach can be seen as closely related to what is sometimes referred to as *career coaching*. To what extent the two forms of career assistance overlap depends on the specific content of the career coaching, which can be highly heterogeneous. Generally speaking, however, career coaching is often more related to helping clients develop certain skills or attitudes that should help them in their career development. It thus more closely resembles what can be called a *career development* intervention. Such a perspective differs from career counseling in the way that helping clients in the construction of meaning and identity through narratives and stories (Savickas, 2012) is not the core aim of career coaching.

It is important to note, however, that the modern approach of career counseling does not attempt to replace the more traditional approaches of career guidance. Indeed, both of them can be combined in career interventions. For instance, helping clients to make a career decision and find an occupation which corresponds to their aspirations and opportunities is a typical approach in a career guidance framework rather than counseling. However, many typical counseling activities (e.g., self-reflection and identity construction) can also be integrated into interventions that focus on improving clients' career decision-making. Therefore, career guidance and counseling are complementary to each other and coexist in career counseling practice without a clear-cut distinction (Savickas, 2012).

Four core characteristics of career guidance and counseling

Across the traditional different approaches to career interventions from career guidance, career counseling, and life design, four core elements represent common typical characteristics: (1) a focus on psychologically healthy clients; (2) a focus on clients' resources and strengths; (3) a relatively short duration of the guidance/counseling process; and (4) considering the client in context (Gelso and Fretz, 2001).

First, career guidance and counseling are not focused on people with pathological disorders (Gelso and Fretz, 2001). Rather, career guidance and counseling aims to deal with problems, challenges, and topics that every person could be confronted with during his or her lifetime (e.g., career undecidedness, unemployment, lack of knowledge about the labor market, job dissatisfaction). The concepts and interventions in career guidance and counseling are thus primarily based on helping psychologically healthy people (Gelso and Fretz, 2001). Also, empirical findings show that people suffering from serious psychological problems (e.g., depression, anxiety, or panic attacks) benefit less from career interventions than clients without these problems (Whiston and Rahardja, 2008). Counselors therefore need to possess the competencies to recognize psychological disorders and to refer such clients to psychotherapy if needed. The therapy of psychological disorders is thus not a goal of career guidance or counseling, nor does it belong to the sphere of typical competencies of a career counselor.

Second, career guidance and counseling traditionally focus on clients' strengths and resources (Gelso and Fretz, 2001). In career guidance and counseling, it is assumed that every person possesses certain resources and strengths that can be activated and taken advantage of to enhance a positive development.

Third, career guidance and counseling typically imply a short duration process. This is also a consequence of the combination of focusing on psychologically healthy clients as well as their resources and strengths. Indeed, as we discuss below when reviewing the effectiveness of interventions, efficacy studies show that career interventions can generate maximal efficacy with as few as five to six sessions (Brown and Ryan Krane, 2000).

Fourth, career guidance and counseling both conceive of clients as embedded in a specific context. Specifically, career counselors take into account how the individual interacts with their environment. Therefore, gaining clarity about personal interests, strengths, and goals is only one aspect of the guidance and counseling process. It is equally important to link these personal factors with the environment. This may imply the more proximal social environment (e.g., how personal interests and goals are influenced by and influence the spouse of the client), as well as the more distal macro-environment such as the labor market (e.g., how personal interests and goals are shaped by and may be realized in the current labor market).

Career guidance and counseling for better career decisions: the CIP model

Ever since its emergence, career guidance has placed a strong emphasis on helping people with their career decisions and overcoming career indecision (Hartung and Blustein, 2002). Until today, research into the environmental and personal factors that create career indecision (Gati et al., 1996), examinations of different career decision-making styles and their effects on indecision (Gati and Levin, 2012), or strategies to cope with career indecision (Lipshits-Braziler et al., 2015), are an important foundation of career guidance and counseling research and practice. One of the most prominent and frequently researched models to assist clients in making better career decisions is the cognitive information-processing approach (CIP) by Sampson et al. (2004). The CIP postulates a model of career guidance and decision-making based on a general process of problem solving, represented in the CASVE circle (named after the starting letters of the five stages of the proposed process). The first stage of the CASVE Model is communication (C), followed by analysis (A), synthesis (S), valuing (V), and finally execution (E) (see Figure 20.1).

During the initial *communication* stage, the current situation of the client is assessed and the discrepancy between the current state and the desired state is clarified. Obtaining a clear understanding of the situation and the current difficulties and challenges of the client is the core task in this phase. Also, counselor and client should define specific and measurable goals for the counseling process as well as identify concrete steps and processes that are necessary to successfully realize the established counseling goals. In this first phase, it is also important to build the foundation for a solid working alliance between the counselor and the client. A clear understanding and mutual agreement upon the goals, the tasks involved in the counseling process, as well as a trusting relationship (i.e., respect, acceptance of the client, and empathy for his or her situation and actions) between the counselor and client, constitute such working alliance (Bordin, 1979).

During the subsequent stage of *analysis*, the client's self-awareness should be enhanced (interests, competencies, goals, personality, values, life situation, influences of the environment). Also, clients should gain a broader knowledge of the working environment and specific vocational possibilities. Clients can receive help in enhancing their reflection about their own person and situation by applying for example psychological assessments (e.g., ability tests, interest inventories), structured interviews, or counseling techniques such as reformulation (rephrasing what the client has said to improve clarity and understanding), summaries (integrating several aspects of what the client said into a more concise and clear statement), or open questions (questioning that requires further elaboration from the client and that cannot simply be answered by "yes" or "no"). Additionally, improving the client's knowledge about his or her vocational possibilities can be achieved, for example, if the counselor provides the client with important information about the labor market or certain occupations. In addition, the client could be encouraged and

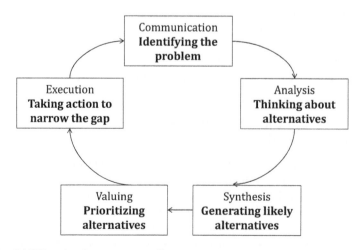

Figure 20.1 CASVE cycle of career counseling
Source: After Sampson et al. (1992).

instructed to look for further career information and the counselor would help the client to evaluate and integrate this information and apply it to his or her current situation.

During the *synthesis* stage, possible solutions for the current career problem ought to be developed, which can be done in two steps. During the first step, as many solutions/career options as possible are developed. This process is called elaboration. Second, solutions/career options not corresponding to the client's identified key aspects of preferred options are filtered out. Through this so-called crystallization process, the client should reduce the large range of considered possibilities to a more manageable number of three to seven alternatives (Sampson et al., 2004). The main purpose of this stage is to get the client to identify a few career alternatives that are both realistic and corresponding to personal key preferences.

During the subsequent *valuing* stage, the options identified during the synthesis stage are evaluated in more detail. Advantages and disadvantages, chances and risk for the client and the environment (e.g., implication for one's spouse) should be discussed and written down in this stage. Based on such a detailed evaluation of each alternative, the client should then attempt to rank the alternatives according to his or her preferences and thereby determine a first and second choice. The main goals of this phase are thus to conduct a profound analysis of the different options and to make a decision about the next career step.

During the final *execution* stage, a plan or strategy to realize the chosen career option is developed. Hereby, it is important to determine specific intermediate goals, to identify and activate resources of the client, to develop strategies for handling drawbacks during the realization of the plan, and to establish concrete next action steps.

The end of the execution stage leads to a return to the communication stage. At this point, the client and counselor should evaluate if the client had overcome the formerly identified discrepancy between his or her current and desired state. Depending on the objectives of the counseling process, this evaluation can take place directly during the last counseling session, or some months afterwards. If it turns out that the desired state has not been reached, the client and counselor can initiate a new counseling cycle by repeating the CASVE process.

Theoretically, this cycle can be completed during one counseling session. However, more likely, several sessions will be needed, especially for clients in complex career situations without sufficient environmental support (e.g., familial support, organizational support), or for clients with few competencies (e.g., job skills) or few internal resources (e.g., self-esteem). Moreover, it is possible that completing a single stage can take several sessions until the aims of this stage are satisfactorily achieved. Finally, it should be said that this procedure is a prototype that does not have to be accomplished in exactly the same way as theoretically suggested. Depending on the client and the career issue, it is possible to change the chronology of the stages. For example, if a client already has clear ideas about possible professions but struggles with the decisions between these possibilities, it makes sense to start directly with the valuing stage. If needed, it is always possible to return to earlier stages, for example, if it appears during the valuing stage that the client needs more clarity about his or her personal preferences (analysis stage) or has insufficiently considered alternative possibilities (synthesis stage) (Sampson et al., 2004).

The life design paradigm of career counseling

Life design has recently emerged as the new paradigm for career counseling in the 21st century (Savickas et al., 2009; Savickas, 2012). Its goal is to initiate activities that foster self-making, career construction, and shape identities (Savickas, 2010). In sum, "life design, from the *project* perspective of social constructionism, views clients as *authors* who may be characterized by autobiographical *stories* and who may be helped to *reflect* on life *themes* with which to construct their careers" (Savickas, 2012). As nine scholars from seven countries introduced life design, they justified the need for a new paradigm by invoking the crisis of "the new social arrangement of work" (Savickas et al., 2009: 240). This arrangement refers to the new social contract between employees and organizations (i.e., careers are own by the individuals) due to new information technologies and globalization processes. Later, Guichard (2015) detailed three main factors that explain the emergence and importance of the life design paradigm. First, Western societies have become a *liquid* modernity, because social structures and institutions no longer maintain their shape for a long time (i.e., solidify) but melt. Thus, they cannot serve as frames of reference for individuals' behaviors any more. As a result, individuals have to define by themselves what their lives mean to them. Put differently, their key personal values become the frames of reference that guide their behaviors and actions.

Second, Guichard (2015) argues that the organization of work and the distribution of jobs have changed from predictable career steps to flexible employment. Concretely, workers are gathered in networks for the duration of a specific assignment only, thus distinguishing between core and peripheral workers (i.e., long-term employees versus those hired when the economic market is good). Similarly, self-employment is increasing, and the responsibility of individuals' career trajectories has shifted from the organization to individuals.[1]

Finally, the third factor evoked by Guichard (2015) is that scientific approaches to studying human behaviors have evolved. Behaviors are seen as less determined by individuals' past experiences and are rather understood in terms of meaning constructing processes (Guichard, 2004). Humans are further viewed as less unified but plural, having been described as speaking with different voices (Gergen, 2009), or as made of a collection of self-efficacy beliefs (Bandura, 1977). Such a plural view further implies that humans are in greater search of giving their life unity, meaning, and coherence. For instance, exploring one's specific life themes (Savickas, 2011) allows increased meaning and coherence of the self.

The life design paradigm reunites constructivist and social constructionism theoretical approaches. While the *constructivist* lens conceives that individuals make meaning of the world through their cognitive structures, the *social constructionism* lens sees individuals as co-constructing meaning through narratives and relationships (Hartung, 2013). Thus, reality is highly subjective, both at the individual (psychological constructivism) and collective (social constructionism) levels. Notably, the *narrative perspective* focuses on careers as stories that define individuals' identities and provide meaning to their life trajectories (Del Corso and Rehfuss, 2011). In particular, three distinct perspectives that include narratives in career theory and intervention have been suggested (Hartung, 2013): career as meaning-making (i.e., work as shaping life's meaning), career as a life theme (i.e., emerging from several career-related tasks), and career as a story. The last form includes an author who tells the story, a specific context of the story, actions to reach a career goal, and resources used to achieve the goal (Hartung, 2013). Specifically, authors build stories about their career experiences because such stories allow them to fulfill personal motives related to purpose (i.e., objective or subjective), value and justification (e.g., being right or good), efficacy (i.e., control), and self-worth (Baumeister and Newman, 1994). Moreover, stories or self-narratives have been argued to help individuals reconstruct their identities during career transitions. Adopting a social constructionist view, Ibarra and Barbulescu (2010) suggested that workers engage in narrative identity work in interpersonal interactions: Based on others' feedback, individuals revise their stories in order to facilitate the expression of their new role identity, which, in turn, fosters adjustment to work transitions.

Further, according to *career construction theory* (Savickas, 2013), careers are constructed as persons make choices in which their self-concepts are expressed, that is, as individuals derive meaning from their vocational behaviors. Specifically, career construction theory has highlighted three key features: (a) vocational personality (i.e., career-related abilities, needs, values, and interests, that foster individuals' reputations among a group of people and define *what* career they construct); (b) career adaptability (i.e., *how* individuals construct their careers, by being concerned about their future as workers, increasing personal control over their vocational future, displaying curiosity by exploring possible selves, and strengthening confidence to pursue their career aspirations); and (c) life themes (i.e., *why* individuals construct their careers, the meaning behind making a specific career choice). As a result, careers are subjectively defined in a coherent and meaningful story that integrates various jobs. Put differently, career experiences from the past, present, and those expected in the future are reunited into a coherent life theme.

Career counseling interventions from a life design perspective

Overall, life design fosters career counseling interventions that make meaning of experiences (Hartung, 2013). This is achieved through autobiographical stories that link individuals' present with their past and future (Savickas, 2012). Specifically, four steps of a life design intervention have been identified see Figure 20.2 (Savickas, 2012, 2015).

In the first step of *construction*, career counselors aim to help a client construct his or her career through small stories. Concretely, Savickas (2015) suggested that after having explored clients' goals for the plot that they would like to co-construct in the career counseling process, career counselors asked five basic questions to foster stories about the origins of the self. Such questions explore clients' favorite book or movie, magazines or television shows, a motto, role models, and early memories. Further, career counselors need to ask clients to describe the circumstances under which they have been disconnected from the current episode of their story (i.e., a tension). Doing so, clients engage in narratives that shape such transitional discontinuations. Second, career counselors and clients *deconstruct* these stories by identifying self-limiting

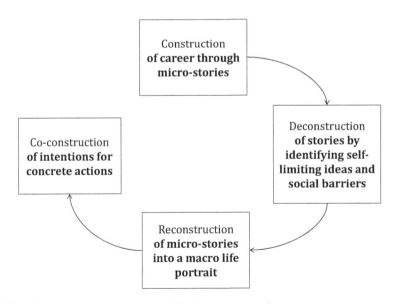

Figure 20.2 Career counseling steps in a life design approach
Source: After Savickas (2012, 2015).

ideas and cultural barriers, which overcome more "life-enhancing alternatives" (Savickas, 2015). Third, career counselors and clients work on a *reconstruction* from micro- to macro-narratives, in order to rearrange stories into a life portrait (i.e., identity narrative). Fourth, the life portrait is revised so that the identity narrative becomes clearer. Such revisions further provide the opportunity to explore clients' emotions and inner thoughts; and represent a means for coping with current problems. This last step is thus referred to as the *co-construction* of intentions, given that a clearer life portrait can be more easily extended into the future and guide concrete actions.

In order to successfully conduct career counseling based on a life design approach, McIlveen (2015) highlighted that career counselors need both basic and enhanced competencies for life design. While the former include general competencies that are needed to conduct career guidance (e.g., psychological assessment, knowledge about the world-of-work), enhanced competencies are specific to the life-design paradigm and allow career counselors to reformulate clients' life stories. Among them, *dialogical interpretation* can be related to conversations involved in the narrative process of an autobiographical storytelling, where career counselors adopt a specific position. Dialogical interpretation prevents career counselors from adopting the position of an expert, as in the case of career guidance. By contrast, career counselors in life designing need to adopt the position of a committed co-editor or co-author, while the client is in the position of the editor or author. Put differently, the professional is the carpenter, while the client is the architect (Savickas, 2015). A second enhanced competency, the *ethic of critical reflexivity*, serves the development of professional skills and the production of new knowledge. Concretely, having space to reflect upon one's practice through supervision allows career counselors to deal with the levels of intimacy and trust necessary to work with clients in the position of a co-author.

Effectiveness of career interventions

General effectiveness

Given the variety of different approaches regarding how career guidance and counseling can be conducted, the question emerges if career interventions have in fact benefits for clients' career development. Over the last decades, it has become well-established that career interventions generally have a positive effect on diverse outcomes of career development for recent overviews see Whiston and Noblin James, 2013; Hooley, 2014; Whiston et al., 2017. Most typically, the success of career interventions is assessed with outcomes such as increased levels of career decidedness, career exploration activities, or career knowledge. The first meta-analysis supporting the general effectiveness of career interventions was carried out by Spokane and Oliver (1983). They showed that clients receiving various kinds of guidance and counseling showed on average a greater improvement in outcome criteria such as career decidedness and career knowledge than 81 percent of a control group without an intervention. Later meta-analyses found a medium effect size of 0.34 for career choice courses for adults (Baker and Taylor, 1998), or mean effect sizes between 0.30 and 0.80 across different career interventions (Brown and Ryan Krane, 2000; Whiston et al., 1998, 2017). The strength of these effects is comparable with the effectiveness of other psychological interventions in counseling and psychotherapy (Whiston, 2002). If we take a conservative value of the effectiveness of career interventions with an effect size of 0.30, this means that the average client after an intervention shows higher values in the assessed outcomes than 62 percent of a control group without an intervention (Whiston, 2002). In a review of the last 45 years of career intervention research, Spokane and Nguyen (2016) concluded that research has made great progress in studying the effectiveness of career interventions. However, they also indicated that, instead of only restrictedly focusing on results and outcomes of an intervention, an enhanced focus on the evaluation of the processes in career counseling is now necessary. Additionally, Spokane and Nguyen (2016) urged future interventions not only to be designed and evaluated for single clients or smaller groups but also for whole populations (for example school graduates, adults from a socially disadvantaged background). Finally, they pointed out that more research on long-term interventions, containing several points of intervention over time, would be needed. Despite these limitations in the current research and needs for future investigations into the processes and effectiveness of career interventions, one can state that diverse kinds of career interventions generally have a positive and significant effect on clients.

Effectiveness of specific types of career interventions

While the general effectiveness of career interventions has been confirmed, several meta-analyses suggest that different forms of career interventions are associated with different levels of effectiveness for the same outcomes (Oliver and Spokane, 1988; Whiston et al., 1998, 2017). Generally, individual counseling achieves the biggest effects per session. However, it is also the most expensive and time-consuming approach. Also, meta-analyses showed that interventions lacking direct support from a counselor (e.g., self-exploration, computer programs) were significantly less effective than interventions that included a direct contact with a qualified counselor (Whiston et al., 1998, 2003, 2017). The most recent meta-analyses on this topic (Whiston et al., 2003, 2017) also reported that various types of interventions are associated with different levels of effectiveness. However, often these differences were not statistically significant. Significant differences in the mean value of effectiveness appeared nevertheless between unstructured group counseling (where there is a freely held discussion about certain topics) and structured workshops, which, according to the analyses of Whiston and colleagues (2003), proved to be significantly more effective. This may be the case because well-designed structured interventions contain more elements that make career interventions particularity effective (see more on this below) (Whiston et al., 2003). Additionally, both recent meta-analyses reported a significant variance in the effects of the career workshops. This suggests that a positive mean effect for a certain kind of intervention (e.g., workshops) does not automatically make all interventions of that kind similarly effective.

Other studies examined the influence of the duration of a career intervention on its effectiveness. Somewhat surprisingly, meta-analyses (Whiston et al., 1998, 2003) found no strict linear relation between the duration of an intervention and its effectiveness. Hence, longer career interventions might not automatically be more effective. The biggest effect size was found for interventions with a duration of 9 or 10 sessions (Whiston et al., 1998). However, another meta-analysis on this topic (Brown and Ryan Krane, 2000) showed that the clients' subjective evaluation of the efficacy of career counseling increased strongly with every session, reached its peak with the fourth or fifth session, and fell dramatically afterwards. Therefore, from the client's point of view, a counseling process with four or five sessions showed the highest efficacy.

These results have many important implications for career counseling practice. They reveal that short interventions also can achieve solid effects if they are well-planned and structured. Thus, structured workshops especially seem to be an effective and cost-effective intervention form for many clients. Furthermore, the results of these studies point to the central role of the counselor for an intervention to be effective. Interventions where clients worked all by themselves, using self-exploration activates or websites, were distinctively less effective than working with a counselor in person. Moreover, the results imply that the biggest effects in the shortest time possible can be achieved by individual career counseling. However, if the focus is on assisting as many people as possible with limited resources, group interventions, specifically in the form of structured workshops, could be applied.

Effectiveness of life design interventions

While most existing intervention research was conducted within more traditional career guidance and counseling frameworks, recent research has started to investigate the effectiveness of interventions based on the life design paradigm. An increasing number of publications have noted the potential usefulness of many life design interventions across various populations, ranging from young (Masdonati and Fournier, 2015) to older adults (Froidevaux, 2018). Some studies reported the effectiveness of life design interventions through increased career adaptability, among Italian middle school students using an online life design career intervention group (Nota et al., 2016), and among South African adolescents using group-based life design counseling sessions (Maree and Symington, 2015). Other studies further reported beneficial results of life design interventions on career decision-making. For instance, group-based life design counseling sessions (i.e., career-story interview) allowed Italian entrepreneurs to decrease their career decision-making difficulties (i.e., lack of information and inconsistent information) and to increase their career decision-making self-efficacy (Di Fabio and Maree, 2012). In addition, life-design group (LDG) settings allowed US undergraduate students to decrease their career indecision and increase their readiness for making career decisions about an academic major (Barclay and Stoltz, 2016). Finally, an improvement in vocational certainty – but not in career maturity – was observed in a case study with a Portuguese adolescent, using life-design counseling (Cardoso et al., 2016). In sum, a high degree of heterogeneity characterizes the life-design interventions that have been evaluated thus far, as they include both face-to-face and virtual sessions, in both individual and group career counseling settings.

Effectiveness of certain career intervention elements

Given the large array of existing career interventions, an important question to be addressed is whether effective career interventions share some common elements. Several studies showed that in psychological counseling more generally, factors such as clients' abilities, strengths, or attitudes in addition to a solid counseling relationship (i.e., working alliance) between counselor and client were vital for the effectives of counseling (Ahn and Wampold, 2001). This suggests that which specific counseling techniques or models are applied seems to be less important for a successful counseling outcome compared to more general factors, such as the quality of the helping relationship between the client and the counselor. In fact, diverse authors (e.g. Corey, 1996) emphasized a real, emphatic, and respectful relationship between the counselor and the client in the sense of Rogers (1951), as the most important factor for the success and effectiveness of any counseling. Supporting the importance of the client-counselor relationship, in career counseling specifically, several studies (e.g. Anderson and Niles, 2000; Masdonati et al., 2009, 2014) found that adult clients considered the emotional support provided by the counselor as well as a positive working relationship as the most crucial factors for the success in career counseling. In sum, the relationship element of the working alliance (Bordin, 1979) seems to be particularly important for career counseling effectiveness.

Despite the importance of the general helping relationship, a meta-analysis (Brown and Ryan Krane, 2000) and a follow-up study by Brown and colleagues (2003) concluded that five elements make a career intervention especially effective:

- Clients reflect upon and write down their career and life goals (e.g., by having an exercise book or by the application of written exercises);

- Counselors provide individual interpretations and feedback to the clients (e.g., based on test results);
- Counselors provide current information about the world of work and support clients in obtaining such information outside of the counseling session;
- Clients learn about effective career behavior by models and mentors;
- Counselors help clients to develop supportive networks to help them achieve their career goals.

However, a recent meta-analysis focusing on a different outcome criterion (i.e., career decision-making self-efficacy vs. career maturity in Brown and Ryan Krane, 2000) could not replicate these findings entirely. This meta-analysis also found that workbooks and written exercises seemed to be critical elements of effective career interventions. In addition, this study found that counselor support, values clarification, and psychoeducational interventions were proven to be specifically effective. Hence, the elements of effective interventions identified by Brown and colleagues (2003) remain an important point of reference when planning and conducting career interventions. However, which elements are most effective might also depend on the specific outcome that an intervention aims to enhance.

Conclusions and avenues for future research

Career counseling as a specific application of psychology and as part of the broader field of counseling psychology represents a varied array of types of career interventions in which diverse groups of clients are supported in various concerns about educational, vocational, and career issues. Among others, the scientific literature on career guidance and counseling contains models that focus on how to structure a guidance and counseling process, how to assist clients in their career decision-making, as well as how to help clients construct a meaningful career identity. Further, the effectiveness of different career interventions is relatively well documented. However, research on career counseling effectiveness has focused mainly on results such as career decidedness, knowledge about careers, or planning clarity. Future research should also increasingly examine how important aspects of modern career theories could be promoted by career counseling, such as a protean career orientation (Hall, 2004), social-cognitive aspects of career self-management (Lent, 2013), or personal and environmental career resources (Hirschi, 2012). Therefore, future research should focus on the effectiveness and processes of interventions based on recent career development and career counseling theories, to identify which kind of intervention achieves what kind of short- and long-term outcomes, with what kind of clients.

This seems especially true for the life-design paradigm. Since its introduction (Savickas et al., 2009), research and practice in career counseling within the life design paradigm has grown rapidly. However, three open questions remain regarding future research in this area. First, as highlighted above, many forms of life design interventions have emerged (i.e., individual and group settings, specific booklets or interviews) and a variety of methods have been used to measure their effectiveness (i.e., questionnaires, thematic content analyses, case-studies). Thus, we believe that it is important to avoid confusion stemming from a growing number of interventions that refer to the life design paradigm but use very different methods and processes. Future research needs to more systematically compare the characteristics and the relative effectiveness of the existing interventions, for example regarding the promotion of client reflexivity (Savickas, 2016). Replication studies of the effectiveness of a specific intervention are further required. Second, despite the initial support of its effectiveness, there is a need to identify specific outcome criteria according to which career counselors may assess whether clients have defined a clearer view of themselves, or have implemented concrete actions that are closer to their life portrait and core values (Cohen-Scali and Kokosowski, 2010). Finally, while career guidance and career counseling are recognized to coexist in career counseling practice (Savickas, 2012), it is necessary to define more precisely the criteria that would determine in which situation, and for which client, it would be more advisable to focus on one or the other approach. For instance, Cohen-Scali and Kokosowski (2010) have argued that life design interventions were not only lengthy and demanding for clients, but that the reliance on dialog and self-reflection might limit their applicability to many populations (e.g., those with lower levels of education or an immigration background) and counseling settings (e.g., short term interventions).

The overall challenge for the future practical application of career counseling is to continue developing professional standards and to apply them over a broad range on a global scale. For this, the profession of career counseling possesses valuable experience over decades and profound research. These advantages should be specifically integrated in career counseling education and practice. Additionally, the training of career counselors based on modern approaches to career development and counseling should be continuously improved and developed. In our view, this should include integrating recent scientific knowledge about career development. This is how career counseling will continue to thrive as a field of research and practice that encompasses many competencies, processes, and lines of scientific research.

Acknowledgement

The contribution of Dr. Ariane Froidevaux was supported by a fellowship financed by the Swiss National Science Foundation.

Note

1 It should be noted here that the popular notion that careers have become highly flexible and boundaryless is increasingly criticized as being based more on conventional wisdom than scientific evidence. For instance, Rodrigues, R.A. & Guest, D. 2010. Have careers become boundaryless? *Human Relations*, 63, 1157–1175, relied on job stability labor data to argue against the collapse of the traditional predictable career model.

References

Ahn, H. & Wampold, B.E. 2001. Where oh where are the specific ingredients? A meta-analysis of component studies in counseling and psychotherapy. *Journal of Counseling Psychology*, 48, 251–257.

Anderson, W.P. & Niles, S.G. 2000. Important events in career counseling: Client and counsellor descriptors. *Career Development Quarterly*, 48, 251–263.

Baker, S.B. & Taylor, J.G. 1998. Effects of career education interventions: A meta-analysis. *Career Development Quarterly*, 46, 376–385.

Bandura, A. 1977. Self-efficacy: Toward a unifying theory of behavioral change. *Psychological Review*, 84, 191–215.

Barclay, S.R. & Stoltz, K.B. 2016. The life-design group: A case study assessment. *The Career Development Quarterly*, 64, 83–96.

Baumeister, R.F. & Newman, L.S. 1994. How stories make sense of personal experiences: Motives that shape autobiographical narratives. *Personality and Social Psychology Bulletin*, 20, 676–690.

Bordin, E.S. 1979. The generalizability of the psychoanalytic concept of the working alliance. *Psychotherapy: Theory, Research and Practice*, 16, 252–260.

Brown, S.D. & Ryan Krane, N.E. 2000. Four (or five) sessions and a cloud of dust: Old assumptions and new observations about career counseling. *In:* Lent, R.W. & Brown, S.D. (eds.) *Handbook of Counseling Psychology.* New York: John Wiley & Sons.

Brown, S.D., Ryan Krane, N.E., Brecheisen, J., Castelino, P., Budisin, I., Miller, M. & Edens, L. 2003. Critical ingredients of career choice interventions: More analyses and new hypotheses. *Journal of Vocational Behavior,* 62, 411–428.

Cardoso, P., Goncalves, M.M., Duarte, M.E., Silva, J.R. & Alves, D. 2016. Life design counseling outcome and process: A case study with an adolescent. *Journal of Vocational Behavior,* 93, 58–66.

Cohen-Scali, V. & Kokosowski, A. 2010. La question de l'opérationnalisation du modèle de la construction de sa vie [Issues about applying the Life designing model]. *L'Orientation Scolaire et Professionnelle,* 39, 87–99.

Corey, G. 1996. *Theory and Practice of Counselling and Psychotherapy.* Pacific Grove, CA: Brooks/Cole.

Council of The European Union. 2008. *Entschließung Nr. 15030/08 des Rates der Europäischen Union und der im Rat vereinigten Vertreter der Regierungen der Mitgliedstaaten vom 21.11.2008: Bessere Integration lebensbegleitender Beratung in Strategien für lebenslanges Lernen.* Brüssel.

Del Corso, J. & Rehfuss, M.C. 2011. The role of narrative in career construction theory. *Journal of Vocational Behavior,* 79, 334–339.

Di Fabio, A. & Maree, J.G. 2012. Group-based life design counseling in an Italian context. *Journal of Vocational Behavior,* 80, 100–107.

Froidevaux, A. 2018. A life design perspective on the work to retirement transition. *In:* Cohen-Scali, V., Rossier, J. & Nota, L. (eds.) *New Perspectives on Career Counseling and Guidance in Europe.* Cham, Switzerland: Springer.

Gati, I., Krausz, M. & Osipow, S.H. 1996. A taxonomy of career decision-making difficulties. *Journal of Counseling Psychology,* 43, 510–526.

Gati, I. & Levin, N. 2012. The stability and structure of career decision-making profiles: A 1-year follow-up. *Journal of Career Assessment,* 20, 390–403.

Gelso, C. & Fretz, B. 2001. *Counseling Psychology.* Belmont, CA: Wadsworth Group/Thomson Learning.

Gergen, K.J. 2009. Relational being: Beyond self and community. New York, NY: Oxford University Press.

Guichard, J. 2015. From vocational guidance and career counselling to life design dialogues. *In:* Nota, L. & Rossier, J. (eds.) *Handbook of Life Design: From Practice to Theory, from Theory to Practice.* Boston, MA: Hogrefe Publishing.

Guichard, J. 2004. Se faire soi [Making oneself self]. L'Orientation Scolaire et Professionnelle, 33, 499–533.

Hall, D.T. 2004. The protean career: A quarter-century journey. *Journal of Vocational Behavior,* 65, 1–13.

Hartung, P.J. 2013. Career as story: Making the narrative turn. *In:* Walsh, W.B., Savickas, M.L. & Hartung, P.I. (eds.) *Handbook of Vocational Psychology: Theory, Research, and Practice.* New York: Routledge.

Hartung, P.J. & Blustein, D.L. 2002. Reason, intuition, and social justice: Elaboration on Parsons's career decision-making model. *Journal of Counseling and Development,* 80, 41–47.

Hirschi, A. 2012. The career resources model: An integrative framework for career counsellors. *British Journal of Guidance & Counselling,* 40, 369–383.

Hooley, T. 2014. *The Evidence Base on Lifelong Guidance: A Guide to Key Findings for Effective Policy and Practice.* Saarijärvi, Finland: The European Lifelong Guidance Policy Network.

Ibarra, H. & Barbulescu, R. 2010. Identity as narrative: Prevalence, effectiveness, and consequences of narrative identity work in macro work role transitions. *The Academy of Management Review,* 35, 135–154.

Kidd, J.M. 2007. Career counseling. *In:* Gunz, H. & Peiperl, M. (eds.) *Handbook of Career Studies.* Thousand Oaks, CA: Sage.

Lent, R.W. 2013. Career-life preparedness: Revisiting career planning and adjustment in the new workplace. *The Career Development Quarterly,* 61, 2–14.

Lipshits-Braziler, Y., Gati, I. & Tatar, M. 2015. Strategies for coping with career indecision: Convergent, divergent, and incremental validity. *Journal of Career Assessment,* 25, 183–202.

Maree, J.G. & Symington, C. 2015. Life design counselling effects on the career adaptability of learners in a selective independent school setting. *Journal of Psychology in Africa,* 25, 262–269.

Masdonati, J. & Fournier, G. 2015. Life design, young adults, and the school-to-work transition. *In:* Nota, L. & Rossier, J. (eds.) *Handbook of Life Design: From Practice to Theory, from Theory to Practice.* Boston, MA: Hogrefe Publishing.

Masdonati, J., Massoudi, K. & Rossier, J. 2009. Effectiveness of career counseling and the impact of the working alliance. *Journal of Career Development,* 36, 183–203.

Masdonati, J., Perdrix, S., Massoudi, K. & Rossier, J. 2014. Working alliance as a moderator and a mediator of career counseling effectiveness. *Journal of Career Assessment,* 22, 3–17.

Mcilveen, P. 2015. A reflexive research approach to professional competencies for life design. *In:* Nota, L. & Rossier, J. (eds.) *Handbook of Llife Design: From Practice to Theory and from Theory to Practice.* Boston, MA: Hogrefe Publishing.

National Career Development Association. 2011. *National Survey of Working America 2011.* National Career Development Association.

Nota, L. & Rossier, J. 2015. *Handbook of Life Design: From Practice to Theory and from Theory to Practice.* Boston, MA: Hogrefe Publishing.

Nota, L., Santilli, S. & Soresi, S. 2016. A life-design-based online career intervention for early adolescents: Description and initial analysis. *The Career Development Quarterly,* 64, 4–19.

Oliver, L.W. & Spokane, A.R. 1988. Career intervention outcome: What contributes to client gain? *Journal of Counseling Psychology,* 35, 447–462.

Rodrigues, R.A. & Guest, D. 2010. Have careers become boundaryless? *Human Relations,* 63, 1157–1175.

Rogers, C.R. 1951. *Client-Centered Therapy: Its Current Practice, Implications, and Theory.* Boston, MA: Houghton Mifflin.

Sampson, J.P., Peterson, G.W., Lenz, J.G. & Reardon, R.C. 1992. A cognitive approach to career services: Translating concepts into practice. *Career Development Quarterly,* 41, 67–74.

Sampson, J.P., Reardon, R.C., Peterson, G.W. & Lenz, J.G. 2004. *Career Counseling and Services: A Cognitive Information Processing Approach.* Pacific Grove, CA: Brooks/Cole.

Savickas, M.L. 2010. Career studies as self-making and life designing. *Career Research and Development,* 23, 15–18.

Savickas, M. L. 2011. Constructing self and identity. In M. L. Savickas (Ed.), *Career Counseling* (pp. 15–35). Washington, DC: American Psychological Association.

Savickas, M.L. 2012. Life design: A paradigm for career intervention in the 21st century. *Journal of Counseling & Development,* 90, 13–19.

Savickas, M.L. 2013. Career construction theory and practice. *In:* Brown, S.D. & Lent, R.W. (eds.) *Career Development and Counseling: Putting Theory and Research to Work.* 2nd ed. Hoboken, NJ: Wiley.

Savickas, M.L. 2015. Life designing with adults: Developmental individualization using biographical bricolage. *In:* Nota, L. & Rossier, J. (eds.) *Handbook of Life Design: From Practice to Theory and from Theory to Practice.* Boston, MA: Hogrefe Publishing.

Savickas, M.L. 2016. Reflection and reflexivity during life-design interventions: Comments on career construction counseling. *Journal of Vocational Behavior,* 97, 84–89.

Savickas, M.L., Nota, L., Rossier, J., Dauwalder, J-P., Duarte, M.E., Guichard, J., Soresi, S., Van Esbroeck, R. & Van Vianen, A.E.M. 2009. Life designing: A paradigm for career construction in the 21st century. *Journal of Vocational Behavior,* 75, 239–250.

Spokane, A.R. & Nguyen, D. 2016. Progress and prospects in the evaluation of career assistance. *Journal of Career Assessment,* 24, 3–25.

Spokane, A.R. & Oliver, L.W. 1983. The outcomes of vocational intervention. *In:* Walsh, W.B. & Osipow, S.H. (eds.) *Handbook of Vocational Psychology.* Hillsdale, NJ: Lawrence Erlbaum Associates.

Statistics, B.O.L. 2016. *Occupational Employment and Wages, May 2016: 21–1012 Educational, Guidance, School, and Vocational Counselors* [Online]. Available: https://www.bls.gov/oes/current/oes211012.htm [Accessed 2016-07-28].

Watts, A.G. & Sultana, R.G. 2004. Career guidance policies in 37 countries: Contrasts and common themes. *International Journal for Educational and Vocational Guidance,* 4, 105–122.

Whiston, S.C. 2002. Application of the principles: Career counseling and interventions. *The Counseling Psychologist,* 30, 218–237.

Whiston, S.C., Brecheisen, B.K. & Stephens, J. 2003. Does treatment modality affect career counseling effectiveness? *Journal of Vocational Behavior*, 62, 390–410.

Whiston, S.C., Li, Y., Goodrich Mitts, N. & Wright, L. 2017. Effectiveness of career choice interventions: A meta-analytic replication and extension. *Journal of Vocational Behavior*, 100, 175–184.

Whiston, S.C. & Noblin James, B. 2013. Promotion of career choices. *In:* Brown, S.D. & Lent, R.W. (eds.) *Career Development and Counseling: Putting Theory and Research to Work*. 2nd ed. Hoboken, NJ: Wiley.

Whiston, S.C. & Rahardja, D. 2008. Vocational counseling process and outcome. *In:* Brown, S.D. & Lent, R.W. (eds.) *Handbook of Counseling Psychology*. New York: Wiley.

Whiston, S.C., Sexton, T.L. & Lasoff, D.L. 1998. Career-intervention outcome: A replication and extension of Oliver and Spokane (1988). *Journal of Counseling Psychology*, 45, 150–165.

21

Teaching and learning about careers

Monica Higgins and Priscilla Claman

Introduction

The prolific leadership scholar, Warren Bennis, originally made the point that *leadership cannot be taught, but it can be learned* (Bennis, 2003). The same could be said for careers. Careers cannot be taught, but they can be learned.

Careers, much like leadership, are fraught with change and uncertainty, are highly idiosyncratic and subject to a myriad of external constraints, as discussed in other chapters of this volume. Over the last decade, careers for young adults in particular have become even more of what could be called an "adaptive" rather than a "technical" challenge (Heifetz et al., 2009), given the truly turbulent times that have struck since the Great Recession in 2007–2009 and since the *Handbook of Career Studies* was last published (Gunz and Peiperl, 2007). As a result, "teaching" about careers, while still attempted in higher education institution classrooms, has had to be supplemented by substantial informal "teaching," rendering the focus on the learner and learning.

In this chapter, we investigate how careers are taught or rather, learned, through different kinds of institutions, including higher education institutions and private sector organizations. Our core thesis is that the last decade has shifted the focus to the individual as the navigator of his or her career – not in the sense of a "protean career," as scholars have debated (e.g., Rodrigues and Guest, 2010), but, rather, necessarily, due to changes in the marketplace. Given these changes, it is even more critical to understand how individuals learn and the work conditions that enable learning in today's career environment. This shift to enabling conditions is consistent with a developmental lens and offers the opportunity for us to incorporate what we know about the science of how people learn.

Given our focus here on learning, we introduce the reader to some core tenets regarding the science of learning from the education and cognitive science literatures. None of these tenets of learning are bound to a specific cultural context but rather come from studies in education and cognition that examine diverse samples of individuals from a range of country contexts (for a review, see Hattie and Yates, 2014). While a departure from traditional careers literature, these insights may provide some grounding for the kinds of programs and initiatives – whether in higher education institutions or in the private sector – that might better enable career-related learning. Indeed, we look at some general trends in the education sector that reflect just these kinds of shifts in building a set of career-ready skills for the 21st century. Further, we look at some trends in the private sector that also echo these tenets and note opportunities for future research. Before delving into the science of learning, we motivate our perspective by reflecting on some of the changes in the current career environment since the last handbook was written over a decade ago.

A decade of change in the career environment

> Careers are always careers in context.
>
> *(Mayrhofer et al., 2007: 215)*

During the more than a decade since the 2007 handbook was first published, many external contextual factors have had an effect on career thinking, teaching, and on career learning. We have chosen these three: the Great Recession, the mismatch between job skills and openings, and technological change.

The great recession

It is hard to overstate the importance of the Great Recession that occurred between January 2008 and February 2010 on jobs and careers, not just in the United States, but around the world. In the United States alone, the jobs lost numbered 8.8 million, twice that of the earlier record for job loss in the recession after World War II (Goodman and Mance, 2014: 3; Goodman and Mance, 2011: 3). The Great Recession was also notable for the breadth of industries that were affected and the unusual 19-month length of the recession (ibid: 8). Job loss was also precipitous. Monthly job losses in the six-month period from October 2008 to March 2009 averaged 712,000 jobs a month (ibid.: 5), flooding the job market with job seekers. So many jobs were lost that the systems that normally help people find work were overwhelmed. Employers couldn't keep up with the applications, phone calls, and inquiries. After all, the recruiters had been laid off, too.

Work, not careers, became the important issue for many. College graduates became one of the most affected groups, a result that persisted in a 2015 study, "nearly half of those young people who attain a four-year degree are struggling in this labor market: 44 percent are underemployed" (Schwartz, 2015: 1). These graduates may "bear a 'scar of unemployment' that lasts for years. They fall behind while others gain experience, many desperately settle for work that requires less skill than they have, and few ever catch up with their peers who were not unemployed" (Hout and Cumberworth, 2012: 2).

Even though employment in the United States has recovered to pre-recession levels, there has been a persisting impact on the long-term unemployed, those without employment for 27 weeks or more. Although long-term unemployment had declined from a high of 45 percent of the unemployed in 2010 to 31.6 percent by the end of 2014, Bureau of Labor Statistics studies show that the effects continue (Kosanovich and Sherman, 2015). As their job skills depreciate, the unemployed become more discouraged and their job search slows down, people become less employable, and "employers may view long-term unemployment as a signal of lower worker quality, thus decreasing the likelihood that a long-term unemployed person is considered for a job" (Bureau of Labor Statistics, 2016).

Although the formally acknowledged period of the Great Recession only lasted a few years, its impact on careers and work lives still reverberates. Long-term unemployed or underemployed are becoming "socially marginalized" (Prasad et al., 2007). Now, with many more individuals in the category of the socially marginalized and the prospects of future recessions always present, what is the role of career teaching and learning?

The mismatch between skills and job openings

The Great Recession increased the mismatch between skills and jobs. By June 2011, a McKinsey survey found that "41 percent of companies planning to hire more workers in the next 12 months have had open positions for six months or more" (Manyika et al., 2011: 77). At the time of the study, close to 14 million Americans were out of work. During the recession, whole industries were deeply affected by lost jobs, among them manufacturing and construction. Education and healthcare were the least affected, but those jobs were out of reach for most of those with manufacturing and construction skills.

Unlike the long-term unemployment problem, the skills-jobs mismatch has received a lot of attention from all levels of educational institutions, companies, and government. Corporations, in particular, have chosen to develop a range of programs to identify, hire, and retain the skills they need for the future. Some of those approaches to the problem will be discussed below. But from a career-learning standpoint, for those who are on the wrong side of the skill-jobs mismatch, it isn't easy to switch from a medium-skilled job to a high-skilled job. Furthermore, the skills most in demand – life sciences, engineering, computer science – take years to acquire.

From the point of view of teaching about careers, how do you direct the career learner toward "marketable skills" when career-self help books abound, promoting self actualization over marketability, such as *Do What You Love, Follow Your Passion*, and others? (e.g., Junttila, 2014).

Technological change

For many decades, technological change has both made some jobs obsolete and created others. But in the 21st century, the impact of information and communication technology is much more one-sided. The advent of algorithms for big data, artificial intelligence, and smart robots, threaten a whole range of occupations, "changing the nature of work across occupations, industries and countries." This research by Frey and Osborne estimated that "47% of the US workforce is at risk of automation as a result of these trends" (Frey and Osborne, 2015: 57).

The trend toward globalization has been facilitated by technological change. Meetings, job interviews, projects, and problems are now handled virtually, with the latest in communication technology. This means that the customer service representative in the Philippines is in competition with the customer service representative in Arizona or Ireland, enabled by technology.

Technology has also made self-employment viable on a global scale, with individuals who sell their handicrafts worldwide on sites such as Etsy, contractors who work from home like the customer service representatives for JetBlue, and the homeowners all over the world who rent out part of their homes as on Airbnb. The need for companies as structures and intermediaries for earning a living is attenuating, as musicians start their careers on YouTube and authors self publish and reach a broad audience with the support of Amazon.

The ultimate atomization of work into small, discrete tasks that are paid like piecework and held together by sophisticated software has led to more crowdsourced work, now commonly used as an adjunct to corporate IT departments and by companies that sell work by the task, such as Uber or Lyft. It is no wonder that self employment has increased, by as much as 50 percent in the years since the beginning of this century in the United States alone. With modern technology, piecing together "gigs" – or pieces of jobs – is a viable option for many in the "gig economy." By 2027, some predict that freelancers will become the workforce majority (Wertz, 2018).

Parallel to that development, is the rise of entrepreneurship as a career – to a record high of 13 percent of adults working in the United States, according to a 2013 Babson study lead by Donna Kelley (as quoted in Pofeldt, 2013). For many entrepreneurs now, the objective is not to found a company that endures the way Dave Packard and Bill Hewlett did with the company Hewlett-Packard, but to start a company and sell it to a larger company, make a lot of money, and then do the whole process over again. The trend toward buying and selling of start-up companies and their products is reflected in the rise of entrepreneurial contests at universities, in the celebrity of serial entrepreneurs such as Elon Musk and Sir Richard Branson, and in the emergence of television shows such as *Shark Tank*.

These technology-enabled changes in the world of work suggest the possibility that individuals may need to learn how to pursue a career with no or little support from employers – for at least some part of their work lives. The technology change issue, in particular, has elicited some creative responses from organizations and educational institutions, some of which will be discussed later. First, however, we shift our attention to some of the core tenets of learning science so that when we do consider these shifts in the careers context, we can understand how current solutions do or do not fit with what we know about how people learn.

The science of learning and its relationship to career education

If we consider seriously the aforementioned changes in the work environment since the previous handbook was written, then it seems appropriate that we understand much more about how people learn to navigate those challenges. As scholars, teachers, and practitioners, we propose that the science of learning will enable us to better support individuals as they navigate their careers, given the aforementioned marketplace shifts.

We note, however, that this emphasis on learning is, in and of itself, not that novel an idea. Indeed, it aligns with what was termed a "developmental perspective" in the 2007 handbook – with linkages to the early work of Freud and Jung and then to Maslow, Erikson, Alderfer, Vaillant, Levinson, and Schein. We can also see elements of this developmental lens in our definitions of "career" over time – for example, as that which encompasses the study of individual change or the passage of time (e.g., Van Maanen, 1977 as reviewed in the 2007 Handbook: 4). The notion that people learn as they grow in relationship to the environment is also evident in recent career research and is echoed in other chapters of this volume (in particular Chapters 6, 14, and 22).

Keeping with this idea that careers require individual-level learning, we offer some key tenets regarding the science of learning. These insights could aid us in helping individuals learn – not just about themselves and what they want to do with their careers – but about how their talents, career goals, and aspirations might align with the world of work that now envelops them. It may assist teaching institutions – whether those be schools or higher education institutions or companies – design more effective ways to engage individuals in career-related education.

While cognitive science is a field unto itself, we pull from the seminal work of education scholar, John Hattie and cognitive scientist, Gregory Yates, who have done scores of studies on learning. John Hattie's (2009) *Visible Learning* book (Hattie, 2009) is a robust review of the collection of research on not just what is in vogue but what actually works when it comes to education and learning. Partnering with Yates, these scholars have published a volume on the major principles and strategies of learning (Hattie and Yates, 2014). Both scholars are based out of Australia. However, the research they draw upon is situated in multiple country contexts and combines studies that draw on diverse samples of participants. Their work is geared primarily toward an education audience and yet, we believe that their insights may be useful to management audiences as well. Here, we highlight three topics on learning science and later, reveal how these are or are not covered in the teaching and learning of careers in education institutions and in private organizations: (a) prior knowledge effects and information overload, (b) the IKEA effect, and (c) multi-modal learning and the social brain. We take each in turn.

Prior knowledge effects and information overload

One of the core tenets of learning science is the idea that people are cognitive misers (De Neys et al., 2013; Kahneman and Egan, 2011). People tend to take cognitive shortcuts when confronted with large amounts of information, especially ambiguous or complex information. Scholars have shown that we experience cognitive overload all the time. Therefore, it is important to consider how information is presented as well as how individuals are motivated to sort through it, particularly when the information presented is highly complex (see Hattie and Yates, 2014).

From this perspective, the issue for complex problems such as sorting through an uncertain career environment is not so much the availability of information as it is how to *process* that information. In the field of organizational theory, this focus on how information is processed has been highlighted by scholars, such as Hansen (1999), who shows that how information is transferred is at least as important as the content and quantity of information presented. In short, more information or more access to information is not necessarily better; sorting mechanisms are critical to learning.

Sorting through vast amounts of complex information – for example, in a job search process – is a problem that can be categorized as requiring something learning scientists refer to as "deliberate thinking." Deliberate thinking is the kind of thinking that requires systematic effort, reflection, and higher-order consciousness (Evans, 2008). Unfortunately, deliberate thinking can be taxing, which results in our taking short cuts or relying on prior schemas when making decisions. As research on memory shows, as information load increases, it becomes not only more difficult to recall but also, less likely to be valued when that information is received in high volume. For example, if asked to recall 12 childhood events versus only 4, people are likely to downgrade their abilities in the higher event-recall task, even though they recalled more tasks (Winkielman et al., 1998). More generally, cognitive science suggests that we are highly selective in what we attend to and that deliberative thinking is a process that we often avoid, even when it is needed.

One way of focusing our attention is to attend to information that connects to that which we already know something about – such as our prior work experience. In the previous handbook, one chapter that touched on this idea of previous work experience influencing current career decision-making was the chapter about "career imprints" (Higgins and Dillon, 2007). In that chapter and building on the work of Stinchcombe and March (1965), the authors argued that prior work experience impacts current schemas about how to lead and make career decisions. In their study of biotechnology executives, the authors argue that prior work experience in healthcare helped these young leaders learn how to lead at the dawn of the biotechnology industry. Unfortunately, however, this prior research did not incorporate learning science in their work and so, did not delve deeply into the mechanisms that might explain the effects they observed. Learning science can help us understand how individuals make sense of uncertain and vast information in a turbulent career context like the one they studied and like the one individuals face today.

Putting these two ideas together – that people are cognitive misers and that they rely on prior experience to sort through overwhelming amounts of information – leads to a challenge, particularly for young adults and for those responsible for teaching and learning about careers: young adults may need to sort through complex information in the career environment and yet they lack the cognitive schemas that come from prior work experience to effectively take those useful short cuts. Further, they may have limited confidence or self-efficacy to gain such knowledge. In particular, the awareness that they don't know what they need to know coupled with a lack of clarity that gaining such knowledge might lead to "success" may hamper their motivation to learn (Hattie and Yates, 2014). This combination of barriers – a knowledge gap and a motivation gap – can, together, impede efforts to invest in the kind of deliberate thinking that is required to learn how to navigate a complex career environment.

Given these challenges that are inherent in the process of learning, particularly when the information presented is vast, uncertain, and overwhelming, what does cognitive science tell us about what might "work"? Of course, there are tactics that are useful in aiding memory retention and recollection in general, such as chunking information into meaningful organizing segments or using mnemonics or imagery to recall what is needed. However, these are techniques that primarily apply to what Ronnie Heifitz might call "technical challenges," those which have a clear cut answer. In contrast, "adaptive challenges" (Heifetz et al., 2009), such as those facing young adults in a turbulent career environment, may require other tactics. We turn next to topics in learning science that could help us better understand what works for these kinds of complex challenges.

The IKEA effect

One of the well-researched findings in the realm of cognitive science is the fact that people tend to value what they have struggled to achieve – whether that be completing a difficult academic assignment or exerting significant effort in order to meet set goals. For example, in a series of studies, researchers showed that individuals who were asked to assemble an IKEA product valued the product they built much more highly than those who were not asked to assemble the same product (Norton et al., 2012). These IKEA-like findings have been replicated many times, which has led to the following arguments about underlying mechanisms: when people are asked to place a value on a difficult task they just completed, their memory is triggered; people then come to recall the effort they exerted, which leads to some metacognitive assessments (e.g., that you had to "take charge" or "be responsible," which could have put some of your "self-worth" at stake, depending on the task). These self-assessments yield more favourable ratings than efforts that do not require such self-investment.

Taking this idea to the context of career decision-making suggests another reason that Ibarra's (1999) notion of "provisional selves" might be useful during the job search. As Ibarra suggested, individuals tend to make career decisions after reflecting upon the experiences of others – as they take on different provisional selves. That is, individuals do not make career decisions by taking in information in the abstract; rather, individuals need to experience different work, as best they can, through the taking hold of schemas that others possess. Building on this idea and integrating now what we know about cognitive science suggests the following: not only may it be useful from a cognitive load perspective to try on different provisional selves during the job search, it might also be helpful as a motivation tool. Trying on different roles requires deliberative thinking. This takes work. It takes effort and so, is likely to be valued. Thus, effort and investment – active investment – may be necessary, particularly in a complex and turbulent career context. This idea brings us to our final insights from learning science – that is, multi-modal learning and our social brains.

Multi-modal learning and our social brains

In addition to understanding how we value that which we put effort into, particularly on difficult tasks, it is important to recognize that when it comes to learning, the mind needs to be active. Cognitive science research shows that when our learning is memorable and so, can be recalled and put to good use, our brains have been active in the knowledge-acquisition process. That is, while we *can* learn when we are passive and not actively doing something, that passivity can be dangerous. Hattie and Yates (2014) caution that passive or implicit learning can have detrimental effects, such as not noticing when errors are being made or not challenging one's underlying assumptions; these can lead to problems in the longer run. As they report, deliberate focus and mental effort are necessary to be able to access prior information effectively, which, as we noted before, is critical to being able to make sense of new ideas and information that come our way – to learn.

Many curriculum-based typologies of how people learn do not take these dynamics into account. Traditional typologies follow a sequence, such as the following: information acquisition, comprehension, application, and evaluation (which then repeats with an assessment based upon what new information is deemed necessary). And yet, that does not appear to be the way that the mind actually works; Biggs and Collis (1982) suggest instead that there are two basic levels of learning – surface and deeper-level learning – and that in order to engage in critical thinking or the deeper level one must first have some knowledge to build upon. Put differently, one can not engage in "critical thinking" absent a subject domain; we need to have something to relate to first. And, if you lack such surface-level information, then mental models can be helpful, as discussed before with the "provisional selves" schema. Mental models can help one come up with creative "if-then" statements about what might happen under certain conditions that could enable one to solve complex problems, such as navigating one's career.

How do we acquire mental models? For years, there has been debate over whether or not individuals have certain preferences for learning or "learning styles" that should be taken into consideration by teachers. And yet, reviews of the evidence to date by cognitive scientists in Britain, Australia, and the United States all suggest that the idea that students learn best when their teaching and learning styles match is "an urban legend of educational psychology" (Lilienfeld et al., 2010: 96). There are many studies that demonstrate main effects for teaching strategies – for strategies that work to help us acquire new knowledge, irrespective of learning style preferences. Thus, preferences exist but they may not be predictive of actual learning (Hattie and Yates, 2014).

Instead, we know, for instance, that "worked examples" are critical for novices in any domain (for recent research in one such domain (algebra), see Star et al., 2015). Since novices don't have prior knowledge to fall back on, "problem-solving" in the abstract is of little use; again, novices need examples. We also know that examples tend to be more powerful when words are accompanied with pictures; multimedia is useful as our minds combine images and words well, especially when these are shown simultaneously as opposed to sequentially. Cognitive load studies have demonstrated that oftentimes instructors fail to do this and instead, pile on information using one modality, such as large amounts of reading for a class, for example, when there are limits to how much individuals can process (e.g., Clark et al., 2006).

In addition to tactics such as employing multi-modal pathways to learning as well as concrete examples that can enhance both information acquisition and retention, research shows that creating a positive social environment is important to learning as well. For example, studies show that group work can be useful not just for social reasons but because it reduces the cognitive load required to diagnose complex problems (Kirschner et al., 2011).

More generally, research shows us that we have social brains in the sense that we learn through our interactions with others and through our observations of others (Hattie and Yates, 2014). Even if we don't know personally that certain professional development efforts, for example, will lead to certain career outcomes, our observations of such connections in the lives of others can help us develop mental models or "if-then" statements that could apply to our own lives as well − or, at minimum, could be tested. Thus "social modeling" is a major vehicle for learning. It is not sufficient to take pencil and paper tests about our career preferences − particularly as young adults − as our brains naturally learn through and with others.

Taken together, these observations from learning science suggest that when it comes to learning about careers, especially in the current career environment, learning is a tricky business. Teaching so that people *can learn* and not just be exposed to information is essential. And yet, the deliberative effortful thinking that is required for learning about complex issues such as careers must take into account our tendency to take short cuts to process lots of new information, our need for mental models that help us make sense of the information we are exposed to, our tendency to value that which we put effort into, and our preference for multi-modal learning and a social learning environment. Many of these factors are or could be incorporated into the teaching and learning about careers − whether that be in education institutions and/or in private sector organizations. We address each of these environments for teaching and learning about careers in turn by examining trends in both environments and the extent to which they do or do not incorporate both marketplace shifts and what we know about the science of learning.

Trends in teaching about careers in the field of education

Although the careers research in organizational and management journals oftentimes focuses on studies of business school students, the field of education more broadly has been reconsidering the teaching and learning about careers in earnest over the last decade. And for good reason. In the education literature, three relatively separate streams of work have taken up this question of teaching about careers either directly or indirectly in recent years: (a) policy makers and experts in the field who see vocational training as a moral and societal imperative, given recent trends, (b) education entrepreneurs who are focused on reinventing schools to meet 21st-century demands for work, and (c) higher education practitioners who aspire to "teach" about careers by changing their curriculum and instructional methods. We take each in turn and relate these shifts, as appropriate, to the aforementioned insights from learning science.

Vocational education pathways to careers

Education scholars and policy makers alike have pointed to the fact that improving the quality of education is at the heart of economic progress on a global scale (Reimers and Chung, 2016). Indeed, quality education is one of the United Nations Sustainable Development Goals, to which 193 countries have committed support. Yet despite the increase in numbers of students in schools worldwide, research demonstrates that the quality of schooling has waned − that it has not led to mastery of core content or higher-order thinking skills, such as those just described as necessary for the current career environment. Further, recent reports suggest that these differences are amplified for those living in poverty (Perlman et al., 2016). Consequently, not only are some students less prepared for a changing career landscape, their education is only exacerbating the gap between what is needed and what students find themselves equipped to handle. This is especially true in underserved communities and despite the increase in schooling across the globe.

In the United States, this realization has led to a shift in some of the ways that students are taught and further, the common wisdom that the goal of early education should be to advance students to higher education, such as college. As Hoffman and Schwartz (2017) argue, despite the fact that US high school seniors surveyed expected to go to college (over 90 percent in 2008), the facts remain that only about a third actually received a four-year degree. That is, there remains a "forgotten half" that has not declined over the years, despite all the emphasis on the importance of a four-year degree, at least in the United States. Clearly, they argue, education systems must change to ensure that schools are preparing students for future careers. In Hoffman and Schwartz, 2017 book, *Learning for Careers*, these policy makers and practitioners call for a response that requires a re-alignment of education institutions' practices with labor market needs. Further, they propose that the "gold standard" of such offerings build upon cognitive science and so, include a thoughtful mix of learning modalities that include real-world learning applications, as can be achieved through apprenticeships (Halpern, 2012).

Internationally, this trend toward apprentice-based work has a long history, particularly in the developed world. However, here too, the challenges associated with bringing these new approaches to scales that require coordination with communities, states, and employers are numerous. Global scholars reflect that even if, for example, improving science education to prepare students for the changing economy should include "inquiry pedagogy" and "project-based learning," there are barriers to change that hinge upon entrenched systems of accountability and compliance that hamper innovation in schools across the globe (Reimers and Chung, 2016). Teachers, many argue, are often unable, not unwilling but unable, to implement such "active pedagogies" (e.g., Arango, 2017) and further, schools are not well-connected to their local communities to do so (e.g, Grino, 2017).

Building effective inter-organizational networks that link the vast and varied student-career initiatives of states, employers, and schools is a novel and complex idea. But, it is also an idea that has taken hold and begun to thrive in places such as Massachusetts and California in the United States (for a review, see Hoffman and Schwartz, 2017) as well as developing countries contexts such as education systems in Chile and Colombia (for examples, see Reimers, 2017) The core idea that youth need to experience, early on, real work that ties in with their academic schooling, in order to develop the skills they will ultimately need for the current workforce ties back directly to the notion of active learning and cognitive overload. As discussed previously, novices, such as young adults, need to develop mental models and schema to reflect upon as they learn – as they navigate their careers in a complex context. And, to the extent these work-based connections are done as classes or cohorts in schools, the efforts similarly tap into the social brain and provide models through social comparison that could similarly help these young adults learn about and prepare for work.

Transforming schooling

A related but separate stream of activity underway in the education sector is rethinking the traditional school-house model that can impact thinking and learning about careers. Researchers such as Wagner (2008) who study the "global achievement gap" argue that traditional style classrooms in which students sit in rows and chairs and then "sit and get" information fails to prepare them well – neither for higher education nor for the global economy.

This angle on the work force problem stresses the issue of how and what is learned in and beyond the classroom. The solution is then tied to the kinds of "complex cognitive thinking" and "deeper learning" that is needed in the classrooms and the workforce today. Therefore, the instruction in schools (or online) must shift, it is argued, to create the kinds of challenge needed to keep students both engaged and motivated while at the same time, learning new skills that will help them be productive, engaged, innovative citizens of the 21st century. This kind of thinking, spurred on by documentaries in the United States such as "Most Likely to Succeed," has created openings in the education reform movement for "flipped classrooms," "project-based learning," and "blended learning" that has created a social movement for shaking up traditional methods of schooling.

Here again, we find examples of action-oriented learning projects, such as that found in new kinds of schools, such as a US-based system of schools called Rocketship Public Schools (e.g., Robinson, 2017) where students learn calculus, history, and the arts, all while working on a theatre production. Similarly, reports from new models of schooling in Singapore as well as China, Chile, and India, have demonstrated that curriculum reform that aims for the cultivation of teaching and learning for the 21st century is not only underway, it is gaining traction (see Reimers and Chung, 2016, for examples).

This kind of active engagement fits well with what we know about the science of learning. That is, young adults not only "apply" what they are learning in terms of knowledge and subject-matter expertise, they use what they acquire while they practice and produce something, and they do so in a social setting. Thus, through specific tactics such as a theatre production or a STEM project, students exert effort, collaboratively, that helps motivate them to acquire and apply new knowledge and to learn in preparation for a changing career context.

Career instruction in higher education

The field of higher education is embarking on a host of instructional changes, some of which are likely to improve the teaching and learning of careers. Similar to trends for childhood learning, there is evidence of innovation that moves away from traditional approaches such as lecture-style instruction. Instead, the push has been for more interactive modes of engagement, some of which mirrors that which is being done in the earlier grade levels. These tactics could and should, if done well, improve the competencies of students that will be useful in the new labor market and in developing global citizens. As Reimers and Chung (2016) argue, the types of competencies needed to navigate the increasing diversity in a global market economy include intellectual openness, adaptability, critical thinking, and teamwork – that is, the kinds of skills not typically addressed through traditional methods of teaching and learning.

Further, there is a renewed emphasis among higher education institutions to offer credit in return for students' engagement in internships, signaling the legitimacy and value of this new mode of learning about careers. Online modes of teaching and learning face different challenges that are too numerous to review here. However, to the extent students are taking classes online while they are working, these online modules offer the obvious advantage of giving young adults the opportunity to more immediately apply what they have learned to their work. And, there has been a growing emphasis placed on project-based learning with consulting projects to give students real-life applications of their coursework as well as exposure to different careers and work experiences that very well may assist them in their career decision-making (Hoffman and Schwartz, 2017). Still, we know very little about the efficacy of these programs and initiatives specifically with respect to individuals' careers – in part, because we have yet to assess learning.

One similarity across these three different trends in the field of education is the ways in which these new approaches address the issue of cognitive overload in the labor market. With pathways shifting and uncertainty high as to what kinds of jobs are open for young adults, it is now more critical than ever that students have the opportunity to learn and to know how to learn prior to entering the job market. Through internships and project-based learning, the argument can be made that even if the knowledge of the specific field they choose for their career remains elusive, they are still picking up skills and receiving feedback that will help them navigate – to, as Donald Schön (Schön, 1983) said years ago, become a "reflective practitioner" or reflect as they practice. And, perhaps, through these experiences, students will be given the opportunity not just to learn but to fail – ideally, in a relatively psychologically safe environment (Edmondson, 1999), before they fully enter the labor force. As the science on learning suggests, while positive self-appraisals are useful in that they can buffer against a host of negative emotions, self-assessment is also critical to learning. Without opportunities for appraisal and feedback, it is possible that, as Hattie and Yates (2014) suggest, students can't self-check or "get real" regarding both the opportunities and challenges they face, making learning very difficult. We argue that these kinds of learning behaviors and skills may be especially important in the current career environment.

Trends in the private sector that enable career-related learning

The three contextual factors that have affected career thinking and learning since the 2007 handbook was published – the Great Recession, the mismatch between skills and job openings, and technological change – have had an impact on career-related learning in practice. Although in the United States, for example, employment appears to be back to pre-recession levels for most people, the same cannot be said for the socially marginalized or those who have difficulty competing in an increasingly high-skilled and global economy (Kosanovich and Sherman, 2015).

In the past 10 years, the private sector has focused on the skills-jobs mismatch and used technology to help resolve the problem. Generally, corporations have ignored the unemployed, considering the unemployed the province of government and social service agencies. An exception to that is the proliferation of joint programs in the United States, for example, between community colleges and local employers targeting the unemployed or the underemployed. Examples include Bunker Hill Community College in Massachusetts, which has a learn-and-earn program that places students with a consortium of local employers, or Farmingdale State College in New York State, which has a natural-gas technician certificate program in a partnership with National Grid, an energy provider. There are examples like these all over the United States (e.g., Hank, 2017). In this, the United States is behind other nations; German companies have been doing this for years (Newman and Winston, 2016).

Corporate career-related programs offered to selected employees

Talent management programs

The understanding that there was an increasing mismatch between available people and job openings and an increasing need for people with advanced technical skills was first called "the war for talent" in a 1998 McKinsey Quarterly, followed by a best-selling business book of that name by Michaels et al. (2001). Today, this concept of a "war for talent" has generated a substantial corporate response called "talent management," a term so widely used that it appears in job titles and descriptions.[1]

The talent management approach educates select employees so that they can learn and develop in their careers in a way that is deemed strategically important to the company. Although "talent management" may vary programmatically in different organizations, it generally includes "talent acquisition" or selection and hiring and various post-acquisition "talent management" activities, such as career and advancement information, training and development, leadership development and career management or development.

All of these new activities are enabled and tracked by sophisticated, cloud-based automated systems (e.g., IBM's Kenexa system) that make it possible to deliver elements of the system and evaluate results globally. One common denominator of the talent management processes is their reliance on the development and use of "competency models" or "competencies." Generally, "competencies" refer to certain individual-level characteristics that are believed to predict success as determined by an assessment of the behaviors of successful performers at the job, or organization level.[2] "Competencies have evolved to be the current best practice in defining criteria for all talent management" (Washington and Griffiths, 2015).

Competency models were first used in the early 1970s to choose junior US foreign service officers. First, the attributes of successful foreign service officers were determined and then candidates with those attributes were selected (Spencer and Spencer, 1993). The same approach is common today in organizations all over the world – in consulting firms like McKinsey, international banks like HSBC and in multinational technology firms such as Tata or Google. The firm hires for "talent" and then develops the talent to fulfill strategic needs.

Once selected for talent management programs, individuals tend to be given a lot of programmatic support for their career development. The very selection process itself exposes them to senior level management who discuss their skills and performance. A personal development plan is frequently a part of the process, with special training and internal or external coaching as well. Socially facilitated learning is usually a part of the program through the use of group work in workshops or through special projects. Further, since talent management programs tend to be organization-wide, the programs provide a natural network of relationships among those selected, so that internal opportunities are known about earlier and with an inside track to apply for them.

From a science-of-learning point of view, talent management programs can deliver far more than information and knowledge about how to develop in one's career. They usually include a social component that motivates participants to learn and grow since these programs tend to operate in a group structure. Further, participants are given a model of superior performance to strive for as well as the coaching and feedback that serve as a sorting mechanism to help them understand what makes for success in their particular circumstance.

Leadership development programs

One way to think of leadership development programs is as highly selective and well-resourced talent management programs targeted at executives and the senior leaders in an organization. Although leadership development programs in the United States predated the Great Recession, they are now common in companies all over the world. As global giants introduce leadership development programs, other organizations feel the competitive necessity to do the same, according to M. Douglas Adams of MDA Associates International. "For example, I have developed and led leadership development programs for major firms in Southeast Asia for the last twenty years, and now small to mid-level firms feel they need have their own leadership development programs to stay competitive" (D. Adams, personal communication, June 24, 2016).

The quality and content of these programs have become much more sophisticated in the last 10 years. The best now employ many of the principles of the science of learning. First, they are based on a competency model of what leadership is, articulated with story examples to explain and reinforce the competencies. This provides the mental model for participants so that they can direct their development toward specific goals and behaviors. These models can be developed from within the organization or drawn from the many available models and programs, such as the one in Kouzes and Posner's (2017) book, *The Leadership Challenge*, which was originally published in 1987.

Leadership development programs generally offer self-assessment instruments, 360-degree assessments by superiors, colleagues, and subordinates, exercises to increase skills, cases, videos, traditional presentation and discussion, and individual coaching. As learning theory suggests, these multi-modal forms of learning speed up the development process by encouraging deeper-level learning and improve participants' ability to solve problems.

Like the talent management programs described above, high-caliber leadership development programs tend to rely on group work as well as multi-modal learning. But unlike most talent management programs, leadership development programs showcase IKEA-effect group projects of substance. These projects can include bringing new products to market, automating functions, or starting a community-based service organization. The results of these projects are traditionally presented to senior executives, which increases exposure and opportunities for learning and mentoring.

Corporate universities

General Electric (GE) considers its Management Development Institute founded in 1956 to be the first corporate university. Many articles have been written about GE's corporate university, as chronicled in the book, *Career Dimensions*, originally published by GE in 1976. It was then in the 1970s that Walter Storey's career programs paved the way for corporate leadership and career development in multinational firms.

By 2011, corporate universities had grown to over 4,000 (McAteer and Pino, 2011). As corporate universities have proliferated, they have shifted from being an open-ended benefit like tuition reimbursement to a targeted benefit directed toward strategic skills. One such example is the partnership between IBM and Northeastern University, which was created to develop a world-wide course in sales.

Technology also makes delivering training globally possible. Corporations can use external university-designed and delivered programs, both online and in classrooms, as a part of their corporate university programs. Corporate universities with a university connection like Northeastern, or INSEAD in France or the University of Singapore are able to offer a full range of programs – online and in person. Some even give course credit towards certificates or even degrees in business administration. Online courses make this targeted benefit available to all. For example, Starbucks offers its employees a free bachelor of arts degree through the online resources of Arizona State University.

From a science of learning standpoint, corporate universities are only as good as their teaching partners in transmitting learning and career information. Corporate universities have been generally open to more employees than talent management programs, and any selection process tends to be transparent.

Corporate career-related programs offered to all employees

Tuition reimbursement and training budgets declined precipitously during the Great Recession, and while they have grown rapidly since, corporate career learning options have migrated toward internal web sites or webinars (Bersin, 2014).

Web-based programs

Many organizations make internal career and job information available on internal web sites. The content may include job openings, information about the hiring and the job posting process, or the application itself. Internal sites work just like the large external job boards, such as Monster (www.monster.com) or CareerBuilder (www.careerbuilder.com), so they tend to focus on jobs, with little information about careers.

When they do include career information, internal web sites often have too much complex information, without the sorting mechanisms critical to learning. Web-based programs alone are inadequate for those who are early in their careers and who lack the mental models or the internal social networks to interpret the information. As learning science suggests, without these baselines to refer to, new information can be too abstract to effectively transform an individual's way of thinking and acting.

Web-based career-related programs have a second problem: they usually do not include senior-level jobs or the informal "how to" knowledge about jobs and careers that people learn from mentors, networks and experience, such as how to present your skills and experience, how to find out what different managers are looking for, or how to be a successful internal applicant. There are some exceptions to this, but generally, these platforms are purely for information transfer or "what" to consider versus "how to" learn what may be most helpful to one's career development.

In an effort to address these problems, it is becoming a common expectation that managers give their direct reports career advice and help them use the internal web site. That is, the managers are oftentimes expected to provide the scaffolding for the employee's career-advancement efforts. This assignment may or may not be within a manager's skillset. It is logical to assume that some managers may not think it is in their best interest to help a key member of their team move on and leave their team.

Webinars

Webinars have in many cases replaced traditional training to address specific needs: Do you want to know how to write a performance review? Onboard a new employee? Hire or promote someone? There is probably a webinar or an employee self-service portal for most of these questions and more. Webinars may increase productivity for the human resources department, but they are much less effective for career learning. The amount and density of information make it difficult for individuals to digest and apply it to complex situations.

In the post–Great Recession environment, career teaching and learning in corporate settings have evolved from the open-access tuition reimbursement and open-enrollment training of the past, to a two-tiered system – excellent programs for the few that follow all or most of the tenets of scientific learning and web-based learning for everybody else. Corporate universities fall somewhere in between, depending on how the courses are designed and delivered and whether there is any coaching involved.

The rise of online career resources

For people seeking information outside of what their own organization offers them, there is a widely used alternative – online career information.

Since the last handbook was written in 2007, more and more information about careers has become available online, whether that information is reliable or not. Usually, these are recruiting web sites with corporate clients. They don't just provide information about job openings as Monster does, or about companies as Glassdoor does, or about people to contact and network with as LinkedIn does. New kinds of online resources are beginning to provide a full range of opportunities for career education that touch many career learning needs.

An unusually complete example is that of TheMuse.com, which purports to have helped over 50 million people with their careers. The site is sponsored by employers who place not just job listings but photographs of their work environment and interviews with their employees to illustrate their company culture. This multi-modal approach could enhance an applicant's ability to truly learn about that job and work environment.

This is not the usual job board with some attached career advice. It integrates many kinds of career services. TheMuse is designed to help users, whether or not they have a clear career direction or were "selected" as having "talent." The site offers a variety of assessment tools, resume templates, interview questions, photo descriptions of work place culture, video interviews with employees, postings on advancement, and other career issues – even career coaching, which assists with the "how" as well as the "what" of career education. The site also connects people with phone-based career counselors, enabling multi-modal forms of learning that are highly interactive.

Still, from a career learning standpoint, what is missing from sites like TheMuse.com are the same things that internal web sites lack: the opportunity for social or group learning and problem-solving applications of IKEA effect-like projects. There is also potential for information overload, given the breadth and complexity of these sites.

Finally, TheMuse often demonstrates limited understanding of current career research. For example, it gives information about what to do at networking events but does not provide an understanding of how to effectively build productive and useful career networks. Sometimes these sites provide information that is inaccurate. For example, although TheMuse has advised against breaking eye contact during an interview to guard against being viewed as untrustworthy, research by Mann and colleagues (2012) shows that breaking eye contact does not indicate that a person is lying.

In summary, in the last 10 years, teaching and learning about careers in organizations has changed as companies have focused intensely on bridging gaps in strategic skills. Today, specific skills training now exists through corporate universities and talent management programs. Also, much more career information is available to individuals, both from internal and external web sites. The widespread current emphasis on competencies gives individuals a mental model of how they need to develop their skills and abilities. New and sophisticated technological tools developed in the last 10 years have made all these corporate offerings available globally and to people with access to basic technology.

Although these developments suggest progress in supporting individuals who must learn how to navigate their careers in an increasingly complex and uncertain marketplace, when the learning sciences are added to the picture, the progress becomes less clear. There appear to be critical elements missing that could make that career teaching and learning even effective, such as applying what we know about the science of learning to "how" one should investigate the marketplace and apply or even sift through these various and expansive sources of information. Chief among the issues presented by these new forms of "teaching" about careers in practice are the problems of information overload in the web-based systems – corporate or online – which lack the sorting mechanisms critical to learning, like groups, mentors, or coaches. For the most part, they also lack the IKEA effect of engaging people in their own learning that increases motivation and commitment.

By contrast, the highly selective programs of leadership development and talent management are much more integrated with learning science and should be much more valuable to their participants. However, with the decline of traditional benefits such as tuition reimbursement and open-enrollment training and development, the best of corporate career education may only be available for the select few.

Conclusion and implications for careers research

The present chapter has highlighted many ways in which the career context has changed and the resultant responses by institutions in the education and private sectors that are charged with helping individuals navigate their careers today. Considering the changing career context, we highlighted the increasing importance of learning, on the part of the individual, to cope with new marketplace needs. And yet, ironically, perhaps, the careers literature as well as the careers field has not incorporated what we know about how individuals learn in either the study of careers or in the practice of helping people navigate this complex and uncertain environment. This is ironic, perhaps, for two reasons: first, we careers researchers have often noted that navigating one's career is complex and requires learning, as demonstrated in prior chapters as well as the previous handbook. Second, we do tend to gravitate toward an integration and acknowledgement of the importance of literature on career development, professional development, adult development and the like. And yet, the cognitive science of learning – if we truly believe that learning is key – has been missing.

Therefore, we see this chapter as an opportunity to both inform readers about some of the knowledge we have amassed around the science of learning and, by reviewing trends in research and the field, to open windows of opportunity for future research and practice. For example, as we notice trends in how education institutions are shifting their teaching and learning activities to incorporate more applied forms of learning to prepare students for global 21st-century skills, we need to understand as well the assumptions behind those models and whether they are "working." Right now, we have little evidence about the conditions under which certain models, such as apprenticeships or even coaching, enhance learning about oneself and one's career. The evaluation is missing. On the outcomes side, for example, we have evidence from the education literature that career-related instruction yields increments in school valuing (Orthner et al., 2013). However, in the careers research, we don't know whether or if the same is true regarding career learning. From the science of learning research, we know that employing multiple modalities (such as words as well as video) enhances transfer of knowledge, that working directly on a project from start to finish (such as assembling an IKEA desk) enhances perceived value in the task, and that social modeling (such as working in groups) assists with complex problem-solving. And yet, we have not incorporated this understanding into how we build out career development programs. Nor have we incorporated research methods that aim to parse out some of these learning mechanisms that could yield greater benefits for career-related learning. With that knowledge and with the assistance of new technology, we could spread those benefits globally. We hope this chapter has provided the motivation and the insights to embark on this new pathway forward.

Acknowledgements

We are indebted for many of the examples of corporate universities to David Abdow Dean, Executive and Enterprise Education at Babson College and former Associate Dean for Executive Programs at Northeastern University's D'Amore-McKim School of Business.

We are indebted for many of the examples of leadership development programs to M. Douglas Adams of MDA Associates International.

Notes

1 For example, even the American Society for Training and Development has become the Association for Talent Development.
2 It is important here to make a distinction between this use of the word, which refers to personal qualities or attributes, and the notion of competence, referring to skill level – a term frequently used in education or in a licensing context.

References

Arango, S.I. 2017. Skills for the 21st century: Perspectives and contributions from active urban school. *In:* Reimers, F. (ed.) *Empowering all Students at Scale*. CreateSpace Publishing.

Bennis, W. 2003. *On Becoming a Leader*. New York: Basic Books.

Bersin, J. 2014. *Spending on Corporate Training Soars: Employee Capabilities Now a Priority*, 4 February. Available: https://www.forbes.com/sites/joshbersin/2014/02/04/the-recovery-arrives-corporate-training-spend-skyrockets/#52a96398c5a7.

Biggs, J.B. & Collis, K.F. 1982. *Evaluating the Quality of Learning: The SOLO Taxonomy: Structure of the Observed Learning Outcome*. New York: Academic Press.

Bureau of Labor Statistics. 2016. An analysis of long-term unemployment. *Monthly Labor Review*, July [Online] https://www.bls.gov/opub/mlr/2016/article/an-analysis-of-long-term-unemployment.htm.

Clark, R.C., Nguyen, F. & Sweller, J. 2006. *Efficiency in Learning: Evidence-Based Guidelines to Manage Cognitive Load*. San Francisco, CA: Pfeiffer Wiley.

de Neys, W., Rossi, S. & Houdé, O. 2013. Bats, balls, and substitution sensitivity: Cognitive misers are no happy fools. *Psychonomic Bulletin & Review*, 20, 269–273.

Edmondson, A. 1999. Psychological safety and learning behavior in work teams. *Administrative Science Quarterly*, 44, 350–383.

Evans, J.S.B. 2008. Dual-processing accounts of reasoning, judgment, and social cognition. *Annual Review of Psychology*, 59, 255–278.

Frey, C.B. & Osborne, M. 2015. *Technology at Work: The Future of Innovation and Employment*. Oxford: Oxford University, UK, Citi Global Perspectives and Solutions.

Goodman, C. & Mance, S.M. 2014. *The 2007–09 Recession: Overview*. Washington, DC: Bureau of Labor Statistics, Division of Current Employment Statistics, Office of Employment and Unemployment, Washington, DC.

Goodman, C.J. & Mance, S.M. 2011. *Employment Loss and the 2007–09 Recession: An Overview*. Washington, DC: Bureau of Labor Statistics, Division of Current Employment and Unemployment.

Grino, P. 2017. Changing science teaching practice in Chile. *In:* Reimers, F. (ed.) *Empowering all Students at Scale*. Create Space Publishing.

Gunz, H. & Peiperl, M. 2007. *Handbook of Career Studies*. Thousand Oaks, CA: Sage Publications.

Halpern, R. 2012. Supporting vocationally oriented learning in the high school years: Rationale, tasks, challenges. *New Directions for Youth Development*, 134, 85–106.

Hank, J. 2017. With innovation, colleges fill the skills gap. *The New York Times*. June 7, 2017 [Online]. Available: https://www.nytimes.com/2017/06/07/education/with-innovation-colleges-fill-the-skills-gap.html [Accessed 22 July 2019].

Hansen, M.T. 1999. The search-transfer problem: The role of weak ties in sharing knowledge across organization subunits. *Administrative Science Quarterly*, 44, 82–111.

Hattie, J. 2009. *Visible Learning: A Synthesis of Over 800 Meta-Analyses Relating to Achievement*. London: Routledge.

Hattie, J. & Yates, G.C. 2014. *Visible Learning and the Science of how we Learn*. New York: Routledge.

Heifetz, R.A., Grashow, A. & Linsky, M. 2009. *The Practice of Adaptive Leadership: Tools and Tactics for Changing your Organization and the World*. Boston, MA: Harvard Business Press.

Higgins, M.C. & Dillon, J.R. 2007. Career pattern and organizational performance. *In*: Gunz, H. & Peiperl, M. (eds.) *Handbook of Career Studies*. Thousand Oaks, CA: Sage Publications.

Hoffman, N. & Schwartz, R.B. 2017. *Learning for Careers: The Pathways to Prosperity Network*. Cambridge, MA: Harvard Education Press.

Hout, M. & Cumberworth, E. 2012. *The Labor Force and the Great Recession*. Palo Alto, CA: Stanford Center on Poverty and Inequality.

Ibarra, H. 1999. Provisional selves: Experimenting with image and identity in professional adaptation. *Administrative Science Quarterly*, 44, 764–791.

Junttila, H. 2014. *Do What You Love: Essays on Uncovering Your Path in Life*. CreateSpace Independent Publishing Platform, Junttila Henry.

Kahneman, D. & Egan, P. 2011. *Thinking, Fast and Slow*. New York: Farrar, Straus and Giroux.

Kirschner, F., Paas, F., Kirschner, P.A. & Janssen, J. 2011. Differential effects of problem-solving demands on individual and collaborative learning outcomes. *Learning and Instruction*, 21, 587–599.

Kosanovich, K. & Sherman, E.T. 2015. Trends in long-term unemployment. *Bureau of Labor Statistics*, March. Available: https://www.bls.gov/spotlight/2015/long-term-unemployment/.

Kouzes, J.M. & Posner, B.Z. 2017. *The Leadership Challenge, How to Make Extraordinary Things Happen in Organizations*. Hoboken, NJ: John Wiley & Sons.

Lilienfeld, S.O., Lynn, S.J., Ruscio, J. & Beyerstein, B.L. 2010. *50 Great Myths of Popular Psychology: Shattering Widespread Misconceptions about Human Behavior*. Chichester, UK: John Wiley & Sons.

Mann, S., Vrij, A., Leal, S., Granhag, P.A., Warmelink, L. & Forrester, D. 2012. Windows to the soul? Deliberate eye contact as a cue to deceit. *Journal of Nonverbal Behavior*, 36, 205–215.

Manyika, J., Lund, S., Auguste, B.G., Mendonca, L., Welsh, T. & Ramaswamy, S. 2011. *An Economy that Works: Job Creation and America's Future*. New York: McKinsey.

Mayrhofer, W., Meyer, M. & Steyrer, J. 2007. Contextual issues in the study of careers. *In*: Mayrhofer, W., Meyer, M. & Steyrer, J. (eds.) *Handbook of Career Studies*. Los Angeles: Sage Publications.

Mcateer, P. & Pino, M. 2011. *The Business Case for Creating a Corporate University*. North Vancouver, BC: Corporate University Xchange.

Michaels, E., Handfield-Jones, H. & Axelrod, B. 2001. *The War for Talent*. Boston, MA: Harvard Business Press.

Newman, K.S. & Winston, H. 2016. *What the U.S. Can Learn from the Way German Trains Its Workforce*, 21 April. Available: https://www.fastcompany.com/3058946/what-the-us-can-learn-from-germanys-work-training-programs.

Norton, M.I., Mochon, D. & Ariely, D. 2012. The IKEA effect: When labor leads to love. *Journal of Consumer Psychology*, 22, 453–460.

Orthner, D.K., Jones-Sanpei, H., Akos, P. & Rose, R.A. 2013. Improving middle school student engagement through career-relevant instruction in the core curriculum. *The Journal of Educational Research*, 106, 27–38.

Perlman, J.R., Winthrop, R. & Mcgivney, E. 2016. *Millions Learning: Scaling up Quality Education in Developing Countries*. Washington, DC: Brookings Instituion.

Pofeldt, E. 2013. US entrepreneurship hits record high, May. *Forbes*, May 27, 2013 [Online]. Available: https://www.forbes.com/sites/elainepofeldt/2013/05/27/u-s-entrepreneurship-hits-record-high/#7a6494e31d79 [Accessed 22 July 2019].

Prasad, P., D'Abate, C. & Prasad, A. 2007. Career issues for the socially marginalized. *In*: Gunz, H. & Peiperl, M. (eds.) *Handbook of Career Studies*. Thousand Oaks, CA: Sage Publications.

Reimers, F.M. 2017. *One Student at a Time: Leading the Global Education Movement*. North Charleston, South Carolina: Fernando Reimers.

Reimers, F.M. & Chung, C.K. 2016. *Teaching and Learning for the Twenty-First Century: Educational Goals, Policies, and Curricula from Six Nations*. Cambridge, MA: Harvard Education Press.

Robinson, J. 2017. Parents must understand growth scores to make sense of student progress. *Tennessean*, September 25 [Online]. Available: https://www.tennessean.com/story/opinion/2017/09/25/

parents-must-understand-growth-scores-make-sense-student-progress/702172001/ [Accessed 22 July 2019].

Rodrigues, R.A. & Guest, D. 2010. Have careers become boundaryless? *Human Relations*, 63, 1157–1175.

Schön, D.A. 1983. *The Reflective Practitioner: How Professionals Think in Action*. New York: Basic Books.

Schwartz, R. 2015. The case for career-focused charter schools. *Thomas Fordham Institute Advancing Educational Excellence* [Online] [Accessed 22 July 2015].

Spencer, L.M. & Spencer, P.S.M. 1993. *Competence at Work: Models for Superior Performance*. New York: John Wiley & Sons.

Star, J.R., Pollack, C., Durkin, K., Rittle-Johnson, B., Lynch, K., Newton, K. & Gogolen, C. 2015. Learning from comparison in algebra. *Contemporary Educational Psychology*, 40, 41–54.

Stinchcombe, A.L. & March, J.G. 1965. Social structure and organizations. *In:* March, J. (ed.) *Handbook of Organizations*. Chicago, IL: Rand McNally.

van Maanen, J. 1977. *Organizational Careers: Some New Perspectives*. London: John Wiley & Sons.

Wagner, T. 2008. *The Global Achievement Gap: Why Even Our Best Schools Don't Teach the New Survival Skills Our Children Need and What We Can do about It*. New York: Basic Books.

Washington, E. & Griffiths, B. 2015. *Competencies at Work: Providing a Common Language for Talent Management*. New York: Business Expert Press.

Wertz, J. 2018. Why the gig economy can be essential to business growth. *Forbes*, January 23 [Online]. Available: https://www.forbes.com/sites/jiawertz/2018/01/23/why-the-gig-economy-can-be-essential-to-business-growth/#aaa6b6d25809 [Accessed 22 July 2019].

Winkielman, P., Schwarz, N. & Belli, R.F. 1998. The role of ease of retrieval and attribution in memory judgments: Judging your memory as worse despite recalling more events. *Psychological Science*, 9, 124–126.

22

HRM/organizational career management systems and practices

Silvia Bagdadli and Martina Gianecchini

The economic and social context in which organizations develop and retain human resources has changed intensely from the years when scholars initially studied and defined career management. During the 1980s and 1990s, companies were competing in steadily expanding markets, which allowed for long-term planning, so the purpose of career management practices like succession planning, job posting and skill inventory was to prepare talented individuals to achieve top management positions in the organization (Gutteridge, 1993). Today, however, uncertainty in the labour and product market requires organizations to be adaptable to volatile business conditions (Doyle, 2000). As several authors observe (Cappelli and Keller, 2014; Bidwell and Keller, 2014), in this uncertain context, organizations manage their workforces with increasing dismissals and external hiring at all organizational levels, especially for generic competencies, a phenomenon which is slowly eroding the monolithic institution of internal labor market (Doeringer and Piore, 1971).

Nevertheless, even in this highly dynamic and competitive context, not all competences are generic and easy portable from one organization to another (Groysberg et al., 2006). There are several competencies, including leadership ones, which are firm specific and difficult to transfer and organizations need to breed them internally. In order to retain those individuals who possess these skills, companies design organizational career systems (Bagdadli, 2007; Bagdadli et al., 2003; Hall and Las Heras, 2009) and use organizational career management (OCM) practices to favour their internal development. The career management of these individuals, either hired from the external labour market or promoted from within, plays an important role in companies' effort to manage human resources.

This chapter defines OCM systems, analyzes the theoretical roots of OCM, looks at OCM practices, shows the link between human resource management (HRM) and career management and illustrates important insights with practical examples from the world of organizations.

Organizational career management systems

OCM systems are concepts present in the two previous handbooks (Arthur et al., 1989; Gunz and Peiperl, 2007). The background literature in the various chapters (Sonnenfeld, 1989;

Rosenbaum, 1984; Slay and Taylor, 2007; Bagdadli, 2007) ranges from economics to career and HRM or strategic human resource management (SHRM).

According to Sonnenfeld (1989) in the first career handbook and to Sonnenfeld and Peiperl in the original work (1988: 588),

> career systems are the collections of policies, priorities, and actions that organizations use to manage the flow of their members into, through, and out of the organizations over time. The career system focuses on the changing, longitudinal issues regarding the creation and maintenance of the firm's membership. It involves (a) entry, which includes human resource planning, recruiting, and selection; (b) development, which involves socialization, training, career planning, succession planning, and promotions; and (c) exit, which includes retirement, layoffs, resignations, and dismissal.

In this chapter, we adopt a narrower definition of 'career system' focusing our attention on those practices aimed to manage people once they have entered the organization. We consider as part of an OCM system those practices that support the development of individuals inside organizations.

Over time, scholars proposed different career system models (e.g., Gunz, 1989; Sonnenfeld and Peiperl, 1988; Lepak and Snell, 1999), intended as frameworks that describe career management practices and how they work together. The most recent career system model is the Human Resource Architecture (HRA) developed by Lepak and Snell (1999) and discussed by Slay and Taylor (2007) in the second careers handbook. Interestingly the authors adopt the generic label of 'HR system' even though the content of the model is essentially career-related: this is one of the cases, recurrent in contributions interested in studying careers, where the terminology varies according to the research domain (HRM or career) of the author. Like the other (few) career system models (e.g., Gunz, 1989; Sonnenfeld and Peiperl, 1988), the HRA is a contingent model.

The HRA model (Lepak and Snell, 1999) offers an interesting angle to understand career systems and practices in contemporary organizations, because it highlights that, no matter whether companies promote from within or recruit from the external job market, there are people with valuable competences that need the most managerial attention and the best possible development practices. In particular, the authors extend previous work by Sonnenfeld and Peiperl (1988) combining the type of competences people possess (in Sonnenfeld and Peiperl's model, the contingent variable was instead the business strategy), with HR and career practices. The classification of individual competences relates to their *uniqueness* and *value*: the former is the degree to which a competence is firm specific or not, while the latter refers to its impact on profit. The higher the uniqueness and the value of competences possessed by an individual, the higher is the level of investment in developmental HR practices made by the company. In such a case, the company will develop an *organization-based* relationship (Tsui et al., 1995) characterized by commitment-based HR practices (Arthur et al., 1994), aimed at enhancing employee skills, motivation and opportunity to perform autonomously. Organizations use these practices and all OCM practices, from training to mentoring, to strengthen the relationship and to increase individual and organizational performance.

The theoretical roots of organizational career management

Career studies tend to be interdisciplinary (Arthur et al., 1989; Gunz and Peiperl, 2007) and the same can be said about the theoretical roots of OCM. In particular, we identify economic, career and HRM literature.

In the economic literature, transaction cost economics (Williamson et al., 1975), and more specifically the conceptualization of the internal labour market by Doeringer and Piore (1971), offers a suitable explanation of the reasons why companies should invest in the internal development of workers. Doeringer and Piore (1971) identify the origin of the internal labor market in (1) skill specificity, (2) on-the-job training and (3) customary laws. 'Firm-specific skills' are acquired through on-the-job learning in one organization and they cannot be used in another organization (Becker, 1962). Williamson (1981) and Williamson and colleagues (1975) state that such specificity explains the failure of external labour market and the need for an internal one. Internal labour markets are organizational career systems defined by specific internal mobility policies and practices: respectively, promotion systems and OCM practices. In addition, the advantage of the internal labour market, over the external one, is reinforced by the 'information impactedness', the degree to which 'relevant information is known by some parties but cannot be costless discerned by or displayed for others' (Williamson et al., 1975: 31). This might induce the use of internal employees instead of contractors and might explain the development of internal pool of talents, as external hiring might be very difficult and risky, due to this information problem. These differences in assessing internal versus external candidates will increase the use of internal labour markets and the use of OCM practices to develop individuals internally. This might be true especially for filling jobs with high variability in performance as Bidwell and Keller (2014) tested in a recent research.

In the career literature, theoretical roots for OCM can be traced in the tension between individual agency and social determinism (see also Chapter 5):

> Running through the entire literature on career is the tension between individual agency, the notion that we are what we make of ourselves, and social determinism. The former perspective, agency, is most evident in the vocational literature [. . .], which is founded on the precept that the individual should find out about his or her individual capacities and match them to the occupation that best suits those capacities.
>
> *(Moore et al., 2007: 30)*

This concept has been developed in I/O psychology literature explaining the determinants of managerial success (e.g., Seibert et al., 2001; Wayne et al., 1997). The latter, social determinism, is instead a strong component of the sociological tradition, being the macro-social structures considered either constraints or enablers of individual actions, such as Durkheim's division of labour, or Weber's bureaucracy and status and class hierarchies (Moore et al., 2007).

Within the career literature, Rosenbaum (1984) proposed another critical contribution that moved the level of interest for OCM from macro-social structures to organizations. In his seminal work, *Careers in a Corporate Hierarchy*, he explicitly asserted the paucity of individual investments in developmental actions, if compared with organizational ones, given that individuals have less resources to invest then companies. In doing so, Rosenbaum departs from human capital theory (Becker, 1964), which posits that individual achievements are the result of individuals' abilities and investments in education and training and that there are no barriers to career mobility, as individuals control the investments that determine their careers. Contrasting these assumptions, Rosenbaum (1984) asserts that managers use signals from the socio-structural organizational context to assess individual abilities, so their assessments are biased by factors like age, career path and the speed of career advancement. In addition, organizations can afford a higher level of investments in training and education than a single individual: such investments being focused on workers who have the potential to grow into leadership positions (Rosenbaum, 1984). In synthesis, with his work Rosenbaum sustains the relevance of organizational investments in fostering individual career development and success.

Figure 22.1 The intersection among HRM, OCM and TM practices

The strategic HRM literature demonstrated an interest in studying the effects of HRM practices (which include OCM practices – see Figure 22.1) on organizational and individual performance. The recent AMO (ability-motivation-opportunity) framework explains that HRM practices exert their influence on performance mainly by motivating individuals to produce more through the intrinsic value of development, enhancing skills and providing opportunities to networking and progress in the internal hierarchy (Boxall and Purcell, 2008, 2016). In particular, among the HRM practices, training is considered skill enhancing activity that fosters human capital (*ability*), developmental performance management, promotions and career development practices enhance employee motivation (*motivation*), and flexible job design activities, such as lateral moves, empower employees to use their skills and motivation to achieve organizational objectives (*opportunity*) (Jiang et al., 2012).

Organizational career management practices

OCM practices are 'activities undertaken by the organization in order to plan and manage the careers of its employees' (DeVos et al., 2009: 58). Research on OCM practices flourished in the 1990s. The main contribution of this research consists in the effort to define a comprehensive list of practices (Gutteridge and Otte, 1983; Gutteridge, 1993; Baruch, 1996, 1999; Baruch and Peiperl, 2000; Eby et al., 2005; DeVos et al., 2009) and assess their adoption in organizations. Moreover career scholars have been interested in studying the effects of OCM practices on subjective career success (Ng et al., 2005) and objective career success (see Bagdadli and Gianecchini, 2019 for a review), but without taking a systemic approach. Table 22.1 shows definitions of main OCM practices.

Table 22.1 OCM practices: definitions

Assessment center	An assessment center consists of a standardized evaluation of behaviors, based on multiple inputs. Assessment center uses multiple trained observers and several techniques. From specific work sample simulations it is possible to evaluate the potential of present or future managers.
Career counseling	Career counseling is the process of discussing with employees their current job activities and performance, personal and career interests and goals, personal skills, and suitable career development objectives. HR staff members, managers and supervisors, specialized staff counselors, or outside consultants can provide this service.
Career planning workbook	Workbooks guide employees individually through systematic self-assessment of values, interests, abilities, goals, and personal development plans.
Career workshops	Career workshops are short-term workshops focusing on specific aspect(s) of career management (such as identifying future opportunities, improving the employability of the participants, or enhancing their career resilience) and aim to provide managers with relevant knowledge, skills and experience.
Development center	Development centers evolved from assessment centers, focusing on the participants' further professional development. The competency profile for the development center is tailored to the organization and/or the specific function and reflects the organization's expectations for the role.
Developmental assignment	Developmental assignments require individuals to accomplish tasks for which they are not fully qualified, such as: job transitions that place managers in new and unfamiliar situations (such as an international assignment); starting up a new part of the business; fixing an operation in trouble; downsizing a business.
Dual ladder	Dual ladder is a parallel hierarchy created for professional or technical staff which enables them upward mobility and recognition without conducting a managerial role. Dual ladder system provides equal status and rewards to equivalent levels in both hierarchies.
Job Posting	An internal recruitment channel through which an organization posts all its available vacancies to give an opportunity for its existing employees who wish to apply to change job.
Lateral moves (job rotation)	Lateral moves are job transitions, which occur at the same hierarchy level within the organization (e.g., between business unites or functions). They aim is to give the individual a breadth of exposure to the entire operation/business activities, increasing his/her cross-functional experience.
Mentoring	Career-management activity in which an individual (the mentor) with advanced experience and knowledge is committed to providing a mentee with personal and professional insights, leading to career growth
Networking	The practice of creating a set of relationships with other members of the organization (having lower, higher or equal social status) aimed at offering resources and career support to the individual.

(Continued)

Table 22.1 (Continued)

Assessment center	An assessment center consists of a standardized evaluation of behaviors, based on multiple inputs. Assessment center uses multiple trained observers and several techniques. From specific work sample simulations it is possible to evaluate the potential of present or future managers.
Orientation programs and induction	A process whereby all newcomers learn the behaviors, attitudes, norms and culture of their new organization. Part of it is formal, led by organizational officials, whereas other aspects are learned in an informal manner, not necessarily in line with organizational formal norms and policies.
Outplacement	Services provided by organizations to help terminated employees find a new job.
Performance appraisal	It is a formal and structured process used to measure, evaluate and influence an employee's job-related attributes, behaviors, and performance results.
Pre-retirement programs	Seminars and workshops to help make employees aware of the kinds of adjustments they may need to make when they retire. The topics include pension plans, health insurance coverage, Social Security and, personal financial planning, wellness and lifestyles.
Succession planning	Deliberate and systematic effort by an organization to determine the possible replacement of every manager within the organization and evaluate the potential for promotion of each manager.
Training and formal education	Activities aimed at providing employees with skills necessary for supporting their professional development. In some cases, organization can select people of managerial and technical potential and sends them on a formal program of study (e.g., graduate or post-graduate courses) as a part of their development path.

Source: Adapted from Baruch (1999, 2003).

We have to note that in the SHRM literature, OCM practices are a subset of HRM practices often generally labelled as career development practices (Jiang et al., 2012). In the human resource development (HRD) literature (Egan et al., 2006), OCM practices are called HRD practices. Although scholars disagree on the exact definition of talent management (TM) (Dries, 2013), TM practices are a group of activities with the purpose of hiring, identifying, developing and retaining persons with high potential. Initially developed in the 1950s, they were

> workforce plans to set direction; sophisticated recruitment and selection techniques for hiring entry-level candidates; assessments of potential (including assessment centers, ability and personality tests, etc.); developmental assignments like job rotations, shadowing, and action learning with coaches; assessments of performance such as 360 feedback and forced rankings; career ladders and succession planning to fill the important jobs.
>
> *(Cappelli and Keller, 2014: 313)*

Nowadays, TM practices can be more generally defined as a subset of OCM practices, dedicated to a special group of individuals, identified as best performers and high potentials. Figure 22.1 depicts differentiation and overlap between HRM, OCM and TM practices.

OCM practices promoted by organizations are different from individual career management activities. Individual career management or career self-management (CSM) refers to the proactivity employees show with respect to managing their career. It includes activities such as collecting information about existing or possible career opportunities, searching for feedback about one's performance and competencies, and creating career opportunities through networking and actions aimed at enhancing one's visibility (King, 2004). CSM thus involves those activities that allow individuals to make a realistic self-assessment of their own talents and capabilities in view of organizational career opportunities as well as concrete actions (e.g., networking, self-nomination, creating opportunities) undertaken to realize these ambitions. In developing their own career, individuals can take advantage of OCM. Therefore, upward progression appears as nurtured by both individual career-specific activities and organizational processes.

From theory to practice

In this section we describe some examples of what companies do in terms of career management systems in order to complement theory with practice and to derive some insights for the career management literature.

We will draw on four large organizations: General Electric, Nissan, McDonald's and Infosys. We chose these companies because they operate in different industries and different parts of the world, so to enhance institutional and cultural variety, and trying to avoid the usual American parochialism (Boyacigiller and Adler, 1991). Among the possible companies, we directed our attention to those which were documented with a plurality of sources – case studies, articles and books – in order to enhance scientific reliability (Yin, 1994). In these companies, most of the practices are dedicated to the best employees and are in fact examples of talent management systems or, in other words, of career management systems dedicated to the best employees. Table 22.2 provides a synthesis of main practices in these four companies.

General Electric case

GE is probably one of the most widely studied organizations when it comes to the career management systems and practices aimed to attract and develop the future GE leaders. Founded in 1892 by Thomas Edison, GE is now a multinational conglomerate, one of the largest in the world, operating in several businesses – oil, gas, health care and finance, to name a few – with around 295,000 employees, around USD 120 billion of revenues in 2017, operating worldwide (180 countries) in several industrial segments (e.g., GE Capital, GE Oil and Gas).

GE is quite well known for its career management system which is interpreted, as in the Sonnenfeld and Peiperl definition (1988), as a complex of policies and practices to manage the flow of people in through and out the organizations and which is clearly including most of the respective HR practices. GE is a very selective organization, which has sponsored meritocracy since the beginning of its history. Consequently, it put great emphasis on the individual performance evaluation in order to identify the best performers with the highest potential who will become the future leaders of the organization. In the following, we describe the main practices that are at the heart of GE career management system.

Performance management

GE identifies their best employees through the performance evaluation system and the assessment of the potential (GE values), segmenting the workforce through a nine-block grid. The

Table 22.2 OCM practices: main companies' features and focus

	GE	Nissan	McDonald's	Infosys
Performance management	Nine grid box Formerly forced distribution App (PD@GE)	Personnel evaluation system based on 'objective appraisal' and 'contribution appraisal'	Performance management system (MBO on leadership behaviour, forced distribution, higher compensation for top 20%, assessment)	360 degree feedback evaluating performance and individual skills
Succession planning	Session C	Nomination Advisory Council (NAC)	Presidents of each area of the world together with corporate staff manager define leadership talent requirements	Infosys Role and Career Enhancement (iRace)
Training	Management education at Crotonville	Global Executive Training program (Advanced and Intermediate) at Nissan Learning Centre Management Institute	Leadership @ McDonald's Program (LAMP)	Infosys Leadership Institute (nine-factor model leadership behaviours and Tier Leadership program)
Developmental assignment	Lateral move, stretch assignment and international assignment	International and trans-functional assignments Nissan Rotational Development Plan		
Job Posting		Shift Career System Open Entry System		
Coaching/ mentoring		Career coaches	McDMentoring program	Future leaders are coached by ILI professionals

discussion around performance with managers is intense and open and, until few years ago, GE used a forced distribution curve known as 'vitality curve'; in 2015 GE moved toward a continuous assessment/feedback from supervisors to employees, managed through an app – PD@GE (performance development at GE). As a part of the performance and development system, GE introduced another well-known and benchmarked system called Session C, which includes the CEO and the HR VP, the business unit (BU) manager and the HR BU manager to discuss individual performance across business units. Session C is an in-depth review of BU leadership and 'it is where the decisions on development, deployment and retention are made and followed through on' (Conaty and Charan, 2011: 48). Session C has several meetings during the year to adjust to new situations and critical issues (i.e., someone to retain) and to calibrate the evaluations of different BUs.

Succession planning

Succession planning follows the assessment process and session C. Due to the deep knowledge of leaders in the organization, successors emerge slowly and the focus is narrowed down only close to succession, to consider as many potential successors for as long as possible.

Training

Extensive leadership training is provided at Crotonville, the J. Welch Learning Centre, a centre admired and benchmarked worldwide. Crotonville is not only a management education centre, but 'it is a driver for management innovation, change and adaptation, a melting pot to bring people and businesses together and the central transmitting station for GE culture and values' (Conaty and Charan, 2011: 56).

Development assignments

Lateral moves, stretch assignments and international assignments are continuously proposed to talents in order to develop specific competencies: managing a mature business, implementing a start-up, managing a difficult unit or a business in crisis and eventually fail, in order to develop coping and resilience.

One-to-one development tools

Networking, mentoring and coaching are used extensively to develop leaders for future positions.

Nissan case

Nissan is a Japanese multinational automobile manufacturer founded in 1933. It is one of the largest automakers in the world with around 137.000 employees and JPY 11.72 trillion of revenues in 2016 (about EUR 97 billion in 2016). Nissan used to be a typical Japanese multinational company with a polycentric approach (Perlmutter, 1969) and its HRM systems were different from country to country. Since 1999, Nissan has been part of an alliance with Mitsubishi Motors and French automaker Renault. As a consequence of this organizational change, Nissan launched a Global Talent Management (GTM) program. It includes a set of OCM practices aimed at identifying and promoting capable human resources from a global perspective in order to utilize them as company-wide assets (Furusawa, 2014). Together with the GTM program, Nissan proposes to all its employees specific career development opportunities (Furusawa, 2014; Yorozu, 2015) that we illustrate below.

Performance management

In 2007, Nissan standardized a personnel evaluation system for managers across the globe. This system is composed of two appraisals, namely an 'objectives appraisal' and a 'contribution appraisal'. According to the 'objectives appraisal' managers are required to set their individual goals and group goals at the beginning of the fiscal year. The results of the objectives appraisals affect managers' incentives, constituting about 20 to 30 percent of their annual base salary. The contribution appraisal, instead, is the extent to which each manager embodies in mind-set and actions the Nissan Way, according to a four-grade rating system. This appraisal affects annual base salary. Outstanding performance in both appraisals is a pre-requisite for promotion.

Succession planning

The core governance body of the GTM program is a personnel committee named the Nomination Advisory Council (NAC). The Corporate NAC is held monthly and chaired by the CEO, with the COO, Executive Vice Presidents and HR Director as its members. It is responsible for approving succession planning for 'Global Key Posts', which are of great importance to Nissan's global strategy. Employees in Japan also have the chance to take on the challenge of a new position through the Shift Career System (SCS) and the Open Entry System (OES). The SCS, which represents a hybrid OCM practice between job posting and succession planning, enables employees to apply for jobs in departments that interest them regardless of whether there is a position immediately available. The OES, which resembles the characteristics of a classic job posting system, allows employees to apply for all openly advertised positions. During fiscal year 2015, 158 employees applied for 102 open posts, and 54 of them succeeded in getting the positions they applied for.

Training

As a part of the GTM program, in 2002 Nissan started a set of training activities called Global Executive Training (GET). GET comprises two courses (Advanced and Intermediate). Each course lasts one year and it is held at Nissan's corporate university in Japan (Nissan Learning Center Management Institute).

Developmental assignments

As a part of managerial development, Corporate NAC approves individual development plans that include international or trans-functional assignments or both, appointments as a pilot (leader) of cross-functional teams or problem-solving activities. New hires with five to seven years of work experience and a MBA degree may be eligible for participating in a specific developmental plan, called Nissan Rotational Development Plan. It is a highly selective five-year program, which includes three to four cross-functional, cross-regional rotations, mentoring and feedback from top executives.

Coaching

As a part of the GTM program, the Corporate NAC appoints a set of 'career coaches'. They are general managers with the mission of identifying individuals with high potential for promotion and proposing a development plan for them as well as making a list of successor candidates for the Global Key Posts.

McDonald's case

McDonald's is the world's leading global food service retailer with almost 37,000 locations in over 100 countries, around USD 23 billion of revenues and a net income of USD 5.19 billion in 2017. More than 80 percent of McDonald's restaurants worldwide are owned and operated by independent local businesspersons. The company employs approximately 375,000 people as of 2016. The company is well known for the opportunities it has given many of its people to grow with the company and to rise (over time) from working as a member of a store crew to its highest executive ranks. After many years of successful management and strong business results, from mid-1990s, McDonald's started to face strong competition from an increasingly diverse set of competitors beyond the traditional quick service restaurants (Williams-Lee, 2008). The competitive pressure culminated in the fourth quarter of 2002, when the company declared the first loss in its history. Before that turning point, the company was already trying to respond to the changes in the business landscape, launching a set of initiatives (starting from 2001), aimed at enhancing the company capabilities for developing local managers and ensuring management continuity throughout its global system (Intagliata and Kulik, 2009; Intagliata and Small, 2005). Below we briefly describe the main career-related practices at McDonald's.

Performance management

Prior to 2001, McDonald's performance management system led to a chronic inflation rating since in contrast with mediocre business results, the system suggested that everyone was doing an outstanding job. As a consequence, there was little meaningful performance and compensation differentiation and a culture of entitlement had set in: employees believed that their past success and associated rewards would guarantee their future success and rewards. In order to change this situation, the top management team asked the HR Department to redesign the performance management system for all staff throughout the company. The main characteristics of the new system are:

- The MBO program, based on six key leadership behaviours, that measure not only 'what' the individual accomplishes but also 'how' they accomplish it;
- The overall performance, evaluated on a 4-point rating scale (exceptional performance, significant performance, needs improvement, unsatisfactory) with a forced distribution of 20, 70, and 10 percent, where those rated in the 'top 20 percent' receive a significantly higher compensation than their colleagues;
- The new assessment of potential, that identifies no more than 20 to 25 percent of managers as 'ready' immediately for a promotion.

Succession planning

In order to redesign the succession planning system, in the beginning in 2003 the presidents of each area of the world (United States, Europe, Asia/Pacific/Middle East/Africa, and Latin America), together with each corporate staff manager (EVP-HR, EVP-Finance/CFO), had to offer a view about their leadership talent requirements. The increased ownership that top managers have taken as a result of this review process was reflected in specific actions that they proactively initiated to respond to the replacement needs that emerged.

Training and development

In June of 2003, McDonald's launched the Leadership @ McDonald's Program (LAMP), aimed at accelerating the development of directors to vice-president positions (Williams-Lee, 2008). The first LAMP, involving 22 directors and lasting nine months, had five key components: an executive assessment, the formulation of an individual development plan, leadership training, a two-week executive education course on global business and culture, and business improvement recommendations presented to the board. Since the successful pilot, the LAMP program has expanded into three parallel programs, based on geographical areas (the Americas; Europe; Asia Pacific, Middle East and Africa). Combining global and regionally based development programs has allowed McDonald's to create a global leadership standard while providing individuals with practical skill development and knowledge that is relevant for their region.

Mentoring

McDonald's considers mentoring a way to develop employees and promote a continuous learning culture. The McDMentoring program gives employees the opportunity to build their competencies through informal and formal mentoring. Every learner is assigned a mentor at every step of development. Together with a 'traditional' mentoring program, McDonald's has introduced a web-based tool used for matching, tracking and facilitating mentor/mentee relationships across an entire organization. The 'virtual mentoring' program provides a virtual environment to encourage Career Engagements (one-to-one), Topical Engagements (group/peer learning/sharing), and Situational Engagements (short-term, special projects).

Infosys case

Established in 1981, Infosys is an Indian-founded global consulting and IT services company with more than 200,000 employees and revenues of about USD 10.7 billion in 2017. Started with a USD 250 angel investment from the founding CEO's wife, Infosys pioneered the 'Global Delivery Model' of writing software for customers in the developed world with talent based in India. The seven founders leveraged each other's diverse business and technology expertise and their shared commitment to ethical practices that stood out in a country notorious for corruption and exploitation. Infosys had always been at the forefront of developing and implementing HR initiatives, recognizing that its employees, or 'Infoscions', were at the heart of its impressive success. Indeed, it had been one of the first Indian companies to grant stock options to its employees and it ranked, for many years, as one of the most attractive employers in India. Below we outline the main practices of Infosys' career management system.

Performance management

The performance appraisal at Infosys is a rigorous and comprehensive process, tied to the future development of the individual skills and capabilities (Cappelli et al., 2010). It encompasses not only the performance, but also the evaluation of individual skills for the tasks assigned to an employee during the assigned period of performance evaluation. In this regard, performance appraisal takes into consideration various performance criteria like timeliness, quality of work, customer orientation, peer satisfaction and performance improvement potential. The process is carried out semi-annually on the basis of 360-degree feedback, with a minimum of six to seven appraisal reports for each employee. The appraisal information is used to identify training courses and other developmental interventions.

Succession planning

In October 2009, Infosys introduced a career planning program called iRACE (Infosys Role and Career Enhancement; Purkayastha and Chaudhari, 2011). iRACE gave employees designations depending upon the amount of domain knowledge they possessed and the unit to which they belonged. With the introduction of iRACE, traditional designations (such as General Manager) were replaced with specific designation, such as Head of Sales for a certain vertical or region. With iRACE, Infosys mapped the competences required for the available positions together with the experience and skill level of the employees. In particular, individuals were assessed according to three criteria: years of experience, past performance, ability to deal with difficult task. The norms of iRACE required employees to have at least six years of experience in technology responsibilities before they could move to heading projects. The employees got the chance to choose between 24 career streams, some of them (called 'career paths') aimed at achieving managerial position, whereas others (named 'career lattices') provided lateral opportunities in different areas of expertise and they aimed at offering high-value roles to technology professionals. iRace represented a relevant change in the Infosys approach to promotions, as criteria included both seniority and (technical and managerial) expertise, whereas employees were used to obtain fast promotions and salary increases as a direct effect of a booming industry. As a consequence, employees had difficulties in understanding rationalization imposed as part of the iRace initiative. They expressed their discontent in terms of a rising attrition rate and badmouthing the company management on social media. In order to understand such strong reactions, some observers outline some critical decisions in the implementation of the program, whereas others consider the business conditions. In particular, as the company enacted iRace retrospectively, several employees were demoted as they could not meet the iRace criteria. In addition, the program had been drawn up during the recession period, therefore employee dissatisfaction and attrition may be also related to the difficulties in business, and not only to the implementation of iRace (Purkayastha and Chaudhari, 2011).

Training and development

In 2001, the firm created the Infosys Leadership Institute (ILI) to systematically grow leaders throughout the senior-most ranks (Barney, 2010; Day and Barney, 2012). ILI developed a nine-factor model of leadership behaviours required for effective performance. ILI selects candidates annually, through customized psychometric assessments, into a high-potential leader program known as Tier Leadership, the duration of which is three years. Tiers are broken into four categories with varying levels of readiness for senior positions. Each Infosys tier leader is assigned a coach who is responsible for providing client feedback, developmental guidance, as well as consulting support.

From practice to theory

The four cases offer insights about career management systems in large multinational companies and allow us to further discuss and advance what we argued in the theoretical part of this chapter. We can identify the following major issues.

First, as clearly emerged from the cases, all the companies designed and developed their OCM practices not in isolation but as a part of a career management system. The system is internally consistent and aligned with the strategy of the company. For instance, as far as internal consistency is concerned, at Infosys the 360-degree feedback is not only a performance management technique but also one element of the nine-pillar model for leadership development: the results of the feedback are used as basis for the preparation of an individual Personal Development Plan. This plan serves as the blueprint to guide the individual in acquiring new skills, also through the support of specialized coaches. As far as alignment with the business strategy is concerned, individual development plans at Nissan include not only international or cross-functional assignments, but also the opportunity to be assigned to companies of the group (e.g., Renault) to learn the respective best practices. The company cases also suggest that the career management systems co-evolve with the business development of the companies: sometimes OCM practices, initially developed for the headquarters staff, are replicated internationally or customized in order to be offered to different segments of the workforce; in some other cases they were developed as a response to company crisis and organizational change.

This systemic approach has an echo in the career literature and in the models of career systems we presented (e.g., Bagdadli, 2007; Baruch, 1999; Sonnenfeld, 1989), although the focus of those models has been theoretical and aimed at relating the career management practices to the organizational structure (Gunz, 1989) or the firm strategy (Sonnenfeld and Peiperl, 1988). Notwithstanding this theoretical effort, the effects of the career systems on individual career outcomes were overlooked not only by the theoretical career literature – with the exception of the seminal work by Rosenbaum (1984) – but also by empirical research. Indeed, the empirical studies mainly tested the effects of single practices on individual career outcomes (e.g., Lyness and Heilman, 2006; Melero, 2010; Singh et al., 2009), but not the effects of a system of practices. Such an analysis would have been beneficial for organizations in terms of evidence-based management (Rousseau, 2006). While testing the effects of a set or bundle of practices is well established in the SHRM research (e.g., Delery and Doty, 1996; Wright et al., 2005), this literature was not interested in analysing the relation with individual career outcomes. Its main focus was instead on the relation with organizational performance (Combs et al., 2006) and with individual performance (Boxall and Purcell, 2016).

A second insight emerging form the cases relates to the centrality of performance management among the OCM practices. Although the performance management systems adopted by the companies have different features, they represent a cornerstone for the managerial development both providing the company with valuable information for promotion decisions and providing the managers with information on the behavior expected from them. As a matter of fact, all the performance management systems illustrated include both objective results and expected individual behaviours and attitudes. The fact that this system is crucial and pivotal to all the OCM practices has not been in the OCM literature which mainly focuses on defining a comprehensive list of practices or on assessing their adoption in organizations (Gutteridge and Otte, 1983; Gutteridge, 1993; Baruch, 1996; Baruch and Peiperl, 2000; Eby et al., 2005; de Vos et al., 2009). Only Baruch (1999: 442) acknowledges that 'among all career and planning management practices, the performance appraisal system is the most fundamental [. . .], if valid and reliable, it may serve as the foundation stone for an integrated career planning and management system'.

A third point from the cases relates to the fact that most of the developmental tools are offered to individuals who are assessed as 'talents'. This shows that career systems not only manage the flow of *all* individuals in and out of the company but, at the same time, also serve to identify the best employees for further growth and development. The latter group receives advanced and mainly one-on-one (mostly coaching and mentoring) interventions. This is in line with the exclusive approach to workforce differentiation (Mellahi and Collings, 2010), confirming its larger diffusion in corporations compared to the inclusive approach (Buckingham and Vosburgh, 2001).

As a fourth point, although the four companies operate in different markets and they have different geographical origins, most of the practices described are present in every company with minor differences. Thus, our cases offer support to a universalistic approach to the development of career management systems. This is relevant to the convergence debate in the HRM comparative literature (Chen et al., 2005; Al Ariss and Sidani, 2016) and with recent findings in global talent management research (Cotton et al., 2017).

Finally, although some of the most advanced companies are trying to have a more 'make or buy' approach to leadership development (Cappelli, 2008; Cappelli and Keller, 2014), these cases show the enduring importance in organizations of career management systems and of internal career management in contemporary organizations.

References

Al Ariss, A. & Sidani, Y. 2016. Divergence, convergence, or crossvergence in international human resource management. *Human Resource Management Review*, 26, 283–284.

Arthur, J.B. 1994. Effects of human resource systems on manufacturing performance and turnover. *Academy of Management Journal*, 37, 670–687.

Arthur, M.B., Hall, D.T. & Lawrence, B.S. 1989. *Handbook of Career Theory*. Cambridge, UK: Cambridge University Press.

Bagdadli, S. 2007. Designing career systems: Are we ready for it? *In:* Gunz, H. & Peiperl, M. (eds.) *Handbook of Career Studies.* Thousand Oaks, CA: Sage Publications.

Bagdadli, S. & Gianecchini, M. 2019. Organizational career management practices and objective career success: A systematic review and framework. *Human Resource Management Review*, 29, 353–370.

Bagdadli, S., Solari, L., Usai, A. & Grandori, A. 2003. The emergence of career boundaries in unbounded industries: Career odysseys in the Italian new economy. *International Journal of Human Resource Management*, 14, 788–808.

Barney, M. 2010. *Leadership@ Infosys*. New Delhi, India: Penguin Books.

Baruch, Y. 1996. Organizational career planning and management techniques and activities in use in high-tech organizations. *Career Development International*, 1, 40–49.

Baruch, Y. 1999. Integrated career systems for the 2000s. *International Journal of Manpower*, 20, 432–457.

Baruch, Y. 2003. Career systems in transition: A normative model for organizational career practices. *Personnel Review*, 32, 231–251.

Baruch, Y. & Peiperl, M. 2000. Career management practices: An empirical survey and implications. *Human Resource Management*, 39, 347–366.

Becker, G.S. 1962. Investment in human capital: A theoretical analysis. *Journal of Political Economy*, 70, 9–49.

Becker, G.S. 1964. *Human Capital.* New York: Colombia University Press.

Bidwell, M. & Keller, J. 2014. Within or without? How firms combine internal and external labor markets to fill jobs. *Academy of Management Journal*, 57, 1035–1055.

Boxall, P. & Purcell, J. 2008. *Strategy and Human Resource Management.* Basingstoke, Hampshire: Palgrave Macmillan.

Boxall, P. & Purcell, J. 2016. *Strategy and Human Resource Management.* London, UK and New York: Palgrave Macmillan.

Boyacigiller, N.A. & Adler, N.J. 1991. The parochial dinosaur: Organizational science in a global context. *Academy of Management Review*, 16, 262–290.

Buckingham, M. & Vosburgh, R.M. 2001. The 21st century human resources function: It's the talent, stupid! *Human Resource Planning*, 24, 17–23.

Cappelli, P. 2008. Talent management for the twenty-first century. *Harvard Business Review*, 86, 74–81.

Cappelli, P. & Keller, J. 2014. Talent management: Conceptual approaches and practical challenges. *Annual Review of Organizational Psychology and Organizational Behavior*, 1, 305–331.

Cappelli, P., Singh, H., Singh, J. & Useem, M. 2010. *The India Way: How India's Top Business Leaders are Revolutionizing Management.* Boston, MA: Harvard Business Press.

Chen, S.J., Lawler, J.J. & Bae, J. 2005. Convergence in human resource systems: A comparison of locally owned and MNC subsidiaries in Taiwan. *Human Resource Management*, 44, 237–256.

Combs, J., Liu, Y., Hall, A. & Ketchen, D. 2006. How much do high-performance work practices matter? A meta-analysis of their effects on organizational performance. *Personnel Psychology*, 59, 501–528.

Conaty, B. & Charan, R. 2011. *The Talent Masters: Why Smart Leaders Put People Before Numbers*. Great Britain: Restoration Hardware.

Cotton, R.D., Dries, N., Bagdadli, S. & Ziebell de Oliveira, M. 2017. Implicit link: Using free association to explore cross-cultural differences in the meaning of talent. *In:* Atinc, G. (ed.) *Best Paper Proceedings of the Seventy-Seventh Annual Meeting of the Academy of Management Proceedings*. Briarcliff Manor, NY: Academy of Management.

Day, D.V. & Barney, M.F. 2012. Personalizing global leader development@ Infosys. *In:* Mobley, W., Wang, Y. & Li, M. (eds.) *Advances in Global Leadership*. Bingley, UK: Emerald Group Publishing Limited.

de Vos, A., Dewettinck, K. & Buyens, D. 2009. The professional career on the right track: A study on the interaction between career self-management and organizational career management in explaining employee outcomes. *European Journal of Work and Organizational Psychology*, 18, 55–80.

Delery, J.E. & Doty, D.H. 1996. Modes of theorizing in strategic human resource management: Tests of universalistic, contingency, and configurational performance predictions. *Academy of Management Journal*, 39, 802–835.

Doeringer, P. & Piore, M.J. 1971. *Internal Labor Markets and Manpower Adjustment*. New York: D.C. Heath and Company.

Doyle, M. 2000. Managing careers in organisations. *In:* Collin, A. & Young, R. (eds.) *The Future of Career*. Cambridge: Cambridge University Press.

Dries, N. 2013. The psychology of talent management: A review and research agenda. *Human Resource Management Review*, 23, 272–285.

Eby, L.T., Allen, T.D. & Brinley, A. 2005. A cross-level investigation of the relationship between career management practices and career-related attitudes. *Group & Organization Management*, 30, 565–596.

Egan, T.M., Upton, M.G. & Lynham, S.A. 2006. Career development: Load-bearing wall or window dressing? Exploring definitions, theories, and prospects for HRD-related theory building. *Human Resource Development Review*, 5, 442–477.

Furusawa, M. 2014. Global talent management in Japanese multinational companies: The case of Nissan motor company. *In:* Al Ariss, A. (ed.) *Global Talent Management*. Cham, Switzerland: Springer International Publishing.

Groysberg, B., Mclean, A.N. & Nohria, N. 2006. Are leaders portable? *Harvard Business Review*, 84, 92–100.

Gunz, H. 1989. *Careers and Corporate Cultures: Managerial Mobility in Large Corporations*. Oxford: Basil Blackwell.

Gunz, H. & Peiperl, M. 2007. *Handbook of Career Studies*. Thousand Oaks, CA: Sage Publications.

Gutteridge, T.G. 1993. *Organizational Career Development: Benchmarks for Building a World-Class Workforce*. San Francisco, CA: Jossey-Bass.

Gutteridge, T.G. & Otte, F.L. 1983. Organizational career development: What's going on out there? *Training and Development Journal*, 37, 22–26.

Hall, D.T. & Las Heras, M. 2009. Long live the organisational career. *In:* Collin, A. & Patton, E. (eds.) *Vocational Psychological and Organisational Perspectives on Career: Towards a Multidisciplinary Dialogue*. Rotterdam, NL: Sense Publishers.

Intagliata, J. & Kulik, N. 2009. McDonald's. *In:* Goldsmith, M. & Carter, L. (eds.) *Best Practices in Talent Management: How the World's Leading Corporations Manage, Develop, and Retain Top Talent*. San Francisco, CA: John Wiley & Sons.

Intagliata, J. & Small, D. 2005. McDonald's corporation: A customized leadership development program targeted to prepare future regional managers. *In:* Carter, L., Ulrich, D., Goldsmith, M. & Bolt, M. (eds.) *Best Practices Champions in Organization Development and Change*. San Francisco, CA: John Wiley & Sons.

Jiang, K., Lepak, D.P., Hu, J. & Baer, J.C. 2012. How does human resource management influence organizational outcomes? A meta-analytic investigation of mediating mechanisms. *Academy of Management Journal*, 55, 1264–1294.

King, Z. 2004. Career self-management: Its nature, causes and consequences. *Journal of Vocational Behavior*, 65, 112–133.

Lepak, D.P. & Snell, S.A. 1999. The human resource architecture: Toward a theory of human capital allocation and development. *Academy of Management Review*, 24, 31–48.

Lyness, K.S. & Heilman, M.E. 2006. When fit is fundamental: Performance evaluations and promotions of upper-level female and male managers. *Journal of Applied Psychology*, 91, 777–785.

Melero, E. 2010. Training and promotion: Allocation of skills or incentives? *Industrial Relations*, 49, 640–667.

Mellahi, K. & Collings, D.G. 2010. The barriers to effective global talent management: The example of corporate élites in MNEs. *Journal of World Business*, 45, 143–149.

Moore, C., Gunz, H. & Hall, D.T. 2007. Tracing the historical roots of career theory in management and organization studies. *In:* Gunz, H. & Peiperl, M. (eds.) *Handbook of Career Studies*. Thousand Oaks, CA: Sage Publications.

Ng, T.W., Eby, L.T., Sorensen, K.L. & Feldman, D.C. 2005. Predictors of objective and subjective career success: A meta-analysis. *Personnel Psychology*, 58, 367–408.

Perlmutter, H.V. 1969. The tortuous evolution of the multinational corporation. *Columbia Journal of World Business*, 4, 9–18.

Purkayastha, D. & Chaudhari, A. 2011. *Infosys Role and Career Enhancement: A People Strategy or Fall from Grace?* Hyderabad, India: IBS Center for Management Research.

Rosenbaum, J.E. 1984. *Career Mobility in a Corporate Hierarchy*. New York: Academic.

Rousseau, D.M. 2006. Is there such a thing as "evidence-based management"? *Academy of Management Review*, 31, 256–269.

Seibert, S.E., Kraimer, M.L. & Liden, R.C. 2001. A social capital theory of career success. *Academy of Management Journal*, 44, 219–237.

Singh, R., Ragins, B.R. & Tharenou, P. 2009. What matters most? The relative role of mentoring and career capital in career success. *Journal of Vocational Behavior*, 75, 56–67.

Slay, H.S. & Taylor, M.S. 2007. Career systems and psychological contracts. *In:* Gunz, H. & Peiperl, M. (eds.) *Handbook of Career Studies*. Thousand Oaks, CA: Sage Publications.

Sonnenfeld, J.A. 1989. Career system profiles and strategic staffing. *In:* Arthur, M.B. & Hall, D.T. (eds.) *Handbook of Career Theory*. Cambridge, UK: Cambridge University Press.

Sonnenfeld, J.A. & Peiperl, M.A. 1988. Staffing policy as a strategic response: A typology of career systems. *Academy of Management Review*, 13, 588–600.

Tsui, A.S., Pearce, J.L., Porter, L.W. & Hite, J.P. 1995. Choice of employee-organization relationship: Influence of external and internal organizational factors. *In:* Ferris, G.R. (ed.) *Research in Personnel and Human Resources Management*. Greenwich, CT: JAI Press.

Wayne, S.J., Liden, R.C., Graf, I.K. & Ferris, G.R. 1997. The role of upward influence tactics in human resource decisions. *Personnel Psychology*, 50, 979–1006.

Williams-Lee, A. 2008. Accelerated leadership development tops the talent management menu at McDonald's. *Global Business and Organizational Excellence*, 27, 15–31.

Williamson, O.E. 1981. The economics of organization: The transaction cost approach. *American Journal of Sociology*, 87, 548–577.

Williamson, O.E., Wachter, M.L. & Harris, J.E. 1975. Understanding the employment relation: The analysis of idiosyncratic exchange. *The Bell Journal of Economics*, 6, 250–278.

Wright, P.M., Gardner, T.M., Moynihan, L.M. & Allen, M.R. 2005. The relationship between HR practices and firm performance: Examining causal order. *Personnel Psychology*, 58, 409–446.

Yin, R.K. 1994. *Case Study Research: Design and Methods*. Beverly Hills, CA: Sage Publications.

Yorozu, C. 2015. *Narrative Management in Corporate Japan: Investor Relations as Pseudo-Reform*. London: Routledge.

23

Policy issues in careers

The case of internal migration in China

Marina A. Schmitz and Soo Min Toh

This chapter seeks to understand how government policy affects careers. To illustrate our argument, we take the example of the role of government policy and its effect on the careers of internal migrants (citizens of a country who relocate, permanently or temporarily, within the country). According to the United Nations (2015: 1) the "global urban population is projected to grow by 2.5 billion urban dwellers between 2014 and 2050, with nearly 90 per cent of the increase concentrated in Asia and Africa." This movement of people has caused many governments to develop policies to capitalize on economic development opportunities while minimizing the ills of mass rural-urban migration or over-concentration of population in certain urban centers. Numerous countries, such as Malaysia, Brazil, Philippines, Indonesia, and India, have over the past decades experimented with, and implemented, various policies that directly or indirectly affect the movement and geographical distribution of workers, and thus their careers, within national borders. Many of these policies adopted have been intended to restrict the movement of people from their place of origin. Such restrictions, in turn, have profound implications for the careers of citizens as they manage the opportunities, challenges, incentives and disincentives they face when relocating.

We choose, in this chapter, to address the case of the Peoples' Republic of China internal migration-related policies. Our choice of China is driven by two main factors. First, China is known as a "tight" nation (Gelfand et al., 2011) with many strict rules that are strongly enforced using severe punishments for non-compliance. It has a strong and highly controlled form of government policy making with respect to internal migration. Furthermore, China's culture of strong in-group collectivism contributes to the fact that local people living in cities view "strangers" or internal migrants from other Chinese provinces or cities with suspicion, and thus affects the employment and social integration of these migrants. Second, China presents a unique context: its immense population and geographical scale, and the large waves of internal migration provide an ideal foundation for our case study. In 2017, China's migrant workers represents the largest proportion of the worlds' internal migrants, reaching a total number of 286 million (National Bureau of Statistics of China, 2018), and thus changing the face of urbanization in China's cities and creates important questions for how careers of migrants and the host communities evolve.

The state, as a major player in the allocation of labor, has the power to be a force of change as geographical mobility in the permanent sense "mirrors the state's spatial development policy and ideological predisposition" (Li and Siu, 1997). One needs to be aware that the state has played and will play a role in controlling the process of migrant workers' flow to the cities. In recent years, the state is also controlling the increasing amount of migration in a more careful and observable way (Su, 2011). The most distinctive feature of Chinese rural-urban internal migration is that it is governed by a *hukou* system, the Chinese household registration which assigns Chinese individuals to their place of origin and grants them specific benefits, such as access to medical treatment, housing, schooling for their children, employment, social insurance, and so forth. This system essentially seeks to restrict the movement of workers within China. This system is unique – as other similarly intended systems found in Ethiopia and South Africa have been lifted due to failure (Deshingkar and Grimm, 2005). Even now, China is reforming the *hukou* system to continue to manage the movements of its people and ensure to the social and economic welfare of all its citizens. However, even when a government exerts very strong control over internal migration there can be many unintended consequences for the people involved, especially when it comes to their careers, which we present in this chapter.

Given this context, there is a need to understand how the careers of millions of migrant workers in China unfold as a result of a policy that constrains the geographical and social mobility of its people. To do so, we review the current state of China's internal migration policies and adopt the Interactive Acculturation Model (IAM) (Bourhis et al., 1997) to understand the acculturation and career outcomes of migrant workers in China (see Figure 23.1). The IAM models a broad range of migrant integration policies in Western (democratic) states and tries to connect it to acculturation strategies which are based on Berry's assumptions in this respective field (e.g., Berry, 1980, 1990). The model predicts that these acculturation strategies which are portrayed as a reciprocal relationship between migration and host community acculturation orientations are essentially a result of the aforementioned migration and state integration policies. As a final outcome, the reciprocal relationship between migrants and host community leads to relational outcomes as products of the respective acculturation orientations. This framework will help us to analyze China's approach to managing internal migration and show how it provides an explanation for the unintended consequences mentioned above. We address, from the IAM model (Figure 23.1) only the aspects of state migration policies, state integration policies, dominant host majority acculturation orientations, migrant communities' acculturation orientations. The IAM usually refers to immigrants, whereas we adopt and apply this model to the *internal* migration phenomenon and would thus use the term migrant. We take account of the perspectives and roles of multiple stakeholders, namely the government (or state), local community citizens, and the migrants and do so in a way that accounts for the different migrant types. Drawing on the IAM also helps us identify the state's and host communities' integration attitudes, as well as the migrants' own integration attitudes. Our analysis reveals that the state's orientation towards migrants affects the relationships between host communities and the migrants and has spillover effects on the careers of migrants. While IAM deals specifically with migration policies, attitudes and acculturation outcomes, it provides an important framework for explaining why migrants' careers vary and where opportunities to improve the outcomes of migrant workers may be found.

As research on migrant workers in the careers and management literature has also made significant strides in the past decade (Carr et al., 2005; Thomas et al., 2005; Connell et al., 2009; Zikic et al., 2010), we seek to contribute to this diverse body of research by casting the spotlight on state institutions and their impact on the career experiences of the *internal* migrant population. By accounting for the perspectives of different actors regarding their effect on migrants' life and especially work domains, we provide a more complete picture than the literature that has previously mainly focused on inequalities and institutional constraints of migrant versus urban

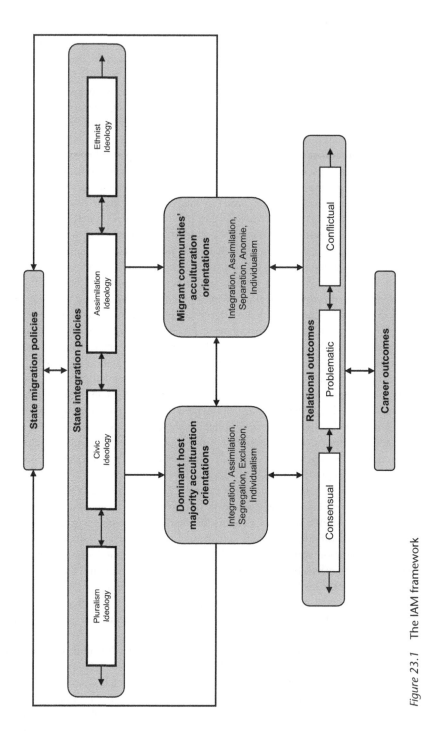

Figure 23.1 The IAM framework

Source: Bourhis et al. (1997: 371), adapted and modified.

population (Nielsen et al., 2006; Chen and Wang, 2015). Accounting for the acculturation attitudes of the different stakeholders should yield greater insight into the acculturation process and the implications for the stakeholders and the migrants' careers. It also allows us more targeted and effective policy recommendations which incorporate the needs of the different stakeholders, thus concluding our chapter.

In the following sections, we discuss China's migrant policy context, followed by China's attitude towards integrating rural-urban migrants. We reveal that China's evolving migrant policies vary in their treatment of different types of migrants – temporary or permanent. We introduce the IAM to situate the integration attitudes of the state, host communities, and migrants, recognizing that the career outcomes of different types of migrants are very much dependent on the attitudes of the different stakeholders. We conclude by offering implications and outlining current and potential challenges posed by diverse stakeholders. We hope to demonstrate that a government policy on migration, albeit internal migration, has significant direct and indirect impact on the career experiences of its population as it not only affects mobility and opportunities, but also the attitudes that the non-migrant populations have towards the migrant population and migrants' own attitudes towards their careers.

State migration policies

State policies on internal migration, largely driven by economic and/or social interests of the state, determine rural-urban migration flows and the possibilities for migrants to settle down in cities. These flows and possibilities in China are uniquely controlled by the *hukou* system. This system was designed to allow cities to benefit from much-needed labor, while ensuring that the influx of workers does not overwhelm public services. However, what it inadvertently created was a social stratification of Chinese workers based on the *hukou* they carry. Initially designed in the 1950s by the Chinese government for internal migration control, the *hukou* system soon became a social institution creating social hierarchies within the population. One's *hukou* was classified in terms of place of origin – either rural or urban – and in terms of socioeconomic eligibility – agricultural or non-agricultural with the latter group being afforded better welfare treatment by the state, and greater employment opportunities than the former. Rural migrants retain their rural *hukou* status even when they migrate to the urban centers. As a result, they are not afforded the same rights and benefits as the local or urban *hukou* holders, facing serious discrimination in their everyday life, including their work life, by the local people, employers, and institutions. Without a resident *hukou* for the urban center that the migrants work and reside in, workers and their families are denied access to many public services, including schools for their children.

Migrant workers fall into two categories – permanent migrants and temporary migrants. In China, the former category of migrants are also termed the "elites" because permanent migrants often are sponsored by the state to hold positions in state-owned enterprises (SOEs), have or seek higher levels of education and training, such as graduate and post-graduate degrees, enjoy more privileges and access to institutional resources, and may often even be better off socially and economically than the native urban population (Fan, 2002). These permanent migrants are also likely to be migrating from other urban centers, instead of from the rural provinces. According to a comparison of Chinese census data, Sun and Fan (2011) found that permanent migrants are usually highly educated, young and employed in prestigious occupations. Thus, the socioeconomic status of permanent migrants is relatively similar to or better than the non-migrant workers in the cities they reside in (Chen, 2011) and they can access employment to a similar degree. The careers of permanent migrants may thus be indistinguishable from those of locals and may sometimes even exceed those of locals who are not as highly educated.

On the other end of the spectrum, "outsiders" are viewed as temporary, or floating, the low-skilled migrant workers from rural areas who are not considered part of the "plan" (Fan, 2002), arriving in urban centers to perform the jobs that the natives or the elites are unwilling to perform. Not unlike Germany's *Gastarbeiter* (guest workers) in the mid-1900s, or the Chinese immigrants in Canada in the 1880s, such migrants are denied permanent urban residency rights and other benefits. In China, this denial results in exclusion from local society because an agricultural *hukou* keeps migrants from gaining socioeconomic status (Kuang and Liu, 2012). Most of the low-skilled, temporary migrants are usually employed in the informal sector, where job security is low and turnover is high (Wang and Fan, 2012). For them, employment is viewed as means to increase income, which, combined with the limited chance of obtaining an urban *hukou* increases job insecurity, fueling the increase of labor turnover rates (Fan, 2002) – which already surpass 20 percent – and building a continuing trend (Jiang et al., 2009).

Regardless, migrants, the "outsiders," using Fan's (2002) categorization, are generally more likely to be disadvantaged compared to natives. In the past, migrants filled jobs that were not popular among the local urbans (Knight and Yueh, 2004) or were not granted consideration for employment in SOEs. In the mid-1990s, many SOEs were not profitable, partly due to overstaffing and thus cuts to their mostly local workforce were needed (Chen, 2011) during the redundancy program launched in the mid-1990s. This further reinforced discriminatory policies, as local workers were considered for employment before migrants. Additionally, most of the contracts were short term (Knight and Yueh, 2004), meaning that migrants had to return to their hometowns if contracts were not renewed.

However, the state has recently modified some *hukou*-related practices and intends to gradually push reforms further to improve the situation for migrant workers. The state government now plans to grant urban residency to 100 million migrant workers by 2020 (He et al., 2015; Liang, 2016). A point system will be used to determine the eligibility for these urban *hukous*. Holders of these *hukous* will then have access to education, medical treatment, employment, housing, and social insurance, equal to the local residents. Furthermore, the former transitional or temporary *lanyin* or blue-stamp *hukou* will also be removed and the categories of "non-agricultural" and "agricultural" will be unified into a single "resident registration" (*jumin hukou*) regardless of the people's urban or rural origin (People's Republic of China Central Government, 2014). These changes are expected to facilitate mobility and integration of migrants in cities, as well as reduce the discrepancies between migrant groups and locals regarding their rights, benefits, and status. Some researchers have acknowledged the constructive strategies the state established to promote and develop migration (Solinger, 1999; Guang, 2005). Additionally, some efforts have been made to protect temporary migrants by setting up job centres, providing free legal services for migrant workers to collect any delayed salary payments, and offering some labour protection (Li, 2006).

That said, criticisms remain, including how these changes might be superficial, insufficient for improving the livelihoods of migrant workers (Goodburn, 2014) or help to reduce prejudice, and how they might actually be implemented across the provinces. There are potentially unintended consequences which undermine the recent efforts being made and thus provoke criticism of state practices (Li, 2005; Goodburn, 2014). For instance, the majority of reforms are likely to target higher educated permanent migrant workers. Most of the temporary migrants are unlikely to qualify for the urban *hukou* under the point system and have little hope to obtain one of the very limited numbers of urban *hukous* available. Further, although several announcements and experimental implementations in certain cities have been made, such as Shanghai, actual implementation and effects remain uncertain leading some researchers to believe that these efforts are insufficient and result in other undesirable outcomes for migrants (Wang, 2006; Lan, 2014).

Further, state laws meant to help migrants may have unintended consequences. The state policies are usually the first step to increasing equal treatment of migrants. For instance, the state has issued instructions for public institutions regarding contact with migrants, such as the "Notice on the management of and services for rural people coming to work in cities" (Reutersward, 2005). The Labor Law in 1995, Mediation and Arbitration Law in 2008, and the new Labor Contract Law in 2008 require written contracts between employer and every employee, limited overtime hours, and a greater role for the trade unions (Wang et al., 2009). These changes empowered the workers to a certain degree. Previously, workers were largely informally employed or only had vague contract statements on a temporary basis (Wang et al., 2009). However, the enforcement of these laws has proven to be problematic and has yielded only a limited positive effect so far. Labor rights can be easily violated if workers found their jobs through personal networks, and are therefore more likely to tolerate mistreatment by the employer due to personal ties and obligations. Some firms even reduce real wages by unilaterally reducing the unit price of production or raising the production target, forcing workers to work unpaid overtime to complete their tasks. Wage arrears and unlawful deduction of wages were the most common violations revealed in the labor inspections (Cooke, 2012). Therefore, despite good intentions, the laws may not be doing enough to fully protect the nations' most vulnerable group of workers – the low skilled, temporary migrants. Nevertheless, the state's policies reveal to us its attitude towards the integration of migrants, and affect the host communities' attitudes towards migrants. We turn to these issues next.

State's integration policies

According to the IAM, four clusters describe a typology of possible ideologies that states hold about the integration of migrants, namely, pluralism ideology, civic ideology, assimilation ideology, and ethnist ideology (Bourhis et al., 1997). The pluralism and civic ideologies respect the private values of migrants while expecting that migrants adopt the public values of the host community. States with such orientations support, and at the very least, do not interfere with the activities of migrants to maintain or promote their cultural, linguistic, ethnic, and/or religious distinctiveness. The difference between pluralism and civic ideologies lies within the fact that civic ideology would in certain cases grant state funding to preserve interests of (mainly) the dominant majority group whereas pluralism would also support the migrant cohorts in regards to funding availability so that they can maintain some of their own cultural distinctiveness while adapting to public values of the host majority. With an assimilation ideology, migrants should adopt the public values of the host community but the state also expects them to abandon their distinctiveness and may impose laws and regulations to restrict the manifestation of this distinctiveness. The ethnist ideology takes this intrusion even further to, in some cases, expect migrants to reject their private values and adapt to the host community's, and in others have no expectations because the state has no intention of ever accepting migrants as rightful members of the host community.

Although the Chinese migrants are ethnoculturally homogeneous to the local population, they generally receive little financial support or official recognition as part of the local population. However, we can observe that the state treats different categories of migrants in a different way, depending on their utilization for the continuous economic growth of the country – the skilled migrants having greater potential for utilization. Regarding temporary migrants, the low-skilled migrants are usually placed within special areas of the cities; therefore, the state *does* interfere with and controls the private values of this group. This can be characterized as assimilation or even an ethnist approach as this geographical exclusion already indicates their standing in society. One could argue that they may never be treated as equal and are thus marginalized. For the skilled group of temporary migrants, the evidence suggests a more civic or even pluralistic approach by the state, to first attract this higher status class and integrate them into the urban cities in the long term. This group perfectly fits into the upscaling plans of the Chinese economy, which relies heavily on a highly skilled workforce to drive innovation. Therefore, the state gives priority to this group in granting urban *hukous* before turning to the lower strata of unskilled temporary workforce that would potentially not net a positive return for the state in terms of advancements in technology and to the economy. Regarding the permanent migrants, low-skilled permanent migrants are still a little better off as they qualified for the urban *hukou* already and are thus entitled to certain benefits not available to temporary migrants. Overall, we may infer that the skilled migrants, both temporary and permanent, are not treated differently from the native urban population.

In sum, China's current integration policy context and attitude could be characterized as a mix of civic and assimilation ideology that varies depending on the type of migrant in question. According to the IAM, the state's integration policies can have a substantial impact on the attitudes of host communities towards migrants, and the migrants' own attitudes towards integration. Thus, we next turn our discussion to the attitudes of host communities.

Dominant host majority acculturation orientations

The model proposes that relational outcomes form the result of certain acculturation orientations of host majority and migrant groups, respectively, being themselves a product of state integration policies which have been outlined above. This fact has also been acknowledged by Berry and colleagues in previous studies (Berry, 1974; Berry et al., 1977). Additionally, the attitudes of the state towards the different groups of internal migrants also influence the attitudes of the dominant group – the host citizens – within the respective Chinese cities or provinces (Bourhis et al., 1997). These attitudes vary depending on the type of migrant – whether they are the low-skilled migrants, or the higher-skilled, higher educated migrants. To help understand the integration attitudes of host communities, we turn to the IAM again. Two dimensions provided by the IAM help situate the acculturation orientation of host community members pertaining to the acceptability of (1) migrants maintaining their cultural heritage and (2) migrants adopting the culture of the host community. Based on the work of Berry and colleagues, this results in a five-way classification of host community members' acculturation orientations towards migrants: integration, assimilation, segregation, exclusion, and individualism. Exclusion means that the host community is not only intolerant regarding migrants' culture but also denies them adopting characteristics of the host culture. Individualism is probably the most ideal way, as this approach goes beyond migrant or local categorization. Members belonging to this category evaluate personal characteristics of individuals rather than judging people on the group they formally belong to. Thus, they will not judge migrants' successful acculturation based on whether migrants maintained their own culture or adopted to the host culture (Bourhis et al., 1997).

Exclusion or segregation

Host community urban citizens, especially those citizens with urban *hukou* at birth, higher educational background, and household income, have a prejudiced opinion about low-skilled migrant workers, often referred to as *nongmingong* (rural workers). According to Wang and Zuo

(1999), they believe them to be "uneducated, ignorant, dirty, and also have high propensities to be criminals," which is also partially a result of the cohort's representation in the media (Wong et al., 2007). Therefore, most of these urban citizens show a high self-identification as a local and a preference to interact only with locals (Tse, 2016). The group boundaries based on the Chinese *hukou*-system are an institutional cause for prejudice against rural-to-urban migrants (Zhang et al., 2014). On one hand, the locals are grateful that the migrant workers perform the less desirable "3D" (dirty, difficult, and dangerous) jobs (Liang, 2016) that they would not deign to do, but at the same time, they despise the migrants for doing those jobs (Fan, 2002; Li, 2005, 2006).

Besides status-based exclusion, migrants are also actively separated because of different skin color, dialect, cuisine, clothes or other regional cultural behavior (Fan, 2002; Li, 2005). Although the culture among the Chinese Han ethnicity is relatively similar, there are still certain behaviors, appearances and dialects that easily distinguish the local from the migrant population. Additionally, locals with lower socioeconomic status show even more prejudice against (low-skilled) migrants since they directly compete with them for the same jobs. This phenomenon is mitigated when migrants are seen to be separated from or marginalized by the rest of society (Yang et al., 2010).

Integration or assimilation

With the increased ambitiousness of urbanization plans, however, we propose that in time, the local and migrant populations will become less distinguishable as migrants become accustomed and integrated into the urban lifestyle. At the intergroup neighborhood level, however, Wang et al. (2016) revealed that contact and support between migrants and urbans exists, which even seems to be stronger in deprived neighborhoods. These ties between local and migrants could further enrich social integration (Yue et al., 2013) and these ties seem to be stronger among the young generation of migrants who also seek more interaction with locals than former migrant generations (Liu et al., 2012). Interestingly, permanent migrants are equivalent to their non-migrant counterparts in terms of earnings (Wang et al., 2013). But this still does not seem to be enough to place these migrants at the same level with the local urbans.

Therefore, this hints at an ambivalent mixture of integration and separation approaches for low- and high-skilled migrants. High-skilled migrants are treated similarly based on their educational attainment, but never fully accepted as insiders when interacting with the local population as they might still be perceived as being different which could be due to limited contact and interaction between the groups. The same logic applies to low-skilled migrants, although the likelihood of integration is far less likely as the local community still looks down on this stratum of migrants and seek little interaction.

Migrant communities' acculturation orientations

According to the IAM, migrants' acculturation orientations include integration, assimilation, segregation, anomie (rejecting both own and the host's cultures), or individualism (seeing themselves and others as individuals).

Integration or assimilation

In our case, according to IAM, low-skilled migrants who reject their own *nongmin* or peasant background, as well as high-skilled migrants, want to shed their migrant status to pursue a city lifestyle similar to the local community, thus characterizing them as belonging to the anomie group. If this group fails to integrate, it can also negatively affect their self-esteem. Most of the younger generation born in the '80s or '90s, the so-called second-generation migrants, are driven to integrate in the city (Huang and Liu, 2016) and become urban citizens. They usually migrate immediately after obtaining a basic level of education in order to seek better living conditions in the cities. Migrants

> "who are socially and culturally adapted, who speak the dialect of the host society, and who have the financial resources to buy an apartment in the city or pursue self-employment are more likely than other migrants to develop a sense of belonging in the city."
>
> *(Wang and Fan, 2012: 746)*

Individualism

This specific cohort often consider themselves neither migrant nor local; therefore, they find themselves in a no man's land, seeking their identity. However, they seem more individualistic and confident to pursue a life that is not shaped by these social categories. They seek their own way to deal with the integration. This individualistic attitude might also be the product of persisting discrimination among the local host community on one side and pride (resulting because of rejection) of the migrants on the other side who were confronted with these barriers and thus left with returning to their original identity as the only choice. Despite their great desire to settle down in the cities, this is by no means easy, as factors such as education, labor market outcomes, and interaction with local urban residents influence their social integration to a great extent (Chen and Wang, 2015).

Segregation

Unfortunately, the assimilation process usually favors the dominant, local group because of its inherent status which goes hand in hand with the institutional control it possesses, therefore leaving the migrant group at levels of lower social hierarchy (Bourhis et al., 1997). Due to this continuing discrimination, the self-esteem of migrants is affected (Kan, 2013), resulting in describing themselves by the term *diaosi* ("loser"). When people face discrimination, they are much more likely to identify with the group of their origin (Padilla and Perez, 2003) and also show less willingness to acculturate because they do not believe that the host society would accept them even if they try. Discrimination might further foster this identification as people retreat within their own groups instead of seeking contact with the discriminating group. It further increases perceived intergroup inequalities and injustice, and creates intergroup conflict. For those who do *not* want to integrate, the environment makes them feel even less welcome while also creating social pressures to make efforts to integrate (e.g. abandon their local dialect) during conversations. They are usually torn between considering the value of retaining their own cultural identity and desiring to seek interaction with the host community.

Relational outcomes

At the moment, there exists a mismatch or discordance between the orientation modes of the host and migrant groups. The majority of migrants want to integrate and live in the cities, whereas the majority of the host community still harbor prejudices against this group and despise them. Accordingly, they rather seek segregation, a clear separation between the two groups without any desired contact. These different combinations of attitudes regarding host community and migrants lead to relational outcomes that are highly problematic and conflictual. Only if both groups select an individualistic approach, can these relational attitudes be consensual (Bourhis et al., 1997). However, the potential clashes between host community and migrants would be more severe for the temporary or low-skilled migrants. This mismatch affects relational outcomes on a social-psychological level – communication, discrimination, acculturative stress, and attitudes or stereotypes (Bourhis et al., 1997). We discuss how this interferes with their careers next.

Career outcomes

As a result of the state's policies on rural-urban migration, and the integration attitudes of the state and the host community, migrant workers often face discrimination, not only in society, but also in organizations. First, they only have limited job choice possibilities, due to certain regulations that have been passed on during the 1990s and early 2000s, excluding them from upward social mobility (Li, 2005) into the desired strata of the urban labor market. Limited access to welfare or social security, delay of wage payment, pay differentials regarding the urban workforce, long working hours and poor working/health conditions, and absence of training opportunities are common issues migrant workers are facing when they come to work in factories located in the coastal cities (Li, 2005; Hartmann et al., 2012). Compared to the local population, the unskilled migrant cohorts tend to be disadvantaged in terms of pay and underrepresented regarding managerial positions they obtained (Knight and Song, 2005).

In general, we observe that the literature is scant regarding the career prospects that migrant workers have. However, job mobility seems to be one of the core issues that have been most often discussed (Knight and Yueh, 2004; Zhang, 2010). It is mostly linked to institutional constraints, explained by using the framework of the segmented labor market. The current categorization of Chinese society seems to be based on occupation (farmers, workers, intelligentsia, managers, and private entrepreneurs), keeping rural laborers or manual workers mostly trapped at the bottom of society (Li, 2005) because of their limited access to education. Migrants differing by educational attainment find themselves in different parts of a segmented labor market, with different possibilities to acquire economic status. Most of the low-skilled temporary migrants are usually employed in the informal sector, where job security is low which in turn increases turnover (Wang and Fan, 2012).

Furthermore, segmented labor market theory, which focuses on job mobility and its barriers, confirms that institutional structures are preventing migrants from attaining favorable jobs. Chen (2011) argues that the segmentation of the labor market, in addition to institutions which constrain mobility between the segments, offers jobs characterized by certain benefits, appropriate pay level, and development opportunities on the one hand and jobs characterized by low pay, bad working conditions, and low job security on the other. Theoretically, the likelihood of upward occupational mobility increases with time. However, Chinese migrants are less likely to escape lower strata work once they assume their first "bad" job (Chen, 2011), as they will not be integrated in the labor market. Hence, for low-skilled migrants, inequalities will persist and for high-skilled migrants they will be reduced over time (Liang, 2016). However, institutional discrimination reduces the number of jobs available to the migrants, increases their job search costs and the cost of losing jobs. Even though migrants take jobs unacceptable to local residents, the effects of this institutional discrimination still constrain migrants in changing jobs (Zhang, 2010). Especially when unemployment is high, temporary migrants are the first to suffer, since government discourages employment of migrants during times of high unemployment and they additionally face increased resentment from the urban population as they are blamed for job losses (Li, 2005).

For poorly educated workers, job mobility is one of the most important factors in improving their income. The voluntary mobility is higher among skilled/educated migrants and higher among younger people with more career options. It also seems to increase with the advancement of labor market reforms (Knight and Yueh, 2004), providing more job alternatives. As the environment is gradually being privatized, this also increases voluntary labor turnover among young locals since the restrictions related to working in SOEs are no longer present. Job mobility, however, has been found to have little effect on the income of highly educated workers, whose income stratification is mostly affected by years of schooling and work experience (Wu, 2011).

In general, the high mobility rates are not only a product of individual characteristics, but also caused by the institutional environment as "prohibition on or impediments to urban settlement, restricted access to skilled jobs, and the system of short-term contracts, may have generated an excessively high migrant mobility rate" (Knight and Yueh, 2004: 659). Usually, migrants start to change jobs more often only after they have stayed in the city for some time and have accumulated enough assets to be able to survive when unemployed (Zhang, 2010). Finally, Zhang (2010: 53) stated that,

> "compared to non-migrants, the migrants have lower or similar job mobility rates, that is consistent with the presence of institutional discrimination against them. If they are found to have higher job mobility rates, that suggests that the supply of jobs which residents will not accept is so large that it dominates the effects of institutional discrimination on migrant job mobility."

Internal migration or talent (Chapter 21, this volume) flow (Carr et al., 2005) could also contribute to bridging the gap between the rich coastal area and the still relatively poor inland provinces. The increase of knowledge that migrants gain during their employment in the coastal area could contribute to their increasing activity in their hometowns (e.g., as entrepreneurs opening their own businesses). In the migrant context, causes of labor mobility are economic, such as the higher wages and higher employment opportunities in the coastal areas. Reasons for returning mostly lie within their personal networks, such as close family ties.

Thus, we conclude that migrants are still embedded in their role as "second-class workers" (Démurger et al., 2009) being deprived of access to certain occupations and equal earnings mostly connected to lower educational status of the young migrants in comparison to their urban counterparts. However, with educational level higher than senior middle school (*gaozhong*), discrimination is significantly reduced, leading to equal opportunities in regards to jobs of migrants and locals (Chen, 2011). At the same time, we believe that high-skilled temporary migrants and low-skilled temporary migrants are subject to a similar level of discrimination although for different reasons. High-skilled temporary migrants increase competition on the labor market and therefore reduce economic security (Esses et al., 1998; Maisonneuve and Testé, 2007) especially for the laid-off workers of SOEs (Wong et al., 2007), whereas low-skilled migrants usually take the jobs the local community in the urban areas are not willing to take anyway. In this vein, the competition caused by temporary low-skilled migrants is usually not considered as serious for locals (Zhang, 2010). In sum, we could say that low-skilled temporary migrants are subject to discrimination because of their low status, whereas high-skilled temporary migrants are subject to discrimination because they pose a threat to locals' occupational attainment opportunities.

Discussion

Theoretical implications

Especially in the Chinese context, the IAM provides a useful framework to analyze the state's and host community's attitudes toward migrant workers, as well as the migrant workers' attitudes about integrating to the host community. This then allows us to speak to the life and work of migrant workers and the career-related outcomes of migrants. We think that this framework is applicable to China, and for other countries that are characterized by a segmented labor market or where the state plays a dominant role. However, a cautious approach is necessary to draw conclusions about generalizability since segmented labor markets models in developing countries are highly diverse (Fields, 2009). For example, this framework could be used to examine why similar policies in other countries like Indonesia and South Africa were unsuccessful in controlling population mobility, even when extreme measures (e.g., destroying unapproved housing, forcible relocation) were used (Msigwa and Bwana, 2014). Although the IAM theoretical framework adopted here has been developed more for individualistic countries, we suggest that it is applicable to the context of collectivistic countries to further enrich careers research (Bimrose and McNair, 2011), being applicable for both internal migrants, as has been shown in this chapter, and immigrants, referring to the original application context of the IAM.

Implications for state policy

The state plays a vital role in reducing discrimination and ensuring fair participation in the labor market and limiting the exploitation of cheap labor by employers (Bimrose and McNair, 2011). As our analysis reveals, China's policies and adjustments to the *hukou* system, despite good intentions, have yielded rather mixed results and do not decrease the existing barriers between migrants and host communities – although recent estimates suggest that migration has contributed 16 percent annually to China's GDP (DeWind and Holdaway, 2005). We would even go as far as to say that the gap between the local and migrant population is increasing given, for example the recent evictions of migrant workers in Beijing, "tearing at the fabric of the city's economy" (South China Morning Post, 2018). They do not go far enough to improve living conditions, training and development, and thus career opportunities in host cities or hometowns for low-skilled migrants that are forced to bear with poor conditions at the host and perform jobs with limited career development prospects, or to return home. Indeed, low-skilled "migrants will not have the luxury of selecting an occupation that best suits their personal profile, abilities and qualifications" (Bimrose and McNair, 2011: 328).

Thus, to enhance the integration of low-skilled migrants, the state could, first, accelerate the formulation and implementation regarding the integration of internal migrants and subsequently further strengthen the integration of disadvantaged migrant groups. This means taking a pluralism or civic approach in the language of the IAM as opposed to an ethnist or assimilation approach that many countries adopt. Institutional and structural barriers still play a major role in the creation of equality, as they are intertwined with individual factors limiting migrants access to opportunities and resources (Chen and Wang, 2015). Although there have been some transformations regarding the *hukou* system in the past 50 years (Chan, 2009), there still is room for improvement, as the majority of migrants are still not able to obtain local *hukou* status at the respective migration destination, reducing their chances in life and work (Solinger, 1999; Wing Chan and Buckingham, 2008; Chen, 2011). If these institutional barriers cannot be reduced, solely providing skill-enhancing opportunities will have no effects, as skills, education, *and* urban background seem to increase job mobility (Chen, 2011). However, as a first step, at least the institutional environment needs to incorporate migrants, as they are neither part of the unemployment statistics nor are they entitled to get help from governmental institutions working with administration of employment opportunities (Zhang, 2010). The lack of good data on internal migration is a problem faced in many countries and hinders the ability of governments to take effective action (Deshingkar and Grimm, 2005).

Second, the attitudes of the local community are still characterized by the locals' unwillingness to accept migrants as part of their community – exclusion or segregation ideology. Prolonged contact might, however, influence both parties to a certain extent, since prejudices can be reduced and an exchange of values and behavior can take place. Chen and Wang (2015) also confirm that in addition to labor market outcomes, interaction with local urban residents is beneficial for migrants' social integration. *Multicultural* ideology on both sides, the dominant, local, and the non-dominant group of the migrants, facilitates intergroup contact via mediation through greater tolerance or lower perceived discrimination (Hui et al., 2015), indicating that both parties have to make one step towards each other. Furthermore, public attitude could be influenced through various institutional means, such as the educational system, public administration, and the mass media (Bourhis et al., 1997; Meeussen et al., 2013) to reduce the urban-rural social dichotomy. Increased media attention could be one way to reduce the deep rooted discrimination by local citizens or institutions such as the police (Li, 2005). An external labor market needs to be built. This influence can further have an impact on acculturation strategies of both groups. The reputation of migrants and thus their economic value from the perspective of the receiving community should be improved (Montreuil and Bourhis, 2001, 2004; Maisonneuve and Testé, 2007; Bourhis et al., 2009).

Third, from a government's perspective, migrants returning home can also be beneficial especially for provinces with a lower economic development status, since the returnees can function as developers of the rural regions by providing capital and engage in entrepreneurship. Thus, local provinces or municipalities can profit from the returnees' resources and knowledge by integrating them in the development of the province (Murphy, 2000; Démurger and Xu, 2011). The central government's policies also influences the attractiveness of migration destinations, as cities with a higher administrative level (ranging from county level to prefecture level, and province level cities) implies more job opportunities in public administration and public service resources (Liu et al., 2015).

Moving beyond the Chinese case: global implications for government policy

What can we learn from the Chinese case? What and how might migration policies, attitudes, outcomes affect migrant careers? What happens when governments have few controls or too many constraints placed on the movement of their own people? Policies that govern internal migration are also in place in other countries and reveal the integration attitudes of the state. Governments like Malaysia, Philippines, and India have adopted resettlement schemes; others like Cuba and Sri Lanka attempted colonization or settlement schemes, building more houses, roads, industry, and basic services to discourage outward migration (Msigwa and Bwana, 2014). Still others, like Canada, adopt policies relating to unemployment insurance, personal income taxes, social assistance, and provincial and federal spending, to induce a more even distribution of migrants across provinces (Day and Winer, 2006). Some of these policies have been shown to be effective while many have been fruitless. What appear to be universal are the perils that accompany rapid and unplanned urbanization and the futility of migration policies when comparative earnings and employment prospects remain the key drivers of migration (Day and Winer, 2006). For instance, internal migration in India accelerated coinciding with India's economic liberation program initiated in 1991 and migration flows followed regional differences in development across its 35 states and Union Territories (Bhagat, 2016). This is further complicated by gender differences in migration in India – with men moving for employment, and women for marriage. As a result of uncontrolled migration, receiving cities and regions often are unable to provide proper living conditions, social security, and basic services for all. This causes migration to be untenable and unattractive to the poorest migrants as well where local governments may enforce strong laws to evict illegal or undocumented migrants. Undocumented Indonesian migrants, for example, who flock to urban hubs like Jakarta are deprived of health benefits, have no formal access to clean water and housing, and are relegated to informal employment arrangements (International Organization for Migration, 2015). As such, many governments around the world seek to manage the flows of their population internally to manage the complex problem of ensuring that people are gainfully employed, their protections and rights assured, while enabling the country's economic prosperity.

The consequences of poor planning and ineffective migration policies are many, particularly when the migrants are low-skill, low-education – a population that cities are unlikely to be able and even unwilling to accommodate because of the high costs of living, already stretched public services, like transportation. Such ethnist attitudes towards migrants in cities where the local governments are hostile to the extent that no rights are afforded to the poor and unskilled migrants, and the public blame migrants for the woes of the cities (Bhagat, 2016), make it really difficult for this category of migrants to integrate and establish their careers beyond working in the lowest levels of the economy and to settle long-term or permanently in these cities. Hence, if the inflow of migrants is inevitable, then governments do need to pay attention to various policies and programs that ensure that the local population are not significantly harmed by migration with respect to a whole host of aspects related to their quality of life, cost of living, and opportunities for their own career development. This may then encourage more open, welcoming, and respectful (i.e., civic or pluralistic ideologies) attitudes of the host cities and enable the employment and social integration of migrants to occur. If this is not addressed, the attitudes towards migrants could become or remain hostile and migrants are likely to face discrimination in employment and unlikely to pursue careers at the host cities for the long term.

Avenues for future research

While migrants continue to be predominantly male, the number of women migrants is not only increasing in China (Yang and Guo, 1999; Sun and Fan, 2011) but can be seen as a global trend of empowering women. Especially in this stream of literature, the employment and social vulnerability of women migrants is a critical issue for study (Deshingkar and Grimm, 2005). Return migration, we think, could also be a vital issue. Migrants' decision to return is a result of policies of the sending and receiving locations, as well as family separation duration (Piotrowski and Tong, 2013; Liang, 2016). As already mentioned in the case of China, the chance of the return migrants to engage in entrepreneurial actions could improve their place of origin and present a career shift (Liang, 2016). The impact of urbanizing villages as well as providing incentives for return on the return and re-integration of migrants would be important to understand.

Conclusion

In this chapter, we relied on the IAM to explain and discuss the interactions between the main players regarding integration, namely state, host communities, and the diverse migrant groups. While China is a unique context, the lessons from the impact of various legal and mobility restrictions, and the integration attitudes of the state, communities, and migrants, policies and attitudes towards migrant workers on the well-being of citizens may be instructive for other nations as they consider the social and employment integration of their own citizens as well as those from other nations.

References

Berry, J.W. 1974. Psychological aspects of cultural pluralism: Unity and identity reconsidered. *Topics in Culture Learning*, 2, 17–22.

Berry, J.W. 1980. Acculturation as varieties of adaptation. *In:* Padilla, A.M. (ed.) *Acculturation: Theory, Models, and Some New Findings*. Boulder, CO: Westview Press, 9–26.

Berry, J.W. 1990. The role of psychology in ethnic studies. *Canadian Ethnic Studies*, 22 (1), 8–21.

Berry, J.W., Kalin, R. & Taylor, D. M. 1977. *Multiculturalism and Ethnic Attitudes in Canada*. Ottawa: Minister of State for Multiculturalism.

Bhagat, R.B. 2016. Changing pattern of internal migration in India. *In:* Guilmoto, C.Z. & Jones, G.W. (eds.) *Contemporary Demographic Transformations in China, India and Indonesia*. Cham, Heidelberg, New York, Dordrecht and London: Springer, 239–254.

Bimrose, J. & McNair, S. 2011. Career support for migrants: Transformation or adaptation? *Journal of Vocational Behavior*, 78 (3), 325–333.

Bourhis, R.Y., Moïse, L.C., Perreault, S. & Senécal, S. 1997. Towards an interactive acculturation model: A social psychological approach. *International Journal of Psychology*, 32 (6), 369–386.

Bourhis, R.Y., Montreuil, A., Barrette, G. & Montaruli, E. 2009. Acculturation and immigrant/host community relations in multicultural settings. *In:* Demoulin, S., Leyens, J.P. & Dovidio, J. (eds.) *Intergroup Misunderstanding: Impact of Divergent Social Realities*. New York: Psychology Press, 39–61.

Carr, S.C., Inkson, K. & Thorn, K. 2005. From global careers to talent flow: Reinterpreting 'brain drain'. *Journal of World Business*, 40 (4), 386–398.

Chan, K.W. 2009. The Chinese hukou system at 50. *Eurasian Geography and Economics*, 50 (2), 197–221.

Chen, Y. 2011. Occupational attainment of migrants and local workers: Findings from a survey in Shanghai's manufacturing sector. *Urban Studies*, 48 (1), 3–21.

Chen, Y. & Wang, J. 2015. Social integration of new-generation migrants in Shanghai China. *Habitat International*, 49, 419–425.

Connell, J., Burgess, J., Fang, T., Zikic, J. & Novicevic, M.M. 2009. Career success of immigrant professionals: Stock and flow of their career capital. *International Journal of Manpower*, 30 (5), 472–488.

Cooke, F.L. 2012. *Human Resource Management in China: New Trends and Practices*. Abingdon, Oxon and New York: Routledge.

Day, K.M. & Winer, S.L. 2006. Policy-induced internal migration: An empirical investigation of the Canadian case. *International Tax and Public Finance*, 13 (5), 535–564.

Démurger, S., Gurgand, M., Li, S. & Yue, X. 2009. Migrants as second-class workers in urban China? A decomposition analysis. *Journal of Comparative Economics*, 37 (4), 610–628.

Démurger, S. & Xu, H. 2011. Return migrants: The rise of new entrepreneurs in rural China. *World Development*, 39 (10), 1847–1861.

Deshingkar, P. & Grimm, S. 2005. *Internal Migration and Development: A Global Perspective*. IOM Migration Research Series 19. Geneva: United Nations Publications.

DeWind, J., & Holdaway, J. 2005. *Internal and International Migration in Economic Development. Fourth Coordination Meeting on International Migration*. New York: United Nations.

Esses, V.M., Jackson, L.M. & Armstrong, T.L. 1998. Intergroup competition and attitudes toward immigrants and immigration: An instrumental model of group conflict. *Journal of Social Issues*, 54 (4), 699–724.

Fan, C.C. 2002. The elite, the natives, and the outsiders: Migration and labor market segmentation in urban China. *Annals of the Association of American Geographers*, 92 (1), 103–124.

Fields, G.S. 2009. Segmented labor market models in developing countries. *In*: Kincaid, H. & Ross, D. (eds.) *The Oxford Handbook of Philosophy of Economics*. Oxford: Oxford University Press, 476–510.

Gelfand, M.J., Raver, J.L., Nishii, L., Leslie, L.M., Lun, J., Lim, B.C., Duan, L., Almaliach, A., Ang, S. & Arnadottir, J. 2011. Differences between tight and loose cultures: A 33-nation study. *Science*, 332, 1100–1104.

Goodburn, C. 2014. The end of the hukou system? Not yet. *University of Nottingham China Policy Institute Policy Papers 2* [Online]. Available: https://www.nottingham.ac.uk/cpi/documents/policy-papers/cpi-policy-paper-2014-no-2-goodburn.pdf [Accessed 12 September 2016].

Guang, L. 2005. The state connection in China's rural-urban migration. *International Migration Review*, 39 (2), 354–380.

Hartmann, P., Schiller, D. & Kraas, F. 2012. Workplace quality and labour turnover in the electronics industry of the Pearl River Delta, China: Contrasting employer and employee perspective. *Zeitschrift für Wirtschaftsgeographie*, 56 (1–2), 58–79.

He, S., Li, S.-M. & Chan, K.W. 2015. Migration, communities, and segregation in Chinese cities: Introducing the special issue. *Eurasian Geography and Economics*, 56 (3), 223–230.

Huang, X. & Liu, X. 2016. Consumption and social integration: Empirical evidence for Chinese migrant workers. *Economics – The Open-Access, Open-Assessment E-journal*, 11, 1–24.

Hui, B.P.H., Chen, S.X., Leung, C.M. & Berry, J.W. 2015. Facilitating adaptation and intercultural contact: The role of integration and multicultural ideology in dominant and non-dominant groups. *International Journal of Intercultural Relations*, 45, 70–84.

International Organization for Migration. 2015. *World Migration Report 2015: Migrants and Cities: New Partnerships to Manage Mobility*. Geneva: IOM International Organization for Migration.

Jiang, B., Baker, R.C. & Frazier, G.V. 2009. An analysis of job dissatisfaction and turnover to reduce global supply chain risk: Evidence from China. *Journal of Operations Management*, 27 (2), 169–184.

Kan, K. 2013. The new "Lost Generation": Inequality and discontent among Chinese youth. *China Perspectives* (2013/2), 63–73.

Knight, J. & Yueh, L. 2004. Job mobility of residents and migrants in urban China. *Journal of Comparative Economics*, 32 (4), 637–660.

Knight, J.B. & Song, L. 2005. *Towards a Labour Market in China*. New York: Oxford University Press.

Kuang, L. & Liu, L. 2012. Discrimination against rural-to-urban migrants: The role of the hukou system in China. *PLoS One*, 7 (11), 1–8.

Lan, P.-C. 2014. Segmented Incorporation: The second generation of rural migrants in Shanghai. *The China Quarterly*, 217, 243–265.

Li, B. 2005. Urban social change in transitional China: A perspective of social exclusion and vulnerability. *Journal of Contingencies and Crisis Management*, 13 (2), 54–65.

Li, B. 2006. Floating population or urban citizens? Status, social provision and circumstances of rural – Urban migrants in China. *Social Policy & Administration*, 40 (2), 174–195.

Li, S.-M. & Siu, Y.-M. 1997. A comparative study of permanent and temporary migration in China: The case of Dongguan and Meizhou, Guangdong Province. *International Journal of Population Geography*, 3 (1), 63–82.

Liang, Z. 2016. China's great migration and the prospects of a more integrated society. *Annual Review of Sociology*, 42, 451–471.

Liu, T., Qi, Y., Cao, G. & Liu, H. 2015. Spatial patterns, driving forces, and urbanization effects of China's internal migration: County-level analysis based on the 2000 and 2010 censuses. *Journal of Geographical Sciences*, 25 (2), 236–256.

Liu, Y., Li, Z. & Breitung, W. 2012. The social networks of new-generation migrants in China's urbanized villages: A case study of Guangzhou. *Habitat International*, 36 (1), 192–200.

Maisonneuve, C. & Testé, B. 2007. Acculturation preferences of a host community: The effects of immigrant acculturation strategies on evaluations and impression formation. *International Journal of Intercultural Relations*, 31 (6), 669–688.

Meeussen, L., Phalet, K., Meeus, J., Van Acker, K., Montreuil, A. & Bourhis, R. 2013. "They are all the same": Low perceived typicality and outgroup disapproval as buffers of intergroup threat in mass media. *International Journal of Intercultural Relations*, 37 (2), 146–158.

Montreuil, A. & Bourhis, R.Y. 2001. Majority acculturation orientations toward "Valued" and "Devalued" Immigrants. *Journal of Cross-Cultural Psychology*, 32 (6), 698–719.

Montreuil, A. & Bourhis, R.Y. 2004. Acculturation orientations of competing host communities toward valued and devalued immigrants. *International Journal of Intercultural Relations*, 28 (6), 507–532.

Msigwa, R.E. & Bwana, K.M. 2014. Assessment of internal migration policies in developing countries: Evidence from Tanzania. *Business and Economic Research*, 4 (1), 32–47.

Murphy, R. 2000. Return migration, entrepreneurship and local state corporatism in rural China: The experience of two counties in south Jiangxi. *Journal of Contemporary China*, 9 (24), 231–247.

National Bureau of Statistics of China. 2018. *Statistical Communiqué of the People's Republic of China on the 2017 National Economic and Social Development* [Online]. Available: http://www.stats.gov.cn/english/PressRelease/201802/t20180228_1585666.html.

Nielsen, I., Nyland, C., Smyth, R., Zhang, M. & Zhu, C.J. 2006. Effects of intergroup contact on attitudes of Chinese urban residents to migrant workers. *Urban Studies*, 43 (3), 475–490.

Padilla, A.M. & Perez, W. 2003. Acculturation, social identity, and social cognition: A new perspective. *Hispanic Journal of Behavioral Sciences*, 25 (1), 35–55.

People's Republic of China Central Government. 2014. *2014户籍制度改革: Hukou-System Reform 2014* [Online]. Available: http://www.gov.cn/zhuanti/2014hjzdgg/.

Piotrowski, M. & Tong, Y. 2013. Straddling two geographic regions: The impact of place of origin and destination on return migration intentions in China. *Population, Space and Place*, 19 (3), 329–349.

Reutersward, A. 2005. *Labour Protection in China: Challenges Facing Labour Offices and Social Insurance*. OECD Social, Employment and Migration Working Papers No. 30. 30th ed. Paris: OECD Publishing.

Solinger, D.J. 1999. *Contesting Citizenship in Urban China: Peasant Migrants, the State, and the Logic of the Market*. Berkeley, CA: University of California Press.

South China Morning Post. 2018. *Migrant Evictions Tear at the Fabric of Beijing's Economy* [Online]. Available: http://www.scmp.com/news/china/policies-politics/article/2126836/how-eviction-beijings-migrant-workers-tearing-fabric.

Su, Y. 2011. The relationship between state and Migrants in the Urbanization: A case of the change on migrant management in Shenzhen: 城市化进程中国家与流动人口的关系 – 以深圳市流动人口管理模式的变迁为例. *Journal of Gansu Institute of Public Administration*, 2, 66–74.

Sun, M. & Fan, C.C. 2011. China's permanent and temporary migrants: Differentials and changes, 1990–2000. *The Professional Geographer*, 63 (1), 92–112.

Thomas, D.C., Lazarova, M.B. & Inkson, K. 2005. Global careers: New phenomenon or new perspectives? *Journal of World Business*, 40 (4), 340–347.

Tse, C-W. 2016. Urban residents' Prejudice and integration of rural migrants into urban China. *Journal of Contemporary China*, 25 (100), 579–595.

United Nations. 2015. *World Urbanization Prospects: The 2014 Revision*. New York: United Nations.

Wang, C. 2006. 农村流动人口的 "半城市化" 问题研究: A study of floating rural people's "Semi-urbanization." 社会学研究, 5 (7), 107–122.

Wang, F. & Zuo, X. 1999. Inside China's cities: Institutional barriers and opportunities for urban migrants. *The American Economic Review*, 89 (2), 276–280.

Wang, H., Appelbaum, R.P., Degiuli, F. & Lichtenstein, N. 2009. China's new labour contract law: Is China moving towards increased power for workers? *Third World Quarterly*, 30 (3), 485–501.

Wang, W.W. & Fan, C.C. 2012. Migrant workers' integration in urban China: Experiences in employment, social adaptation, and self-identity. *Eurasian Geography and Economics*, 53 (6), 731–749.

Wang, X., Oropesa, R.S. & Firebaugh, G. 2013. Permanent migrants to cities in China: Hukou origin and earnings among men in an era of economic transformation. *Migration and Development*, 2 (1), 37–56.

Wang, Z., Zhang, F. & Wu, F. 2016. Intergroup neighbouring in urban China: Implications for the social integration of migrants. *Urban Studies*, 53 (4), 651–668.

Wing Chan, K. & Buckingham, W. 2008. Is China abolishing the hukou system? *The China Quarterly*, 195, 582–606.

Wong, D.F.K., Li, C.Y. & He, X. 2007. Rural migrant workers in urban China: Living a marginalised life. *International Journal of Social Welfare*, 16 (1), 32–40.

Wu, Y. 2011. Labor market segmentation, job mobility and the two-track model of Chinese urban workers' acquisition of economic status: 劳动力市场分割、职业流动与城市劳动者经济地位获得的二元路径模式. *Social Sciences in China*, 32 (3), 74–86.

Yang, H., Tian, L., Van Oudenhoven, J.P., Hofstra, J. & Wang, Q. 2010. Urban residents' subtle prejudice towards rural-to-urban migrants in China: The role of socioeconomic status and adaptation styles. *Journal of Community & Applied Social Psychology*, 20 (3), 202–216.

Yang, X. & Guo, F. 1999. Gender differences in determinants of temporary labor migration in China: A multilevel analysis. *International Migration Review*, 33 (4), 929–953.

Yue, Z., Li, S., Jin, X. & Feldman, M.W. 2013. The role of social networks in the integration of Chinese rural – Urban migrants: A migrant – Resident tie perspective. *Urban Studies*, 50 (9), 1704–1723.

Zhang, H. 2010. The hukou system's constraints on migrant workers' job mobility in Chinese cities. *China Economic Review*, 21 (1), 51–64.

Zhang, X-X., Zheng, J., Liu, L., Zhao, X. & Sun, X.-M. 2014. The effect of group boundary permeability on intergroup prejudice: The case of rural-to-urban migrants in China. *Journal of Pacific Rim Psychology*, 8 (02), 53–61.

Zikic, J., Bonache, J. & Cerdin, J.-L. 2010. Crossing national boundaries: A typology of qualified immigrants' career orientations. *Journal of Organizational Behavior*, 31 (5), 667–686.

Part V
Commentary

24

Two modest ideas for future research on careers

Douglas T. (Tim) Hall

When I ponder the state of the world today, as well as the state of research on careers, I am struck with the great progress we have made since 1989, when Michael Arthur, Barbara Lawrence, and I published the *Handbook of Career Theory* (Arthur et al., 1989). And the impressive works in this volume are certainly a testimony to that idea. But at the same time I have an uneasy sense that we as careers scholars have underappreciated the significance of the far greater contributions that we could be making.

I am writing this the day after the *New York Times* published an op-ed article by a senior official in the Trump administration stating that members of the president's senior staff are actively working to monitor and moderate any extreme or potentially harmful decisions that the president might take. This is in the context of a worldwide phenomenon of populist anger, political and social division (waves of immigration in numerous low-income countries, debates over immigration policy in wealthier receiving countries, Brexit, dramatic political upsets usually won by young newcomers, etc.). There is an atmosphere of popular distrust of political leaders around the world, with many people feeling that nobody is looking out for them, and their seeing that most of the benefits of economic prosperity are going to the top 1 percent of earners in their countries. This extreme unequal distribution of wealth around the world is growing, as are the social tensions it sows.

At the heart of this popular economic and political discontent are people's feelings about their careers. When people are unhappy about their jobs and income, when you add the time dimension, this means they are despairing about their careers – with a lack of hope and no aspirations for the future. What do career theory and careers research have to offer to people who feel left behind in this way?

We know from our research that some of the causes of career despair are job dissatisfactions that can be linked to any of the following conditions: underemployment, unemployment, inadequate skills, blocked opportunity, inadequate information about better opportunities, discrimination, economic injustice, work-family conflict, workplace inflexibility, impoverished environments, poor management, lack of support, poor education, poor transportation, no hope for retirement, and so forth.

So this brings me to the first of my modest proposals – that we focus more of our research on factors in the work and social environment that could be significant for improving people's aspirations and attainments for their careers. Let us have some debate and scholarly conversation about what would be the most career-enhancing factors in the economic, political, social, educational, and organization environment, and let us strive for some consensus as researchers that research should focus on these factors. Just as we have a "Big Five" in personality theory that has helped to focus research on these dispositional factors, let us together identify a "Career Big Five" that would let us discover how to provide more of these career-enhancing experiences to workers around the world.

An example of career-enhancing research would be the studies in Belgium and the Netherlands on the positive benefits of publicly supported career counseling for workers' self-awareness and sense of personal agency (e.g., Verbruggen and Sels, 2008). Access to this kind of resource has the potential to yield big gains in positive career self-direction. We have seen a blossoming of this "positive careers research" over the last 10 to 15 years, with major outputs such as the *Handbook of Career Sustainability* (De Vos and Van der Heijden, 2015).

A related example of collective and concerted effort is the 5C project (i.e., the Cross-Cultural Collaboration on Contemporary Careers www.5C.careers). The first phase, a qualitative study, illuminated the meaning of career success in 11 countries, yielding both universal meanings of success and those that were unique to certain countries (Briscoe et al., 2012). The current phase is a survey which covers more than 30 countries. The 5C project has identified a model of influencing factors (both in the person and in the environment), intervening factors, and key career outputs. And here, too, the effort was to identify high-impact influencing factors and key career outcomes that, if present, would lead to feelings of career hope and engagement. As an example of this research, one current study is looking at career employability, an important factor in a person's sense of hope for the future. Not surprisingly, the study, which included over 9,000 employed individuals, found that in all countries employability tends to drop as the person ages. (Thus, it would not be surprising if these older workers also hold more negative attitudes about admitting immigrants into their countries.) However, on the positive side, the study showed that these decreases in employability with age are mitigated by the presence of organizational career management practices (Dello Russo et al., 2018). The career model that was agreed upon by the members of the 5C project is an example of a group of scholars holding discussions over time, working collaboratively as a group, and agreeing on what would be high-impact research questions.

My second modest proposal is that we extend our time frame of attention and give more attention to the final phases of the career and the transition from work into retirement. Some chapters in this volume pick up on this theme, even if only in passing – and we need more work like this. In the current careers literature we tend to focus more on how people enter careers and become more engaged in them, as well as at how career experiences interact with our other spheres of life. These are all certainly important, and I have focused on these issues as much as anyone, but as populations age in many parts of the world, we also need to learn more about how people *disengage* from work and find meaningful engagement in a path with a heart in their retirement years. We know how strong the socialization is from a succession of career and life transitions during the person's working years. What happens when the work component of life suddenly stops? What takes its place? How does a person's identity change when employment is taken out of what Daniel Levinson (Levinson et al., 1978, 1986) called the life structure? Leaving the work role creates a "hole" in the person's "life map." What fills in that gap? What other related changes in life structure take place?

There is an irony here: retirement is seen as a stage with a lot of freedom, ability to be agentic, to chart one's own path. But this is often experienced not as freedom but rather liminality, being betwixt and between – which is usually not viewed as a positive experience. Why is it that some people see this as a time of great opportunity and expanding horizons, while others just feel lost? Dispositional factors, such as having a strong protean career orientation (Briscoe et al., 2006), may account for some of these differences, and past experiences with major transitions may also enhance the person's adaptability in the retirement transition (Karaevli and Hall, 2006).

One promising concept to explore is how people find meaning in retirement. Wang et al. (2014) propose a recursive identity learning process in retirement, in which the person explores new options, engages in trial activity, reflects on the outcomes, and then revises his or her identity. And then after many small and large trial-and-error experiences, a new retirement identity can emerge. In a satisfactory adjustment to retirement, the person finds meaning (Hall et al., 2013). A useful way of describing this positive identity state in retirement is what Jonsson et al. (2001) called having a "meaningful occupation": "Evidence from [our] longitudinal study indicates that a special type of occupation[1] – *engaging occupation* with six constituents – was an important determinant of retirement satisfaction". (424; emphasis added). This means engaging in activities with the following qualities:

- Infused with positive meaning
- Intensity
- A coherent set of activities
- Goes beyond personal pleasure
- Occupational community
- Analogs to work.

When people find a "path with a heart" (Shepard, 1984) in this way, they have achieved a life structure that has the two qualities that Levinson (1978; 1986) saw as indicators of a successful life transition: viability (effectiveness in terms of the demands of the world) and satisfactoriness (meeting one's own needs). At this point they have become the agent of their own destiny. As Crary and colleagues describe it (Crary, 1982; Crary, Pazy & Wolfe, 1988; Crary, Hall & Kram, 2018), they have moved from the position of tenant to *architect* (or from object to agent) of their life structure.

What is it that enables some people to proactively seize upon the freedom offered by retirement and design a life structure that provides the rewards of high suitability and viability, while others experience this freedom as a liminal state lacking in meaning? For some people who have been socialized by decades of responding to the expectations of others they may be in a state of learned helplessness when they have high autonomy. In such cases, people must learn to recognize their own internal signals and needs and to become comfortable following their own path. For other people the challenge might be having a wealth of competing personal interests, and for them the task might be personal self-exploration and gaining greater self-awareness regarding their path with a heart. As Erich Fromm (1994) pointed out decades ago, there is a learning process in moving from *freedom from* (external control) to *freedom to* pursue one's own path. This is the learning process that many of us have to navigate as we move from employment to retirement and design our own life structure. Careers scholars could provide a great service by helping people learn to set their own course at this stage of life. Given the scope of processes such as this retirement transition, more large-scale, collaborative, cross-cultural research designs could provide the model for future research in careers.

Note

1 The word "occupation" is not used here in the sense of "job" or "profession," but rather in reference to being occupied with meaningful activities in retirement.

References

Arthur, M.B., Hall, D.T. & Lawrence, B.S. (eds.) 1989. *Handbook of Career Theory*. Cambridge: Cambridge University Press.

Briscoe, J.P., Hall, D.T. & Demuth, R.L.F. 2006. Protean and boundaryless careers: An empirical exploration. *Journal of Vocational Behavior*, 69, 30–47.

Briscoe, J.P., Hall, D.T. & Mayrhofer, W. (eds.) 2012. *Careers Around the World: Individual and Contextual Perspectives*. New York and Oxon: Routledge.

Crary, L. 1982. *Patterns of Life Structure: Person-Environment Designs and the Impact on Adult Lives*. Unpublished doctoral dissertation, Case Western Reserve University.

Crary, L.M., Hall, D.T. & Kram, K.E. 2018. *Processes and Patterns of Life Structure Changes in the Retirement Transition*. Contribution to a symposium, T. Amabile, L. Bailyn, L. M. Crary, K.E. Kram & D.T. Hall, Navigating retirement life: Retirement attitudes, transitions, and experiences, Symposium presented at the Academy of Management Meeting Chicago, 13 August.

Crary, L.M., Pazy, A. & Wolfe, D.M. 1988. Patterns of life structure and variability in self. *Human Relations*, 41, 783–804.

de Vos, A. & van der Heijden, B.I.J.M. (eds.) 2015. *Handbook of Research on Sustainable Careers*. London: Edward Elgar.

Dello Russo, S., Bosak, J., Apospori, E., Chudzikowski, K., Ferencikova, S., Hall, D.T., Parry, E., Andresen, M., Bagdadli, S., Dickmann, M., Gianecchini, M., Kase, R., Lazarova, M. & Reichel, A. 2018. *Still Feeling Employable with Growing Age? Exploring the Moderating Effects of OCM Practices and Country-Level Unemployment Rates in the Age-Employability Relationship*. Unpublished technical report, ISCTE-iul, Lisbon, Portugal.

Fromm, E. 1994. *Escape from Freedom*. New York: Holt (Owl Books Edition).

Hall, D.T., Feldman, E.R. & Kim, N. 2013. Meaningful work and the protean career. *In:* Dik, B.J., Byrne, Z.S. & Stever, M.P. (eds.) *Purpose and Meaning in the Workplace*. Washington, DC: The American Psychological Association.

Jonsson, H., Josephsson, S. & Kielhofner, G. 2001. Narratives and experience in an occupational transition: A longitudinal study of the retirement process. *The American Journal of Occupational Therapy*, 55, 424–432.

Karaevli, A. & Hall, D.T. 2006. How career variety promotes the adaptability of managers: A theoretical model. *Journal of Vocational Behavior*, 69, 359–373.

Levinson, D.J. 1986. A conception of adult development. *American Psychologist*, 41, 3–13.

Levinson, D.J., Darrow, C., Klein, E., Levinson, M. & Mckee, B. 1978. *The Seasons of a Man's Life*. New York: Knopf.

Shepard, H.A. 1984. On the realization of human potential: A path with a heart. *In:* Arthur, M.B., Bailyn, L., Levinson, D.J. & Shepard, H.A. (eds.) *Working with Careers*. New York: Center for Research in Career Devel.

Verbruggen, M. & Sels, L. 2008. Can career self-directedness be improved through counseling? *Journal of Vocational Behavior*, 73, 318–327.

Wang, L., Hall, D.T. & Waters, L. 2014. *Finding Meaning During the Retirement Process: Identity Development in Later Career Years* [Online]. [Accessed 2018-09-11].

25

Toward a work-home perspective on career studies

Jeffrey H. Greenhaus

The *Routledge Companion to Career Studies* contains chapters on an impressive array of topics within the career domain, and the individual chapters are insightful and comprehensive in their coverage of the literature on their respective topics. The breadth and depth of the chapters provided an opportunity for me to examine the extent to which the contemporary literature incorporates what Ellen Kossek and I refer to as a work-home perspective on careers, that is "a lens through which to examine careers that explicitly recognizes the interdependencies between individuals' work and home domains" (Greenhaus and Kossek, 2014: 363).

Certainly, the topics covered by many of the chapters – occupational choice, career counseling, the dark side of careers, and career outcomes, to mention a few – are relevant to a work-home perspective because of the inherent connections between the work and home domains that are embodied in each of these areas. However, most of the chapters in the book did not systematically examine the work-home interdependencies potentially relevant to their topic. This is not to suggest that the family or home domain was not mentioned, but rather that the cross-domain connections were not, in my opinion, strongly emphasized as a central element of the particular topic under investigation. This is *not* a criticism of the chapters, which were of uniformly high quality, but rather an observation about the current literature, which generally does not place work-home relationships on center stage in attempting to understand a career phenomenon.

Greenhaus and Kossek (2014) argued that the changing composition of the workforce (more women, dual-earner partners, and single parents), increasingly demanding jobs that are flexible in the timing and location of work, and feelings of job insecurity in an uncertain work environment require employees to make frequent career decisions that can affect (and be influenced by) their family life. They illustrated the value of adopting a work-home perspective by examining how such a perspective might inform four active research areas within the career literature – career self-management, career success, global careers, and sustainable careers – and suggested an agenda for future research in each of these areas.

Because each of the four areas may benefit from the adoption of a work-home perspective, they concluded that careers "can be better understood by considering how employees' home lives influence and are influenced by these four elements of many contemporary careers" (2014: 380). They also suggested that a work-home perspective can help explain the influence of sex and gender on contemporary careers, and that the adoption of a work-home perspective can provide insights into additional career phenomena that they did not discuss in their article. I next offer my opinions on the relevance of a work-home perspective to several of the topics included in the *Routledge Companion to Career Studies*.

- Home or family issues can be critical factors in the *selection of an occupational role* (Powell and Greenhaus, 2010) and the crafting of the role to achieve more balance (Sturges, 2012). Because the pursuit of different occupations has implications – financial and psychological – for family life, it is not surprising that family considerations (such as the presence of young children at home and spouse supportiveness) can play a significant role in the selection of an occupation or career field, especially for women (Powell and Greenhaus, 2010). A work-home perspective on occupational choice would show how work- and home-related characteristics combine to influence the initial selection of a career field as well as the decision to undergo a career change. That college students in the midst of choosing an occupation engage in multiple role planning regarding how they will combine their work and family commitments in the future (Basuil and Casper, 2012) reinforces the importance of incorporating work-home issues into *career counseling* interventions as well.

- The *mentoring* literature has focused almost exclusively on the impact of mentorship or mentoring functions (psychosocial and career) on protégés' work-related outcomes, such as advancement, income, and job satisfaction, and "has been relatively silent on whether mentors can affect protégés' success in balancing their work and family lives" (Greenhaus and Singh, 2007: 519). As more employees – men and women – seek a satisfying level of balance, it is critical to understand the effect (positive or negative) that mentoring can have on the achievement of balance. Greenhaus and Singh (2007) have suggested that mentors who adopt a "work-family lens," that is, who believe it is their responsibility as a mentor to attend to protégés' work *and* family needs, enact career and psychosocial support with the aim of helping their protégés' balance their work and family responsibilities. This type of mentoring support can lessen protégés' work-related demands and increase their work-related resources so that they experience less work-family conflict, more work-family enrichment, and ultimately more balance between work and home. A work-home perspective on mentoring would seek to understand the factors that encourage a mentor to adopt a work-family lens and the process by which the adoption of this lens affects protégés' success at work and at home.

- Research on the *antecedents of career outcomes* has placed considerably more emphasis on work-related factors than on home- or family-related factors (Greenhaus and Kossek, 2014). Nevertheless, there is growing evidence that critical career decisions and outcomes – starting one's own business (Brown et al., 2006), employee turnover (Sicherman, 1996), working long hours (Humbert and Lewis, 2008), and career success (Mayrhofer et al., 2008) – can be affected by family-related factors such as child-rearing motives, extensive family responsibilities, and having a self-employed spouse. As a result of the disproportional emphasis on work-related determinants of work decisions to the near exclusion of family-influenced work decisions (Greenhaus and Powell, 2017), researchers are missing an opportunity to gain a more comprehensive understanding of the broad range of factors that affect career decisions and outcomes. Moreover, because the impact of family circumstances on work-related decisions tends to be stronger for women than men, it is critical to understand the gender-related constructs that explain the tendency of women more than men to factor family considerations into their work decisions (Powell and Greenhaus, 2010).

In sum, I believe that there is considerable merit in adopting a work-home perspective to the study of careers because the interdependencies between the two domains can shape career decisions, patterns, and outcomes, and can shed light on the similar and unique career experiences of women and men. Although the work-home interface has been firmly entrenched in the organizational behavior literature, it has not been systematically applied to the study of critical career phenomena. I encourage scholars to consider the implications of a work-home perspective for career topics in which they have particular interest and to develop theory and conduct research that can provide insights into the multiple strands of life that affect the enactment of the careers of women and men in contemporary society.

References

Basuil, D.A. & Casper, W.J. 2012. Work – family planning attitudes among emerging adults. *Journal of Vocational Behavior*, 80, 629–637.

Brown, S., Farrel, L. & Sessions, J.G. 2006. Self-employment matching: An analysis of dual earner couples and working households. *Small Business Economics*, 26, 155–172.

Greenhaus, J.H. & Kossek, E.E. 2014. The contemporary career: A work-home perspective. *Annual Review of Organizational Psychology and Organizational Behavior*, 1, 361–388.

Greenhaus, J.H. & Powell, G.N. 2017. *Making Work and Family Work: From Hard Choices to Smart Choices*. New York: Routledge.

Greenhaus, J.H. & Singh, R. 2007. Mentoring and the work-family interface. *In:* Ragins, B.R. & Kram, K.E. (eds.) *Handbook of mentoring at work*. Thousand Oaks, CA: Sage Publications, 519–544.

Humbert, A.L. & Lewis, S. 2008. 'I have no life other than work' – Long working hours, blurred boundaries and family life: The case of Irish entrepreneurs. *In:* Burke, R.J. & Cooper, C.L. (eds.) *The Long Work Hours Culture: Causes, Consequences and Choices*. Bigley, UK: Emerald, 159–181.

Mayrhofer, W., Meyer, M., Schiffinger, M. & Schmidt, A. 2008. The influence of family responsibilities, career fields and gender on career success: An empirical study. *Journal of Managerial Psychology*, 23 (3), 292–323.

Powell, G.N. & Greenhaus, J.H. 2010. Sex, gender, and decisions at the family→work interface. *Journal of Management*, 36, 1011–1039.

Sicherman, N. 1996. Gender differences in departures from a large firm. *Industrial and Labor Relations Review*, 49, 484–505.

Sturges, J. 2012. Crafting a balance between work and home. *Human Relations*, 65, 1539–1559.

26

The past, present and future of 21st-century careers

Gerard A. Callanan, Maury A. Peiperl, and
Michael B. Arthur

Several years ago, the editors of *Time* magazine declared 1989 to be the year that, in retrospect, "Changed the World." In making this assertion, the magazine documented a number of historic events, including the fall of the Berlin Wall, which effectively ended the cold war and the bloody protests in Tiananmen Square, where more than a million protesters challenged the Chinese government. On a lighter note, 1989 saw the broadcast premier of the iconic television show *Seinfeld*, which ushered in a new brand of sitcom entertainment. Beyond these memorable events, for researchers interested in the study of careers, 1989 was notable for another reason – it was the year of publication for the *Handbook of Career Theory* (Arthur et al., 1989).

At the time of its publication, the *Handbook* served as a primer on the major issues and challenges that confronted researchers in the study of individual careers. Over the course of the three decades since the *Handbook's* original release, as Bidwell, Briscoe, and Anderson affirm in Chapter 12 of this *Companion to Career Studies*, much has changed in the employment world. These changes include major geopolitical shifts, a globalization of commerce, the arrival of the Internet and further technological disruptions, fresh challenges in workforce diversity and work-family accommodation, and – not least for career scholars – stark alterations in employment relationships. In recognition of these changes, this chapter begins with a description of exogenous factors that have altered the nature of work and workforce deployment covering the interdependent topics of (a) the loss of job permanence and (b) globalization, spurred on by technology, over the past three decades. Next, we discuss how these factors have influenced individual careers and career decision-making, in both positive and negative ways, and affirm the need for individual ownership of careers to maintain employability. The chapter concludes with a section titled "Where Next for Careers?" which is also offered as an agenda for future careers research. Throughout the chapter, we draw disproportionately on information from the US context; we therefore invite readers from other parts of the world to relate the ideas to their own situations.

Exogenous factors

For convenience we separate our discussion below into interdependent factors associated with (a) the loss of job permanence and employment security and (b) changes brought on by globalization and attendant technological developments.

Loss of job permanence and employment security

Over the past 30 years, a major shift in the nature of employment patterns and relationships has occurred on a global scale. This shift involves the movement from jobs and careers based on the assumption of some level of permanence in the employment relationship to one where there is an expectation of low (or no) permanence (Kalleberg, 2009). Moreover, this transformation accelerated in the years after the Great Recession of 2008–2009 (Katz and Krueger, 2016; Valletta and van der List, 2015; Kroft et al., 2014). This rise of impermanent employment, and the introduction of technology to support it, has brought about new terminology to describe the new arrangements. This includes terms such as gig employment, precarious work, app-enabled workers, on-demand workers, and a revitalization of such existing terms as contract work, part-time service work, and freelancing (Bureau of Labor Statistics, 2018a; Horowitz, 2015; Kalleberg, 2009; Kuhn, 2016). Although the Bureau of Labor Statistics (2018a), Cappelli and Keller (2013a), and Spreitzer et al. (2017) offer in-depth descriptions for these terms, they all generally fall under the broad categorization of "alternative work arrangements." Further, regardless of the specific classification, the common theme in all of these terms is a lack of permanence in the employment relationship (Callanan et al., 2017).

Katz and Krueger (2016, 2017) and others (Board of Governors of the Federal Reserve System, 2018) have highlighted the degree of the movement toward impermanent work affiliations in the United States. During the time period between 2005 and 2015, Katz and Krueger estimated that individuals involved in "alternative work arrangements" in the United States grew by approximately 9.5 million, moving from about 10 percent of the total workforce to nearly 16 percent. On a net basis, they concluded that this increase in the number of people in alternative work arrangements accounted for virtually all of the job growth in the US economy during that 10-year period (Katz and Krueger, 2016). In addition, the percentage share of US workers who report income from self-employment continues to rise, and is substantially higher than in previous decades (Board of Governors of the Federal Reserve System, 2018; Katz and Krueger, 2017). Beyond the United States, the European Union experienced similar results of employees taking on non-permanent jobs in far greater numbers in the post–Great Recession environment (Eurofound, 2015).

The ongoing increase in impermanent and alternative work arrangements reflects a number of concurrent economic, technological, global, and social forces (Spreitzer et al., 2017). Perhaps the most significant of these is the overall decline in job security experienced by workers in the United States and throughout other economically developed parts of the world (Brochu and Morin, 2012; Keim et al., 2014; Lee et al., 2018; Shoss, 2017).

Pressures to compete (and to maximize value to shareholders) through greater efficiency and more flexible work scheduling resulted in the well-documented change in the psychological contract between employers and employees. The longer-term relational focus, which had its heyday in the decades following World War II, was based on mutual loyalty, full-time employment, and job security that was often guaranteed through the presence of strong trade unions. Beginning in the 1980s, that form of psychological contract began to lose sway. It was supplanted by the shorter-term "transactional" bond that emphasizes economic exchange, whereby employment is based on the mutual provision of economic benefit to the employer and the worker (Cappelli and Keller, 2013b; Ng et al., 2010; Rousseau, 1995). The steep decline in private sector and blue-collar trade unionism since the 1980s certainly influenced the shift in the psychological contract. White-collar trade unionism – especially in the public sector – grew over this period, but is now in a tenuous position, at least in the United States, given court decisions outlawing compulsory membership.

This shift in the psychological contract, with the attendant decline in job security, has taken place without full consideration of the consequences to employees' career aspirations or its effects on the relationship between work and non-work domains. When individuals repeatedly enter into and out of jobs (or "gigs") they can be in a state of perpetual career decision-making. Each new potential work arrangement brings a choice of whether or not to accept the job. The choice implies a recognition of the attendant opportunity costs of continuing to pursue short-term rather than longer-term and possibly full-time employment (Callanan et al., 2017; Mas and Pallais, 2016). Under this scenario, an individual's career can become a series of economically necessary jobs without regard to whether they collectively fulfill longer-term career aspirations or allow for any balance between work and family domains (Callanan et al., 2017).

Globalization and technological change

Over the history of industrial society, technological changes have played a deterministic role in defining the nature of work and the types and locations of jobs. Today, technological developments in such areas as communication, production, and artificial intelligence (AI), are dramatically altering the employment landscape (Autor, 2015; Colbert et al., 2016; Holland and Bardoel, 2016). These tend to influence jobs and careers in three primary ways: (a) allowing for the establishment of nascent business applications and industries, thereby creating new employment opportunities; (b) eliminating occupations and career paths through a process of "creative destruction"; and (c) leading to the establishment of novel ways of working for the employee as well as changes in tasks and expectations from the employer (Ewing, 2017; ten Brummelhuis et al., 2012; Bughin et al., 2010). Each of these influences is discussed below.

With regard to emerging business applications, the establishment of an "app-enabled" workforce is the result of instantaneous and mobile communications technology in conjunction with revised methods of work deployment (Manjoo, 2015). The rapid development of smartphone technology has led to more "on-demand" job openings in which employer needs and worker availability can facilitate movement from one assignment to another. However, many technology-driven, impermanent jobs result in restricted opportunities for planning and uncertainty over the number of hours to be worked or the compensation to be received (Board of Governors of the Federal Reserve System, 2018; Henly and Lambert, 2014). A further concern for US workers is that impermanent, technology-based positions often offer few (or no) employee benefits, such as healthcare coverage, unemployment insurance, or family friendly programs.

With respect to creative destruction (Schumpeter, 1942), rapid advancements in technology have led to the elimination of many occupations with low skill or entry requirements (Acemoglu and Restrepo, 2017; Agrawal et al., 2017; Cortes et al., 2016; Ewing, 2017). These include first-level customer service personnel, toll booth operators, bank tellers, grocery clerks, parking attendants, travel and insurance agents, and salespeople (Abram, 2010). In addition, "knowledge-based" occupations historically protected from technological displacement, are also undergoing job loss as advanced technology and AI eliminate tasks, services, and occupations with a high human component – such as call centers – in their delivery (Cortes et al., 2016; Frey, 2015; Bremmer, 2018).

Advanced communication technology also offers alternatives for the location and timing of where and when work is performed. One-fourth to one-fifth of all workers in the United States are estimated to be performing some or all of their work at home (Bureau of Labor Statistics, 2017, 2016; Irby, 2014). A reduced physical presence in a defined work location can facilitate an improved balance between the work and non-work domains, reduce the stresses associated with commuting, and lead to increased job engagement and satisfaction (Masuda et al., 2017; Allen et al., 2015; Vega et al., 2015; Golden et al., 2013; Leslie et al., 2012). However, communication and monitoring technology that "electronically tethers" the employee to the employer can also produce time demands which in turn cause conflict between work and non-work domains (Butts et al., 2015; Diaz et al., 2012; Matusik and Mickel, 2011; Piszczek, 2017) and impair work performance due to physical disconnection from the workplace (Lanaj et al., 2014; Leslie et al., 2012).

Perhaps the most controversial and debated outcome of globalization is the outsourcing of jobs from industrialized countries to less developed ones (Bachmann and Braun, 2011; Bremmer, 2018). The process of outsourcing has resulted in both lower and higher skilled jobs being transferred to countries where the labor costs are comparatively low and skills can be clustered for productive efficiency. For workers in the United States, for example, offshoring has resulted in a mass outflow of jobs, especially in manufacturing (Acemoglu et al., 2016). According to data from the Bureau of Labor Statistics, since the late 1980s, US manufacturing's percentage share of total non-farm employment has been cut in half, from roughly 17 percent in 1989 to about 8.5 percent 30 years later (Bureau of Labor Statistics, 2018b).

The decline in the availability of low- and medium-skilled occupations in economically developed countries ought to be offset by a commensurate increase in occupations that demand higher skill levels (Cappelli, 2006). However, a labor mismatch occurs when there is an inadequate supply of skilled workers (Canon et al., 2013). Much evidence suggests a lack of synchronization between the skills required by higher tech occupations and the skills currently possessed by workers in the United States and in other parts of the world (Jaimovich and Siu, 2012; Şahin et al., 2014; Bremmer, 2018).

Implications for careers

New working arrangements, advancements in various forms of technology, and the ongoing globalization of business functions (despite increasing protectionist trends) have fundamentally and dramatically altered the ways by which people undertake and fulfill employment responsibilities (Barley et al., 2017). In turn, these environmental changes require individuals to take a more conscientious, holistic, and employer-independent approach by claiming *career ownership* (Arthur et al., 2017; Greenhaus et al., 2019). Moreover, the proliferation of impermanent work positions carries both negative and positive implications for individuals as they attempt to manage their careers and their responsibilities across work and non-work domains.

Negative implications

On the negative side, the implications are all concerned in some way with the loss of traditional long-term employment. "At-will" employment practices offer no assurances a worker will be able to continue on a set career path within any one employer or industry (Callanan et al., 2017), and prolonged lack of employment stability can be seen as a sign of career indecision or lack of ability (Caza et al., 2017). Variable work schedules can interfere with life events such as child care and medical appointments (Henly and Lambert, 2014; Lambert et al., 2012; Martin et al., 2012). Lack of job permanence also means loss of the certainty of a paycheck, insecurity over benefits such as child and elder care, and potential interference with the ability to make long-term life choices concerning marriage, family, children and elder care, home ownership, and retirement (Callanan et al., 2017; Fleming, 2017; Hannagan and Morduch, 2015; Petriglieri et al., 2018).

Technological connections to one's work can also place uncomfortable demands on the individual, preventing any clean demarcation between work and personal or family time (Eddleston and Mulki, 2017; Noonan and Glass, 2012; Kossek et al., 2015). On a broader level, technology is widely implicated in the acceleration in alternative work arrangements, and the movement of blue- and white-collar jobs out of industrialized sectors of the world, with potentially long-term sociological consequences (Gabe et al., 2018; Kalleberg, 2009). Job insecurity can lead not only to monetary loss but also to the loss of identities, roles, and expectations tied to one's job and the security in that job (Shoss, 2017). There is a further challenge that people who lose jobs often are insufficiently educated or trained to attain higher-skill jobs (Bachmann and Braun, 2011; Gabe et al., 2018; Goldin and Katz, 2010; Jaimovich and Siu, 2012). In turn, for individuals and organizations seeking to meet the job demands of a high-tech economy, career management becomes exceedingly difficult (Greenhaus et al., 2019).

The broader social implications of these environmental factors are becoming more pronounced. Specifically, increased job insecurity and occupational displacement can lead – absent strong social policies to prevent this – to greater wage inequality, labor market polarization, and the socioeconomic bifurcation of societies in the industrialized world (Autor, 2014; Autor and Dorn, 2013; Autor et al., 2017; Bachmann et al., 2016; Chetty et al., 2017; Gabe et al., 2018; Cortes, 2016; Parker, 2014; Temin, 2017). The world of work and employment in advanced regions of the globe has gravitated toward a two-tiered structure (Cortes, 2016; Parker, 2014; Pew Research Center, 2015; Temin, 2017). In the United States, less educated and lower-skilled workers tend to be concentrated in industries such as retail, wholesale, and food services, where there are commensurately higher levels of impermanent work and with lower job security (Board of Governors of the Federal Reserve System, 2018; Fusaro and Shaefer, 2016).

Positive implications

On the positive side, the impermanence of work positions points in an entirely new and potentially favorable direction. Moreover, the enduring value of that direction depends on both individual career owners and the social institutions – communities, organizations, and governments – that contribute to the shaping of career opportunities (Best, 2018; Mazzucato, 2018). We cannot point to future research that has yet to be written, but we can argue three major factors will influence these career opportunities. A first factor is the demise of the factory system and all that it has meant to employment practice. The Luddite Martyrs of the early 1800s were right to fear the factory, and the broad demeaning of occupations and family life that followed. Weaving was the first of many occupations weakened or displaced by the factory system, and the teamwork of household sheep-rearing and wool-making on the family farm was also lost to industrial progress. For many, the factory system brought on both a deskilling of work and the relinquishing of worker control over their careers (Freeman, 2018). The changes described above may present an opportunity to reverse both of those processes.

A second factor is the growth of an interdependent global economy. It is an interdependence that many experts have believed holds the key to both global peace and prosperity. For example, statistics from the World Bank (World Bank Group, 2018) bear witness to an impressive growth in per-capita income and intergenerational economic mobility in China, India, Vietnam, and other developing nations through this global interdependence (Tarzi, 2016), even though there are questions as to whether the benefits from that growth have been shared equally. Yet, at the time of this writing we are witnessing political forces, described to involve "nativist" thinking, seeking to loosen this interdependence. The prospective loss of global prosperity, and of a broader peace to sustain it, stands in sharp contrast to career ownership ideals. Our opportunity is to engage in debates on behalf of free and fair trade (as opposed to bilateral trade deals that limit people's access to career opportunities) (Luckhurst, 2018).

A third factor is the emergence of innovation as a critical determinant of future work arrangements. It used to be thought that innovation brought broad benefits, and that the middle class was largely immune from any disruption. However, a 1996 *New York Times* (1996) report on "The Downsizing of America" signaled that innovation was now reaching the middle classes. Social psychologists Karl Weick and Lisa Berlinger (1989) have forcefully argued that innovators themselves are highly vulnerable, since their employment only takes place one project at a time. Others have argued there will be necessary delays between layoffs and new job opportunities while the effects of innovation get absorbed (Ford, 2015). We need to help people own the possibility of those delays, so that the overall effects of innovation can be enjoyed by all. In these circumstances, career ownership may be a necessary but incomplete driver of effective change. Governments, at all of local, regional, and national levels, can play a role in helping workers take time to transition and retrain between jobs. Further, individual support systems can play a role in helping people re-establish themselves in new work roles.

Where next for careers?

In looking ahead, we first point out five longer-term implications for career studies, then conclude by taking an even longer-term view of where careers have come in order that we might think as broadly as possible about where they may be going.

First, in the spirit of this volume and of the interdisciplinarity that rightly permeates career phenomena, we would posit that careers researchers, if their work is to be of practical value, are destined to study the interplay between micro and macro phenomena. Further, as Gunz, Mayrhofer and Lazarova discuss in Chapter 2 of this *Companion to Career Studies*, the contextual embeddedness of careers and the related demands that are placed on career actors need to be fully recognized. Without individual-level understanding, careers research has little to offer career owners. Without a deep appreciation of macro-level context, anything it does offer them will likely be impractical, or worse, inapplicable.

Second, even the most successful organizational career model is unlikely ever to become a template for most people's careers. Few enough long-term career paths still exist, although we could highlight certain global companies – Nestlé, for example – that develop their top talent over many years across a variety of disciplines, geographies, and business areas. But beyond the fact that such systems only persist in a minority of companies, we would also point out that they can apply only to a minority of employees within those companies, as the majority will at some point come off of the path, either through their own decision or by a lack of job permanence or by losing out in the "tournament" for advancement. Thus organizational career systems, while perhaps interesting to study and to develop, are becoming less and less broadly applicable, and research will continue to follow suit.

Third, and likewise, a global career (Peiperl and Jonsen, 2007) is still much more likely to be accomplished at the individual level than within an organization, even the most successful. Thus, as referenced by McKouen, Shaffer, and Reiche in Chapter 19 of this *Companion to Career Studies*, the study of boundary-spanning and border-crossing – already well-established areas of career research – will need to continue, taking more and more into account the evolving global landscape.

Fourth, the longstanding organizational career concepts of entry and exit now apply across more and more diverse employment arrangements, and not in a uniform or even comparable way. Given that it continues to become more and more common for individuals to experience breaks in employment for a variety of reasons, including family, formal learning, health, exploration, reconnection with a changing system, and so forth, careers research needs to take this "new normal" in stride and embed it in future studies of all kinds – not only studies about entry, exit, work – non-work, and/or career breaks.

Finally, we would advocate a greater focus on the value of "weak ties" and infrequently activated networks as important paths to career enactment, from gigs to start-ups to long-term employments, for example. Beyond focusing on how to develop weak ties into strong ties, or on existing structures and "structural holes" as techniques for understanding career paths, we recommend focusing on the kinds of career innovation and change that emerge from diverse, dispersed networks rather than on employment that may result from strengthening connections with existing structures/organizations.

The very long-term view

The trends described in this chapter, and particularly the norms of long-term employment so clearly challenged over the past few decades, relate to the time since the Industrial Revolution, and to the developed world which brought it about and has reaped the most benefit. Although this is the only world most Western career-owners and their research subjects have known, it is hardly a norm in long-term historical or evolutionary terms. Consider, for example, the primarily agrarian societies that pre-dated the Industrial Revolution and still persist in some parts of the world. What can we say about individual careers in this context that represents so much more of human history? It is clear that career paths, or at least, long-term career paths as such did/do not exist in these societies, and that individuals living in them have always had to (1) develop their own skills, (2) work when necessary – that is, more or less constantly, (3) deal with the needs of family without the support of any employer, and (4) cope with whatever external shocks (war, weather, famine, disease) arise without recourse to benefits or other protections obtained through long-term employment (Wolf, 2015). Furthermore, as alluded to by Briscoe, Dickmann and Parry in Chapter 18 of this *Companion to Career Studies*, depending on where one lives in the world, the idea of career will make more or less sense. Even in what we can describe as developed countries, the concepts of individual careers or of the "boundaryless career" (Arthur and Rousseau, 1996) will not apply evenly given cultural and/or geographic limitations (Thomas and Inkson, 2017). Thus, it is essential to specify the contexts in which we are researching or advising, to be clear about any differences between them, and consequently to be explicit about the limited applicability of our work.

In summary, human beings have not yet evolved to the point of being optimal owners of individual careers – or as Nicholson (2007: 570) once put it, to the point of getting "beyond career illusions and delusions." Nor have we yet managed to develop a world in which even the concept of career development is universally understood, for in the contexts in which large proportions of humanity find themselves, just as would have been the case throughout most of human history, it would make no sense even to try. And when we seek to understand, analyze, and advise on individuals' careers, we must therefore be clear about the geographical, cultural and temporal contexts, and thus the limitations, of what we advise and advocate. While we are at it, careers researchers might also consider advocating for a more just and open career context, for the 21st century and beyond.

References

Abram, S. 2010. What you aren't seeing anymore: Has technology changed our learners' futures forever? *Multimedia & Internet*, 17, 20–22.

Acemoglu, D., Autor, D., Dorn, D., Hanson, G.H. & Price, B. 2016. Import competition and the great US employment sag of the 2000s. *Journal of Labor Economics*, 34, S141–S198.

Acemoglu, D. & Restrepo, P. 2017. *Robots and jobs: Evidence from US labor markets*. National Bureau of Economic Research, NBER Working Paper No. 23285, 1–91.

Agrawal, A., Gans, J.S. & Goldfarb, A. 2017. What to expect from artificial intelligence. *MIT Sloan Management Review*, 58, 23–26.

Allen, T.D., Golden, T.D. & Shockley, K.M. 2015. How effective is telecommuting? Assessing the status of our scientific findings. *Psychological Science in the Public Interest*, 16, 40–68.

Arthur, M.B., Hall, D.T. & Lawrence, B.S. (eds.) 1989. *Handbook of Career Theory*. Cambridge: Cambridge University Press.

Arthur, M.B., Khapova, S.N. & Richardson, J. 2017. *An Intelligent Career*. New York: Oxford University Press.

Arthur, M.B. & Rousseau, D.M. (eds.) 1996. *The Boundaryless Career: A New Employment Principle for a New Organizational Era*. New York: Oxford University Press.

Autor, D.H. 2014. Skills, education, and the rise of earnings inequality among the 'other 99 percent'. *Science*, 344, 843–851.

Autor, D.H. 2015. Why are there still so many jobs? The history and future of workplace automation. *Journal of Economic Perspectives*, 29, 3–30.

Autor, D.H. & Dorn, D. 2013. The growth of low-skill service jobs and the polarization of the US labor market. *American Economic Review*, 103, 1553–1597.

Autor, D.H., Dorn, D., Katz, L.F., Patterson, C. & Van Reenen, J. 2017. Concentrating on the fall of the labor share. *American Economic Review: Papers & Proceedings*, 107, 180–185.

Bachmann, R., Bechara, P. & Schaffner, S. 2016. Wage inequality and wage mobility in Europe. *Review of Income and Wealth*, 62, 181–197.

Bachmann, R. & Braun, S. 2011. The impact of international outsourcing on labour market dynamics in Germany. *Scottish Journal of Political Economy*, 58, 1–28.

Barley, S.R., Bechky, B.A. & Milliken, F.J. 2017. The changing nature of work: Careers, identities, and work lives in the 21st century. *Academy of Management Discoveries*, 3, 111–115.

Best, M.H. 2018. *How Growth Really Happens*. Princeton, NJ: Princeton University Press.

Board of Governors of the Federal Reserve System. 2018. *Report on the Economic Well-Being of US Households in 2017* [Online]. Available: https://www.federalreserve.gov/publications/report-economic-well-being-us-households.htm [Accessed 6 June].

Bremmer, I. 2018. *Us vs. Them: The Failure of Globalism*. New York: Portfolio, Penguin.

Brochu, P. & Morin, L-P. 2012. Union membership and perceived job insecurity: Thirty years of evidence from the American general social survey. *ILR Review*, 65, 263–285.

Bughin, J., Chui, M. & Manyika, J. 2010. Clouds, big data, and smart assets: Ten tech-enabled business trends to watch. *McKinsey Quarterly*, (August), 1–14.

Bureau of Labor Statistics. 2016. *24 Percent of Employed People Did Some or All of Their Work at Home in 2015* [Online]. Available: https://www.bls.gov/opub/ted/2016/24-percent-of-employed-people-did-some-or-all-of-their-work-at-home-in-2015.htm [Accessed 8 July].

Bureau of Labor Statistics. 2017. *American Time Use Survey – 2016 Results* [Online]. Available: https://www.bls.gov/news.release/pdf/conemp.pdf [Accessed 27 June].

Bureau of Labor Statistics. 2018a. *Contingent and Alternative Employment Arrangements – May 2017* [Online]. Available https://www.bls.gov/news.release/pdf/atus.pdf [Accessed 7 June].

Bureau of Labor Statistics. 2018b. *Employment, Hours, and Earnings from the Current Employment Statistics Survey (National)* [Online]. Available: https://data.bls.gov/pdq/SurveyOutputServlet [Accessed 10 June].

Butts, M.M., Becker, W.J. & Boswell, W.R. 2015. Hot buttons and time sinks: The effects of electronic communication during nonwork time on emotions and work-nonwork conflict. *Academy of Management Journal*, 58, 763–788.

Callanan, G.A., Perri, D.F. & Tomkowicz, S.M. 2017. Career management in uncertain times: Challenges and opportunities. *The Career Development Quarterly*, 65, 353–365.

Canon, M.E., Chen, M. & Marifian, E.A. 2013. Labor mismatch in the great recession: A review of indexes using recent US data. *Federal Reserve Bank of St. Louis Review*, 95 (May–June), 237–271.

Cappelli, P.H. 2006. Churning of jobs. In: Greenhaus, J.H. & Callanan, G.A. (eds.) *Encyclopedia of Career Development*. Thousand Oaks, CA: Sage Publications.

Cappelli, P.H. & Keller, J.R. 2013a. Classifying work in the new economy. *Academy of Management Review*, 38, 575–596.

Cappelli, P.H. & Keller, J.R. 2013b. A study of the extent and potential causes of alternative employment arrangements. *ILR Review*, 66, 874–901.

Caza, B., Vough, H.C. & Moss, S. 2017. The hardest thing about working in the gig economy? Forging a cohesive sense of self. *Harvard Business Review Digital Articles*, 2–5.

Chetty, R., Grusky, D., Hell, M., Hendren, N., Manduca, R. & Narang, J. 2017. The fading American dream: Trends in absolute income mobility since 1940. *Science*, 356, 398–406.

Colbert, A., Yee, N. & George, G. 2016. The digital workforce and the workplace of the future. *Academy of Management Journal*, 59, 731–739.

Cortes, G.M. 2016. Where have the middle-wage workers gone? A study of polarization using panel data. *Journal of Labor Economics*, 34, 63–105.

Cortes, G.M., Jaimovich, N. & Siu, H.E. 2016. Disappearing routine jobs: Who, how, and why? *National Bureau of Economic Research*, NBER Working Paper No. 22918, 1–42.

Diaz, I., Chiaburu, D.S., Zimmerman, R.D. & Boswell, W.R. 2012. Communication technology: Pros and cons of constant connection to work. *Journal of Vocational Behavior*, 80, 500–508.

Eddleston, K.A. & Mulki, J. 2017. Toward understanding remote workers' management of work – family boundaries: The complexity of workplace embeddedness. *Group & Organization Management*, 42, 346–387.

Eurofound. 2015. *Recent Developments in Temporary Employment: Employment Growth, Wages and Transitions*. Luxembourg: Publications Office of the European Union.

Ewing, J. 2017. Robocalypse now? Central bankers argue whether automation will kill jobs. *The New York Times*, 28 June. Available: http://www.nytimes.com.

Fleming, P. 2017. The human capital hoax: Work, debt and insecurity in the era of uberization. *Organization Studies*, 38, 691–709.

Ford, M. 2015. *Rise of the Robots: Technology and the Threat of a Jobless Future*, New York: Basic Books.

Freeman, J.B. 2018. *Behemoth: A History of the Factory and the Making of the Modern World*. New York: Norton.

Frey, T. 2015. 101 endangered jobs by 2030. *Journal of Environmental Health*, 77, 40–42.

Fusaro, V.A. & Shaefer, L.H. 2016. How should we define low wage work – An analysis of using the current population survey. *Monthly Labor Review*, 139(October), 1–11.

Gabe, T., Abel, J.R. & Florida, R. 2018. Can low-wage workers find better jobs? *Federal Reserve Bank of New York Staff Reports*, No. 846, April, 1–35.

Golden, L., Henly, J.R. & Lambert, S. 2013. Work schedule flexibility: A contributor to happiness? *Journal of Social Research & Policy*, 4, 107–135.

Goldin, C. & Katz, L.F. 2010. *The Race Between Education and Technology*. Cambridge, MA: Belknap Press of Harvard University Press.

Greenhaus, J.H., Callanan, G.A. & Godshalk, V.M. 2019. *Career Management for Life*, 5th ed. New York: Routledge.

Hannagan, A. & Morduch, J. 2015. Income gains and month-to-month income volatility: Household evidence from the US financial diaries. *US Financial Diaries Project*, October, 1–28.

Henly, J.R. & Lambert, S.J. 2014. Unpredictable work timing in retail jobs: Implications for employee work – life conflict. *ILR Review*, 67, 986–1016.

Holland, P. & Bardoel, A. 2016. The impact of technology on work in the twenty-first century: Exploring the smart and dark side. *International Journal of Human Resource Management*, 27, 2579–2581.

Horowitz, S. 2015. Help for the way we work now. *The New York Times*, 7 September. Available: https://www.nytimes.com.

Irby, C.M. 2014. All in a day's work: Overcoming telework challenges. *Monthly Labor Review*, 137, 1.

Jaimovich, N. & Siu, H.E. 2012. The trend is the cycle: Job polarization and jobless recoveries. *National Bureau of Economic Research*, NBER Working Paper No. 18334, 1–53.

Kalleberg, A.L. 2009. Precarious work, insecure workers: Employment relations in transition. *American Sociological Review*, 74, 1–22.

Katz, L.F. & Krueger, A.B. 2016. The rise and nature of alternative work arrangements in the United States, 1995–2015. *National Bureau of Economic Research*, 1–19.

Katz, L.F. & Krueger, A.B. 2017. The role of unemployment in the rise in alternative work arrangements. *American Economic Review*, 107, 388–392.

Keim, A.C., Landis, R.S., Pierce, C.A. & Earnest, D.R. 2014. Why do employees worry about their jobs? A meta-analytic review of predictors of job insecurity. *Journal of Occupational Health Psychology*, 19, 269–290.

Kossek, E.E., Thompson, R.J. & Lautsch, B.A. 2015. Balanced workplace flexibility: Avoiding the traps. *California Management Review*, 57, 5–25.

Kroft, K., Lange, F., Notowidigdo, M.J. & Katz, L.F. 2014. Long-term unemployment and the great recession: The role, composition, duration dependence, and non-participation. *National Bureau of Economic Research*, Working paper 20273, 3 (June).

Kuhn, K.M. 2016. The rise of the 'gig economy' and implications for understanding work and workers. *Industrial and Organizational Psychology*, 9, 157–162.

Lambert, S.J., Haley-Lock, A. & Henly, J.R. 2012. Schedule flexibility in hourly jobs: Unanticipated consequences and promising directions. *Community, Work & Family*, 15, 293–315.

Lanaj, K., Johnson, R.E. & Barnes, C.M. 2014. Beginning the workday yet already depleted? Consequences of late-night smartphone use and sleep. *Organizational Behavior and Human Decision Processes*, 124, 11–23.

Lee, C., Huang, G-H. & Ashford, S.J. 2018. Job insecurity and the changing workplace: Recent developments and the future trends in job insecurity research. *Annual Review of Organizational Psychology and Organizational Behavior*, 5, 335–359.

Leslie, L.M., Manchester, C.F., Park, T-Y. & Mehng, S.A. 2012. Flexible work practices: A source of career premiums or penalties? *Academy of Management Journal*, 55, 1407–1428.

Luckhurst, J. 2018. *The Shifting Global Economic Architecture: Decentralizing Authority in Contemporary Global Governance*. Cham, Switzerland: Palgrave Macmillan.

Manjoo, F. 2015. Uber's business model could change your work. *The New York Times*, 28 January. Available: http://www.nytimes.com.

Martin, J.E., Sinclair, R.R., Lelchook, A.M., Wittmer, J.L. & Charles, K.E. 2012. Non-standard work schedules and retention in the entry-level hourly workforce. *Journal of Occupational and Organizational Psychology*, 85, 1–22.

Mas, A. & Pallais, A. 2016. Valuing alternative work arrangements. *National Bureau of Economic Research*, Working Paper 22708, 1–63.

Masuda, A.D., Holtschlag, C. & Nicklin, J.M. 2017. Why the availability of telecommuting matters: The effects of telecommuting on engagement via goal pursuit. *Career Development International*, 22, 200–219.

Matusik, S.F. & Mickel, A.E. 2011. Embracing or embattled by converged mobile devices? Users' experiences with a contemporary connectivity technology. *Human Relations*, 64, 1001–1030.

Mazzucato, M. 2018. *The Value of Everything: Making and Taking in the Global Economy*. London: Allen Lane.

New York Times. 1996. *The Downsizing of America*. New York: New York Times Co.

Ng, T.W.H., Feldman, D.C. & Lam, S.S.K. 2010. Psychological contract breaches, organizational commitment, and innovation-related behaviors: A latent growth modeling approach. *Journal of Applied Psychology*, 95, 744–751.

Nicholson, N. 2007. Destiny, drama, and deliberation: Careers in the coevolution of lives and societies. *In:* Gunz, H. & Peiperl, M. (eds.) *Handbook of Career Studies*. Thousand Oaks, CA: Sage Publications.

Noonan, M.C. & Glass, J.L. 2012. The hard truth about telecommuting. *Monthly Labor Review*, 135, 38–45.

Parker, N. 2014. Divergence: Wealth and income inequality in the United States. *EconSouth*, 16, 1–5.

Peiperl, M. & Jonsen, K. 2007. Global careers. *In:* Gunz, H. & Peiperl, M. (eds.) *Handbook of Career Studies*. Thousand Oaks, CA: Sage Publications.

Petriglieri, G., Ashford, S.J. & Wrzesniewski, A. 2018. Thriving in the gig economy. *Harvard Business Review*, 96, 140–143.

Pew Research Center. 2015. *The American Middle Class Is Losing Ground: No Longer the Majority and Falling Behind Financially* [Online]. Available: http://www.pewsocialtrends.org/2015/12/09/the-american-middle-class-is-losing-ground [Accessed 9 December].

Piszczek, M.M. 2017. Boundary control and controlled boundaries: Organizational expectations for technology use at the work – family interface. *Journal of Organizational Behavior*, 38, 592–611.

Rousseau, D.M. 1995. *Psychological Contracts in Organizations: Understanding Written and Unwritten Agreements*. Newbury Park, CA: Sage Publications.

Şahin, A., Song, J., Topa, G. & Violante, G.L. 2014. Mismatch unemployment. *American Economic Review*, 104, 3529–3564.

Schumpeter, J.A. 1942. *Capitalism, Socialism and Democracy*. London: Harper & Brothers.

Shoss, M.K. 2017. Job insecurity: An integrative review and agenda for future research. *Journal of Management*, 43, 1911–1939.

Spreitzer, G.M., Cameron, L. & Garrett, L. 2017. Alternative work arrangements: Two images of the new world of work. *Annual Review of Organizational Psychology and Organizational Behavior*, 4, 473–499.

Tarzi, S. 2016. The third world and relative gains from global trade: An empirical comparative analysis of developed versus developing countries. *Journal of Global South Studies*, 33, 11–48.

Temin, P. 2017. *The Vanishing Middle Class: Prejudice and Power in a Dual Economy*. Cambridge, MA: MIT Press.

Ten Brummelhuis, L.L., Bakker, A.B., Hetland, J. & Keulemans, L. 2012. Do new ways of working foster work engagement? *Psicothema*, 24, 113–120.

Thomas, D.C. & Inkson, K.C. 2017. *Cultural Intelligence: Surviving and Thriving in the Global Village*, 3rd ed. Oakland, CA: Berrett-Koehler.

Valletta, R.G. & Van Der List, C. 2015. Involuntary part-time work: Here to stay? *FRBSF Economic Letter*, (8 June), 1–5.

Vega, R.P., Anderson, A.J. & Kaplan, S.A. 2015. A within-person examination of the effects of telework. *Journal of Business and Psychology*, 30, 313–323.

Weick, K.E. & Berlinger, L.R. 1989. Career improvisation in self-designing organizations. *In:* Arthur, M.B. & Hall, D.T. (eds.) *Handbook of Career Theory*. Cambridge: Cambridge University Press.

Wolf, M. 2015. *The Shifts and the Shocks: What We've Learned – and Have Still to Learn – From the Financial Crisis*. New York: Penguin.

World Bank Group. 2018. *GDP Per Capita Growth (Annual %)* [Online]. Available: https://data.worldbank.org/indicator/NY.GDP.PCAP.KD.ZG [Accessed 18 June].

Index

For Product Safety Concerns and Information please contact our EU
representative GPSR@taylorandfrancis.com Taylor & Francis Verlag GmbH,
Kaufingerstraße 24, 80331 München, Germany

Printed and bound by CPI Group (UK) Ltd, Croydon, CR0 4YY
08/05/2025
01864329-0005